ADRIAN LEVY and CATHY SCOTT-CLARK are award-winning investigative journalists and film-makers who have worked as foreign correspondents, writers and producers for the *Sunday Times*, the *Guardian* and Channel 4's *Dispatches*. They won the One World Media award for foreign reporting in 2005 and were selected as One World Media Journalists of the Year in 2009. They are currently working on their fifth book, about the 2008 attack on Mumbai. For more on *The Meadow* and the authors please see www.clarkandlevy.com

From the reviews of *The Meadow*:

'A compelling account of the 1995 kidnapping of six westerners in Kashmir that may have sparked the rise of Islamic terrorists … Bravura reporting. Levy and Scott-Clark are nonpareil investigators'
Sunday Times

'A staggeringly well-researched new book by two respected journalists'
PANKAJ MISHRA, *Bloomberg*

'A superb probe … This riveting book reminds me of the best of western journalism, which in its heyday produced works of contemporary history, for it unravels every complex detail of a tragic and misunderstood story … Beautifully written'
RADHA KUMAR, *Outlook*

'Compelling. The authors argue that the incident paved the way for the kind of terrorist tactics and kidnappings that have now become common from Pakistan to Afghanistan to Iraq. More controversially, their meticulous investigation concludes that Indian security forces knew where the hostages were throughout the ordeal, but declined to rescue them – and even sabotaged negotiations for their release – to prolong the adverse international publicity for Pakistan'
Washington Post

'Levy and Scott-Clark deserve a lot of credit for recognising the kidnapping as the start of a new chapter. [They] produce some first-rate repo   uthorities' response
l Magazine

'I haven't read anything more terrifying than *The Meadow*, a narrative non-fiction book about a bunch of hapless tourists who go to Kashmir only to get kidnapped by militants – reading this will prepare you for a genuine worst-case holiday scenario' *Wall Street Journal*

'Gripping ... raises many questions that need answers'
Hindustan Times

'A terrific and scary story' *Spectator*

'Unputdownable. The authors bring us up close to the bone-chilling developments of the militancy-torn state ... superb reading'
India Today

'Heartstopping. *The Meadow* is clearly destined to become a land-mark narrative ... its publication is in itself an achievement in the exacting process of putting together the history of that tortured valley' SANJAY KAK, *The Caravan*

'The authors have exposed the glaring faultlines in the Indian state's handling of the Kashmir issue ... This fascinating book should be read by our policymakers and the lay-reader' *The Pioneer*

'Levy and Scott-Clark have pieced together a multi-stranded narrative ... a meticulous, cold-case investigation based on a mountain of offi-cial paperwork, revitalised by a key layer of new testimony ... a grip-ping and often emotional read' *Literary Review*

By the same authors

*Deception: Pakistan, the United States and
the Global Nuclear Weapons Conspiracy*

*The Amber Room: The Controversial Truth About
the Greatest Hoax of the Twentieth Century*

*The Stone of Heaven: The Secret History
of Imperial Green Jade*

ADRIAN LEVY AND CATHY SCOTT-CLARK

The Meadow

Terrorism, Kidnapping and Conspiracy in Paradise

WILLIAM COLLINS

William Collins
An imprint of HarperCollins *Publishers*
77–85 Fulham Palace Road
Hammersmith, London W6 8JB

This William Collins paperback edition published 2013

1

First published in Great Britain by Harper*Press* in 2012

A catalogue record for this book
is available from the British Library

Maps © Malik Sajad, kashmirblackandwhite.com

ISBN 978-0-00-736817-4

Typeset in Minion by G&M Designs Limited,
Raunds, Northamptonshire
Printed and bound in Great Britain by
Clays Ltd, St Ives plc

MIX
Paper from
responsible sources
FSC™
www.fsc.org
FSC® C007454

FSC™ is a non-profit international organisation established to promote
the responsible management of the world's forests. Products carrying the
FSC label are independently certified to assure consumers that they come
from forests that are managed to meet the social, economic and
ecological needs of present and future generations,
and other controlled sources.

Find out more about HarperCollins and the environment at
www.harpercollins.co.uk/green

For all of the injured, the dead and the missing

The headlights filled the road. Everyone cried out for mother and father's love and as the doors to the ascent opened the ballad began again. For his disappeared love he went from hole to hole, grave to grave, searching for the eyes that don't find. From gravestone to gravestone, from cry to cry, it went through niches, through shadows, and it went like this.

FROM RAÚL ZURITA, *SONG FOR HIS DISAPPEARED LOVE*, TRANSLATED INTO ENGLISH BY DANIEL BORZUTZKY (ACTION BOOKS, NOTRE DAME, INDIANA, 2010)

CONTENTS

ILLUSTRATIONS

The route to the Meadow, photographed by Hans Christian Ostrø shortly before he was kidnapped. (Marit Hesby)

Julie and Keith Mangan and Catherine Moseley trek towards the Meadow in early July 1995. Photo by Paul Wells. (Bob Wells)

Cath, Keith and Julie trek towards the Meadow. Photo by Paul Wells. (Bob Wells)

Setting up camp en route to the Meadow. Photo by Paul Wells. (Bob Wells)

Hans Christian Ostrø being made up for his *kathakali* dance graduation show in Sreekrishnapuram, May 1995. (Marit Hesby)

Ostrø on board *Montana* houseboat, Dal Lake, Srinagar. (Marit Hesby)

The Heevan Hotel in Pahalgam. (Courtesy *Conveyor* magazine, Srinagar)

The wives and girlfriends of the kidnapped men leaving the first press conference at the Welcome Hotel in Srinagar on 13 July 1995. (Agency photo)

Rajinder Tikoo, Inspector General of Crime Branch at the time of the kidnappings. (Undated photo, courtesy *Kashmir Times*)

Members of the al Faran kidnap party. (Courtesy Maqbool Sahil)

One of the first hostage photographs, taken by al Faran outside the herders' hut from which John Childs had escaped in the early hours of 8 July. (Agency photo)

Lt. General (retired) D.D. Saklani, Security Advisor to the Governor of Kashmir. (AP)

John Childs reunited with his daughters on 15 July 1995. (Agency photo)

Childs shortly after his rescue. (Agency photo)

A picture of the hostages and their captors that was delivered to the Srinagar Press Enclave on 14 July 1995, shortly before the first deadline expired. (Marit Hesby)

Hostages photographed inside an unidentified herders' hut, probably in the Warwan Valley. (Marit Hesby)

The Warwan Valley, where the hostages were held for eleven weeks. (Authors' archive)

Sukhnoi village. (Authors' archive)

Indian security forces question shepherds about the whereabouts of the hostages. (AP Photo/Qaiser Misra)

Don Hutchings, supposedly injured following a botched Indian security force operation. (Authors' archive)

Hans Christian Ostrø's corpse at Anantnag police station in south Kashmir. (Marit Hesby)

The hostages soon after they arrived in the Warwan Valley. (Marit Hesby)

Two views from Mardan Top, at the southern end of the Warwan Valley. (Authors' archive)

David Mackie and Kim Housego were seized by Pakistan-backed militants in June 1994 and held for seventeen days. (AP)

Letter written by Hans Christian Ostrø to his family and the Norwegian Embassy shortly after his capture. (Marit Hesby)

Ostrø arranged for several batches of photographs, on which he wrote cryptic clues as to the hostages' condition and location, to be smuggled out of the Warwan. (Marit Hesby)

The contents of Hans Christian Ostrø's money belt, recovered from his tent at Zargibal. (Authors' archive)

Press conference given by Jane Schelly and Julie Mangan, Srinagar, July 1995. (Authors' archive)

Photograph of Paul Wells thought to have been taken in the wooden guesthouse in Sukhnoi village, Warwan, where the hostages were kept for several weeks. (Bob Wells)

Photograph taken by al Faran in August 1995 that served as a prelude to 'proof of life' conversations that followed. (Authors' archive)

In the years following the kidnapping, the families of the hostages announced several rewards for information leading to the return of their loved ones. (Bob Wells)

Jehangir Khan, a commander of the pro-government renegades. (Javid Dar, 2008, courtesy of *Conveyor* magazine)

Kashmiri women passing an Indian Central Reserve Police Force patrol. (Faisal Khan, 2011, courtesy *Conveyor* magazine)

The last confirmed photograph of the hostages. (Bob Wells)

Identity card of renegade field commander Basir Ahmad Wagay, aka 'the Tiger'. (Authors' archive)

Renegade commander Azad Nabi, call-sign 'Alpha'. (Authors' archive)

Naseer Mohammed Sodozey, a treasurer of Harkat ul-Ansar (the Movement). (Authors' archive)

Omar Sheikh, from London, arrested in Pakistan in 2002 in connection with the kidnapping of Daniel Pearl. (AP)

Masood Azhar in Pakistan in January 2000. (AP)

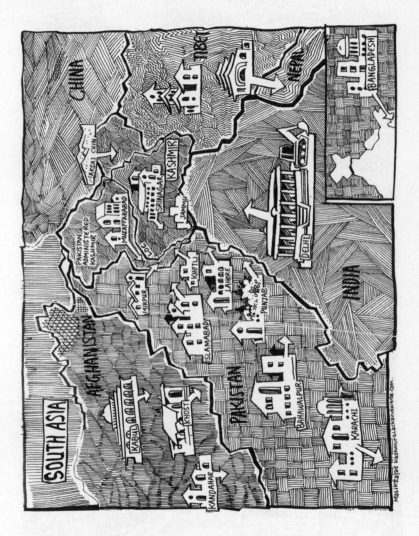

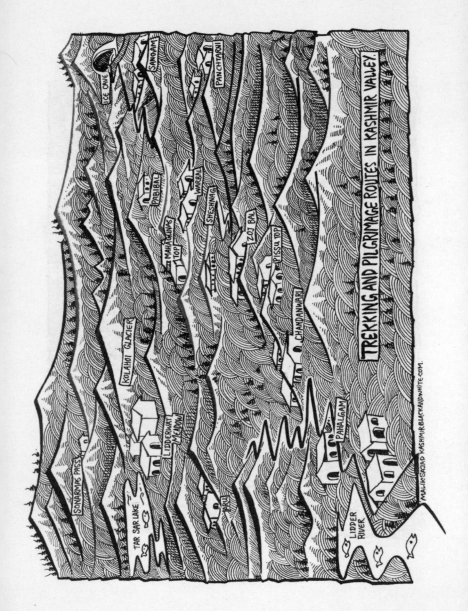

TREKKING AND PILGRIMAGE ROUTES IN KASHMIR VALLEY.

ICE CAVE
SONAMARG
PANCHTARNI
PABIBAL
WARSAL
MAHAGUNAS TOP
SHESHNAG
ZOT PAL
PISSU TOP
KOLAHOI GLACIER
CHANDANWARI
SONAMARG PASS
LIDDERWAT CANYON
PAHALGAM
TAR SAR LAKE
PAYL
LIDDER RIVER

MALIKSAJAD.KASHMIRBLACKANDWHITE.COM.

SONASAR PASS

PAHALGAM

SUKHNOI

AISH MAQAM

SEER

WARWAN VALLEY

INSHAN

TRAMSAR PASS

ANANTNAG

MARDAN TOP

ANANTNAG DISTRICT
JAMMU AND KASHMIR.

MATI GAWRAN

MALIK SAJAD KASHMIRBLACKANDWHITE.COM.

DRAMATIS PERSONAE

THE HOSTAGES

John Childs – a forty-two-year-old explosives and ordnance
   engineer from Connecticut, USA
Dirk Hasert – a twenty-six-year-old student on a gap year from Bad
   Langensalza, Germany
Kim Housego – a sixteen-year-old British boy, kidnapped while on a
   family holiday in Kashmir in 1994
Don Hutchings – a forty-two-year-old neuropsychologist and
   mountaineer from Spokane, Washington State, USA
David Mackie – a thirty-six-year-old British film producer,
   kidnapped in 1994 alongside Kim Housego
Keith Mangan – a thirty-three-year-old electrician from
   Middlesbrough, England
Hans Christian Ostrø – a twenty-seven-year-old actor and director
   from Oslo, Norway
Paul Wells – a twenty-four-year-old photography student from
   Blackburn, England

THE WIVES AND GIRLFRIENDS

Anne Hennig – Dirk's girlfriend, a student
Julie Mangan – Keith's wife
Catherine Moseley – Paul's girlfriend, a social worker
Jane Schelly – Don's wife, a PE teacher and mountaineer

THE FAMILIES

Joseph and Helen Childs – John Childs' parents, from Salem, upstate New York, USA

Marit Hesby and Anette Ostrø – Hans Christian's mother, a travel agent, from Oslo, Norway, and his younger sister, a film-maker then based in Stockholm

David and Jenny Housego – former *Financial Times* South Asia Bureau Chief, and his wife, a businesswoman, parents of Kim Housego

Claude and Donna Hutchings – parents of Don Hutchings, from Coeur d'Alene, Idaho, USA

Charlie and Mavis Mangan – Keith's retired father and his mother, a school dinner lady, from Brookfield, Middlesbrough

James and Joyce Schelly – Jane Schelly's parents, from Orefield, Pennsylvania, USA

Robert and Anita Sullivan – Julie Mangan's parents, from Eston, Middlesbrough

Bob and Dianne Wells – Paul's parents, from Blackburn

WESTERN DIPLOMATS AND INVESTIGATORS

Philip Barton – First Secretary at the British High Commission, New Delhi

Tim Buchs – Second Secretary at the US Embassy, New Delhi

Frank Elbe – German Ambassador to India

Sir Nicholas Fenn – British High Commissioner to India

Tore Hattrem – Political Officer at the Norwegian Embassy, New Delhi

Gary Noesner – lead hostage negotiator of the FBI's Crisis Negotiation Unit

Commander Roy Ramm – hostage negotiator, head of Scotland Yard's specialist operations

Arne Walther – Norwegian Ambassador to India

Frank Wisner – US Ambassador to India

J&K POLICE AND OFFICIALS

IG Paramdeep Singh Gill – police chief who instigates his own al Faran inquiry

DSP Kifayat Haider – police officer with operational responsibility for Pahalgam

SP Farooq Khan – the first STF chief

General K.V. Krishna Rao – former chief of the Indian Army and Governor of Kashmir

DG Mahendra Sabharwal – Kashmir police chief

SP Mushtaq Sadiq – officer leading the al Faran Squad

Lt. General (rtd) D.D. Saklani – Security Advisor to the Governor of Kashmir

IG Rajinder Tikoo – Crime Branch chief, who leads the negotiations with al Faran

SSP Bashir Ahmed Yatoo – senior Kashmiri police officer seconded to Kashmir State Human Rights Commission to investigate unmarked graves in 2011

THE KASHMIRI PRESS PACK

Mushtaq Ali – photographer for AFP. Rescued Kim Housego and David Mackie in 1994, and worked closely with Yusuf Jameel in 1995

Yusuf Jameel – the BBC's Srinagar correspondent, instrumental in digging up the story behind the 1995 kidnapping

THE JIHADIS

'The Afghani' (Sajjad Shahid Khan) – the Movement's military commander, a veteran Pashtun fighter from the Afghan–Pakistan border

Master Allah Baksh Sabir Alvi – retired schoolteacher and father of Masood Azhar

Masood Azhar – the jailed General Secretary of Harkat ul-Ansar (the Movement for the Victorious), from Bahawalpur, in the

Pakistan Punjab, who later became the head of Jaish-e-Mohammed (the Army of Mohammed)

'Brigadier Badam' – pseudonym for a senior ISI officer who was instrumental in establishing the ISI's proxy war in Indian Kashmir

Maulana Fazlur Rehman Khalil – Masood Azhar's mentor in Karachi. The spiritual leader of the Movement

Nasrullah Mansoor Langrial – famed *jihadi* commander from Langrial, Pakistan, chosen as deputy to the Afghani and known in *jihadi* circles as 'Darwesh'

Omar Sheikh – former student at the London School of Economics, who became a kidnapper for the Movement in 1994. Also involved in the 2002 abduction of American journalist Daniel Pearl

'Sikander' (Javid Ahmed Bhat) – southern commander of the Movement, from Dabran village, in Anantnag, Kashmir

Naseer Mohammed Sodozey – a senior fighter in the Movement, captured in April 1996 and forced under torture to incriminate himself in the 1995 kidnappings

'The Turk' (Abdul Hamid al-Turki) – field commander of al Faran, a veteran *mujahideen* fighter of Turkish ancestry

Qari Zarar – Kashmiri deputy commander of al Faran, from Doda, in Jammu

THE PRO-GOVERNMENT RENEGADES

'Alpha' or 'Azad Nabi' (Ghulam Nabi Mir) – renegade commander based in Shelipora, above Anantnag

'Bismillah' – Alpha's deputy, based in Shelipora

'The Clerk' (Abdul Rashid) – Alpha's district commander, based in Vailoo, above Anantnag

'The Tiger' (Basir Ahmad Wagay) – Alpha's field commander, based in Lovloo, above Anantnag

ABBREVIATIONS

AFP – Agence France-Press

BJP – the Bharatiya Janata Party, a conservative Hindu nationalist
political party

BSF – Border Security Force, a paramilitary outfit raised by India
after its war with Pakistan in 1965 and later employed in Kashmir
on counter-insurgency operations

CRPF – Central Reserve Police Force, the paramilitary police
inducted into Kashmir to fight the insurgency

DG – Director General of Police. The force's chief

DIG – Deputy Inspector General of Police

DSP – Deputy Superintendent of Police

HM (Hizbul Mujahideen: 'the Party of the Holy Warriors') – a
Kashmiri militant outfit, formed in 1989, heavily backed at first
by Pakistan

HuA (Harkat ul-Ansar: 'the Movement for the Victorious') – a
group formed in Pakistan in 1993 by the combination of three
jihad fronts, including Harkat ul Mujahideen, to rally insurgents
fighting India in Kashmir. Designated as a terrorist organisation
by the US in 1997

HuM (Harkat ul-Mujahideen: 'the Order of Holy Warriors') –
formed in Pakistan in the mid-1980s by Maulana Khalil to fight
the Soviets in Afghanistan. The precursor of Harkat ul-Ansar

IB – Intelligence Bureau, Indian domestic intelligence

IG – Inspector General of Police

IPS – Indian Police Service

ISI – Inter Services Intelligence directorate, Pakistan's military intelligence agency

J&K – Jammu and Kashmir

JKLF – Jammu and Kashmir Liberation Front, formed in Birmingham, UK, in 1977; one of the first militant outfits to mount an armed struggle against India in Kashmir

JKSLF, or SLF – Jammu and Kashmir Students Liberation Front, also known as the Students Liberation Front. Formed in Kashmir in 1987

LoC – Line of Control, the 406-mile-long 'ceasefire line' that separates the Indian and Pakistan sections of the divided state of Jammu and Kashmir

POK – Pakistan Occupied Kashmir, as the Indians sometimes refer to the section of the state administered by Islamabad

RAW – Research and Analysis Wing, Indian foreign intelligence

RR – Rashtriya Rifles, an Indian Army force of specialist counter-insurgency troops, formed in 1990 to fight the insurgency in Kashmir

RSS – Rashtriya Swayamsevak Sangh, a Hindu paramilitary movement founded in 1925 to oppose British colonialism

SHRC – State Human Rights Commission, an Indian government body that investigates allegations of human rights abuses

SP – Superintendent of Police

SSP – Senior Superintendent of Police

STF/SOG – police Special Task Force, later renamed the Special Operations Group, founded in 1993 to fight the insurgency in Kashmir

PROLOGUE

On 1 May 2011, a Prowler electronic-warfare aircraft, taking off from the USS *Carl Vinson*, jammed Pakistan's radar systems, silence spreading like emulsion over the Islamic republic. At fifty-six minutes past midnight on the morning of 2 May, two American stealth Hawks, ferrying a team of US Navy Seals, hovered over a walled compound in the spick-and-span garrison town of Abbottabad, seventy-two miles north of Islamabad, the Pakistani capital.

Over the next few minutes, Operation Neptune Spear came to a head, achieving, with only a dozen shots fired, what John Brennan, President Obama's chief counter-terrorism advisor would call the 'defining moment' in the war against terrorism.

Winkled out of his hiding place by cruising satellites capable of measuring the length of a man's shadow from six hundred miles up, while down on the ground a medical-aid camp established to counter polio in Abbottabad had been subverted to sniff out residents' DNA, the elusive Osama bin Laden had finally been tracked down, a decade after 9/11. As he reached across his bed for his AK-47 he was shot dead, 'decapitating the head of the snake that is al Qaeda', according to Brennan.

One chapter in a story of our times had come to an end.

Sixteen years earlier, in the heights of the Indian Himalayas, where the mountains gather in a half-hitch to encompass the troubled valley of Kashmir, a crime was committed whose nature and cruelty presaged the age of terror Osama would go on to marshal.

In July 1995, high in the mountains of Kashmir, six Western trekkers – two Britons, two Americans, a German and a Norwegian – were seized by a group of Islamic guerrillas who demanded the release of twenty-one named militants imprisoned in Indian jails in exchange for their lives. At the head of the list was Masood Azhar, a portly cleric from Pakistan.

Masood Azhar's early career mirrored that of Osama. Growing up in Pakistan's eastern Punjab province in the seventies and eighties, Masood, the spoiled favourite son of a wealthy landowner, had lacked for nothing – much like the privileged young Osama, whose well-connected family made its fortune constructing palaces for Saudi royals. Educated in an Islamist hothouse in the frenetic port city of Karachi, in Pakistan's deep south, Masood graduated to become the mouthpiece for a guerrilla outfit that would, like Osama, gravitate to Afghanistan to fight the occupying Soviet Red Army to a standstill.

When Moscow retreated from Kabul in 1989, Masood and his unemployed fighters had converged on northern Africa, looking for new causes. They found Osama there too, well before 'the Sheikh' had been flagged up on Western watchlists. Together, Masood, a stubby firebrand, whose hypnotic patter had already propelled thousands into battle, and Osama, the lean and pensive fugitive whose deep war chest had bought matériel and men, began to direct Afghanistan veterans in a new fight against the West.

They struck first in broken Somalia in 1993, where America was bogged down in a peacekeeping mission, Masood and Osama arming Islamists with rocket-propelled grenades that brought down two US Black Hawks in the battle for Mogadishu, leaving nineteen American soldiers dead and seventy-three wounded in a bloody débâcle. Masood was soon travelling again, this time to Britain, where he raised more funds and recruited *jihadi* sleepers who would wait the best part of a decade before attaining notoriety in both the West and the East.

However, in 1994, while Osama was consolidating his front in Sudan and Yemen, buying a commercial airliner and shipping weapons and gold around the world, Masood became temporarily unstuck while sowing the seeds of insurrection in Kashmir. Slipping into India on false papers, hoping to galvanise a flagging local Muslim insurgency, he was captured by the Indian Army. It was this event that led to the kidnappings of July 1995.

The fate of Masood, and the bloodshed and intrigue that engulfed the six Western trekkers, would shape much of the epoch that followed. In the mountains of Kashmir that summer, Masood's gunmen experimented with the tactics and rhetoric of Islamic terror, unveiling to the world extreme acts and justifications that would soon become all too familiar.

Finding and squeezing Western pressure points, testing foreign governments' sensibilities and resolve, this hostage-taking would enable Masood and his men to refine their methods before they combined forces with Osama's al Qaeda, soon assisted by the black-turbanned Taliban when they came to power in Afghanistan in 1996.

It would only be a short leap from the kidnappings in Kashmir to suicidal assaults in Srinagar, New York, Washington and London, in which many thousands would die or be injured. Three months after 9/11, India accused Masood of being behind a brazen raid on its parliament in New Delhi, an assault that was broadcast across the subcontinent, just as the Twin Towers had fallen before a live TV audience around the world.

In 2002, Masood's bodyguard and one of his British recruits adapted tactics honed during the Kashmir kidnapping to abduct Daniel Pearl, a *Wall Street Journal* reporter, and to film his horrific beheading. Masood himself, like Osama, slipped from public view, becoming a shadowy *éminence grise*. In 2004 he welcomed several British Pakistanis back to the land of their forefathers, and in the terrorist training camps of north-west Pakistan he helped them plan for the mayhem they would unleash in London in July 2005, when four near-simultaneous suicide bombs went off in the heart of the heaving capital, killing fifty-two and injuring more than seven hundred.

In 2006, another of Masood's British protégés manipulated *jihadi* recruits from the West to mount a complex plot to bring down multiple airliners over the Atlantic with liquid bombs smuggled aboard in soft-drinks bottles. Many more plots in India, the US and the UK were narrowly thwarted, saving untold lives. By the time Osama bin Laden was run to ground in Abbottabad, many others from al Qaeda's top table had perished too. Apart from Masood Azhar.

He continues to thrive, flitting today between Pakistan's borders and his old home in Punjab. Four of the tourists seized in Kashmir in the summer of 1995, whose abduction foretold a new age of terror, simply vanished. Their bodies were never found, and their case was forgotten. Until now.

When the book was first published it provoked a storm in India, with the government challenged by national newspapers and cable news networks to respond, New Delhi giving the *New York Times* a date by when it would. That day came and went. However, lawyers in Kashmir representing the Association of Parents of Disappeared Persons (APDP), an organisation representing some of the estimated 8,000 Valley dwellers who are said to have vanished after being taken into the custody of the Indian security forces, picked up the baton. The organisation filed a petition with the Indian government's Human Rights Commission in the spring of 2012, alleging that the army and government had deliberately misled the investigation into the kidnappings and withheld information. They also suggested that a criminal network had been formed between the kidnappers and government militiamen that worked together to keep the hostages hidden from view. They demanded the case file be made public and that senior policeman be called in for questioning. On April 17, the commission agreed to review the seventeen-year-old case, triggering headlines around the world, from *Fox News* in the US to the *BBC* in London.

By July, the police had declined to react to the judge's request to produce the Al Faran file, with the Inspector General warned by the commission that action would be taken against him. Finally, on August 13, five months after the case was listed, the J&K police Crime Branch submitted its official response. They claimed that the master file, containing key evidence, 'went to ashes due to a fire incident'. The case is ongoing but the army and intelligence services are immune from investigation and will escape the probe.

CATHY SCOTT-CLARK AND ADRIAN LEVY
London, April 2013

ONE

Packing

They weren't the type to brag. But Jane Schelly and Don Hutchings had been to many places, far more than most of their friends. Soon after getting together back in 1985, they had concluded that in this life there was no point treading water. With no children between them, Don, forty-two, and Jane, forty, had made the most of their shared wanderlust, embarking on six ambitious foreign expeditions in the past eight years. Now, on a summer's evening in late June 1995, Jane was packing once again, surveying the items laid out around the bedroom of their large, high-ceilinged cedarwood home in the Pacific north-west, ticking them off on a checklist: money belts, passports, tickets and travellers' cheques, a well-thumbed edition of the Lonely Planet *Trekking in the Indian Himalayas*, preparing for their latest foreign foray with the clinical confidence of the well-travelled. Memories flitted back and forth – Switzerland, Bolivia, Turkey, India, Nepal. They lived for the wilds, preferably high up in some mountain range. She loved her job as a physical education teacher at a local elementary school, but Jane lived for these summer voyages.

It was a passion for the outdoors that had thrown her and Don together, and as she got ready for another adventure she found herself thinking how strange it was that they had turned out to be such a perfect fit, as back at the start she had not been at all sure about him, and had not thought there would ever be a *them*. Nowadays she loved Don's strong, calm demeanour, this dependable climber with a sinewy frame and a rugged beard, who brought

1

others through risky situations with a joke and a squeeze of the arm.

On their wedding day in 1991, Don described them as climbing partners. 'When you're tied to someone with a rope,' Jane would later say, 'you get to know them very well, and you learn about trust.'

At home they were sober, law-abiding citizens, from solid backgrounds: her father had been a scoutmaster, his a cattle rancher. Out in the wilds, they were both risk-takers. Don had hacked up Mount McKinley in Alaska and taken a tumble at Montana's Rainbow Falls. Jane had traversed the volcanic glacier fields of Mount Rainier and taught cross-country skiing at Spokane Falls Community College. On a clear day, Rainier, the highest peak in the Cascade Range, was just about visible west of Spokane, a laid-back, outdoorsy sort of city on the eastern fringes of Washington state, where the couple lived and worked. 'The Mountain', as people called Rainier, with its three peaks, Columbia Crest, Point Success and Liberty Cap, served as a constant reminder of why they were there. 'Mount Rainier had a special meaning for him,' said Jane. Don had been brought up in Spokane, whose motto was 'Near Nature, Near Perfect', and the mountains, lakes and woods grounded him like no other place, he said.

Most weekends Don and Jane went out of town. They'd head for the Cascades or the Rockies, whose peaks delineated the skyline to the east and north, trekking, skiing or kayaking with friends, many of them doctors and nurses who had trained or worked with Don, a neuropsychologist, or were old classmates from Spokane's Shadle Park High. On weekday nights Jane liked to cycle with her fellow teachers and friends from the Spokane Mountaineers, whose eight hundred or so members belonged to the region's oldest outdoor association. 'What we did was *with* the Spokane Mountaineers and *through* the Spokane Mountaineers,' she says. For two years she had served as club president, one of the first women to do so, and everyone quickly learned not to get on her wrong side. 'Don't bullshit Jane,' the Mountaineers whispered. Don, as fit as a man a decade younger, joked that he was the First Husband.

Once a month a group of Mountaineers would gather at Jane and Don's, in the Spokane Valley suburb of Northwood, to plan the next club outing over an exotic dinner. The shady wooden house on stilts with verandas back and front, surrounded by Ponderosa pines, its large sunken living room painted blue and red to match a rug the couple had bought in India, was filled with photos of Jane, smiling or waving against a snowy backdrop, and mementos from the couple's foreign voyages: Tibetan rugs and prayer flags, tribal masks and recipe books from some far-flung place or other. It was an easy spot to hang out, Don's golden retrievers, Homer and Bodhi (short for *bodhisattva*, an enlightened being in Buddhism), sprawled across the floor, Jane walking visitors around her latest botanical acquisitions, displayed in pots along the red-brick path that wound around their garden, Don conjuring some Indian or Thai recipe in the kitchen. 'You move the flowers around so often you ought to put them on roller skates,' he used to joke out of the window.

In the summer, most of this close-knit group went further afield, and this year Jane and Don were heading back to the Himalayas, which they had explored twice before. The world's largest mountain range was a place you could visit time and again, and still know little about it, Don told friends. This time Jane was packing extra carefully, as she had a gut feeling that things might get choppy. They were heading for the mountains of Kashmir. From what they had read, this trip would come with additional risks, as the ranges lay on a political fault-line: a disputed border between warring neighbours India and Pakistan. For the past six years the state had been enmeshed in a local insurgency that pitted Muslim rebels calling for independence against the Indian security forces, which accused them of being in the pay of Pakistan.

Unsettling stories of political and religious turmoil had recently emanated from there, and for several weeks Don and Jane had debated whether to go at all. But they had done their homework, listened to other people's views and read widely, before concluding that this was, like so many others they had negotiated, a risk worth taking. And now Jane was surveying their kit with a sense of anticipation.

Don's royal-blue fleecy climbing hat, his blue Gore-Tex Moonstone walking trousers with the black inset panels above the knee, an extra-thick blue Patagonia top. On top of the pile she laid thermal underwear, lightweight T-shirts and rainproof gear. As she ticked off the items, Jane thought how among the many things that had drawn her to Don was something that others found galling: his impulse to order. They were both inveterate list-makers. Hers were invariably practical. His were a mix of function and aspiration, scribbles on yellow legal pads that he left scattered around the house: skiing once a year, cooking the *perfect* Indian meal, semi-retirement by the age of fifty (which only left another eight years to get his work–life balance sorted out) and, most importantly, an annual mind-expanding and physically demanding expedition. Climbers are like that, he would say. Embracing order so as to cope with the disorder, fetishising the planning in order to counter the random. It was the same with their equipment. Although he said he hated technology, he always bought the latest climbing gear and gadgets. And she loved laying it down, cleaning it, counting it out. This time especially, they needed to get the preparation right.

There was a satisfying rhythm to Jane and Don's life. He was 'the philosopher', she 'the shipwright'. He sought experiences, while she wrangled with logistics. Prepping for these trips, Don always beefed up on the region's spirituality and history, while Jane wanted to know how many hours it would take to climb to a particular col. At home, he cooked. She rearranged the garden. He took the photos. She put them into frames. He wanted a crystal ball. She preferred a new set of skis. On holiday, he talked to most anyone, while she took notes and crammed little keepsakes into her rucksack. She was capable and devoted to Don, whom privately she called 'sweetie', while publicly she remained fiercely independent, retaining her maiden name. The students at Arlington Elementary viewed her with a mixture of bafflement and awe. 'Stimulating the nation's young hearts and minds,' she said to herself every morning in mock-declamatory style before setting off for school.

4

With her tight brown curls and turned-up nose, at first glance Jane had an impish air. But to those who knew her well, she was the more driven of the two. Among their circle, many had watched, doubtfully, as Jane had made her first attempts to infect Don with the travel bug. She had gone on foreign-exchange trips at school and travelled across the United States from her native Pennsylvania before pitching up in the Pacific north-west. She was already an explorer, and wanted to partner up with someone who felt the same way.

Don was many things, but until Jane came along nobody would have described him as a man of the world. He was of pure north-west country stock, his father, Claude 'Red' Hutchings, having been a tough-talking Idaho cattle-rancher, originally from Coeur d'Alene in the neighbouring county. Don was closer to his mother, Donna, a nurse, and there was a bond between mother and son that had its roots in the loss of his twin brother, who had died at just three days old. But Red had been intent on shaping his surviving son's earliest memories. Almost as soon as Don could walk, Red had him in the saddle, dressing him in a cowboy hat and boots. Sitting astride his own palomino, Don would accompany his father on week-long 'gentlemen on horseback' rides, as he called them, into the wild. But Don wasn't cut out to be a cowboy.

Instead, a freak accident helped him find his niche. After flying through a car windscreen during high school, he spent months in hospital being put back together. 'With cuts from ear to ear, tongue damage and teeth knocked out, he thought he looked like Frankenstein,' said Jane. When he had recovered, Don determined to help others who had also been to the brink. He would follow his mother into the health-care sector. As soon as he was old enough he grew a beard, to conceal his scars.

After school and a BSc from Washington State University, Don opted for neuropsychology, a specialism that appealed to a man who had had many months to explore his inner self while in hospital. For a while it seemed as if he would be a student forever, gaining a Masters and then a doctorate, never straying too far from home. But eventually he made a break, taking up a position as a hospital psychologist in Lancaster, Pennsylvania, on the other side of the country. He married for the first time, a psychology student from West Virginia, and together they attempted to renovate a thirty-acre abandoned farm in Pennsylvania. Both projects failed in the end, and Don returned alone and disconsolate to Spokane in 1984.

He found a job as a neuropsychologist at the Sacred Heart. Scott Earl Bently, a former patient who had suffered a severe head injury and paralysis in a car accident, was in awe of him: 'Don was the catalyst that moved my life away from institutionalised health care to a life of happiness and freedom by integrating me back into society and by remaining my friend, talking with me about hiking, camping, climbing, and other things we were both interested in. I'll never forget him for that, and I thought then he would remain my friend for my entire life'. Such was Don's enthusiasm for this esoteric field that the hospital was persuaded to open a dedicated head injuries unit, the first in the region. Soon other local hospitals did the same, bringing Don on board as an advisor.

But the mountains remained his passion. After returning from Pennsylvania he had joined the Spokane Mountaineers, finding a release at high altitude. Soon he was signing up to ice-climbing seminars, instructors' workshops and winter-camping seminars, and learning Telemark skiing. At five feet eight he had been too short to fulfil his dream of becoming a professional basketball player or footballer, but here was something he could do. Within a few months he was elected to the club's climbing committee, soon becoming its chairman. One climbing friend described his 'unbeatable combination of moral fibre that is absolute high-carbon steel'.

Don had not been looking for romance, but through the club he met Jane Schelly. Born and brought up in Orefield, a small town in Pennsylvania's Lehigh Valley, Jane had left the flat landscape of the east as soon as she got out of college in 1976, and headed for the wilderness of the Pacific north-west. She had earned a reputation for fearlessness, and could outpace many of the men in the club. Luck ran in her favour too, said climbing friends: 'Jane is the type who always lands on her feet.' She and Don had their first tête-à-tête waist-deep in the Jerry Johnson Hot Springs near Lolo Pass, during a club trip to Idaho in October 1984. 'Don and I sat in the hot pool and chitchatted,' Jane remembered. 'He didn't tell me for many years that he thought, "That's the woman I'm going to marry."' Afterwards, Don signed up to a country ski class Jane was running out of Spokane Falls Community College. They dated 'a bit', but Don was wary of messing things up again, and they did not come together until the following October. 'We took the same hot springs trip, and clicked,' says Jane.

Behind Don's practical façade Jane discovered a romantic, who took her away from school on Friday nights: bed and breakfast on the bay at San Francisco; Point No Point on Washington's Kitsap Peninsula; an inn in Oregon overlooking the Columbia River. 'I just couldn't imagine finding someone as good as Don,' says Jane. 'He was a very gentle and sensitive person.'

Don soon became a leader, arranging 'crazy weekends', pitching himself and other club members into 'endurance stunts', like the time he bivouacked up the East Ridge of Wyoming's 13,775-foot Grand Teton to watch the Northern Lights. 'Don got me so fired up about ice climbing,' recalled Bill Erler, a close friend. 'We'd just motor up stuff.' He also gained a reputation as a man who could operate under extreme pressure. Don 'always tried to do more than his share', and was 'a talented and stable force', according to club member and friend George Neal. Inevitably there were knocks and scrapes, like the winter's day at Montana's Rainbow Falls when Don fell and sprained his ankle. Telling the rest of his group to go on without him, he had dragged himself down across a rockslide and to his car, risking permanent injury.

Jane bided her time, waiting for the right moment to widen their horizons. It came in 1988, when they spent four weeks trekking on the arduous Annapurna Circuit in Nepal, in the shadow of Mount Everest. It was Don's first big foreign trip, and only the second time he had left the US. He could not get enough of the Himalayas, which sparked a fascination in him with all things Asian. Soon his upstairs office in Northwood was crammed with books about climbing in the subcontinent, Tibetan Buddhism and Indian philosophy, yoga and meditation. Most evenings he could be found sprawled across the living-room floor, surrounded by books and maps, Indian music tinkling out of the speakers, plotting the next foray to the East.

The only problem was synchronising their lives. While Jane had the long summer school holidays, Don could never take more than two weeks off. For a while they turned this into part of the adventure, Jane going on ahead and rendezvousing with Don at some distant destination, like the time she toured alone around Thailand and India, having arranged to meet him outside a post office in the northern Indian state of Himachal Pradesh. When Don quit his job at the Sacred Heart to set up Spokane's first independent neuropsychology practice, he did it mainly so he and Jane could spend more time travelling together.

They got round to marrying in 1991, a home-made affair in their back garden, literally tying themselves together with climbing ropes looped into a double fisherman's knot. It could have been corny, but that was Don and Jane, bound to each other by the things they loved. The act, for Jane, 'symbolised the dependence of each of us upon the other'. Afterwards, Don gave a set of Tibetan bells to the chaplain in thanks. For their honeymoon they returned to the Himalayas, this time visiting Ladakh, a solemn, arid mountain landscape dotted with prayer flags and Buddhist monasteries in India's far northern Jammu and Kashmir (J&K) state. Don came home mesmerised by what they had seen, and also by what they had heard of another nearby destination, the Kashmir Valley, that lay three hundred miles to the west, a place of ancient gods with a landscape shaped by hunters and poets.

Four summers later, Jane was packing for the Kashmir Valley. This trip would be a culmination of many things: ten years of climbing, ten years being together, almost a decade of foreign exploration. They had decided there was no better location in which to celebrate.

* * *

The journey was well within their physical capabilities. Jane had worked it out. The twelve-day trek would, they hoped, fill their heads and hearts. If the maps were accurate – Don had struggled to find anything half decent – they hoped to cover over a hundred miles, which seemed about right for the kind of weather and the severity of the inclines they expected to encounter.

Don read how the wilderness of glacial chutes and iridescent mountain lakes had a way of punishing trekkers, while serving as home to hard-pressed nomadic *gujjars*, *dards* and *bakarwals*, the native herders, hunters and cowboys who wore kohl round their eyes to ward off evil spirits, their children bound to the backs of their ponies with rope. Through a silent landscape they moved in slender single-file convoys to summer pastures of lush, flower-filled valleys and on to the high Himalayas, a medieval caravan of maroon robes and scarves. Up high, the temperatures careened from the seriously sub-zero to the high forties. There was a dry heat that cracked skin, and a wet cold that blistered everything. Sometimes the wind dropped, only to slam into you like a pantechnicon.

But then, many times before Don and Jane had started off from somewhere beneath a cobalt sky, only to end up in a white-out. Jane had read that it was not exceptional for the highest passes in Kashmir to become blocked by snow even in summer. At times they might need to double back. She knew that, warming and cooling, dehydrating and freezing, the mountains would be punishing, but their years of experience should get them through the worst of it. In Kashmir, where the rich pastureland typically remained frost-free from May to September, they would probably walk for ten hours a day. In the upper reaches, where they would have to negotiate fields of scree that would punish their ankles and knees, they might go down to eight hours. But they had time.

Their destination was a high-altitude ice cave called Amarnath that was dedicated to Lord Shiva, the Hindu god of destruction and trans-formation. A giant, gaping hole, it looked as if a meteorite had slammed into the side of a mountain. While Amarnath was virtually unknown in the West, it was revered across India as an ancient Hindu pilgrimage site, to which hundreds of thousands of devotees flocked annually. Some came by foot, others by pony, a few on their hands and knees, the least able piggybacking on local guides, everyone scrabbling to scale the mountains so as to demonstrate the depth of their faith.

Don was drawn by the collective act of devotion, and loved the idea of going on Shiva's trail, but he and Jane intended to arrive at the end of June, before the main pilgrimage season began the following month. That way they would have the route to themselves. After Amarnath they would head west, following the ice-water streams down to the lush pasture of the Lidderwat Valley, where mountain flowers gorged on snowmelt, according to the guidebooks. There they would pitch their tents at a legendary campsite that travellers simply referred to as 'the Meadow', a velvet green cleft at a little over ten thousand feet, with an icy river running through it and enveloped on all sides by conifer forests. There was something prosaic, minimalist even, about the sound of the Meadow. Don and Jane looked forward to pitching camp up high, surrounded by aromatic mountain pasture.

By late evening, Jane had placed tidy little heaps of possessions all over the bedroom floor. Now she slid each one of them into a separate waterproof pouch, working on a maximum load of fifteen kilos per person. Using the vacuum cleaner, she sucked the air out of each before slotting the shrivelled jellyfishes they now resembled into the new frameless purple-and-red Sundog daypacks she and Don had bought during a recent club trip to Montana. For Jane, packing was an art, the trip broken down into components, each of them carefully arranged like evidence at a crime scene, then layered in a bag that just might save you one day. Plasters, antiseptic spray, teabags, Don's favourite Snickers bars; and should she bring some more Imodium? Could you get Imodium over there? She did not know, and threw in an extra packet.

The most important thing was her journal, in which she would note down the route, the ascents, the views, as well as snippets of lore picked up from locals and information on flowers and plants.

Sometimes she enjoyed the quiet moments after dusk just as much as the walking, a time to lounge across their sleeping bags making notes, with books scattered around, her head propped against Don's flat stomach, their limbs heavy from exertion. This was a real existence, the living that gave purpose to life.

Batteries, waterproof bags, first-aid kit, rolls of film; she counted the final items off her list. Don's post-expedition slide shows at the house had become a tradition among the Spokane Mountaineers. They were nothing flashy, just a chance for Don to cook, try out the latest micro-brewery beers and give a talk. He loved to share what he had seen. Some people didn't get that Don and Jane were just who they appeared to be. They had no interest in getting one over on anybody, or crowing about their far-flung adventures. There was no edge to them. Their lives were about getting out and making it back sufficiently healthy to tell others what they had experienced.

As she finished packing, Jane reminded herself to remind Don about his black-and-yellow Casio altimeter. He would be sorely disappointed if he got halfway over Mahagunas Top at fifteen thousand feet, only to realise he'd left it at home in a bedside drawer.

Finally she stood back and surveyed her handiwork, pondering the things that were not yet sorted out. Was this really a good time to go to Kashmir? What did they actually know? They had both had a gnawing sense of unease that had kicked in after they had bought the tickets, as they read that the region was in a state of flux, a worrying instability that became more real to them with every new snippet of information they gleaned from newspapers and magazines.

Don knew from his research that as a geographical and spiritual crossroads between the Arab world to the west, China to the north and the tropical subcontinent of India to the south, Kashmir had always been steeped in one conflict or another. Its recent troubles stemmed from the Partition of India in 1947, when the predominantly Muslim principality, whose residents longed for independence, had been split in two after both India and the newly founded Pakistan claimed it. Since then the two countries had fought three wars in their attempts to gain the other's share, in 1947, 1965 and 1971, with the

Muslim population of the Kashmir Valley caught between the aspirations of the warring neighbours, and held in a firm grip by the Indian government in New Delhi.

In the years after the 1971 conflict, Kashmir had settled down for a time. Srinagar, its summer capital, became a place of pilgrimage for Western backpackers, the valley eulogised by the likes of Led Zeppelin, whose music evoked a mystic kingdom of the mind, a lyrical paradise wreathed in hash smoke, drawing in thousands of visitors who put up on intricately carved wooden houseboats moored on the city's tranquil lakes, Dal and Nagin. Between the lotus gardens, floating markets and bobbling villages glided some of the world's most persistent salesmen, touting shawls woven from antelope hair, almond biscuits, semiprecious stones, papier-mâché boxes and sticky gobbets of dark *charas* from their hand-painted *shikara* boats, against a backdrop of the jagged Zabarwan mountains.

But these days Kashmir had an undercurrent of tension, especially after reports that New Delhi had rigged the state assembly polls of 1987, so as to box in the independence lobby. This ham-fisted act of muscle-flexing had gone largely unnoticed in the West, but had led to an explosion of protests in the state that had developed into an armed insurgency. For the past six years, bloody clashes had been erupting between Kashmiri Muslim youths calling for freedom from India, and the Indian security forces sent by New Delhi to neuter them. India accused Pakistan of exacerbating the dissent. Pakistan slammed India for triggering a revolution through its brutal crackdowns, as army bunkers rose up on the street corners of Srinagar, and post offices and cinemas were requisitioned as barracks and interrogation centres.

What little news leaked out had served to deter much of the foreign tourist trade. Rather than Kashmir, stoners and their disciples, adventurers and refugees from the West now headed for India's Parvati Valley, or far south-west to the beaches and freshwater lagoons of Goa and Kerala. The number of tourists visiting the mountain state shrank from eighty thousand a year in the mid-eighties to fewer than ten thousand in 1994, leaving the houseboat owners destitute, dreaming of a time when their paradise had paid the bills.

Jane and Don knew they would have to be careful. But then, ascending a mountain was no different. 'We did a lot of preparation before we left,' Jane said. 'We knew there was some turmoil in Kashmir, but we had been in northern India in 1991, and what we had heard about the Kashmir area from various people was that … there were no problems trekking in the areas where we were most interested.' But in those days it was difficult to find up-to-date and accurate information about such a remote area without actually going there. 'Don had recently purchased a computer for work, but he hated technology and we were not on email yet,' Jane recalled. 'Thus, we had limited access to news of that area.' Jane and Don decided to leave for Kashmir with maps in hand, ready to switch destinations should they become spooked by the ground realities.

A few nights before they left for New Delhi, Don took out a notepad. 'The Don Hutchings yellow-legal-pad method of decision-making', as friend George Neal called it. The biggest 'pro' was the weather. Don's work commitments meant they could only trek at the end of June that year, and for a maximum of two weeks. That ruled out possibly safer destinations like Nepal, which would be lashed by monsoons at that time. For Jane, there was also Kashmir's flora, which she had read was second to none: wild mountain strawberries, lilac and forget-me-nots.

The obvious 'con' was the unrest. What to say about that? Don made a list.

1. According to the limited information they had been able to pick up, the trouble was largely restricted to the northern and western portions of the Kashmir Valley, close to the border with Pakistan, far from where they intended to trek in the mountains rising to the east of the valley.
2. None of the violence had been aimed at foreigners.

'We had heard consistently that as long as you stayed out of the central part of Srinagar, the summer capital, out of the old part of the city … there were typically no problems,' Jane said. Although they would have to fly in to Srinagar, they planned to stay only as long as it took them to negotiate a taxi ride south to the hill-station town of Pahalgam sixty miles away, the starting point for many treks.

Don and Jane invited some Spokane Mountaineers over for a farewell dinner. They were leaving with open minds and a back-up plan, they told them. Mount Rainier was probably far more taxing than anything they would encounter in Kashmir, Don said, reminding them that in 1981 an ice plug had fallen from above, entombing eleven climbers traversing the Ingraham Glacier on the mountain's eastern flank, the worst mountaineering accident in American history. And Don and Jane had erred on the side of caution once before, and regretted it. Having travelled to La Paz in Bolivia so as to climb to Machu Picchu, they had been warned away by local officials, only to discover from other climbers that the route had been safe.

'We're going to look into it,' Don told his friends as he bade them goodbye. 'We'll ask the authorities there: the Indian government tourism bureau and the American Embassy. We'll see what they have to say.' He had already tried to call the Indian Consulate in San Francisco several times, but had been unable to get through. He had another worry too. Jane had recently injured her shoulder, and part of the reason they had decided to head for Pahalgam was because they had read that there they could hire ponies to carry their equipment. 'That was the first choice, as I wouldn't have to carry a heavy pack,' Jane said. They promised to make some final checks upon arrival in New Delhi. 'It only seemed logical that the Indians would know best what was safe or unsafe.' For a seasoned traveller like Jane Schelly, asking people on the ground for advice seemed the logical thing to do.

India even confuses Indians. And in June 1995, a 48°C heatwave was cooking everything, including the roads, chewing them up, licking deep concave bowls into the tarmac, while the humidity that made the night queen blossom like nowhere else in the world also peeled the stucco off buildings. Jane had taken the sensible precaution of ringing ahead and booking a hotel with air-conditioning for the two nights they intended to stay in New Delhi.

But nothing had prepared them for the wall of opportunists waiting in the arrivals hall of the old Indira Gandhi International Airport, all of them with an idea, and an address. A traveller needed a rude strategy to deal with them, a fixed plan to stick by, a determined walk that gave not a scintilla of encouragement to the waiting crowd. Weakness was punished. Politeness was exploited. Indecision was manna for the middle man. Born-and-raised New Delhi-ites blanked strangers and brushed aside enquiries from touts. Surrounded by the throng, Jane and Don found their contingency plan failing the minute they arrived in New Delhi on 25 June 1995. The chaos bowled them over.

Weakened by 'thirty-five hours in the air', as Jane put it, no sooner had they collected their luggage than they were lured into a conversation with reps from a private-accommodation agency and convinced that their pre-booked hotel was a bad choice. Hustled off to a different place in another part of town, Jane and Don began their Indian journey in confusion. It happened to everyone, Don said afterwards. It was no big deal, Jane murmured. They had seen this sort of thing before.

The phone in their hotel room did not work, and the next morning Jane and Don headed out into the mêlée of New Delhi's streets. A taxi they had not ordered was waiting to take them to a private tourism agency they did not want to do business with. 'We knew there was another scam going on,' recalled Jane. 'But we said to ourselves, "OK, we'll go and we'll listen, but we'll be watchful."' At the agency, the staff proved helpful, and seemed knowledgeable about Kashmir. They assured them it was safe. The main focus of the insurgency, as Don and Jane had already heard, was far away, concentrated in the western portion of the valley near where Pakistan began, a ceasefire line so disputed that neither side could agree to call it a 'border'. Instead, it was known as the Line of Control (LoC).

This sounded reassuring. But they wanted a second opinion, and set off for the government tourism office. 'They didn't deny there were problems,' Jane said, but the general message was the same: the insurgency was very localised. Stay out of downtown Srinagar and everything would be fine. Most importantly, the trekking areas were safe. Finally, they spent an hour trawling backpacker hangouts, searching for anyone who had just returned from Kashmir. There were plenty, and those they spoke to had all had a trouble-free time. 'They seemed to love it, and gave glowing reports of the beauty,' said Jane.

Even though both of them were now flagging, Don insisted on one more stop. They took a ride to leafy Chanakyapuri, New Delhi's diplomatic enclave, to get advice at the US Embassy. 'It was closed for lunch, and we were intimidated by the long lines of people,' Jane said. 'It was hot as heck – we were jetlagged, and had been told at the Indian government tourist office that the area was OK for tourists.' They gave up, and returned to the hotel. 'If there had been a red flag at any point, then we would have researched further,' said Jane.

As Jane Schelly and Don Hutchings began to plot their Kashmir plan in the spring of 1995, Julie and Keith Mangan, from Teesside in the north-east of England, were packing for the trip of their lives, one that would also lead them to the Meadow. Casting their eyes around the world for somewhere to explore in the run-up to their tenth wedding anniversary, Julie and Keith, both aged thirty-three, had decided on India. This would be their first time in the subcontinent. In fact, it would be their first exotic trip together anywhere, a holiday they had long promised each other, having married at a time when they had been too broke to have the kind of dream honeymoon they had both wanted.

India, and Kashmir in particular, sounded very far from the close-knit and hard-working Teesside city of Middlesbrough, where Julie and Keith had grown up. With its flinty vistas of pipelines and cooling towers, it wasn't pretty, but Middlesbrough people seldom left. They worked in the vast foundries and industrial plants of companies like

British Steel. Among them had been Keith's father, Charlie Mangan, a British Steel plater whose punishing working life had left him with a miserly pension and a host of chronic ailments.

Julie and Keith loved their families, and they loved the north-east. They scorned people who denied who they were, people who over-wrote where they came from. But they needed a change. Keith had hankered to see the world since he was nine, an itch he had got when he had gone to Lake Garda in Italy on a school trip. His mother Mavis, a school dinner lady originally from Brambles Farm council estate in the east of the city, still had photos of him larking around at the water's edge with Neil Jones, his best friend. It hadn't been the greatest adventure in the world, but it had set something off in Keith, and after he married Julie he had got her thinking about travelling too.

Middlesbrough had seen its best days. When Julie and Keith were growing up in the seventies it was impoverished and struggling. Times were tough for everyone, including Julie's parents, Anita and Robert Sullivan, who lived in Eston, a working-class suburb to the east. Keith's parents had moved to up-and-coming Brookfield, in the south, where they lived with their three sons in a tidy post-war bungalow, its pristine garden being Charlie's pride and joy.

Julie and Keith had met as fifteen-year-olds at the local compre-hensive, Bertram Ramsey. Keith was not particularly interested in Julie, but that changed when he bumped into her again five years later, inside the blue double-doors of Madison's, a dive of a nightclub in Middlesbrough town centre, better known to locals as Mad Dog's, where a famed cloakroom attendant called 'Queenie' took the coats. Julie, full of life, her hair a cascade of brown curls, and Keith clicked in a way they had not at school. By then, lanky Keith, the oldest of Charlie and Mavis Mangan's three boys, had set himself up as a self-employed electrician, one of a group of school pals who had all gone into trades. Julie already had a sensible head on her shoulders, and she could see that unlike many other young men she knew, Keith was determined to do something with his life.

His mates described him as level-headed and laid-back, 'a good bloke to have around in a storm', while his father Charlie, who had barely ever left his native Teesside, was proud of his eldest son's inquisitive nature, saying to anyone who would listen that Keith 'soaked up new experiences like a sponge'. Keith was also, Julie now noticed, tall and good-looking, sure of himself but not arrogant. When they met at Mad Dog's she was working in Clinkards, a Middlesbrough shoe shop. Chatting in a corner by the bar, they found they had many friends in common. By the time Keith celebrated his twenty-first birthday six months later, on Boxing Day 1982, at the Central pub on Corporation Road, Julie knew she had found the man she wanted to marry. Keith made her laugh. He was dependable and loving. And both of them had a geeky thing for *Star Trek*.

Three years later, they became the first in their group to tie the knot. The wedding was a traditional affair of red carnations and frothy white chiffon at St Barnabas church in Linthorpe. Their white-leather wedding album shows Keith, dressed in a silver suit and winklepickers, towering above his new bride. After a make-do honeymoon, Julie became the daughter Mavis Mangan had never had. Straight-talking and easy-going like her new mother-in-law, Julie enjoyed a laugh, and embraced her new family, ringing up Mavis for a chat most days, always starting the conversation the same way: 'Hello, Mrs Mangan, it's Mrs Mangan here.' That's why Charlie and Mavis were so taken aback when Julie and Keith announced out of the blue in 1989 that they were leaving for London. Nobody in either family moved away, especially south.

But Keith and Julie lived for each other now. Leaving their home in Ingleby Barwick, a residential estate south of Middlesbrough town centre, they rented a small flat in Tooting, south London. It was a big wrench for both of them, leaving a real neighbourhood where they were surrounded by friends and family to live far away, among strangers. Middlesbrough was always only a phone call away, Julie would say to herself whenever she was alone, but in a new city as vast and anonymous as London, she struggled to make friends.

To start with, the Tooting flat didn't look much, but Julie tarted it up. Keith, already planning their next jump, hopefully to somewhere hotter, put his energies into developing his business, and began picking up contract work all over Europe. It wasn't the kind of travelling he had had in mind: without Julie, just a bunch of lads who rarely saw anything but the inside of one project or another. But the money was good, and he started to save. Left behind in Tooting, Julie wasn't going to sit on her hands. She trained as a nursery nurse, took cake-decorating classes and got herself a job.

In 1994, Julie and Keith got the break they were looking for when a Sri Lankan friend invited them to Colombo to meet his family. At first it was just pub talk, a crazy idea bandied about over a few pints. But the more they thought about it, the more they realised they wanted it. They didn't have kids yet. They had worked hard, saved well, and now they were ready to leave it all behind. It wasn't intended to be a permanent break, just eighteen months travelling around the world, chasing new experiences. Sri Lanka would be a soft landing for the voyage into the unknown. Just the thought of giving up Tooting for the South Asian island sent a shiver through both of them. From there, they could go anywhere. In early 1995 they took the plunge. They bought two rucksacks, matching petrol-blue his-and-hers bomber jackets, walking boots and travel guides. They went back up to the north-east on the train to break the news. So far only a couple of destinations, Colombo and New Delhi, were definite, but the climax to the trip would be dinner in front of the Taj Mahal on 3 August. That would be a proper tenth-wedding anniversary, Julie and Keith told their family and friends. In Eston and Brookfield, there were stunned faces.

Julie and Keith Mangan's leaving bash at the Ship, a pub in Eston, around the corner from Julie's parents' house, was a proper drunken affair, even if afterwards they had a last-minute wobble. But they had already bought the tickets. Keith had sold his electrical business to a schoolmate. They'd given notice on the Tooting flat, and Julie had resigned from work. It was too late to turn back. A few days later they pitched up in Colombo, jetlagged and initially overwhelmed by the heat. But it did not take them long to realise they had made the right decision. They had the run of the golden beaches of Galle. Their Sri

Lankan friend was there to show them around, and they gorged themselves on seafood. The first few weeks flew by so easily that Julie persuaded Anita to come over. Going home full of stories, Anita worked on Mavis and Charlie Mangan too. Keith's parents had barely ever left the north-east, but now they all made plans to meet up in Sri Lanka in one year's time. Before then, there was so much to do. Julie and Keith were ready to explore.

Having talked to other travellers, they locked on to Kashmir. What struck them when they entered the Indian Consulate in Colombo were the posters. 'Paradise on Earth', one declared above a photograph of rosy-cheeked Kashmiri women picking saffron in a crocus-filled meadow beneath a dramatic, snow-capped Himalayan skyline. Emblazoned across another scene of gaily-painted wooden *shikaras* skimming across Dal Lake were the words 'Garden of Eden'. As the sweat trickled down Julie and Keith's backs, the images of Kashmir's spectacular peaks seemed to offer the prospect of welcome relief from the humidity of Sri Lanka. The Kashmiri people were welcoming, they were told, while the floating hotels of Dal Lake provided luxury for only a handful of rupees a night. Julie and Keith were keen for a change of scene.

They were going to Kashmir. They did not know where in Kashmir. They did not know anything about Kashmir. Perhaps they would stay on a houseboat before heading off on a mountain trek. Nothing too exhausting, just far enough to see the flower-filled pastures they had been reading about in the Lonely Planet guidebook – and of course the Meadow. It sounded idyllic. But when Keith rang home to wish his father a happy sixtieth birthday and mentioned their plans, Charlie was horrified, and did his best to dissuade him. Mavis tried to reassure her husband. 'Keith's a sensible lad,' she said. 'He wouldn't go off the beaten path.' 'Ring the British Embassy if you get into trouble,' was all she could think to say to her son.

In June 1995, Paul Wells, a twenty-four-year-old photography student from Blackburn, Lancashire, was also packing. He had planned a life-changing trip to the Indian subcontinent, but he didn't want to be alone. He had spent much of the spring trying to persuade his reluctant girlfriend, Catherine Moseley, to come with him.

Paul had just inherited a Nikon camera and a small cash legacy from his grandfather, and he intended to use them to put together a photographic project that he hoped would launch his career as a photojournalist. For several months he had been searching around for the right location, and after seeing *Desert in the Sky*, a TV documentary about the Buddhist kingdom of Ladakh, the same place Jane Schelly and Don Hutchings had visited in 1991, he knew it was where he would go. He had loved the film so much that his mother, Dianne, had recorded it, and still has the video today. 'He was fascinated by the eagles turning on the thermals,' said Dianne, who remembered Paul sitting in the family home in Blackburn, watching the film over and over again. 'It was another world to me, but the isolated mountain region appealed to Paul, who'd developed a fascination with spirituality and reincarnation.' Bob, Paul's father, said: 'Once he'd seen that bloody film, he was determined. He was off buying maps and guidebooks.' He also spent £800 on photographic equipment. 'After he latched on to something, there was no stopping him. That was our Paul.'

Paul wanted Cath, as he called his girlfriend, to go with him, but she was not grabbed by the idea. She was busy, she told him, committed to her demanding social-work job. Then there was the expense. 'He told her he would cover all the costs out of his legacy,' said Bob. 'Paul saw it as one "last big holiday" before they moved apart. He hoped to be able to spend some time together before Cath went off to study in another part of the country, and he just nagged at her until she gave in.' By the middle of May 1995, the trip was on. 'In the end, she did a trade,' remembered Dianne. 'She'd come, as long as they went to the forts and palaces of Rajasthan, in western India, after he'd got the Kashmiri mountains out of his system.'

Paul had always loved exploring. 'Walking, climbing up things, hanging off things,' was how Bob put it. 'Walking is in our family's blood. Paul just stuck at it, and always went further than the rest of us.' When Paul was growing up, the family moved around regularly, following Bob's work at Debenhams department store, where he managed the gents' suit department. Dapper Bob, originally from the West Country, had taken the family to Scotland, and then to England's north-west. For Dianne, originally from Ealing in west London, it was an unsettling existence. 'To be honest, wherever I was, was too far away from family and friends,' she says. When they finally set up home in a modern cul-de-sac on the Pinewood estate in Feniscowles, a suburb of Blackburn, she had been delighted. They would not move again, Bob promised.

Paul enrolled at Feniscowles Junior School. Of the three Wells children, he was always the reckless one. 'He spent more time outside the head teacher's office than in the class,' recalled Bob. 'There was no telling Paul. If he had any idea in his head he just went for it.' But soon after moving to Blackburn, Paul formed a steadying bond with Dianne's father, Grandpa Seymour. With the Lake District on their doorstep, Seymour introduced Paul to hill walking, climbing and orienteering. Soon the young boy and his grandfather were off most weekends, walking a section of the Pennine Way, or climbing Low Fell or Helvellyn.

By the time Paul was a teenager, he was struggling academically at Darwen Vale High School. But he could happily guide a party up Scafell Pike, and family photos show him standing tall in an Aertex shirt against the hills, walking socks wrinkled around his bony ankles, his face sun-bronzed, his hair wind-ruffled. He dreamed of following in the footsteps of Chris Bonington, Britain's most famous mountaineer. A former army instructor, Bonington had led a life that Paul wanted to emulate. While Dianne thought he was studying upstairs in his bedroom, his head was with Bonington, on Everest and K2. 'The walls of his room were covered in pictures of the Himalayas,' says Dianne. 'He had all Chris Bonington's books, and would read them obsessively.'

Paul's parents knew he wouldn't get the grades to go to university. He didn't care. After leaving school he followed in Bonington's footsteps, seeking out an outward-bound training course sponsored by the armed forces. But, reckless as ever, he abandoned it in favour of a last-minute climbing holiday in Spain. For two weeks he trekked alone through the El Chorro gorge in Andalusia, coming back with a new idea. 'That time alone gave him pause for thought,' says Bob. Grandpa Seymour always carried a camera, and Paul loved tinkering around in his darkroom. In the autumn of 1994 Paul signed on for a Diploma in Photography at South Nottingham College, finally moving out of home at the age of twenty-three. '"Paul Wells, the photojournalist" – he liked the sound of that,' said Bob. 'He was always backing the underdog, getting into the wild. It was the perfect career for him, and he chanced on the idea all by himself.'

It was in Nottingham that Paul hooked up with Catherine Moseley, an art graduate from Norwich whom he met at a gig in Rock City, a venue whose manager liked to call it 'an oasis of alternative culture in a desert of Gaz-and-Shazness'. Cath was a willowy blonde social worker at Base 51, a drop-in centre for troubled Nottingham teens, and her romance with Paul was intense. Paul was not afraid to speak his mind. He was only ever going to be himself. Two years older than him, Cath was quieter, having grown up in middle-class Norfolk. Paul was smitten, and as far as his parents could see, Cath too was committed to their having a real life together.

When Grandpa Seymour died unexpectedly just before Christmas 1994, Paul was 'crushed', according to his father. But after the funeral Paul picked himself up and went back to college in Nottingham, taking his younger brother Stuart along as a flatmate. With the money his grandfather left him, he could afford his first real taste of foreign adventure. All he talked about that spring was the Ladakh plan. And he had kept going on at Cath: 'Please come away with me to India. It will change our lives forever.'

Even though she had finally said yes, Cath was still nervous as summer approached. She called tour agencies in Nottingham, and went so far as to contact the Foreign Office for its latest advice on travelling to India. Ladakh was part of the troubled Jammu and Kashmir state, she was told, but this eastern sector had been untouched by the conflict that rumbled on further west.

The cheapest way for Paul and Cath to travel from New Delhi to Ladakh was to take a bus to Srinagar, a grinding thirty-hour trip, before getting a connection along the Kargil road to Leh and finally to Ladakh, another two days' journey. Like Jane Schelly and Don Hutchings, they were told that the riskiest part of the trip was the time they would have to spend in Srinagar. If they wanted to avoid travelling through the Kashmir Valley there was a more circuitous route via Himachal Pradesh, to Kashmir's south. Or they could fly. Since the last option was too pricey, and no one in the UK appeared to know much about the first two, they decided to make their decision in New Delhi.

Towards the end of the summer term, Cath booked the flights and a hotel in New Delhi. 'She got their jabs sorted, too,' says Bob. 'Paul even went to the dentist and got his fillings fixed.' As they waved Paul and Cath off from Manchester Airport on 15 June, Paul's parents felt a pang of fear. Dianne wondered when she would see him again. 'Don't worry,' Bob reassured her, putting an arm around her shoulder. He was pleased that his son was at last sorting himself out. 'Paul can look after himself. He's a strong lad.' For Dianne, the only saving grace was that Cath was going with him.

Jetlagged and dehydrated, Paul Wells and Cath Moseley arrived at Indira Gandhi International Airport on 16 June. As Jane Schelly and Don Hutchings would nine days later, they fell prey to a tout. This one convinced them that people were rioting in the street near their pre-booked hotel, and that he should take them somewhere safer instead. Panicked and sweating, they agreed, only to find themselves deposited at the entrance to Paharganj, a swamp of squalid backpacker hostels opposite New Delhi railway station.

Lost, Paul and Cath lugged their overstuffed rucksacks past dusty roadside stalls displaying joss sticks, scarves and fake silver. Eventually they found the hotel the taxi driver had recommended, a tumbledown establishment where a handful of teenage boys lay snoring on the floor behind the reception desk. Paul and Cath gingerly stepped over them, trying to block out the pungent smells, and headed for their room.

Over the next couple of days, as they acclimatised to the heat and the lack of sanitation, they tried to make the best of it, buying home-spun Indian *kurtas* and quizzing young travellers over banana pancakes and coffee laced with condensed milk about routes to Ladakh. The owner of their hotel turned out to be a Kashmiri, and offered to book their onward trip for a small commission. They opted for the bus to Srinagar, a journey that would involve travelling north across the New Delhi plains and into the Punjab, before striking north-west to Jammu and the Pir Panjal mountains, taking them, according to their map, alarmingly near to fractious Pakistan. As they left, the hotel owner pressed a handful of his relatives' business cards into their hands, 'Just in case you want to stay in Kashmir.'

John Childs was heading towards the Meadow too, although he did not know it yet. By the time Jane Schelly and Don Hutchings, Keith and Julie Mangan, Paul Wells and Cath Moseley had arrived in New Delhi, the forty-two-year-old chemical engineer from Simsbury, Connecticut, had already been in India several weeks, although his experience of the subcontinent could hardly have been more different from theirs. Childs, an introvert and a deep thinker, a wiry figure whose hangdog expression belied his quick wits and dry humour, was not joining any hippy trail. When he wasn't in his running gear he was happiest in a suit and tie addressing executives in New England boardrooms. He worked for an American weapons manufacturer, Ensign Bickford, and had come to India to tour explosives plants in and around West Bengal. His schedule had been put under the micro-scope and mulled over for many months – nothing he did was uncon-sidered, and all too often he tended to see the worst in everything. But then, he was the kind of man who had learned to celebrate his own fatalism. He had worried about this journey for several months, but in the end he had decided to go for it. It would be his first foreign trip for the firm he had joined the previous February, and he hoped that at worst, even if he was struck down with dysentery, it would take his mind off the messy divorce that he feared was going to put a distance between him and his much-loved daughters, Cathy, six, and Mary, five. There was another upside to the visit. After the work was done, he hoped to get in some trekking on the company's account. And as John was a self-confessed 'cheapskate', born watching the nickels and dimes, this was a boon. 'I never go anywhere without someone else paying,' he liked to say.

However, from the moment he landed in Calcutta, John, who had grown up surrounded by suburbia on Long Island, New York, the second son of churchgoing Joseph and Helen Childs, found the teeming subcontinent oppressive. India was a chaotic mix of vinegary odours. He couldn't eat the food. He felt as if he could bench-press the humidity, it weighed so heavily on him. Not widely travelled, he was overwhelmed by the surface details that the locals did not seem to notice, the 'noise and filth', as he put it. He also found it more difficult than he had expected to communicate with his Indian counterparts, even though they were all supposedly 'talking the same language', and he knew in an instant that he had nothing in common with the Western travellers who milled around the Saddar Street backpacker area, close to his five-star hotel. John had gone straight from school to college, and then into his first job. He couldn't see the point of putting off the inevitable by travelling aimlessly around the globe. He was always uneasy around people like that.

After Calcutta, John's colleagues had driven him several hours into the industrial heartland of Bihar, a state that even Indians call the Wild West because of its reputation for corruption and chicanery. He was appalled by the grime-cloaked factories, staffed by hordes of impoverished workers who toiled in atrocious conditions: 'Coming from the land of the free, I could not take in how people could live and work like that.' His final work destination was Gomia, a town in southern Bihar where an enormous explosives factory was operated by the British chemical giant ICI. The plan was that he would work there with local managers and technical staff on improving the quality of the explosive materials they supplied to Ensign Bickford.

By the end of June, John's work was done, and as he had planned, he had a week in hand. Back home in Simsbury he was an endurance athlete, proud of the fact that he ran four or five miles around the local school track every day. He climbed and skied too. Doing business just down the road from the greatest mountain range on earth – he had seen the Himalayas on the flight over to Calcutta and been staggered by their jagged heights – had been one of the reasons he had agreed to make this trip.

But where in the Himalayas should he go? He had thought about doing part of Nepal's challenging Annapurna Circuit, the mountain trek Jane and Don had completed in 1988, and there were regular flight connections between Calcutta and Kathmandu. But then he came across the adverse weather reports, just as Jane and Don had: 'When I set about looking into it, I realised pretty quickly it was the wrong time of year for Nepal. The monsoon ruled this option out.' The 'real treat' of seeing Everest was now out of the question, but running his finger along the range to the west he could see other options: 'All the guides said the same thing. June and July was the best time of year to visit Kashmir.' Wherever he ended up would be an adventure, he thought, as he zeroed in on the trekking routes in the Kashmir Valley.

Was it safe? John was no authority on the region, but even he knew that Kashmir was troubled by a simmering war he was 'vaguely aware of' from the occasional news report. However, the descriptions and photographs he studied of the treks around Pahalgam, to the south-west of the summer capital, Srinagar, were inviting. Was it possible to reach the mountains without being caught up in the state's insurgency? He was still feeling fragile as a result of the divorce, and he had two confused young daughters back home, about whom he had worried constantly since arriving in India. The last thing he needed was to screw things up by getting himself in a tight spot on the other side of the world. He rang his mother, who was still his main confidante, in Salem in upstate New York. 'Check things out with the locals,' she said. 'They'll know what is and isn't safe.'

John sounded out several of his Indian colleagues at the Gomia plant. 'Half of them jumped straight in. They said I was crazy. They said there was a war going on. Didn't I know? There had been some kind of kidnapping involving Westerners the previous summer too.

But the other half said it was fine to go, and the 1994 incident had been quickly resolved with no one hurt.' Like every other discussion he had had since arriving in India, this one quickly dissolved into a confusing roundabout of conflicting arguments, with everyone talking over each other.

Most vocal were a couple of Kashmiri staffers. They were in the camp that firmly believed he should go. Over a cup of tea, they told him alluring stories of the challenging trekking, the wildlife and the wildness around Pahalgam. It was a world away from the troubles, they said, 'a paradise on earth that everyone should experience at least once in their lives'. All Kashmiris knew, they insisted, that the insurgency was restricted to the LoC and to militant-infested towns in the north of the valley like Kupwara, Sopore and Baramulla. No one had any interest in getting tourists mixed up in a local dispute. The militancy had been rumbling on for six years already, and Pahalgam remained thronged with trekkers.

These two employees seemed credible and likeable, and they gave John numbers for local contacts: guides, hotels and taxi drivers, many of whom they were related to and said they trusted completely. Eventually, even the cautious John was persuaded, and he arranged a six-day excursion through his hotel. Taking account of flight connections, that would give him four days' trekking, which was just about enough. 'In life, you go to many places and you have to make many judgements about your own safety,' he said. 'And my judgement at that moment in time was that Kashmir would be OK.'

As their plane approached Srinagar airport on 26 June, Jane Schelly and Don Hutchings had heart-stopping glimpses of the Himalayas bursting through the clouds, and a lattice of orchards, conifers and villages sprinkled across the dun-coloured Kashmir Valley. After bumping down on the runway, the plane rumbled past rows of Indian Air Force fighter jets, military transporters and camouflaged helicopters. Here were gun emplacements and corrugated-iron hangars, all of them draped in olive-green netting. Sentries in foxholes, machine-gunners in pillboxes, zoomed in on the plane. Jane and Don immediately forgot the reassuring news they had just read in the paper: US Ambassador Frank Wisner, accompanied by his daughter, had returned from a fly-fishing trip to Pahalgam. This place looked like a war zone.

But as they stepped down onto the tarmac, the cool air was a joy after New Delhi. Up ahead, beyond the exit barrier, what looked like a thousand sombre male faces, many of them bearded, most of them smoking, eyed them. Aquiline noses, cat-green eyes, skin so fair that many seemed more Aryan than Don or Jane – some Kashmiris could have passed as Europeans. The noise was overwhelming: a helicopter whumping somewhere above them, tour guides shouting to get their attention.

As Jane and Don stood by the ancient, flaking luggage carousel, a police official sought them out and took their names, passport details and notes on their itinerary. 'Foreigner registration,' he said by way of explanation, tapping a laminated label on his clipboard. 'What a madhouse,' Jane recalled. 'It was an absolute nightmare … I had to open and taste my sealed pack of Western Trail mix to show it wasn't poison or a bomb. The absolute bizarreness of the whole process almost made it entertaining.'

Outside, the full scale of the Indian military operation in Kashmir hit them: a chaotic jumble of sandbags, concrete barriers and barbed wire, the roads jammed with armoured vehicles of all descriptions: trucks, pickups, tanks, around which scores of heavily armed soldiers milled. It took an hour to get through the checkpoints encircling the airport. Barrelling into town, their taxi passed yet more bunkers and pickets, out of which dark-skinned Indian soldiers peered, their guns aimed at Kashmiri men and women who walked solemnly along the broken pavements, heads cast downwards.

Gigantic piles of decomposing trash were everywhere, with sleeping pi-dogs lying on top of them. Not a windowpane seemed intact. Shops were barricaded or boarded up. Long avenues lined by trees were choked by every kind of machine of war imaginable. At one point the driver slammed on his brakes to avoid an oncoming army convoy, a vast column of khaki lorries with soldiers riding atop them, their faces obscured by black bandanas, who beat canes on the side of the taxi, drumming everyone out of their way. 'Welcome to Kashmir,' he muttered under his breath. Jane and Don said nothing. 'We hadn't expected things to be this bad, no way,' Jane said.

Then she and Don caught a glimpse of the mountains ringing the city, and the hairs rose on her arms.

TWO

A Father's Woes

For most of his working life, Master Allah Baksh Sabir Alvi had been a teacher of religious studies at a government school in Bahawalpur, Pakistan, lecturing indifferent boys in what had once been the influential capital of a Rajputana princely state, a glittering city lorded over by a Muslim *nawab* and his entourage. Nowadays Bahawalpur was a chaotic sprawl of back-street mosques, low-lying mud-brick compounds and potholed roads, on the banks of the Sutlej River. Deep in the heart of the scorched southern Punjab, it was encircled by fields of cotton, sugarcane and corn, and these days it was ruled by a small circle of feudal landowners or *zamindars*, industrialists and entrepreneurs, who squeezed all they could out of the impoverished majority.

The only thing everyone had was faith. Here and there, down traffic-choked streets and back alleys, was a multitude of mosques and *madrassas* (religious schools). When Master Alvi was growing up there had been a few dozen *madrassas* in the city, and perhaps only two hundred throughout Pakistan. By the time he retired there were twenty thousand across the country, some consisting only of breeze-block classrooms, others gathered around the marble apron of grand mosques. Like most people in Bahawalpur, whether by profession or dint of the especially charged atmosphere of religiosity, Master Alvi spent his days praying, reading and discussing the Koran.

Most Bahawalpuris were conservative Sunni Muslims, their faith shaped by Deobandism, an austere revivalist sect that had emanated more than a hundred years earlier from Deoband, a town over the

31

border in the Indian state of Uttar Pradesh. Many living in Bahawalpur today originated there, but were forced to flee India at Partition in 1947. Millions of Muslims had abandoned their ancestral homes in the central plains of India and its former princely states as stories spread that the new India would welcome only Hindus. Families were torn apart, villages destroyed and hundreds of thousands massacred, former friends and neighbours killing each other, sending thousands of trains speeding east and west, carrying a tide of people to an uncertain future. In the years that followed, while India flourished, life in the new nation of Pakistan became ever harder. Supporters there of Deoband became increasingly sectarian, their tone and demeanour echoing that of the oasis-dwelling Wahhabis of Saudi Arabia, who championed a return to the medieval life described in the Koran.

Master Alvi and his circle were as literal-minded as you could get. Known among more liberal neighbours as the 'no-doubters', they were certain about everything, especially matters ecumenical. Alvi and his followers believed that every form and facet of Islam that was not of the Deobandi-infused Sunni school was contemptible. These opinions were passed down through the family like a gold watch. But while the Alvis sought security and comfort in an age that no longer existed, the world outside Bahawalpur was changing fast. And in the summer of 1995, Master Alvi confided in his friends that for the first time since Partition, nothing seemed certain.

He had read how Islam was under attack in many places around the world. In former Yugoslavia, Serbs were massacring Bosnian Muslims in a genocidal onslaught. In the Caucasus, Russia had launched a war against Chechen Muslims, leaving many thousands dead. Most distressing, as it was nearer and involved a people he regarded as his closest brothers and sisters, was the Muslim uprising over the border in Indian Kashmir, which was being put down by hundreds of thousands of Indian security forces, turning the Kashmir Valley, once regarded as a jewel, into one of the most heavily militarised regions in the world.

Master Alvi had more personal worries concerning Kashmir, too. The 'rock' of Kausar Colony, as he was known to his neighbours in the comparatively well-to-do community where he lived, by whom he was regarded as a matchmaker, troubleshooter, arbitrator, religious pundit and general go-between, a man who was trusted, loathed and envied in equal measure (like all big religious fish in small barrels), Alvi had a serious problem that needed fixing. One of his sons, his favourite, Masood Azhar, the third boy of eleven children, had gone missing in Indian-administered Kashmir.

Although Master Alvi still thought of him as his 'golden child', Masood was actually twenty-seven, short-sighted and a squat five foot two inches tall. Sporting an oversized pair of aviator shades and a luxuriant beard, Masood had, much to his father's delight, embraced the family business of 'no doubting' with great enthusiasm, becoming the scourge of all *kufrs*, or unbelievers, including Muslims who did not adhere to the Deobandi way, such as Shias, whom he once described in a pamphlet as 'cockroaches'. Masood was not handsome or charming – his siblings teased him for being a 'little fatty', according to a relative. One brother joked, in an aside that was passed around Kausar Colony, that with his head swathed in an Arab *keffiyeh* and his body robed in a white cotton shawl over traditional white *kurta* pyjamas, Masood looked like a 'fundamentalist pupae'. But when he opened his mouth, something happened. Elaborate bursts of English, Urdu, Persian and Arabic flew out, arpeggios of assertions that, despite his somewhat high-pitched delivery, stopped people in their tracks.

Masood had the gift of the gab, something that had first been noticed at the age of four, when he recited lengthy tracts of the Koran at the local *maktab* (Islamic elementary school). After winning prizes for public speaking, he had caught the eye of a relative who taught at Darul Uloom Islamia Binori Town, a wealthy mosque and *madrassa* a short bus ride from downtown Karachi, Pakistan's largest city, five hundred miles south of Bahawalpur, on the Arabian Sea. One of the largest religious seminaries in Pakistan, Binori Town was widely recognised as among the world's most influential centres of Deobandi ideology.

To Deobandis, Binori Town, with its vast, sprawling campus, dusky pink towers, delicate, white-topped minarets and grand gateway, was *Paris*. Since its foundation in the 1950s by the religious scholar Yusuf Binori, members of every faction of the biggest Sunni religious-political party in Pakistan, the Assembly of Islamic Clergy, had vied to study there. Having one's son among its 3,500 students was considered a blessing that would markedly raise one's standing in the community.

In 1981, a year after twelve-year-old Masood had been enrolled and Master Alvi had received the necessary plaudits, the *madrassa* began taking its students down a new path, one that would transform the course of Masood's life. Exciting dispatches had begun arriving from Afghanistan, sent by three recent Binori Town graduates who, styling themselves 'The Companions of the Afghan People', had headed up to Peshawar, in Pakistan's North-West Frontier province, a gateway to neighbouring Afghanistan, where they had joined the *mujahideen* fighting against the Soviet Red Army that had occupied Kabul eighteen months previously. This anti-Soviet campaign was being secretly funded by the US government through the CIA, and run on the ground by its Pakistani counterpart, the Directorate of Inter Services Intelligence (ISI). Pakistan's premier intelligence agency was a secretive organisation, with enormous resources, whose skilled agents, never publicly identified, were universally feared for spying on, abducting, torturing and executing Pakistanis, as well as ruthlessly meddling in the affairs of the country's neighbours. Now in Afghanistan, knee-deep in America's battle to temper Moscow's regional ambitions, the ISI made sure that it got a grip on the recruitment and training of those Pakistanis who went there to fight, as well as on the Afghani tribes being trained to mount resistance.

The three graduates from Binori Town had undergone basic training, supervised by military instructors borrowed from the Pakistan armed forces and the ISI, and paid for by the CIA, before being sent through the Khyber Pass to do battle with the Red Army. Stories of the Companions' bravery in Khost and Kandahar were read aloud at

Binori Town after Friday prayers, entrancing many students, including Masood Azhar.

By the time Masood was fifteen, in 1983, one of the three Binori Town graduates had been martyred in Afghanistan, another had vanished, presumed dead, while the third had become a famed warrior with the *nom de guerre* 'Saifullah', or Sword of Islam. Reports of his continuing exploits spurred on a second generation of graduates from his old alma mater, who streamed up from Karachi to the Afghan border by bus, lorry and cart. Some of them joined Harkat ul-Mujahideen – the Order of Holy Warriors – a movement of Afghanistan-bound *mujahids* that had been established by Binori Town scholar Maulana Fazlur Rehman Khalil.

With his belly-quivering rhetoric, Maulana Khalil rang the bell for *jihad* so loudly that thousands volunteered for battle from the Karachi mosque complex; with Master Alvi's help, many more came from *madrassas* across the southern Punjab. Soon Maulana Khalil and Master Alvi's efforts had drawn the attention of the ISI, which noted that the Holy Warriors were making a significant contribution to their Afghan operation. According to the indiscreet Alvi himself, the ISI began to finance the Order. A former student claimed that cash stuffed inside jute rice sacks was delivered to the main canteen at Binori Town mosque. Convalescent centres for wounded fighters were opened nearby. Some of the ISI money was used to extend the large network of affiliated *madrassas* all over Pakistan, especially in the lawless tribal areas of the north-west, where Pashtun tribesmen liked to say they had been 'born to fight'. Money aside, the system was soon self-sustaining. Those who survived Afghanistan, coming back to Karachi as *ghazis*, or returning war heroes, gave inspiring speeches to students during lessons and at Friday prayers, priming the next generation for a holy *jihad*, while Binori Town was guaranteed a steady stream of willing new pupils from across Pakistan, most of whom arrived as six-year-olds who were then steeped in a deeply conservative curriculum tinged by the ethos of the Dark Ages.

* * *

Among the thousands of students, Masood Azhar stood out. He quickly gained a reputation for his oratory prowess and religious fervour. Maulana Khalil, who visited Binori Town regularly, came to hear of him. 'He thought I had talents that needed growing,' Masood later reflected solemnly, when, at the tender age of twenty-five, he put pen to paper and wrote down his life story for other students to read. 'Had this not been my path since I was a child?'

By the time Masood reached ninth grade, Maulana Khalil announced that he would be sent 'for *jihad*' with other students from his class. Masood was unnerved. He had always been an 'indoors' child, preferring the company of his mother and siblings to the tough neighbourhood boys who played cricket in the street. Since becoming a teenager he had been desk-bound, and had grown used to the creature comforts of Binori Town, preferring a rickshaw to walking, and growing fat on plates of tender *nihari*, the spicy meat stew that many Pakistanis regard as their national dish. The prospect of roughing it in a desert training camp in Afghanistan horrified him, he wrote candidly. He managed to wriggle out of the trip, writing later that 'I could not participate physically because of my studies. [Instead] I sent a few of my relatives including one of my brothers for *jihad*.'

However, when Masood graduated in 1988, aged twenty, Khalil again offered him a place at a *mujahideen* training camp. This time Masood could not refuse, and a few weeks later found himself at a Holy Warriors base in Yawar Kili, a sprawling mud-brick compound in the bronze desert outside the southern Afghan border town of Khost. Camp Yawar, with its subterranean classrooms, dormitories and bomb shelters carved from the bedrock, came as a severe shock to a young cleric more accustomed to air-conditioned prayer halls. Swarming with brawny recruits, who scrambled on their hands and knees under nets and peppered distant targets with bullets, it was run by Saifullah, the Binori Town graduate turned *mujahid*, whose abilities were by now legendary. Although he was pleased to meet a warrior about whom he had heard so much, Masood, exhausted by his three-day journey by pickup and pony and overwhelmed by the 50°C heat, confided to his private journal that he was 'appalled' by what greeted him.

Overweight and short of breath, Masood failed to make it through the forty-day basic training. But as the young man had been sent with the personal blessing of Maulana Khalil, Saifullah could not return him to Karachi uninitiated in battle, so he dispatched him to the front line anyway. Needing to relieve himself in the middle of the night, Masood emerged from the dugout where his unit was sleeping and forgot, in the darkness, to utter a password to the guards. Believing that Soviet-backed Afghan forces were mounting an ambush, they opened fire, and Masood received a bullet wound to the leg. Saifullah was horrified, and arranged for Masood to be stretchered back to Karachi immediately, accompanied by one of his most trusted lieutenants. The calamitous story was reported to the ISI, whose agents still recall reading it incredulously. For a lesser recruit, this incident would have signalled an ignoble exit from the world of *jihad*. But Master Alvi was too important a figure in the Deobandi movement for his son to be cast aside. After recuperating, Masood was asked to become editor of *Sadai Mujahid* (Voice of the *Mujahid*), the Holy Warriors' weekly magazine and recruiting officer.

Masood enthusiastically embraced his new position. It gave him a chance to spread his message to a far wider audience, and he let his imagination run wild, creating in one edition a fantastical story of how a young *mujahid* named Masood, who was filled with a passion for *jihad*, had been cut down by a Russian sniper, but bravely struggled back to his trench. 'This left a lasting impact on me and caused a revolution in my heart and mind,' Masood wrote, imagining himself as the semi-fictional character in the narrative. 'That's why I resolved with Allah to spread the message of *jihad* (besides waging practical *jihad* at every opportunity).'

Available for five rupees outside mosques and bookshops throughout Pakistan, Masood's magazine became a smash, selling tens of thousands of copies every Friday. In its pages he wove a spell around the battle being fought in the dusty mountains of Afghanistan, concluding later, in an unpublished memoir, that his words had been responsible for 'the spread of the *jihad* task on a vast scale'. A speaking tour followed, visiting '*maktabs*, *masjids*, streets and bazaars of

Karachi ... without ever taking a holiday'. Soon Masood was in demand all over Sindh and the Punjab, too, where he was introduced, often with his father Master Alvi at his side, as a war veteran who 'ignited fire in the hearts of the people'.

Wherever he went, the Russian sniper story preceded him, and after a while he began using it to explain his pronounced limp. Despite his youth, the twenty-one-year-old Masood was now addressed with the epithet '*Hazrat*', the respected one. But by 1989, with the conflict in Afghanistan on the wane, and Soviet forces retreating from Kabul, Masood was at a loose end. Many battle-hardened Afghani *jihadis* and their Pakistani counterparts had begun spilling over the border into Peshawar and Quetta, the capital of Pakistan's south-western Balochistan province. Tens of thousands more set up home in Karachi's outer suburbs. For a time it looked as if the Holy Warriors would stagnate completely – until a spook with a new project emerged from the woodwork.

Privately he was known as 'Brigadier Badam' because of the almond milk he drank like whisky, in shots from small glasses, having given up alcohol during the dry years of the Afghan *mujahideen*. An ISI veteran with more than thirty years' service, the Brigadier had been one of those responsible for distributing the CIA's cash for the past decade, US dollars that had been flown into Islamabad, stacked up on wooden pallets. The Brigadier, who is now retired, although he continues to dabble in politics and religion, knew back then how to get the most from his money. One day it would be a truckload of Kalashnikovs for a tribal elder who was running out of steam, and the next a wad of banknotes for an unruly *mujahideen* commander complaining about the carnivorous Soviet front. He had become an expert in unconventional warfare, and knew how to build and maintain a private army. He also had some ideas about how to redeploy the Holy Warriors, sending them to fight for a new cause that would benefit the Islamic Republic of Pakistan.

Ever since the Soviets had begun withdrawing from Afghanistan, with refugees flooding into Peshawar, fearful of what would replace the Red Army, Pakistan had been secretly preparing, in the words of General Zia-ul-Haq, the country's most recent military dictator, to 'make something of Kashmir'. Now the eyes of the army and the ISI had been drawn by the fortuitous events taking place on the other side of the LoC. The local insurgency had just exploded there, with hundreds of thousands of people rising up in the Muslim-dominated valley. 'Pakistan's security agencies, the army and the ISI, would never pass up an opportunity to make India, the perennial enemy, bleed,' Badam said.

In the Brigadier's mind was an idea to send battle-hardened veterans from the Afghan war over the border into Indian-administered Kashmir to boost the insurgency. Almost as soon as it had come into being following Partition in 1947, Pakistan had felt that it had got the dirty end of the stick. The new Islamic republic was awkwardly formed of two halves: West Pakistan, the area west of India that is the Pakistan of today, and East Pakistan, the region east of India that is now Bangladesh. Maps of the subcontinent resembled two green Muslim batwings encircling a great saffron-coloured Hindu heart. A deep sense of insecurity settled over the divided country, an unfading paranoia about the bigger, wealthier and better-armed India that sat in the middle.

In its hurry to leave the subcontinent, Britain had left such haphazard borders that the two new countries began fighting over territory immediately. One of the most contested areas was East Pakistan, where a sizeable proportion of the population wanted independence, and the Himalayan principality of Jammu and Kashmir, whose Hindu monarch had sided with India against the wishes of his Muslim subjects. The deal that Maharaja Hari Singh had signed with India's last Governor General, Lord Mountbatten, had resulted in the mountain kingdom being divided up like spoils: a small portion of western Kashmir, Gilgit and Baltistan going to Pakistan, while Hindu-dominated Jammu, the Muslim Kashmir Valley and tiny, Buddhist Ladakh remained with India. Later, Pakistan had gifted bits and pieces to China, which went on to seize another slice from India. Ever since, India had continued to claim all of Kashmir while holding just over

40 per cent of it, while Pakistan, administrating just under 40 per cent, wanted it too, but publicly insisted that every Kashmiri had the right to decide his or her own destiny,

The two countries had fought many times over these disputed territories. The most serious conflagration came in December 1971, when Indian Prime Minister Indira Gandhi had ordered an assault on East Pakistan, which had ended after barely two weeks, with the Pakistan Army forced into a humiliating surrender at Dhaka racecourse. Pakistan had never recovered from what it regarded as a deeply shameful moment in its young history, and ever since, its military leaders and the ISI had been searching for the right lever to pull so as to reassert themselves. Now, in 1989, with the war in Afghanistan coming to a close, tens of thousands of pumped-up Muslim guerrillas at a loose end and Kashmir boiling up of its own accord, it was obvious to Brigadier Badam (and many others he served with) that their moment had come.

According to a journal written by Masood and later seized by Pakistani federal investigators, the Brigadier approached Maulana Khalil in Karachi with a proposal. The ISI was prepared to offer $25,000 a month to the Holy Warriors to find fighters to wage war in Kashmir, a sum that could rise dramatically if Maulana Khalil achieved anything like his success in Afghanistan. The Brigadier added, Masood recalled, that there was money to spend because for years the ISI had been siphoning off American cash intended for Afghanistan and putting it into a contingency fund to aid rebellion in Kashmir. To date, Pakistan's activities there had been restricted to reaching out to the leaders of Kashmir's indigenous freedom struggle, clandestine meetings often being staged in Saudi Arabia, where participants met under the cover of going on *Haj*.

There had been the odd ISI-sponsored incident in Kashmir, like the time in 1983 when India had played the West Indies in a one-day cricket international at the Sher-i-Kashmir stadium in Srinagar, and spectators were paid to shout abuse and hurl eggs at the Indian players. A series of bomb blasts across the Kashmir Valley, paid for by the ISI, had led to riots and government buildings being put to the torch.

Some places, such as the southern town of Anantnag, at times became ungovernable. But the Kashmiri groups, Badam complained, had a habit of going their own way, preferring to mount their own campaigns, calling for freedom and independence from everyone, rather than incorporation into Pakistan. In the eyes of the Holy Warriors, whose ranks were now bloated with war-hungry Pashtuns and dutiful Punjabis, the Kashmiris – infused with their mountain ways and Sufi-inspired traditions – were insufficiently bloodthirsty. 'The Kashmiris were just too moderate,' Masood Azhar wrote in the *Voice of the Mujahid*, 'to mount the kind of total war that was needed if India was to be unseated.'

What Kashmir needed to tip it over the edge, according to Brigadier Badam, was a fully-fledged infiltration across the LoC. India's superior military might meant Pakistan was unlikely to win a conventional war. So, rather than sending its own soldiers to die, Pakistan would manage the action from the sidelines, officially distancing itself, claiming that the upwelling of violence over the border was a spontaneous Holy War, a '*jihad* for freedom'. It was a neat plan that Badam had borrowed from his recent experience of working with the Americans in Aghanistan. As Masood later wrote, it would be 'a steady stream of volunteers crossing over'. The Holy Warriors was just the kind of organisation the ISI needed to see the plan through, a tried and tested group of Islamist fighters loyal to an ISI-friendly *emir*, or leader (Maulana Khalil), with an established recruitment base (Binori Town, the Pashtun heartlands and the southern Punjab), a well-oiled training infrastructure (Saifullah's Camp Yawar) and a mouthpiece to rally its followers (the *Voice of the Mujahid*). The candle on this cake was Masood Azhar, someone capable of getting the youth hot and bothered.

After Maulana Khalil agreed terms, the military operation escalated rapidly, Badam recalled, with young men from places like Bahawalpur and Peshawar, trained by Saifullah and armed by the ISI, infiltrated into Indian Kashmir at high altitude in cells of six to eight, their passage masked by artillery bombardment from regular Pakistan Army units stationed along the LoC. Once they were on Indian soil,

Kashmiri guides helped bed them in before they mounted hit-and-run operations across the valley.

India was taken aback by the sudden rise in violence. The tipping point came in December 1989, when militants kidnapped Rubaiya Sayeed, the twenty-three-year-old daughter of India's Home Minister, threatening to kill her unless India released five leading Kashmiri fighters from jail. Within five days the New Delhi government capitulated, and Rubaiya was saved. Believing the security situation in Kashmir was running out of control, India suspended local government, imposing Governor's Rule and New Delhi's writ on the citizens of Kashmir. The man they sent in to stamp out the unrest was Jagmohan Malhotra, a confidant of the Gandhi dynasty who had served in Kashmir before.

On his first day, 19 January 1990, Governor Malhotra ordered a curfew across the valley, while the Indian security forces mounted a crackdown, local parlance for mass house-to-house searches. In the lanes and alleys of Srinagar's old town, usually a whirl of rug merchants, horse-drawn carts and young boys scurrying about with trays of tea and freshly baked bread, everything was brought to a standstill as residents were strip-searched, soldiers battering down ancient wooden shopfronts, toppling wagons of dried fruit, searching for explosives and weapons, arresting residents without warrants or warnings, making the summer capital seethe.

On Malhotra's second day, Indian security forces opened fire on unarmed demonstrators, defying the curfew to spill out over Gawakadal, a rickety bridge over the Jhelum River in downtown Srinagar. New Delhi eventually conceded that twenty-eight people had been killed, and promised an inquiry that was never convened. However, international human rights groups claimed that the true death tally was almost double that, and survivors gave harrowing accounts of how they had clung to life by hauling corpses over themselves as police officers walked through the scene of the slaughter, finishing off anyone who was still breathing.

The following month, as New Delhi reacted to the mounting violence in the Kashmir Valley by dissolving the state assembly, Brigadier Badam in Pakistan implemented the second part of his plan, a vivid, week-by-week description of India's heavy-handed response to the Pakistan-backed putsch, written by Masood in his *Voice of the Mujahid*. He wanted to ensure that people across the Muslim world read about Kashmir's pain. Masood wrote up a storm, describing how in March 1990 'forty unarmed Kashmiris were shot by Indian forces as hundreds of thousands marched for independence'. In May, after militants assassinated Mirwaiz Maulvi Farooq, a moderate religious leader, Masood recorded vividly how Indian forces shot dead a hundred mourners at his funeral.

By October 1990 Jagmohan Malhotra was gone, replaced as governor by Girish Saxena, a former head of India's Research and Analysis Wing (RAW), the equivalent of the ISI. Five years earlier, Saxena had orchestrated a plan designed to smash an insurgency and pro-freedom movement in the Indian Punjab, the brutally effective 'Operation Blue Star' that left an estimated 1,500 civilians dead. Under his rule the bloodletting in Kashmir increased. After the army was sent in to quell a riot in the market town of Handwara, fifty miles north-west of Srinagar, 350 ancient houses and shops were burned down. Fifteen charred bodies were pulled from the ruins.

By now there was a multitude of Indian security forces operating in the Kashmir Valley, ranging from regular army to newly created reserve forces, paramilitary police as well as regular police, Special Branch, CID and a range of armed units attached to the intelligence agencies RAW and the Intelligence Branch (IB). The Handwara incident was blamed on the Border Security Force (BSF), a paramilitary outfit raised after the war between India and Pakistan in 1965. By 1990 more than a third of its 240,000 strength was deployed in Kashmir on counter-insurgency operations.

It was not just the paramilitaries who were excessive. 'Are they animals?' Masood demanded in February 1991, after reporting on events in Kunan Poshpora, a village close to the LoC where at least twenty-three women were raped, an attack blamed on the 4th

Rajputana Rifles, an army unit that had the distinction of winning two Victoria Crosses during the Second World War. It wasn't as if these incidents were few and far between, Masood reported. Two months after Kunan Poshpora he wrote up 'a Kashmir family story' from Malangam. It told how seven members of one Kashmiri family were shot dead, before their corpses were tied to military vehicles and towed down from the mountains by the BSF (116th Battalion). When their remains were later handed to police, the deaths were recorded as due to their having been 'caught in the crossfire', although the only shots fired had been Indian. Masood wrote about the 'crossfire' excuse again in June 1991, after Indian security forces killed seventeen unarmed civilians, all of whom supposedly died inadvertently, during a gun battle in Srinagar's Chotta Bazaar.

Blood and more blood. With Maulana Khalil's recruits striking indiscriminately across the valley, the indigenous militants fighting too, and a reeling India responding chaotically, Masood revelled in the region's descent into savage war, with his focus firmly fixed on atrocities committed by the Indian side. In January 1993, soldiers gunned down more than fifty unarmed civilians in Sopore, a rebellious town surrounded by apple orchards in north Kashmir, where insurgents had killed two Indian paramilitaries. Afterwards Sopore was set on fire, with most of its wooden buildings being destroyed and an unknown number of residents burned to death. Amnesty International sent a delegation to Kashmir. In Pakistan, Masood drew his readers' attention to a subsequent report that documented '706 cases of custodial killings' by Indian forces. 'Disappearances, routine torture of detainees so brutal that it frequently results in death, rape of women during search operations, and extrajudicial executions of unarmed civilians, often falsely labelled as having been the result of "encounters" or as having occurred in "cross-fire"' was how Amnesty expressed it. A few days after the delegation departed, Hriday Wanchoo, a vocal Kashmiri human rights campaigner, was abducted and shot dead by unidentified gunmen in Srinagar.

* * *

As far as Brigadier Badam and the ISI were concerned, their proxy war in Kashmir was going better than expected. India was on the back foot, and unrest was spreading daily through the valley. But according to Masood's account, seized by Pakistan federal investigators, the Brigadier was concerned about the burgeoning number of militant groups operating in the Kashmiri theatre over which the Pakistanis had no control.

In a dizzying process of *jihadi* mitosis, there were now more than a hundred Islamic front organisations – the Prophet's This and the Army of That, the Fight-for-Something-or-Other and the Battle-of-Some-Such, nominal names for notional outfits whose members on average had a battlefield life expectancy of less than six months. India did not bother to detail each of these groups' inconsequential allegiances, since to them the only good *jihadi* was a dead one. But Brigadier Badam could see that a large number of the smaller outfits were home-grown Kashmiri groups, which felt no allegiance to the ISI, while even Pakistan's purpose-made militias were increasingly difficult to control from afar. He was also aware that a significant amount of the Holy Warriors' monthly Kashmir stipend was now unaccounted for. Worse still, some of the pro-independence Kashmiri groups were gaining the upper hand around the valley, going against the ISI's plan to turn the Kashmiri freedom struggle into a campaign for Kashmir to become part of Pakistan.

In early 1993, Brigadier Badam returned to the Binori Town mosque to meet Maulana Khalil again. According to two others who were present, and also to Masood's impounded journal, the Brigadier said he wanted to consolidate the military campaign. He came with both a stick and a carrot, producing evidence that the Holy Warriors had stolen ISI cash, but adding that he was prepared to overlook this misdemeanour, and even to 'expand the monthly stipend to $60,000', in exchange for a radical restructuring. To streamline matters and push India over the edge, the ISI wanted to construct one overarching *jihadi* outfit from its three largest existing fronts. The Holy Warriors would be central, and Masood, still only twenty-five, would leapfrog the established order by being made – to the consternation of many

in the room – General Secretary of the new-look group that was opti-
mistically named Harkat ul-Ansar, the Movement of the Victorious.

The military success of this unified front would rest on the shoulders of one man, Sajjad Khan, who had been chosen to be the
Movement's chief of military operations. A hoary military tactician
from the Afghan–Pakistan border who had made his name battling
the Soviets, he was better known by his *nom de guerre*, 'the Afghani'.
He was such an important ISI asset that rather than risk infiltrating
him over the heavily patrolled LoC, Brigadier Badam suggested he
cross into India through the porous border with Bangladesh. After
losing its precious eastern territory in 1971, Pakistan's security agencies had forged strong links with Bangladeshi *jihadi* groups that now
promised to oversee all arrangements for the Afghani's safe passage.
General Secretary Masood Azhar was tasked with accompanying the
Afghani, giving him a personal send-off.

They flew together to Dhaka, the capital of Bangladesh, in
December 1993. It was an embarrassing reunion for Masood, since
the Afghani had seen him at his lowest, having arranged for him to be
evacuated from Camp Yawar back in 1988 after the notorious friendly-
fire incident. He knew the truth behind Masood's 'battlefield limp'.
But, ever dutiful, the Afghani said nothing of this during the journey
to Bangladesh, and Masood reflected in his journal that after handing
his charge over to another Binori Town old boy in Dhaka, he returned
to Karachi 'filled with enthusiasm for the new Kashmir operation'.

The Afghani reached the Kashmir Valley in the first week of 1994,
after travelling west through Bangladesh and the Indian state of West
Bengal before crossing India's northern plains towards the western
Himalayas. Now he headed for Anantnag, the largest town in south
Kashmir, a militant stronghold where India's writ was as worn as an
old ten-rupee note. He recovered from his epic journey in a safe house
that the Movement of the Victorious had established in Chhatargul,
an isolated village of stone cottages and cedars tucked into the dark
green folds of the Pir Panjal mountains, one hour's journey east of
Anantnag, a windswept landscape of pines and glacial debris

populated mostly by *gujjar* herders, Pakistani and Kashmiri militants. At night this eyrie was engulfed in blackness, bar the occasional flare of a kerosene lamp. Here, life had barely changed in hundreds of years. And despite the spread of Islam, the inhabitants of these outlying areas remained wary of the mystical spirits said to roam the forests at night. The stillness was punctuated only by the sound of wild animals, black bears and deer, rustling through the undergrowth, or the mournful tolling of goat bells.

From here, using his contacts in the established ISI-backed militant groups and local herders as guides, the Afghani pressed on further east into no man's land, where the snow lay thick on the ground. Travelling mostly at night to avoid attention, heavily armed and wreathed in multiple layers of scarves, he familiarised himself with the landscape, the language and the local customs, seeking out recruits, friendly hamlets and safe locations for munitions drops. Over cups of sweet black tea sipped beside smoky hearths, nervous villagers whispered how hard life was under Indian occupation, the men sitting cross-legged around the Afghani while their wives and children watched from behind a kitchen curtain, holding their headscarves tight, one end clenched between their teeth. The Afghani learned that these days the Indian security forces largely policed these upper reaches of Kashmir from the air, and that the poverty-stricken inhabitants, who survived on government rations in winter and on pulses and whatever vegetables they could coax into life from the thin mountain soil in summer, could easily be persuaded to side with the insurgency.

Soon he reached Lovloo village, high up beyond the Daksum road. This hamlet was a wild frontier, whose inhabitants reeked of wood smoke in winter and whose palms were stained with walnut juice from harvesting in the late summer. They rarely left the safety of their stone villages and farms. From here it was more than two hours' walk to a doctor, an hour to the nearest school. There was no electricity and no proper road, but this route was the back door into the Warwan, a remote stretch on the other side of the Pir Panjal range whose name means 'green valley', a place so remote that no one held control. In the summer the Warwan lived up to its name, a lush, perfectly formed thirty-mile-long glacial valley, with tiny settlements huddled along its flanks. But the Warwan was a soulless place in winter, most passes in and out being blocked by snow, its steep slopes trapping its few intrepid inhabitants for up to six months of the year. It was the perfect location for Pakistani and Kashmiri militants to lie low, and in recent times it had seen a steady increase in the numbers of foreign militants too.

Slowly, the Afghani seeded cells along the route to the Warwan, trudging through the snow for hours at a time to reach the remotest settlements, knocking on ancient wooden doors to find frightened families huddled around meagre fires. He made his way as far as Pahalgam, the famed trekking station, favoured by Western trekkers, sealing allegiances as he went with promises of weapons and money from Pakistan, deals that were settled over huge mounds of steaming rice and pickled vegetables, laid out on cloths rolled out over the floor, all the time gathering together a ragtag army to join the Movement's ranks. Some were veteran Kashmiri fighters who had been exchanging fire with the Indians long before 1989, and had a wealth of knowledge about their opponents' tactics and firepower. Others were Pashtun *mujahids*, recently arrived from over the LoC, trigger-happy and pumped up, their wild, unwashed hair and beards swathed under dun-coloured scarves. Then there were the boys and men from Punjab and Karachi, Master Alvi and Maulana Khalil's *madrassa* protégés, religiously conservative, militarily inexperienced but immersed in this new *jihad*, their uniforms, new tan-and-blue *kurta* pyjamas that the Kashmiris called 'khan dress', making them stand out from the locals, who back then preferred jeans and trainers. Finally, to get them through the mountains safely and to ensure there was sufficient food and a refuge at the end of the day, the Afghani recruited a network of helpers from Kashmir's tough mountain tribes, the *gujjars*, *dards* and *bakarwals*. These herders and hunters had no interest in *jihad*, although many had grown to despise Indian brutality, but they knew these mountains better than anyone. Universally feared by suspicious villagers, it was said their rejection by the mainstream meant they would do anything for money.

However, one crucial brother was missing. Key to the Afghani's military plan had been his chosen deputy, a Pakistani field commander called Nasrullah Mansoor Langrial, a gutsy fighter who had been running rings around the Indians in Kashmir for the past year, setting bombs and booby traps, mounting hit-and-run operations on Indian bases and patrols. Nasrullah and the Afghani were men of the same breed, the former being a farmer's son from the Punjabi village of Langrial, a community of impoverished and religious *jati* tribesmen. Like many Pakistani families, Nasrullah's parents made so little from the fields they rented from the local *zamindar* landlord that they had sent their son to a nearby Deobandi *madrassa*, where he was educated for free and inculcated with the merits of *jihad*. He had proven an eager pupil, and after graduating he had headed for Camp Yawar. There, in the deserts of Khost, the gangly youth Nasrullah had been transformed into the *mujahid* Langrial. With his lion's beard, smiling face and tall, lean frame, he led from the front, eschewing marriage and home comforts for a life of *jihad*. It had been the same story with the Afghani, and the two men had fought together on many occasions, Langrial attaining the name in *jihadi* circles of 'Darwesh', the smiling and happy narrator of a *hadith*. But now, in January 1994, a courier came to the Afghani with news. Langrial had been caught in an ambush in Kashmir, and was being held by the Indian security forces.

The Afghani reeled. He told his comrades that they must risk everything to free his brother in *jihad*. He immediately diverged from the ISI plan and entered Srinagar, where he launched a reckless and savage frontal attack on security forces in the Elahi Bagh quarter of the city, the firefight (on 16 January 1994) lasting thirty hours. The Afghani had hoped to take prisoners to trade for Langrial, but he was lucky to escape with his own life. Three days later he tried again, this time kidnapping an Indian major, Bhupinder Singh, but the authorities refused to negotiate. In his fury, the Afghani executed the Indian officer and then went into hiding, leaving the Movement's embryonic cells to melt into the dense pine forests.

When Brigadier Badam heard the news from Indian Kashmir, he was furious, Masood would later write. He immediately sent for

Maulana Khalil in Karachi, and warned him that this was not the streamlined operation the ISI had paid for. 'A number of messages were sent to the chief commanders in Kashmir to join hands. We did not, however, receive any confirmation of our orders,' wrote Masood. Someone senior from the Movement would have to travel to Kashmir to get the Afghani back on course. The obvious choice was General Secretary Masood Azhar, who in recent times had been travelling widely, acting as Maulana Khalil's roving ambassador and chief fund-raiser abroad, armed with a range of doctored passports provided by the ISI. Whatever his private thoughts about going to India, Masood hid them, writing vaingloriously in his journal: 'It was my duty in the organisation to maintain unity among the *mujahideen*, and it was felt necessary that I needed to be there to fulfill this job. Heads had to be brought together, prayers must be said.'

But although Masood's message rang clear in the ears of fighting men like the Afghani, the editor of the *Voice of the Mujahid* was not a fighting man. Once before he had demonstrated his lack of judgement in a live-fire situation, and this would be his first foray back onto the battlefield.

In late January 1994, as Masood said his farewells, his father, Master Alvi, worried that his son was not ready to grab *jihad* by the throat. 'Was he not better leading from Karachi?' Master Alvi wrote in a desperate letter to one of Masood's brothers, later seized by Pakistani investigators. The ISI was too busy concocting a cover story to listen. Masood was now Wali Adam Issa, a Portuguese businessman. The Movement's contacts in Britain had obtained a stolen Portuguese passport through the *maulvi* of a mosque in east London, and the ISI had had it stamped with Pakistani, Indian and Bangladeshi visas. Everyone was convinced that this mission was well within Masood's capabilities, as he had already travelled widely around Europe and the Horn of Africa, even assisting another merging *jihad* general in Sudan, Osama bin Laden, the son of a Saudi construction tycoon, who had fled there from Afghanistan.

Masood Azhar arrived in New Delhi on 29 January, via Dhaka, on a Biman Bangladesh fight, in a newly tailored Western suit, his beard trimmed, he would write, 'to resemble those worn by captains of industry' he had seen in the pages of *Time*. He had clipped his finger-nails and remembered to shower and use anti-perspirant, but the Indian immigration official still stared him down. Within minutes, his new nylon shirt was soaked with sweat. He didn't look Portuguese, the officer observed. Masood would later write that he had wondered if the man 'could smell Bahawalpur' on him. Luckily, he had practised his response. He was originally from Gujrat, in Pakistan's Punjab, but had left for Portugal some years before. The officer looked down at his screen. He scrutinised the passport again, and waved Masood through.

Masood headed for the five-star Ashoka Hotel in Chanakyapuri, the kind of hushed, moneyed place that asked no questions as long as the bills were paid. Delighted, he unpacked his bag and called his contact, a Kashmiri carpet exporter. This man was an old hand. He brought Masood some hot bread and *nihari*, made that morning at Karim's in Old New Delhi. 'Eat,' he told him, according to Masood's written recollections. 'Relax. No need to hurry. The Kashmir plan is running a little late.'

Masood the tourist. His first stop was naturally the town of Deoband, a three-hour journey east in Uttar Pradesh state. Afterwards, he browsed Old New Delhi's Islamist bookshops and visited roadside shrines to long-dead *maulanas*. He went shopping in New Delhi's Connaught Place, buying boiled sweets, woollen socks, a bottle of talcum and a small brass bell that he thought would be useful when he came to convene his first *majlis*, or council meeting, with the *muja-hids* of Kashmir. What did you buy for fighting men, he wondered. He found a place selling compasses, and bought a dozen as presents for the field commanders.

Finally, on 9 February, after twelve days of shopping, eating and waiting, they were ready for him. Wearing his comfortable *kurta* pyjama suit and skullcap as if he were a returning *haji*, Masood flew to Srinagar. As soon as he arrived he was thrown into a panic by the lines of khaki-clad security men, and he began shaking as a Kashmiri policeman with a clipboard approached him, having spotted the Portuguese passenger on the flight manifest. 'Foreigner registration,' the officer demanded, taking down Masood's details. He felt horribly exposed, but emerged from the airport unscathed.

During the taxi ride into the city the sheer scale of the Indian military presence became clear to Masood for the first time. The sight of Kashmiris with their pony carts cowering beside the road as vast army convoys thundered past made him shake with fear. Thinking back over all those speeches and newspaper articles he had written, it dawned on him that the reality was far worse than he had imagined: he had 'never seen more miserable-looking people anywhere in the world'. Srinagar in February was dark, dank and freezing, the dirty brown ice sludge on the roads splattering the people on the pavements. Locals hung around braziers filled with burning rubbish while Indian soldiers looked on enviously, shivering at their positions, dressed in balaclavas, winter-issue coats and oversized galoshes. Most shops had their shutters rolled down, and parts of Dal Lake were frozen over. There was not a tourist to be seen. Shuddering, as he wrote later, Masood searched for the Qasmia *madrassa* in downtown Srinagar, following the instructions he had memorised. That evening, safely indoors, as he sat beneath a quilt warming his hands on a Kashmiri *kangri* or charcoal burner, the Afghani slipped in.

They would leave at first light, the fighter announced, heading south for Anantnag. The leaders of the three militant groups that had merged to form the Movement would be waiting for them in the forest near the isolated village of Matigund, a difficult journey east of Anantnag along unmetalled mountain roads, a four-hour drive from here, possibly six, depending on the snow and the Indian security presence. 'Before we left, one of the local Kashmiri *mujahids* gave me his *pheran* [Kashmiri cloak] to wear,' Masood wrote later. 'The Afghani also got two hens, which he kept in the boot of the car.' Since they were going into the hills, the Afghani explained, they might have to fend for themselves. Only then did it occur to Masood that he 'might have to fight'.

* * *

At Matigund, Masood, by now exhausted, was greeted with salt tea and unleavened *lavash* by 'Brother Raees', a Kashmiri militant who explained that he was right-hand man to Sikander, the Movement's local District Commander. Sikander had proved himself a trustworthy lieutenant to the Afghani, but he was not present: 'He had skidded on the ice on a mountain road and crashed his motorbike.' He would attempt to reach them some time the next day.

Fifteen *mujahids* were waiting in the village house that had been commandeered for the *majlis*. Bearded and wearing an assortment of khaki uniforms and tribal dress, they were led by Abu Ghazi, a veteran tactician and weapons expert who had previously been based at Camp Yawar in Khost. He was now chief trainer at the Movement's main camp in Kashmir, concealed a stiff one-and-a-half-hour walk east, far beyond the point where the electricity pylons and telephone lines ended. Sixty recruits were currently there, Ghazi said as he gratefully accepted a wad of cash that Masood had brought from his ISI benefactors. 'We saluted them warm-heartedly and soon a *majlis-i-jihad* [*jihad* council] was in full swing,' Masood wrote.

The men, who had been fighting for their survival in the pine forests, were greedy for news, and they pressed forward as Masood began to speak. 'What an exhilarating scene it was!' he noted. 'In front of me and around, were faces shining with the spirit of *jihad*. Decorating the chests of these young men were magazines and grenades, and within them burned high the flame of courage and bravery. They cradled their Kalashnikovs in their laps like babies. Some of them had rocket launchers as well as carbines that they had seized from the Indian Army.'

Mesmerised by the surrounding weaponry and the proximity of men at his beck and call, Masood spoke uninterrupted for several hours, explaining why they needed to come together while all around him held a respectful silence. Out in the surrounding forest, he was informed, militants acting as lookouts also listened in via their radio sets. 'Their presence was vital where they were, and so they had to content themselves by listening to us over the airwaves.' At 2 a.m. Masood was politely interrupted. The brothers had not eaten all day.

'Our historic meeting ended when one of our companions informed us that the dinner is served (one of the two hens).' Dishes of gravy and chicken were set down beside a pile of cold *girda*, a striated Kashmiri flat bread. Afterwards, as the fighting men stretched out, Masood got up. 'I quietly took up one of the Kalashnikovs and started downstairs, to join the *mujahideen* on guard. Halfway down, in the darkness, I felt the weapon in my hands … It was cocked, and the bullet was in the chamber. A feeling of ecstasy descended upon me. My joy knew no bounds as I held the loaded gun in my hands.' There were no older siblings to make fun of the 'little fatty' now.

Outside, the night sky seemed overburdened with stars. You rarely saw them in polluted Karachi. 'It was the wee hours, a cool breeze was blowing,' wrote Masood, imagining himself as a fighter. 'Praise be to God who granted me an opportunity to perform guard-duty on the front of Kashmir.' Here, on the front line of a holy *jihad* in Kashmir, he could finally expunge those stinging memories of his embarrassing departure from the battlefield at Khost.

At daybreak, the Afghani sprang a radical plan. Since there was still no sign of Commander Sikander, Masood should deliver the Friday sermon at the Jamia mosque in Anantnag. This was a unique opportunity, and it would be a defiant act, demonstrating to the Indians, who would hear about it later, that the Movement was capable of bringing its General Secretary to the heart of south Kashmir under their noses. Masood was unsure, but the Afghani reassured him, saying the town's people had risked much by supporting the Movement, and he needed to give something back.

Reluctantly, Masood agreed. Leaving the guards behind, he, the Afghani and Sikander's deputy Raees walked down to the car. But half an hour into the journey the vehicle spluttered and died. Masood panicked. Miles from anywhere, they set off on foot until they spied a village, where they commandeered an auto-rickshaw. 'Raees got seated with the driver while I and the Afghani settled in the back,' Masood wrote. Just before they reached Anantnag, the rickshaw driver noticed a BSF truck driving at speed behind them. 'Army!' he yelled. But it was too late. They were totally encircled.

Raees was ordered to run for it, his weapon clanking beneath his *pheran*. 'As the soldier tried to search him he threw one man down, let off a grenade and made it to the woods,' recalled Masood, who remained frozen to the spot, aghast at the sight of the Indian para-militaries running towards him, firing off their weapons in all directions. For a few moments the Afghani sat calmly, holding Masood's hand, until they were hauled into the snow, chained and thrown into separate trucks. 'The Indian soldiers were beside themselves with joy,' Masood wrote. 'We were blindfolded, our hands tied behind our backs. A crowd soon gathered there, and I could hear them cheering "*Jai Hind! Bharat mata ki jai!* [Hail India! Victory to Mother India!]" We had no choice but to pray.'

Khundroo Army Camp, protected by 2nd Rashtriya Rifles and located close to the headquarters of the Indian Army's 21 Field Commandos, was a twenty-minute drive south of Anantnag. The signboard by the gate proclaimed 'If Paradise is on Earth it is here, it is here', but those who lived nearby thought of it differently. Like every other army, paramilitary and police camp in the valley, Khundroo had its interrogation centre, that consumed the daily intake of the detained, holding them for weeks or months without reference to the courts. Far away from the prying eyes of international human rights delegations, the Geneva Convention did not apply here, and the Afghani knew many comrades who had emerged from here and camps like it lame, broken and shamed. Masood had written countless column inches about prisoners who had been tortured or killed in detention centres, hung upside down, whipped, burned with blowtorches, electrocuted, near-drowned, their wounds rubbed with chilli, many of them vanishing altogether. He had never expected to find himself inside such a place, and he was terrified.

When an officer accompanied by plain-clothed agent arrived to begin their questioning, Masood shrank back and let the Afghani take the lead. 'It was indeed a spectacular scene,' Masood recalled later, emboldened by the passage of time. 'His eyes were sparkling dangerously.' The Afghani announced that he had a confession to make, but only in front of a senior officer. Someone found 'an old Colonel with the red dot on his forehead, which the filthy Hindus consider to be blessed'.

'Congratulations!' announced the Afghani without fear. 'Today you have gained great success. I am the commander of the Movement.' The Indian soldiers exchanged glances. 'But this scholar accompanying me has nothing whatsoever to do with the *mujahideen*. He is a visitor to this country. I kidnapped him. In all likelihood his prayers were answered when you arrested me, otherwise I would have held him until I got a ransom.'

According to his own later account, Masood swivelled to look at the Afghani before the penny dropped: 'In every era there have lived pious slaves of Allah who have chosen to drink the cup of death in order to save their fellow brothers.' For the next two days the Afghani was 'tortured horribly', but revealed nothing. Yet somehow 'the Indian Army discovered a hole in the story'.

In fact, according to the Indian interrogation transcripts, when Masood's turn came he broke down within thirty minutes and blurted out the truth: he had not been kidnapped at all. The Afghani was furious, and this time could not bring himself to forgive Masood. Now, after twelve days in Khundroo, both of them would face long prison sentences. Many months later, when Masood and the Afghani were reunited in Ward One of Tihar jail in New Delhi, where India housed the men it regarded as its most feared terrorists, the commander refused even to acknowledge his General Secretary. 'Here, for the first time we developed differences,' Masood later wrote circumspectly. 'After four months the situation changed; he came to me and asked me to forget everything, as it was harming the freedom movement.' The Afghani kept silent about their time together in Kashmir, even after Masood began telling other prisoners his life story, concocting a new explanation for his pronounced limp, which he now said was the work of Indian interrogators.

* * *

It was quiet in Kausar Colony, Bahawalpur. Two of Masood's brothers were away in Afghanistan, fighting alongside the emerging Taliban. A sister, Rabiya Bibi, would soon join them, doing welfare work for this force of dour students led by Mullah Omar that would soon capture Afghanistan, while another brother was running the Movement's Bahawalpur recruiting office.

Master Alvi should have been happy. Most of his family were doing holy work. Apart from Masood. He was desperate to secure the release of his golden child. He travelled to Karachi to see Maulana Khalil, and together they had gone to pay their respects to Brigadier Badam of the ISI. 'Do what the Afghani did when Langrial was taken,' the Brigadier told them. 'Kidnap someone important, preferably foreign. Make it an embarrassment for India. It's the only sure way to get him back.' Master Alvi was unsure. What did he know about kidnapping, let alone foreigners? But he was certain of one thing. The Movement owed his son.

THREE

The Meadow

'Paradise on Earth', declared the sign beside the old Jammu and Kashmir tourist reception centre on Residency Road, a short rickshaw ride from Lal Chowk, Srinagar's main shopping bazaar, with its cake shops and dressmakers, *kurta*-sellers and papier-mâché emporiums, behind which sprawled alleyways and lanes faced on either side by rickety wooden and stone structures. Plastic-chair depots blended into office supplies, and then came an entire street selling computers shorn of their inner workings, before you reached car parts, bath taps and telephones. Here was a Sikh *gurdwara* and an Islamic welfare association, hotels selling hot buttered toast, *seekh kebabs* and Lipton's tea, while in the lanes below suited businessmen and Kashmiri house-wives picked their way around overloaded handcarts.

But it was the large signboard that attracted Jane and Don's attention that morning. It might have convinced the increasing number of Indian tourists coming from the cow belt that all was peaceful here, the dark-skinned holidaymakers from the south who were all keen to do their bit to reinforce the government's writ in Kashmir. But it struck Don and Jane as odd, given what they had seen so far: the occupation of everything by the security forces, including this tourist centre, which was surrounded by razor wire, sentries and bunkers.

Inside, there were no tourists. The deserted corridors smelled of bleach and someone else's lunch. Asking for information on trekking routes at reception, Jane and Don were half-heartedly directed to a room where they found two Kashmiri officials sipping tea beneath a whirring fan that agitated the curling edges of posters depicting

Kashmir's many beauty spots. The men seemed delighted and surprised to have visitors. One jumped up, proffered a hand and introduced himself as Naseer Ahmed Jan, 'of the J&K tourist police'. Immediately he launched into a speech about the dangers of travelling alone in the mountains. It was the first voice of caution Jane and Don had heard since arriving in India, and it immediately grabbed their attention. There was a possibility of thieves, he said, sizing up their reactions, and a real chance of getting lost. They should be clear that the weather up in the mountains was unpredictable. For these reasons – and to ensure that they found the *best* routes and the *right* campsite – it was imperative that they take along a recommended guide.

Jane knew a sales pitch when she heard it. She was not surprised when Mr Jan introduced the colleague sitting by his side as being able to arrange a taxi to Pahalgam, as well as find ponies. 'He tried to give us many reasons why we shouldn't go on our own, why we should hire someone to go with us. It was inappropriate,' said Jane. She and Don got up to leave. Looking perturbed to have lost out on an opportunity, Mr Jan handed them his card. 'Call me,' he said weakly as the other man followed them out, still talking silkily: '*You choose the price. Only pay me what you feel I deserve. The decision is yours …*' Out in the street, Jane and Don concluded wearily that they would only have to go through the same performance with someone else at the trekking station. Why not get it over with? 'We were persuaded,' Jane said. 'The guide then said he would hire the pony-men.' Without really thinking it through, they had been hustled into committing to the Pahalgam option.

Seven days earlier, just before midnight on 21 June, Julie and Keith Mangan had lugged their belongings to the Inter State bus stand in New Delhi, where they were to board a coach to Kashmir. After three months in Sri Lanka, the British couple were bronzed, and they had become deaf to the mayhem of the subcontinent, feeling like old Asia hands. As they were settling into their seats on the Srinagar-bound bus Julie spotted two other Westerners, who with their blue-white skin and hassled expressions seemed to be fresh off the plane. Pushing their way through the crowds, with bags and tickets tumbling around them, the young couple were being trailed by a crowd of coolies, children and *chai-wallahs* who had sniffed out an opportunity. It was Paul Wells and Catherine Moseley, who had survived the experience of staying in the backpacker district of Paharganj and were now heading for Ladakh, having decided to take the cheapest route, by road via Srinagar, after the owner of their guesthouse arranged the tickets for them, taking a healthy commission. 'Do you need help?' Julie shouted over the hubbub. The young woman surrounded by beggars whipped around at hearing the English voice, and seeing Julie standing on the steps of the bus waving, burst out laughing. Cath was finding the whole India thing mind-boggling.

Once they were safely aboard, Julie introduced herself and Keith, and made a gentle jibe about Cath and Paul's lack of experience. More than twenty-four hours on an Indian bus would see to that, she joked. Had they come prepared, Keith asked, listing the necessary provisions for the trip: toilet roll, Imodium, real mineral water. 'Test the seals before you buy, or face a lifetime on the shitter' was the mantra of the travelling Westerner in those days, since so many water bottles were actually filled from the nearest unfiltered tap. Cath told them she and Paul had signed up to another forty-eight hours of travelling beyond Srinagar. As the bus roared out of New Delhi, passing pavements where homeless children slept beneath the fierce glow of halogen lights, Cath and Paul began to relax.

Despite the age difference, the Mangans chatted easily with the young backpackers. Keith, Julie and Paul discovered that they were all from the north of England, and they swapped stories from home and away. Having been in South Asia for so many weeks, Julie and Keith were familiar with the road trick of building casual relationships with other travellers. Leaving the hot colours of the Indian plains behind, the bus, keeling ominously, headed into the Pir Panjal, a mountain range in the lower Himalayas that separated the Kashmir Valley from the rest of India. By that afternoon, 22 June, they were in the foothills and the two couples knew pretty much everything there was to know about each other.

That night, as the last light faded, they headed through the dank Banihal Tunnel, the only road route connecting Kashmir to the rest of India. At times of heightened tension this road would be blocked by the army, sealing Kashmiris in, but just now it was open, although at its end an army checkpoint loomed like a giant mousetrap. Welcome to Paradise, the couples thought to themselves as the waiting Indian soldiers waved flashlights in the gloom. The bus came to a halt, and all the passengers were ordered off and made to stand in line with their passports and identity documents to hand. As the only Westerners on board, Keith, Julie, Paul and Cath were taken over to a small cabin that served as the local office of the J&K tourist police. There they were asked seemingly endless questions, their details noted down in longhand in lined ledgers, the pages bookmarked with elastic bands. Keith wondered if anyone ever read them afterwards.

Most of the other passengers on the bus were Kashmiri, born broke and destined to spend their lives trapped in the valley; or if they could get the papers, compelled to be permanently in transit, travelling the vast subcontinent the cheapest way possible, carrying plastic suitcases full of shawls, business cards and trinkets. It was thirty-four hours to Calcutta from here, and forty-two to Goa. More than two thousand miles lay between Kashmir and Pondicherry, in India's deep south-east. They were willing to ply even these far corners of the subcontinent, eking out every opportunity to make a small profit. Behind the hut where Paul, Cath, Keith and Julie were being questioned, they glimpsed Indian soldiers trampling on the Kashmiris' possessions. They were probably checking for contraband, weapons or explosives, someone murmured. After all, a nation had every right to protect itself.

Half an hour later they were back on board, rumbling north along National Highway 1A in the dark. From here on they would be in the bowel of Kashmir, as locals called it, the valley cupped by a sinewy lining of mountains. The road was quiet, but every couple of miles they passed sleeping army encampments, their whitewashed gates and watchtowers rising above walnut orchards and saffron fields. Along the camp perimeters, the bus's headlights lit up chain-linked fences strung with empty whisky bottles, a crude intruder alarm designed to give the sentries a few minutes' warning of a guerrilla attack. Quite a party the soldiers must have had, someone joked.

Finally disgorged at Srinagar bus station in the early hours of 23 June, the two British couples were glad to be stationary at last, and gulped in the cool air. Around them brightly painted buses revved and rattled into life, while local women jostled to board them for distant towns and villages – Kupwara, Handwara, Baramulla, Pulwama – their arms overflowing with children, shopping bags and live poultry. A few of the women wore black *abayas* or pale-blue *burqas*, but most only covered their heads with scarves. 'Good Luck', the hand-drawn signs above the bus drivers' cabins read. It all felt very foreign, but Keith, Julie, Paul and Cath were soon distracted by the breathtaking mountains that ringed the city, the crest of peaks clear in the crystalline early-morning light, a delicate, craggy line of snow-tipped summits meeting a sapphire sky.

However tense they felt about being in the much-talked-about hotbed of Srinagar, Paul and Cath had already decided they were going nowhere in a hurry. Over the course of the journey, Julie and Keith had talked them into staying a night or two, and as they collected their luggage from the belly of the bus, a heckling crowd of houseboat owners massed. There were so few tourists and too many berths. Soon they were surrounded by jabbering touts, who pressed laminated photos and testimonials into their hands. Eventually the British tourists plumped for the *Holiday Inn*, an intricately carved wooden houseboat on Dal Lake. The name raised a laugh, and the owner, a middle-aged man called Bashir, had a friendly face and promised electricity *and* hot water.

Bashir led them to his friend's waiting taxi, and as they drove through the city the houseboat owner pointed out the centuries-old wooden houses owned by Pandits, the valley's indigenous Hindu inhabitants, who claimed to trace their history back thousands of years. These days their homes were locked, deserted and collapsing, the owners having fled Kashmir as the local war had become tinged with sectarian savagery. Could they stop? Bashir said he'd explain about the Pandits later. In the old city quarter of Nowhatta they passed the minarets of Jamia Masjid, built by Sultan Sikander in the fifteenth century, one of Srinagar's most significant mosques, that could hold thirty thousand worshippers. Was it worth visiting? Bashir said he could not stop. Now was not good. He would show them its magnificent courtyard and hall of 370 wooden pillars 'another time'. Wrestling their way through the back streets of Maisuma to Lal Chowk, he pointed to the ancient, delicately carved fretwork of the wooden shrine to Shah-e-Hamden, which he said contained 'the secrets of all Islam', and which would be wonderful to visit another year, for reasons he would tell them later. Bashir was finding it difficult to disguise his nervousness at having foreigners in the car, although outside the market hawkers, mothers with young children shopping for cheap Chinese blankets, old men reading newspapers pegged outside a shop, seemed oblivious to the heavily armed Indian soldiers milling all around them.

Paul and Cath could not get over the overwhelming security presence. The place was heaving with armed men and their bullet-marked, rock-battered military vehicles. Julie too was intimidated. Everything, from the old cinema to the old post office building, from the sports stadium to Raj-era hotels and villas, had been cloaked by vast khaki nets, while beside every fortified army camp and pillbox some New Delhi-*wallah* had pasted yet another colossal hoarding declaring, 'If Paradise is on Earth, it is here, it is here'. Perhaps this also related to another time.

Everyone's mood lifted when they pulled up on Boulevard Road, with its bakeries, *shikara* moorings and photographic studios that had last been decorated in the sixties. To the left of them Dal Lake shimmered, and beyond, through the haze, the mountains unfurled. Bashir pointed to a houseboat 150 metres out in the water, and whistled for a *shikara*. One skimmed over, and they settled beneath its curtained canopy as the boatman rowed them like a Kashmir gondolier, humming a *lol-gevun*, a local love song. Boys dressed in jeans and Western T-shirts waved from passing skiffs. An old man in a skullcap drew up. 'Chrysanthemums, madam?' he asked the women. 'Silver? Shawls?' They found themselves smiling as they shooed him away, having finally arrived somewhere that felt gentle and evocative. Everyone was reassuringly attentive. 'Welcome to your home!' cried Bashir as the *shikara* glided to a halt at the *Holiday Inn*. The entire family had gathered to greet the guests. Cath and Paul were overwhelmed, and Julie and Keith thought it the most beautiful place in the world. Their eyes were drawn to the pink and purple lotus flowers that covered the water's edge. 'It sent tingles down your spine,' Julie recalled.

Inside, the *Holiday Inn* was a confection of cut-glass chandeliers and carved walnut, with a panelled corridor leading to six spacious double bedrooms. For the next few days they would stay in style, waited on hand and foot as if they had been transported back to the time when the British fled roasting Delhi for the cooler mountainous climes, and these boats had first been built. Bashir's unseen wife produced steaming *gusturba* (boiled Kashmiri meatballs), *pilau* rice and curd flecked with *jeera*. His sons carried it all to the polished dining-room table in chipped porcelain servers. At night the rooms were heated by wood-burners, the bedsheets warmed by a 'winter wife', the universal Kashmiri term for a hot-water bottle.

After a day, none of them wanted to leave, as life on the lake floated by. Paul and Cath lay on the boat's decked roof, writing postcards home. 'Dear Mum and Dad,' Paul wrote in green ink, 'It took us 30 hours to get here and I (oops!) *we* are now staying on a houseboat for £3 a night. I'm sitting on the roof of the houseboat writing this to you. Srinagar is very nice but there are political problems. It's a bit like N. Ireland.' For Bob and Dianne Wells back in Blackburn, the fact that their son was writing postcards seemed to be a sign that he was settling down. 'Paul was never one to put pen to paper,' Bob says. 'Kashmir must have made a significant impression on him.' While Paul and Cath lazed, Julie and Keith hired a skiff to explore the shallow lake brimming with floating allotments, exploring the broken camel-back bridges and pontoons of a Mughal Venice that had run out of luck, snapping photographs of each other to send back home: Keith taking the oars as they set out across a silvery expanse of water, Julie grinning happily in a white T-shirt, her hair bunched up, making her look years younger.

In the evenings they all met in the carpeted living room of the *Holiday Inn* to compare stories. On the first night Bart Imler, a solo Canadian traveller, introduced himself. He was looking to team up with another party and go trekking somewhere near Pahalgam. When Bashir overheard the discussion, a sell began, softer than chamois. He got out his oversized photo album, and started leafing through pictures of tourists waving against the striking backdrops of Sonamarg, Gulmarg and Aru, smiling foreigners sitting astride tough little mountain ponies, sooty faces around a campfire at night, trekkers with their arms around each other. There were dozens of satisfied comments in the guestbook, too: 'Dear Bashir, we thank you and your family for being so welcoming and kind and giving us the holiday of a lifetime. We will be back soon.'

It didn't take long for everyone to cave in. Paul and Cath would postpone Ladakh so they could all climb to the Kolahoi Glacier, a high-altitude ice sheet in the mountains above Pahalgam which Bashir described as one of south Kashmir's must-see destinations. The expedition would take three days up and two days down, with a stop-off in the Meadow. Had they heard about the Meadow, Bashir asked, getting out more photographs. Keith and Julie recalled seeing photos of it in the Indian Embassy in Sri Lanka: a campsite where the grass was as soft as *shahtoosh*. Snow leopards ran wild up there, Bashir said, along with the burly Himalayan black bear, while the forests were alive with hangul stags, chiru antelopes, monal pheasants and even the odd (and very rare) blue sheep. Their guides would provide everything. They would fish for trout, fried in butter and Kashmiri almonds on a roaring fire, and tether milk and beer bottles to rocks in the rushing river to keep them cold.

Was there any danger? There were no real risks, Bashir assured them, adding that the price was extremely reasonable. He would take them there himself, along with his handpicked party of guides and pony-*wallahs*, who all seemed to be brother-cousins or cousin-cousins.

They knew secret picnic sites, and the most beautiful back routes that other trekkers would not have heard about. The others were convinced, but Julie still wanted one more opinion. The following morning she took them all to the Jammu and Kashmir tourist reception centre on Residency Road. Mr Jan was waiting, sipping tea. 'Don't do the trip,' he warned them. They listened intently. 'Only go if you have a good guide.' Just by chance, he had such a man. He introduced his colleague, who he assured them came at a good price. The Westerners knew a scam when they heard one, and told Mr Jan they had already done a deal with Mr Bashir. Seeing that there was nothing in it for him, Mr Jan showed them out, handing over his business card as he did so. 'Call me if you have any troubles,' he said brightly.

John Childs flew in to Srinagar on 30 June, carrying a sleeping bag, a tent and a small backpack. He was determined to get his trip up and going as soon as he touched down. He knew roughly where he wanted to go, and had maps and trekking contacts from the factory workers in Bihar, although he had not yet rung them to make firm arrangements. As the other Western passengers dispersed, leaving him standing alone by the luggage carousel, he suddenly realised that he had not really thought this through: 'Signs of war were everywhere. Sandbags, soldiers, tanks and guns of every possible description. I was a little overwhelmed.' Although he worked in the weapons industry, and could identify the make, model, bore and clip capacity of pretty much any gun from a distance, he had never handled one in a conflict situation, or even really thought about the realities of war. 'I should have just turned around, got back on the plane to New Delhi and listened to the voice inside my head.' But stubborn John got talking to a taxi driver instead, who offered to take him to his hotel for what seemed an honest fare. He wasn't interested in seeing Srinagar, other tourists or the inside of a houseboat, he told the driver. He just wanted to have a good sleep at the hotel he had booked from New Delhi, and to get going first thing in the morning.

After a circuitous trip through downtown Srinagar, during which John saw a lot more razor wire, the taxi driver pulled up at a patch of waste ground. 'Sir, your hotel seems to have been knocked down,' he said, eyeing John in the rear-view mirror. Incredulous, John attempted to get out of the car. 'It's not safe here, sir,' the driver insisted, ushering him back in. 'I am not lying to you, sir. This area has been appropriated by the army. It happens all the time. There are militants in this district, and the security forces are building here to beef up security. You should stay on the houseboats, that is the only safe place for tourists, and not city-centre hotels.' John sat back down. He had no way of knowing if the man was telling the truth or not. The hotel had been his only pre-planned arrangement in Kashmir, and now it seemed to be gone. Or was this even the right address? It sunk in that he did not know anyone here, or even if it was safe to call the numbers the factory workers had given him.

The driver reassured him. 'Sir, please, I am a tourist guide. Stay with my family tonight and we will help you make your onwards arrangements in the morning. I will not charge you.' Within minutes John had been driven down to Boulevard Road, where his bags were tossed into a waiting *shikara*. 'I was embarrassed and angry. Before I knew it, I was being rowed down these little waterways accompanied by a man I had only known for thirty minutes who might well be planning to slit my throat as soon as we got round the next corner. I knew I couldn't do a damn thing about it.'

His mood lifted a little when they arrived at the houseboat, which, just as the driver had promised, was luxurious and welcoming. The men of the household, all dressed in brown *pherans* and smoking heavily, quickly surrounded him, while the women dispersed to cook him 'a Kashmiri *wazwan*'. What were his trekking plans, the men wanted to know. 'Kolahoi? Aru? Sonamarg? Tar Sar? Sheshnag? Chandanwari?' When they found that he had nothing in mind, they began bidding for his cash. 'They showed me letters from foreigners who had been on successful treks with them.' Afterwards there was a lavish banquet and all the houseboat's wood burners were lit. Relaxing a little, deciding he had little option other than to go with the flow – a difficult decision for a planner like John – he bartered with the men until they reached a price: US$300 for a four-day trek, with food, guide and a pony-*wallah* thrown in. Within half an hour, two men appeared. The guide was a lean, mournful-looking Kashmiri with a pencil moustache, who introduced himself as Dasheer. He talked John through where they could walk and what he would see, recommending the Lidderwat Valley, with a stop-off at the Meadow. Had he heard of it? 'One of the most beautiful campsites in the world.' John quizzed him about trekking times and elevations, and concluded that the man knew what he was talking about. That night, for the first time in several weeks, John slept soundly, dreaming of his girls back home and of the mountains to come.

They set off by taxi down Highway 1A just after dawn on 1 July. John spent most of the journey batting away questions fired at him by Dasheer, the driver and the pony-*wallah*, Rasheed, all of whom chain-smoked, filling the cab with fumes. What was America like? How did he get into the weapons business? How much was he paid? Did his company sell guns to India? Did he know how poor Kashmiris were? Unused to being bombarded at such close quarters, John buried his head in his guidebook, so he did not see the locals queuing at check-points to be body-searched, their *pherans* held aloft, as his vehicle, with its conspicuous passenger inside and its tourist permit glued to the windscreen, was whisked past them. He barely noticed the relent-less caravan of military traffic that dominated the road. But as soon as they turned off the main highway at Anantnag, and started heading north-east towards the mountains, everyone fell silent as the car manoeuvred around several large craters in the road. 'Mines,' the driver said by way of explanation, glancing at John in the rear-view mirror.

John was dismayed, but the driver seemed unconcerned, laughing as he used his entire body to force the wheels around another hole. Military convoys were constantly on the move nowadays, he said as they careered around another, ever since the Indian Army had taken over the holy village of Aishmuqam. Once it had been most famed for its hilltop temple, the last resting place of a fifteenth-century Sufi saint, or *rishi*, called Zainuddin. It was venerated by the boatmen of Kashmir, who would take their children there to cut off their first lock of hair. 'If this was done elsewhere, the child would die or become blind,' explained Dasheer, who had been born on a houseboat himself. Should they stop to have a look, John asked. Earnest Dasheer shook his head. Like many of Kashmir's ancient mountainside pilgrimage spots, which held special meaning for Muslims and Hindus alike, the Aishmuqam tomb had attracted visitors for centuries, but these days people were frightened of the notorious army garrison and signals headquarters that lay in its shadow, and of the anti-government militants who constantly sniped at them.

When John said he had been assured that all the trouble spots in Kashmir were far away, to the west of the valley, his companions exchanged glances. Were they just trying to scare him, he wondered as he stared out at the crocus fields on either side of the road. Maybe it was the Kashmiri factory workers in Bihar who had lied? If so, what else had they not told him? What about the kidnapping of the foreigners the previous year? He asked his companions if any of them knew anything about it. The men shrugged, lit up cigarettes and began speaking to each other in Kashmiri.

At Aishmuqam there was nothing much to see of the army camp, and John's fears lessened as they entered a gentler landscape, a terraced valley of lush green paddies. 'Kashmiri rice,' the driver declared, pointing towards the fields, where young girls and old women stooped over the ripening crops while their men looked on, smoking cigarettes. 'The finest in subcontinent. Twice the price of Punjabi rice. Doubly delicious.' But nowadays, he continued, it was mostly exported to rich Indians to the south: 'Locals cannot afford to eat it.' Dasheer and Rasheed shook their heads. The road started to climb again, following the flank of an ice-melt river in which ancient boulders had been worn flat.

By the time they reached the confluence of the East and West Lidder rivers, between which the trekking station of Pahalgam sprawled across a flat grassy plateau, they were at nearly nine thousand feet. John took in the view: gentle pine-topped ridges folding into one another as far as the eye could see. Pahalgam's canny tourist and guide agencies had long ago dubbed the town 'the Gateway to the

Himalayas', although its charming old wooden quarter was gradually being swallowed up by modern modular concrete hotels. But it was not the town planning that drew people here, John thought. And it certainly was not the golf course. He had laughed when they had passed its cratered fairways. On a fine day like today there were stunning glimpses of the snow-covered foothills beyond. From here, trekkers climbed north-east towards Sheshnag and Amarnath, or north-west to the Meadow, the mountain village of Aru, Kolahoi Glacier and the three high-altitude lakes Tar Sar, Mar Sar and Son Sar.

Just as John was beginning to feel excited for almost the first time since arriving in India, several small heavy objects rattled against the car, one of them clattering into the windscreen. 'Stone pelters!' yelled Dasheer, diving for cover. Panicking, John ducked too. Was this some kind of militant attack, he wondered, spotting that the rocks were being thrown by a group of young Kashmiri men outside the bus station. As he lay down on the back seat, his companions shouted at them in Kashmiri. Soon the car was completely encircled by furious-looking trekking guides, and at one point it seemed certain a full-blown fight would erupt. What the hell was going on, John asked. 'They're jealous that we picked you up in Srinagar,' Dasheer shouted to him. 'They say we've stolen their trade. Life here is hard, you see. Don't worry. This happens all the time. Everything will be OK once we're up in the mountains.'

After a few minutes the crowd drifted away, and John asked to get out of the car. He was becoming concerned that everything he had heard about Kashmir was unreliable. He could still turn back, he told himself; but then he gazed at those distant mountains once more. He wandered off, still nervous, but hoping to ask other travellers for tips. The further he walked into the town, the more alarmed he became by the air of decay that hung over this place. Pahalgam was empty, a single road fringed by wooden shop-houses, some offering trekking services, and not a soul to be seen in any of them. John passed the ornamental park and gardens, the police station and a couple of grander-looking hotels down by the river, the Heevan and the Lidder Palace. Where were all the tourists, he wondered, the throngs of people he had been told about by the factory workers in Bihar. The only visible Western faces were in yellowing photographs pasted in travel-agency windows. But every few yards there was a sorry huddle of trekking guides, all of whom would rush over at the sight of a rare Western visitor. These days it seemed all they could do was dream of a time when they had had all the work they could handle, carrying clanking cooking stoves up and down the mountain paths to glittering shrines illuminated with *ghee* lanterns and burning sandalwood.

Sick of the relentless attention, John waved off the last huddle and strode down the road in search of his companions. Dasheer had made arrangements for them to stay in a cheap hotel on the outskirts of the town. 'I seem to recall it didn't really have windows,' John said. 'At the time I felt I was semi-camping already. But soon I would come to think of it as luxury.' As he bedded down for the night, he tried to forget about the worryingly negative aspects of his trip, and focused on the next day. The three of them would set out at dawn the following morning for the Lidderwat Valley. They would head for Kolahoi Glacier, the three lakes of Tar Sar, Mar Sar and Son Sar, and would set up camp in the Meadow. He was determined to enjoy his holiday, whatever the cost. His company was paying, after all.

By 2 July, the day John Childs set out from Pahalgam, Jane Schelly and Don Hutchings had been walking at high altitude for several days. They too had been concerned by the cratered road up from Anantnag – 'a horrendous, horn-honking mad dash' – and the ghostly appearance of Pahalgam. But once they had departed the town along the eastern route, following a well-worn track beside the East Lidder River, heading into the heart of the Betaab Valley and towards Amarnath Cave, their misgivings were left behind. 'It was glorious shirt-sleeve weather,' says Jane. The temperature was in the seventies. The scent of pine and lilac filled the air. The skies were clear, and the meadows alive with grazing sheep. Due to an unusually late thaw, the wildflowers were only just coming out on the hillsides, springing up with extra vigour because of the snowmelt. Little streams wound between pollarded willows, their crystal-clear water flowing between banks of vivid green moss and over beds coloured like autumn leaves. Jane was delighted. 'Everything was perfect. Good food. The guides, Bashir and Sultan, were good. All we saw were the local shepherds.' The only disconcerting sight was the occasional army jeep charging past them.

The first day, their guide, Bashir, had suggested they take noon *chai* with a *gujjar* family. It was a tourist stunt, but Jane didn't care. This was a way for these people, who had little, to make a few rupees, and for visitors to see how they lived. Jane and Don followed Bashir's lead, and sat dunking rolled-up pieces of salty *girda* bread into sugared tea. The family's hut, or *dhoka*, set back from the main trekking path among the pine trees, was constructed of four sturdy trunks around which stone walls had been built, using mud as a mortar. Someone had pushed little strands of wild plants into the cracks, allowing them to cascade down the walls. The family sat mute, smiling. They spoke no English, and the guide said they did not speak Kashmiri either, but had their own dialect. Don took a few snaps, and Jane asked Bashir to identify some of the local flowers, and wrote their names down in her journal. Noonday *chai* would become a welcome part of their routine.

Later, after zigzagging back and forth over the East Lidder on little wooden pony bridges, wild lilac bushes perfuming the air, they reached Chandanwari, a village Hindu pilgrims called Amarnath base camp. Famous for its snow bridge, a semi-permanent glacial sheet that spanned the river, this was as far as army vehicles could reach. From now on the route consisted of a trekking path that climbed sharply, and Indian soldiers had to proceed by foot to their positions in the heights. Although the military presence was by no means over-whelming, there were still troops everywhere. Don and Jane reasoned that security was a good thing. The soldiers gave them no trouble, and soon they had left them behind, walking through pastures filled with violets, primulas and anemones, and spending their first night in the open steeped in air flecked with blossom. They sat with their books and journals by a gurgling stream, while Sultan, the pony-*wallah* who also doubled as their cook, prepared pots of *daal*, rice and curried vegetables on a kerosene stove.

After eating, Jane and Don talked a little to the guides about their families, who lived in Aru, a village near the Meadow. 'You will come to our homes,' they said. 'You will have a meal with our families.' But behind the smiles, Bashir and Sultan seemed sad, as if they knew that this business that had come their way would not be sufficient to mend Kashmir's problems. Jane and Don had been quick to spot this, and it unsettled them. Whenever the guides talked together in their own language, over the pots and pans or with the ponies, they seemed to be arguing. 'Life is hard these days,' Bashir commented one evening, trying to spark up a conversation. 'Why have people stopped coming?' Jane asked, and probed them about any danger from militants. Bashir frowned. There was no militant activity in these parts, he mumbled. She must be sure to tell her friends back in the United States. 'You are our friends, your friends are now our friends too.' When the conversation dried up, Bashir and Sultan drifted off for a smoke. Jane and Don contemplated the valley as the darkness deepened, the roar of the river swelling and spreading. Above them rose the sombre masses of the snow-topped mountains, and meteorites streaked across the sky behind the seven snowy peaks of Sheshnag to the north-east. From this vantage point, the two Americans could see why these mountains, so closely connected to each other, were said to resemble the writhing heads of a mythical *naga*. This untamed beauty was worth coming to Kashmir to see. But they couldn't help wondering if they would ever understand the crisis that had blighted the state.

The next day they hiked to nearly ten thousand feet, clambering across a field of moraine over Pissu Top. Don looked back, taking pictures along the valley. They dropped down into Zargibal, a wind-blasted stone hamlet, and a little further on they spent another night in the open, listening to their campfire crackle.

Up with the sun, they headed for Wavjan on the third day, over-looking the velvety waters of Sheshnag Lake and a slew of glaciers that ballooned out before them like pegged laundry. Blue irises grew all around. Jane asked Don to take some pictures, as she doubted if the specimens she picked would survive the trip back home. From here, Bashir told them, they would have to make it over Mahagunas Pass, before descending into the meadows of Panchtarni, the last place they would camp before trying for the Amarnath ice cave. Don had read that the cave was the supposed site of a tryst between the Hindu god Lord Shiva and Parvati, his divine consort, the place where he had explained to her the secrets of immortality. Bashir said a pair of mating doves had overheard, transforming the cave into their eternal dovecot. Inside was a shrine built around a giant ice *lingam*, a phallic stalagmite that represented Shiva's potency. During the holy Hindu month of *Shravan*, between the full moons of July and August, when devotees made their annual *yatra*, the *lingam* was said visibly to wax and wane.

Eventually, still walking well, despite a few aches, over fields of scree, they reached Mahagunas Top at fifteen thousand feet. With rippling layers of geology exposed all along the bare ridgelines, and the glittering Himalayas spread out ahead, the landscape inspired them to forget the weariness they had begun to feel in their calves and knees. After Don, thinking of the post-trip potluck dinner they would arrange back in Spokane, got as many shots as he could, they headed for Panchtarni, the confluence of five streams, and the last camp before the holy cave itself.

Amarnath was a hard three-hour walk from there, the culmination of the *yatris'* pilgrimage, at the end of a well-worn path that wound its way at a forty-five-degree angle through a gigantic glacial amphi-theatre, where the bedrock rose hundreds of feet on either side, caus-ing the trekkers' footfalls to echo. When Don and Jane reached their destination the following morning, the giant cavern, more than 150 feet high and open to the elements, carved deep into the side of the mountain, was an overwhelming spectacle. The final approach was a zigzagging path, and Jane and Don could imagine how the cave had inspired stories of the gods for many hundreds of years: the *Rajatarangini*, a twelfth-century Sanskrit chronicle of the kings of Kashmir, had recorded how Aryaraja, a monarch who had ruled around the time of Jesus Christ, had worshipped a phallus formed of snow and ice 'in the regions above the forests'.

After reaching the mouth of the cave and catching a glimpse of the giant ice *lingam*, filling their lungs with the sandalwood incense left by pilgrims, Don and Jane began to retrace their steps along the mountain path before branching off along a little-used track Sultan had told them about. 'We didn't do a "V" all the way back to Pahalgam, but instead cut across due west at around the area where the streams come into the East Lidder River from the north,' Jane says. 'That would have put us a little south of the village of Barimarg.' There were trails all over the place, and the guides knew the routes. They were heading for the Lidderwat Valley and the Meadow, where they would spend the night before pushing on north-west, along a high-altitude route to the difficult Sonarmas Pass, at eleven thousand feet. Near here they would spend their last night in the mountains. A few hours beyond lay Sumbal, a village on a metalled road, from where a taxi would take them back to Srinagar.

Carpeted with white daisies and blue gentians, the Meadow was spellbinding when they reached it at the end of that afternoon, exhausted after a full day of walking and climbing. Bashir and Sultan set the tents up as usual, choosing a pitch in what they described as 'the Upper Camp', near a couple of empty *dhokas*, whose roofs were grassed over for insulation. They made a point of positioning Jane and Don's tent close to the blue ice water, so they could hear it where they lay.

The couple fell asleep early, Jane complaining of toothache. The next morning, 3 July, they woke feeling glum. Just one more yomp to the high-altitude lake, Tar Sar, lay ahead of them. The adventure was coming to an end, although Jane's toothache almost made her quit early: 'I thought it was just a seed that had got stuck and so I ignored it, and we went ahead.'

The day John Childs set out on his trek up the Lidderwat Valley, heading for the Meadow, British tourists Keith and Julie Mangan, Paul Wells and Cath Moseley, accompanied by their new Canadian friend Bart Imler, arrived in Pahalgam with the *Holiday Inn*'s owner Bashir, who introduced them to their guides and pony-*wallahs*. True to his word, Bashir had arranged a full team: ponies, a cook, guides, and two extra teenage boys, brought along for 'emergencies'. But there would be none of these, Bashir had assured them, his words ringing in their ears after the alarming drive down from Srinagar, the road pitted with constant reminders that there was a major military operation going on in the Kashmir Valley.

Now that she was here before the mountains, Julie was excited, and grateful that she would not have to heft her cumbersome kit. The party set off in bright sunshine, Julie and Cath in shorts and T-shirts, small daypacks slung over their shoulders, following the same track up the Lidderwat Valley that John Childs had taken at daybreak. Bashir was chatty, passing on titbits about the flowers and wildlife. The pony-*wallahs* asked where they came from, what life was like in the UK and where they had been so far on their travels. As they made their way out of the town, heading north-west up a gentle incline along a path that followed the route of the sloshing Lidder River, Paul got out his camera and began taking photos of the nomadic shepherds tending their flocks, men whose entire lives were spent wandering with the seasons, their burnished faces topped by wool caps, inset with tinsel and mirrored fragments to catch the sunlight.

Apart from the occasional herder, the group had the valley to themselves. For a while they walked in silence, listening to the cries of a hawk on the thermals high above their heads. Paul snapped his walking companions: Julie, wearing a bandana and baseball cap; bow-legged Keith, sporting a natty woollen waistcoat, bought from an insistent *shikara* salesman; Cath striding along with an improvised walking stick, happy for the first time since she had arrived in India. Ahead was the hulking mass of one of the smaller peaks.

'It was as if God had given us a piece of paradise,' Julie recalled. It was everything the posters had claimed. Kashmir had won her round. The mountains rose ever higher, thickly cloaked in red pines that grew so densely that the absence of light below the canopies ensured that nothing grew in the warm mulch of crushed leaves and cones around their bases.

After a few hours they stopped for lunch at Aru, which marked the end of the drivable road. Spongy, lush grass lay beneath their feet. A clutch of wooden houses served as *chai* stalls and guesthouses. This was their last chance to buy sweets and biscuits. They sat down to vegetable curry and rice before heading out of the village, on a less well-defined path than before. Paul snapped a couple of shots of the dilapidated 'Milky Way Tourist Bungalow and Cafeteria' on the outskirts of Aru. It looked like a set from a spaghetti Western. Bashir mumbled that he didn't like the place, and ushered them past. Something bad had happened here, he said. The owners were not good people. He would explain another time.

The path headed up through the pine forest at a precipitous gradient before swinging down to rejoin the Lidder. After a couple of hours they broke out of the conifers and into an expanse of grassland, a glacial valley that smelled of clean washing and star anise, where the wind blew the grass into eddies. Bashir said they had at last reached the Meadow.

Julie and Keith reached for warm jackets, while Bashir and his crew pitched the tents. There were a couple of other small groups already camping here, among them Jane Schelly and Don Hutchings, but Julie and Keith, conscious of everyone's desire for space, chose not to go and poke around. People could come down later, drawn by the camp-fire, if they wanted to talk, they reasoned. Instead, the Mangans wandered over to the stony banks of the Lidder, taking sips from the ice-cold water while Bashir's team clanked around, setting up the kitchen. They had brought everything they would need: big blackened cooking pots and pans, kerosene stoves, and enough food to feed a cricket team. One of the boys was sent off to forage for wood while Bashir set a fire in a ring of stones left by some other trekking party. By the time the tea had boiled the Westerners had settled around the fire, hungry and footsore. Tomorrow they would head for the glacier, travelling light, leaving most of their kit behind. The Meadow was that kind of place, Bashir said. It wasn't like back home in Blackburn or Middlesbrough, he joked, where you had to leave the lights on all night to keep the burglars guessing. But, just to be safe, he would leave a couple of his boys to guard the camp while they did the eight or nine hours up and down. They would take food for the journey, but there was nowhere to stay at the top. Julie wasn't sure she'd make it all the way, but she'd give it a try. The Meadow was already proving hard to leave.

The next day, at dawn, Keith, Julie, Paul, Cath and Bart slowly made their way on towards Kolahoi base camp, a gentle climb at first through a vast, sweeping glacial valley, its floor littered with large boulders deposited by ancient ice floes, a solemn, eerie landscape that rose on either side towards sheer granite cliff faces high above. Here and there wild ponies grazed, tiny specks dwarfed by the rugged land-scape. Dotted around was the odd *gujjar* settlement, a row of tiny stone shelters that jutted out of the hillside. Occasionally the party met the families who lived in them. They were dressed in scarves and robes, the men with brightly hennaed beards, the women with tightly bound hair, their children riding on the ponies along with the pots and pans.

A few hundred metres short of the base camp, an opaque mist had settled, limiting their visibility, though the sun shone through it with a glare that was trying to the eyes. Then the dark granite of the Kolahoi peak suddenly became visible, with the Zanskar mountains just visi-ble behind. The party paused to take it all in. Ahead, they could see there had been an ice-fall, with huge seracs below the peak. To the left was the glacier itself, a frozen torrent of water, an iced-over moment that looked as if it could fracture at any time, sweeping them away. Then there were the crevasses that they imagined lay ahead, having heard stories that they regularly consumed sheep and ponies. In the distance they thought they could make out tiny figures climbing the fluted ice ribs and hanging glaciers. 'Indian soldiers,' said Bashir matter-of-factly. They came here to train before being deployed to the army's most vertiginous bases at Siachen, at 18,700 feet. Paul took rolls of film, switching from black-and-white to colour. After their six-hour ascent they stayed at the summit for some time, taking in the panorama below, and the vapour trails above that seemed to be almost within reach. 'I think at that point Paul must have realised he was very pleased that he had come to Kashmir,' Bob Wells mused later. 'Although it wasn't Ladakh, it was just about as foreign and awe-inspiring as he could imagine a place to be.'

Later, their legs stiffening as the afternoon clouds rolled in, signalling that the temperatures would soon plummet, the group picked their way back down to the Meadow. Julie was finished well before she got back to the camp, and slumped down inside the entrance of her tent to examine her badly blistered feet. Bart too had had enough. In the grip of a vicious headache, he suspected he was suffering from altitude sickness, and went off to lie down without eating.

That night, the others sat around the fire, planning. It had been quite a day, the best since arriving in Kashmir. Some of them, exhilarated by what they had achieved so far, talked of going up to Tar Sar the following morning. Keith was keen, but Julie put the kybosh on it. This was her first attempt at serious trekking, and Kolahoi was enough. Tomorrow, she was staying put. Paul and Cath were also tired, and opted to explore closer to the Meadow. Keith was alone in wanting to try to see the mountain lake. He would follow the track up for a while, he said, just to find out what was up there. 'A big, strapping lad', as his mother Mavis called him, he thought he could make it there and back in seven hours. He would probably be back by mid-afternoon, definitely by dinner, he promised Julie.

John Childs had also arrived at the Meadow. 'It was truly peaceful,' he remembered. He had asked his guide Dasheer to set up his tent on a hillside, away from the other tents gathered down by the river. He had come here to push himself through the wild mountains, and he wanted to do it alone: 'I was going to go down and say hello, but it just didn't happen. I'm a very quiet, shy and private kind of person.' While the Kashmiris prepared camp, John walked up to the woods behind his tent, following a herders' path through the creaking pines. Somewhere up above he could hear dogs barking. Perhaps it was a remote *gujjar* settlement, he thought as a family of herders appeared through the trees. On seeing him they instantly scurried off into the undergrowth. 'Although we were way up in the mountains there were people everywhere,' he said. 'It felt like nothing happened around this valley without everyone knowing about it.' When he headed back down later, tired and hungry, he noticed that more tents had been pitched in the Meadow, but he was glad to see that his was still several hundred yards from its nearest neighbour. Unlike Calcutta and Bihar, which he had found suffocating, here there was plenty of space. It looked as if he had chosen the perfect spot for a two-nighter.

Dasheer pondered John as he prepared their evening meal that night. He had torn up the track from Pahalgam, from where they had set out at daybreak, barely speaking a word the whole way. Most foreigners walked at half the speed of a Kashmiri, and many of them struggled to adjust to the altitude. But John had been at his shoulder all the way, making Dasheer work harder than he was used to. Three hours from Pahalgam to Aru, with two more to reach the Meadow. He could probably make it to Tar Sar and back with half a day to spare, Dasheer guessed. The Kashmiri guide admired the steely American, even if he could not say that he liked him. John seemed to him to cut a lonely figure. Kashmiris like to be surrounded by friends and family, but this American sought out no one's company other than his own. He had not given Dasheer a chance to get close, and after exchanging pleasantries at dinner he retired to his one-man tent.

Jane and Don packed up and left the Meadow at dawn on 3 July, without meeting either the British party or John Childs. They wanted to get as much out of their last two days as possible, pushing to the head of the Lidderwat Valley and then branching north-west along a path that took them over a series of precipitous ridges. 'It was the best day's trekking we had, some of the most spectacular scenery we had seen on the Kashmir trip,' Jane says. They began their descent, heading east through a sweeping valley to a remote campsite at Sekhwas. 'I remember camping and seeing the moon in the sky next to what might be the 13,450-foot Yarnhar Peak.' They were lucky to have caught it, Jane thought as she tracked wisps of light cloud moving across the plush darkness.

They woke on the morning of 4 July, daunted by the knowledge that by evening they would be back in Srinagar. Breaking camp, they headed out west along the same route they had taken the previous day to Tar Sar, but this time they continued towards the Sonarmas Pass.

For the whole trip Jane had kept a record of their route, and now she added this final journey to the map, tracing it in black felt-tip pen. As they ascended, Don photographed the wildflowers. 'The meadows were still somewhat soggy from recently melted snow (not all of it was gone), and the wildflowers including creeping phlox were amazing,' Jane recalled. Then some *gujjars* up ahead waved them down. The normally solitary herders were feared by many Kashmiris, who treated them like tinkers. This group talked for a time to Bashir in Urdu. He nodded, then turned to the foreigners. The *gujjars* had said the pass ahead was choked by snow, he told them. There was no way through. But there was something about his manner that made Jane and Don uneasy. They needed compelling reasons to abandon a route. Bashir suggested they should return to the Meadow, and camp there for one more night before descending to Pahalgam early the next day.

Don and Jane did not want to retrace their steps. Was he sure the information was accurate, Jane asked Bashir. She and Don were experienced ice climbers, who could make it over most things. Sultan, silent at first, claimed he was worried about his pony falling, while Bashir appeared uneasy. Was it laziness, or was he being over-protective, Jane wondered. Or was there something else to the story? Was he pushing them into another part of the mountains on the instructions of some unseen hand or authority? Don and Jane debated it. They were paying the guy, so he should do as they wished. 'But if the pony got injured we'd be responsible,' Don reasoned. 'In the end,' said Jane, 'we had to take Bashir at his word.'

As they irritably started their descent, a young Danish couple came up the path towards them, travelling alone. They stopped and chatted in English. When Don and Jane explained what their guides had told them about the blocked pass, the Danes said they would take their chances. They had no ponies to hold them back, and were experienced climbers. Jane never saw them again, 'But I think about them even to this day. Turning back would be the worst decision of my life.'

Shortly after, Jane and Don had another chance encounter, meeting a tall young British trekker, walking alone with a daypack. He introduced himself as Keith Mangan from Teesside, and said he was on his way up to Tar Sar. It was truly stunning, they said, well worth the effort. Keith said his wife, Julie, was waiting for him at the Meadow. They were heading back there, they replied. 'Tell her I'll be back later,' Keith said with a wave before heading up the path.

Within a couple of hours, Jane and Don were back at the Meadow. The Upper Camp was crowded, but they easily found Julie, sitting outside her tent. 'We met your husband,' Jane told her. They chatted for a few minutes, until Don looked around for Bashir and Sultan. They had agreed to pitch camp here, but the guides were already heading down out of the campsite, seemingly in a hurry. Jane and Don gave each other a *look*. Bashir knew something that he was not sharing. 'We felt that he was being evasive,' says Jane. But, nearing the end of a glorious trip that had buoyed their spirits, they followed anyway. They were tired, Jane's tooth throbbed and she was actually looking forward to going home.

Twenty minutes later they stopped beside a newly-built log bridge that marked the start of the Lower Camp. Bashir and Sultan were already busy getting the tents up. Jane went down to the river to relax while Don attempted to wash their socks and T-shirts in the icy water, doing his best to work up a lather. She caught up with her journal. It was 4 July, Independence Day. She realised this was the first time she'd thought about it all day. 'What would all our friends be doing back in Spokane?' she wondered. The great thing about leaving home was the warmth of returning, she thought. Don was already talking about what he would tell the Spokane crew. She started to write one last sentence about the day: 'So we agreed to come back the same way we had come,' she began, before she was interrupted.

FOUR

Home

The name chosen for the operation was *Ghar*, the Urdu word for 'home'. It reminded everyone of the objective – getting Masood Azhar back to Pakistan. And from the moment of its conception in January 1995, one candidate emerged as the man to handle it.

His Pakistani handlers called him, flippantly, 'the Kashmiri'. But in his native Kashmir, where their name meant nothing, he had many others. His parents had named him Javid Ahmed Bhat. School friends dubbed him 'Dabrani', after his village, Dabran, a few miles outside Kashmir's unruly southern town of Anantnag, an hour and a half's drive from Srinagar.

Javid was a stocky boy who lived in a two-storey brick house near the village's communal wash-house – a stone-lined pond where everyone cleaned their linen – and close to the ramshackle store, with its cardboard boxes of five-paisa chews, so congealed that you had to eat them with the wrappers on.

The Bhats were an educated family, Mr Bhat having been a quality-control officer in the district's agriculture department. Javid had done well enough to qualify for the government college in Anantnag, where he studied engineering. It always seemed to his neighbours that he would be somebody, one of the few who would escape the village, with its spinach-green houses and stone-and-mud lanes that tracked the saffron field. Dabran sat in a quiet copse of walnut and *chinar* (an oriental plane tree), surrounded by terraces of paddy. In high summer the village was dappled in light, and in winter it was frozen to the bone. In the daylight hours Dabran bustled along, while at night, like most villages in the valley, it coiled up like a fern, its residents locking shutters and barricading doors against the regular Indian security-force patrols that clattered through conducting cordon-and-search operations. Ostensibly, they were trying to catch militants, but they had become vengeful, with windows being smashed and possessions thrown into the mud, doors stoved in, sons and fathers taken away to an uncertain fate, women and girls hauled into dark places where bored soldiers, a long way from home, assaulted them.

As a child, Javid had lived for the spring, when he could finally prise open his bedroom shutters and oil his cricket bat, hand-carved from cheap Kashmiri poplar by an uncle. A pace bowler and a robust batsman, a thinker and a leader, it was no surprise to anyone in Dabran that this boy who others loved to be with had a loyal following by the time he was sixteen. He was a dependable friend, but also a worry to his family.

At college he joined the J&K Students Liberation Front (SLF), the youth wing of the *azadi* or 'freedom' movement that had taken root in campuses across Kashmir as a reaction to India's clumsy rigging of the state elections in 1987. For Javid, the SLF was also a vent for his fear and anger at all that he had seen his neighbours and family endure. He quickly moved up the ranks of the organisation, acquiring another name, Saifullah, to shade his political activities, while his alter ego pushed forward silently, attaining a BSc in engineering.

As the screws tightened around the valley with the introduction of Governor's Rule in December 1989, the SLF debated how to respond. Like students the world over, they were at the forefront of street protests, but some among their ranks wanted to take up arms and fight. 'Is it worth marching any more?' Javid had asked one day at a meeting convened to arrange a demonstration. He had been reading about radical German students who had taken up arms and formed the Red Army Faction in 1970. His intervention stopped all of them in their tracks. 'Holding placards won't stop the bloodshed. We are at war,' he continued. In April 1990, with calls for Kashmir's *tahreek*, or armed struggle, gaining momentum and being fuelled from over the border by Brigadier Badam and the ISI, Javid became part of a breakaway SLF bloc that took the plunge following the arrest of several student activists. India would only withdraw, so the argument went, if Kashmiris were willing to make it too costly for them to stay. Javid's group abducted the Vice Chancellor of Kashmir University and his elderly assistant while they were on their way to Friday prayers. They also snatched the general manager of Hindustan Machine Tools from downtown Srinagar. Their aim was to use the captured men to bargain the release of the jailed activists. A line had been crossed.

The Indian government refused to negotiate, throwing the SLF into a panic. What were they to do now? For days there was a standoff, until reports emerged that the Vice Chancellor and his assistant were to be freed anyway, at Padshahi Bagh, a beauty spot close to Anantnag town. The news was greeted with widespread joy, but as the two hostages clambered through the short grass, heading for freedom, they were shot in the back by unseen gunmen. The third hostage was cruelly killed too, his body dumped in the Srinagar neighbourhood of Batamaloo.

Many in the valley were shocked by these executions. Ordinary Kashmiris and regular SLF members rose up in disgust, pointing out that Indians were always pleased to see Kashmiris killing each other, as it saved them the trouble. Such actions only benefited the oppressor, said the mainstream SLF leadership, denouncing the breakaway faction that Javid had joined. Although he was unconnected to the abductions and killings, he refused to criticise those who had carried them out. 'They are not *darshit gar* [terrorists], they are *mujahids*,' he told his friends. 'Don't shy away. We have to meet this terror head-on. Remember the massacres of Gawakadal, Sopore and Handwara.' The bloody events would mark the beginning of Javid's withdrawal from mainstream Kashmiri society, and while some in the SLF went underground, he sought out more militant comrades. If India was to be beaten, then all the old ways, of soft-edged politicking and mystical faith, had to be replaced by a razor-sharp Islamic identity. The only way to purge India from the valley was through *tahreek*, Javid declared. He signed up with the Ikhwan Muslimeen, the Muslim Brotherhood, a group of religiously conservative Kashmiri *mujahids* who had been sizing up the massing Indian security forces. As he took up arms, he was a long way from the schoolboy Javid Ahmed Bhat, or the jaunty cricket player Dabrani. But in his own mind he was not yet far enough.

In the summer of 1990, on the run from the Indian security forces after the Brotherhood had been bloodied in an encounter in Anantnag, Javid unexpectedly stopped by to see his family in Dabran, shinning in through the kitchen window. 'No need to worry,' he said, at which his mother and father froze in fear. For Kashmiri parents, said Mr Bhat, these four words meant just one thing: their child was going 'over there'.

'We knew then that he was heading for Pakistan. He kissed us and he was gone. Then we heard absolutely nothing.' For months, hundreds of young men across the valley had been disappearing over the LoC, heading for training camps. But terrible reports soon seeped home of boys, too young and inexperienced to evade the hardened Indian border forces, being cut down the minute they crossed back over into Kashmir. Those who made it further into the valley were also being culled, as India stepped up to the growing militancy. After a while Javid's parents started mourning, hoping someone would be kind enough to bring his body home to be buried in the village cemetery, a shady spot near a line of knock-kneed *chinars*. But no news came. 'To be honest, there were times when I would have claimed any body – just so we could say it's done,' said his tearful mother.

In Javid's absence, the pocket handkerchief of scrub that made up Dabran cemetery rapidly filled with 'martyrs'. One third were boys of Javid's age, friends with whom he had played cricket in the summer holidays, killed by the Indian Army while serving one *tahreek* organisation or another, some of them home-grown, some funded from across the LoC. Another third were boys who had had no connection to the militancy whatsoever, but were killed just for coming from Dabran, which for many in the Indian security forces was crime enough, given the village's links to Javid and other up-and-coming figures in the *azadi* movement. The remaining third were unknowns, mostly gunned down by the Rashtriya Rifles (RR), a new specialist counter-insurgency force raised by India's army chief in May 1990, whose ruthlessness would change the face of the conflict beyond recognition.

Made up of soldiers seconded from other parts of the Indian Army and paid extra, the original six battalions of the RR – motto *Dridhta aur Virta*, meaning 'Strength and Bravery' – had been created as a counter to Brigadier Badam's ISI operation. But soon the RR, which would have forty thousand men in Kashmir, the largest dedicated counter-insurgency force in the world, was as renowned for its reckless lack of precision as for its ingenuity and valour. In Dabran and other villages across the valley, the bodies of those it had killed, who it described as 'foreign militants', were dumped at the local police post, without justification or documents. Most were Kashmiri civilians who had been abducted by the RR and summarily executed, but no one was brave enough to take it to task. Instead, Dabran's cemetery became a place to bury the evidence, and for collective mourning. Everyone in the village had someone 'over there', so the Dabranis clubbed together to pay for the last rites and the burial shrouds of these unclaimed corpses, hoping the same civility would be accorded their kin, should their bodies be found on Pakistani soil.

One day early in 1995, six years into the insurgency, while snow settled on the single track through Dabran, a stranger banged at Mr and Mrs Bhat's front door. His face was obscured by an unkempt beard and a *pakul*, the flat woolly cap favoured by the Afghan *mujahideen*, and the couple were terrified until he spoke. Then Mrs Bhat fell to her knees. It was Javid, the son who in her mind's eye she had buried. After the hugging and kissing, and the pouring of *namkeen* (salt tea) from the thermos, Javid cleared his throat. 'I am not Javid any more,' he told them, adding that he did not have long to explain. He was with some men with guns, on their way to carry out an important mission. Right now they were stationed outside as lookouts.

'Where have you been?' asked his father, wanting a souvenir of his son, a fragment to fill the void of waiting. In Pakistan, Javid told him.

And Afghanistan. Sipping his tea, he explained that while serving in the Muslim Brotherhood he had come across a *mujahid* who had mesmerised him, an implacable, smooth-skinned man nicknamed Supahi al-Yemeni, or 'the Warrior from Yemen', who rarely broke into a sweat. Supahi had said that he bottled up his fear. The proof was that in an engagement with the enemy he always remained standing even under heavy fire, trading bullets until his Kalashnikov glowed in the dark. Everyone had been a little afraid of Supahi's self-control and recklessness, which were daunting qualities for young Kashmiri recruits so raw they still dropped their weapons and tripped over guide ropes at night. But Javid had been drawn in as Supahi told him of his experiences as a veteran of many wars. Believing that in Javid he had found a like-minded soul, Supahi convinced him to undergo specialist training. In the summer of 1990 they had taken a bus to Uri, a town in western Kashmir, then climbed high up to the LoC and crossed over with a few dozen other boys, following a toe-tingling midnight scramble so close to Indian Army camps they could hear the soldiers guffaw. When they finally reached the other side they were exhilarated, calling out '*Naraay takbir, Allahu akbar!*' (Cry out loud, God is great) before sliding down the snowy slopes on their trouser bottoms, like boys in the park. Eventually, as the temperature dropped further, Javid had arrived in Muzaffarabad, the capital of Pakistan-administered Kashmir, his face tinged with blue.

Small tent villages run by religious organisations encircled Muzaffarabad, the capital of what all Kashmiris dreamily eulogised as 'Azad', or Free Kashmir, the region over the LoC that was administered by Pakistan. Now it had the appearance of a refugee camp and the smell of a rubbish dump. Uniformed instructors, who everyone murmured with respect were members of the ISI or from the Pakistan military, taught Javid how to strip down a Kalashnikov and assemble a rocket launcher. Once a week he ate slivers of fatty mutton; the rest of the time it was cold bread, rice and *daal* scoffed down while squatting on the ground. They dug latrines day and night, but raw sewage flowed everywhere, and wild dogs converged to pick at the garbage left rotting in the open. However, for the first time in his life, surrounded by pious and like-minded youths, Javid felt alive, and over the weeks he spent there the camp was deluged with new recruits from his side of the Line of Control.

'Somehow, between prayers, and from one week to the next, thousands of boys came over,' Javid told his father as he sat cross-legged on the carpeted floor of the living room of his childhood home in Dabran, a flock cushion wedged behind his back and a Chinese rug thrown over his legs. 'Within a month there were barely enough weapons to go around, only one Kalashnikov for every seven volunteers.' They counted out bullets, sharing the few they had equally between them all. Soon there were no live-fire exercises at all. Although Pakistan had planned this secret Kashmiri revolution, it had been taken aback by the speed with which it had spread, and the demand for arms and training. What had started as a dribble of fighters had become a torrent, with one group of 1,800 young men rumoured to have crossed over the LoC in a single day. Wedding caterers from Rawalpindi had to be brought in to cook for the ISI's massing Kashmir militia. 'No one teaches you how to prepare for a revolution,' Javid told his father. 'Which books should we read? It was chaos.'

While Pakistan tried to come to grips with the forces it had set in motion, Javid moved up the ranks. Many boys were sent back over into Indian Kashmir after just a few weeks of basic guerrilla-warfare training, but Javid, with his BSc in engineering, was picked out. Supahi suggested he accompany him over another mountainous border, this time the ranges that divided Pakistan and Afghanistan. Working their way between boulders on ponies bowed by the weight of bursting saddlebags carrying munitions and banknotes, they eventually reached Camp Yawar, the *jihad* factory of the Holy Warriors where Saifullah, the warrior former student from the Binori Town *madrassa* in Karachi, had trained thousands, the place where Masood Azhar had endured his night-time humiliation. By the time Javid arrived it was capable of housing up to 1,800 recruits, and with strictly assessed diploma courses and a postgraduate programme, Yawar had evolved into a college of war. Here, Javid told his father, were serious-minded revolutionaries. His first lesson had been to accept that he was no longer a Kashmiri, but an Islamic fighter who would respond to any call to perform holy *jihad*, the world over. 'First Kashmir, then Palestine,' he recounted. Mr Bhat stared back at his son, fearing that he understood all too well what this meant.

Yawar's core curriculum was based around three pillars: *Haj Habi Tablighi* (religious indoctrination), *Tarbiyat* (training) and *Jihad* (the holy fight). Two kinds of courses were offered: the basic one-month guerrilla-warfare starter (the one Masood had failed in 1988), and a three-month specialist course that included modules in explosives, encrypted communications and counter-intelligence. From this second course, students graduated as fully-fledged *jundullahs*, or soldiers of Allah. The best would be picked out for further training as commanders, learning how to manage men as well as weapons, and how to plot and execute operations. Javid completed this final course, becoming an ordnance specialist, handling explosives for the first time and also learning to create highly volatile home-made incendiaries by mixing textile fixatives with petroleum jelly. He was taught how to manufacture mines, IEDs and booby traps, and shown how to transform a battery-powered doorbell into a remote detonator.

In April 1992, Javid was ready. He was appointed district commander for Anantnag, part of the Holy Warriors' high command structure in south Kashmir, and was launched back across the Line of Control into India, repeating his first treacherous mountain journey in reverse. His base would be a newly-established Holy Warriors camp in the remote forests east of Anantnag, where he and his father had once hunted musk deer.

From now on, Javid Ahmed Bhat of Dabran took on another identity: 'Sikander', the Persian name for Alexander the Great. He chose it because he believed it befitted a *mujahid* with an understanding of justice, capable of compassion as well as bravery. And the Kashmir operation he had been sent to mastermind began well, as he mounted audacious operations against Indian patrols while recruiting hundreds to the cause, like-minded boys he had searched out from among former neighbours and friends, who were sent over the LoC to be trained and armed by the ISI. However, it was not long before there were breakaway factions. Everyone in Kashmir had an opinion about everything, and even these splinter groups split again to form new cells. Too many Kashmiris wanted to be king, Sikander complained to his closest comrades. Far away in Pakistan, Brigadier Badam realised this too, as he surveyed the rapidly disintegrating ranks of militants. He knew they would have to be consolidated if the insurgency was to begin to bite.

In the autumn of 1993 Sikander was one of the Holy Warriors' senior Kashmir commanders who received a message that their group was being subsumed into the unified ISI-backed outfit Harkat ul-Ansar, the Movement of the Victorious. A new chief of military operations was coming to the valley to whip everyone into shape: the Afghani. Sikander told his father that initially he had been worried. While he was an important commander in south Kashmir, in the eyes of Islamabad he was but a small cog. He needed to prove himself all over again.

Things had gone well. From the moment they met in January 1994, the Afghani could see that Sikander was brave and committed. He also came with the blessing of Langrial, the Afghani's old comrade, who had sized up the bright young Kashmiri at Camp Yawar and crossed the LoC with him in 1992. Langrial and Sikander had even conducted a few successful operations together in Kashmir. The Afghani was quick to appoint Sikander his lieutenant.

Shortly after the Afghani's arrival, however, news broke that Langrial had been caught. Sikander was among the first to volunteer to bring about Langrial's freedom. He was a central figure in the brazen thirty-hour firefight in Elahi Bagh in Srinagar on 16 January, from which he and the Afghani only narrowly escaped alive. Sikander was there too when the Afghani abducted Major Bhupinder Singh, the Indian Army officer who was supposed to be exchanged for Langrial. And Sikander was also present when that plan foundered, and the Major was executed. He told his father that his role in this killing had 'saddened him'. He was more than happy to kill Indian troops in battle, but the cold-blooded execution of an unarmed man breached his moral code.

However, in February 1994, when the Afghani learned that Masood Azhar was coming to south Kashmir on a mission to get the ISI's Kashmir operation back on track, it seemed only natural that Sikander should be put in charge of all security arrangements. He selected the remote village of Matigund, high above Anantnag, as the place where Masood would deliver his first address, an event that the ISI hoped would draw a line under the Langrial affair.

However, the visit had gone disastrously wrong, with Masood and the Afghani being captured. As District Commander of Anantnag, Sikander felt he had failed both the Movement's Chief of Military Operations and its General Secretary, who were both now in Indian hands. He had been charged with their security, and he should have been there to protect them. But, like a schoolboy, he had fallen off his motorcycle on the way to the *majlis*, and therefore had not been in the room to voice his concerns at the ill-advised plan for Masood to give the Friday sermon at Anantnag. Sikander imagined he was now a laughing stock. He felt as if he had to restore his reputation and exact revenge.

Immediately after the arrests, Sikander began blasting the first Indian patrol he found, strafing, bombing, hurling grenades and risking the lives of all those around him. This led to mass round-ups and crackdowns, in Dabran and elsewhere, although when Masood heard about it later, he was impressed, writing 'Commander Sikander attacked the Indian Army for fifteen consecutive days.'

In his mind, Sikander had to rectify the mess, but those around him were alarmed by his actions. Eventually he was disarmed by his fellow Brothers and forced to take refuge in a safe house in remote Lovloo village, high up in the Pir Panjal mountains, until he cooled off. 'I was brought down to earth,' he told his parents.

In the early summer of 1994, plans arrived from Pakistan for an audacious plan, backed by the ISI, to free Masood, the Afghani and Langrial. Sikander was to run it, and he received instructions that he was to conduct another kidnapping. As he related this story to his parents Sikander seemed uneasy with it, and skimmed over some events. All he would say was that he had been told to seek out foreigners, rather than well-connected Indian nationals or army officers. Western hostages could be used to exert pressure on the Indian government to release the prisoners, he had been advised.

Sikander had hastily put together a kidnap party that in June 1994 seized two British hostages, Kim Housego, who was only sixteen, and a thirty-six-year-old video producer, David Mackie, both of whom had been trekking with their families in the hills above Pahalgam. They were held in the Pir Panjal mountains for seventeen anxious days, while Sikander's group attempted to negotiate with the Indian authorities.

He finished this story abruptly, his father recalled, claiming that it had ended well for the hostages and badly for him. Although he had put together enough supplies and armed protection to hold out in the mountains for months, influential voices on the other side of the Line of Control had ordered him to end the operation. The government of Benazir Bhutto in Islamabad had come under intense international pressure after Kim Housego's father, a former British journalist based in New Delhi, launched a noisy public campaign to save his son, claiming that the group holding him had links to the Pakistani establishment. Soon after, with the Pakistani Prime Minister demanding that the hostages be freed, Sikander had been forced to hand the two Britons over to Kashmiri journalists at Anantnag. He had vowed never to get tangled up with foreigners again. 'It wasn't like transporting bullets or rice,' he told his father. Human cargo was prickly and temperamental. Hostages required kilos of meat to eat, and were capable of shredding their captors' nerves. Furious foreign governments were difficult for Pakistan to ignore. All of Sikander's men had been 'deeply affected' by the operation, finding the stress of living in close physical proximity to their unpredictable Western charges far more taxing than fighting in the woods and villages.

Now, in January 1995, after various other abortive plots to secure Masood's freedom had been proposed, a new order had come from over the Line of Control. A few days previously, a courier known as 'Zameen' had arrived from Muzaffarabad with news that a high-level delegation was on its way from Pakistan, bringing instructions, approved by the ISI, that would lead to Masood and the Afghani being freed. Sikander said that all he knew was the code-name: Operation Ghar.

Draining his tea, Sikander kissed his family goodbye. 'The end is not yet written,' he told them as he pulled his *pakul* down over his head before vanishing into an indigo night speckled with snow. If Mr Bhat had known that this would be the last time he would ever see his son, he would have asked Javid what he meant.

Sikander headed for the Heevan Hotel, a three-storey wood-and-tin building on the banks of the Lidder River in Pahalgam, the nearest thing the trekking town had to luxury. It was a journey of just thirty-five miles, but it took Sikander a couple of days, as he was a wanted man and had to travel by foot and pony, sticking to the remote mountain ridges, frequently doubling back on himself to ensure no one was following. Popular with wealthy Indian honeymooners and executives, and the odd Western trekker doing India-lite, the Heevan, the police suspected, had become a refuge for senior commanders in the Movement, with several members of staff under scrutiny for having contacts with the insurgent group. The police knew that Sikander had stayed there on several occasions. He did not mingle with the paying guests, who enjoyed large, comfortable mustard-yellow bedrooms with TV, air-conditioning and hot showers. Instead, the *mujahid* from Dabran slipped in through a kitchen door around the back, and occupied a disused storeroom in the attic, with a view of the blackness of the pine forest behind and up to the glistening Pir Panjal and the raucous Lidder River gurgling down below, clearing his head.

There word reached Sikander from Zameen, the ISI messenger. Operation Ghar was to involve yet another kidnapping. Sikander told two confidants that, even worse, Zameen had said his targets would once again be foreigners, so as to heap pain on India by international-ising the Kashmir crisis, drawing Western embassies into the fray. Why do this again, Sikander had asked, but Zameen was a messenger and had no idea. All he had been told was that Sikander was ordered to capture European or American specialists working on infrastructure projects in the region, people of consequence from powerful corporations that would work hard to get them released. To avoid a repeat of the embarrassing climbdown of the previous year, the Movement was to create a front organisation to carry out the kidnappings, making it harder for the Indian security forces to anticipate their tactics and easier for Pakistan to disguise its involvement. More significantly, the captives were not to be concealed in the Pir Panjal. Instead, they would be spirited over the LoC into Pakistan, a treacherous journey of more than a hundred miles, mostly by foot, sometimes by pony, a marathon of mountain passes and peaks that, if successfully traversed, would surely secure the release of Masood and his jailed colleagues.

Three weeks later, at the end of February 1995, Sikander heard from Zameen again. Most of the kidnap team had crossed the LoC. Right now they were camped in the snow-covered forests past Uri, the last Indian-administered town on the old Muzaffarabad road. The party consisted of twenty-four 'brothers', as the *mujahids* referred to one another. They had been organised into an outfit called 'al Faran', a name randomly chosen by someone in Islamabad that had vague Islamic connotations, being a mountain in Saudi Arabia. Some of the team were Punjabis from Bahawalpur, Masood's hometown; others were drawn from the *madrassas* of Karachi; more than a dozen were Pashtuns from either side of the Afghan border. All were war veterans, and among them was 'the Turk', whose real name was Abdul Hamid, a *mujahid* of Turkish ancestry who had fought just about everywhere. Sikander knew him, and was immediately worried.

The Turk had a reputation as a *kal kharab*, a crazy guy. He had been flitting back and forth between Kashmir and Pakistan for a couple of years, and Sikander had seen him in action on many occasions. There was no denying he was a brave and experienced *mujahid*, having also survived battles in Sudan and Somalia, even fighting with the Somali warlord Mohamed Farah Aideed, and rumoured to have been part of the detachment of foreign Islamic shock troops involved in the so-called 'Black Hawk Down' incident of October 1993, a badge of honour in the world of *jihad*. Two US helicopters had been brought down after rocket-propelled grenades were fired into their tails, triggering the notorious battle in which nineteen American soldiers died and many hundreds of Islamic militiamen were killed or wounded. He was also said to have been in Bosnia and the Caucasus, setting ambushes for Russian troops (who he had also slain in large numbers in Afghanistan for much of the 1980s).

Sikander knew that the Turk would be difficult to lead, and even harder to follow. Coupled with his legendary temper was a deep religiosity, a spirituality that comforted simple fighting men, although his commanders had found it often swamped his strategic vision.

There was some good news. Sikander's role was to make sure that Operation Ghar was supported in every way possible once the team had entered his theatre of south Kashmir, but he was not expected to travel with the al Faran brothers day-to-day, so handling the Turk would fall to al Faran's Pakistani field commander, Mohammed Hassan Shafiq. An alumnus of the Darul Uloom *madrassa* in Khanewal, Punjab, another offshoot of Masood's grand *madrassa* in Karachi, Shafiq had trained at Camp Yawar at the same time as Masood, graduating with honours, and had joined the Holy Warriors as a senior commander with the *nom de guerre* Abu Jindal, roughly translated from the Arabic as 'the Killer'. Since early 1994 he had been fighting in Kashmir with the Movement, regularly crossing the LoC with newly trained fighters, weapons and explosives. Sikander knew him as cool on the battlefield and ruthless in his dealings with the enemy. Abu Jindal, Sikander was certain, was equipped to keep a lid on his deputy. He was renowned for his battlefield vision, even if the Turk's eyes were often cloaked by a crimson rage.

There was something else about the kidnap team that pleased Sikander. Some of its members were Kashmiris, who had been included for their local knowledge, contacts and allegiances to local insurgent groups who might be called on to assist the operation. It was also important to make sure al Faran had a genuine *azadi* element to it, so the Indian government could not turn the kidnappings into a political issue, blaming Pakistan for interfering on Indian soil.

The most senior Kashmiri was Qari Zarar, an old hand from Doda, a district in Jammu, the southern half of the state. Zarar had been recruited primarily for his mountaineering skills. He could read a track like no one else, but his nerve had been called into question. Sikander worried about him. The Pashtuns had an expression, which translated as 'last man standing', that referred to a man's courage under fire. Whenever a Soviet helicopter gunship had roared overhead in Afghanistan during the 1980s, its auto cannon spitting out three thousand rounds a minute, the first person to hit the deck would be thrown out of the unit, and the last would be made the leader. Although he had not fought in Afghanistan, Zarar was thought of as having 'a mouthful of dirt'. Beside him would be a sixteen-year-old novice, also from Doda, a teenage *gujjar* boy who Zarar called *beta*, or son. This boy was rumoured to be so green he barely knew how to shoulder a rifle. But he did have hidden uses, Sikander was advised, including a thorough knowledge of the secret shepherds' routes through the high Pir Panjal and into the deadly Warwan.

Sikander could not quite put his finger on it, but for some reason he was still filled with anxiety. The team was an awkward mix of men and boys, with different allegiances and priorities, some too weak, in his opinion, to see things through, others too strong-willed and unpredictable for such a delicate operation. Having been in the business of kidnapping several times already, including direct experience of holding Western hostages, this was not the unit Sikander would have chosen. But he was not in overall charge, his authority having been significantly weakened by the loss of the Afghani and Masood, as well as the failure of the Housego and Mackie operation. It was too late to gripe or turn back. But in March 1995, as he awaited the team's arrival in south Kashmir, busying himself concealing weapons, ammunition and food in the horseshoe of hills above Anantnag, Sikander received some alarming news.

Instead of making their way directly to Anantnag, as had originally been intended, the al Faran party had been forced to divert to the ancient citadel of Charar-i-Sharief, in Badgam district, twenty miles south-west of Srinagar. Heavy snow and rain had hampered their passage down from the LoC, and when they reached the valley they encountered heavier Indian patrols than had been expected. Unable to push on, they had decided to consolidate at Charar-i-Sharief, a wooden medieval settlement, closely stacked on a knife-edge of a hillside, which was known to strongly support the militancy. As far as the Indian security forces were concerned, the town was a vipers' pit of enemy gunmen at the best of times, and in March 1995 thawing militants from many different groups were known to have converged there, holing up in and around Charar's main attraction, a wooden mausoleum and prayer hall that had been erected in ancient times because of a story that the flying coffin of Sheikh Noor-ud-din Wali, a famous *rishi*, or saint, who had attracted a vast following in the fourteenth century, had descended from the heavens and chosen Charar as its final resting place.

The arrival in Kashmir of the remains of Noor-ud-din had had an enormous impact on the region, gradually transforming it from Hinduism to Islam. Noor-ud-din, who had spent his last years living in a cave, surviving, it was said, on only one cup of water a day, had even been chosen as Kashmir's patron saint, a decision that had infused the region with its unique flavour of Sufism. This holiest of shrines had become a place of pilgrimage for devotees from across the subcontinent. Relics of the Sheikh's life and death were guarded inside a complex decorated with chandeliers and ancient Persian rugs, and surrounded by a maze of inns and food halls, markets and boarding houses – a Kashmiri Lourdes, flocked to by hundreds of thousands of worshippers of all faiths, especially the sick. More importantly to the insurgents, all approaches to the shrine could be observed, making it the perfect redoubt, with the added advantage that the reverence it inspired made the Indian security forces tiptoe around its boundaries.

When the brothers of al Faran arrived seeking refuge in Charar-i-Sharief in March 1995, they discovered they were not the first. Ahead of them was a group of Kashmiri and Pakistani insurgents under the command of Haroon Ahmed, a mercenary from Peshawar. Known to his men as 'Mast Gul', or simply 'the Major', he had come over to boost the Kashmiri insurgency, working for Hizbul Mujahideen (HM), the largest of the indigenous Kashmiri militant groups, which had also been lavished with cash and weapons by the ISI. Now Mast Gul had stockpiled munitions in the holy of holies. 'I had hoped to lure India into a direct attack,' he said later, 'bringing about a battle in this holiest of cities that would make the entire *ummah* [Muslim world] rise up in hatred.'

The Indian security forces were aware of this plan, and instead laid siege to the town. The brothers of al Faran found themselves stuck in the middle. Although the Movement (Pakistani) and HM (Kashmiri) were rivals, they shared a common enemy in India, and both had a loyalty to the Kashmiri freedom movement and the ISI. So when Mast Gul told them, 'You will fight with us,' Abu Jindal's boys could not refuse him.

The Movement had intended for the Operation Ghar party to arrive in Anantnag quietly and well-rested. But at Charar-i-Sharief they were press-ganged into another man's operation. In Anantnag, Sikander became frantic on hearing this news. It was already mid-March. The hostages should have been seized by now, yet every morning he read in the papers of the siege hardening.

The frozen spring thawed into early summer, and still there was no let-up. Sikander was about to send word that a new team should be sent from Pakistan, when in the early hours of 10 May 1995, two explosions rocked Noor-ud-din's shrine. He saw the footage for himself, broadcast live by local and international TV channels that had gathered on a neighbouring hillside to watch events. It showed how the ancient wooden edifice crackled and smoked before flames licked through it, panicking the Indian security forces that ringed it, who tried to douse the flames, at the same time keeping a lookout for Mast Gul and his men. But the HM fighters never emerged, and the soldiers failed to extinguish the fire. By dusk the security forces were surveying a dismal scene: more than two thousand ancient homes destroyed, along with the shrine itself. The footage was broadcast everywhere.

A powerful story spun its way across continents that the Indian Army had deliberately torched the shrine in order to smoke out the HM cell. This was vehemently denied by India, which insisted that the militants holed up inside had done the deed themselves. However, given their track record in Kashmir, the Indian security forces were now plausibly framed. Almost as demoralising, Mast Gul and most of his men had slipped away through the choking smoke. Abu Jindal, the leader of the al Faran kidnap party, had not been so lucky. He had been captured, and a third of his men killed. Even before commencing Operation Ghar, the brothers were leaderless and down to sixteen.

Two weeks later Mast Gul emerged triumphant, staging an impromptu press conference on 26 May from a new hideout, in which a senior HM commander presented him with a 100,000-rupee reward for his 'heroic deeds' in escaping the siege at which 'India had brazenly levelled one of Islam's most historic sites'. Only later did he confess to supporters in Peshawar that it had in fact been his boys who struck the match. 'I did what India could not,' he said, recounting how they had poured thick black lines of gunpowder around Noor-ud-din's shrine before setting it alight.

Sikander's bile rose as he read about Mast Gul's speech. He knew he had to come up with a salvage plan. Operation Ghar was now three months behind schedule, and had lost sight of its original targets: the foreign engineers. By the time the depleted kidnap team made it to the rendezvous point near Anantnag, it would be June. They would be fractious, exhausted and rudderless. Sikander took a decision. They needed to settle on easier prey, he told his comrades, forgetting all of his previous reservations. The summer trekking paths around Pahalgam would soon be attracting a trickle of foreign tourists. He had done this once before, he told his men. Through gritted teeth, he said it would be as easy as picking walnuts.

FIVE

Kidnap

Sitting on the riverbank, her journal open on her lap, Jane Schelly glanced up at the two Kashmiri guides squatting by the stove. Vegetables and rice again, she thought, her heart sinking. Bashir and Sultan were squabbling. Something was wrong. This was their last night together, and if she was honest, she was looking forward to saying goodbye. She was grateful for all the humping of kit, the cooking and the renditions of Kashmiri love songs, and even the convoluted accounts of local lore and the circular stories that started but never ended. However, there had been a subtle but significant shift in relations earlier in the day as a result of the argument over the 'snowblocked' pass. 'I now realised that I no longer trusted them,' Jane recalled. That was the nub of it. Or maybe it was just her tooth, which continued to ache. 'Note to self: call the dentist when we get back,' she remembered thinking as she watched Bashir lecturing Sultan on the best way to dice onions.

She shivered in the coolness of the dusk and thought about going to the tent to get an extra layer of clothing, but her feet were throbbing from the long day's trek. It was just past 5 p.m. on 4 July, and the sun had already sunk behind the ridgeline, leaving the campsite several degrees colder than when they had arrived. Instead, she wrapped her fleece more tightly around herself and went back to her journal, to finish describing the aborted attempt to cross the Sonarmas Pass.

Then, an indeterminate flickering drew her eye. Struggling to focus in the fading light, she thought she saw a group of figures approaching. They appeared from a clump of pine trees. Had they been spying on her, watching the camp, she wondered. She didn't have time to think about it now, as they were heading straight for her, walking and then trotting. It was the antelope and the lion, a moment of precognition.

Trying not to stare, Jane estimated that there were a dozen of them, dressed in an assortment of long robes and shawls, like medieval warriors. Some wore dark indigo turbans, others flat woollen caps, and their hair and beards were long, their skin dark and unwashed. As they drew closer she saw that some were wearing military-style green-and-khaki tactical vests. For a moment she thought they might be mountain police, but although she and Don had passed the occasional army patrol, she had never seen men like this. She looked about, but there was no one else around, just her, Don, Bashir and Sultan. She glanced over at Don, still down at the river. He had seen the strangers too, and nodded down at his soapy hands as if to say, 'Let's not draw attention to ourselves.' Don would work this out, she reassured herself.

As the men neared, Jane saw they were stained by sweat and dirt, as if they had been out in the wilds for many days. Beneath their shawls they carried rifles and coils of ammunition. Were they some kind of irregulars, a part-time government unit deployed in the mountains? One of them called out to Sultan, who looked up, utensils clattering to the ground as the man barked questions in what Sultan recognised as Pashto-accented Urdu, his language and tone instantly marking him out to any local Kashmiri as a foreign *muja-hid* from the Afghan borders. Sultan tentatively answered, '*Angresi*,' the Urdu word used for all foreigners, regardless of where they come from. The armed men moved closer, and motioned for Don and Jane to go over to their tent. Jane stared hard at the one who seemed to be the leader, but he remained emotionless, almost aloof, his face swathed in a rough indigo-coloured scarf. She looked over at Sultan and Bashir. Had she been right to doubt them, she wondered. 'Have we been set up?' she asked herself. The gunman gesticulated with his rifle. They were to be silent. Jane did her best to remain calm, although a rage was rising within her. Was this the reason Bashir and Sultan had been so eager to come to the Lower Camp, because they were accessories in this robbery or whatever it was? As she watched the men quiz the guides further, she thought about her money and travellers' cheques that were lying inside the tent along with Don's camera. She needed to get in there and conceal everything.

Bashir came running over. 'Passports,' he urged, sweating, and with a panicked look in his eyes. 'Who are they?' Don muttered under his breath. Bashir didn't reply. Seeing the foreigners hesitate, the leader's eyes settled on Jane and Don. 'Just give me, *please*,' Bashir insisted, thrusting out his hand. 'He seemed genuinely afraid,' Jane recalled. As she retrieved the passports from their tent, she considered pushing their cash inside one of the sleeping bags, but decided against it. She sat back down, and saw an itinerant *gujjar* stroll into the camp, carrying a basket of flat *lavash* bread, an incongruous moment of normality given the events of the past few minutes. Seeing the armed party a few seconds too late, the *gujjar* was unable to beat a retreat. He flinched as one of them beckoned him over, then grabbed a handful of *lavash* and stuffed it roughly into his vest. 'This will be a test,' thought Jane. When the gunman reached inside his *kurta* and produced some money to pay, she felt relieved. He was not a robber after all. But what did that make him?

After studying the passports, most of the armed group, including the leader, broke away, heading off up the Meadow, leaving behind only two sentries. Two guards and four prisoners. She and Don had not exchanged anything more than meaningful glances about what was happening, but she knew he was thinking the same thing as her. Could they overpower them? But the men were heavily armed, and even if they could escape, it would not be without serious injury. It wasn't worth it.

It began to drizzle, and in an unexpected act of compassion the men gestured for Jane and Don to put on some warmer clothes. Sit down, they motioned. Jane and Don sat and watched as the strangers unravelled their turbans and laid them out on the ground along with their weapons. Then they stooped to wash their hands in the river before prostrating themselves in prayer.

Paul Wells and Cath Moseley were waiting for dinner at the Upper Camp. Cath felt more content than at any time since they had reached India, and this was the kind of environment that suited Paul: up high in the wilds. He took snaps of their camp, black-and-white images showing the party's three tents lined up in a row; Julie and Keith, Paul and Cath, with Bart Imler between them. In one shot, Keith Mangan, who had just got back from Tar Sar, can be seen rummaging around in his tent while Julie looks on, dressed in her warm sweatpants, hand on hip as if slightly irritated by the mess he is making. Exhausted, cold and footsore, Keith had come back elated at the end of the afternoon, saying that the scenery had been stunning, and while he was up there he had heard about a breathtaking high-altitude campsite at Sekhwas. Julie knew what he was getting at. 'No way,' she said, her feet still aching.

At around 6.30 p.m., just as they were getting ready to join the others for food, Julie turned to see a group of strangers approaching their camp. Wearing robes and turbans, they were dragging Julie and Keith's guide Bashir with them. Clearly terrified, Bashir called out that the gunmen wanted to see everyone's passports and that they had to obey their orders. Who were these men, Keith asked, but there was no reply. 'They had guns,' said Julie. 'We were surrounded.' Everyone handed their passports over, then, following mimed instructions, sat down in a semi-circle. Gripping Keith's hand, Julie was filled with a burning sense of dread as one of the armed men used his rifle to prod through their tent. He moved on, eventually finding Bart Imler, who had spent the day wrapped up in his sleeping bag, still complaining of sickness and a headache. What was wrong with him, the gunman asked via Bashir. Bashir said he had altitude sickness. What nationality was he? 'Canadian,' the sick man croaked, trying to sound as feeble as he could. The gunman threw a strip of pills at him and barked, 'Take these,' before walking away. They clearly wanted the tourists alive.

It was almost dark, but the newcomers seemed in no hurry. Whatever this was, Julie sensed, it wasn't an impulsive bushwhacking. Possible scenarios flashed through her mind: the women raped, the men lying with their throats slit. All the time she could hear dogs yelping in some distant *gujjar* encampment. How could they sound the alarm? She held on to Keith. Perhaps these strangers were forest rangers, she thought weakly. Just then, one of the younger ones, who couldn't have been more than sixteen, gestured with a knife at Julie and Cath. She froze, but Bashir explained, 'They want you to dress properly.' T-shirts and running shorts were inappropriate, the boy had said. Julie and Cath fumed, but went off to get changed. Then everyone was ordered over to the two *dhokas*, where more gunmen were guarding a group of Kashmiri schoolboys who had arrived noisily in the Meadow that afternoon. Julie had watched them setting up their tents on the other side of the river, joking and larking about. Whatever she and her friends had got themselves into, these local boys were in it too, she thought. Somehow, that reassured her.

But as the minutes ticked by while the leader established everyone's nationality, turning the previously immaculate campsite into a tip, Julie felt as if the blood were draining from her body. She couldn't breathe: it felt like the period of intense discomfort that is the precursor to full-blown panic. 'I am going to die,' she recalled thinking. 'This is a firing squad.' Would they end up digging their own graves, she wondered. Keith squeezed her hand. At least they would die together. But no shots were fired, and the gunmen remained calm. They ordered the Westerners to sit down, handed back the women's passports and began rifling through all the tents again, stripping them of valuables. So it was just a robbery. Then two of the armed men marched off up the hill towards the tent belonging to a Western trekker no one had talked to: John Childs.

He was sleeping when they reached him. 'That day, my fourth day of trekking, I had been to the highest elevation and had got altitude sickness. I was flat out. The first thing I knew about what was going on outside was when I woke to find a man pointing a gun into my tent. He told me to get up, and outside I saw another gunman.' When

John shouted at the man to get out, a gun was shoved in his face. He instantly recognised it as a Kalashnikov. As he scrambled outside he grabbed his passport, and was ordered to hand it over. He felt the weight of his money pouch beneath his shirt. It was filled with all his cash and credit cards. 'They're not getting that as well,' he thought to himself as one of the gunmen led him down the hillside, still hazy from his sleep. Ahead of him he saw a large group of long-haired *mujahideen*-type figures guarding a handful of seated Westerners. He glanced back to see if there was any way of escaping up the hill, and caught sight of the second militant searching his tent for valuables. Had they staked out the woods too? 'I saw him take my Canon camera with my social security number etched on it. He stole my sunglasses, too. I was furious.' Could he make a run for it? If not now, then when?

John sat down beside the other foreigners, and took in his captors. 'I could see that they were armed to the teeth with knives, semi-automatics and handguns. From that moment on I knew this was very bad news, whichever way I looked at it. Some of them were just kids, but the older ones had Kalashnikovs that looked like they had seen some battles. They were very nervous about the Indian Army coming into the camp, apart from the one who was evidently the leader. He did all the talking. He kept things calm. He carried himself with authority. He had a bearing that told me he was serious about this operation, whatever it was, a stillness of having experienced real fear and survived it.'

As he waited in silence for their captors to explain their next move, John ran over the past twelve hours in his head. Something came to him. That morning, Dasheer, his guide, the only Kashmiri he had grown fond of (although Dasheer had not seen any evidence of it), had urged him several times to break camp and move back down to Pahalgam a night early. 'At the time I thought he was trying to con me, get back to his family early, take a day's money for a trek that would now not happen, and we argued. "This is bullshit," I told him. This was my holiday, and I wanted all of the nights camping I'd paid for. But then it suddenly became clear to me. Did all the locals know that something was going down? The jungle drums, that kind of thing. I'm utterly convinced that Dasheer tried to save me by getting me out of the Meadow, but I'd been too stupid and arrogant to listen.' John had read about crimes like these in Colombia or Ecuador. 'But this kind of thing only happened to someone else.'

With all the foreigners corralled beside the river, the leader turned his attention to the Kashmiri schoolboys, who, clearly of no use to him, were marched into the larger of the two *dhokas*, followed by all the other Kashmiris on the campsite, except for Julie's guide Bashir. 'We could see the schoolboys being pushed into the hut, no one saying a word, like a silent movie,' recalled Julie. After a brief scuffle to secure the door, the leader began barking questions in rudimentary English at the foreigners, helped by Bashir. 'Are any of you in the army? Do you work for your governments? Are you married?' What were the right answers, Julie thought, panicking. Were there any? Did religion matter? Who was fighting whom? Everything she knew about Kashmir had left her mind as soon as they had been surrounded. She struggled to recall what the local troubles were about. Was there a way of answering that would safeguard their lives? They were not cut out for this. John Childs, who had still not looked up at the others, muttered a prayer under his breath.

All the time the leader thumbed the passports: British ... American ... Canadian.

A decision was made. The leader pointed his gun: 'You, you and you.' Paul Wells, Keith Mangan and John Childs stood up. 'This is it,' John thought as he was led back up to his tent to retrieve his walking boots and padded trekking jacket. 'You complete idiot. Why the hell didn't you just turn around and go home at the first sign of trouble? Now you're going to die. You're going to be shot in this hellhole and you're never going to see your girls or your parents again.'

The women froze. Where were the men being taken, Julie demanded of Bashir as the gunmen searched the camp for a last few possessions to steal, including their travellers' cheques. The leader answered for him. The group's commander was waiting in Aru to question them, he said. 'Israeli spies are operating in the valley. Your husbands are now suspects. Bring some warm clothes.' Spies? It sounded too ridiculous to be true. As the gunmen started to move away, Keith was still frantically searching for his jacket in their tent. They were not prepared to wait a moment longer, Bashir said. Julie took off her jacket and pushed it into Keith's arms. 'Take mine,' she said, looking her husband in the eyes as he was pulled away. Then she locked eyes with the teenage gunman. 'Leave him alone, he's just an electrician from Teesside,' she wanted to scream in his face.

'No harm will come to your men,' the leader said, as Julie and Cath began to cry. 'After their passports are checked, they will return in the morning.' Cath and Julie watched Paul, Keith and the silent John (whose name they still did not know) being frog-marched down the Meadow and into the dark. 'I didn't even have a chance to say goodbye,' Julie said. 'They just took off down the river, the ten armed men, and our three.'

Julie and Cath huddled in silence as the rain drizzled. 'I don't think they're coming back,' Cath said finally. 'Don't worry,' said Julie, fighting back her tears, 'they *are* coming back.' Outwardly confident, inwardly she was falling to pieces. 'I wanted to believe they would come back,' she recalled. Saying it out loud might make it come true. '"They will bring them back; of course they will bring them back," I was saying to myself, while all the time what you're really thinking is, "I bet they don't."'

It was almost 8 p.m. by the time Jane and Don saw the armed party returning from the Upper Camp. They had been gone for more than two hours, and now they seemed to have other foreigners with them. As the party got closer, Jane recognised Keith. She caught his eye and he acknowledged her, but his previously happy-go-lucky face was now sober and worried. She did not recognise Paul Wells, with his straggly ponytail and goatee, or John Childs, a gaunt-looking man who refused to make eye contact with anyone, his face swivelled to the ground. Childs, she recalled, as she rewound this moment over and over again in her mind, was the one who most struck her. He looked a wreck. He would vividly remember the episode too. 'My mind was absolutely clear. I knew what was going down. I understood at that instant that we were being marched to our deaths. I knew that I would never get out of this unless I took drastic action. I felt, instinctively, that I could trust no one, and that the only way to save myself was to take matters into my own hands. What everyone else deduced was not my concern.'

Seconds later, before Jane could take in what was happening, one of the gunmen came over. Her guide Bashir translated. 'He says that Don must dress warmly. He is going to Aru with the others. There is a senior commander waiting to question them about being Israeli spies.' Jane's head whirled with questions. 'For the love of Pete, we had no idea what this was all about,' she recalled, searching for meaning in the eyes of Don's captors.

Doing what he was told, Don went into their tent and put on his blue Gore-Tex fleece and trousers, his blue hat and a Patagonia fleece. He was already wearing his yellow-and-black Casio altimeter, and decided to keep it with him, but as he emerged he handed Jane a pile of clothes. 'These are yours,' he said forcefully. She knew what he was doing. He had concealed their documents in them, and, typical Don, he was worrying about her. He also glanced down at a pair of shoes by the door, where he had just hidden their cash. 'He suspected they were going to loot the camp and that he might not be coming back any time soon,' said Jane. 'I don't recall actually saying goodbye. We just looked into each other's eyes.' Now was not the time to cry.

As Don and the other three hostages were led off into the night, it began to rain. A wave of helplessness washed over Jane. Just before they reached a log bridge, where during daylight hours a villager from Aru ran a teashop, the leader turned to look back at her, before ordering the party off the trekking path and up the left-hand flank of the valley. As they scrambled up the bank, Jane recalled that she had been instructed to go to the Upper Camp and stay there for two hours, while Bashir and Sultan had been told to remain by the tents. Taking one last look at the kidnap party as they disappeared into the silent shadows above her, she started walking in the other direction, up the Meadow. She must not put Don and the others at risk, she said to herself. She must do what she had been ordered. If they played by the rules, the armed party might feel compelled to do the same.

When she reached the Upper Camp half an hour later, plodding silently through the gloom, she heard sobbing coming from a tent. Inside it she found Julie Mangan, whom she had briefly chatted with earlier in the day. Beside her was Cath Moseley, a blonde young Englishwoman she had not seen before. The three of them sat together in Julie's tent as the rain drummed on the flysheet. 'I just sat there as Keith walked away,' Julie said. She was crying, 'This has really happened. This has really happened.' Jane, the eldest among them, told the others they were in it together, and should stop thinking about what had been done, and start working out what to do next. Should they follow the gunmen's instructions, or should they raise the alarm? Jane reckoned they had no choice, as sentries might be watching from the forest. To go against orders might worsen their loved ones' situation. Julie and Cath nodded, grateful for her composure and barely able to speak. A compromise was reached. 'If Don, Keith and Paul had not turned up by dawn, we agreed we would all walk back down to Aru, and if we could not find them there we would continue on down to Pahalgam and seek help,' said Jane.

At 10 p.m., Jane returned to her own tent at the Lower Camp. Julie had tried to convince her to stay, but Jane secretly hoped that Don would make it back. If anyone could, Don would, and she wanted to be there just in case. As she walked alone in the moonlight, the landscape took on a new, more menacing hue. Dark silhouettes of trees surrounded her. In the distance, the bleating of a goat sounded like a child's cry. All the worries they had talked through before going on this trip came flooding back. She wished they had never come to Kashmir. But now she was in this predicament, she would have to deal with things as Don would deal with them, logically, methodically and rigorously: 'It was pointless wasting energy on regrets.'

As she entered the camp, her heart sank. Sultan and Bashir were nowhere to be seen. And Don's camera, the daysacks they had bought on last year's club trip to Montana, all the things she had carefully folded up on their bed and packed back in Spokane barely two weeks before, were gone.

She crawled into the wreckage of her tent and pulled something warm over her. The silence she had once craved now deafened her. She ran over what had happened, trying to piece it together. She should not panic – Don would find a way out of it. In a fix on an ice wall, bivouacked on a summit ascent or beaten flat by sculling snow, he always did. And anyhow, things always looked brighter in the morning.

At first light, Jane heard voices. Don! She looked at her watch. It was only 4 a.m. Heart thumping, she poked her head out of the tent. The first rays of the sun were gilding the ridgeline, and a party of Kashmiri teenagers was passing through the campsite. One of them came over and introduced himself as Khurram Parvez, a student from Srinagar. He spoke good English, asked if she was all right, and explained that he and his friends had been in the Upper Camp too, and had spent the night locked in a shepherd's hut. They had just broken out, leaving several foreign trekkers behind. She told him her husband had been taken, and that she wanted to wait here a little while longer, in case he returned. She asked him if he understood what was going on.

Khurram had some ideas. Before being locked up, he had spoken to one of his captors. 'He talked to us in broken Urdu,' Khurram recalled. The man's accent suggested he was Pashtun. 'He was abrupt. He asked us where we were from. When we told him Srinagar, he said, "Why are you trekking when your brothers are dying, fighting the Indian Army?"' Khurram could tell that this was not a rhetorical question, and the man expected answers. Fearful that whatever he said would anger him, Khurram had replied that he and his friends were students.

'Then all of us were asked to line up. My friends were scared. My cousin and I continued trying to talk. We asked one of these guys, "Where are you from?" He said, "Dar-e-Khyber [the Khyber Pass, in Pakistan]." I asked them which militant group they belonged to. He replied, "Harkat ul-Ansar."' Khurram had felt a chill. He knew the Movement was a Pakistan-backed militant group, but to Jane the name meant nothing.

Khurram told Jane they would raise the alarm. She nodded, and returned, dazed, to her tent. She must have dozed off, because the next time she looked at her watch it was 6.30 a.m., and Bashir and Sultan were back, boiling up tea. Her frustrations exploded. Where had they been, she demanded. What did they know about the men who had taken her husband? Were they in on this? Unshaven, with black circles round their eyes, they appeared to be terrified, and Sultan looked as if he was about to burst into tears. The gunmen had ordered them to run into the forest, Bashir told her. They had obeyed, frightened that if they did not they would be killed. 'Sorry, sorry, so sorry,' they both kept repeating. Kashmiris were all too intimate with the cost of the militancy, although Jane did not know that yet.

Where *was* Don, she wondered. He should have been back by now. She had to get her head together. She went down to the riverbank. She scanned the ridges and forests. 7 a.m., 5 July. Nothing was moving apart from a *gujjar* family on a goat track high above her. She'd give it another half hour, then she would move. Suddenly she saw a figure walking up from the direction of Aru. Was it Don? She ran down towards the man, her heart thumping. But as she drew nearer, she pulled up quickly. It was a Kashmiri wearing a *pheran*. He waved, but she did not return the gesture, suddenly unsure of him. When he reached her a few minutes later he introduced himself as Dasheer, John Childs' guide. In the chaos of the previous evening she had not noticed him among the party that had returned from the Upper Camp before taking off with Don. The gunmen had ordered him to come back with a message.

Dasheer handed Jane a damp note, explaining that the commander of the group had written it. She snatched the piece of paper, but found it was in Urdu. Frustrated and shaking, she handed it back and asked Dasheer to translate it. Addressed 'For the American Government Only', it listed twenty-one prisoners the gunmen wanted freed in return for Don, Keith, Paul and John. The deadline was 14 July, nine days from now. The note threatened: 'accept our demands or face dire consequences. We are fighting against anti-Islamic forces … Western countries are anti-Islam, and America is the biggest enemy of Islam.'

For the first time, Jane realised that something life-changing had just happened: 'That's when it really hit me.'

Where was her husband right now, she asked, struggling not to cry. Dasheer had no idea. He'd been sent packing by the commander, and had last seen the kidnap party heading over a high-altitude ridge. 'What about Aru?' she asked, thinking of the story they had been told of the commander waiting to check passports. They hadn't gone there at all, Dasheer replied. 'It was like a really bad dream,' says Jane. 'I went into some kind of trance.' But even in her heightened emotional state, she instinctively knew what to do. She would summon up all the courage and stamina she had developed over years of climbing, descend to Pahalgam and whip the authorities into action, and as quickly as possible. But first she would have to marshal the others, Julie Mangan and Cath Moseley. 'Come on!' she shouted at Dasheer, intending to hike back up to the Upper Camp.

As she packed up what was left of her belongings, Jane heard voices: Julie, Cath and others from the Upper Camp had come down to her. They had heard nothing from anyone in the past twelve hours. There was a Japanese tourist and an American woman with her teenage daughter who had also been staying at the Upper Camp, but had not been targeted. When Jane showed them all the note and explained what it said, Cath started crying. Julie was already numb. Bart Imler, the Canadian, was so weak he could barely walk. They all had to leave the Meadow, Jane said, right now. 'It's imperative we reach someone in authority from the British or American embassies as soon as possible.'

'Walking out was a terribly difficult thing to do,' Jane recalled. 'It was hard to leave the site. It was hard to see Bart, the young Japanese fellow, the American woman, and to know they were coming out and Don wasn't. It wasn't anger, but maybe envy. That they were lucky and we weren't. "Why us?" I kept thinking. "Why Don?" What had we done? It wasn't that I wanted anyone else to be taken. It was just hard to imagine why … that we were the ones with the bad luck that day.'

* * *

5 July 1995 was an idyllic, sunny day, but none of them were taking in the landscape. Following the silvery twists and turns of the Lidder River, Jane Schelly, Julie Mangan and Cath Moseley retreated from the Meadow as quickly as they could. Along the way they gathered witnesses and other trekkers. 'It's not safe,' they told every passer-by. 'People have been abducted. Don't believe what the tourist officials tell you.' Every herder or villager they saw on the path represented a potential kidnapper or spy.

On the way down they stopped off at Aru, the village where they had been told Don, Keith, Paul and John would be taken for the so-called passport checks in the middle of the night. The story seemed even more unlikely given what Dasheer had recounted of the previous night's journey. Nobody in Aru admitted to knowing anything about foreign fighters passing through in the company of four Westerners. And the villagers shrank back in fear when Jane tried to engage them in conversation: 'We hoped to get some information, a sighting or a direction, but there was nothing.'

By the time they reached Pahalgam at around 2 p.m., after six hours' trekking, they were tired and footsore. More than fifty people were now in their party, a motley caravan of ponies, heavily laden trekkers, worried guides and hennaed village elders who filed solemnly down the main street, past the empty trekking agencies, bakery and souvenir shops, the mouldering craft emporiums and general stores, with their bright strips of bunting made of multi-coloured crisp bags that crunched and rustled in the breeze. Many shop owners pulled down their shutters, seemingly anticipating what was to come.

The centre of town was already in an uproar, news of the abductions having come from Khurram Parvez and his friends. The kidnapping of a local for money was so regular an occurrence these days that it barely raised an eyebrow. But meddling with foreigners' lives broke the unspoken code of Kashmir. Whatever people's private thoughts about the beliefs and behaviour of those who came here from abroad, foreigners were the valley's bread and butter, and seizing four of them was unthinkable. The large group of loud Westerners drew nervous crowds, while taxi drivers, desperate for trade, tried to secure fares down to Srinagar, and hotel agents attempted to block-book their rooms. 'It was bedlam,' recalled Jane.

She, Julie and Cath pushed their way into a phone booth, only to find that the line was down. They found another which was working, and as a dozen faces pressed against the glass outside she rang the US Embassy in New Delhi. Two American citizens had been abducted, she tried to explain calmly on a line that echoed and whined. She gave their names and Don's passport details, and said that her brother-in-law Donald Snyder, a Republican member of the Pennsylvania House of Representatives, could be called upon to help. She said the only thing she knew about the other American man who had been seized was his name: John Childs. Next, they phoned the British High Commission, and relayed a similar message: armed Islamic militants had kidnapped two Britons and were demanding the release of jailed activists. The phone line seemed to howl in sympathy. The officials appeared to understand through the static, and said they would put their emergency protocols into action, dispatching representatives by the next available flight, which would not be until the morning. It was imperative that the women report the abductions to the local police, they were advised, and file an FIR, a First Information Report, officially registering the incident. That way a criminal inquiry would have to commence immediately. Then they should head, quickly, to the sanctuary of the United Nations office in Srinagar.

Jane asked if she could be alone, and made the hardest calls of her life. Fearing she would finally break down, she rang her parents, Joyce and James, in Orefield, Pennsylvania, and, knowing the news would terrify them, told them calmly and methodically where she was and what had happened. She then called her older sister Nancy, and asked to speak to her brother-in-law, Donald. He promised to get straight on to the US State Department. Finally she called her husband's family in Spokane and Coeur d'Alene. Struggling to understand, they were horrified.

Afterwards, gasping for air, Jane went outside while Julie rang her mother in Middlesbrough and Keith's parents, Charlie and Mavis. Hearing Julie's distant voice calling, 'Mavis, Mavis, is that you?' Keith's mother knew something was wrong. Where was the usual joke – 'Hello, Mrs Mangan, it's Mrs Mangan here'? Julie explained how Keith had been kidnapped by 'Kashmiri rebels', along with another Brit and two Americans. The four men had been taken off somewhere into the mountains, and the rebels had issued a note demanding the release of twenty-one prisoners. It was a confused, rambling story, and Mavis struggled to keep up. Putting the phone down, she turned to her husband and cried.

Lastly, it was Cath's turn to ring her family in Norwich and Paul's parents in Blackburn. Bob was stunned when he took the call: 'What the hell am I going to tell Dianne?' She had been against this trip from the start. 'I thought it was the worst day of my life,' says Bob. 'But it was just the beginning.'

Pahalgam police station, a brick-and-plaster building with a curling tin roof, nowadays ringed with sandbags, sentries and coils of razor wire, lay at the split in the road just north of the bus station, where the Lidderwat Valley route peeled off to the north-west and the East Lidder River road headed north-east to Amarnath. It was thronged with constables and clerks when Jane, Julie and Cath arrived to file their FIR at around 3 p.m., accompanied by several other trekkers from the Meadow who wanted to report the theft of their money and possessions. They fought their way inside, passing a morbid tableau of photographs of corpses, each one an unidentified victim of the conflict or of some mountain misfortune whose body had been recovered, each one an unexplained tragedy. Unsure what to do with the Western party, a constable ushered them into a small, humid anteroom filled with mismatched chairs. On the table lay a couple of the previous day's newspapers, carrying excerpts of a speech by Frank Wisner, the American Ambassador in New Delhi, to mark Independence Day. 'I can think of no better way to celebrate our own Independence Day than to reaffirm the commitment of the US to a long-term relationship with India that will serve our common interests and protect our common ideals,' he was quoted as saying.

After some time Jane, Julie and Cath were shown into the Deputy Superintendent's office, with constables, head constables and sub-inspectors squeezing in behind them. By this stage Jane was 'feeling physically ill'. Someone was dispatched to find the tea-boy and buy some *girda* bread before the proceedings could begin. The women only wanted to get on with filing their report. 'Wait, wait,' the policemen responded, trying to be hospitable, coaxing a fan into life by poking bare wires into an electric socket. 'I remember as many people looking on as could possibly fit in,' says Jane. Noticing the jumble of dusty files piled up on shelves behind the Deputy Superintendent's desk, she wondered if their FIR would end up there, unread and unactioned.

Eventually the women were informed that the Deputy Superintendent, the senior officer responsible for Pahalgam police station, was 'not available'. Where was he, Jane asked. 'Out of station,' said someone unhelpfully. They were told that a Duty Inspector would take down their story instead. His belly flopping over the bright silver buckle of his police-issue belt, the officer entered the room and, without looking at the women seated before him, began talking in Kashmiri to the assembly of constables. Some of them laughed and joked. One of the women asked what was going on. Shuffling papers in his logbook, the Inspector ignored her. Jane felt her frustration welling up again. All these minutes wasted gave the kidnappers another half-mile up into the mountains. Why could they get no one's attention? Julie wanted to scream, 'Men's lives are hanging by a thread! Can someone please just take some notes?' All over the station phones began trilling as news of the kidnappings spread across the police network. No one answered them. A constant stream of men brought files and bits of paper for the Inspector to sign. 'I was in such a stupor I have no idea of his name,' Jane says, 'but I do remember lots of carbon paper.'

The women tried to be as helpful as they could. The Inspector eventually began, taking down their names (spelt wrongly) and details of their itinerary to date (mangled), confirming locations and trekking routes on a large hand-drawn map of the area on the wall. To the accompaniment of constant mutterings from the gathered mass of junior ranks, he asked about their guides, who had melted away the moment the women had entered the police station, except for Dasheer, who was being restrained in another room. Jane had made up her mind that Bashir and Sultan were innocent of any involvement, and her suspicions had turned instead to the itinerant herders they had met on the paths: 'There had been lots of *gujjars*, *bakarwals* and locals moving about.' Ignoring her, the Inspector issued orders to bring the guides and pony-*wallahs* in for interrogation. Looking at him, Jane feared for them.

Finally, the Inspector asked about the kidnappers. 'Julie, who was very artful, drew sketches of many of them,' says Jane. 'We turned these over to the Kashmiri police, but later on nobody was able to find them again.' She had been thinking as if this was *Crimewatch*, on which an identikit picture might help crack the case, rather than Kashmir, where the insurgents were so numerous that few files were kept on any of them, only thousands of photos of mutilated corpses that were displayed in a morbid black museum at the headquarters of the Rashtriya Rifles, images the army used to propel new recruits into battle and to show off to visiting politicians from New Delhi.

It was only when Jane disclosed that she had a handwritten note from the kidnappers that the babble quietened. Tangible evidence. The women were taken off to a larger room, with benches pushed against one wall on which sat rows of unopened files. 'Please show me the note,' the Inspector demanded. Jane was reluctant, having seen him scrunch Julie's sketches into a drawer. In any case, it was addressed to 'the American Government'. He insisted, and grabbing it, zeroed in on the demands, especially the list of twenty-one prisoners.

His finger hovered over the name 'Masood Azhar', and he raised an eyebrow. The Afghani too. A dry cough. Then he found Langrial, the warrior revered by Pakistani *jihadis* as 'Darwesh'. He glanced at Jane, and asked if she knew anything about these men. She shook her head. They were all main players in the Movement, he said, adding that it was a Pakistan-backed militant group, as he saw that they did not understand him. Masood Azhar was the outfit's chief ideologue, he thought, and had been captured in Kashmir the previous winter. India would never give him up. Did they realise this was an exceptionally serious situation? Growing desperate, Jane pointed out that the letter had been signed 'al Faran'. The Inspector shrugged, saying he had never heard of it.

The Inspector turned on her. What had they been doing up there? Didn't they know the mountains were crawling with militants? This was the second kidnapping they'd had to deal with in a year. Jane could not believe what she was hearing. Why hadn't they been warned by the tourist police, government officials, the guides, the pony-*wallahs*, the soldiers who had waved to them, or the local police who had seen them leave? What did he mean by 'the second kidnapping'? The Inspector frowned before explaining that the previous one had involved 'a pair of Britishers', but it had worked out all right. It had taken place in June 1994, near Aru, and the two foreigners involved had been released unharmed. He couldn't remember their names, but he was sure Masood Azhar's outfit had also been behind that episode.

The situation was even worse than the women had thought. An unknown militant group was demanding the release of twenty-one Muslim terrorists, men that India would never hand over. Nothing in Jane's well-ordered world had prepared her for something of this magnitude, or the double talk and deception that had got her here. She needed Don and his legal pad. She wanted to get out of this stifling office and away from this Inspector who gave the impression of not caring about her husband or the other three hostages. Extracting the kidnappers' letter, along with an inky copy of the FIR, the women hailed a ride to Srinagar.

As they drove back down a road she had never expected to see again, passing the Aishmuqam shrine before turning onto National Highway 1A at Anantnag, Jane was numb. If things had gone to plan, she and Don would have been back in Srinagar by now, shopping and relaxing, having left the mountains via the village of Sumbal. 'Later on, I drove by car past where that valley meets the road, and was heartsick knowing that we might have exited there,' she recalled. 'I really could have just cried.' Instead, she was sitting in a taxi with two British women she barely knew, but whose lives had become inextricably linked with hers by the events of the past twenty-four hours.

It was dark by the time they got to the city, and the Pahalgam taxi driver had trouble locating the office of the United Nations Military Observer Group for India and Pakistan (UNMOGIP), which the women had been advised to head for. Since 1949, UN observers had maintained a low-key presence in Srinagar, supposedly monitoring the Line of Control, the ceasefire line between India and Pakistan. But most of the time they were not permitted even to leave their office, a Raj-era blue-and-white mansion, ringed by high fences and *chinar* trees, that resembled a British *sahib*'s summer residence.

Inside, the UN staff made it clear that getting tangled up with the kidnapping was the last thing they needed. Their presence in Kashmir was already on a knife-edge. The chief said the women could stay at the local UN guesthouse for two days only. He explained that the previous year he had been involved in negotiations for the release of Kim Housego and David Mackie, an episode that had tarred UNMOGIP's relations with New Delhi for months after. They could not afford a repeat of the situation. 'Everyone seemed to know about this previous kidnapping except us,' Jane thought as they headed off to the guesthouse.

By midnight on 5 July there had been no further word from the kidnappers, and nothing of consequence from the Indian authorities either, although at the UN compound the women had at least been able to use a satellite phone to update their families. 'Julie just cried and cried,' recalled her mother Anita Sullivan. In Blackburn, Paul's father Bob was threatening to get straight on a plane and 'march into the mountains myself'.

No one slept well that night. Jane stayed up late, doing what she always did in an emergency: the debrief. She wrote down every detail, lest she forgot a crucial snippet of information, banishing any feelings of regret the moment they crept into her mind: 'It was a very uncertain time. We hadn't been informed about how the Indians intended to respond to the kidnapping, although we hoped that they would do their best to secure the release of our loved ones as quickly as they could.' Julie lay awake too, haunted by those grimy bearded faces, the guns that smelled of cold tar and grease, Keith walking off into the rain. Cath could not get to grips with the hell her holiday had become, and regretted ever agreeing to the plan.

By the time they woke up the next morning, exhausted and frightened of what the day would bring, a large pack of Kashmiri photographers and journalists had massed at the guesthouse entrance, and pictures of Don, Keith and Paul were being splashed across the world. In Middlesbrough, the headline in the local paper read: 'KIDNAPPED: Rebels Seize Tourists on Dream Trip'. Mavis and Charlie Mangan were photographed sitting on the sofa in their front room, and the paper had got hold of a picture of Julie and Keith taken on the day of their leaving party, both of them grinning from ear to ear, arms wrapped around each other. 'Julie rang from Kashmir last night in total shock,' Mavis told a reporter. 'I wanted to jump on the first plane out there, but I couldn't do anything. We don't know much about these kidnappers, only that they are Kashmiri rebels.' Charlie added, 'I didn't want him to go out there because of the dangers, but this is what he wanted to do.'

The paper reported that Philip Barton, from the British High Commission in New Delhi, was now in Srinagar, 'giving assistance to the Indian authorities'. A High Commission spokesman said Barton would be 'taking what action he can', but that the tourists should not have been trekking anywhere near Pahalgam: 'It is a particularly dangerous area because of previous kidnappings. We have advised tourists not to travel there and that has been our policy for some time.' There was also an ominous-sounding comment from a Foreign Office spokesman: 'We will do what we can.' The families, who had been actively assured by everyone that it was safe to travel to the region, bristled.

The women's mood lifted a little when they heard that the embassies' representatives had arrived. Then two young diplomats walked in, looking significantly younger than them, thought Julie and Jane. Philip Barton, a thirty-one-year-old political officer, recently posted from Venezuela, told Julie and Cath that he had been to Kashmir a few times. But he had limited contacts, due to the restrictions the Indian government placed on foreign diplomats visiting the region. Taking the two British women to one side, he assured them that the Foreign Office would do all it could. It was already talking to Scotland Yard's specialist hostage-negotiation team, and the Indians had promised the British that 'a massive search was under way'. He seemed keen to keep the Indians happy, impressing on Julie and Cath the need to say as little as possible about the kidnapping to the media. The more publicity was given to the incident, the more the kidnappers would be convinced their captives were valuable, and the harder they would bargain before releasing them.

What had they been doing in the mountains, Barton asked gently. Had they not seen the warnings about Pahalgam, which was considered to be particularly dangerous because of the previous kidnapping and ongoing militant activities? For some time the Foreign Office had been advising tourists not to travel there. Crying, Cath and Julie explained that Indian officials had told them the opposite. Barton, sensing a clash of opinions, backed off. Instead, he went off in search of a secure phone line.

Tim Buchs, a Second Secretary at the US Embassy, seemed unsure too, according to Jane. He had only recently arrived in India, and this was only his second visit to Kashmir. The first had been the previous month, when he had helped organise the Pahalgam fishing trip for Ambassador Frank Wisner. It had turned into something of a catastrophe, he admitted, with Kashmiris reacting testily to Wisner's much-publicised and ill-advised claim that the valley was 'tired' of the militancy. Buchs had learned from that experience that nothing said or done in Kashmir was inconsequential. Jane sensed that this unhappy experience would determine Buchs' and the other diplomats' actions now: 'I don't know if all the decisions they made were right or wrong. I constantly think of all the things I might have done differently, and only wish I knew then what I know now. It's easy to find fault, to blame and second-guess.'

Buchs asked Jane if she had seen the latest State Department advisory. Dated 25 November 1994, it read: 'In July 1994, an American tourist was fatally shot in Srinagar, and in June 1994 militants held two British hikers hostage for 18 [sic] days before releasing them. These recent events demonstrate that the Kashmir Valley remains a dangerous place where terrorist activities and civil disturbances continue.' Jane shook her head, explaining how she and Don had gone to the US Embassy in New Delhi but had been put off by the heat and the enormous queue. No matter, Buchs said. What mattered now was getting her husband back. He told her the in-country FBI agents had already been briefed, and that a second specialist team was shortly to arrive from the FBI offices in Quantico, Virginia.

Anything she could tell him about the circumstances surrounding the kidnapping would help, especially if she had any understanding of why they had been targeted. Jane had been thinking about nothing else. 'I think we were scouted,' she replied. 'There were *many* people in the valley at that time, but the militants didn't want the American women, the Japanese man or some of the other nationalities we passed – they were going, I think, for American and British men, and knew where to find them.' She was convinced now that the kidnappings had nothing to do with their guides, Bashir and Sultan, telling Buchs, 'They seemed very afraid of both the militants and the police.'

Buchs told Jane he would help her the best he could. He explained that Kashmir was currently under Governor's Rule, and visiting the current incumbent, retired Indian Army chief General Krishna Rao, would be his first stop. Informing her that there were a dozen officials from the Indian security agencies asking to interview the women, he promised to act as liaison, so as to minimise the number of times they would have to retell their stories. But right now, he said as he got up to leave, his most immediate concern was tracing the family of the other American hostage, John Childs. No one knew anything about him, since he had been travelling alone and his passport was with the kidnappers. Throughout their meeting Buchs seemed nervous, Jane thought, and to be playing things by ear. But who else could she place her faith in?

* * *

Deputy Superintendent Kifayat Haider, the police officer responsible for the Pahalgam area, got the call about the kidnapping a few minutes after Jane, Julie and Cath had walked into Pahalgam police station on the afternoon of 5 July. He was, for once, at home with his family in Srinagar, squeezing in a few days off before the chaos of the annual *yatra* pilgrimage from Pahalgam, during which he and his officers would be responsible for the security of hundreds of thousands of Hindu devotees heading for the Amarnath Cave. That would no doubt be a four-week marathon of round-the-clock intrigue, threats and violence, so he had been glad to take a break – one that had now been interrupted. But Haider was philosophical. 'Immediately I got the message, I knew this was a serious situation. And there was no point bitching about losing holidays. This was a policeman's lot. Transferred willy-nilly. Called to duty at the strike of a match. Some dealt with it by drinking or screwing around. Others played golf. But no one ever got used to the pitch-and-putt of life in the force.' The great Superintendent Farooq Khan, Haider's role model, a Muslim officer who had been the first to lead a police anti-terrorist unit, liked to say the stress was enough to kill a man if the militants didn't get him first. 'And this from someone who had killed more than most since the troubles first bubbled over in 1989,' Haider reflected.

From the moment he received the call, Haider was acutely conscious of a significant fact: since the foreigners' FIR had been lodged at one of his police stations and the kidnapping had taken place in his district, he would get first shot at running this significant criminal inquiry. He knew also that as the victims were Western tourists and the alleged perpetrators Pakistani militants, it would not be long before a multitude of Indian security agencies were crawling over it too, not to mention the army. But with more than twenty years of service under his belt, many of them spent in the dirty business of counter-insurgency, tracking militant groups across the valley, coaxing villagers to give up vital information or dragging it out of them, he sensed that this was his moment to shine.

Appointed six months previously as DSP of police district Bijbehara (a town twenty minutes north of Anantnag), with a zone of responsibility that extended east to Pahalgam and beyond, Haider was aware that his background, although never publicly spoken about, imposed limits on his career. A Shia in a predominantly Sunni department, his religious beliefs (although he kept them to himself) would restrain him from ever getting higher than Senior Superintendent of Police, unless he got lucky. He had already begun to stamp his mark on his new district as a cogitator and agitator. Brusque and with a short fuse, the DSP was intolerant of slackness. Appearances were important to him. Chestnut brogues on his feet, brown baton tucked beneath one arm, khaki shirt sleeves rolled up to the elbow, revealing muscly, hairy forearms, his trouser seams as crisp as a new five-hundred-rupee note, Haider wanted everyone to know that he was taking the force by the scruff of its neck and dragging it into the modern age, regardless of sectarian prejudices.

The old-style policing, remote, heavy-handed and mendacious, would yield nothing in these days of insurgency. He intended to encourage the people of his new district to tell him what they knew, holding open-door sessions of the 'You scratch my back and I'll scratch yours' variety: the worthy and the poor ushered into his grand office to stand, caps in hand, before the acreage of his spotless glass-topped desk. Working out what people needed so he could provide it in return for information, once ensconced in Bijbehara DSP Haider had formulated a judgement on each and every case, however trivial, in exchange for fealty and intelligence. An old boy of Burn Hall School, the prestigious missionary establishment in Srinagar, this was Haider's formula for staying ahead. 'Doing humbly our task, to seek knowledge and light,' as the school song went.

As Haider prepared to leave for Pahalgam, he summoned a staff officer to give a précis of what was coming down the police radio, hoping his men in the field had not failed him. 'Did they find anyone to write up the FIR?' he asked. The staff officer said it was waiting on his desk. 'How about the witnesses, were they made comfortable?' There was no information available. 'First impressions,' the DSP murmured to himself, imagining how the foreign women must have felt in the furnace of Pahalgam police station. He hoped someone had found them some chairs to sit on, and had thought to turn on the fan.

Fiddling with his slim gold lighter, he bellowed for his driver. 'Fucking get a move on!' Grouchily, he pulled a Classic cigarette from the packet and glanced down to see how many he had left. Two hours from Srinagar to Anantnag, then three more from Anantnag to Pahalgam – if they didn't get tangled up in army manoeuvres. And he only had eighteen cigarettes, which worried him, as did the number of hours during which every piece of evidence could be corrupted or lost by incompetent subordinates, all fat fingers and sticky boots. The best he could hope for was that the capable Duty Inspector had remembered to offer the foreigners a cup of tea, and that his constables had not ogled the women too much.

Sitting in the back of his government issue white Ambassador car, the DSP applied himself to the bare facts. 'Who or what the hell is al Faran?' he wondered, contemplating the name on the kidnapper's note. Haider had spent the best part of his career tracking Kashmiri and Pakistani militant outfits, and prided himself on having a deep understanding of the etymology of the militancy – he could spend hours berating his friends with the philosophical differences between the Jamaat-e-Islami Pakistan and the Jamaat-e-Islami Hind. But this name threw him off-course immediately. For years he had studied the competing ideologies of Hizbul Mujahideen and the Movement, but al Faran meant nothing to him. He could cite at least ten things that divided Mast Gul (the HM commander and leveller of the holy city of Charar-e-Sharief) from Sikander (the bomb-maker from Dabran who had roared up the Movement's ranks). But al Faran? He could not summon up one iota of intelligence about where it had come from or what it stood for, which led him to only one conclusion. It did not exist.

Pleased with himself, having calculated that al Faran was merely a front for someone or something, Haider reached Pahalgam after nightfall, striding into his police station and waking up the constables. 'Bring in the witnesses!' he shouted, meaning Jane Schelly, Julie Mangan and Cath Moseley. 'They took off in a taxi,' the Inspector mumbled, unnerved by the sudden appearance of his senior. Haider exploded. 'What kind of screw-up is this? Preserve the crime scene and all evidence!' he shouted. He sat down at his desk grumpily, lighting up a cigarette before studying the brief FIR. This was a crime in the mountains, and it would need mountain people to solve it. 'And few are better placed than me to conduct such an operation,' he said to himself.

In his school days, Haider had trekked the Pir Panjal many times with his teachers. He liked to say that he could still draw a map from Pahalgam to the Line of Control via Kishtwar or Gulmarg, naming all the passes, concealed lakes and glaciers in between. He had grown to empathise with the impoverished groups that populated this harsh landscape, especially the *gujjars*, living as they did on the margins of society. They were like the Romany people of Europe, he would say. Insular and paranoid, they lived off their animals and from portering during the *yatra*. He understood their rich culture and social dynamics, as well as their migration patterns. He knew how to draw them out. Then there were the *bakarwals* and the *dards*, armed with their home-made knives and rifles, who most Kashmiris denigrated as thieves and murderers. 'It was partly the prejudice of the urban classes, muddled with a grain of truth,' said Haider. *Dards* had become renowned mercenaries, acting as trackers and hit-men for the security forces. 'But they'd just as easily work for the other side, if the money was right.' This was the privilege of the outsider.

As he pondered how he would roll out his operation, the DSP caught sight of a stack of *yatra*-related paperwork piled up on his desk. What about Amarnath? How would it affect things? This kidnapping could not have come at a worse time, he thought. He was under no illusions about the difficulties he would face over coming days. For the past four years this Hindu religious procession had been targeted by Pakistan-backed Kashmiri militant groups calling for *azadi*, freedom from the yoke of New Delhi. But this year the Indian government had negotiated ceasefires with all but one of these outfits, and saw it as imperative that the *yatra* went off without a hitch. In just a few days Pahalgam and the hills surrounding it would be thronged with hundreds of thousands of Hindu pilgrims heading for the sacred cave. And keeping them safe, whatever he thought of the religious cheerleaders behind them, was his task.

What Haider always came back to was that before the uprising of 1989, the Kashmir Valley had been home to tens of thousands of Kashmiri Pandits, the indigenous Hindus with ancient roots in the state, and all communities had lived peaceably. The valley was crammed with *masjids*, shrines, temples and *gurdwaras*, representing each and every faith. 'Even the bloody Jews staked claim to one tomb or other,' the DSP liked to say. But since the troubles, the militancy had been turned into a nasty religious war by unseen hands in New Delhi and over the LoC in Islamabad, transforming the annual pilgrimage to the cave into not only an article of faith, but also a way of underscoring the Hindu government's writ on Muslims in the valley. If the pilgrims' arrival at the cave said New Delhi was winning, stopping them with bombs, mines and guns was a favourite militant tactic to show the *azadi* movement still had clout. Either way, Haider's district had become a focal point for the terror, and this year, with the pilgrimage certain to be larger than ever, he girded himself for fireworks.

There were many agitating groups that needed to be watched closely. On the Hindu side there was the Rashtriya Swayamsevak Sangh, a right-wing religious and nationalist paramilitary volunteer force and welfare organisation that ran schools and programmes supporting Hindus all over the subcontinent. A Hindi mouthful, the group was known to everyone by its initials, the RSS, and its members were a regular sight in towns and villages across India, exercising in their tan shorts, caps and white shirts, like ageing boy scouts. Whether the *yatra* was officially on or off, RSS volunteers were always thick on the ground in Pahalgam during the pilgrimage season, urging devotees to come, saying they were not afraid to face the bullets and the bombs, as Kashmir was an integral part of India, and the Amarnath Cave their holiest shrine.

This year, things would not reach a climax until the full moon of 10 August, the most auspicious date on which to reach the cave, although a showdown in Pahalgam before then already seemed likely. According to Haider's Duty Inspector, the RSS had arrived in town, and in force. 'How will the pilgrimage impact on the kidnapping, and vice versa?' the DSP wondered again. Would the priorities of New Delhi – to make sure the *yatra* went ahead unhindered – place the safety of the pilgrims before everything else? Or would a crime committed in the heights of the Pir Panjal compete for its attention, given the nationalities of those who had been kidnapped?

As Haider pondered these matters, an enormous explosion rattled his windows. *Whoomf!* His desk was shaken. Baton in hand, he raced out of the station, leading from the front. *Whoomf!* More blasts bellowed, with the unmistakable deep bark of IEDs. Pahalgam's bus station had been wrecked, and five people had been killed outright, with twenty-three badly injured. Among the dead were a police constable and several newly-arrived *yatris*. It was already clear to Haider that he had a breakaway Islamic militant faction on his hands, who were against the ceasefire. And in the mountains, he thought, was another as yet unidentified faction, holding four Western prisoners.

On hearing the blasts RSS volunteers emerged from their lodgings, bamboo canes or *lathis* at the ready. Screaming crowds fleeing the explosions ran straight into them, and the RSS battered every Kashmiri they could spot. Hauling out local Muslim shopkeepers, breaking heads, the RSS rumbled through town. 'Pahalgam's going to hell already,' thought Haider. The delicate balancing act of matching Hindu aspirations with Kashmiri sensibilities had been thrown off-kilter even before the *yatra* had started, unless DSP Haider could rein in the saffron vigilantes and stop the Islamic fanatics behind the bombings.

Back at the station, he contacted police headquarters in Srinagar. 'I need men!' he shouted into the radio. He got them from the Central Reserve Police Force (CRPF), a paramilitary militia deployed in Kashmir since 1990 to bolster the regular police in tackling counter-insurgency. Their commanding officer agreed to loan him 140 men. He was explicit in his orders: 'If Haider says kill, you kill.'

SIX

The Night Callers

The Kashmir press pack had got wind of the kidnappings just moments after they had happened. Among the first to hear was Yusuf Jameel, the BBC's man in Kashmir, who received a call on the evening of 4 July, shortly after Don Hutchings, Keith Mangan, Paul Wells and John Childs had been led out of the long grass of the Meadow at gunpoint. Srinagar-born, with more than a decade's experience, Yusuf was professionally unflappable.

Many people in the valley knew Yusuf. A teacher's son, he had graduated from Kashmir University with a degree in political science, to become a polished reporter who found it easy to cross the social, religious and cultural divides between East and West, and New Delhi and Srinagar. Equally at home in his tweed blazer or *shalwar*, he was someone who could make sense of the complexities of the Kashmir conflict for BBC listeners around the world. As a result of his prominence and accessibility, he got calls, often anonymous, from all sorts, including gunmen with uniforms and without, mostly urging secrecy.

Since 1989, being a journalist in the valley had become a deadly business. Apart from working in Kashmir's brimming hospital emergency wards, where corpses collected like pencils in a jar, there was no other profession that brought a person so close to death on a daily basis. Reporters like Yusuf, working from their lair in the Srinagar Press Enclave, a warren of small, smoke-filled offices set back from Residency Road in the heart of the city, steered a delicate path around the demands of the militants, with their guns and cudgels. Simple revolutionaries, Pakistan secessionists, Kashmiri nationalists and puritanical *mullahs* of every flavour and colour, from the hennaed to the greying, every one of them wanted to be depicted by the BBC as a leading man. It was the same with the Indian security forces, who similarly jostled for airtime and prominence, from the portly police officers bulging out of their khakis to the sallow-skinned Intelligence Bureau agents.

But even this old hand was disturbed by the night-time conversation that took place on 4 July, many hours before anyone else had heard about al Faran, and Jane, Julie and Cath had scrambled down to Pahalgam.

'*Jameel-sahib? Vaaray?*' the caller had started politely, asking after Yusuf's health. The journalist thought he recognised the voice, its Kashmiri diction with a southern burr, but the man did not volunteer a name. '*Vaaray,*' Yusuf replied cautiously. Yes, thanks, he was well.

'How can I help you?' he asked, hoping that here was a good story, but worried too that he knew the voice, and that it was one that always presaged grim news.

'*Aghwa karne wala,*' said the caller, using the Urdu word for kidnapper. Yusuf's news antennae pricked up at the thought that he was being tipped off to a live abduction of some kind. 'Details,' he replied respectfully, realising that this caller sounded like Sikander, the Movement's Anantnag commander. A key player in the insurgency rocking south Kashmir, he was one of the most wanted men in the valley. Unwilling to come to town unless it was a dire emergency, Sikander needed his mouthpieces in the media, and for a time he had called up Yusuf.

However, the BBC man was surprised, and a little frightened, to hear from him now. Their last conversation had been more than a year back, in June 1994, and it had not ended well, with Sikander physically threatening Yusuf for failing to report some story or other. 'So why is he renewing contact with me now?' Yusuf wondered.

'*Ghayr mulki,*' said the anonymous caller. The phrase meant 'foreign'. Yusuf bit his tongue and wondered: 'This could be a very significant story. Do I have it to myself?'

The caller spilled some more details, saying that the abduction of the foreigners was the work of 'al Faran'. Like everyone else who heard this name, Yusuf frowned, as he jotted it down on his pad. He suspected that this group must be either a blind or an offshoot of a better-known faction. In an insurgency that had disintegrated into many hundreds of outfits, prompted by spies from Pakistan and India who encouraged dogfights and jealousies by sponsoring sectarian hits and fomenting betrayals, this was by no means unusual. 'Anyhow,' Yusuf thought, 'whoever's behind the kidnapping doesn't really matter just yet. It was enough that there had been a crime.' He knew the news would trigger a feeding frenzy: foreigners (for which he read tourists) abducted at gunpoint, no doubt while trekking in the mountains of Kashmir, the only place to which a trickle of backpackers still came. He spared a momentary thought for the unsuspecting holidaymakers, whoever they were, unfamiliar with the local terrain and language, uninitiated in the pervasive terror of the valley, hauled from their tents by masked men speaking a Babel of languages.

The caller recapped. Four foreigners trekking above Pahalgam had been seized at gunpoint by a militant outfit calling itself al Faran. There would be dire consequences for the hostages unless the Indian government agreed to free twenty-one Muslim prisoners incarcerated in Indian jails. The man rattled off a long list of names, and stressed that the clock was ticking.

After he had hung up, Yusuf wondered how he should proceed. Reporting these kinds of incidents in Kashmir carried considerable personal risks. Twice, over the years, masked men had lobbed grenades at his office and his home, unhappy about one of his bulletins. Another aggrieved group had demanded he appear before its *qayadat* (leadership council), or face execution. A third had denounced him as a collaborator just for reporting the outspoken views of a junior Congress minister, Rajesh Pilot.

Threats came from all sides. Back in the summer of 1990, soldiers from the 11th Gurkha Rifles had abducted him from Srinagar and transported him several hours away to remote Uri, far from friends and contacts, for interrogation. There was no point in his blaming whoever had made whatever unsubstantiated allegations the Indian Army was now acting upon. In those early days of the militancy, becoming a suspect was as unavoidable as catching a cold. All it required was for a needy contact to haemorrhage the names of everyone he could think of while being dangled by his ankles, with a funnel shoved up his rectum. And then his whole neighbourhood was incriminated. This was a favoured method of the security forces – petrol, preferably laced with chilli powder, decanted into a naked, upended prisoner. After thirty gruelling hours in the hands of Lt. Col. Bhanwar Singh, Yusuf somehow talked his way free, having to make his own way back to distant Srinagar. But in a dirty war you learned not to take things too personally.

Nine months ago the Indian security forces had got him again, beating him viciously as he covered a protest by the Daughters of the Nation, a fringe women's group lobbying for strict adherence to Koranic law, demanding that women completely cover up. For centuries, Muslim women of all ages had walked with their faces uncovered in Kashmir, having little truck with Islamists or their garb. But after the attack on Yusuf some people came to the conclusion that maybe the Daughters were right, and only by concealing their entire persons within an Afghan *burqa* would they be protected from a state so pathological that it was happy to see a BBC man thrashed in broad daylight.

Yusuf had been hospitalised for four days. Afterwards, friends in the Press Enclave had warned him to get out of the valley and let things simmer down. But he had stayed. Not long afterwards Ghulam Mohammed, a well-liked freelancer, had received a night visit from the Indian Army's Punjab regiment and been asked to write up a heroic tale about the recent slaying of two militants. Ghulam had told colleagues that his research revealed that the dead men were in fact blameless locals who had been killed in cold blood. The soldiers were furious, warning Ghulam that there would be repercussions, and days later the journalist lay dead, shot in his own parlour, along with his eight-year-old son. The front pages of the next morning's papers were printed black all over in protest at the killings.

Still, there was no shortage of Kashmiris wanting to do what Yusuf did. The reason lay flapping in the wind on the walk up to Amira Kadal, the arched bridge that linked Residency Road to Srinagar's central market. On any morning, come rain or snow, newspaper vendors laid out titles in a fan on their handcarts. A literate state of loquacious inhabitants, gripped by an emergency in which every form of communication was often withdrawn as a form of collective punishment, had become fixated by news. Yusuf kept the voice of Sikander in his head as he prepared a late-night dispatch.

Yusuf Jameel and Sikander had spoken many times, and had met at least twice. The first time had been early in 1994, when Sikander had telephoned the Press Enclave to rant about the arrest of Nasrullah Langrial, the notorious Pakistani militant who for more than a year had been careering around the valley causing mayhem. Six weeks previously the Indians had finally caught up with Langrial, and Yusuf had reported the incident, telling colleagues afterwards that the arrest of such a high-profile Pakistan-backed *mujahid* would 'result in bloodshed'.

The Movement would do whatever it could to spring their man, Sikander had warned then. He had also asked Yusuf to come to a mountain hideout, promising him a scoop. Heart in mouth, the BBC stringer had eventually agreed to meet him at an isolated rendezvous. Nothing ventured, nothing gained, he had said to himself. Which is all well and good somewhere like London or New York, where at worst you might lose a handful of banknotes on a wasted lunch. But here in Kashmir, if things went wrong someone was likely to find his body thrown into a gutter behind the cemetery in Anantnag. For security, and in case there were any picture opportunities, Yusuf had taken along his great friend Mushtaq Ali, an Agence France-Press photographer.

Following detailed instructions, the two had climbed up through the steep woods rising to the east of Anantnag, eventually arriving at a remote col somewhere near Chhatargul village, where a tall, bearded young Kashmiri introduced himself as Sikander. Alongside him were other fighters: one called the Turk, another called the Afghani, and a Yemeni who was referred to as 'Supahi'. At the time, Yusuf and Mushtaq had had no idea of the significance of these men, or of the aspirations of the newly launched Movement. But just as Sikander was beginning to explain what all this was about, chaos had broken out. 'Run!' Sikander had screamed, pointing to a glint high up on a mountain ledge that Yusuf had assumed was just sunlight bouncing off some long-abandoned shrine. 'Telescopic sights!' Sikander had bellowed as he headed for cover.

Yusuf and Mushtaq had run for their lives, following the gunmen into the pine trees. Here, to their shock, they found several miserable-looking Indian soldiers tied to each other. 'Sikander told us that these men had just been captured at the water gardens of Verinag.' He was referring to the former holiday retreat for Mughal Emperors, south of Anantnag town. One of the prisoners was identified as Major Bhupinder Singh, whom Sikander intended to trade for Langrial. Following Sikander's instructions, Mushtaq had taken some photographs, and he and Yusuf returned to Srinagar to break the kidnapping story. After New Delhi had refused to budge, Major Singh had been photographed once more, this time dead and face-down in an open sewer.

Barely a month later, Yusuf had been called to a press conference in Badami Bagh, Srinagar's army nerve centre south of Dal Lake, a vast encampment of razor wire, whitewashed lookout towers and sandbags that ran alongside Maulana Azad Road and extended into the forests of Shankarashariya, the pointed hill that sat beside Dal Lake. Badami Bagh was named after an almond orchard that had once grown there, but these days all Kashmiris knew it as BB Cantt: headquarters of the Indian Army 15th Corps, the force responsible for maintaining law and order throughout the whole of Jammu and Kashmir. Now it was the security forces' turn to gloat. A gleeful Corps Commander, Brigadier Arjun Ray, had a surprise. His troops had just captured Masood Azhar and Sajjad Khan, aka the Afghani, two key players in the Movement, a relatively new ISI-backed militant group that the Indian Army described as being 'intent on spreading chaos through the valley'. Yusuf says: 'The army was understandably in a back-slapping mood over the arrests.' That evening he received an anonymous phone call with another angle on the story. His voice shaking and incoherent, the caller had warned that the Movement would respond. Yusuf knew at once. This was Sikander, and his message presaged a fifteen-day bombing spree.

When Yusuf next heard from Sikander it was June 1994, and this time the young militant was calmer, and sounded pleased with himself. He revealed that the Movement had just kidnapped two British tourists from the hills above Pahalgam. One was a sixteen-year-old schoolboy, Kim Housego. The other was a video director from London called David Mackie. 'Now,' Sikander warned Yusuf, 'their lives are hanging by a thread unless Langrial, Masood and the Afghani are freed.'

The Movement had crossed a line. Up to now, most home-grown Kashmiri militants had agreed that targeting foreigners would destroy any hopes Kashmir had of returning to its former incarnation as a haven for backpackers and trekkers once this war was over and done with. Until the kidnapping of Housego and Mackie, this understanding had largely been adhered to, barring two deviations very early on in the conflict. A couple of Swedish engineers had been captured back in March 1991 by the Muslim Janbaz Force, a Kashmiri outfit, but had been released unharmed after ninety-seven days. Three months later, eight Israeli tourists were seized from a houseboat on Dal Lake. This incident had quickly degenerated into farce, with the tourists snatching the kidnappers' weapons and all escaping, except one who was fatally wounded.

As Yusuf wrote up his story on the kidnapping of Housego and Mackie, wondering why Sikander had broken the unspoken rule, he had an unexpected visitor in the Press Enclave. It was David Housego, whom Yusuf had known from his days as the New Delhi bureau chief for the *Financial Times*. Now retired, David had remained in the city to run his own business. David and Yusuf were men of the same mould, the Englishman having been a much-admired reporter with influential contacts across the subcontinent and a wide circle of loyal

Indian friends. Now David explained that he wanted Yusuf to help kick up a stink in order to try to free his son Kim, who had just been seized with David Mackie while the family was trekking to celebrate David's wife Jenny's fiftieth birthday and Kim's impending departure for Britain, where he was about to start boarding school.

Yusuf grabbed his notebook, and David described how he, Jenny and Kim had been held up on their return from a day trip to the Kolahoi Glacier. Having camped in the Meadow for a night, just as Jane and Don, Keith and Julie, Paul and Cath and John Childs would do a year later, they had packed up and were walking down to Aru when three men carrying Kalashnikovs stepped out from the trees to block their path. David's initial assumption was that they were Kashmiris from one of the groups he had interviewed during his many trips to the state for the *Financial Times*. But without saying a word, one of the men had put his hand in David's pocket and taken his money. 'The leader then said, "We are looking for Israeli spies. No harm will come to you,"' David told Yusuf. 'He told us we would be escorted down to Aru to have our passports checked. We would wait for his return that evening.'

At Aru, the Housegos had been taken to the Milky Way Tourist Bungalow, the run-down-looking establishment Paul Wells had photographed a year later, until his guide had urged him to move on, filled with a wariness that he chose not to share with his guests. Here the Housegos found another British couple, David and Cathy Mackie, who had been woken in the middle of the night by armed men who had raided the Milky Way. David told Yusuf, 'The Mackies watched our arrival from a first-floor balcony, and said they had been told they would be released that night, after the militants moved out of the village.'

While they waited, David Housego got a closer look at the gunmen. 'I could tell from their language and dress they were Afghanis and Pakistanis from the frontier, one of the Islamic fundamentalist groups that had been thrown up by the Afghan conflict.' He worried that such men might be ruthless. 'Night came. There was still no sign of us being set free.' More militants arrived. 'We began to feel apprehensive.'

After dinner, David and Jenny Housego and Cathy Mackie were called one by one into another room, on the pretext of writing down their names and addresses. 'It was only when the door was locked behind us that we realised that my son and Cathy's husband had been separated from us.'

In the middle of the night, David heard what sounded like the militants moving out. Restless and exasperated, at 4.30 a.m. he broke down the door of their room to find they were alone. 'We searched the village, going with growing despair from house to house. No sign of Kim and David.' Instead, they found a note in Urdu, left behind in the room where Kim and David Mackie had been. It demanded the release of three men: Masood, the Afghani and Langrial. The names had meant nothing to David.

At Pahalgam police station, where they reported the kidnapping, just as Jane Schelly would do thirteen months later, the Duty Inspector had 'burst into tears', setting Jenny off too. Afterwards the party had come down to Srinagar, 'Cathy walking barefoot as her shoes had been stolen', where the well-connected David had called up the Chief Secretary of Kashmir, the state's most senior bureaucrat, who was a personal friend. Afterwards he had visited the offices of Rajinder Tikoo, the Inspector General of Kashmir Zone, one of the valley's most senior police officers, and had spoken on the phone to Brigadier Arjun Ray, the army chief at BB Cantt. 'Ray made it clear there was no question of prisoners being released,' David told Yusuf. The Brigadier also said the army would not launch any rescue operation that would put the hostages' lives at risk. David's best bet was to try to get friends to bring pressure on the Pakistani government.

He suspected New Delhi would do little to secure the hostages' freedom unless its hand was forced. He also believed that if the story was widely publicised, Kashmiris would not stand by while Westerners were sacrificed in the name of their liberty, especially when a blameless teenager was involved. His explanation complete, David glanced around Yusuf's office. 'That's them!' he had suddenly shouted, pointing excitedly to Mushtaq Ali's photographs of Sikander, the Turk, the Afghani and Supahi. 'They're the ones who seized us two days back in the Meadow!' Now Yusuf knew something no one else did: that the Movement was behind the hostage drama, and Sikander was personally involved. He promised to help David any way he could.

Kim Housego and David Mackie would endure seventeen agonising days in captivity as pressure was heaped on the Movement and Pakistan's civilian government. Yusuf Jameel had sent regular updates to the BBC, while David Housego did rounds of interviews, visiting Brigadier Ray and Rajinder Tikoo at his headquarters in the Batamaloo neighbourhood of Srinagar. At one point it looked as if the hostages would be killed, after Qazi Nisar, a highly influential *mirvaiz*, or chief cleric, in unruly Anantnag who had publicly agreed to help the families by acting as an intermediary was shot dead by masked gunmen. Some newspapers reported that the Movement had executed the priest, to stop him embarrassing them into surrender. The militant outfit issued a furious denial, insisting that Qazi Nisar was the victim of the Indian intelligence forces.

When Yusuf Jameel went down to Anantnag to cover Qazi Nisar's funeral, he was not sure which of these stories he believed. 'But whatever the truth, it was murky. And the hostages were still out there.' The entire grief-stricken town ground to a halt as hundreds of thousands of mourners came out to bear the cleric's coffin on high. Yusuf spotted Sikander in the crowd, surrounded by masked men. A furious Sikander strode over to him. 'He blamed the media for the Movement being tarnished with Qazi Nisar's killing. He said I had to set the record straight.' Sikander demanded that the BBC run a piece right away, carrying his views. Yusuf refused, telling him that the one rule he stuck to in dealing with the army and militants alike was never to report anything under duress. A mob began to close in on the BBC man and his colleagues, young men instructed to pelt them with stones, forcing them to run for a waiting car which was damaged in the fusillade.

This time Sikander had really scared Yusuf, who vowed that he would not meet the Movement's district commander face to face again. But a few days later he had received another breathless middle-of-the-night call, instructing him to go to a roadside shrine between Anantnag and Aishmuqam, on the route up to Pahalgam. 'I knew at once it was Sikander. He claimed that the hostages were about to be released.' But Yusuf worried that he was being set up. He was torn. 'I owed it to my good friend David Housego to do anything I could to help rescue his son,' he said. But he owed it to his own family not to risk his life.

In the end, a compromise was reached. His photographer friend Mushtaq Ali volunteered to go for him. He too had the advantage of knowing Sikander personally, through the Major Bhupinder Singh affair, but he wasn't wrapped up in the unpleasantness of the Qazi Nisar killing. Everyone would buy the pictures if Kim and David were released. Mushtaq set out, taking another photographer for back-up. Following Sikander's instructions, they drove to the shrine, parked in a nearby poplar nursery and waited for a man to arrive carrying a watermelon, as agreed by Sikander.

Finally, a man had duly emerged with his fruit, and led a tense Mushtaq and his colleague to an empty building. They waited there for several hours, until Kim Housego and David Mackie arrived. It was a moment Kim would never forget: 'Two rickshaws had taken us through the centre of town to a forest. We walked for a couple of minutes and saw journalists appearing from an empty house clicking with their cameras.' After seventeen days of being moved around the Warwan Valley and Anantnag, Kim could not believe it. He sat down, 'shaking with anxiety', to be photographed by Mushtaq Ali. The Movement had coached him on what to say, and he repeated the story. 'At the end the militants talked together and then announced that we would be freed to go with the journalists. "You shall be missed around here," the masked commander said to me.'

As a parting gesture to cap the surreal mountain hike, Kim was given a gift, a clock that bore an inscription comparing the Indian Army to the Nazis: 'Teacher – Hitler; Pupils – Indian Occupational Forces; with Best Wishes to Kim Housego from Harkat ul-Ansar International'. A few minutes later a grinning Mushtaq Ali emerged from the building, his arm around Kim's shoulder. Before taking the former hostages back to Srinagar, where their families were waiting, Mushtaq joked with Sikander's emissary, asking if they could now eat the watermelon. The militant shook his head, and cracked the fruit open to reveal a hand grenade concealed inside. 'My instructions were to kill you all if we were betrayed,' he said, before discarding the melon and vanishing into the woods.

The story of the kidnapping did not end there. Still determined to win the freedom of Masood, the Afghani and Langrial, the Movement had struck again, this time in New Delhi in October 1994. Sikander had not been involved in this operation, as the Movement had instead used a British-Pakistani recruit, Omar Sheikh, who had been educated at the London School of Economics, and who used his familiarity with Western ways to lure three British and one American backpacker away from their guesthouses in the travellers' enclave of Paharganj opposite New Delhi railway station, where Paul Wells and Cath Moseley would later stay. The Movement had issued a ransom note demanding the release of the three imprisoned militants, this one signed by a fictional group, al Hadid, meaning 'the blade'. However, the plot was foiled when police investigating an unrelated report of a burglary stumbled across Sheikh's hideout, leading to his capture and the freeing of the hostages, some of whom told of being chained to the floor, an indication of the increasing violence being meted out by an ever-hardening Movement.

After the New Delhi kidnapping there had been a lull. Until now: 4 July 1995, and this call from someone Yusuf was certain was Sikander. He cast his eye down the list of twenty-one names dictated to him. Here was the proof he was looking for. This time round the kidnappers were making the same demands as before. They wanted Masood, the Afghani and Langrial freed. And beneath their names was that of the British recruit Omar Sheikh, who was currently languishing in the high-security wing at Tihar jail, in New Delhi. It was clear to Yusuf what was going on: al Faran was the Movement, and the Movement was al Faran. Sikander, whose *jihadi* career to date had involved three separate kidnappings, had launched the Movement's third serious attempt to win the freedom of Masood

Azhar and his comrades. But for now, as Yusuf prepared to file to the BBC, he kept most of this to himself. He needed to back up his surmises. Instead, his report would stick to the bare bones of the story.

Dirk Hasert and Anne Hennig, a young German couple taking a break from their college studies in Erfurt, the capital of the German state of Thuringia, knew none of this when they reached Dal Lake in Srinagar on 4 July. They had met as students a year earlier, during a film screening at Erfurt's Anger Kino, and had come on holiday to Kashmir to widen their horizons.

Anne was a couple of years Dirk's junior, but they had hit it off straight away, sharing a love of art-house movies and a desire to get away from the decaying eastern side of reunified Germany. Dirk had grown up in Bad Langensalza, an insular medieval city near Erfurt. The youngest and most rebellious of Christa Hasert's three children, he had found it claustrophobic and depressing.

Dirk had longed to turn his back on what he saw as the dead-end Eastern Bloc. While his older brother Berndt and sister Birgit followed a more conventional route, he buried himself in magazines smuggled in from the West, imagining what it would be like to travel. After just scraping through his *Arbitur* exams, the German matriculation, Dirk made what his brother Berndt called 'a break for freedom', moving to the big city of Erfurt, where he chose vocational training over university. Berndt said: 'Dirk didn't stick at anything, and spent his days casting around Erfurt for something more fulfilling.' Then, in November 1989, the Berlin Wall fell, setting the twenty-year-old free.

Dirk immediately got a passport, saved up to buy an InterRail card and embraced his new freedom, pushing his budget as far as it would stretch, at one stage reaching Turkey. Gradually he stopped calling his siblings altogether, although he still contacted his mother once in a while. She was too old to change, he said: 'Too much water under the bridge.' She would never move away from Bad Langensalza.

At twenty-five, Dirk tried to figure out how to raise more money, in order to travel further and for longer. He went back into education, getting onto a degree course in social education at Erfurt Polytechnic. That summer, 1994, before college started, he had made his most adventurous trip yet, a solo voyage to Iran and Afghanistan. 'Everything he saw transformed his view of the world, sparking a fascination with religion, politics and spirituality,' Berndt said. Dirk began his studies that autumn energised, and fell for an ethereal first-year student, Anne Hennig. 'The region fascinated him,' she recalled. 'It was all Dirk would talk about for hours.' She shared his curiosity, but was not so driven to explore. He was particularly interested in Islam, captivated by the way devout Muslims *lived* their religion, unlike Christians. Having coaxed Anne into coming with him on his next big adventure to witness Islam in its raw state, much as Paul Wells would talk Cath Moseley into going to Ladakh, Dirk began planning their trip for the following summer. After reading up on Asia and poring over maps, they agreed on Kashmir.

Stopping off in New Delhi at the end of June 1995, and feeling nervous about travelling to the valley, they had gone to the government tourism office to get advice. 'Dirk was very careful,' reflected Anne. They were given the usual reassuring story: 'Stay out of downtown Srinagar and you'll have the holiday of a lifetime.' 'And it looked like paradise in the travel guides we saw,' said Anne, although like everyone else they were shocked when they flew in to Srinagar airport. 'It was suddenly machine guns, razor wire and sandbags.' As the J&K tourism police at the airport quizzed them – names, passports, hotel, itinerary – and Anne looked out into a crowd of unsmiling bearded faces, she began to get cold feet. 'There were threatening signs,' she said, worried by the overwhelming military presence.

However, once they reached Dal Lake, life slowed down on the calming waters. The people were open, the mountain views uplifting. They tried once again to pin down the facts, calling at the J&K state tourism office on 5 July, the day after the kidnappings. 'Everyone assured us it would be OK,' said Anne, unaware at the time that just a few blocks away in the UN guesthouse Jane Schelly, Julie Mangan and Cath Moseley were going through hell explaining their partners' abductions. Dirk and Anne were advised by a policeman, Nasser

Ahmed Jan, to head for Pahalgam, 'which was where other Westerners were happily going'. He said he would contact them if the situation changed, and waved them out, even though the newspaper on his desk was reporting the Pahalgam abductions and that the day before DSP Kifayat Haider had, unsuccessfully, recommended to his superiors that the trekking routes above Pahalgam be cleared of all Western holidaymakers.

Dirk and Anne were on holiday. They were not reading newspapers. They had asked officials for their views, and had heard nothing about the kidnapping of Don, Keith, Paul and John. On 6 July, the day news of the events in Kashmir was broadcast around the world, Dirk and Anne left Srinagar at dawn, taking the bus to Pahalgam, just missing the breaking story. Pony-*wallahs* and guides crowded around them when they arrived in the trekking town around noon. Instead of telling them to turn back, men who were desperate for business vied with each other to describe the wonderful sights the German couple would see camping beyond the ridgelines. No one mentioned Jane, Julie and Cath's dramatic arrival in Pahalgam the previous day.

Dirk and Anne started out the next day, following in the footsteps of Jane Schelly and Don Hutchings along the Amarnath route. Up in the mountains it was 'incredibly quiet and peaceful', Anne recalled. But at the mountain village of Chandanwari they were slightly disconcerted to see droves of Indian soldiers. 'It was certainly irritating that so many military people were around, but who could take notice of that in such a magnificent landscape?' Anne said. Coming from a country that had been divided, the couple had lived with uniforms their entire lives, and they were advised that these troops were preparing for a Hindu pilgrimage whose route needed securing. The soldiers themselves did not stop to talk, but just waved at the foreigners, ushering them on and up, higher into the mountains. 'There was no reason to worry,' said Anne. 'There seemed to be everything to live for.' So they pressed on, camping on the night of 7 July just outside Chandanwari, going to bed early since they had dawn plans. As they lay in each other's arms they talked about Pissu Top, the high-altitude pass they hoped to cross the following day. And of Zargibal, a small hamlet of stone houses and a mountain stream where it was said one could pitch a tent and get a near-perfect view of the seven peaks of Sheshnag. How glad he was that they had made it this far, Anne remembered Dirk whispering to her, just before they fell into a deep sleep.

SEVEN

Up and Down

8 July, just after midnight. Was he the only one awake, John Childs wondered. As he lay huddled under a couple of thin horse blankets next to his fellow captives, it was difficult to say. Just like every other night they had endured, the hostages were hemmed in on all sides by clumps of wheezing, scratching and snoring insurgents, more than a dozen men and boys in total. Their Kalashnikovs were stacked against the walls, while they kept their pistols and knives jammed into their waistbands or close at hand throughout the night. The situation was as close to a nightmare as John could imagine, cooped up at uncomfortably close quarters in a pungent, smoke-filled *gujjar* hut somewhere in the Kashmiri mountains, who knew how many miles from safety, with no sign of rescue. For the past four days and nights his every move, his every bodily need, had been controlled by these rough strangers, who he had begun to hate with a passion. 'I came from America, the land of the free,' he said. 'And now I had to ask some idiot kid with a rifle for permission to urinate, to speak, even to wash my hands before eating. I was stunned by the loss of freedom. This is what struck me most. The thing that pained me.' But having got over his self-pity, John was determined to get out.

After four days in their company, he was still not sure who his captors represented, or what they wanted. They appeared to be some kind of *mujahideen*, like the turbanned gunmen he'd read of fighting in Afghanistan. Two of them claimed to be veterans, without saying which conflict they had fought in, or on what side. Some of the younger ones had let the odd fact slip during unguarded moments.

One said he came from Gilgit, which John knew was somewhere in the Pakistani mountains. Another said he was from 'the tribal areas', which probably placed him on the Pakistan–Afghanistan border. Other than that, there had been little talking. The leader had seen to it that his men kept their distance and said little. 'Shut up, keep quiet!' he had barked every time he caught the hostages exchanging whispers, gesturing with his pistol.

One thing was clear. These men had known no life other than the mountains or the battlefield: washing only to pray, defecating wherever, charging up mountains in plastic sandals, spending the evenings obsessively cleaning their weapons. 'Some of the younger ones were just teenagers,' said John. They made a few attempts to ask about cricket, bands, life in Britain and the US. John had decided right at the start to smile through it, and not to be the one who caused trouble. 'I didn't want that responsibility, I didn't want to anger my captors. I just wanted out of this. I left the bolshiness to Paul.'

But on the inside, John was fighting himself. 'All I kept thinking was how stupid I'd been, too proud to accept I'd made a mistake in going to Srinagar, too arrogant to turn around when it was staring me in the face that this was *not* an appropriate holiday destination. Now I was stuck, and as far as I was concerned, no one was coming to rescue us.' He could not block out the thought that less than a week earlier he'd been in a suit and tie in Calcutta, pondering a break in the Himalayas. Now he was trapped, and distrustful of everyone – including, if he was honest, the other hostages. How could he rely on men he did not know?

John focused on the kidnappers, trying to work out the pecking order and their rituals, noticing how reverentially they acted around the leader. 'He was sinister-looking, with a long, narrow face, a hawkish nose and an expression that gave nothing away. Unlike some of the others, who got excitable or panicked, the leader was cool, and spoke near-perfect English. Fair-skinned, with a long beard and hair, he had a stillness about him that, enhanced by his aquiline profile and robes, gave him the aura of an educated aesthete. He seemed to have come from privilege, but to have been brought down by war to something more basic.' John felt that this man had chosen his path, and that he was capable of anything. Many years later John would say that every time he saw a picture of Osama bin Laden he was reminded of al Faran's leader.

Now he lay studying the primitive eaves of the shelter, roughly hewn from red pine, sawn and hacked into lengths which it must have taken many men and animals to haul to this spot. He had had enough of the last four arduous days, walking and climbing endlessly, with nothing more to greet them at the end of another twelve hours than a smoky hut and a clump of rice. Back home, running for miles, trekking into the mountains or taking a bike ride through the woods, setting up an impromptu campsite, were all voluntary experiences. But a route march at gunpoint through these high mountains, up flanks and over icy ridges with vertiginous sheer drops on either side, was punishing.

The hut they were currently housed in, which they had reached at dusk the previous evening, was split by a wooden partition into two dank rooms, devoid of furniture, each of them barely six feet square, the walls and ceiling scorched black by wood smoke. Its miserable male occupants had spent the early evening guarding the rough corrugated-tin gate of the compound, before coming inside to squat on a patchwork of rugs thrown over the impacted earth, from where they watched the hostages with fascination. The women and children remained out of sight in the second room, boiling up tea on a wood fire, rinsing metal bowls and talking in soft whispers.

The wind breached the nicks in the rough stone-and-earth wall, fanning the embers in the firepit. Earlier, two women who could have been mother and daughter had been forced to make dinner for all of them, eking out a meal for everyone from their meagre rations: ash-flecked rice, *lavash* and some kind of vegetable that resembled spinach and that had got the locals very excited when the leader had produced it. Spotting a small bowl of home-made butter in one corner, the younger gunmen had fallen on it, dipping their bread into it, gobbling it all up then taking it in turns to run a forefinger around the bowl. John had felt sick as he ate, hiding pieces of bread in his socks and padded trekking jacket before pushing the rest away. Sitting by the fire, watching the militants through the haze, he had thought, 'I have to get out of here.'

He studied the sleeping hostages. He and Don had bonded a little. Two Americans *in extremis*. But the British pair, Keith and Paul, were different to him in outlook, experience and nature, almost as foreign as the kidnappers. They believed, naïvely, in the generosity of others, and in the importance of acting collectively. No doubt they would try to form some kind of escape committee if they had the chance, whereas he had calculated that he would have to capitalise on whatever chances arose, because they would be infrequent. 'The Indians will save us,' they had said. John had shaken his head in disbelief. They had been abandoned to their fate the minute they had been kidnapped. 'There would be no rescue. In my mind we were totally alone.'

John had always been the one who'd unflinchingly confronted unpopular thoughts, even at the cost of making friends. He knew that saying these things out loud would have made him sound mean-spirited. But all he wanted was to live. He needed to see his mother, his father, his daughters again. He believed in the power of his imagination. That was what would get him out of here.

By the faint light of the embers of the fire he could see his sleeping comrades' faces, pinched with exhaustion. How much ground had they covered over the past seventy-eight hours? Twelve hours of walking and climbing every day, stopping only to pray and at dusk. His, Keith and Paul's beards were beginning to show, which he was sure would please their captors, as it made them less obviously foreign. He felt bad about what he was starting to plan, and knew it would have an impact on the other hostages. 'But I had no other option. I chose to live. And I knew if I didn't do it now, I would die.' Everything depended on the number of sentries outside, and how alert they were. John was banking on the fact that no one would be rising for another three hours, until the 4 a.m. prayers. His stomach knotted in spasms. He was not sure if it was fear, dysentery, altitude sickness or a parasite. Whatever it was, he would use it to his advantage.

He got up and silently wound his way, boots in one hand, between the sleeping bodies. Gingerly pushing the tarpaulin door-flap aside, he emerged into the cold night air of the mountains: wood smoke, pine resin and snow. A sentry who was sitting beside the entrance to the compound looked up. John acknowledged him, then grimaced and gripped his stomach, as he had done many times over the past days. The sentry nodded and went back to cleaning his weapon. John walked out of the compound, counting three more guards dotted about in the trees, all of them in various states of slumber. He knew there were more sleeping in the next hut. Gripping his stomach again, he groaned gently before stumbling into the woods and finding a place to squat. He shivered and watched, taking in the scene.

Somewhere nearby, a river was gurgling. He drew himself a mental map. Why hadn't he gone home after Calcutta? He berated himself yet again, thinking about his daughters, Cathy and Mary. Did they know he was missing yet? Probably not. News travelled slowly in what he saw as the swamp of India. Here he was, in a deadly Himalayan scrape, with his trousers around his ankles. But he had to try to quell the self-pity, and do something. His captors had become more blasé with every mile under their belt. Head up and inhale, he said to himself. Above him the sky was dark and cloudy. Perfect, he thought. An overcast night would make it easier to travel unnoticed. A few minutes later he stood and hauled up his trousers. It was not yet time. Was he prevaricating? No, he had a plan. He had a simple idea that would change the course of the next forty-eight hours. But it was not yet late enough. He stumbled back into the sour-smelling hut.

Four days earlier, when they had first been marched up the mountainside away from the other campers in the Meadow, all John Childs had dwelled on as the rain poured down his neck was how unbelievably stupid he had been. If he had heeded Dasheer's advice he would have been back in Pahalgam by the time the gunmen had entered the Meadow. He would have read about the incident in the newspaper as he boarded his plane to New Delhi, and told his work colleagues back in New England about his scrape with death. From the moment he had awoken to find a militant standing in his tent he had come down on himself hard: coming to Kashmir had been 'the biggest screw-up of my life'.

The hostage party, with Dasheer tagging along at the leader's insistence, had climbed for a couple of hours through a pitch-black forest, slippery and prickly, the rough path made treacherous by moss-covered rocks on which their feet skidded, twisting ankles and jarring knees.

John, who was still feeling the effects of walking at high altitude for seven hours the previous day, struggled to keep up. And all the time there was a gun muzzle knocking the small of his back, reminding him of the consequences of lagging. His rigid mountaineering boots, designed for crampons, scraped another layer of skin from his heels as negative thoughts crowded into his mind. His socks were wet with blood. He had to fight his pessimism, and dig deep to find his fitness, or the route and his fatalism would kill him.

'Stupid, selfish idiot,' he said under his breath over and over, convinced he was about to die, looping into a self-destructive cycle. Now his daughters, his parents, the people he loved most in the world, would have to deal with his death, telling their friends he had gone off to Kashmir on a selfish adventure. His parents would go to their graves without seeing their son again. Would anyone ever find his body? Would there be a funeral? Then there was his sister Barbara and her children. And his younger brother Richard. All these lives messed up by his reckless decision to go trekking in the most dangerous location in the world.

The red flags had been obvious from the minute he touched down in Srinagar. Why had he not heeded them? Watching the younger militants racing up the hillside ahead of him, clearly exhilarated by their catch, John felt like hurling himself off the side of the mountain. He was so angry that even after several hours of climbing, he couldn't bring himself to look the other hostages in the eye. What must that look like to them? Shame? Pride? Bitterness? There was no point worrying about how the others saw him. He seldom cared about the impression he made. By the time they had scaled the ridge, hundreds of metres above the Meadow, all of them were soaked to the skin and depressed.

They reached a plateau where grass gave way to stones. Numb and cramped, they had finally reached the snowline, and the temperature dropped by many degrees. In the moonlight, John could see an expanse of boulders and pebbles rising above them, glacial detritus that would have been hard to clamber through in daylight, let alone at night. The only trees were charred black as if struck by lightning, or perhaps they had been burned by *gujjar* herdsmen. Either way, they stuck out of the granite like vandalised telegraph poles, giving the landscape an apocalyptic feel, as if all around had been carpet-bombed. Ahead of them was a sizeable *gujjar* settlement. Even though it was late, the family who lived in the biggest hut emerged as their dogs began to bark at the party's approach.

John wondered if this would be a chance to send a message for help, but his heart sank as an old man walked over to the kidnappers' leader and embraced him. 'What the hell? They knew we were coming,' he said to himself. 'This has all been pre-planned. Dasheer was right to try to get me away from the Meadow. He knew something too. Everyone in the valley knew a kidnapping was about to happen. Except us.' The growing feeling that he was the victim of a conspiracy almost crushed him once more. 'I could feel myself ebbing.' He looked over to Dasheer, sodden and sorry-looking in his ripped *pheran*. The guide held John's gaze for a moment, then cast his eyes downwards as if he understood that John knew too. Just beyond Dasheer was Don, his fellow American and the nearest to him in age, although John had no idea of the names of any of his fellow captives at this stage, having spoken to none of them.

'Keep calm,' Don murmured under his breath, winking. 'We'll find a way out of this.' John doubted it.

One of the kidnappers motioned them forwards into the nearest *dhoka*. They sat around the fire, Keith and Paul shuffling together, John beside Don, the hostages already separating into their national groups, British and American. A couple of rough blankets were thrown in their general direction, and then the militants turned their backs. As he stared into the flames, John could not remember ever feeling so tired: 'I was as limp as a child.'

5 July, dark and early. A dozen gunmen were crammed into the hut with them, along with a handful of *gujjars*. All of them were talking animatedly in languages John did not understand. He and the other sodden hostages sat to one side, in a sad, steaming puddle. There was no commander waiting for them here. The Israeli spy story had just been a line to get them away, a clumsy cover for whatever this really was: pure banditry, or worse.

Dasheer was given a note and told to return with it to the Meadow. 'What's going on?' John blurted out. What did it say? Dasheer came over and tried to reassure him in English that there was nothing to worry about, that he was going to get help. But there was a flicker of fear in his eyes. Dasheer shoved the note inside his *pheran* and stumbled out of the hut. John watched him walking away through the rain. Without his guide, he felt strangely bereft. The Kashmiri had been his constant companion over the past four days. He hoped he would hurry straight back to Srinagar and raise the alarm. That was what John would have done, given the opportunity.

He lay down, grateful at least not to be walking. He tried to listen in to the intense conversation between the old man and the militant leader. At one stage he thought he heard the word 'hostage' in English. After what seemed an age, Don called over to the gunmen, breaking the Westerners' silence. They had been walking for hours, and had missed their evening meal. He mimed eating and drinking. 'OK, *chacha*,' said one of the younger gunmen, calling Don 'uncle'. John noticed that they spoke to Don as if he was an elder, drawn to his kindly face with its close-cropped beard. Afterwards, Don had whispered to the others: 'Smile. Keep your faces open. It's much harder to kill a smiling face.'

Later, the leader had turned his attention to the hostages. 'We are Islamic fundamentalists,' he announced. John could not help but smile. Back home, fundamentalism meant an idea taken too literally, bent out of context. But here it seemed simply to be an expression of commitment. 'Our guns are for the Indian Army,' the man continued. 'With your help we want to release our supreme commanders from Indian prisons. You are our guests. We wish to treat you as such.' Could they then have something to eat and drink, Don asked again. The leader spoke to one of the other men and nodded before leaving them in the hut.

'Guests.' 'Hostages.' John rolled the words around his mind and recalled the factory workers in Bihar talking of peace-loving 'Kashmiri separatists', at which their Hindu colleagues had risen up and damned Kashmiris as Islamic terrorists. Sensing John's anger, Don whispered, 'Sit tight. We'll work something out together.' Indian soldiers were crawling all over the mountains because of the pilgrimage to Amarnath, and Jane and the other women would soon raise the alarm, if they hadn't already. By tonight, Don reassured him, they'd all be back in Srinagar, telling everyone about their adventure. Keith, the older Englishman, nodded. 'He was calm and stoic throughout,' said John. Paul smiled too, although he gave little away. His father Bob said: 'Paul was probably enjoying himself at the start of it. Kashmir. Islamic terrorists. Paul Wells, the hostage. He was living a real adventure.' Paul's only regret, his father guessed, would be that he no longer had his camera, which had been stolen by one of the gunmen. They were now using it to take pictures of each other.

5 July, daybreak. It was only when John noticed dawn leaching through the gaps in the walls of the hut that he realised he had been asleep. The militants stood, hands raised to their faces, thumbs touching ears and palms facing outward as they intently recited '*Allahu akbar,*' oblivious to everything, then dropped to their knees and prostrated themselves, transported by prayer. Outside, dogs barked and someone could be heard sweeping the rough ground. Villagers were all around. Did they know hostages were in here? As they lay in the half-light, they were able to take in their shabby surroundings. The stone hut consisted of just one room, with a fire in one corner and bedrolls and blankets piled up in another. From the beamed ceiling hung assorted plastic bags containing dry food. The women of the family were nowhere to be seen.

A young *gujjar* boy entered, nervously carrying a tray of steamed rice, tea and *lavash* bread, and placed it before the hostages. As they tore into it, John could hear a cacophony of voices outside. In the moonlight the night before, he had been able to make out quite a sizeable compound, with several huts protected by a rough perimeter wall. Now he could hear children running about and babies crying. Somewhere a man hawked and spat, and a woman was singing a lullaby. From the direction where the animals were tethered came the sound of tinkling sheep bells. As he munched his way through another tasteless mouthful of starch, John's mind whirred. During the night he had slept in fits and starts, his mood wavering from despair to anger. This morning he had woken with a new sense of determination. 'I knew there was only one way out of this. I had never been more focused in my life.'

Just as the Westerners were draining their tea, several militants rushed in and ordered them to put on their boots. They emerged into the burning sunlight, not knowing what was coming next. The brightness of the sun reflecting off virgin snow was almost blinding. John was disorientated. 'Where are my sunglasses?' he mumbled to one of the guards. 'You stole them. Give them back to me.' Don rushed over to calm him: 'Don't make them angry. It'll just make life harder for all of us. We need to keep them relaxed and work on a plan.' He showed John how to rip a piece of cloth and fashion it into two strips that he tied around his head, leaving just a narrow slit to see through. They looked like Tuareg sand people, but this crude invention worked. All the time, Keith and Paul, who remained slightly apart from their American comrades, watched in silence.

A few minutes later, the kidnappers ordered the hostages to line up with them in formation: the leader and two other gunmen at the front, then Don, the strongest of the hostages, followed by two more gunmen, then Keith, two more gunmen, then Paul, with John, who was still weak and was now limping, as his rigid boots had shredded his heels, followed by the two youngest militants, who were armed only with knives. 'We would walk like that every day, for twelve hours,' said John. 'In a line, straight up the mountains. They kept us moving constantly.'

Ten minutes after leaving the *gujjar* compound, the pace quickened as the militants got into their stride. 'We went over the top and down into the next valley,' said John. Those gunmen who had stolen sunglasses were wearing them, while the others winced in constant pain as the glaring rays flared up in their faces, burning their retinas. Water coursed through the gravel around their feet, snowmelt was finding its way downhill, and plump white vultures circled above them like unmanned drones.

Yet more gunmen were waiting for them ahead. 'This is a sophisticated operation,' thought John as he tried to keep up, determined to take everything in, to consider all possibilities for escape. He had not mentioned these thoughts to the others. In his heart he knew he would not. John Childs had always been a one-man band: 'I just was not a team player. I knew from stuff I'd read that turning inwards to find an inner freedom was the one thing that might help me survive captivity. I had to work this out for myself and in my own head. I had to develop a strategy for dealing with the crisis and I had to create an opportunity to escape.' As time passed, the guards seemed less focused on keeping the marching party in formation, and for a time John deliberately lagged behind to see how long it was before they noticed. 'But my foot was giving me hell, and I knew I wouldn't get very far, even if I legged it. The kidnappers were faster than all of us. As the weakest in the party, I would have to do something that gave me a head start.'

He trudged on. Paul was in front of him, cursing under his breath. Keith, who was also having problems with cramp and blisters, was in the middle. Up front, Don was striding ahead. He seemed to be dealing with the physical exertion the best of all of them, despite being the oldest. John was momentarily envious. Back home in Connecticut, he prided himself on his fitness. He could feel his competitive hackles rising. But then, Don had been in the mountains longer than him, and had had more time to acclimatise to the thin air. 'No time for excuses,' John said to himself.

As the sun dropped behind a ridge, the hostages crossed a picturesque valley, urged on by the kidnappers, who did not want to linger in the icy bottom. 'Shame I forgot my camera,' Keith joked. Some of the tired fighters peeled off, to be replaced by others. They passed no other trekkers, only skinny herders with their goats and sheep. 'One of them stopped us and spoke to us in English,' said John. 'He asked why we'd been *arrested*.' John froze. Finally he replied, 'We've been kidnapped. We're being held against our will.' The man nodded and carried on down the path. A short while later, another herder stopped to greet his brother, who had been commandeered to guide the kidnap party through a dense forest. 'I knew there was no chance of either of these men raising the alarm,' John said. 'Everyone knew, but no one would do anything about it.' In the remote Kashmir heights, where everyone minded his own business, the hostage-takers were safe.

Just before dusk, the party stopped at another *gujjar* settlement, high above the snowline, this one consisting of three tents made watertight with frayed plastic sheeting. As on the previous evening, the family who lived there during the summer months seemed unfazed by the Westerners' arrival. The militants had created a sophisticated network up here, suggesting that they had been operating in this area for some time. 'Another thing the tourist people forgot to mention,' Keith murmured wryly.

After the leader had gone out, the younger kidnappers talked around the fire with their captives for a few minutes. 'Don said our odds of survival were better if we formed a bond,' said John, who asked one of the kidnappers if he knew how to arm-wrestle. 'He didn't understand what I was talking about, so I showed him, and of course I let him win.' Later, with the leader seated back among them, the kidnappers ate and talked among themselves, their guns lined up against the wall in a row, giving John, Don, Keith and Paul a chance to have their first substantial conversation. 'I said for the first time out aloud that I could not see anything good in this situation,' said John. 'Don was with me. He wanted to get out of there just like I did. But he was more patient. For him, it was a matter of the right plan and the right time, whereas I was anytime and anyhow.' Keith and Paul were both against the idea. 'They wanted things to pan out naturally. They had a sense of right and wrong, and they felt that if we hung back, the

Indians would rescue us.' It seemed to John that a rift was forming in the group. That night passed agonisingly slowly for John as he mulled over what to do.

6 July, daybreak. In the early hours, John began contemplating stealing a gun and making a break for it. 'The further we got from the Meadow, the more blasé the militants had become,' he said. On one occasion they had left the hostages alone in a hut with all the guns stacked against a wall. 'I had never handled a Kalashnikov, but I knew how it worked.' The previous evening he had gone outside to urinate, and as he came back in he casually picked up one of the weapons, as if he needed to move it to get by, to see how their captors would react. 'It was much heavier than I thought, but as I suspected, nobody blinked an eye.' What worried him now was whether he could remember the sequence on the selector switch. 'Click it in a certain direction and it took off the safety. Click it again and you found the weapon's mode: single shots or bursts. Click it the wrong way and the whole clip would fall out, clattering on the floor, alerting the gunmen. I just didn't trust myself that I knew which way to push it. I put back the rifle. I just could not take the risk.'

As they moved out that morning, climbing higher and higher, John was filled with self-loathing. Another chance had slipped by. Was he too much of a coward to do this? What kind of opportunity was he waiting for? 'When you watch a movie, the hero always gets out alive,' he reflected. 'But when it's real ...' They trudged on through the snow, heading for an enormous ice ridge that glinted like a razor. Soon they were skidding across it, unable to find any grip. 'They just pushed us on and on. We slithered. That day was Keith's turn to get altitude sickness,' said John, who watched the kidnappers attempt to drive the ponies up a near-vertical ice wall while ignoring Keith's plight. 'There were militants pulling and pushing from below. If our situation had not been so dire, it would have been funny. Keith was reeling.'

John too was in a bad way. His heels were burning, worn to the bone by his hard boots. He longed to take them off and plunge his feet into the snowmelt, but the only time the kidnappers ever stopped was to drink, piss or pray. 'Then they set off again. Up. Up. Up.' By the time they stopped that night, at another tented encampment, everyone was exhausted. And Keith was ebbing. Don asked the kidnappers if they had any medicine, but there was nothing. Don, John and Paul watched, bemused, as one of the gunmen was sent off across the mountainside to catch a sheep. This youth was not country-born, and the animal easily gave him the slip, darting between the boulders. But then another militant joined the pursuit, cruelly knocking the sheep out with his rifle butt. They dragged it over, grabbed its head and drew a long blade across the skin of its throat. An arc of blood sprayed out, the four hostages transfixed by the scene. The animal snorted and whiffled as life surged from the flapping wound in its throat.

John shrank back. For the next hour he could barely watch as the two militants dismembered the animal, stuffing bloody body parts and skin into rucksacks. 'I was utterly convinced now that this would be my fate too.'

Later, after the *gujjar* women had roasted parts of the sheep over a smoky fire, John refused to eat. He was starving, but he couldn't get the animal's horrific end out of his mind: 'As far as I was concerned, they had staged a mock execution.' After dinner, he crouched in a dark corner of the hut, huddled silently against the wall under a dirty blanket, his body warmed by a small clay *kangri* pot containing hot coals. The militants gorged on the animal as if it was their last supper, while Don, Keith and Paul chatted quietly.

Don, as usual, remained rational. The sheep-slaughtering had been brutal, but they had to eat, and meat would build up their strength. Keith murmured that it would only be a matter of hours before the Indians launched a rescue attempt. But for John, who said nothing, the event had been a turning point. He felt he had glimpsed what the militants were capable of. He tried to talk to the two British hostages about escaping, but they were still for waiting. The kidnappers had enough weapons to kill an entire village, Paul whispered. Counting the sentries outside the hut, there were now well over twenty militants in the party. 'I hope you've got your map with you,' joked Keith. Talking about escaping was fruitless, the two British hostages felt.

Anyhow, they'd be rescued. There would be Indian soldiers. Helicopters. 'There won't,' said John.

After dinner, the militants sated, everyone had fallen asleep apart from John. His girls would surely have been told of his abduction by now. Distressing snapshots of the past few days came into his head: a huge cache of ammunition he had caught sight of high in the mountains, and the two-way radio set through which the leader had communicated with his distant controllers. The kidnappers were well supported, fairly disciplined and equipped for the long haul, John concluded. It could go on like this for weeks, and then end bloodily. He watched the militants rouse themselves for the last prayer of the night; standing, hands cupped, the fire casting shadows that weaved and ducked, as the men praised the greatness of God. For a few minutes John got down on his knees too. 'If they could pray, then so could I. But I wondered what kind of God would condemn us to this fate.'

7 July, dawn. 'We were up as soon as it was light,' said John. As they came down from the ice pass of the previous afternoon, the landscape softened a little. They paused to rest beside a river. On the far bank, between colossal red pines that stood erect as organ pipes, the occasional stone shelter could be seen.

John's heels were cut to the bone. But as he sat on a log in the early-morning gloom, contemplating whether he would be able to get through another day, he spotted something that took his mind off the pain completely: Don was wandering off. 'I'd just watched him tell the guards he wanted to pee, as we had been instructed, and then he walked away at speed. This was it. I could see what was in his mind. I could see him go. Don was off. No mistaking it.' John sat immobile, his heart in his mouth. No one else had noticed apart from him. Don was gathering pace and confidence as he got further away from the tents. He was almost out of view. 'I wanted him to do it,' said John, 'but I knew that if Don got away it would be the end of my chances. In one way I was willing the militants to look up, to spot him and bring him back. That's the unspeakable truth.' Eventually one of them did just that, spying Don some way off and shouting to him to come back. 'Don knew he'd been caught. He simply stopped, acted nonchalant, and turned. Pretended nothing had happened. He waved as if it was the most natural thing in the world. Then he walked back into camp. We exchanged glances, but we never spoke about it.'

That day, John was convinced the leader drove the hostage party even harder, as if to punish them all for Don's offence. Keith hobbled along, delirious and dehydrated. John kept pace with him, limping on his butchered feet. When they stopped, John calculated that they had gone ten precipitous miles or more, which was like thirty on the flat. It was almost three days now since the Meadow, all of them spent walking, the nights passed in muttony shelters or flapping tents. John felt as if he was losing his mind.

Some *gujjar* children brought them bread and rice. John sat and ate alone, away from the other hostages, forcing the food into his mouth with his fingers, and secretly pushing some down his socks. 'I had to act while I still had a chance,' he said. As usual, the leader sat by himself on a log, his expressionless eyes focused on the fire. John stood and walked over to him. Everyone in the party stilled. The leader's hand moved to his weapon, but John sat down anyway. He pulled out a photograph of his children. Don had done his thing; now it was John's turn. 'I just want to go home to my daughters,' John said, looking deeply into the leader's eyes as he handed over the photograph. He was the only hostage with kids, he said. 'The leader looked at my daughters' faces. He studied them, but handed the photo back to me with the look of a soldier who had learned to bury his true feelings.' John returned to his previous position, watched by the other three hostages. There was no winning the kidnappers over.

Late in the afternoon, the party crossed a wide valley with a trekking path and a substantial river running along its base. Suddenly Don became agitated. Looking up and down the valley, he whispered that he knew where they were: 'Hey, I know this place. Jane and I walked up here just last week.' They were crossing the main trekking route to Amarnath Cave. John did not share his excitement. If the kidnappers were prepared to bring the hostages in circles, and this close to a busy tourist trail, they were clearly feeling secure. As they plodded on towards a group of huts a few hundred metres up the left flank of the valley, and within sight of the path, Don whispered that he estimated that from here it would be a simple twelve-hour trek back to civilisation. Even less to the army camp at Chandanwari, where they could raise the alarm. Keith and Paul nodded. John, who had seen tents and white-skinned travellers in the distance, said nothing. By the time they stopped at a *gujjar* hut protected by a high wall, his mind was working overtime. 'Everyone was exhausted. The leader promised us that the next day we would be resting here. But I now worked on a plan.'

For the first time since being snatched from the Meadow, the hostages knew roughly where they were. This was, John concluded, his moment, if he could overcome certain problems. Between where they were now and the Amarnath trekking route lay several *gujjar* settlements. Having watched the kidnappers buy food and exchange information with local herders, he distrusted them. Each *gujjar* household represented a potential klaxon, an intruder's footfall setting off a cacophony of dogs. But John kept his thoughts to himself. Night was closing in, and as they huddled together for warmth on the apron of the filthy hut, John, Don, Keith and Paul talked about the things in the world they missed most.

8 July, 2 a.m.: an hour since his last toilet visit. John sat upright. Now was his time. He eased himself out from under the blanket, trying not to nudge or knock anyone as he lumped some clothes into the shape of a sleeping body. His comrades and the guards inside the hut slept as he tiptoed between them, his boots over his shoulder. John felt a pang of remorse for his fellow hostages. Don had been generous, and Keith was a straight-up guy. Paul was likeable, if hot-headed: 'He was just about ready to kill everyone by the time I left them.' They deserved better, but Don's actions of the previous morning had convinced John that it was every man for himself: 'Due to my weakened physical condition I was certain that I would be the first to be killed if the

kidnappers' demands were not met.' He took in his sleeping companions one last time. 'I will seek help and come back for you,' he said under his breath. Then he turned. Slipping on his boots without tying the laces, his trekking jacket over his shoulder and gripping his stomach as if he was contorted with cramps, he pushed aside the tarpaulin door, opened the tin gate and, nodding at the dozing sentry, walked into the night air.

Seconds later he was squatting down behind a tree, heart clattering. 'So far so good, the sentries having presumed once more that another bout of diarrhoea had kicked in.' But then, looking down, he realised his white jacket would make him an easy target in the dark for a gunman. 'No, no, no,' he thought. All the dates and dried fruit and bits of bread and balls of rice he had been squirrelling away over the past four days and nights were stuffed in its pockets and lining, but he had no choice but to discard it, along with his emergency supplies.

He hung the coat on a bush and moulded it into a human shape, hoping it might win him a few extra minutes. Then he grabbed a handful of dirt and rubbed it over his face and into his hair, turning his grey skin streaky brown. He took a deep breath. And then he bolted.

At first he loped gently, crouching, lupine, trying to minimise his footfall as he put a little distance between himself and the militants. Then he became upright and, forgetting his torn feet, ran full tilt, pelting towards a copse, arms pumping.

His walking boots were still unlaced, and in the darkness he kept tripping over them. Should he stop to tie them up? No. Don't stop. He was sure he could hear the sentries behind him, crashing through the undergrowth, clattering over the pebbles, the alarm raised when he had failed to return from the bushes. There was no time to stop now. As he tore on in his heightened state, the undergrowth smashed and crashed around him like cymbals and snares. Could they hear him? He was sure they could. Now his metabolism picked up, releasing adrenaline, nutrients, glucose, cholesterol, his heart thudding as he began to climb. This was the idea he had put all his hopes in. Up, and not down. Down to the trekking path and the white-skinned campers was the obvious way an escaping hostage would go. He was heading up, in the opposite direction, where nothing lived. Only a fool would climb higher into the deep freeze. Breathing deeper and longer, John could no longer feel his destroyed feet, as blood drawn from his skin and gut flooded his muscles and tissues. 'My head was filled with the desire to live.' Up higher and higher, colder and colder. Without the jacket he was freezing, his blood chilling as he pushed himself on.

His stomach churned. He told himself that this was a by-product of fear, and that one's outlook was always different at fourteen thousand feet above sea level. The pain was better than the spasms caused by his dysentery. His eyes dilated as they became accustomed to the darkness. The big expanse of night had shades, and was mottled light and grey. He could see the trees above as he climbed through the Jurassic dark that clung to these ancient woods and ridges. He tried to imagine himself running around the school track in Simsbury on a calm spring day, putting himself anywhere rather than here.

Suddenly something shimmered in the corner of his vision. John almost screamed out loud before realising that a vortex of birds had lifted up ahead. His sudden stop meant that he jammed his foot, twisting his ankle. The throbbing pain was almost too much to bear, and he stopped to take off his boots. He had to give his heels a break. Hobbling along in his socks, he found himself clear of the last few trees and crossing open, stony ground. He could see the trekking route far below, snaking alongside the icy East Lidder, tents dotted here and there. He thought he could see the hut where his companions were being held too. But much as he wanted to reach out to his own kind of people, he could not, would not, go down. He was still certain that someone was behind him, and he knew he would never be able to outrun his pursuers if he stopped now. He could hear stones clattering. Turning his back on a route he knew led down to the safety of Pahalgam, he pushed on even higher, shouting at himself as he went: 'You need to climb, further up! Hand over hand when the legs don't work! You need to get higher before dawn breaks! Go, John, go!'

Three minutes. Five minutes. Twenty minutes. Boots back on. Screaming pain. Many, many minutes. Gradually the hollow tap of his soles on stones and gravel became a crunch as they crackled on frosted grass, and then a cindery rasp as they broke the crust of snow. Now he was really cold. An abrasive wind whipped through his thin Gore-Tex shirt, stinging his back and chest. He had to rest for a moment. Ahead, he could see that a vast sheet of ice had partially melted and come away from the rock, forming a peeling sheet. 'I climbed inside, wedging myself down into the bottom, cupped between the rock and the ice so nobody could see me.' Bathed in sweat and shivering with cold, he ate a morsel of the last of the stale *lavash* bread he had concealed in his socks. But he knew, as his heartbeat slowed and his skin prickled, his fingertips darkening, that if he stayed here he would die.

After some time he struggled out again. 'I ran up a ridge as fast as I could, until just before the sun came up. From my eyrie up there, I now had a view back down the way I had come.' He decided to stop. By his reckoning, two hours had passed since he had left the *dhoka* beside the Amarnath route. He guessed that he had to be well above fifteen thousand feet. To the east, he could see the seven magnificent peaks of Sheshnag. He could also see that the horizon was beginning to bleed red. In less than an hour, sunlight would hit this spot where he crouched. 'I decided to stay here until the end of the day, then after dark I would work my way back down.'

However, a disturbing thought crept over him as he sat up there, struggling with his bearings and the wind-chill. He tried to envisage the map. 'Take in your general position from the dawn,' he murmured, willing himself to remain conscious. Later, he reassured himself, he would be able to check his direction by looking at how the moss grew on the trees, since it disliked direct sunlight and thrived on the northern sides of trunks. But, dehydrated, hypothermic and disoriented by his quick ascent, he came to the conclusion that he was no longer in India at all, and had strayed into Pakistan: 'This was as bad as things could get.' The more he thought about it, the more certain he became. After all, it was not as if there was a wall dividing the two nations at this elevation. All of his effort, and he had simply run into the arms of his enemies, the land of fundamentalism and betrayal. His mind was racing.

A noise from below rose towards him. It sounded like a scratch or a rasp. Maybe he was imagining it, but in an organic landscape of wood and stone, he thought he had recognised the sound of gunmetal on rock. Someone was out there, looking for him. They were armed, and not far away. 'Come on, John,' he said to himself, summoning his last molecules of strength. 'Make a move.' He inched further along the ridge, his more badly injured right foot dragging behind, crawled, wriggled, and then clambered to his knees. Then pushed his bruised and tender frame upright, hand over hand, and dug in behind a larger rock to shelter from the spanking wind. The only sound he could hear was the shrill descending whistle of the bearded vultures circling above.

Back in the *gujjar* hut, Don, Paul and Keith were under armed guard. A sentry had raised the alarm at around 3 a.m., twenty minutes after John had failed to return from his nocturnal toilet trip. When they had discovered the white trekking jacket hanging limply from a bush, the whole hut had been turned over as the militants searched frantically for him, ripping at clothes, hunting for concealed weapons and ammunition, looking for any clues as to his plans. Having screamed himself hoarse and sent his bloodhounds off down the mountain in search of the American, al Faran's leader made a call on the radio.

Sikander, waiting at a secret location down in the valley, had taken it. The Indian government had not yet made contact, and there was much debate going on across the border in Pakistan about how long they should wait before ramping up the pressure. Sikander now found himself listening in disbelief as the Turk told him that the worst had happened. One of the Americans had run off, and a desperate hunt was under way, the Turk's men heading towards Chandanwari, sure that the hostage would have headed straight back down the mountain towards the nearest village. Sikander didn't need to point out that an American hostage was worth twice as much as a European, and now, just four days in, they were down to one of them.

Sikander blamed himself for putting the Turk in charge. After the siege and the inferno at Charar-e-Sharief there had been no time to find another commander to lead Operation Ghar. From the start Sikander had been worried about this decision, concerned that the *mujahid*'s explosive temper, fanaticism and lack of discretion made him a liability. Now here he was, listening to a man he had never trusted, a fighter supposedly renowned for his cunning and strength, explaining how his well-trained team had been outwitted by an American civilian, a stranger to these parts, even before the hostage drama had picked up pace. Sikander would relate this night's events over and over to two close comrades, citing it as the point at which events tilted against them, and repeating what he had told the Turk over the radio that night: 'Make up for it. Make it right.'

Sixty miles from where Sikander sat, wrestling with how to get Operation Ghar back on track, a military chopper lifted off the tarmac at an air force base near Srinagar, carrying the Governor of Kashmir's Security Advisor, Lt. Gen. D.D. Saklani, a regal and highly decorated retired military officer. Dismissing the ground crew with a practised flick of the wrist, Saklani smoothed back his silver hair as he silently counted the multiple crises that preoccupied him that morning, 8 July. Four Western hostages were being held by Pakistani militants somewhere up in the mountains, and there were now an estimated 150,000 *yatra* pilgrims ascending to Amarnath, seemingly undeterred by the deadly bomb attack in Pahalgam three days before. In response to that incident, the vigilantes of the Hindu RSS were still charging around the trekking town, showing Kashmiri civilians their cudgels. And that, Saklani thought, was before he even got to grips with what he wearily described to close friends as 'the everyday hatch, match and dispatch' of life in this wartorn valley, in which he seemed cursed to have served most of his professional life.

If he was to prioritise, the *yatris* presented the biggest headache. New Delhi had made it crystal clear to him that this year's pilgrimage had to go off without a hitch, as much for political reasons as humanitarian. For Saklani that meant making sure all elements of the security protocol were in place and working, and he had sweated blood to ensure this. Truces had been hammered out with virtually all of the militant outfits in the valley, in return for taking down some prominent Indian security-force bunkers and pickets in Srinagar. Only the Movement – which he already regarded as one of the most troublesome ISI-sponsored Pakistani outfits – had defied him, angry that despite its repeated demands, security barriers still surrounded Hazratbal, a lakeside mosque in Srinagar, one of the state's holiest. It had been subjected to an extended siege in October 1993, since when the security forces had guarded it. Saklani recalled thinking that he 'half expected them to throw a spanner in the works'.

And now a group of foreigners had been kidnapped in the mountains above Pahalgam by an unknown outfit that Saklani suspected was an offshoot of the Movement. This suggested that his security measures were not working. Was the bombing at the bus station down to them too, he now wondered. 'Damn them,' he cursed under his breath as the helicopter lurched upwards, following the silvery rope of the Lidder River towards Pahalgam. A militant column was within striking distance of the pilgrims. What had happened to the army operation to pacify the area? There was no point passing the buck.

Looking down at the wild terrain, the endless gullies, the high-altitude meadows and jagged peaks, most of them obscured by shadow and dense forest, Saklani told himself that the task he had been given was an unrealistic one. Not even an army of the size that India had mobilised in Kashmir over the past six years could police this inaccessible landscape. This situation was never going to be resolved by a military operation. Whatever happened in these mountains would be determined by politics. He shuddered at the thought, before glancing down at the papers in his lap. According to police records, there were still thirty-five foreign backpackers out here somewhere, who would have no idea about the kidnappings. How would he find them? As Security Advisor to the Governor of Kashmir, he would feel the heat if any more went missing, especially from New Delhi, where Prime Minister P.V. Narasimha Rao's fragile Congress Party minority government was already on the ropes, with national elections due next year and the rising tide of violence in Kashmir weakening his authority by the day.

Prime Minister Rao had come to power in 1991, promising to expose and combat Pakistan's sponsorship of terrorist atrocities on Indian soil. For four years he had stood his ground, but increasingly Pakistan-backed terrorists in Kashmir had been pushing him onto the back foot, as was being noisily trumpeted by the right-wing Hindu nationalists of the Bharatiya Janata Party, India's largest opposition group. The BJP cited the failure of Indian security forces to protect the Amarnath *yatra* for four years running as evidence that New Delhi was barely in control of the valley, so a successful *yatra* and a firm hold over events in Kashmir over the next weeks and months would determine Rao's fate in the elections that were due in April 1996. Saklani quietly cursed the police and tourism officials who had allowed trekkers to go into the hills in the first place. There was a war going on, and he was constantly mopping up after abductions, bomb-ings, skirmishes. What had they been thinking of? Were they engulfed in some kind of collective act of wish-fulfilment, hoping that by allowing holidaymakers to head off into the mountains the war would vanish?

Saklani knew better. He had served in Kashmir in 1961, 1962 and 1965. By the early 1980s he had risen to the rank of brigadier, and served in the Military Operations Directive at Army Headquarters. Promoted in 1985 to major general, he had spent another two years in Kashmir, keeping an eye on Chinese troops massing on its border. From 1987 to 1992, as Major General (Operations), he had been placed in the army's Northern Command (in charge of Jammu and Kashmir state), and acted as Chief of Staff to the Lieutenant General, where he once again focused on Kashmir.

Saklani had fought against Pakistan in 1947, 1965 and 1971, accru-ing an impressive collection of medals, and considered he knew his neighbour's feints and wiles well. Having chalked up more than forty years of service, he had retired in 1992 with a plan to spend his remaining years at Mhow, a garrison town created by the British that had become home to the Indian Army Signals Corps, the Combat School and the Infantry Training School. Mhow was less a city than an idea, a nerve centre whose name was actually an old British-era acronym for 'Military Headquarters of War'. What better place could there be for a man of war to slow down, living monastically in a simple apartment above a carport, spending his last years teaching, mingling with a new generation of warriors in the pleasant climate of India's central plains?

But in January 1993 he had got a call from South Block, the Raj-era Secretariat Building in Lutyens' New Delhi that housed the Indian Ministry of Defence. 'Sir, we've got a job for you,' Saklani recalled an ingratiating voice saying. Didn't these defence *babus* read the bulletins, Saklani had thought. He had retired. 'It's a prestigious posting, sir.' He was out of it, he replied, finished with service. Down went the phone, but South Block had called again: 'Come up to New Delhi.' Saklani was done with the ministry, he said as forcefully as he could. He was committed to Mhow. Down went the phone. 'The third time South Block rang, it was an order.' A man of service, he packed a small bag, leaving behind his batman and his Spartan quarters, arranged even in retirement with simplicity and order: toothbrush, comb, shaving kit, soap. Cup, saucer and tea caddy, maps, magazines and an ashtray. A lifetime at war meant he had few possessions to take with him.

He was to assume the position of Security Advisor to the Governor of Kashmir. Back in a place he swore he had finished with, he had arrived in Srinagar to find a dinner invitation from Governor Girish Saxena, an old and much-admired friend. The one reason Saklani had finally accepted this job, which he had never sought and did not relish, was Saxena. Working for him would be an honour. India's most accomplished spy chief, Saxena had run the country's foreign intelligence service, and had not only advised prime ministers but been widely credited in military circles for hardening up the country's defence posture, as well as dealing with India's internal uprisings, with bloody gusto. 'It was after dinner,' Saklani recalled, 'after I had agreed to stay, that Saxena let it drop. He was leaving Kashmir right away.' Saklani tried to conceal his feeling that he had been 'stitched up'.

There was no going back. There would also be no new governor for six weeks. Saklani had spent that time 'on a recce', touring the fractious state, becoming 'more and more incredulous at just how appalling things were'. Despite the sheer number of soldiers, paramilitaries, police and intelligence agents, India's tactics in Kashmir were piecemeal and confused: 'So many different outfits were operating in the valley and following their own agendas that it was almost impossible to coordinate them.' Caught off-balance by the flood of Kashmiris taking up arms from 1989 onwards, and the enthusiasm with which Pakistan had come to their assistance, India had thrown all it could at the militancy, without much forward planning. Now, in their attempts to control territory and win over sources, the military, police and intelligence services were tripping over each other. The only messages being received by the international community were of Indian aggression and human rights abuses. Such stories were being energetically promulgated by Pakistan, with several articulate young *maulanas*, including Masood Azhar of the Movement, detailing incidents with unnerving accuracy and dedication. Yet as far as Saklani was concerned, the situation in Kashmir was a simple matter of terrorism stoked by Pakistan. The devastating truth was that twelve thousand innocent people had been killed in the five years since Pakistan had started meddling, and that these days there were nine times more terrorism-related incidents in J&K than anywhere else in the world, most of it, in Saklani's eyes, engineered by the ISI.

'If I was going to make any impact,' Saklani said, 'I would have to make significant improvements in the way the security forces worked together and the way we told the Kashmir story.' He went to work at it in the early spring of 1993, establishing a five-storey home-cum-office off Church Lane, at the heart of a heavily fortified government compound squeezed between the parched Sher-i-Kashmir cricket stadium and the Radio Kashmir complex. He quickly became accustomed to being woken by the plock and phut of live rounds breaking his windowpanes, fired by militants from across the Jhelum River. But having lived his whole life under arms, a few wake-up calls did not bother him, and he soon established a routine. Between 8 a.m. and 10 a.m. every day he saw members of the public, as he believed in keeping one door open, even as through the other the security forces rumbled with catch-and-kill instructions. At 10 a.m. he instigated a Unified Command, a daily meeting attended by all sections of the security services, from the police Crime Branch, Special Branch and CID to the uniformed departments, the army, paramilitary police and domestic and foreign intelligence. After four years on a war footing, it was the first time many of these agencies had even sat down face to face.

In March 1993 General K.V. Krishna Rao had arrived to replace Saxena as governor. Formerly India's Chief of Army Staff, General Rao was one of the most influential military figures in the subcontinent. His greatest source of pride was his command of a division that had liberated much of what would become north-eastern Bangladesh during the 1971 war with Pakistan. Since retiring in 1983, 'the Iron General', as Saklani called him, had gone on to 'restore peace' in some of India's most troublesome border areas: Manipur, Nagaland and Tripura. This was his second stint in Kashmir, and he was coming at it with a firm resolve to sort things out and stymie Pakistan's operations in the valley.

The two generals' mettle and the Unified Command had been tested almost immediately at Hazratbal, literally 'the Majestic Place', a marble lakeside mosque in Srinagar said to house a single hair of the Prophet Mohammed's beard, a holy relic encased in a phial of gold. In October 1993 Hazratbal had become a haven for militants, who trusted that no government would want to be seen to defile a place so holy in order to evict them. Claiming to have received intelligence that these gunmen intended to steal the beard relic so as to inflame the feelings of India's 120 million Muslims, Kashmir's new governor ordered a siege of the mosque by two battalions. In 1963, the last time there had been rumours that the relic was under threat, Kashmir had been plunged into sixteen days of tumultuous rioting. Now an armed cordon surrounded the holy site, with eighty-six worshippers (and alleged militants) holed up inside, while PM Narasimha Rao in New Delhi faced by-election battles in four states where the Hindu nationalist BJP was gaining ground. On the eighth day of the siege, a Friday, thousands of Muslims headed for mosques across the valley to pray and protest, only for the Indian forces to open fire at Bijbehara, north of Anantnag, leaving fifty men and boys dead, and two hundred wounded.

Pictures of the massacre heaped more pressure on PM Rao. In Srinagar, a horrified Saklani brokered long rounds of talks with all involved in the Hazratbal siege, and these negotiations eventually ended the standoff a weary three and a half weeks after it had begun. This was seen as a victory for both the Security Advisor and New Delhi, whose objective all along had been to stamp their authority on a lawless holy place. To make sure things did not blow up again, a military bunker was set up outside the mosque. This inflamed the Movement, which would cite it as the reason for not observing the ceasefire of 1995, and attacking the Amarnath pilgrimage.

But in November 1993, Saklani had been elated at the outcome of Hazratbal. Three days later he was certain the tide was turning in India's favour when news broke that Langrial, the famed Movement commander, had been captured. He told the officers gathered before him at the Unified Command meetings that the Movement was on the ropes, and his confidence seemed justified as the outfit struggled to reassert itself with the botched kidnapping and execution of Major Bhupinder Singh, an act of brutality that New Delhi was glad to hold up as proof positive of Pakistan-inspired barbarism.

In February 1994, after the Movement's Kashmir commander, the Afghani, had been captured along with its General Secretary, Masood Azhar, Saklani had told the Governor that the outfit was all but neutered, since its most significant operatives were now behind bars. He had visited Masood in jail, to see what made him tick: 'He sat there, very calm, his beard neatly combed, in a cell of twenty or so fighters, pleasantly chatting with me, telling me all that he had thought and done. Talk, talk, talk. He was such a talker. He told me how a Russian sniper had taken potshots, leaving him with a limp.'

However, in June 1994 it was Saklani's turn to feel the heat. The Movement hit back, abducting Kim Housego and David Mackie from Aru, and demanding the release of Masood, the Afghani and Langrial. For more than two weeks New Delhi and the families of the hostages had pulled in opposite directions, David Housego urging action, while the huge military machine whose priorities were the annual Amarnath pilgrimage and roasting Pakistan was inclined to do nothing radical, fast. When the two Westerners had been released Saklani celebrated, although in truth he was not sure how it had happened, or if New Delhi was entitled to take any of the credit. As he saw it, this was David Housego's single-handed triumph (and the army's secret shame). And by the year's end, although Saklani still felt India was winning, the official figures told a grim story: 6,043 killed in terrorist-related incidents in just twelve months, the worst year on record. More than four times as many civilians were dead as members of the security forces. Just to drive the knife in further as far as the locals were concerned, 75 per cent of the fatalities were Muslims. Every night he went to bed in his plain bedroom in Church Lane, General Saklani quietly cursed Girish Saxena.

Looking down through the helicopter's window late on the afternoon of 8 July 1995, Saklani surveyed a steady stream of Hindu pilgrims. Army patrols were in position, and hundreds of Rashtriya Rifles were bedding down at Chandanwari, just in case things got choppy. He had spotted a few Westerners too, trekking or camping. But there wasn't much he could do, other than circle above them. He'd inform the police of the locations when he got back to Srinagar, and they could send constables up on foot. He dictated some notes to his bagman, Altaf Ahmed, a police security official who worked in his office, and who was sitting behind him. A small man, Altaf did not attract attention, but he was capable of recalling everything anyone said and did.

Now that dusk was drawing in, Saklani turned to his pilot, Group Captain Jasminder Kahlon, and ordered him back to base. Kahlon was an ace, possibly the best India had, and Saklani liked being out with him and Altaf. 'Just then, the Group Captain spotted a lone figure near Pissu Top,' Altaf recalled. Swooping down, they saw it was a man, roughly dressed and limping badly, making his way down the mountainside beside a stream. 'We thought he was some kind of Paki infiltrator,' said Altaf. 'His face was pitch-black.' Saklani remembered: 'I told Altaf to load a weapon and take that boy out.' Kahlon advised caution. Something was not right. The man was flimsily dressed, without any kind of coat or backpack. He did not look like a *mujahid*. His face was striped with mud. But who else would be up here, and take such fright at seeing an Indian helicopter? What was a man in civvies doing at this altitude? 'I can't get in any closer,' Kahlon said. 'The downdraught might blow him over the edge, or the rockface might take out one of our rotors.'

On the ground, John Childs had been thrown into utter panic by the sight of the helicopter. 'I had heard it first from a distance, heading down the valley along which I was making my descent. I was in really bad shape, and I thought I might be hallucinating. Without me seeing it, it seemed to turn around as if to leave. "Just my luck," I said to myself. "They've found the hostages, and here I am left trying to escape on my own."' A few minutes later John heard the helicopter returning, and suddenly it reared up on him from over a ridge. 'I was terrified. It was a big military thing, with gun muzzles poking out of the window and men dressed in uniform.' In a split second John had convinced himself it was the Pakistanis, who had been searching for him on behalf of the kidnap party. He burrowed down behind a rock.

Inside the cabin, Saklani and Kahlon glimpsed the man's face. 'He was of European complexion,' Saklani recalled. 'That's not a militant!' Altaf shouted. Kahlon butted in: 'He's foreigner. Let's get him.' He delicately moved the chopper so its tail faced the man on the ground, showing him the saffron, white and green of the Indian Air Force insignia. John recalled the moment: 'Stupidly, I was running away (as if I could get away!) when I saw them swing it around so I could see the flag of India.' Saklani beckoned him over, but in a confusion between East and West, John thought he was being instructed to lie flat on the ground.

Then, with his usual poise, Kahlon gently brought the helicopter down, resting one of its runners on the hillside as delicately as if he were placing a glass of water on a mat. John said: 'It was an incredible feat. One of the runners was still floating in the air, and the rotors were whipping just inches from the rock.' Saklani threw the door open, and screamed above the rotors: 'Now! Now! Now! Come now! What are you doing here?' John shouted: 'I was abducted! Save me! Please!' Saklani couldn't believe it: one of the hostages. 'Oh the gods, this is a miracle, this is a miracle from the gods!' he shouted.

The helicopter stayed steady just long enough for Altaf to haul John inside. As they rose high in the sky, the vast landscape merged into one enormous, crinkled canvas. John looked down through the glass, exhausted and panting, trying to identify his route. 'We have to go back for the others!' he shouted, worried that with every second that passed he risked lose his bearings. Saklani smiled, ignoring him. 'You're safe now,' he told him. 'We're the good guys.'

The minute the helicopter touched down in Srinagar, news of John Childs' recovery broke in the press. Jane Schelly, Julie Mangan and Cath Moseley saw a television newsflash at the government guesthouse where they were now staying, next door to Saklani's complex. 'Hostage released. It was the best news we could have possibly hoped for,' recalled Jane. As far as they understood it, John had been given up by the kidnappers, which meant there was a chance that the others might be freed too. Jane, Julie and Cath were delighted, but couldn't help also feeling jealous. They had to talk to John fast. He was the bridge to their missing partners.

But how to get to him? Since arriving at the government villa from the unwelcoming UN guesthouse, they had been pretty much cut off from the outside world. None of the reports they saw, generated by Embassy staff or from General Saklani's office, carried any of the details that the BBC's Yusuf Jameel had put together in the Press Enclave. Nothing at all was coming from the kidnappers' camp. For the past four days Jane, Julie and Cath had been left to dwell on every possible gruesome and bloody scenario: death, gunshot wounds, grenade injuries. But they had been given no hard facts at all, not even been told who al Faran was. And the vacuum had been filled with a torrent of rumours in the local Kashmir and Urdu-language press: one of the hostages had been fatally injured after falling down a crevasse; all of them had been smuggled across the border and were in Pakistan; the kidnappers had pledged to shoot the hostages if the Indians launched any kind of rescue attempt.

Jane, Julie and Cath were at sea. The only people they had talked to regularly were their families back home and the diplomatic liaison officers Philip Barton and Tim Buchs. Barton was still struggling to find a secure phone line, and had brought them very little news from the Indian side, bar the repeated mantra that a 'massive search' was ongoing, while Buchs was wrapped up in trying to assist John Childs, with more senior US State Department officials said to be flying up from New Delhi.

Surely finding John would lead to the location of the others, Julie reasoned. What was his physical condition, they asked. The diplomats confessed that they knew no more than the women did, as he had not yet been debriefed. They saw on the news that John had been transferred by ambulance to army headquarters, where it was expected he would receive medical treatment.

A few hours later, General Saklani emerged to make a brief statement. John Childs, he said, was in remarkably good health given his recent ordeal, and was 'an excellent witness'. But by the end of the day, the women had still not got anywhere nearer him. And then the story suddenly changed: John Childs hadn't been released by the kidnappers. He had *escaped*. This revelation, with all its terrible possible consequences for those left behind, winded Jane, Julie and Cath.

John Childs was overwhelmed by the attention, surrounded by crisp officers and attentive diplomats. 'From the moment I reached safety I kept saying to everyone, "Look, I can take you to the place, it's near the Amarnath pilgrimage route. Jane knows the place too, she was there a week ago, but we have to move quickly, before the kidnappers get the hostages away." I said it to the Governor's advisor who picked me up, and to the US State Department people who greeted me in Srinagar. To the army and FBI. But nobody was listening.' It seemed to John that everyone just wanted him to shut up, with the FBI and the State Department being the most forceful. 'They arranged for a satellite phone so I could call home, for which I was very grateful. But they warned me not to say too much about my rescue to anyone. As far as I could see, they were trying to stop me shooting my mouth off, and said they intended to get me out of Srinagar as quickly as possible. I can only guess they were thinking more about their relationship with India than about the hostages and our ordeal.'

Weak and still disorientated, John did not argue. Instead, he did what he always did when he felt threatened: retreated into his shell. As the hours ticked by, a gnawing realisation washed over him. 'I saw that I was not going to be able to help the others at all, and I knew full well that my escape would have made our captors more livid and vengeful.' It was a shocking realisation that would never leave him. As the diplomats and officials fussed around him, he began to contemplate the truth of the situation: that he had traded his life for theirs. The others would have done the same, he told himself at one point, thinking back to Don's attempt to slip off. But there were no happy endings and no clean-cut choices in a dirty war – that much he had learned from his brief, claustrophobic time inside the *gujjar* hut. Explorers and adventurers of all kinds knew as much: that there will come a time, whether on the exposed face of some crag or lost in the wilderness, when the choices you have to make will ultimately challenge your humanity. Most of all, he was dreading meeting Cath, Julie and Jane, who he knew would have a million questions. He owed it to them to tell them as much as he could, but to make matters worse his gut was still in spasms from the aftermath of his physical ordeal. He was sick, weak, injured and confused, and desperate to get back to his predictable life in Connecticut.

Finally, on 9 July, as they hung around the government guesthouse feeling 'hollow and lost', as Julie put it, Jane caught sight of a thin, limping man being led into the compound, surrounded by a sea of American and Indian officials. He was barely recognisable as the man she had met in the Meadow. He was covered in cuts and bruises, both feet were heavily bandaged and he seemed overwhelmed. Someone brought him over. He was shaking uncontrollably, and Jane thought she could only imagine what he must have been through. The instant he saw the women's expectant faces he shrank back, unable to make eye contact.

The women tried their best not to crowd him, seeing from his physical condition (and guessing at the mental scars) that he had gone through hell. 'Was anybody injured?' Julie asked. 'No,' he replied in a barely audible whisper. The women squeezed in a little closer. The other hostages were in relatively good spirits, he continued, although Keith was suffering from altitude sickness as a result of them being made to climb over a very high pass. Jane asked how they were bearing up psychologically. She brightened visibly when John told her that Don had become a bridge between them and the kidnappers, the most capable man he had ever met. 'He told me that the militants called him *chacha*, or uncle,' Jane recalled. Despite his age, they had been impressed by his agility and speed on the mountain paths, John added. They had also commented on the fact that he wore a beard, joking that he must secretly be a Kashmiri Muslim. 'It was just such a huge relief to know he was OK,' said Jane.

John told them how they had walked long distances at extreme elevations, sometimes at night. The most frightening thing had been the fear of falling. However, they had all survived relatively unscathed, and had been provided with some food. Staying in the *gujjar* huts had been a miserable experience that John had no wish to repeat, he said, but the kidnappers had in the main been polite and accommodating. 'What do you think are their chances of a release?' Julie asked, getting to the point. It was the question the Indians would never answer, and the one John had dreaded being asked. He could not bring himself to tell the women that he believed he had fled as they were being marched to their death. He was 'reasonably optimistic', he said quietly. The al Faran leadership had 'promised' none of them would be harmed. But his heart was not in it.

The conversation petered out. A brusque woman from the US Embassy bustled over, saying it was time for John to leave. Just before the FBI and Tim Buchs whisked him away, Jane took him to one side. 'She asked me how I had escaped, and I told her I'd taken advantage of my sickness and the darkness. She asked me how Don had felt about escaping, and I said that he felt as I did, that it was the only way out. Jane then looked deep into my eyes and said gently, "Why couldn't you just bring Don with you?" I was silent. I was bowled over by this, the hardest question of all. It was impossible to look her in the eye and tell her the truth. I could have. But I didn't.'

Jane, Julie and Cath returned to their quarters feeling more alone than ever, certain that John Childs' actions had significantly reduced their loved ones' chances, although no one in authority would confirm it. Julie rang home to update her mother, trying to keep things upbeat. 'The American told her that no one had been harmed in any way,' Anita said. 'They were being fed and well looked after. It was not knowing if he was hurt that was the most distressing. Julie had been crying, worrying about him being hurt. Now she knew at least he was all right.'

But back in Srinagar, sitting glassy-eyed before the television, the women were confronted by another newsflash. A young German woman, Anne Hennig, looking ashen and terrified, was telling reporters in Pahalgam, between heavy sobs, how she had just scrambled down from Chandanwari, the mountain village that served as the first-night stop for the Amarnath pilgrims. A group of gunmen had appeared from nowhere that morning, and abducted her boyfriend in broad daylight from a trekking path, she said. She had no idea where they had taken him, or who they were. What was his name, a reporter asked. 'Dirk,' she said. 'Dirk Hasert, a twenty-six-year-old student from Erfurt. Please help him.'

A few hours later, a petrified Anne joined Jane, Julie and Cath in Srinagar. The women flocked around, trying to comfort her. They knew exactly what she was feeling. Another room at the government guesthouse was now occupied, as they were all plunged into despair.

* * *

Across Church Lane, between the *chinar* trees, a soft light was still on in the second-floor bedroom of a five-storey building. A low-watt bulb burned into the early hours, illuminating a frugal room in which an old man sat at a bureau, his grey-haired head cupped in his hands. General Saklani understood exactly what was going on. An al Faran search party looking for Childs had scooped up the next best thing.

EIGHT

Hunting Dogs

On 8 July, almost fifteen miles above Pahalgam, in a clutch of stone huts known as Zargibal, a single column of militants arrived, travelling head to tail like hunting dogs. Sitting in a tree-filled dip at nine thousand feet, a couple of hours' trekking distance from where John Childs had escaped his captors, the hamlet served as a way station for pilgrims heading for the Amarnath Cave. The gunmen's arrival must have been sometime after 11 a.m., as a local *chai-wallah*, Abdul Bhat, who operated a seasonal stall here, recalled that his stomach was rumbling, but lunchtime prayers had not yet been called.

At first he thought they were Indian Army soldiers, but when he saw their clothes, a mixture of ragged, unwashed *kurtas* and second-hand khaki, he realised straight away that they must be 'guest *mujahideen*', as Kashmiris respectfully called foreign militants. Trying not to stare, he guessed they were most likely members of the Movement, since these days this mountain area was their heartland. For the past two years it had felt as if Sikander and the Afghani were everywhere. But, he wondered fearfully, what were the *mujahids* doing *here* now, in broad daylight, with soldiers all around?

Mr Bhat was as much for *azadi*, or freedom for Kashmir, as the next man, members of his family having gone 'over there' in 1990, entering Pakistan-administered Kashmir to train at ISI camps. But if these gunmen were caught in Zargibal they would be shot on sight, and the hamlet destroyed by the security forces for harbouring them. Mr Bhat had no idea that these were militants from the al Faran kidnap party, driven to take extraordinary risks by the Turk, who was determined to recapture the escaped American hostage, to rescue both his reputation and the fortunes of Operation Ghar.

The gunmen were desperate, having been out on the mountainsides for eight hours, first going down to Chandanwari and then back up the trekking route in the direction of the cave, with John Childs still nowhere to be seen. Silently, Mr Bhat cursed them. 'Anyhow, they'll be dead sooner rather than later,' he thought as he brought down his hatch, striking the bolt. Kneeling so he could not be seen, he held his breath. He didn't want any trouble.

He was clutching a cup of green tea in the dark when a sharp knock made him jump. Someone shouted in heavily accented Urdu through the wooden slats: 'We're looking for a foreigner. American.' Mr Bhat froze. He could tell from the voice that this man was probably a Pashtun from the Pakistan–Afghan border, where the most feared fighters of all originated. He squeezed his eyes shut. 'He might be limping,' the man continued. Mr Bhat said nothing. 'We've seen a tent.' He gulped. The *tent*. They were talking about the one pitched just outside the village belonging to a blond, curly-haired foreigner. He had arrived two days back, and everyone in the village had taken to him. As Mr Bhat blurted out, 'I can't help you,' he wondered if there was anything he could do to help the outsider. He was not an American. He was no one's enemy. Should he raise the alarm? Should he try to signal to the foreigner to beware? 'We'll be back for you later, *dada*,' the militant snapped, before bringing his rifle butt down on the hatch with a loud thwack.

The foreigner in the tent had arrived alone on the afternoon of 6 July, saying he was on his way up to the Hindu cave. He had stopped for tea, surprising Mr Bhat, who had never spoken to an '*angresi*' before. Most of those who passed through were in the company of guides and pony-*wallahs*, who steered them straight to Pissu Top and then on to the cupric blues of Sheshnag Lake. But this traveller had sat down and chatted in broken Hindi, a language Mr Bhat knew a smattering of too. The foreigner had asked for the date of the full moon, and Mr Bhat had replied that it was not until 12 July, six days' time. 'Then I'm too early,' the blond man had said with a grin. 'Hans

Christian,' he continued, introducing himself with a proffered hand. 'I am Hans Christian Ostrø from Oslo.' Mr Bhat touched his heart. '*Aadaab*,' he said, by way of a Kashmiri greeting. Well, that's what a Kashmiri Muslim would say to a Hindu, but Mr Bhat was unsure what customs this blond-haired outsider kept. He followed Hans Christian to the edge of the hamlet and watched, amazed, as he quickly erected a black one-man tent close to the trekking path. 'Hans,' he had said to himself, trying not to stare too much at that blond hair.

Over the next two days, Hans and Mr Bhat had got into a pattern. Hans would rise at dawn, and set off on his own up the mountains, towards Sheshnag or on a circuit around Mahagunas Top. In the afternoon he returned to drink Lipton *chai* with Mr Bhat and chat about the world. He was a natural entertainer. 'I remember him picking up two five-gallon jerry cans of fuel, balancing them on either end of a pole that he spun around his head,' Mr Bhat recalled. The villagers gave him the nickname *nar gao*, 'the Ox'. At night, Hans had cooked for himself. A vegetarian, he shunned the mutton-based Kashmiri diet. A few locals, Mr Bhat among them, had come over to his fire to watch. He whittled wood for them, making whistles and toys, and let them handle the large army knife he kept tucked in his belt, explaining that it was a bayonet that he had kept after recently concluding his military service. He pulled a hard-man face, turning red and making everyone laugh. 'He said he would defend us against the Indian soldiers who slunk through daily, stealing chickens and throwing their weight around,' Mr Bhat said. He had even aped attacking one passing army patrol from behind, clowning behind the Indian soldiers, who seemed not to notice him, in what the villagers regarded as a suicidal gesture.

'The Ox', they called him, but there were many sides to Hans. On his second night he had called everyone together and started to dance in a jerky, classical Indian style. Afterwards he explained that he was Bhima, son of the Hindu wind god, and that he had the strength of a hundred elephants. Bhima's job was 'to protect the pious so they could live in the forest without fear', he told them earnestly. This was *kathakali*, he explained, a dance from Kerala, in India's far south. He had been studying it before coming up here, and after this trek he was going home to Oslo to put on a show. His first venture as director/producer/promoter. It reminded the village elders of the *bhand pather*, the travelling Kashmiri folk players who had wandered the valley back in the days before the war, when Muslims could enjoy a Hindu pageant without feeling like traitors.

As the guest *mujahideen* party moved off, Mr Bhat was sure it was not Hans they were looking for, but hoped the foreigner would have the sense to run anyway. There was another thump on his hatch. He winced. 'Hello, Mr Bhat. You in there? It's Hans Christian. What's going on?' Mr Bhat wanted to cry out, 'Run away! There are gunmen here!' But as he strained to peer through the gaps in the wooden shutter, he saw the gunmen running back. They knocked Hans to the ground. 'Hey, what's up?' Hans yelled as somebody took a swing at him. Mr Bhat cursed his own cowardice. He watched as the *mujahids* grappled with the foreigner, who put up an impressive fight, throwing off the first two who came at him and felling a third with some deft punches: left, right and then the belly. A fourth militant was about to shoot when someone slapped him, shouting that they needed to take this man alive. 'Hans fought like a black bear,' Mr Bhat recalled. 'He whipped out his army knife and took cover behind a hut.' For the next hour there was a standoff, with the foreigner and his knife pitched against half a dozen heavily armed militants. For a while it looked as if Hans might even outsmart them, but then Mr Bhat saw two men working their way behind him. They clubbed his legs from beneath him with a shovel, and Mr Bhat watched, horrified, as several militants sat on Hans's chest, roped his arms together and dragged him down to his tent, which they rifled through before leaving the village, climbing towards the heights.

After they had gone, Mr Bhat came outside, and for the first time in many years he swore out loud. '*Chacha-chod!*' he spat, using the Kashmiri word for uncle-fuckers. 'I hate this fucking war!' he shouted to his neighbours as they made their way out of their hiding places towards the tent Hans had pitched to face the seven peaks of Sheshnag. A pair of flip-flops still lay on the ground, as if someone was asleep inside. Mr Bhat peered in, hoping that he had somehow got it all wrong, and Hans would be smiling back at him. But clothes were strewn around, photographs torn and jumbled, a packet of instant porridge, a small gas stove and a bottle of honey. A jar of Horlicks had been emptied onto the sleeping bag.

Mr Bhat tried to make things tidy, although in his heart he knew that Hans would not be returning. Hidden beneath a brown woolly hat he found a Norwegian edition of *Opening Doors Within*, a volume of meditations by Eileen Caddy, a British New Age guru, and a book of poems by Khalil Gibran. Mr Bhat could not read in any language, but from the bottom of the sleeping bag he fished out a bulging black notepad with red linen trim. Written in Norwegian, the first page read: 'The books of Katharsis Theatre, Hans Christian Ostrø'. Beneath was a biro sketch of a dancing figure, arms raised, with a budding rose drawn over its heart. Intense currents of swirling script raced across and up the sides of the following pages, interspersed with more biro scribbles: ghostlike faces, lips, hands and eyes. The writings, mostly in Norwegian with a few English words scattered about, were a combination of jottings about *kathakali*, notes on Hindu myths, diary entries and quotes from the great Indian polymath Rabindranath Tagore. Interspersed between them were private, deep-felt thoughts about regrets, old girlfriends and missed opportunities. Mr Bhat deduced that these things were personal, and shut the book immediately.

That night, he called everyone in the hamlet together. What should they do, he asked nervously. 'Keep quiet,' a few of them suggested, pointing out that any admission that *mujahids* had been here would only bring a harsh response from the security forces. An elder tut-tutted and hissed 'Cowards!' Mr Bhat said they needed to report this abduction to the police. The blond foreigner had been travelling alone, and if they didn't raise the alarm it could be weeks before anyone knew he was missing. 'He lived with us, we owe him,' Mr Bhat said. 'Think about his family.' Someone seconded the motion: 'Tell the police. The DSP down in Pahalgam is a bastard who could talk an antelope into eating its young, but he is even-handed compared to the army.' Someone remembered the DSP's name was Kifayat Haider. Everyone had to forget the beatings, the scorn and threats, bile and petty insults they had received at the hands of police constables. They should stick their necks out for the Ox.

But the following day, nothing happened. Nobody went down to Pahalgam, and the tent was left where it was, mournfully flapping. Mr Bhat tried to call another meeting, but nobody came. Not until the morning of 10 July was a lone messenger delegated to make the climb down to Pahalgam, carrying the foreigner's abandoned possessions. Braving the police station, he spoke to a Duty Inspector, who noted down receipt of the tent and its contents before sending an urgent message down the police radio to DSP Kifayat Haider in Bijbehara.

'Another foreigner abducted at Zargibal.' Haider was horrified. Just that morning he had been watching the television news in his office and seen the press conference held by General Saklani at which John Childs had said a few words. Haider contacted the control room in Anantnag, and checked with police headquarters in Srinagar too, but no one could understand what the information from Zargibal meant. It must have been a duplicate report, they said in Srinagar: 'We already know about the German, Dirk Hasert, the fifth hostage. He was taken on the morning of 8 July at 7 a.m., trekking on the path just north of Chandanwari.' But, after checking and rechecking, it appeared that militants searching for John Childs had grabbed Dirk Hasert at 7 a.m. on 8 July, and had then run into another foreigner in Zargibal around midday. Haider confirmed that there were two more missing trekkers, both seized after Childs was rescued, although no word had come from the al Faran kidnap party confirming that it was them who had carried out these new abductions.

The DSP was beside himself. He was already two days behind, since the villagers in Zargibal had failed to report this latest abduction until now. 'The worst of it was the wider implications. There were still thirty-three trekkers out there in the hills, and evidently the column of insurgents had begun picking them off one by one.' There were now five hostages in the mountains. 'How many more are going to be taken before we get this under control?' Haider screamed at no one in particular.

As the senior police official responsible for the area in which the kidnappings had taken place, he was responsible for investigating the crimes, establishing who had committed them and finding the kidnap party. A day earlier he had received express orders to that effect from General Saklani's office, and these were now updated to inform him that police constables would have to be taken off *yatra* duties to track down the remaining thirty-three trekkers who had not yet been accounted for. As Haider understood it, the army would be responsible for leading the search teams for the missing backpackers, as they were already deployed in the mountains to secure the *yatra* route. But then, this was Kashmir, and as always the division of responsibilities was 'as clear as a murky Mughal lily pond'.

Haider barked questions about the new Zargibal hostage into the phone: 'Nationality? Name? Next of kin?' Who the hell was this sixth captive? But no one in Pahalgam knew. He had been travelling alone, and the militants had taken his passport and wallet: 'It seemed he had not followed the rules stipulating he had to register his route with Pahalgam tourist police on his way through. Or the police had failed to follow the rules and register him, which was more likely. Either way, we did not have much to go on.' Incandescent, the DSP decided to drive up and take charge at the crime scene.

But at the police station in Pahalgam there was nothing new, just the tent and some books that Haider decided he would look at later. He drove on up to Chandanwari, the village where the single-track road ended, close to where the German Dirk Hasert had been seized two days earlier. Thousands of *yatris* were congregated around the perimeter of the local Rashtriya Rifles base, sporting balaclavas and tank tops to withstand the coolness of the Kashmiri summer, many of them wearing hired brown plastic booties, slipping and sliding all over Chandanwari's famous ice bridge across the East Lidder River. For most, it was the first snow they had ever touched or seen, and snappers made bundles of rupees selling the pictures as souvenirs, while entrepreneurial Kashmiri boys hired out sledges so pilgrims could hurtle down the slope.

Haider pressed past them on foot, skirting around the sooty ice sheet, littered with discarded Thums Up cola bottles and Amul ice-cream wrappers. He intended to search the spot where Dirk Hasert had been taken and then hike the five miles on to Zargibal, scene of the sixth mysterious abduction. Only two sharpshooters accompanied him, as no one could spare more men. But as he progressed, he was surprised to see no evidence of any kind of army search operation, contrary to the claims Saklani had made on television. Perhaps they were already higher up, he thought, giving them the benefit of the doubt as he marched on purposefully. After all, the heights were the army's domain all year round, with some bases overlooking the Line of Control at up to sixteen thousand feet, manned even in the deepest winter.

As he continued climbing, there was still no sign of a search. Then he was abruptly halted by an Indian Army patrol. 'I'm DSP Haider from Bijbehara,' he said, proffering his police ID, expecting to be ushered through. The soldiers would not budge. 'Let me pass,' he demanded. 'I'm sorry, sir, we have orders. No one can come through,' they replied. An incredulous Haider swore that he would get them disciplined. Then a Rashtriya Rifles Major strolled over. 'There's a cordon,' he said firmly. 'We're not allowing anyone beyond it, other than army officers, sir.' Haider insisted. There were two new kidnappings he needed to investigate. 'Please go back, sir,' the Major told him. Haider decided there was no point wasting more time arguing up here with junior ranks. He would climb down to Pahalgam and make a complaint to army HQ and the Governor's office before returning to his criminal investigation, coming at it from a different angle, one that tapped into his knowledge of the mountains and their inhabitants.

If he could not go into the mountains, others would go for him. After the abductions of Don Hutchings, Keith Mangan, Paul Wells and John Childs, Haider had taken it upon himself to open an informal office away from the main police station in Pahalgam, inside an anonymous shop house up the road towards Chandanwari, to which visitors could come without being stigmatised for entering police property. He had sat in the gloom of the shop for an hour a day, dressed in his civvies, instigating a system of casual rewards for any tribal mountain men who dared call in, promising to buy them ponies and goats in exchange for titbits of information. 'I'm not offering you money, but if your horses have died or you lost some cattle on the high pass, come and tell me,' the wily policeman said. A pony here. Two goats there. It did not cost much, and snippets flowed in: 'One *gujjar* told me the hostages were in Sheshnag, moving around on a track high above the *yatra* route. Another said that one of his relatives had been forced at gunpoint to cook a meal for the hostages, and that they had seemed to be in good health, since they complained about the food.' Then Haider picked up something he had not been expecting, something that went a long way to explaining why the army cordon in the hills above Chandanwari had stopped him. A local hunter whispered (in return for two ponies) that two days back, a Western female trekker had approached the RR camp at Chandanwari to say she had witnessed the abduction of Dirk Hasert. Instead of taking her seriously, an RR major had sexually assaulted her. Senior officers had been sent into the mountains to hush her up and investigate the errant major. Now an operation was in place to prevent anyone knowing the shame that had befallen the RR, which was why Haider had been barred from climbing up to the scene of the second kidnap.

'I could barely believe what I was hearing,' said Haider. 'We had several crises on our hands, and yet an army officer was acting like an animal with a valuable female witness.' Over the next twenty-four hours, Haider would lodge an official complaint with the army about withholding vital eyewitness statements, his report making it clear that he knew about the incident in Chandanwari. 'I intended to let rip with the higher-ups,' he said, emboldened by the power of holding such a useful bargaining chip, but unsure if it would elicit any information about the female eyewitness. The army was a world unto itself.

Then the DSP gleaned another revelation from his Pahalgam Duty Inspector, one that did not work in his favour at all. The previous day a team of detectives from the police Crime Branch in Srinagar had been spotted in Pahalgam, roughing up residents and taking a particular interest in the Heevan Hotel. Haider was mortified. He thought he was the sole police investigator. Nobody from headquarters had thought to inform him that others had been drafted in too. He knew that once Crime Branch, the specialist criminal investigation department of Jammu and Kashmir Police, got its hands on a case, the local officers were pushed to the margins. Was he about to be manoeuvred out of the biggest investigation of his career? If his new mountain sources got wind of this development, they'd disappear in an instant. Haider sat back at his desk in Pahalgam police station, deflated. He smoked a couple of Classics, and wondered about the Heevan Hotel. Why had Crime Branch gone there, he asked himself. Was there some connection to the kidnapping?

Before he went there to check, he remembered what he did have to himself: the contents of the tent that belonged to the sixth kidnap victim. They were packed into a large black holdall: books, dried food, clothes and some other personal items. No different to any of the bags that ended up in police hands in Pahalgam after being stolen from trekkers by unregistered pony-*wallahs*. But then he spotted something the Duty Inspector had missed. The DSP was after all an educated man, and an avid reader. Here was writing and references to places that led him to deduce that the sixth victim was from Norway, and that he had been in India for several months. Delighted to have something new to report, he informed Srinagar of his discovery. He then called up his friend, BBC man Yusuf Jameel, in the Press Enclave. He would need all the help he could get in identifying the missing tourist as quickly as possible. Yusuf prepared a late-night dispatch.

The following morning, 11 July, Tore Hattrem, a young diplomat based in New Delhi, was watching the television news from his desk in the political section of the Norwegian Embassy in Chanyakapuri when a report came on about a sixth tourist being abducted in

Kashmir. 'When they mentioned local police were saying the missing man was a Norwegian national, I immediately had one thought: it was the traveller I had met here a week earlier, an intense young man with piercing blue eyes.' He had been memorable, not just because very few Norwegians went to Kashmir these days, but also because he had been extraordinarily upbeat about his trip.

Hattrem had first come across this man conducting a conversation with the Embassy receptionist in Malayalam, a language from India's southern state of Kerala. 'He explained he'd been in Kerala for five months, learning *kathakali* dancing. He said it had been a tough experience, because of the language.' Having recently completed his 'graduation dance', he was now qualified as a *kathakali* master. Tore had been impressed. He had been in India much longer than the young man, but had not seen much beyond the compound walls. The man enthused about an up-and-coming *kathakali* performance he was planning in Oslo. He had also written a play. 'The theatre's booked,' he said. 'You must come. It's my first big bash.'

The visitor told Tore that he was going to spend his last days in the subcontinent trekking up to Amarnath Cave in Kashmir. Was it safe, he had asked. Now, with the news blaring in his ear, Tore remembered that he had replied that he had never visited this region, and didn't feel qualified to answer. He had called over a colleague, but he did not know what the two had discussed. What was the young man's name, he now asked himself. He was sure he had left a photocopy of his passport. It should be on record somewhere.

When Marit Hesby wanted to get away from it all, she and her husband John went down to her family's wooden summerhouse near Tønsberg, Norway's oldest settlement, dating from AD 871. It was a friendly town, a little over an hour south of Oslo, and they had a black clapboard cabin overlooking the southern reaches of the silvery Oslofjord. Without telephone or television, it was a place to absorb the black-granite landscape and the indigo sky. Tønsberg was pitted with memories for Marit, since she had been born there, and her parents still had a house close by. She also had many happy memories of bringing her children here, although these days she lived and worked in Trondheim, in the far north of the country, and they were far away.

On 11 July 1995, Marit and John were just about to sit down for dinner with some old friends at the Tønsberg summerhouse when there was a knock at the door. Marit's neighbour was there, apologising for disturbing them, but she had just heard some worrying news on the television about a Norwegian man taken hostage in Kashmir. She didn't want to panic anybody but wasn't Marit's son Hans Christian there right now? 'I just froze in an instant,' Marit recalled. Everyone loved the charming, animated Hans Christian, and he left an indelible impression on all who met him. 'Yes,' she said quietly. She had last spoken to him two weeks back, when he had called from New Delhi, excited at just having just left the Norwegian Embassy with a green light to go to Kashmir. 'He told me they had said not to worry, to call them if there was a problem.' He was heading up to Srinagar as soon as he could get a flight, he said before saying goodbye. 'I didn't know the first thing about Kashmir.'

Returning to the table, her face blanched, Marit had a sinking sensation, a feeling she would later describe as a mother's intuition. She had felt the same a year earlier, when Hans Christian had been travelling alone in South America, camping in the Bolivian mountains. He had been sleeping in his hammock when armed police had arrested him during a raid on a coca plantation. He had nothing to do with the drug dealers who ran it, but in his usual dreamy way he had camped in the plantation by mistake. 'Ever since he had been a little boy he always seemed to land himself up in some scrape or another,' Marit said. 'He was just too trusting and too curious.' Trying not to panic, she found an old radio in a cupboard. 'I said to my guests, "I have to put the news on to listen." We heard the same report as our neighbours. A missing Norwegian in Kashmir. I remember saying to my friends, "Why are they not reporting the age?" If they had reported the age then we would know at least if it could have been Hans Christian or not.'

Marit knew her twenty-seven-year-old son had arrived in Kashmir by 30 June, because she had received a postcard from him a couple of days back with that date. It depicted Dal Lake, and bore a character-istically upbeat message: 'Hello! My last little hello from India. Himalaya is fantastic. I'm going to hire a guide and a pony and go into the Buddha cloister. I'm looking forward to enjoying the mysticism and peace of the mountains. It's good to be here with the people and the mountains. I'm coming home on 31 July with SK150 from London at 20:00. Looking forward … HCO.'

Marit's friends reassured her. Hans Christian had been in India for six months, and he knew how to look after himself. They were sure that the missing man was someone else's tragedy. Soon after, Marit's brother, who was staying at another family cabin nearby, called round. He too had heard the news. She asked to borrow his mobile phone to call her ex-husband, Hans Gustav, a bank manager who lived in Oslo. He would know what to do. 'Have you heard?' Marit asked him, strug-gling to stay calm. 'Do you think Hans Christian is in trouble?' Hans Gustav had sighed, exasperated. 'Don't be stupid, there's hundreds of Norwegians up there. Call the Ministry of Foreign Affairs in the morning if you're worried.' Hans Christian had been their perfect first baby, conceived at the end of her husband's accountancy exams in the spring of 1967, when the young couple were living in Oslo. When a little sister, Anette, had come along two years and four months later, Marit thought her family was complete. But the call to her ex-husband demonstrated what had been wrong with their marriage from the start. She had felt things, Hans Gustav had dismissed them. She had had ideas, he had undermined them. That was why they had split when the children were young.

Marit's dinner guests left: 'They thought I needed time alone to deal with what was happening.' She walked into the snug box-room that Hans Christian shared with Anette when they came here for family reunions: two wooden bunk beds still made up with their childhood duvets. A cushion lay on top of each, hand-sewn with flow-ers from a mountain meadow. He was looking forward to returning to Tønsberg, he had told her in that last call. He wanted to bring some friends over, eat pizza and drink beer beside the freezing water and then maybe go for a dip. Marit looked at a set of shelves Hans

Christian had filled with childhood mementos: his old Seiko watch and Iggy Pop badge; a photo of him in his beloved Manchester City football strip, his arm strapped up after he had broken it during a match; another photograph of him cuddling his pet hamster, which he had named Harald Hanssen. He had pestered her for months, picking up stray dogs every time they went on holiday, saying that all his school friends had animals, so why couldn't he too? For a while she'd held out, saying they wouldn't be able to go away on holidays if they had a pet to care for. 'But of course he had won in the end.'

She looked around the room at other family photos: two blond-haired kids, Hans Christian and his sister, ringlets, scraped knees, short socks, always together. Where was he now?

Marit Hesby had always been afraid that Hans Christian's wanderlust would get him into trouble, but she felt some responsibility for sending him down that path. She was a travel agent, and when the children were small the family had been entitled to a free foreign holiday every year. 'Did I cause him to be permanently unsettled?' she wondered, thinking how on these family holidays he had often got into trouble. 'He was just so trusting and generous with everyone, always wanting to go off to talk to the locals.' On one trip to Turkey, something had happened between her son and a group of locals. 'He'd gone off on his own. When he came back, he said he wanted to go home straight away. He wouldn't ever talk about it.'

Although she had worried that India was too much for her intense, easily led son, she had helped him plan the trip, and contributed to the cost of his air ticket. For the last few years he had been a constant source of worry to her, and she hoped that in India he would at last find peace. A sunny, happy child who loved records, films and the theatre, he had gone through a difficult period during his teens, dropping out of school and leaving home at the age of seventeen, having come up with a hare-brained scheme to pay his way through theatre school by travelling around Norway selling books: 'In his mind, he'd already been accepted by the National Theatre.' There was no dissuading him, even when reality took over. Despite several attempts, the prestigious theatre school in Oslo did not offer him a place. 'He was crushed. It was the only thing he ever wanted to do, and afterwards he sank into a deep depression.'

Hans Christian had begun smoking too much hash and hanging out in Oslo squats with people Marit didn't know. But he still loved acting, and at the age of twenty his life took a new turn when he was cast in an Ibsen play after volunteering at a free theatre school. Reinvigorated, he joined a circus workshop, and there he met Gry, a trainee social worker. In 1991 they married and set off for an extended honeymoon in Amsterdam. When the money ran out he sang in the streets with his guitar. Back in Oslo, things seemed perfect. Hans Christian won a couple of bit parts in Norwegian movies, and he and Gry moved into a one-bedroom flat and got a kitten they called Tingaling (Tinkerbell). They even talked about having children.

But in 1992 Hans Christian was forced to do his national service, something he had been putting off ever since dropping out of school. Not one to do anything by halves, he chose the hardest option, an arduous survival training course in the far north of Norway that took him away for months. The posting had a devastating impact on his relationship, and in the spring of 1993 he and Gry split. Broken, Hans Christian lost his head in meditation and Eastern spirituality. 'He grew his hair, gave up meat, eggs, alcohol and smoking. The split with Gry marked the beginning of his fascination with India.'

That autumn, unemployed and rootless, Hans Christian joined another free theatre school, this one run by the government for out-of-work actors. Through it he was introduced to Lars Øyno, a classically trained actor who had turned his back on traditional theatre to run an avant-garde group, Stella Polaris. Lars was looking for volunteers to take part in a play he was preparing for the 1994 Winter Olympics, to be held at Lillehammer. His particular interest was in putting on complex, audience-challenging performances, like the plays of Antonin Artaud, the French playwright and advocate of the Theatre of Cruelty. Hans Christian was transfixed. 'He saw that theatre could be a weapon, a way of life,' Lars recalled. 'After rehearsals, he'd sit there with his big black notebook, writing furiously.'

In September 1993 Hans Christian travelled to Gjøvik, the town where the Lillehammer performers were rehearsing. Lars was planning an ambitious outdoor interpretation of a Nordic myth that involved using Lillehammer's streets as the stage, with actors playing troll-like creatures and rappelling down a corn silo. Hans Christian was in his element. 'He was frantic at the start,' said Lars. 'Very strong, just out of the army. He wanted to rappel free-style, without a safety rope. He was almost too strong physically, and always ready to go. But I kept saying to him, "If you don't start calmly, breathing freely, relaxed physically, you'll injure yourself."' At one point Lars banished him from the set after he refused to take direction. But he was back in time for the final show, pushing the boundaries as always.

Meeting Lars changed Hans Christian's life. After the performance in Lillehammer, in February 1994 he returned to Oslo and started casting around for something more challenging than his unemployed actors' workshop. Soon he realised there was nothing to keep him in the city any more. Gry and many of the friends they had made together had moved on. His younger sister Anette was away at film school in Stockholm, and his mother was remarried and living in Trondheim. Hans Christian booked a trip to Peru, Brazil and Bolivia to study under a physical-theatre teacher to whom he'd been introduced by Lars at a party. To fund the trip he sold his vast record collection: Peter Gabriel, Led Zeppelin, David Bowie, the Waterboys.

The trip to South America was Hans Christian's first time out of Europe. It started badly, when he arrived to find Lars' teacher friend wasn't there. Making the most of the situation, he used his time to learn about the Incas, visiting their remote jungle temples, fascinated by their beliefs, especially reincarnation. 'I have had some fantastic visions,' he wrote in one letter home. 'Visualising light pouring towards the earth. The earth has opened itself unto all the light and turned into a lotus of light.' For Hans Christian, this vision was 'a sign of grace, that everything is well and that new life will continue to sprout and grow on the compost heap'. Exploring spirituality and seeing more of the world were becoming as important to him as his desire to be on the stage.

Inspired by Lars, Hans Christian returned from South America determined to establish a theatre group. He applied for a scholarship, set himself up at an artists' commune in Oslo and launched his group, Catharsis, in December 1994. Despite the doubts of some around him, he planned an ambitious production that would draw from an exotic mix of Aristotle, Artaud and Andrei Tarkovsky, the Russian director whose film *The Sacrifice*, shot on a Swedish island, he adored. He was so sure of himself that he went ahead and booked a venue, the Black Box Theatre, for 21 October 1995. With the pressure on, he needed inspiration. It would have to be something foreign and extreme, originating in a part of the world far from Norway.

In the run-up to Christmas, Hans Christian toyed with the idea of going back to South America. He also thought seriously about Bali, where Artaud had studied the island's ritualised dance. But then he met an actor friend of Lars who had recently spent time in southern India studying *kathakali*. Hans Christian knew that this was it. He'd already been thinking about India as a source of inspiration after coming across the poems of Rabindranath Tagore – while he was in Peru, he'd written to friends that one day he wanted to interpret them theatrically. 'He'd told me once, [Tagore] is a man who Artaud would really have liked to have met,' recalled Lars.

'Hans Christian told me he was heading to India on New Year's Eve,' said Marit. 'I was a little scared for him.' But by the end of December he was on the plane to New Delhi with his guitar. 'I kept telling myself that he'd become more grounded and serious. I hoped he would be OK,' said Marit. Before leaving, Hans Christian and Anette posed for photographs with their mother, wearing traditional Norwegian felt hunting outfits she had bought them for Christmas. Marit gave him a fifty-krone note to put in his money belt. 'On his way home from Bolivia in 1994, he had run out of money and had to walk thirty miles home from Oslo airport,' she recalled with a smile. This time she wanted him to be better prepared.

'I felt very responsible,' said Lars Øyno, who met up with Hans Christian one last time shortly before he left Norway. 'He went to India as a result of Artaud and his philosophy. And I had introduced him. But at the time I was very happy to have planted that seed.'

Despite his mother's misgivings, Hans Christian had landed on his feet in India, living a pared-down existence with a well-respected family of orthodox Brahmins in Sreekrishnapuram, a Keralan village draped in bougainvillea. The habitually erratic Hans Christian slowed down and embraced the frugal lifestyle as an antidote to too much freedom. Up at 7 a.m., he would train for six hours with his *kathakali* master. After lunch he meditated and read until village children came to play with him, pestering him to tell them fairy tales from back home in his 'troll voice'.

Most evenings he sat with the Namboodiri family around the duck pond, strumming along to their Malayalam songs with his guitar. In letters back home to Norway, he described how they had given him a new name, 'Hamsa', meaning Swan, *kathakali*'s royal messenger. The village of Sreekrishnapuram was his 'Garden of Eden'.

'It's nice to be here,' he wrote to his grandfather Ole Hesby. 'It's hot, they are really friendly people. They're not too pushy. There are many exciting things to see and do. Also there is much poverty. Love HC.' Soon the young Norwegian was walking barefoot and wearing a sarong. Sometimes he was homesick. 'I am doing big jumps and have big blisters,' he wrote to Ane Ostrø, his paternal grandfather. 'I give you a big hug and am longing for home.'

When the austerity got too much, Hans Christian took trips up into the hills, hiking in the cool air around the tea plantations of Munnar. Never one to pass up a new experience, he wrote that he had had an opportunity to try 'hot coal running'. He befriended a local Keralan photographer, George, who lived in Cochin. Over cold beers they would discuss spirituality, meditation, women and Hans Christian's plans to introduce *kathakali* to Norway. They also shared books, Hans Christian giving George a copy of Khalil Gibran's *The Prophet*, a fictional account of a traveller who lectures a group of men about life and the human condition as he prepares to make his journey home after twelve years away. George still has it.

But after five months, Hans Christian was ready to go home. 'Katarsis Teater and Kerala Kalakendra Proudly Presents a Kathakali Night' proclaimed the flyer he produced in English and Malayalam for a performance he would give before he left Kerala. Hundreds came, curious to watch him play Bhima, a Hindu immortal of 'great stature and unimaginable strength' who was a brother of Lord Hanuman, the monkey deity. Hans Christian paid George to photograph and video the performance, and afterwards the verdict in Sreekrishnapuram was that it was the best graduation show they'd seen in years.

All that was left for him to do now was to visit Kashmir. The night after the show, he discussed his plan with the Namboodiris. They were appalled, warning him that Kashmir was a terrifying place of murderous *jihadis* and Pakistani *fidayeens*, or suicide bombers. Hans Christian almost came to blows with the Namboodiris' eldest son after he accused them of being small-minded. They responded that they were Hindu Indians, and knew more than him about the truth of Kashmir. 'I will go anyway,' Hans Christian retorted. 'If anything happens to me, it will be according to my fate.'

A few days later, the family tried again to dissuade him. A famed *kathakali* teacher was coming to stay in the village, and they urged Hans Christian to stay longer and train with him. Almost persuaded, Hans Christian tried to change his Air India ticket, but was unable to do so. He rang his mother. 'I tried to buy him a new one so he could stay on in Kerala,' she recalled, 'but I couldn't find him a seat anywhere.' Instead, he bought a rail ticket, packed his Bhima costume and sent it back to Norway by ship.

Around midnight on 11 July 1995, the Norwegian Ministry of Foreign Affairs reached Marit's brother on his mobile. 'As soon as it rang I knew it was Hans Christian who was missing,' said Marit. The family needed to supply a recent photograph, as the police in Kashmir were struggling to identify the missing trekker. 'Kidnapped!' Marit said. 'It was like a wicked dream.' His twenty-five-year-old sister Anette, who was in Stockholm, got the call at two o'clock the next morning. 'This is not happening,' she thought. 'It's a joke.'

On 12 July Marit awoke to find reporters outside the house, and her son's photograph all over the front pages. She panicked. 'My elderly mother was in hospital. My father would be sitting at home alone watching television.' Marit rang him, but before she could speak he said he had news for her, as he had just received a postcard from Kashmir. 'So this card is the last one,' Hans Christian began. 'Now I'm in the mountain country. Here, it's extremely fantastic ... On the photo here, I have gone without a guide, this is at eight thousand feet. I am so happy you gave me the equipment (sleeping bag, etc). Please look after yourself. Give *mormor* [granny] a big hug. PS. I'm coming home on the night of 31 July 1995 ... See you soon. HC.' He had supplied a caption for the place he was writing from: 'Mountain beauty of Pahalgam'.

NINE

Deadline

If a car says anything about its owner, BBC man Yusuf Jameel's battered motor said that while he was sufficiently affluent to have a vehicle (which set him above most Kashmiris), he was insufficiently corrupt for it to be a flashy trophy. In an impoverished valley where most working people could not conceive of ever being able to afford any set of wheels, the journalists who rode around town in brand-new Tata Sumos and Mahindras, and whose children were enrolled in top-notch private schools, were all rumoured to have been paid by warlords, religious leaders, intelligence agencies or politicians who expected the right words to be written and broadcast. While the finger of suspicion pointed at these men with their inexplicable wealth, Yusuf's modest ride meant he had few detractors.

As he drove to work on the morning of 12 July, Yusuf's head was filled with worries about the day ahead: the captives and the *yatra*. The previous day, all hell had broken loose in Srinagar when the news of a sixth kidnapping filtered down from Pahalgam. The phones at the red-brick Press Enclave, tucked in a cul-de-sac behind Residency Road, had been ringing for hours. Dozens of foreign news teams were already ensconced in the city, just around the corner at the dingy Ahdoo's Hotel, where every telephone was tapped by one Indian agency or another, or a ten-minute drive away at the dour Welcome, a two-storey modernist beehive overlooking Dal Lake. The Western media were ravenous in their attempts to identify the sixth victim, hiring Kashmiri journalists, boosting their thin local salaries. By the time a name had emerged on 12 July – Hans Christian Ostrø, from

Norway – these local stringers were set running to gather what they could, in the absence of any comments from the silent Indian authorities or the terrified family in Oslo, where Hans Christian's father, Hans Gustav Ostrø, was fielding all approaches.

It was now more than a week since the kidnappings of Don Hutchings, Keith Mangan, Paul Wells and John Childs, yet there had been nothing more from the kidnappers: no reaction to John Childs' escape on 8 July, and nothing to confirm that 'al Faran' was behind the abductions of Ostrø or Dirk Hasert. All there was was a deadline, issued in the original al Faran demand Jane Schelly had brought down to Pahalgam, that now had just forty-eight hours to run. Two days in which to release twenty-one prisoners, or the five remaining hostages, representing four nationalities, would face unspecified 'dire consequences'.

Arriving at the Press Enclave, Yusuf toyed with his personal theory, sparked by Sikander's call on the night of 4 July, that al Faran was nothing but a subsidiary of the Movement, and that the kidnap party holed up in the hills was the same one that had been behind the two 1994 episodes. He wondered what to do with this potentially significant nugget. Nothing, for the moment, he decided. He still needed to work it up into something more substantial.

Tonight was the full moon, which signalled the official start of the pilgrimage to Amarnath Cave. Many reporters and photographers were heading to Pahalgam, both to catch the action and in the hope of picking up some titbits on the kidnappings. But Yusuf was going nowhere. He opted to stay put in Srinagar, judging that he would get more from his contacts on the phone than he would drinking tea in Pahalgam's expensive tourist cafés. In the absence of a view from inside the kidnappers' hideout, with Sikander remaining frustratingly silent, Yusuf spent the morning ringing round his police contacts.

Kashmiri reporters had a precarious relationship with the law. Hindu officers, and many of the senior Muslim higher-ups, viewed them as either untrustworthy or as spies for militant outfits. They were typically characterised as propagandists, hecklers and agitators, whipping up hysteria in the valley with their unhelpful reports on police massacres, brutal army crackdowns and bloody cordon-and-search operations. But then, the police, whose ranks were dominated by Kashmiri Muslims except among the top tier – the Director General was invariably a Hindu, a New Delhi appointee – had their own problems: hated by the local population for being in the pay of New Delhi, and viewed as untrustworthy by other parts of the security apparatus, including the army, that were more firmly tethered to India.

Journalists like Yusuf, attached to one of the world's most prestigious international broadcasters, occupied an awkward spot somewhere in the middle. He needed his police contacts, and there were many senior officers in the force who wanted to be heard, either 'on the record' or anonymously, for whom the BBC provided an incomparable platform. Among them was DSP Kifayat Haider at Bijbehara, a close contact Yusuf respected, and who he guessed would be at the centre of things right now. But today Haider was tight-lipped and in a strange mood. He claimed it was the combined stress of the *yatra*, his ongoing investigation of the bombing at Pahalgam bus station and the pressure of keeping a lid on the vicious response of the RSS: 'He told me he feared the entire shooting match might go up in flames.' 'Talk to Crime Branch,' Haider had suggested, bitterly referring to the team that had been sent up to Pahalgam by police headquarters, which he worried was deliberately undermining his role. There it was, out of the bag: a turf war between a good local officer like Haider and the specialists from Srinagar who had been drafted in over his head.

These days Crime Branch, which took responsibility for all non-militancy-related wrongdoings in the valley, was under the control of Rajinder Tikoo, a corpulent, philosophical Inspector General who Yusuf liked. Until the previous February, Tikoo had been IG of Kashmir Zone, the most senior operational officer in the valley, and had had dealings with the press on a daily basis. 'IG Tikoo was his own man, someone who knew everything but told only what he wanted to,' says Yusuf. Tikoo had a reputation for being articulate, irreverent and tricky, but Yusuf was hopeful that on this occasion he might be forthcoming. The IG took the journalist's call straight away, but said little of substance. 'I'm afraid there's nothing I can say to you, Jameel *Sahib*,' he said, adding cryptically, 'Try elsewhere.'

Yusuf thought he knew what Tikoo meant. He was referring to his opposite number in the CID, Gopal Sharma, the valley's police intelligence chief. Sharma had risen unobtrusively through the ranks. He had influence and information, but he was regarded as 'a model of discretion', rarely entertaining the press pack. It came as no surprise when he politely refused to speak to Yusuf.

Moving down his contact list, Yusuf tried the usual slack-lipped deputy and assistant superintendents dotted around the valley. But they were also unforthcoming, leaving Yusuf to conclude that everyone's silence had been ordered. The whole valley was bottled up, it seemed, including the militants, who were also saying nothing.

He contemplated the photographs on his wall: Sikander, the Afghani and the Turk, taken by his friend Mushtaq Ali. Was Sikander sitting up there in the mountains in some *gujjar* hut with the hostages? Or hiding with them in a safe house in the heart of Anantnag town? Frustrated, Yusuf contemplated calling the Governor's Security Advisor, General Saklani. But Saklani, Yusuf concluded, was all about control, and was unlikely to take some theories for a spin.

The army? Under normal circumstances, the army and its allies spoke to no one apart from their own kind, unless it was to threaten, chastise or clarify. And at the moment the army was a problem for Yusuf especially. Just two months back he had been given a vicious dressing down by the military over one of his reports about Charar-e-Sharief, the wooden shrine town that had gone up in smoke. The army was furious that he had repeated claims by residents that it was they who had burned it down, although Yusuf had even-handedly reported the army's rejoinder that the Hizbul Mujahideen commander Mast Gul, holed up inside the shrine, was actually responsible. Unfortunately for Yusuf, the BBC editor who had cobbled the package together before it was broadcast in London had erroneously illustrated it with footage from another country altogether, showing Muslims under attack in Bosnia. It was a lazy mistake, but in the eyes of a paranoid Indian Army it looked as if the BBC was propagandising, leaving Yusuf exposed. The BBC bureau in New Delhi was warned by an anonymous caller that their man in Kashmir was in serious trouble.

But this morning, sitting with his Lipton *chai*, Yusuf placed that threat in a mental drawer alongside the others, preferring to focus on the present situation. Without any help from the police or the army, he would do what all good journalists did to drum up information: take in the wider scene. He would concentrate on tracking down where Hans Christian Ostrø had stayed when he first arrived in Kashmir, ringing everyone he could think of in the trekking areas with a working phone line. Who had accompanied Ostrø? Yusuf had picked up the scent of what John Childs and Jane Schelly also suspected, that pretty much everyone in the Lidderwat Valley had known that the Movement was on the lookout for Western hostages on the afternoon of 8 July. Had a casual acquaintance of Ostrø's given details to the kidnap team? Had Ostrø also been set up?

After a few calls, Yusuf discovered from sources in the tourism office that the Norwegian had spent his first couple of days in Kashmir on the *Montana* houseboat, one of the hundreds of floating hotels moored in Dal Lake. Taking a *shikara* out over the water, Yusuf tracked down Abdul Rashid Mir, the *Montana*'s owner, who was clearly terrified of the consequences of being wrapped up in a kidnapping, having heard from relatives in Pahalgam that all the pony-*wallahs* and guides who had been hired by the unfortunate trekkers were now undergoing intense questioning.

Eventually Yusuf coaxed Mir into talking. He confirmed that he had picked Ostrø up at Srinagar airport on 28 June, two days after Jane Schelly and Don Hutchings had arrived, a week after Julie and Keith Mangan, Paul Wells and Cath Moseley, and two days before John Childs. Ostrø and Mir had got chatting that night on the houseboat, Ostrø telling him how shocked he was at the security presence in the valley, and asking about the conflict in the region. Over cups of sweet *khawa*, green tea flavoured with saffron, almonds and cardamom, they had discussed Kashmir's recent history, Ostrø noting some of it down in a black notebook that Mir remembered he carried everywhere. The houseboat owner quickly realised Ostrø wasn't like other tourists. Likeable and energetic, he wanted to know everything and anything about the people he was living with. 'He was never bored,' Mir recalled.

In turn, Ostrø had regaled Mir's family with stories from home, telling them he had come to India after a gruelling stint in military service and the breakup of his marriage, and that the light in Kashmir reminded him of the far north of Norway. He played with Mir's children, telling them Norwegian fairy tales. He asked Mir to take photographs of him in the regal surroundings of the houseboat, pictures that were later processed by the Kashmiri police after the film was recovered from Ostrø's abandoned tent. In one, taken in the *Montana*'s intricately carved sitting room, dominated by a vast copper samovar, Ostrø sits on a sofa, dressed in a cream cotton shirt unbuttoned to the navel, looking relaxed and bronzed. He had grown a beard, and wrote in his notebook that he was thankful the necessity of remaining clean-shaven for his *kathakali* make-up was over. Ostrø also took pictures of Mir and his family in the functional portion of the boat where they lived, Mir smoking and looking pinch-faced with his young wife and two children beside him on the mattresses where they slept on the floor. Today the pictures are in an album kept by Hans Christian's mother Marit Hesby, along with her son's last letters and postcards.

The houseboat owner was disappointed when Ostrø announced two days after arriving that he was leaving for Amarnath, alone. Mir had tried to talk him into taking a guide, concerned about the commission he would be losing – and a little worried that this 'likeable but naïve' foreigner would get into trouble. But the Norwegian was firm. 'I have my knife,' he laughed, waving his army-issue bayonet. 'I'll be fine.' Ostrø had also made some checks, visiting the Indian government tourism offices in New Delhi and the J&K tourist office in Srinagar, where a tourist policeman had done his best to sell him the services of a guide. He showed Mir the officer's card: Nasser Ahmed Jan. 'Call me if you have any trouble,' Jan had said, as he did to everyone, handing him the business card. Mir said the same as

Ostrø boarded the Pahalgam bus. 'I told him, "Good luck. Make sure to come and stay with us on the way back down."'

Ostrø arrived in Pahalgam on 1 July, the same day as John Childs. The next morning Childs, Ostrø and the party consisting of Julie and Keith Mangan, Paul Wells and Cath Moseley had separately trekked up to the Meadow, all of them leaving at different times and camping in different locations. The photographs recovered from Ostrø's unprocessed film showed several mountain beauty spots where he had stopped en route.

Childs had headed to Kolahoi on 3 July, as Jane Schelly and Don Hutchings had set out north-west for Tar Sar, while as far as Yusuf could establish, Ostrø had returned to Pahalgam, meaning that he was lucky enough to be out of the Meadow when the kidnappers struck the following evening. In Pahalgam he had stayed at the Lidder Palace, a wooden hotel overlooking the town's golf course beside the East Lidder River. Its owner, Yaqoob Sheikh, had rented the foreigner a tent, keeping his Air India ticket for London as a guarantee that he would return it in a fortnight's time. Sheikh also tried to rent him a guide, but he had refused, saying he wanted to be alone. He spent most of the following day, 4 July, writing postcards to his family and wandering around Pahalgam taking snaps, coming back at around 10 p.m., a few hours after events unfolded in the Meadow.

The next morning, 5 July, Ostrø had woken at 6 a.m., according to Sheikh, and left Pahalgam by seven, saying he was eager to reach the heights above Chandanwari. He had taken a ride in a jeep taxi part of the way up the East Lidder River route, a journey he also photographed; the films were eventually handed over to DSP Haider, who later gave them to Ostrø's family. What this told Yusuf was that Ostrø had gone from being charmed to becoming the most unlucky hostage of all. If he had stayed just a little longer in Pahalgam, or had overslept that morning, he would have witnessed the emotional arrival of Jane, Julie and Cath in the town to report the kidnappings in the Meadow. In his eagerness to get into the mountains, he had missed them by a few crucial hours.

On the evening of 5 July Ostrø had pitched camp in the country-side outside Chandanwari. He left the next day before 7 a.m., heading for Sheshnag. He had stopped off for tea in remote Zargibal, to and from which no news travelled fast, and where no one would hear about the kidnappings for days to come. Zargibal was in a different time zone, villagers joked: clocks there were set forty-eight hours behind those elsewhere in the valley. 'It was a second stroke of bad luck for Hans Christian Ostrø that he had not pressed on to Amarnath as originally planned,' says Yusuf. Ostrø had stopped to make friends, settled a while, and then, like Don, Keith, John, Paul and Dirk, had been caught in the wrong place at the wrong time.

12 July, 11 a.m. Yusuf pored over a trekking map of the Kashmiri Himalayas, trying to work out how far the kidnappers and their hostages might have got in the last four days. In the absence of police intelligence, everyone in the Press Enclave was doing the same, working on the assumption that the main kidnap party could not have been far away when Dirk Hasert and Hans Christian Ostrø were seized between Chandanwari and Zargibal on 8 July. If they had set out at full pelt from the heights above Zargibal on the afternoon of 8 July, as soon as Ostrø had been captured, walking and climbing a maximum of ten miles a day, they could be anywhere within a forty-mile radius by now. That gave searchers a circle whose diameter was eighty miles long, which meant covering an area of five thousand square miles – if anybody *was* actually searching.

Just as Yusuf was contemplating the difficulty in finding the hostages, and the necessity of a negotiated settlement with al Faran, the phone rang: '*Vaaray chivaa.*' He jumped, recognising the southern burr instantly, took a deep breath, and kicked the door shut. Sikander. The message was brief: a packet was coming. The usual drop-off. Then the phone went dead. Yusuf sent Farooq Khan, a *Kashmir Times* photographer, out to do the collection. Several hours later he returned to the Press Enclave clutching a manila envelope. It had been deposited by the wayside from a passing motorbike at a busy crossroads opposite Jamia Masjid, the most important mosque in Srinagar. These days, anonymous drop-offs were considered by the militants to be far safer than a traceable phone call or a meeting. For now, it looked as if the Press Enclave was ahead of the Jammu and Kashmir Police.

Yusuf ripped open the envelope. Inside were two almost identical photos. The first, in colour, showed Don, Keith and Paul, their hands looped together with flimsy-looking twine, making their detention appear a symbolic affair. The twine's ends were loosely held by heavily armed militants, whose faces had been scratched out, although their figures were clearly visible, giving away some identifiable clues: a woolly Afghan *pakul* cap, bodies swathed in blankets worn over *kurta* pyjamas, suggesting that they were somewhere high and windy. Their wild, straggly hair and uncombed beards harked back to the days of the Afghan *mujahideen*, givng the entire composition a theatrical rather than a menacing air.

Keith Mangan sat at the centre of the group, showing a week's worth of stubble and still wearing his wife's purple bomber jacket. To his left was Paul Wells, his long hair hanging loosely around his shoulders. After more than a week of trudging, sleeping rough and bad food, there was no mistaking his look of resignation: this was no longer a game. To the right of Keith was Don Hutchings in his trademark blue fleecy hat and Gore-Tex trousers, looking drawn and tired. Was he still *chacha* (uncle), Yusuf wondered as he pondered these by-now familiar faces, or were the stresses and strains of their continued incarceration since John Childs' midnight flit beginning to grate on them all? The three of them sat on a bench against the dry-stone wall of a *dhoka*, staring placidly, putting up with being posed for a photograph probably taken with one of their own cameras.

The second photo showed the same *dhoka* and the same rope trick, but this time two new hostages had been squeezed into the line-up: Dirk Hasert, in a white sweatshirt, loose trousers and walking boots, at one end, his hair shorn, a modest goatee beard, his head tilted slightly to the right; at the other end, Hans Christian Ostrø wearing a white-and-purple batik shirt he had bought in New Delhi, his expression irritable, as if he was still coming to terms with being roughly handled in Zargibal.

Yusuf could only draw one conclusion, which was confirmed many years later by John Childs when he studied these pictures together for the first time. They had probably been taken on the same crucial day, 8 July, the first being snapped on the morning of John's escape, and the second after the search party had returned later from Chandanwari and Zargibal, with two new captives to replace the one who had slipped away. 'I could almost hear the kidnappers talking when I saw the second picture,' John said. '"We lost one, but never mind, we got two more."' The pictures also gave a glimpse into what had been unfolding up in the mountains. Yusuf reasoned that the *dhoka* in the photos must have been the one from which John fled. Don, Keith and Paul must have sat there all day, waiting for the search party to return, unsure of their fate. It was a crucial piece of evidence. Armed with this picture, John Childs could possibly lead a search party back to the location, or identify it from a helicopter. There were many such huts on the mountains, but given what was known about the likely route taken by the kidnappers, searchers could whittle them down if they got a move on.

Yusuf pressed his contacts to find out where John Childs was. The information that came back shocked him: Childs was on his way back to the US. Yusuf and the other journalists could not believe it. Knowing nothing of John's repeated attempts to get an army search team up into the mountains within minutes of his being rescued, the local journalists simply concluded, like many others involved in the drama, that the American could not wait to return to his loved ones. And John, being John, kept his mouth shut: 'I just ran away from all the journalists. I did not want to tell my story, or how I was pushed out of town despite asking to be taken back into the mountains.'

One of the few still in Srinagar who knew the truth was Saklani's police liaison, Altaf Ahmed, who later claimed that he and Saklani had wanted to go along with Childs' plan as soon as they rescued him from the ridge above Pissu Top. 'We all said, "Let's go over the hills to find the location of the others,"' he said many years later. 'But as soon as we got Childs back to Srinagar, a woman from the American Embassy arrived and made it very clear that they were taking him out. "We're leaving in twenty-four hours," she told us. And we had no choice about it.' To Yusuf, it didn't really matter whose version was right. The plain fact was that the only living link to the remaining hostages was gone.

As well as the two photographs, there was a note inside Sikander's envelope that rammed this point home. Signed 'al Faran', for which Yusuf read the Movement, it stated that the five hostages would be killed in the next thirty-six hours if the Indian government failed to release the twenty-one militants listed on the scrap of paper that had been handed to Jane Schelly on 5 July. Reading the message, Yusuf was reminded of a similar demand he had seen back in June 1994, after Kim Housego and David Mackie had been seized. But this time the language was more aggressive, with the kidnappers directly threatening to kill the hostages. Did this reflect pressure on Sikander to make things work, second time around? Yusuf was worried about this confrontational stance. New Delhi did not deal with confrontation well, and there seemed little room to manoeuvre. However, he was a journalist, and this was a big story. He had to stop worrying and get on with his job, preparing a report based on this letter drop – and then wait for the fallout.

That night, at his villa down Church Lane, beside the Jhelum River and the cricket ground, General Saklani called a meeting of the Unified Command. As they scraped their chairs across the polished parquet, there was only one item for discussion among the generals, inspector generals and director generals: the fate of the five hostages still in the mountains. Even before the unexpected appearance of the photographs of the hostages, things had become increasingly fraught as a result of the seizure of Hasert and Ostrø. There were now four foreign countries involved, where before it had only been the British and Americans. That meant four diplomatic liaison officers in Srinagar, all levelling questions on behalf of the families, and submitting formal requests for a phalanx of back-up staff waiting in

New Delhi to travel to Srinagar: hostage negotiators, search-and-rescue teams, intelligence officers, military advisors, psychiatrists, medics. Saklani told the meeting he had spent the best part of the afternoon fielding calls from the chiefs of mission in the Indian capital.

He had other irritants. Having forced the pace over the evacuation of John Childs from Srinagar, the US Ambassador, Frank Wisner, was now throwing his weight around concerning Don Hutchings, demanding the right to send in a Delta Force rescue team, the Special Operations Group of the US military responsible for counter-terrorism. He also requested that an FBI unit be allowed to travel north to comb the valley for evidence, with a view to trying the kidnappers at some stage in a US court, given that American citizens had been targeted. Hindu nationalist politicians from the BJP were protesting about sovereignty and Indian pride, making it unlikely that the American requests would get far with Prime Minister Narasimha Rao. And that was before the Indian Army weighed in, pointing out that if anyone was going to launch a military operation or a rescue mission it would be Indian-managed and Indian-led. The army was Saklani's family, and he knew what the view would be from the canteen in Mhow: 'It was India's prerogative to deal with the kidnappings. India had a mature army and a full-fledged democratic political system. It did not need assistance or coaching or mediation from old colonial masters or new-money powers.'

To further complicate matters, Saklani also had the world's media on his back. Srinagar was overflowing with news crews, all of them demanding updates. In the absence of any official responses they were issuing increasingly damaging reports, based on speculation and rumour. One, quoting an unnamed source, asserted that the hostages were in danger of being shot by Indian 'hunter killer' patrols who, it was claimed, had been sweeping the mountains in preparation for the *yatra* pilgrimage.

Back in the UK, that particular story had become front-page news. Julie Mangan's mother, Anita Sullivan, reacted furiously: 'These reports are being put out to frighten the families and help the captors get their demands.' Saklani had had the British Ambassador on the line just that afternoon.

You could not make up publicity this bad, Saklani told the gathered security chiefs. At the start he had been happy to 'let the hares run', as he liked to say, allowing idle speculation, however wild. But now he had a responsibility to make sure that on the international stage India looked as if it had this situation under control. They all did, he said. They would have to give the foreign and local media something to chew on. He proposed putting up the wives and girlfriends in a big, emotional press conference that would also give them a chance to speak directly to the Kashmiri people, something the women, frustrated at the lack of progress, had been demanding for days. A press conference would give Saklani the opportunity to straighten things out and reiterate the official line that everything that could be done was being done. The idea was mooted, rejected, beaten up, thrown out, and finally voted back in again.

The following morning, 13 July, in the Church Lane guesthouse where they were staying, hidden from view behind bunkers and roadblocks, Jane Schelly, Julie Mangan, Cath Moseley and Anne Hennig prepared to face the world's media, in the knowledge that the deadline set by al Faran was now just twenty-four hours away.

It would be their first time out of the restricted zone in days. Since 7 July, home had been a large tin-roofed villa overlooking the Jhelum River to the back and the Sher-i-Kashmir Cricket Stadium in front. Moth-eaten tiger skins were nailed up on the walls of the veranda, and the sitting room was decorated with embroidered calico Kashmiri curtains, tablecloths and cushions. Altaf Ahmed, who called in on them several times a day, always attentive and polite but never giving anything away, as Jane recalled, had advised them that it was not safe to leave this time capsule and wander around Srinagar. So they had sat and waited, sometimes in the dark, due to the regular power cuts which also deprived them of the local news channels. Altaf had arranged for them to receive a full set of newspapers, flown in from New Delhi every day, but the women spent most of the time playing catch-up. Prevented by Saklani from talking to any journalists, they knew nothing of what Yusuf Jameel and others had been piecing together about the kidnap team and its previous incarnations, or the background of its leaders like Sikander. Instead, they had been forced to wait and fret, imagining the very worst. Now, as they prepared to meet the world's press, they felt disorientated and agoraphobic.

The women had dressed in modest, loose-fitting clothes for the press conference. Jane wore a plain, short *kurta* shirt and dark trousers; Cath and Anne silk tops and baggy trousers, in Cath's case paisley print; Julie chose silk pyjama bottoms and an ethnic-print top. A diplomatic liaison officer escorted them to the Welcome Hotel on the shores of Dal Lake, the location chosen for the press conference. In the foreground were the lines of wooden houseboats on which some of them had stayed when they had first arrived in Srinagar, and off to the right was a great expanse of water that sparkled all the way to the Zabarwan mountains. But Jane, Julie, Cath and Anne did not notice the panorama. Instead they were shepherded into a dark meeting room that was stiflingly hot despite the fans blowing full tilt. Julie was horrified to see cameramen and photographers lined up just inches from the table behind which they were to sit, which was covered by a jumbled mass of microphones and tape recorders. Only the thought that this harrowing event might help secure Keith's release got her through.

Many of the foreign correspondents noted how haggard the women looked. 'They took their places, trembling,' wrote the *Guardian*'s reporter. General Saklani called the room to order as the women sat behind a row of tissue boxes, Julie already teary. 'It felt like an inquisition,' says Jane. She was the first to speak, her deliberate voice silencing the room. 'We are innocent bystanders,' she said, as the flashbulbs flared off her glasses. 'We just want them back safe as soon as possible.' She gripped Julie's hand and nodded, 'Your turn.' Tears rolling down her face, Julie squeezed out a few words: 'In the name of God, let our loved ones go. We miss them terribly.' Biting her lip to avoid breaking down completely, she glanced up at the sea of faces. As the shutters snapped, catching the moment she finally made eye contact, her face crumpled.

Next, Cath leaned forward, her long, blonde hair falling over her face like a veil, her voice barely above a whisper. 'This is very hard for me, but I just wanted to say how worried I am about Paul and the other hostages.' She hesitated. 'We have no quarrel with the people of Kashmir or Islam, so I appeal to the people holding our loved ones to let them go.' They were also here to appeal on behalf of the family of Hans Christian Ostrø, she said, who had not yet flown over.

Anne spoke last, staring defiantly into the cameras. 'We came here as tourists,' she said, 'to see this beautiful place. We have made many friends among the Kashmiris and have been treated with great kindness.' But inside she felt bitter that these people had now let her down, and were doing nothing as far as she could see to help them recover their loved ones, she recalled.

Saklani, who had been silently hovering in a corner in a slate-grey suit, his arms folded, chin resting on his thumb and forefinger, stepped forward to issue a statement on behalf of the Governor, calling for the immediate release of the hostages. And then it was over. The four women were ushered back through the hotel's sombre dark-wood reception to a waiting Ambassador car, while more photographers crowded around them; their shots showed the women with eyes downcast, each one with a tissue in her hand.

Footage of the press conference was broadcast around the world, as Saklani had intended. It received most attention in the home towns of the five hostages: Oslo, Middlesbrough, Blackburn, Erfurt and Spokane. In Middlesbrough, Keith's mother summed it up for all the relatives who could only read the headlines and wait for the next phone call when she told local reporters, 'Julie did very well. If these men have a heart they will release them all. Goodness knows how we have coped, we just take each day as it comes.'

The endless days and nights of waiting were taking their toll on Keith's parents. Mavis had barely been to bed in more than a week because of the knot she felt deep in her stomach. Since 5 July she and Charlie had pretty much refused even to leave the house, and instead sat side by side on the sofa, clutching hands, ears glued to the BBC World Service. If they had to go out for shopping, they'd done it in shifts. To keep himself occupied, Charlie had been doing DIY jobs, and cutting and recutting the lawn. 'It's like we are in a jail,' he told his local paper, the *Evening Gazette*, on 11 July. Keith's younger brother Neil, a nurse at Whitby Hospital, had taken time off work to help out. 'It's been a rollercoaster – all emotional ups and downs,' he said.

The general public were not allowed into the Church Lane compound, a smart enclave of Srinagar that had been commandeered by the authorities years back and was now bounded on three sides by high walls and fences, with the river forming the fourth barrier. Inside, the leafy mile-square zone consisted of a network of lanes, where white-shirted civilian staff and military officials in their light summer uniforms strolled among a legion of sweepers, drivers and body-guards. The sounds of downtown Srinagar floated in over the sand-bags and the chain-link fence: Jane recalled that every morning they were woken by the call to prayer from a nearby mosque. But the compound was an oasis of calm in the midst of the frantic city choked with handcarts, *tongas*, two- and three-wheelers, the miserable stray dogs covered in open sores, the army patrols in their carapaces of body armour.

For Jane, each day was harder than the one before. She spent much of her time with her journal, noting everything down. 'Day Two', 'Day Three', 'Day Four', she wrote at the head of the page, going on to describe her feelings, the weather and what she and the others had learned from official and unofficial sources. The worst thing was the interminable waiting, the four of them cooped up with nothing to do except speculate about what might happen, and attempt to keep their worst fears at bay. 'No one got a good night's sleep in those early days,' said Jane. She tried to deal with her anxiety by exercising in the garden, or doing a circuit of Church Lane, every morning before the others rose. 'Jane was already emerging as amazingly strong,' recalled Altaf Ahmed. 'She was the leader, while the others were destroyed by events.'

Then, in this period of no news, Julie took an unexpected call. A British man called Paul Rideout, who had rung the High Commission in New Delhi to offer advice, had been put in touch, the Embassy staff having decided he had something worth saying. Julie listened, stunned, as Rideout described how he had been caught up in a similar hostage crisis the previous year. Was it the Housego/Mackie kidnapping, she asked him. No, Rideout replied, he knew next to nothing about that. He went on to describe another incident, which none of the women had been told about, that took place in New Delhi in October 1994.

Rideout and a friend, Chris Morston, had arrived in New Delhi on 12 October 1994, staying at Hotel Namaskar, in the capital's backpacker quarter of Paharganj. Two days later, at the Hare Krishna Restaurant, they had got chatting to a young man called Rohit Sharma, who spoke fluent English with a London accent. 'He was quite tall, about six feet, medium build, with a short, neat beard, a gap between his front teeth, and wore glasses. He said he was brought up in Wanstead, and that his father was an import-exporter. His sister was doing medicine at Oxford, and his younger brother was still at school. He said he was doing a masters in political science at the London School of Economics.'

Rohit had been charming and bright, a welcome face from the UK in a bewildering city. Over a game of chess he explained that his uncle had died, leaving a house in the family's ancestral village, a few hours east of New Delhi in the neighbouring province of Uttar Pradesh (UP). He had come over to India to see it, and invited Paul and Chris to go with him. 'On 16 October Rohit came to our hotel around 11.30 a.m. The three of us walked to the New Delhi railway station where a light-blue Suzuki van bearing a UP numberplate arrived. Then we drove out of New Delhi.' After two and a half hours they had lunch at a place Rideout thought was called Cheetal. 'Then we drove for hours, once stopping briefly for drinks, and reached the town of Saharanpur around 7 p.m. We were asked to come inside a house and take a rest, while a jeep would come to take us to the village. We walked into a room lit by candles.'

Suddenly, four men with guns appeared. 'Rohit told us we had been taken hostage by the *mujahideen*, and would be held till the release of eleven of their men who were in prison.' Paul and Chris's hands were tied, then they were led into a room where another foreign man was chained up. They were told his name was Rhys, and that he was also British. 'We were chained too, at the ankles. Rohit left, allowing us to speak to Rhys for ten minutes.' When Rohit returned, he started preaching at them. 'He said, "The British cabinet is run by Jews, and so is America." He hated Jews more than anything.' The next day, Rohit promised them they would be freed in a month. 'He said his group was also responsible for the kidnappings of David Mackie and Kim Housego in Kashmir.' They wanted their leaders back: Masood Azhar, the Afghani, Langrial and others.

A few days later, a fourth tourist had been captured: an American, Bela Nuss. All of them had been lined up against a wall and photographed, flanked by Kalashnikov-wielding kidnappers. Julie thought of the shots of Don, Keith, Paul, Dirk and Hans Christian that had recently been published. Letters were written to the British High Commission, the US Embassy and the BBC, the group calling itself 'al Hadid'. The Indian government was given seventy-two hours to release the prisoners or face 'dire consequences', a chilling phrase that Julie was well acquainted with.

Had they escaped like John Childs, Julie asked, feeling overwhelmed by this sudden rush of new information. No, Rideout replied, they had been rescued, and it had been by pure chance. On 31 October one of the kidnappers' hideouts, where the American Bela Nuss was being held, had been discovered by a local police patrol investigating an unconnected robbery at the farmhouse next door. Nuss was able to tell the police the location of a second house, where the others were found the following day. All the kidnappers were caught, including Rohit Sharma, who confessed under interrogation that his real name was Omar Sheikh, and that he was the son of a Pakistani immigrant to Britain. Sheikh really had grown up in Wanstead and been educated at the LSE, but during his studies he became involved in fund-raising for Bosnian Muslims, and in August 1993 he had met a preacher he named as Masood Azhar, who recruited him for the Holy Warriors, sending him to Camp Yawar in Afghanistan for military training. Masood had spotted Sheikh's potential. Amiable as well as audibly and visibly Western, he was the perfect lure.

When Julie put the phone down, she felt sick with worry. All four women understood the implications of Rideout's story. Not only had there been another recent kidnapping that no one had informed them about, there appeared to be so many similarities between the three incidents that it seemed the same group was behind all of them. Almost worse was the revelation that a British university student of Pakistani origin was connected to them, and that he had been recruited in London. Somehow this made the group behind the abductions seem more sinister and tangible, able to reach from alien Pakistan, via Afghanistan and Kashmir, to England. Julie went to bed that night terrified. Had they also been stalked in New Delhi, picked out at their hotel or on the bus? Was there a British connection to the abduction of Keith and Paul? How far did the reach of this group extend, given that it had recruited in the UK? What about their parents – could they also become targets? Whichever way the pieces were arranged, the prognosis looked grim and nowhere seemed safe.

Julie rang her mother Anita, and 'just cried and cried'. The *Evening Gazette* ran a front-page headline: 'I'll Stay Until Keith is Freed'. The women called their embassies to point out the similarities between the kidnappings, and to demand an explanation for why they had not been told about them. They were advised not to draw too many conclusions, since there was no proof that the same gang was involved in all three abductions. This confused Jane, Julie, Cath and Anne, who wanted to believe it, but were unaware that the diplomatic liaison officers were repeating what they had been told by the Indian Ministry of Home Affairs. 'Right from the beginning the strings were being pulled from New Delhi,' said Altaf Ahmed. 'Those of us dealing with the hostage-taking on the ground in Srinagar were not in control.'

* * *

All four of the women knew that 14 July, the day the deadline expired, would be the hardest of all, one long countdown to midnight. Jane tried to stop the others clock-watching. They should write letters to their loved ones, she suggested, addressing them to post offices near to where they might be being held. Since the second night, she had been preparing packages for Don – a few little luxuries: soap, a toothbrush and a book. A sympathiser in the postal service or in a village somewhere might try to get things to the hostages, she reasoned.

At three o'clock that afternoon, just nine hours until the deadline expired, the Press Enclave in Srinagar received a call about another photo drop. Later, the journalists crowded around the photograph: five solemn-faced trekkers squatted before a spectacular mountain backdrop, a crest of sharp peaks that someone speculated looked like Sheshnag. Behind the captives stood eight militants, their faces partially obscured by shawls, their guns raised. The message was clear: the hostage party had moved into the heights, which placed them at least forty or fifty miles north-east of Pahalgam, a hard five- or six-day trek from the nearest town. Yusuf Jameel had an idea: maybe they were heading for the Warwan, a remote valley parallel to the Lidder Valley that was so difficult to reach that most trekking guides in Pahalgam never went there. He had heard rumours that militants were using the Warwan Valley as a back door into Anantnag town, in south Kashmir. He had another reason to think of the inhospitable Warwan. Kim Housego and David Mackie had almost certainly been held in the remote valley, judging by the detailed description of their route they had given after their release. And his experience of the past six years told him that once militant outfits had a route or an arms cache or a safe house that they trusted, they would use it over and over again.

Yusuf and his friend Mushtaq Ali scanned the hostages' faces in this latest photograph. Keith, on the left, still wearing Julie's purple bomber jacket, had a resigned expression. Next to him was Dirk, now wearing a borrowed trekking jacket to ward off the falling temperatures. In the middle was Hans Christian, still in his white-and-purple batik shirt, and beside him crouched Paul, hugging one knee, his hands pushed into his sleeves to protect them from the chilly air. To the far right sat Don in his fleecy blue climbing hat and Gore-Tex trousers, a gun muzzle grazing his chin, quietly self-contained. When she saw the picture in the newspapers the next day, Jane noticed straight away that he was no longer wearing his black-and-yellow Casio altimeter. Small things could sting you. 'They must have stolen it from him,' she thought, and worried about what else they might have taken.

Yusuf and Mushtaq turned their attention to the kidnappers. Most of them had scarves wrapped around their faces to disguise their identities, but Yusuf was certain, judging by their sizes and shapes, that Sikander was not among them. It was possible to match some of the figures who had appeared in the earlier two photographs. The face of one militant of middling height which had been scratched out in the first pictures was now partially visible in the latest one. He was easily identifiable because of the distinctive white-and-red-striped band he wore around his waist like a belt, over fawn-coloured *kurta* pyjamas and a military-style coat. Another long-haired militant in a black *kurta*, a bayonet fixed to the end of his Kalashnikov, whose profile had been just about distinguishable in the first set of shots, was now standing front-on, making his height and build easy to judge. They were making mistakes, Yusuf thought, if anyone with a sharp eye among the authorities was bothering to look.

But his overriding feeling on seeing this new picture was how young the kidnappers looked. They reminded him of the thousands of teenage Pakistanis who volunteered to fight in Kashmir, only to be mown down shortly after they crossed into Indian territory, even as the Pakistani army laid down covering fire. These kids, lured into a fight unprepared, had an estimated life expectancy of less than twelve weeks.

Some of the al Faran team did not look as if they were cut out for tough weeks up in the mountains. Only the one at the centre of the picture stood out. Taller, paler-skinned, more self-assured than the others, he had a grey scarf wrapped over the lower part of his face, and was raising his Kalashnikov to the sky: a real man of war. Maybe he was an Uzbek or a Chechen. A growing number of them had been heading for Kashmir since the end of the Soviet–Afghan conflict. The kidnappers would need veterans like him if they were going to see this one through.

Over in Church Lane, a phone rang in General Saklani's office. It was the Security Advisor's public line, a number that was often printed in Kashmiri newspapers. Altaf Ahmed picked it up and heard a curt, accented male voice demanding to speak to Saklani, and no one else. Altaf motioned to his boss, who was sitting at his vast glass-topped desk.

The General grabbed the handset. At first there was no sound but heavy breathing. Then came a question: had India agreed to the demands? It was someone purporting to be from al Faran. Saklani said nothing. The voice at the other end of the line reminded him that in only a few hours the deadline would run out, and told him they would be forced to start killing the hostages unless the prisoners were freed. Saklani closed his eyes. 'Let's slow things down,' he said. He was an old hand at prevarication. 'Thank you for thinking of me, and for calling. But you've contacted a tiddler. I'm too far down the food chain. I'll need to speak to the Governor, and he'll have to call New Delhi, and from New Delhi a view will be taken. And then New Delhi will call us, and we'll pass it up the line. You must call back in two hours. I'll put my best man on this. Call back on this number. One hundred and twenty minutes.' He had them, he thought. Al Faran wanted to negotiate, and that meant they didn't intend to kill anyone – yet.

Saklani shouted at Ahmed, 'Get Tikoo!' He was referring to the head of Crime Branch. This *was* a job for the Kashmiri police.

Midnight in India was 8.30 p.m. in Norway. The deadline was at hand. Hans Christian Ostrø's close-knit family had gathered at a private address in Oslo. His mother had come up from Tønsberg, his sister Anette had flown in from Sweden, his maternal grandfather Ole Hesby had been brought over by car, and his grandmother had been collected from the hospital. All of them were now sitting with Hans Christian's estranged father, Hans Gustav, around a phone, the number of which had been given to the Norwegian Ministry of Foreign Affairs and the Norwegian Ambassador in New Delhi. 'Nothing. There was nothing,' recalled Anette. 'I was staring at it, willing it to ring. But no news came. We decided to stay up through the night, because we were certain Hans Christian would be awake too. Awake and, knowing him, plotting.'

TEN

Tikoo on the Line

Rajinder Tikoo, the Inspector General of Crime Branch, known in Kashmir as the 'IG Crime', was a fleshy man with a quiff of sleek brown hair. Classically educated, Tikoo was as at ease among the Elizabethans as in the abstract universe of pure maths, but he was also capable of the rough stuff, and was regarded within the force as a pro interrogator. Tikoo was a subtle thug and an elitist democrat, a remorseful tyrant and a scientific plod. Among his staff there were committed loyalists who would do anything for him. But he also had his enemies.

Curious Tikoo, who regarded himself as something of a Renaissance man, had two favourite hangouts, both of them on Maulana Azad Road, a main thoroughfare that cuts across Srinagar city. The first, his official place of work, was in the west, a pipe-tobacco-scented office in Srinagar's Crime Branch headquarters, overlooking Jehangir Chowk, one of the city's most choked traffic intersections, in the shadow of the Budshah Bridge flyover that crosses the Jhelum River. Like much of the infrastructure available to the Jammu and Kashmir Police, this low-lying, cream-coloured brick structure topped by a ruby-red tin roof dated to the days before Partition in 1947, and had barely changed since then. The phones were erratic, the electricity intermittent and many of the windows were broken (making the building miserably cold in winter, when most of the authorities decamped to milder Jammu). Every inch of space was crammed with files, their pastel-coloured cardboard covers and loose sheaves of paper bound together with leather straps and string.

Tikoo's office opened directly onto a wooden veranda that ran the length of the building's frontage, giving its inhabitants a bird's eye view over the guard posts, reinforced walls and nests of coiled barbed wire, designed to keep out militants, mortars, mobs or anyone else with a grudge. Although caretakers did their best to keep Crime Branch spruced up, arranging straggly hibiscus plants in blood-red pots, Tikoo preferred the view from his other regular haunt, the club-house of the Kashmir Golf Club, which lay at the other end of Maulana Azad Road, in the eastern part of the city. Most weekends, IG Tikoo could be found there, or out on the fairways that were surrounded on three sides by a canal fed from the Jhelum River and nearby Dal Lake.

That was where Altaf Ahmed found Tikoo after his boss dispatched him to track down the IG Crime a few hours before the kidnappers' deadline expired. 'The Security Advisor has an urgent message for you,' Altaf said cryptically. 'It's a sensitive job.' He had to go to Saklani's office in the Church Lane zone immediately. Tikoo felt put out. He and Saklani were well-acquainted, but they were not friends. In fact, Tikoo suspected that the Security Advisor had no friends. In the IG's mind, the Security Advisor was simply a piece of New Delhi-engineered artillery, a man enslaved to the chain of command, some-one who spoke army-ese, a cocktail of Dickensian English and military acronyms that characterised a life spent in itchy puttees, while the IG Crime loved trashy detective fiction, his pipe, his whisky and his golf magazines.

Luckily, as far as Tikoo was concerned, up until now their worlds had remained largely separate, the IG getting on with the gritty busi-ness of running down Kashmiri militants and criminals, while Saklani counselled the Governor from the tranquillity of the Church Lane zone. 'What the hell does Saklani want with me now?' Tikoo thought.

He called his driver. A white Ambassador swept up to the front porch of the clubhouse and three armed bodyguards in crisp uniforms, cradling semi-automatics, sprang out and saluted. Tikoo slid onto the back seat, lined with white terry-towelling to soak up the summer humidity. Inside, the car smelled of gun oil and naphthalene.

There was another problem with Saklani, Tikoo said to himself as his driver carved up the traffic, forced by a cumbersome one-way system to make thirty minutes of a ten-minute journey. Like most Kashmiris, Tikoo regarded the Security Advisor as the public face of the notorious 'Governor's Rule', the system that had upended local democracy back in 1990, replacing the authority of the elected State Assembly with the say-so of one New Delhi-appointed apparatchik, the implication being that Kashmiris could not rule themselves. Coming from a family of Pandits, the ancient sect of Hindu Brahmins that claimed thousands of years of uninterrupted connections to Kashmir, Tikoo resented this blanket assumption. With their aquiline noses and pale complexions, Kashmiris (native Pandits and Muslims alike) liked to say that their DNA was in part derived from Alexander the Great, who invaded the subcontinent in 327 BC, reaching as far as modern-day Taxila, now over the Line of Control in Pakistan. Kashmiris also believe that the snow-scented air and the aromatic herbs that infuse the local Himalayan waters might also have contributed to the difference between their looks, mores and manners and those of the Indian masses, baked and boiled on the plains to the south.

Since it had been invoked five years back, in Tikoo's opinion Governor's Rule had only served to stoke rebellion among Kashmiri nationalists, by making their case that New Delhi was acting like a colonial power, denying Kashmiris their right to self-determination and encouraging misrule by the New Delhi-*wallahs* sent up from the south, whose soldiers and security apparatus indiscriminately brutalised local people. As a result of Governor's Rule, many aspects of life in Kashmir were now dictated from afar. Government offices were filled with Indian appointees, and Kashmiris complained that they were treated like second-class citizens: unemployed, ignored, corralled, harassed, with anyone who protested imprisoned or silenced for good. 'A curious feature of Governor's Rule,' Tikoo used to lecture his Kashmiri friends as they strolled down the fairway, 'is that transparency is not available. Governor's Rule is a one-horse show. Governor is at the top.' He would drive his point home, selecting a club from his bag. 'A few advisors like Saklani are below. These people call the shots and issue statements left and right, without even verifying the facts, because they know they are not accountable to the people of Kashmir. Rule of law is bypassed. The courts are manipulated.' His playing companions would nod.

Under Governor's Rule, Tikoo maintained, it was the spies who really governed. 'A standard intelligence set-up will only give inputs, while the outputs come from the political set-up, who decide what to do with the hunches, whispers and surmises.' Tikoo liked to describe how in Western democracies intelligence agencies only advised, while the buck stopped with the politicians, who decided whether to act or not. 'But now with Governor's Rule, the intel boys feed and direct the powers in New Delhi, giving them the what-could-be-happening *and* suggesting the what-should-be-done. They are the research, the advisors and the implementers. What's the policy? It's the spies' policy.' This was not, Tikoo would say, harking back to his Jesuit education, what Plato had intended when he wrote *The Republic*, the thesis on the nature of justice and democracy that he had studied at school.

And now here was Saklani sending orders. Tikoo repeated Altaf's words: 'It's a sensitive job.' He already had a demanding job, having been made the IG Crime Branch just four months back, sporting the single star above a crossed sword and baton on his epaulettes. The new posting, which meant he was in charge of all major criminal cases, was one that he relished after twenty-five years' service. With his remit to investigate serious crimes – murderous, mercantile, political, religious and secular, as well as wrongdoings that crossed borders – he did not need any more duties, unless he was offered the position of Director General of Police, which he hoped to become some day – but that was not in the gift of Saklani.

Waved through the security cordon at the top of Church Lane, Tikoo's Ambassador came to a halt in the gravel outside Saklani's office-cum-residence, where the Security Advisor was waiting for him on the steps. 'We only have two hours,' Saklani said, looking anxious. He immediately turned to walk into the building, beckoning Tikoo to follow. To Tikoo, Saklani seemed to be stringing out the orders without explaining the context, like Sadashiv Amrapurkar hamming it up as Commissioner What-Not in *Mohra*, the Bollywood smash from the year before. 'The phone upstairs will ring,' said Saklani. 'My security officer will pick up the receiver and pass it to me. He is not to be allowed to talk to the caller. Understand? I will introduce you. And then you take over.' Tikoo did not understand. As they mounted the wooden stairs to the first floor, Saklani finally spat it out: 'Al Faran. They have made contact and want to negotiate. You will be our point man with them. Find out what they want. Get to the bottom of this nasty business.'

Tikoo felt trapped, and wondered how to react to the order that would involve him conducting telephone negotiations with the outfit that had kidnapped the Western trekkers. As IG Crime Branch he had followed events closely over the past ten days, and had dispatched his best team up to Pahalgam to have a sniff around, sidestepping the Deputy Superintendent of Bijbehara, Kifayat Haider (an officer he believed was too self-regarding), on whose patch the crimes had been committed.

Now Tikoo was being thrust into the hot seat, just a few hours before the midnight deadline set by al Faran. He feared that he was being set up as the fall guy, given little time to do the job properly, but taking the blame if the whole thing went belly up. 'For God's sake,' he started to say, forgetting where he was, 'why don't you get the Int. Chief to do it?' he said, referring to Gopal Sharma. The twilight world was Sharma's speciality, and he was better placed to understand the nuances thrown up by any dialogue with al Faran (he was also somebody Tikoo would not mind throwing to the wolves). 'The Int. Chief is tied up right now,' responded Saklani, tightly. 'You are the right man, that is to say the *best* man.' He paused before delivering the *coup de grâce*. 'The hostage-taking is a crime, a crime of the tallest order. As Inspector General of Crime Branch it is your duty to take the lead.' For a minute the two men stared at each other. Then Tikoo backed down. 'He was my senior. I had no choice.'

* * *

One hour to go. Tikoo, feeling 'more nervous than I had been in years', wondered what he would say to the kidnappers. He had been in the force since 1970, and now felt as he did back then when he first graduated into the elite Indian Police Service with three all-important letters following his honorific, rank and name: Shri ASP Rajinder Tikoo, IPS.

Thirty-five minutes to go. Saklani was still talking on the phone with some other army-*wallah*. Was there actually going to be a briefing, Tikoo wondered. 'Time was ticking, and I was worried that no one had told me what the government line was. What were we willing to offer? How were we to respond if the kidnappers said they were already killing hostages?' He was not a trained hostage negotiator, although over the years he had had some experience of dealing with kidnappers. But then, he didn't believe in over-preparation. He was an instinctive detective who vested much in hunches, and whose contribution to the force had been as a moderniser and galvaniser, qualities he now tried to tell himself had directly led to his being here, waiting for Saklani to get off the phone.

Twenty minutes to go. Why was he here? To Tikoo this assignment looked like every other job he'd ever been given by New Delhi: 'a bear trap'. He suspected that Saklani might be distancing himself from the messy front end, with all its potential hazards and pitfalls, letting a Kashmiri take the fall. Although, he thought, it was something that a Kashmiri should even be in on such a high-level operation. When the militancy had taken hold in 1989, the Kashmiri police force had been shattered by it. Ramshackle, underfunded and poorly armed, fighting with Second World War carbines and First World War strategies, it had initially been overwhelmed by the tens of thousands of highly motivated Pakistani and Kashmiri fighters flooding into the region, armed with Pakistani semi-automatics and American RDX explosive. Kashmiri police officers and constables were required to crack down on a local nationalist movement that in many instances was led by neighbours and former schoolfriends. Many policemen with deep roots in the community found their loyalties painfully divided, and some defected to the militants. Without proper training, or protection, and labouring beneath a weak leadership, those who elected to fight for the state sometimes responded to the insurgency with a terrible malice and ill-discipline.

Tikoo had been in the police control room on 20 January 1990, when the security forces shot up demonstrators near the Gawakadal Bridge in Srinagar, and he remembered watching, with a lump in his throat, as scores of corpses on stretchers were brought inside. Later many officers had cut out a passage from an Indian commentator, Balraj Puri, that was stuck on the office wall. 'It was no longer a fight between the militants and the security forces,' Puri had warned, 'but a total insurgency of the entire population.'

Rather than bolster the flailing Kashmiri police force, New Delhi had shipped in several hundred thousand outsiders from the CRPF, dark-skinned Indian paramilitaries with no affinity for the valley who, Tikoo thought, proved even more indiscriminate in their use of violence. By the last days of January 1990, Tikoo had counted at least 130 unarmed demonstrators shot dead, with the Indian paramilitaries shooting the wounded too. Srinagar's Bone and Joint Hospital was dubbed the Hospital for Bullet and Bomb Blast Injuries. 'That was when the law enforcers had begun fighting each other,' he said, recalling how hundreds of local cops had trained their guns on the CRPF. Senior police chiefs referred to it as 'the Mutiny', while others more kindly called it 'the Strike'. Either way, over a tense few days the Kashmiri police had their guns taken away, and the incoming Governor, Jagmohan Malhotra, publicly derided Kashmir as 'the valley of Scorpions'.

Ten minutes to go. How they had all hated that label. How demoralised the Kashmiri-born upper echelons of the force had become. For a clever patriot who was also a Kashmiri, watching New Delhi appointees leapfrog the local officer class had been too much for Tikoo to stomach. Bullying figures, with no local knowledge, they had thundered around the state throwing up dust, spilling blood and talking loudly in Hindi to people who didn't understand the language. Tikoo and his golf buddies took to calling these New Delhi-planted police and intelligence officers 'the East India Company', like the English merchants who set out to establish a monopoly over trade in the Far East in the early seventeenth century. 'They knew about as much about the Kashmir imbroglio as I did about my wife's recipe for *tandoori* fish made from singara netted in the Baghilar Dam,' said Tikoo. In return, the outsiders despised the Kashmiri police cadre too, suspecting them of collaborating with Kashmir's uprising. They dubbed Tikoo and his local colleagues 'the Pakistanis'.

Any misfortunes that beset the East India Company were celebrated by the Pakistanis as proof of New Delhi's failings. Tikoo cited one much-derided episode concerning a planned celebration for the centenary of India's elite Intelligence Bureau (IB), which oversaw domestic spying across the subcontinent. In Kashmir, it was decided that the public would be invited to a party and a lecture. IB agents and their helpers were pressed into fly-posting announcements across the valley, inadvertently identifying themselves and their bases along the way. Thankful for this unexpected windfall, the militants were able to pick off a string of IB spies and their proxies in quick succession. 'When the killing stopped there were thirty-nine dead, including four leading agents,' Tikoo recalled. The IB's Kashmir intelligence network would take years to recover.

'The Pakistanis' had also found it hard not to celebrate in January 1992, when the police chief of Kashmir, a brusque Indian called Jitendra Saxena, narrowly survived being blown up in his own office by his Kashmiri stenographer.

Five minutes to go. Finally, in 1993, there had been a sea change as a result of a potentially calamitous event: the army's ill-advised siege of the lakeside mosque at Hazratbal. It had started disastrously in October that year, when the siege had set in and Indian security forces had slain scores of unarmed demonstrators elsewhere in the valley who were protesting against the operation. The Kashmiri police backed a controversial strategy to offer everyone inside the mosque an amnesty, on condition that they agreed to being interrogated by local officers. This plan, which led to the peaceful defusing of the crisis, and the saving of the mosque, made everyone believe a little more in the judgement of the constabulary. Rajinder Tikoo, who by then was a senior officer, claimed to have had a personal hand in the matter, and used the momentum it provided to propose something more radical and permanent. Instead of relying on the heavy-handed CRPF, he suggested the police should raise a roving mobile unit of sharpshooters, made up of Kashmiri officers. They could be deployed to crack sieges and counter gunfights, thus placing Kashmiris, for the first time, at the forefront of counter-insurgency operations. He even suggested a name: the Special Task Force (STF).

Although the East India Company had privately scoffed, Security Advisor Saklani and the Governor had liked the idea, since Indian security forces were already overcommitted in the region, and pitting Kashmiri against Kashmiri was always preferable to losing Indian men. Saklani was heard to say that the plan demonstrated Tikoo's ingenuity, and by the time he was promoted to IG Kashmir Zone in February 1994, the STF was a reality. Selecting as its leader a respected and gruff Kashmiri Muslim police officer, Superintendent Farooq Khan, who had worked his way up through the ranks and was known as a straight dealer, Tikoo pitched the STF to his men: anyone who joined could keep the weapons or communication equipment they seized from the enemy. 'It was an incentive that worked,' Tikoo reflected. 'However, the STF became a *Dirty Dozen* kind of a thing, and we attracted all the encounter specialists, the gang bangers and violent guys.'

By the time Tikoo had become IG Crime Branch in February 1995, the STF was well on the way to becoming a mobile killing force. Two hundred men had now been signed up, and the sight of one of its white Gypsy jeeps thundering into a village was enough to terrify residents. The police's sledgehammer was also proving difficult to control, with the STF facing mounting allegations that it was settling scores and syphoning off booty wherever it roamed, its officers associated with multiple claims of rape and murder. In remote areas where Indian Army camps and STF bases often sat side by side, it was also forming unofficial allegiances with the army that worried the regular police force. But the conception and execution of the STF idea had brought Tikoo recognition as an innovator, and as a bridge between the Pakistanis and the East India Company. Were these the qualities that had got him to the negotiating table with al Faran, he wondered. Or was he being punished?

Then the phone rang. It was midnight on 15 July.

Security officer Altaf Ahmed passed the handset to his boss, as had been planned. 'I have my IG Crime here,' Saklani told the caller. 'Why don't you talk to him? He is one of the most experienced in this field.' He passed the handset to Tikoo, mouthing: 'Arrange the next call in your own lodgings, and not in my office.' Putting the phone to his ear, Tikoo heard the familiar hiss and whine that told him this was a local call. He and the kidnappers' intermediary were probably sitting in Srinagar within a mile of each other.

The room was empty, barring Tikoo. There was nothing but a yawning silence on the other end of the line. 'These things were very ticklish, and hostage negotiation is not everyone's cup of tea,' says Tikoo. 'If you fail to engage immediately, you have destroyed the whole thing in the first twenty-four hours. My way of working was a little different. I didn't have a rulebook. But I was rather shaky at first, thinking, how will I descend to the terrorist level?'

'Hello, my friend,' he began tentatively, taking a note of everything said. 'What can I do for you?'

Earlier, he had had a brief conversation with Saklani. '*Sahib*, how should I do it? What do I do?' Saklani had replied, 'You're a good conversationalist. You go your own way, and try to drag it out as long as possible.' That was all, there would be no script, and no analyst to assist him. 'No markers, no "This is our considered policy. You stop at such and such. You offer this. You do this thing, yadda yadda yadda." So I made it up as I went along.'

At last a voice came over the line, spitting Urdu words like cherry pits.

'You release our people, otherwise we will kill … this thing … you know. Finish them. We will, each of them, kill … murder … them. Do you understand? We will be true to our word.'

Jotting down these words, Tikoo was annoyed. Nobody had spoken to him like this in a long time. He tried to slow things down, mindful as he did so of the imminent deadline. 'Look, my friend, these things are not done in such an abrupt manner. We are not selling vegetables. I am not asking you the price of potatoes. You go slow. What do you want?'

He imagined the caller concealed somewhere, perhaps above an embroidery shop in the maze of Khanyar, a pro-militant quarter of the old city, every fibre in his adversary's body tensing as he spoke to the enemy. 'This is the first base: we're talking,' Tikoo said to himself, before he was brought back to reality.

'Release our people. It's simple. Don't treat us like we are fools. The consequences will be horrible. Don't make us show you. We are not afraid to die.'

Tikoo had to find a way to extend the deadline. 'Who are your people?' he asked. There had been a list of names delivered as long ago as 5 July, but Tikoo decided to make the man spell it out. 'There are hundreds of *people* in the jails. You tell me. Which "*our people*"? There are hundreds of thousands of *our people.*'

'*A humdilallah* [by the grace of God], we have given you the list.' The man was not ready to play games.

Tikoo tried another tack. 'You are ringing me. You made this call. I am now authorised to talk to you, so can you *please* tell me, for God's sake, how do we start? OK: "these people". Who is the first? Who is the second? Who is the last? Which category? How did you choose them? Do you get me? I am trying to sort this out. I don't want you to have to kill. Look, this conversation is now fifteen minutes old. I am sure you would like to break off and call me tomorrow. You call me at another number, and I will try to get permission to help you.' He gave the caller his home telephone number. 'Call me later, at 3 p.m. And at my home. You give me an order for who we release, etc. We can end this. We can sort this out. You and me.'

There was a long pause. 'By the grace of God, good night.'

He had done it. Had he done it? The intermediary had not said no, so Tikoo thought he had just got himself another twenty-four hours.

'Good night,' Tikoo said, noticing how sweaty his hands were, and folding up his notes. Suddenly he was back in the plain surroundings of Saklani's bedroom. He rushed downstairs, eager to share the news. But the Security Advisor was preoccupied with another matter, and simply showed Tikoo the door. 'Keep up the good work, old chap,' he said. The IG Crime slid back into his white Ambassador, and was driven to his bungalow on Transport Lane, just north of Maulana Azad Road, behind the Holy Family church.

Outside his front door was a little-used exercise bicycle. He was going to have to get back into shape, he recalled thinking. He was surprised at how that disembodied voice had got under his skin. It was the kind of voice he heard in jail cells and holding centres every day. But the telephone conversation, where neither of them could see the other, had felt perilous. Five lives hung by the copper telephone wire, and upon his canny knack of 'walking into a shitstorm' with no gloves, or even a hat.

The modest rooms he shared with his wife were all civil-service-issue brown beams and cream walls. A bathroom was off to the right, and his golf bag leaned against the wall in one corner. The dressing table in front of him faced a large window: 'We looked out onto a brick wall. Beyond that wall was another. And then the wide-open greens of the SP College playing fields. So I almost had a view.'

For Jane, Julie, Cath and Anne, who knew almost nothing about the back channel, other than that it had just commenced, every day felt as if it could be the last. They were relieved by the news from their liaison, Altaf Ahmed, that the deadline had been nudged back an inch, but to them it still felt as if a gigantic boulder stood before the mouth of a cave in which the captives were being held. Then on 15 July Saklani asked them to hold another press conference, 'so as to encourage al Faran to keep talking'. The women had only just recovered from the first one, but they reluctantly agreed, so long as Saklani could find a less formal and formidable venue this time.

Suzanne Goldenberg, a foreign correspondent for the *Guardian*, grabbed a seat in the garden of the state guesthouse. How exhausted they look, she wrote as they took their seats in a shady corner, and wondered if any of them would stand the pace. Cath set things off, reading from a script: 'We are glad to hear from al Faran that the five hostages are in good health. But we repeat that the five are merely innocent tourists and are not responsible for the situation.'

Goldenberg could not take her eyes off Julie, who rested her head on Jane's shoulder, tears brimming. Anne stared at a vanishing point beyond the garden, as if she was in another time and country. All of them looked bewildered. Were they aware of what Indian intelligence had advised the press, Goldenberg wondered. In her report, she would write: 'In the past two months, tension in the Kashmir Valley has risen after the destruction of Charar-e-Sharief.' She noted also that one spy had told her: 'After Mr Childs' escape the remaining hostages had been stripped and beaten ... they had since been forbidden to sleep in their clothes. Shoes, too, had been confiscated.' She had heard from local journalists that there were said to be sixteen men guarding the hostages, some of whom were believed to have been involved in the 1994 kidnappings of Kim Housego and David Mackie. The story doing the rounds this morning was that officers from IB and RAW, India's domestic and foreign intelligence agencies, were linking the two events, even as New Delhi and Western diplomats were not. The spies, Goldenberg wrote, gave the impression of knowing intimate details about the kidnap drama, such as the beatings supposedly administered to the remaining hostages after John Childs' escape. She suggested that this was either a crude attempt to blacken the Kashmiri militant outfits, or an indication that India had assets close to the captives. Perhaps they were readying themselves for a raid.

16 July, 3 p.m. Tikoo's phone rang. He grabbed the receiver, hoping that something from the women's press conference, which he had watched on the television news that morning, had reached the Pir Panjal mountains. 'Hello, my friend,' he began, reassured that the caller had rung at exactly the agreed time. 'What can I do for you?' He was off again, sight-reading and completely on his own, with no analysts standing in the wings, or psychologists listening in to offer another view. Only Tikoo, his new adversary, and a notepad – although he presumed that IB would be listening in from somewhere.

'We want our comrades freed. Do not mess us around. There are lives at stake. Have you consulted? When will our demands be met? We need answers now!'

There was a different tone to the voice. The intermediary sounded tired, irritable and out of breath, as if he had had to run to make the call in time.

Tikoo, hoping to extend the deadline again, tried a different tack. 'OK, my friend. I've been asking around. I've done the groundwork, but there are problems. Suppose I have to get someone from a prison in Rajouri, another from a prison in Jammu, someone else from Srinagar, or Agra, or Jaipur. How many people? What numbers? I need to know all the details, an order and a place to start. I told you this. A name to be the first. Have you brought the list and ordered it?'

In the silence that followed, Tikoo decided not to ask the man's identity, tempted as he was. Deep down, as a specialist in intelligence and a lover of minutiae, he wanted to trade names and do a verbal handshake. 'I must not put him off,' he thought. 'I wanted to say, "Are you the commander? The deputy commander?" So on and so forth.' But he was concerned that this might make the man feel threatened.

'You already have our demands,' the caller said sullenly. Tikoo wrote every word down. His notes would be stored on file in Crime Branch headquarters.

The IG pressed home his advantage. 'Well, my friend, what can I do? We must discuss some priorities with your demands. I told you to bring the list.'

'I will ring back,' said the caller grumpily. 'You have until tomorrow. We will not kill the tourists until then. We will talk, and if you have concrete news then we can make progress.'

Was this what Tikoo was supposed to be doing? He had no idea, as no one had told him. But he rang off elated at having extended the deadline once again. If the authorities were looking for a way out, planning a raid, gathering intelligence, then he was playing his part. During the next call, on 17 July, he would pry a little, he told himself, gently applying pressure. This was becoming a passive-aggressive interrogation, and he was rather good at those. 'We had our methods.

You may call it hot and cold, or good and bad. But I was pinpoint accurate at leveraging, and I knew how to squeeze a man.'

He was starting to feel that this crime could be solved. 'Earlier we had done the same with Mr P.K. Sinha, an esteemed MLA [Member of the Legislative Assembly] from Bihar state, who had got himself kidnapped in Kashmir while on holiday,' Tikoo recalled, referring to an incident that had taken place in May 1993. 'It began all blood and death, with "cut off his head". By Day Three the kidnappers told me: "Look, sir, we are in a bad shape. Make a raid and make it look like we put up a fight, and we will leave the MLA out in the field for you."' Tikoo had worked his magic, and the captors had reduced their demands to just two: 'We'll settle for some ammo and a couple of bulletproof jackets. Throw that in, and the useless politician is yours.' Tikoo had done it, without telling anyone: the Bihari had walked free. The kidnappers kept their dignity. No one was the wiser. He hoped he was doing it again.

ELEVEN

Winning the War, Call by Call

The price of being in the negotiator's chair was that IG Tikoo knew little about how the police criminal inquiry into the kidnappings was progressing. Since 14 July he had been relieved of his normal duties, and only caught glimpses of what his officers were up to if he bumped into a colleague on the golf course or in the clubhouse.

These days he gleaned most about the case from television. He learned from the morning news that John Childs had been flown out of Kashmir on 10 July. Five days after that he was back in the United States, sweeping up his two daughters at Bradley International Airport in Connecticut, the string on the money pouch he had kept around his neck throughout his ordeal visible inside his shirt in the television footage. Tikoo was astonished: 'Letting go of your main witness went against every rule in the book.' Childs too had been perplexed by the speed with which he was hustled out of India, and told his family as much.

Tikoo began to dwell on the other potential obstacles that might impede the progress of this inquiry. The longer things ran on, the more chance there was of 'a Kashmiri screw-up', as he called it, a situation where internal conflicts led to an external crisis. Such things were normally triggered by the proliferation of army, paramilitary, intelligence and policing outfits in the valley, one of the most heavily militarised areas in the world. Despite Saklani's Unified Command, which brought the heads of all of these security outfits together daily, the vicious competition between them continued, something that could potentially undermine the case.

From the start, Saklani had made it clear that the Indian Army was to be in charge of all efforts in the mountains to resolve the crisis. But the *yatra* pilgrimage was in full flow, with 150,000 Hindus heading for the Amarnath ice cave. Tikoo worried that protecting their security would distract the army from the plight of the five Westerners, forcing it to slow down or even stop its investigation until the pilgrimage was completed in early August, losing valuable weeks. The army, he believed, also had a problem with its temperament and methods. Although it was adept at eliminating militants and disrupting their networks, it was less comfortable with operations that demanded subtlety, or at taking a back seat while a peaceful solution was negotiated.

If the army was headstrong and unwilling to play second fiddle, India's primary domestic and foreign intelligence agencies, IB and RAW, were slippery and opaque. Their intelligence was largely withheld from the local police, shared mostly in high government circles in Srinagar and New Delhi, and revealed only when it served the spooks' (and India's) agenda, which at the moment was to highlight Pakistan's meddling in the valley and its involvement in acts of terrorism. Tikoo had watched as IB and RAW agents jumped on the kidnappings, making sure they became global news, with Pakistan portrayed as a state sponsor of terrorism. Tikoo went back to his paradigm about Governor's Rule, in which intelligence both fed government with secrets and devised policy based on those secrets, making him worry that agents would feel they had little to gain by wrapping the case up quickly.

Was he being too cynical? He hoped so. He was wishing he had never begun this exercise, which was making him spiral into depression. He had to finish what he had started, and he mulled over how beneath the carnivorous army and the foot-dragging spies were the paramilitaries of the Indian CRPF and the BSF, both of which were bull-headed and also distracted by the *yatra* effort. These men's primary skills involved raw firepower and indiscriminate brutal encounters, regardless of collateral damage (or evidence of guilt), which could lead to the five Westerners becoming victims of an ill-thought-out mountain assault. At the very bottom of the pile was the Kashmiri police, which, unable to rely on the help of any of the groups above it, would have to create its own streams of intelligence, battering down doors and knocking heads together, playing to its strength, that of being the only truly grassroots agency that understood how Kashmiris thought and acted.

Meanwhile, as the various agencies 'stovepiped' information, bickering and sniping, the kidnappers' clock continued to tick. And it would fall to Tikoo to explain to al Faran's frontman on the line, whoever he was, why no decision on its demands was forthcoming. For this reason, Tikoo had decided to keep a transcript of all their conversations. He had a feeling that later on, he might need to defend himself.

Finally, he contemplated the potential repercussions of his necessary prevarication. Tikoo feared that it might lead to a slaughter in the mountains. He had been deliberating about the likelihood of a so-called 'show kill', the execution of one of the hostages early on in proceedings, an act calculated to demonstrate that al Faran had the guts to follow through, and would not tolerate being messed around. Death was a powerful tool, and many times Pakistan-backed militant groups had shown that they were willing to kill hostages, such as the shooting in cold blood of the Vice Chancellor of Kashmir University and his assistant in 1990 together with the general manager of Hindustan Machine Tools, and the execution of Major Bhupinder Singh in 1994. Both of those murders had involved the Kashmiri militant known as Sikander, who Tikoo strongly suspected was behind these latest kidnappings. 'I tried to put all these phantoms to one side,' he recalled. 'I had to keep my mind clear for the job at hand.' The next deadline was fast approaching, and he needed to reassure al Faran's intermediary that he remained open to all suggestions. Even if that was untrue.

If Tikoo was burdened by too much knowledge, it was very different for the wives and girlfriends of the hostages, still in the dark about these top-secret back channels, and oblivious to everything else that was going on behind the scenes. Even his role as government negotiator had been kept from them, as had the method of communication

The route to the Meadow, a photograph taken by Norwegian trekker Hans Christian Ostrø shortly before he was kidnapped on 4 July 1995.

(Left to right) Julie and Keith Mangan together with Catherine Moseley trek towards the Meadow in early July 1995. PHOTO BY PAUL WELLS.

(Left to right) Cath, Keith and Julie trek towards the Meadow. PHOTO BY PAUL WELLS.

Setting up camp en route to the Meadow, Keith and Julie standing by their tent in the foreground. PHOTO BY PAUL WELLS.

Hans Christian Ostrø being made up as his character Bima for his *kathakali* dance graduation show in Sreekrishnapuram, May 1995. Ostrø spent five months training to be a *kathakali* master in southern India before travelling to Kashmir in June 1995.

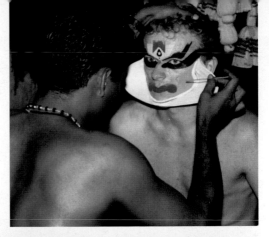

Hans Christian Ostrø on board *Montana* houseboat, Dal Lake, Srinagar, where he stayed shortly before he was kidnapped.

The Heevan Hotel in Pahalgam. Kashmiri police alleged that 'Sikander', al Faran's commander, was sheltered here, unbeknown to the hotel's owners.

The wives and girlfriends of the kidnapped men leaving the first press conference at the Welcome Hotel in Srinagar on 13 July 1995. (Left to right) Cath, Jane Schelly (wife of Don Hutchings), Julie, Anne Hennig (girlfriend of Dirk Hasert). An unidentified diplomatic liaison officer accompanies them.

Rajinder Tikoo, Inspector General of Crime Branch at the time of the kidnappings.

Members of the al Faran kidnap party.

One of the first hostage photographs taken by al Faran. It was shot outside the herders' hut from which American hostage John Childs had escaped in the early hours of 8 July 1995. The remaining three original hostages (left to right) Don, Keith and Paul are flanked by new hostages Dirk Hasert (left) and Hans Christian Ostrø (right), both seized on 8 July. The photograph was delivered to reporters in Srinagar on 12 July.

Security Advisor Lt. Gen. D. D. Saklani briefs police officials before they begin an aerial search for the five Western hostages on Tuesday, 18 July 1995. Saklani had found American John Childs in the same helicopter the week before.

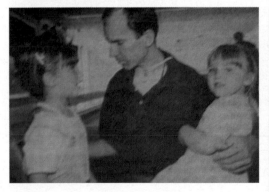

(Above) John Childs reunited with his daughters Cathy and Mary Childs at Bradley International Airport, Connecticut, on 15 July 1995. (Right) Childs shortly after his rescue. The skin on both his heels had worn away to the bone during his fifteen-hour trek to freedom through the mountains.

A picture of the hostages and their captors that was delivered to the Srinagar Press Enclave on 14 July 1995, shortly before the first deadline expired at midnight. Investigators concluded that the kidnap party was now moving up beyond the snowline in a north-easterly direction, possibly heading for the remote Warwan Valley.

Hostages photographed inside an unidentified herders' hut, probably in the Warwan Valley. (Left to right) Hans Christian Ostrø, Dirk Hasert, Paul Wells, Keith Mangan, Don Hutchings.

The Warwan Valley, where the hostages were held for several weeks.

Sukhnoi village, looking south, where the hostages were held for eleven weeks in a guesthouse on the edge of the village.

Indian Border Security Force soldiers question *gujjar* shepherds about the whereabouts of four hostages on Saturday 8 July 1995. A fifth and sixth hostage, Dirk Hasert, from Germany, and Hans Christian Ostrø, from Norway, were taken that day, as police would later discover.

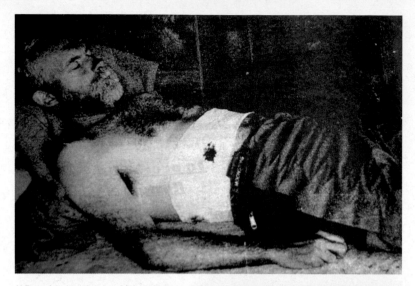

Al Faran falsely claimed on 21 July 1995 that two hostages had been injured following a botched Indian security force operation, and later issued photographs appearing to show an injured Don Hutchings (pictured here) and Keith Mangan.

Hans Christian Ostrø was beheaded in the early hours of 13 August 1995 by the leader of al Faran, Hamid al-Turki. His corpse was later taken to Anantnag police station in south Kashmir, where it was photographed.

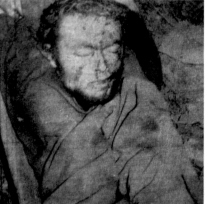

The hostages soon after they arrived in the Warwan Valley. In an attempt to identify their location, the FBI studied this and other pictures for evidence of plants that grow only in specific locations of the Himalayas.

A view from Mardan Top, a treacherous pass at the southern end of the Warwan Valley over which the remaining four hostages were marched in the second week of September 1995, across the Warwan and towards Inshan.

Another view from Mardan Top.

(Left to right) David Mackie and Kim Housego were seized in the same area by Pakistan-backed militants in June 1994 and held for seventeen days, with some of the hostage-takers involved going on to carry out the 1995 abductions.

Letter written by Hans Christian Ostrø to his family and the Norwegian Embassy in New Delhi shortly after his capture. It is unclear how this letter was smuggled out, but it eventually reached his mother Marit Hesby, who was staying at the Embassy.

Ostrø arranged for several batches of photographs, on which he had written cryptic clues as to the hostages' condition and location, to be smuggled out of the Warwan.

The contents of Ostrø's money belt, recovered from his tent at Zargibal and eventually returned to his family.

Press conference given by Jane Schelly and Julie Mangan, Srinagar, July 1995.

Photograph of Paul Wells thought to have been taken in the wooden guesthouse in Sukhnoi village, Warwan, where the hostages were kept for several weeks.

Photograph taken by al Faran in August 1995, after Ostrø's beheading, that served as a prelude to 'proof of life' conversations that followed. (Left to right) Keith Mangan, Don Hutchings, Dirk Hasert, Paul Wells.

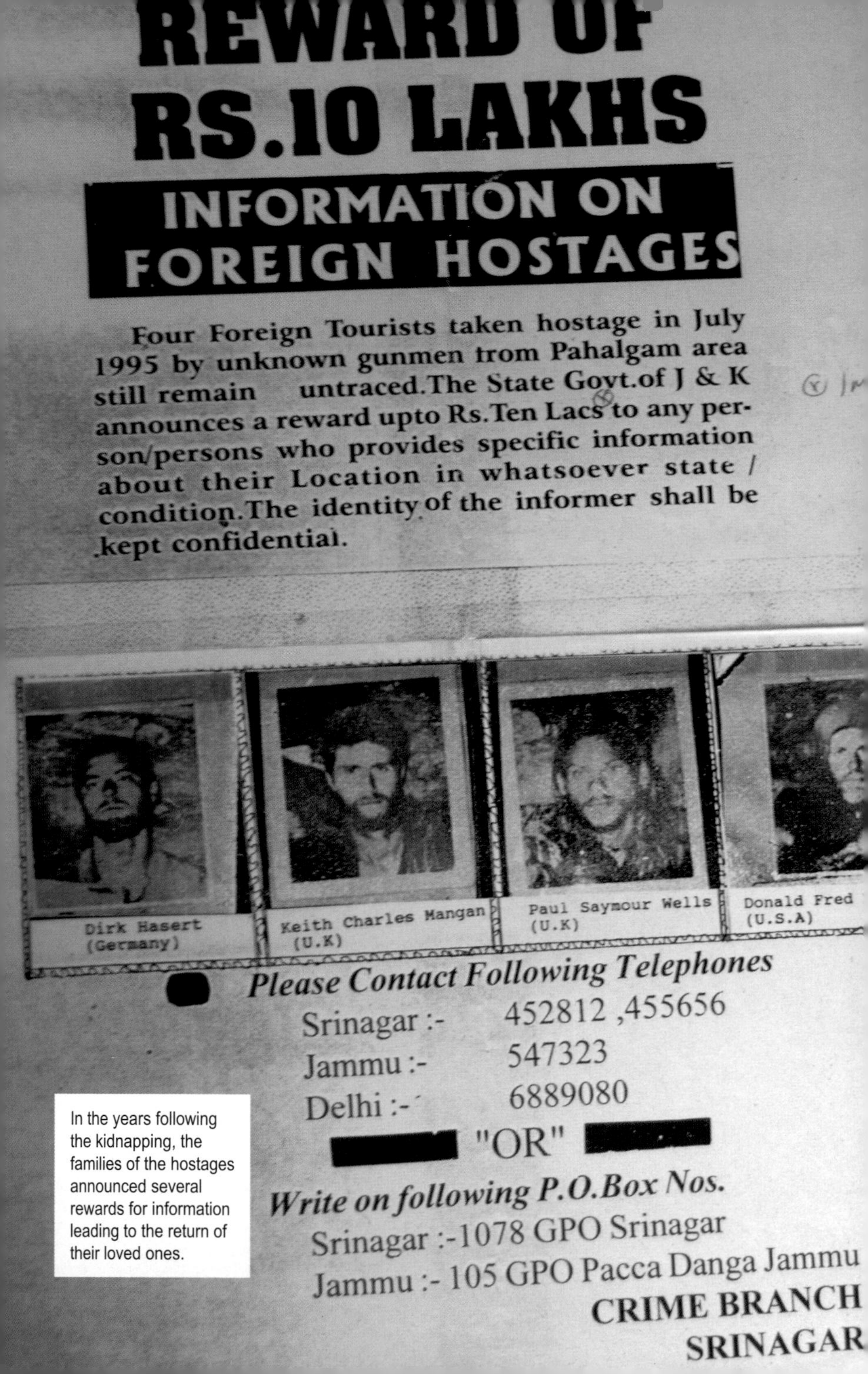

REWARD OF RS.10 LAKHS

INFORMATION ON FOREIGN HOSTAGES

Four Foreign Tourists taken hostage in July 1995 by unknown gunmen from Pahalgam area still remain untraced. The State Govt. of J & K announces a reward upto Rs. Ten Lacs to any person/persons who provides specific information about their Location in whatsoever state / condition. The identity of the informer shall be kept confidential.

| Dirk Hasert (Germany) | Keith Charles Mangan (U.K) | Paul Saymour Wells (U.K) | Donald Fred (U.S.A) |

Please Contact Following Telephones

Srinagar :- 452812 ,455656

Jammu :- 547323

Delhi :- 6889080

"OR"

Write on following P.O. Box Nos.

Srinagar :-1078 GPO Srinagar

Jammu :- 105 GPO Pacca Danga Jammu

CRIME BRANCH SRINAGAR

In the years following the kidnapping, the families of the hostages announced several rewards for information leading to the return of their loved ones.

WE ARE PROUD TO BE INDIANS. GET THEM BY THEIR BALLS HEARTS AND MINDS WILL FOLLOW.

Jehangir Khan, a commander of the pro-government renegades, semi-retired but still afforded bodyguards by the state, at one of his bases in Kadipora, Anantnag, in 2008.

Kashmiri women walk back from market in 2011, passing an Indian Central Reserve Police Force patrol.

The last confirmed photograph of the hostages. (Left to right) Paul Wells (squatting), Dirk Hasert, Keith Mangan and Don Hutchings. When it emerged in February 1996, the families were told by Indian investigators that it had been taken the previous month. Western investigators believed it was much older, and dated to September or October 1995. There was much discussion about the identity of a fifth figure, whose shoulder can be seen on the far left, and why he had been cut out of the photograph.

Identity card of Basir Ahmad Wagay, aka 'the Tiger', a field commander for the pro-government renegades whose territory spread from Lovloo to Mati Gawran, in Anantnag district.

IDENTITY CARD

1.   It is certified that Basir Ahmad Wagay S/O Ghulam Mohd Wagay R/O Desu Daksum (Kokernag), Dist – Anantnag (J & K), Belt No 38 is working with 36 RR Bn (GARH RIF), C/O 56 APO and is attached to Vailu Coy.

2.   Identification mark:- A mole on neck.

Date.........

No ....

Unit   : 36 RR (GARH RIF)

Date   : 05 Jun 2005   (Signature of issuing auth)

Renegade commander Azad Nabi, call-sign 'Alpha', whose real name was Ghulam Nabi Mir. One of the most powerful renegades, he led pro-government militias in the hills above Anantnag.

Naseer Mohammed Sodozey, a treasurer of Harkat ul-Ansar, captured by Indian security forces in April 1996 and allegedly forced to confess that the hostages had been killed by the Movement on 13 December 1995.

Omar Sheikh, from London, arrested in Pakistan in 2002 in connection with the kidnapping of Daniel Pearl.

Masood Azhar (right) in Pakistan in January 2000, shortly after he was released from an Indian jail, after Pakistani militants, including one of his brothers, hijacked an Indian Airlines jet, forcing it down in Kandahar, Afghanistan, and holding the passengers hostage. Having led the Movement, he now formed a new *jihadi* group – Jaish-e-Mohammed – accused of the kidnapping and murder of *Wall Street Journal* reporter Daniel Pearl in 2002.

and the investigations of the police and the intelligence agencies into al Faran. In the meantime the women clung together, buffeted by rumour, and hustled frenetically from place to place by obsequious diplomats and dissembling Indian officials, their anguish rising by the hour. The one finding it most difficult to cope, he had heard from Saklani's bagman Altaf Ahmed, was Julie Mangan, who over the last thirteen nights had frequently woken sweating and panicked, grateful to have escaped from another nightmare about Keith being shot, maimed, tortured or killed. Like Tikoo, all of them searched for news of John Childs, back home in Connecticut, but he was keeping a low profile, refusing all requests for television interviews, saying he was worried that too much talking would put the remaining hostages' lives at extra risk. Outwardly he seemed cold, as if all he cared about was getting his normal life back: his nine-to-five job at Ensign Bickford, his daily five-mile run around the school athletics track, and spending time with his daughters. But inwardly he was in turmoil. 'I could not forget a minute of my ordeal,' he said years later. 'Every single second of those four days in captivity was etched onto my memory forever, along with the faces of my comrades. I did not go a minute of the day without thinking of them, what they must be going through, how I had failed to go back and rescue them as I had promised myself. But what could I do? The answer was nothing.'

In Washington DC, Tikoo read in the papers, the US State Department was also, publicly at least, taking a back seat. He found this difficult to believe, given its previous determination to hustle John Childs out of Kashmir. 'Who's in charge on the ground in Kashmir?' State Department spokesman Nicholas Burns was asked at a press conference a few hours before the second deadline expired. 'The Indian government,' Burns replied. 'It most definitely is, and we are working with them.' Tikoo put the newspaper down and closed his eyes. 'Who's in charge?' he asked himself.

Fifty minutes before the latest deadline expired at midnight on 17 July, an envelope arrived at the Srinagar offices of the Associated Press. Given the sensitivity of the timing, it was passed straight to

General Saklani. IG Tikoo, who had not spoken to al Faran's intermediary since the previous day, jumped into his Ambassador. Arriving in the Church Lane zone, he found Saklani's Police Liaison Officer tightening the spools of an audio cassette, and took a seat in one of the many straight-backed chairs lined up before the Security Advisor's glass-topped desk. Tikoo could see that al Faran was adopting a tricky twin-track approach: when the secret telephonic negotiations looked as if they were faltering, it would present its case to the world at large on tape.

A dozen police, army and intelligence officials milled about, shaking hands and exchanging meaningless pleasantries before everyone was enveloped in cigarette smoke. When Western diplomats had described the situation as 'a war of nerves' several days back, Tikoo had scoffed. Now, as Saklani took his seat, Tikoo felt it in his gums. The Security Advisor nodded at Ahmed, who flicked a switch. As the brittle fuzz of the tape filled the room, Tikoo closed his eyes and felt the heat drain from his hands.

'I am Don Hutchings,' said a slow, deliberate American voice. It was the first time Tikoo had heard one of the hostages speak, and he was surprised how affected he was by it. 'We have walked many days and nights, crossing rivers and mountains, and I am tired.' Tikoo's mind wandered out of Saklani's office and up to Pahalgam, following the right fork in the road towards Chandanwari, where the track ran out and the mountains rose up. Amarnath, Sheshnag, Kolahoi … how far had the kidnappers dragged these poor men, he wondered.

'The *mujahideen* have been OK with me. Jane …' All those present were listening intently, wondering how this would play when the women heard it. 'Jane, I want to let you know I am OK. I do not know [if] today I will die or tomorrow I will die. I do not know what will happen. I appeal to the American government and the Indian government for help.'

That was not what IG Tikoo wanted Jane Schelly and the others to hear right now, but the tape would have to be shared with them. If he got the chance to see her beforehand, he would say that Don's speech sounded awkward, and had the ring of having been scripted. It was possible to find some reasons for hope in the American's words, Tikoo thought. Hutchings had sounded strong. He might have been exhausted by the pace of the forced trek, but he seemed calm, making the threat to the hostages' lives seem a little more distant. Tikoo had a more profound insight too: 'Just as we had put the families on show at the press conferences to try and elicit a change of heart from al Faran, the kidnappers were putting the hostages up to the world, reminding us what was at stake.' He closed his eyes again, listening to the hum of a break in the recording.

Another voice, also speaking English, but with a different accent: 'My name is Hans Christian Ostrø.'

Tikoo's first thought: Ostrø was one of two hostages who should not have been there. If the army and police had been doing their jobs properly, all backpackers would have been evacuated from the mountains as soon as the first kidnappings had been reported. After nine days in captivity, this was, incredibly, the first confirmation that al Faran was holding Ostrø. 'I am from Norway,' he said. 'I was taken a week ago and ever since then I've walked over many mountains, high mountains and pastures. I saw lots of nice nature. I appeal to the Norwegian and Indian governments to do anything they can to release us because we don't know when we will be killed. I appeal especially to the tourist office because everybody there told me that this place was safe. An officer there gave me his card and said I could call him if there was a problem. Well, I am calling now.'

That was Kashmir all over, the punch-drunk valley that misspoke the truth. Tikoo knew Nasser Ahmed Jan, the smooth-talking tourist police official to whom Ostrø was almost certainly referring. He had become an inveterate salesman, wishing the war away in a myriad of languages. Tikoo reflected that Kashmiris, desperate for a change in their fortunes, had become untrustworthy friends and guides.

He looked up to see that everyone in the room had bowed their heads, trying to extract meaning from every syllable. The messages, if a little stripped of emotion, were identical in structure, and succinctly got al Faran's perspective across. The hostages were, as yet, unharmed, but that could change at any time. How long did they have, Tikoo wondered.

He knew that in part the answer would be dictated by, of all things, the weather. In the mountain passes the summer still blazed, and the kidnap party could stay high and hidden for several weeks to come. But having worked in the Pir Panjal, he knew a thing or two about the impact on the body and mind of the first deep frost of the year.

Another reedy voice issued from the cassette player. 'We are very tired, but the *mujahideen* are treating us very well.' It was Paul Wells. 'But if the Indian government doesn't sort out this situation we will be killed. Catherine, I hope to see you soon.' Wells sounded desperate, and Tikoo grimaced in the knowledge that all of the women's hearts would be squeezed when the tape was shared with them.

Straight after Paul Wells came another British voice, this one stronger and more forceful. 'I'm from England,' Keith Mangan said defiantly. 'For the moment I'm a little poisoned in my stomach ...' The same clunky sentence construction, as if he was reading from a script.

Tikoo imagined the hostages sitting in a smoky *gujjar dhoka* rehearsing what the kidnappers wanted them to say, talking among themselves in rapid English about whether they would be able to slip in a few clues as to their location or their real condition. But there appeared to be none, only five disconnected voices that helped fill in some of the gaps in Tikoo's mental chart of their characters. It was a little game he had been playing in the small hours, constructing a matrix of the inside workings of the hut, creating hierarchies and possible relationships from what he had learned about the five hostages, information culled from press reports and what had filtered back to him from the Crime Branch interrogations of pony-*wallahs*, guides, hotel and houseboat owners, most of whom had by now been pulled in.

In Tikoo's mind, Don Hutchings was at the top, a calm man with profound resources. A climber and explorer, Hutchings had proven himself capable *in extremis*. He understood how debilitating fear could be, and acted as a bridge builder and a peacemaker. And Tikoo suspected, incorrectly, that as an American he would probably be the most altruistic, trying to ensure that his fellow hostages survived, possibly at his own peril. If he had been allowed to debrief John

Childs in detail, he would have known that Don had been the first to try to make a break for it. Tikoo tried to assess Hutchings' potential weaknesses, correctly judging that he might rely too heavily on the goodness of men and on 'doing the right thing'. He had, Tikoo thought, an inclination to act pastorally when it came to the others.

Tikoo rightly had Keith Mangan pegged as man of physical strength, but more canny and street smart than Hutchings. Mangan was mature, stoical and likeable, according to what his wife, family and friends had said in reports Tikoo had scanned in Transport Lane. He was a practical and resourceful character who was used to looking after himself, and stood a good chance of coming out of this intact.

In his imaginings, Tikoo got Paul Wells spot on. As the youngest hostage, in the middle of his list, he saw him as physically capable but emotionally immature, prone to anger and unpredictable actions, likely to be feeling isolated as the novelty of his capture wore off. Tikoo hoped one of the others, Keith Mangan probably, had taken him under their wing.

More isolated still, Tikoo estimated, was Dirk Hasert, the only one among them who did not speak English. The IG suspected that Hasert, just a year older than Paul Wells, was similar in outlook and maturity, reaching out to befriend the militants during the initial thrill of capture, but withdrawing as the likelihood of an early rescue faded with the passing days. The only captive who could strike up a meaningful conversation with Hasert was Hans Christian Ostrø, who spoke German. Tikoo hoped the Norwegian had drawn the young student from Erfurt into the group.

Tikoo had the Norwegian down as a wild card, a man who was capable of anything, and who according to the friends who had spoken to the Norwegian press, and the villagers up in Zargibal (many of whom had been brought in for questioning) was adept at physical posturing and psychological provocation. Tikoo was sure that Ostrø would repeatedly try to escape, and would certainly not stick to any scheme he disagreed with. On the emotional front he was said to be susceptible to rapid mood changes, from euphoria to depression. Tikoo feared for Ostrø especially.

The tape fizzed, and was ejected. There was a letter too, Saklani announced, and started to read it out. 'We made contact with the Indian government three days ago,' he began, looking at Tikoo. 'But the government does not seem to be prepared for any *purposeful* talks.' Tikoo frowned, knowing that he had not yet been able to establish any kind of meaningful relationship with al Faran's negotiator. '[The hostages] can be killed at any time after the expiry of the deadline. We will not extend the deadline again.'

Since the tape had been recorded, the deadline had expired, so this was zero hour, which meant the hostages' lives were under imminent threat. Tikoo had to get on top of his role as negotiator, and also to deal with a bombshell from Saklani, who in the last forty-eight hours had told him in the strictest confidence something the Indians had withheld from the women: there would be no prisoner releases. New Delhi had ruled it out. Tikoo's heart had sunk in the knowledge that he could never let al Faran suspect this. He had to string them along to keep the hostages alive, find something to occupy them, and conjure a solution that would be palatable to New Delhi.

The next telephone conversation was slated for 11.30 the following morning. As he bade General Saklani goodnight, IG Tikoo felt as if he was in a free-fall zone in the war of nerves. From here on in, anything could happen.

Back at home in Transport Lane, Tikoo's wife was waiting with his warmed-up dinner: some chicken and rice. He wasn't hungry, and sat at his dressing table contemplating his unused computer, a bulky grey box that dominated the room. He had always wanted one, and a couple of years back had bought this one second-hand in New Delhi. There had never seemed to be time to use it – until now.

Just as he was about to boot it up, thinking it would be a welcome distraction, since he had run out of Alistair MacLean novels, a worry surfaced, something that hit him so hard he kicked himself for not having thought of it before. Although it had not been discussed, he assumed the intelligence agencies were covertly monitoring al Faran, and probably attempting to trace the telephone number the negotiator was calling on. Suddenly distressed, Tikoo called for his driver. 'I went back to my people right away and to the Security Advisor. I said, "For God's sake, don't go for a raid." I told them, "Look, I know the tendency is to trace the caller's location and then ambush. That's what I would do in any normal circumstance. But that way you will *not* get the hostages freed. Possibly you might get this fellow, the messenger. More likely, as per normal, the messenger will escape, and then you'll kill the innocent householders. And if we are honest, you will probably slaughter the neighbours too, and that, with the greatest respect, is the most certain way to lose the case. Bang. End of story."'

He arrived back home after midnight, reassured that he had convinced General Saklani of the sensitivity of the situation, but still concerned that he was too remote from the decision-making process to be sure the message had got through to all those who needed to know. For a while he sat in the gloom, smoking his pipe, thinking about going to bed, until the phone rang.

He was not expecting anyone at this hour. 'Who is this, please?' he asked tentatively, willing the caller to go away.

'We have a question,' the caller said politely. It was al Faran once more. 'Are you drawing this out so as to track us down? What I mean is, is this line bugged?'

Tikoo ran his hands through his hair, smiling to himself: al Faran had had exactly the same thought as him. Great minds. If only this man knew what Tikoo had just been discussing with General Saklani. 'My friend, I give my solemn assurance that nobody will disturb you,' the IG said. 'As long as we are talking to each other, you are safe.'

Tikoo tried another tack, using this opportunity to broaden the relationship. 'How are the guests? Are you treating them well?' 'Guests' was a word that Tikoo knew had great significance to Pashtuns and Afghans, tribal peoples steeped in traditions of hospitality and respect.

He pondered the identity of his night-time caller. This man's education had been restricted to the prayer book, and he was definitely not from the valley. Those clipped 't's' and 'r's' – it was a familiar accent, but he could not quite identify it, and in his mind's eye he had raced up and down the Pakistani districts hugging the Line of Control searching for a place name. Then he had it. Mirpur. That was it. Most likely this man was from the Mirpur-Kotli belt, in the southern part of Pakistan-occupied Kashmir, or POK, as Indians referred to it, making it sound like catching a dose. The accent of Mirpur was as distinct as the area itself, a region that had become known as 'Little Britain'. Thousands had emigrated to England from there in the sixties, impoverished farmers who worked in the cotton and wool industry and returned as rich as kings. The intermediary was a Pakistani, and from Mirpur.

'What do they eat?' asked the al Faran man. Tikoo smiled as he wrote the words down. He realised how much the kidnappers must be struggling with this alien situation, faced with trying to keep these Westerners alive and comfortable. They were tribal men who had spent their lives on the battlefield in Afghanistan or eking out an existence along the Pakistan–Afghan border. They had only ever known a diet of rice, bread, *ghee*, the odd vegetable and occasionally a fatty lump of meat. And they had never met anyone who was different.

'Friend,' replied Tikoo, 'don't give them this *mirch* [chilli], you know.' In the tape recording Tikoo had listened to earlier that night, Keith Mangan had described having stomach problems. 'Not too much red chilli. They can't eat that. Give them, you know, meat and potatoes, but without spice.'

There was a pause as the intermediary took this in. Emboldened by his new paternal position, Tikoo filled the gap with an extemporised attempt to get a real conversation going: 'I've been reading.'

'Yes?' The caller seemed unnerved by the change in tone.

'Tell me, where has it been provided in the Koran that you are killing innocent bystanders?' This was a risky tactic Tikoo had wanted to try from the start, confronting the intermediary with the fact that the Koran outlawed the killing of innocents. He had regarded it as essential to study the Koran, as had many of his ancestors, who travelled widely in predominantly Muslim lands and never stopped educating themselves. One great-great-grandfather, Diwan Nandram Tikoo, had been Prime Minister of Afghanistan at the time of the Second

Anglo–Afghan War, and before Partition Tikoo's father had been a successful tycoon in the real-estate business in Bombay, to which he had moved from Kashmir. Despite his deep sense of his Kashmiri identity, Rajinder Tikoo had spent much of his childhood in Bombay, being schooled at St Xavier's, a strict Jesuit academy where he had stood out as a gifted pupil with a voracious appetite for learning. As an adult, back in the valley, he had come to despise those who manipulated the ill-educated, like the so-called religious men who used Koranic justifications for bloodshed.

There was no answer from the caller.

'And these people are Christians. Do you know? They are *Ahl al-Kitāb*,' Tikoo pressed on. The term meant 'People of the Book', adherents of religions like Christianity and Judaism that had revealed testaments. Showing off, Tikoo spiced things up a bit with a reference to his own religion, Hinduism. 'Look, I am a non-believer. This is true. I am an idolater. Undeniable? I am an anathema to you. You kill me, it's OK. Sure, my friend, you butcher me. But these people, they are practising Christians. They are neither involved in the war, nor are they supporters of it. You are holding them and threatening to kill them, and for that you risk damnation. Am I right?'

There was a long silence, which left Tikoo worrying that he may have overstepped the mark. 'Maybe talking Islam with the *mujahideen* doesn't cut any ice,' he thought. He had been too hasty, too cocky, he realised. What had he been thinking? After all, these people had had sophisticated counter-intelligence training in Camp Yawar, where they had probably been instilled with a strident self-belief and instructed to avoid debates on philosophy, that were probably psychological ploys aimed at demoralising the faithful.

It was too late. The silence told him that the caller had hung up. Rajinder Tikoo cursed his arrogance and dropped the handset into its cradle.

The Inspector General sat back in his chair, looking at his uninspiring surroundings. When would the intermediary call back, he wondered anxiously. While he waited, he watched the local news bulletins, hoping not to see reports of Western bodies being fished from the Lidder River. Over in the corner, his computer's green-and-white screen blinked at him.

He had to get a rhythm going. Two deadlines had already passed with no progress made. In three days' time three of the hostages would have endured seventeen days of captivity, the same as Kim Housego and David Mackie in 1994. Would the seventeen-day rule apply again? The theory had cropped up in today's newspaper, but he thought it unlikely. He wondered what the hostages' partners knew about the 1994 incident and about what he was trying to do, as well as the limits placed on him by his government. 'I wished I could slip out and share my impressions with them.' But Saklani's orders had been explicit: the women were off-limits; and Tikoo's role, and any information gleaned from it, were classified. Everyone was to be kept at arm's length.

Depressed at this thought, Tikoo cast around the room for something to distract him. Someone had dropped off a well-thumbed Clive Cussler novel, *Sahara*, and as he began to read, inhaling the aroma of printer's ink and dust, his shoulders dropped a notch. This promised to be just the kind of rollercoaster he needed to take his mind off reality.

The next day, 19 July, started as well as could be expected, with Tikoo playing a round of golf before returning to Transport Lane. Halfway through his first pipe of the day, the phone rang.

'*Sub bakhair*,' he said, delivering an Urdu good morning. He was in a better mood, having spent half the night thinking through his tactics, and deciding that he was not going to pose as the intermediary's friend at all, but go at it from another angle, becoming 'how this man sees me'. This was Tikoo all over: a thinker. He had gone to university in Bombay, graduating in 1965, at the age of sixteen, with a science degree. A single-minded and highly inquisitive teenager, he had decided to work for his country. 'But since I had to be twenty-one to compete in India's elite civil service exams, I amused myself for the next couple of years, gaining an MSc in pure maths and an MA in British history.' Armed with a degree and two postgraduate qualifications by the time he was twenty, Tikoo was bored, 'and still too young for entrance to the civil service'. But he was not too young to sit the highly competitive Indian Police Service entrance exam. By the time he returned to Kashmir at the age of twenty-one in 1970, he had found himself with a vocation he had never previously considered. Before he knew it, the accidental policeman was an assistant superintendent.

Now, with more than two decades of service under his belt, the IG launched his opening gambit: 'Look, you have your 786. Well, from now on I am 108.'

'What? What is this?' The caller was perplexed. 'I have him on the back foot,' Tikoo thought to himself.

Tikoo knew that in Pakistan, 786 was sometimes used as a substitute for the opening phrase of the Koran, 'In the name of Allah, the merciful, the compassionate', since Islamic numerologists argued that the Arabic letters added up to that value. He explained to the intermediary that for Hindus the number 108 had similar significance: Lord Ganesh and Lord Shiva had 108 names; the Hanuman Chalisas were to be recited 108 times; there were 108 ways to represent the universe in the Vedic system; 108 beads in a Hindu rosary; 108 ancient *Upanishad* texts; 108 holy places associated with Lord Vishnu; and Sati's body split into 108 pieces when she heard that her husband, Lord Shiva, had been insulted. 'And so on and so on,' Tikoo said.

'My point in all of this is simple,' he continued with a flourish. 'The way you love Islam, I love my religion. I have a conflicting point of view. We should accept our differences and get on.'

Tikoo stared at the window, and waited for the caller to mull these thoughts over. He tried to conjure the smell of Lidderwat, that unique combination of moss and mutton.

Then the caller responded: 'OK, 108, I thank you.'

Tikoo's fingers did a silent jig on his dressing table. 'That clicked with him, you see?' he recalled. 'I realised that to reason with a person hung up on fundamentalism does not get you anywhere. For every quote that you have, he gives you a counter-quote, a chapter this and verse that. To accept that we were enemies was a first step in the right direction.'

He spoke again. 'Choose a name, my friend. Come on, we should be civil with one another.'

'OK,' said the caller, laughing. '*Mera naam Jehangir hay.*' My name is Jehangir.

'Be careful what you wish for, Mr Jehangir,' said Tikoo, taking advantage of the first moment of shared levity. 'Jehangir is a jolly good name, but let me tell you that particular Mughal ruler might have been the Conqueror of the World, but he was famed for creating one of the first systems of criminal justice, that hunted down the callous and cruel.'

The line went dead, but Tikoo was still smiling broadly.

The following morning seemed never to end. Tikoo was nursing a sore head, and for a while he thrashed around on his exercise bike before playing minesweeper on the computer, having found the game on the hard drive. 'Boom boom: it was amazing how these things exploded.' But after fifteen minutes or so he had tired of such child's play.

Just as he was thinking about the families, for whom this was Day Sixteen, or 20 July in the calendar of the free, the phone rang. He grabbed it, and waited eagerly for his opposite number to speak.

'Jehangir here,' the intermediary said coldly. Tikoo could sense that something was wrong.

'Mr Jehangir, my friend, how are you?' he said brightly, trying to lighten the mood. But just as he was about to launch into a speech, the caller interrupted him.

'You have violated your word, and you will be blamed for the consequences. You want their deaths on your hands? How stupid do you think we are?'

What the hell was going on? 'Calm yourself please, my friend. Please, Jehangir, tell me what has happened.'

'There was a raid.'

'What? Where?'

'You betrayed me, and now there will be a price to pay.'

'I tell you, I know nothing,' Tikoo replied as calmly as he could, although his mind was racing back to the late-night conversation he had had with Saklani a couple of days ago. 'Please tell me. Explain to me what has happened, and then give me a day to find some answers. Ring me tomorrow, and I will get to the bottom of this.' The line was already dead.

Tikoo called for his driver. Had the army found the kidnappers' hideout and tried to free the hostages by force? If so, he could not believe that he had not been warned. Down the lane by the Holy Family, he drove through the dappled sunlight and out onto Maulana Azad Road, where IG Tikoo looked longingly through the rusty fence of Srinagar Golf Club at the freshly watered fairways. There had been no announcement of any rescue attempt, so he hoped Jehangir was talking of a lesser incident – maybe the raiding of the house of an al Faran sympathiser, or the discovery of a hidden weapons store. Turning right, Tikoo's Ambassador raced past the Tourist Reception Centre where the oft-quoted Mr Jan worked. At the top of Church Lane the vehicle was stopped before being waved through the security cordon.

They pulled into the Security Advisor's compound. Tikoo found General Saklani seated at his desk, doling out ten-rupee notes to a long line of distraught women and old men clutching pictures of their missing sons, who they claimed had last been seen alive in army custody. 'Out, out!' he said, shooing them all away. 'We are not to be disturbed!' he shouted at Altaf Ahmed.

Tikoo relayed the message he had just received from Jehangir, telling Saklani, 'You gave me an assurance.'

The Security Advisor raised a hand to calm him. 'A raid?' he said, with a look that suggested he did not know anything either. 'Give me some time. I'll make some calls.'

Tikoo excused himself and called for his driver, a dozen possible scenarios whirling in his head. 'I had been in this business long enough to know that toast always landed butter-side down,' he recalled. Whatever had happened would have serious implications for his role as negotiator, assuming the hostages were not already either free or dead. While he waited nervously for Saklani's explanation he was driven aimlessly around Srinagar, trying to calm himself by recalling the city in the days of his grandfather, before the bunkers and sandbags, when it was still possible to glimpse how the wooden maze of the old town might have looked.

When he returned to the government compound an hour later, Saklani was smiling. A wave of relief washed over Tikoo. 'From the look on his face I knew that at the very least the hostages were still alive.' The information from Saklani's comrades at army headquarters in BB Cantt was that a team of paramilitaries from the BSF had got intelligence about some Pakistanis holed up in Khanyar, a militant stronghold in Srinagar's old city, and had raided a house there. By the time they got inside, the place was empty, but they subsequently discovered that a phone line in the building was the one al Faran had first used to call Tikoo. 'Just a routine op. No one knew that our man was in there,' Saklani said. 'A left-hand-right-hand kind of a thing. No one communicating. My apologies, but I'm sure you can smooth things over.'

That night, Tikoo tossed and turned as he tried to work out what had really happened. He had a finely tuned ear for these things. This was not, in his mind, what the cops called a 'Pink Panther kind of thing', the phrase they used to describe the countless cock-ups that went on in Kashmir. The only logical conclusion he could come to was that the army, accidentally or otherwise, had discovered Jehangir's hideout and decided, despite Saklani's assurances, to chance a raid. He fumed. For Tikoo, this was proof that the army regarded these five foreigners, none of them VIPs or politicians, as less important than their task of wresting control of the valley from the militants. How much more careful would the authorities be, and how much heavier would these five lives weigh if this kidnapping was unfolding in Europe, Tikoo thought. There, a different gravity existed, facilitated by peace and development, in which every single human being, encased in a complex tapestry of lifelong medical, social and financial records, from blood types to library borrowings, was important, and distinguishable from the throng.

The hostages were still out there, and Tikoo's job had been made significantly harder. How was he going to mend the broken bridges with Jehangir? And how, he wondered, would al Faran respond? To date it had been a tit-for-tat relationship. Firstly, Saklani had put up the partners at the press conferences, and al Faran had then put up the hostages, first in the form of the photographs, then their taped messages. Now the bungling security forces had raided an al Faran safe house, what would the kidnappers' reaction be?

While he waited for the phone to ring, Tikoo dug around among some cardboard boxes and pulled out an old tape recorder. He was not prepared to be the fall guy, should anyone from New Delhi conducting a post mortem on the affair be searching for a Kashmiri to hang out to dry. His written transcript was no longer enough. From now on, he would record everything that was said in this room and on the line to al Faran – as an insurance policy. Having concluded that the army must have been listening in to the calls before making the decision to raid the house in Khanyar, Tikoo wanted an end to that damn leaky telephone too. He would have to find a new way of communicating with the kidnappers that protected both sides.

The IG called up one of his most trusted officers, Superintendent Farooq Khan, the man he had placed in charge of the STF. Later that day Khan sent a man round to Transport Lane with a box. Inside was a Kenwood VHF two-way radio that the STF had seized from a militant cell it had eliminated in downtown Srinagar. It was still working, and Tikoo had decided that the talks, if they could be resurrected, would have to continue by these means. Such communications were far harder to trace. A roaming band of hostage-takers would almost certainly have the same kit. Tikoo pushed a phono cable into the Kenwood, inserted the other end into his tape recorder, and sat back.

For more than twenty-four hours there was nothing except the monotony of the cream walls and the bricked-up view. The day dragged by, punctuated with filling and refilling his pipe from a rapidly emptying tobacco pouch, a bout on the exercise bike followed by minesweeper. Then, on the afternoon of 21 July, Day Seventeen, the telephone rang. Tikoo began to explain about the VHF set, and which frequency they should use, and the code they would then employ to change frequencies, but Jehangir started shouting, 'There's been an encounter!' He used the army word for an exchange of fire between troops and militants. Tikoo paled as Jehangir continued: 'Hostages are injured. You … have … blood … on your hands.'

'My friend, my friend Jehangir, it is not possible,' said Tikoo. He could hardly believe that even the Indian Army would conduct another raid, targeting the kidnappers' hideout. Before he had a chance to ask anything more, the connection went dead. Panicked, Tikoo tore round to Saklani's office. He found the Security Advisor busy with some army officers, discussing the *yatra*. 'Saklani seemed genuinely surprised to see me. But on seeing the state I was in, he cleared his office and asked me to explain.' Then he picked up the phone to army headquarters. 'I sat there watching his reaction as he made a succession of calls,' Tikoo remembered. 'But there was nothing, no information about any kind of operation involving the hostages, either in Srinagar or in the mountains.' General Saklani said he would go and speak to the Governor, and that they should meet again that evening. Confused, Tikoo went back to sit by the silent radio in Transport Lane.

Later that night, Saklani told him there were no reports of a raid of any kind connected to the hostages. But the story would not go away. Instead of calling Tikoo, al Faran delivered a message to the Press Enclave, claiming that the Indian Army had attacked the kidnappers and that two hostages were seriously injured. The Press Enclave printed and broadcast the information. Jane, Cath, Julie and Anne learned the news from their diplomatic liaison officers.

'We were absolutely silent and aghast,' Jane recalled. 'We had only recently heard the recording of their voices, which was a major boost. It just didn't seem possible that they might now be injured. Our thoughts were: what sort of wounds do pistols, machine guns and hand grenades cause? How would you get them to a safe place, on

horseback or on a litter? Would they be in shock? Would Don be critically injured? So many thoughts and concerns that I actually felt
physically ill, a feeling I hadn't had to such a degree since the night
and the morning that Don was actually taken.'

An official public statement had to be made. An Indian government spokesman emerged to issue an emphatic denial of 'any gun
battle between the security forces and the kidnappers'. At the state
guesthouse in Srinagar, the women, their nerves shredded, did not
know what to believe, but felt relieved. 'Although I still wanted proof
that they were safe,' Jane wrote in her journal that night, exhausted by
the day's events, which she likened to being lurched around in a fair-
ground ride, '[the government statement] was reassuring.'

That weekend, Jane spent most of her waking hours doing some
serious thinking. The longer this went on, the more she felt like a
punchbag, soaking up every incident, claim and feint without being
able to do anything. In just over a week's time her and Don's tickets
home would expire, and even before the story of the raid had broken
she had been toying with going back, hoping to better serve Don's
cause by lobbying from the US, where she could use her brother-in-
law Donald Snyder's political connections to get some serious attention. 'By Monday, 24 July, which was Day Twenty-One of Don's
captivity, I awakened, as it always seemed, at 4 a.m., the time of the
morning prayers,' she wrote. 'I was able to go back to sleep but at 6.30
a.m. I was back up and my mind was busy turning things over and
over.' Jane had decided she had reached the end of the line in Srinagar,
where she felt she couldn't do much more. She and the other three
women were also coming under increasing pressure from their
embassies to relocate to New Delhi, 'simply because we wouldn't be as
at risk as we were in Srinagar'.

To-ing and fro-ing in her mind, Jane wondered, 'If New Delhi, then
why not Spokane?' There at least she could start sorting Don's life out.
Although colleagues were covering for him, he was long overdue back
at work, and a neighbour was looking after their dogs. She could not
go on like this. Jane felt certain that if she did go back, Don would
respect her decision, and she would also be comforted by her family

and friends. But on the other hand, if the situation changed, and Don emerged from captivity physically or mentally injured, 'I would want to be there quickly, and from Spokane it's nearly a thirty-five-hour trip.' She did not want to miss the moment Don was set free, and knew 'Don would be disappointed if I were not there, or feel that I had bailed out'. The last thing she wanted was for him to feel she had deserted him. She would have to sit tight for now.

For several days there was nothing. Then, on 4 August, another envelope arrived at the Press Enclave.

Yusuf Jameel ripped it open, and out slid colour photographs of Don Hutchings and Keith Mangan lying in a *gujjar* hut, bloodied and injured. Don's eyes were closed and he was stripped to the waist, his midriff bandaged with white gauze, with what looked like blood seeping from a gunshot wound. Keith too had his eyes tight shut, his chest exposed. He lay on a tartan blanket, with a broad ribbon of blood-stained white bandage across his breast. What looked like an intravenous drip was attached to his right arm, and pills were scattered around.

A tape clattered out of the envelope. Yusuf pushed it into his cassette player. 'I do not have the strength to speak much,' said an American voice that was evidently Don Hutchings', 'but I think Keith is critically ill with many wounds in his broken leg. We have no medicines.' Also in the envelope was a note in Urdu. Hans Christian Ostrø, Dirk Hasert and Paul Wells were also sick: 'For the last three days they have stopped eating. Unless immediate treatment is given they might die and for that the Indian government will be responsible.' The note continued that the governments of Britain, America, Norway and Germany had a responsibility to put pressure on India to get on with meaningful negotiations. As a sign of good will, al Faran was unilaterally reducing its demand on prisoner releases from twenty-one men to fifteen, but Masood Azhar remained a priority, top of the list.

Al Faran appeared to want a resolution, thought IG Tikoo when he heard the news. But would any of the hostages live long enough to see it through? Or was this just a ruse, the mocked-up after-effects of a non-existent encounter, calculated to turn the knife and keep New Delhi hopping? Not even he knew.

The photos and the threats felt real enough to the hostages' families waiting overseas. In Eston, Middlesbrough, Julie Mangan's mother Anita noted that Julie and Keith had been planning to celebrate their tenth wedding anniversary at the Taj Mahal on the day before the photos emerged: 'She's devastated. We all are. We have done nothing but cry since Saturday.' A local Teesside radio station obtained the pictures before the families, and called Keith's mother, asking if she wanted to see them. 'Of course I said yes, and so they, the people from the radio station, came out to the house. "Is this your son Keith?" they wanted to know. And I said, "Yes, this definitely is Keith." It looked so authentic in the black-and-white version they had.' The Mangans were so worried they called the Foreign Office, which by now had appointed a family liaison officer. 'A Family's Agony' ran the headline in the Middlesbrough *Gazette* above the picture of Keith lying injured. 'I don't know how we're coping,' Mavis said, describing this time as the 'days from hell'.

In Spokane there were shocked headlines too: 'Hostage Shot, Critically Ill, Rebels Report'. Don and Jane's friends – climbers and walkers, doctors and psychologists – passed around copies of the photos to scrutinise. On the waistband of Don's walking trousers it was just possible to make out the label 'Moonstone', confirming to them that this was really Don. But the peaceful expression on his face and the pristineness of the bandages suggested to some in the Spokane medical community that the pictures were faked. There was also something odd about the positioning of Don's right hand, which was in the foreground of the picture. The fingers seemed to be at an unnatural angle. A sign-language expert in Spokane suggested that he could have been signalling 'I'm OK.' In Middlesbrough, Charlie Mangan was also not so sure about the photographs when he saw them in colour for the first time: 'You could tell that the blood looked like Tabasco sauce, and the needle in his arm was not stuck in.'

Back in Transport Lane, Srinagar, IG Tikoo studied the photographs in a newspaper. He thought he knew what this was all about: retaliation for the BSF raid on the house in Khanyar. He could see that the bodged operation had given al Faran a fright, and the kidnappers wanted the families (and New Delhi) to suffer too. In this they had succeeded. Mavis Mangan recalled: 'If those men holding our son wanted us to feel the terror, they did with that, they certainly did. This was real terror.'

Tikoo's confidence ebbed. Nothing felt certain any more. He did not even know if he could trust Saklani. He thought long and hard as he contemplated the photographs reproduced in the paper. This was the essence of what terrorism truly meant: powerlessness and not knowing. Al Faran was working the grey space between ignorance and speculation. What, he wondered, was his side *really* doing?

TWELVE

The Golden Swan

Marit Hesby woke with a start on the night of 12 August. An air-conditioner hummed above her head, and she could see from the clock that it was just past midnight. She was still on Norwegian time, although she'd been in New Delhi for three days. She'd never be able to get back to sleep now, she thought, so she tried to recollect her dream: something to do with cats. That worried her. Whenever she dreamed about cats it signalled a momentous event in her son's life. Where was Hans Christian right now, she wondered. He was strong and resourceful, she told herself, trying not to think of where he might be sleeping, as she lay in the plush cotton sheets of the Norwegian Embassy.

He could survive this. Later, the experience would become one of the family stories recited every Christmas, like the one about him and his girlfriend struggling home from school summer camp five hundred miles away without a krone in their pockets.

Marit had arrived in New Delhi on her son's thirty-third day in captivity, her journey prompted by the ambush photos. In Oslo she had woken to see the brutal images of Keith and Don lying bandaged and supposedly bloodied on the NRK morning news. Horrified, she had called Anette, who had already flown out to India with her father Hans Gustav on 18 July. Anette confirmed that there was a possibility that a secret army rescue attempt had gone wrong, but the Indian authorities were so unforthcoming that anything was possible. 'Later, people said the pictures were fake, but it didn't make any difference to me,' said Marit. 'I just knew I couldn't sit by in my cosy little life any longer while my boy was out there suffering.'

263

Marit had joined Anette and her ex-husband in New Delhi just in time to contribute to an emotional appeal by the families of all the hostages that would be placed in key Kashmiri newspapers. Jane, Julie, Cath and Anne had by now relocated to New Delhi at General Saklani's request. Although it was a relief to be out of Srinagar, they all felt unnervingly removed from whatever was happening in Kashmir. 'We make a compassionate appeal to you for the unconditional release of these innocent tourists,' their joint statement began. For Marit, it was better than sitting at home pasting newspaper articles about the kidnapping into a scrapbook for Hans Christian to read when he came home, which was how she had filled up her time until now. Somebody must know something, they had all hoped. Someone would feel a pang of guilt.

And somebody had felt something. A couple of days after the advertisement appeared, the Norwegian Embassy handed Marit a copy of a letter from her son, sent by fax from Srinagar. Somehow, he had managed to write it without his kidnappers knowing, and then to discard it, hoping it would be found. Incredibly, having withstood the beating sun, rain and possibly frost, as well as grazing animals and curious village children, it had been discovered by someone who understood its importance and who had then risked the wrath of militants and the suspicions of the Indian security forces to ensure it reached the authorities.

Marit felt an intense surge of emotion as she saw her son's trademark chaotic handwriting, and she struggled to suppress the image of him held hostage. He had written in English, knowing that, unlike Norwegian, it was widely spoken in Kashmir. 'My dear family, I am fine,' he wrote. 'I keep on believing in the good in people. My biggest concern is what you think and feel. Please be strong because I am. Love from Hans Christian.' Ever the optimist, Marit thought, marvelling at these words that had come from nowhere. This letter was clearly written by her son. As was its second half. In the midst of this crisis he was addressing the Embassy in his pernickety way: 'I must ask you for a favour. When I was taken hostage by the Mujahadin [sic] there was a thick black notebook in my tent. It is ¾ full of handwriting in Norwegian. It contains three months worth of drama and poetry. I have booked the Black Box stage in October and this book is absolutely necessary for the play. (I don't want anything in the book published, if found. It's private.) My name and address stands on the first page and I have promised a $50 reward if lost.'

Marit was relieved that he was still focused on the performance he had been planning all these months. He clearly believed he had a future. 'Please help me,' the note ended, 'contact the Indian army etc. Please keep the pressure on the Indian government. Their officials in three tourist offices *guaranteed* that my trek was absolutely safe. *Nobody* told me the Mujahadin had been in this area for *six* years. Thank you very much. Hans Christian.'

Marit read and reread the astonishing letter, tears pouring down her face. Soon afterwards, more artefacts materialised: a black kitbag, held for weeks by the police in Pahalgam, that was filled with the contents of Hans Christian's tent. Unzipping the bag, Marit was overwhelmed by the smells of incense and pine resin. She sat with her daughter Anette, pulling out the contents one by one, inhaling the aromas of the place from where Hans Christian had been taken, a brown woollen hat that he had brought back from Peru, his army issue string vest, and a pair of broken old sunglasses he had had since his teens. She also found the large black notebook; she would keep it safe in her room. At the very bottom of the bag was her son's money belt. Rigid with dried sweat, it was curved by the shape of his body. When she felt it, it was as if she was running a hand along his abdomen, as she had done when he was six years old, bathing him in the family's home in Tromsø. Inside the money belt was his old student ID card from 1990, Hans Christian adopting a well-practised 'academic pose' in the photograph: head tilted at an engaging angle, eyes staring quizzically into the camera, his fingers clasping his chin as if deep in thought. At the time it was taken, it had made her laugh. Now it just reminded her of his absence and her loss, making her wish she had been as engaged in his life as she now was in his disappearance. There were also his driving licence, Imodium tablets, business cards from hotels and shops in Cochin, New Delhi and Srinagar.

Folded up along with his yellow-fever certificate she found little slips of paper bearing Hindi or Kashmiri phrases written phonetically with English translations: 'They reminded me of when we had moved to the far north of Norway when Hans Christian was six, and he had charged straight over to the house next door, eager to learn the local dialect from the neighbours' son.'

Inside a zipped compartment at the back of the pouch was a tightly folded piece of paper. With a finger Marit worked it free, starting to sob a little as she guessed what it was. She pushed and twisted it until it eventually came loose: the fifty-krone note she had given her son the night before he went to India. Now he had no bus money to get home.

Another startling packet from the mountains arrived a few days later. Again there was no indication of how it had been assembled, discarded, found and delivered, filling Marit with conflicting feelings of pleasure, pride and pain. This one consisted of another letter and nine snapshots. Was someone in the kidnap party assisting her son? Marit could not guess. Had he recruited some villager somewhere to his side? He had always been capable of springing surprises, but even so, she was amazed that he could be so prolific and brazen, risking everything to alert the outside world to their plight, while the other hostages apparently remained silent (apart from the tape recordings). She felt as if she could feel his determination coursing through the lines of text. The photos were copies from a set he had already sent home of his *kathakali* graduation performance in Kerala back in May. She wondered why he had smuggled them out now, until she turned them over. On the backs of each he had annotated the images, again in English. 'I am Hamsa, the gold swan who threw away a wheel,' he had written on one. The messages were cryptic and oblique, the kind of dreamy prose he'd adopted in his teens, but imbued with snatches of his new-found world of *kathakali*. From postcards he had sent home earlier, Marit knew Hans Christian's teachers in Kerala had named him Hamsa, the ancient swan character of *kathakali* who epitomised equilibrium, the mystical pearl-eater who was able to throw off the troubles of the physical world, symbolised by the wheel, channelling thoughts to the eternal.

In the picture, Hans Christian was dressed as Hamsa. 'Good night,' he had written underneath the message. 'Good night, my lovely boy,' Marit said to herself.

Her son was a magpie, picking up snippets of knowledge everywhere he went. Hamsa was a key figure in ancient stories of love, separation and reunion. Was that her son's message, she wondered, desperate to comprehend his intended meaning. Was this a sign to his family that he would struggle until he was back with them? Or was it meant to indicate that he would not *stop* struggling, regardless of the danger? One way was imbued with hope, the other was reckless. However Marit took it, he seemed not to care about the risks he was taking. But that was Hans Christian all over.

A second photo was covered with dense notes: 'On little eyes which still can look but understand little of the complicated processes which regulate human relations, I am quiet ...' This showed Hans Christian's frustration at not being able to reach out to his abductors, she thought. 'Hopelessness and meaninglessness take over where love should have been blooming.' Did this mean that, unable to convince them away from their prejudices, he was exhausted and heading for a confrontation? 'I still believe in the world's meaning and achievement. But I am understanding by living the opposite.' He remained engaged, even as his energies were sapped and he was becoming drained by his time in captivity, Marit thought.

She read on nervously, often finding his writing obscure. 'Like a storm of wild, sick horses, caught in a corral, they have been running in panic,' he wrote. 'The hooves smashing against bare granite, the white is in their eyes.' Had they all fled from something? Had there been a firefight, with al Faran battling the Indian security forces, and the hostages trapped in the middle? Her mind cast back to the haunting photographs of Don Hutchings and Keith Mangan. Or was Hans Christian saying he had clashed with his guards? 'They pull and draw in all directions, the wheels are lifted above the ground and make flashes together with the lightning. Thunder booms like machine guns.' It sounded like a battle. Her eyes played over the next sentence: 'I am tied up under the wagon. Stones and grass cover my body.' She prayed that this was not literal, and that he was not lying in some wooded encampment, trussed like an animal.

'I'm cold and calm even if rats are jumping up and hanging off my skin.' His words were getting darker with every line, but Marit could not tear herself away. 'Nearly all the horses are fallen and are drawn by the two left. One horse is falling over against the wagon. Everybody is dead. I am alive.' Something terrible had happened. What was it? She needed to know. She read the next lines aloud: 'Winter does not wait to start, summer does not wait to end, the mist does not come with advance warning, but people who give in are slaves in time and place.' That must mean Kashmir's changing seasons were beginning to impact on the kidnappers. 'Only people make stars in the snow.' Up in the high passes, winter was on its way, endangering the lives of those struggling to survive its bleakness. 'Only people take their own lives.' He was expecting a showdown.

Marit knew her son. He would never take his own life. But she was not so sure he would not sacrifice himself to save his fellow captives. Generous and reckless, he had always put others first. 'I will refuse to eat and die,' he wrote here. He had started a hunger strike in an attempt to force the kidnappers' hands, she was sure of it. 'Their not eating strike was short, we moved and now I am exhausted ...' The others had done the same, but had folded too soon, and they had been moved as a result. Or was it just him? Then, the first mention of something concrete: '0.24' – it looked like a time, just past midnight, but there was no date. When he was young, she had often found Hans Christian writing under his duvet in the middle of the night, and she imagined him, cold and hungry, doing the same now.

The penultimate coded message was the worst. 'My searching battery is flat. I, who can vibrate around the whole world, have little spirit left. There is little joy left over.' It must have been a very bad day indeed. 'Little humanity. But I need to fight and I need to escape. I'm not dead, even if I can kid myself that I am ... I still want to be a human being ...' The force within him was still strong. 'I will escape if I can. I will not eat.' It was hard to go on, but she turned to the last letter. Thankfully, this one seemed more hopeful: 'You are a light wind of gold dust, spreading down into the river of my life. You are the most beautiful, concrete earthly thing in my fantasies. Your body and your soul shine out from your being. I'm very awake now. I'm more awake than for a long time.' *A light wind of gold dust.* Marit was heartened to see that her son had not yet lost what the family called 'the glow in his soul'. But then she came to the last line: 'I'm in mortal danger, surrendered to people without balance or God.'

Marit desperately wanted to talk with the other families about these letters. But Arne Walther, the Norwegian Ambassador, had asked her not to share the contents of the package with anyone. It was a protective measure, he had said. Marit told Anette that she felt this was dishonest. 'Everyone was telling us to keep quiet and let the Indians get on with their job,' Anette recalled. 'The American Embassy said it. The FBI came to see us and said it. Arne said it. It didn't seem right, and went against our instincts. But we were so inexperienced that we went along.'

Fingers of light poked through the curtains in Marit's room at the Embassy. Hearing bulbuls twittering in the bougainvillea, she knew why her son loved India. When he was free again, she would take time to enjoy it with him. Today, 13 August, would be a better day, a good day, she told herself as she got up and set off on an early-morning stroll around the Embassy garden. Frank Elbe, the German Ambassador, had invited the hostages' partners and family members over for Sunday lunch.

Deputy Superintendent Kifayat Haider was enjoying a calm Sunday. Finally the *yatra* was over, and he was down in Srinagar with his family. But he was finding it hard to unwind. When the message was relayed to him from Aishmuqam communications centre that officers were needed to attend a crime scene in his district, he was quietly glad of something to do. Women gathering firewood high up in the Shael Dar forest, north-east of Anantnag, had discovered a body. It was a mortuary trip, but he could do with stretching his legs. So, gathering three armed constables, he drove out in a white police Gypsy jeep. A guide who knew where the body lay would be waiting at Seer, a village on the banks of the Lidder River.

At Anantnag, the party took the Pahalgam road, crossed the iron bridge over the Lidder at Martand and followed a track along its right bank. As the Gypsy climbed beneath the shadows of deodars, the constables sitting on either side of Haider gripped their rifles. Occasionally the jeep scattered a few straggly children and stray dogs, but otherwise they seemed to be alone. Lighting a Classic with an ostentatious flourish, Haider was actually a little nervous. Ahead was Logripora, the final resting place of Zain Shah Sahib, the patron saint of the Lidder Valley. His shrine in an ancient tree trunk had once been a popular place of pilgrimage, but since the area had become dense with militants, hardly any worshippers came.

A few miles short of Aishmuqam, the jeep reached Seer, where a bent old man in a *pheran* and white skullcap was waiting beside the road. Motioning to a steep incline up through the dark pine forest behind him, he said the quickest way to where the body lay was on foot. Haider elected to go with him, while the constables took the long way round in the Gypsy, agreeing to meet them at the top, in Panz Mulla village. Early-morning mist shrouded the trees, and everything was still as the DSP and the old man climbed up the hillside without talking. Eventually, after more than an hour, they emerged at Panz Mulla, a settlement of dilapidated *dhokas* where 220 families lived in a state of near-constant siege, preyed on by the security forces that came up here to hammer militants hiding in the woods. Smoke rose from several chimneys, but there was no welcome party or cup of *chai*. The villagers were frightened, and these days they barricaded themselves inside when they knew trouble was coming.

They were not stopping here anyway. The old man motioned Haider to keep going. 'Vail Nagbal,' he said, referring to another village two miles further on. The nearest police station was now twenty miles back. Haider felt for the reassuring grip of his pistol in its holster, and followed. But Vail Nagbal came and went, and still the old man didn't stop. This was much further into no man's land than Haider had intended to go, and he was becoming more worried. At last they reached a clearing in the forest, and then he saw it: something lying on the ground, surrounded by small bundles of firewood.

Haider took in the crime scene. He had been to so many of these since the militancy had flared up that he felt nothing at first, although some things stood out. The corpse was dressed in mismatched olive fatigues, with green sweat pants underneath baggy *shalwar* trousers, and its arms and legs had been trussed with rough twine. The head was missing. 'It made the scene appear as some kind of nasty execution.' From the large maroon stain on the ground beneath the body, death had been caused by decapitation at this very spot. Haider poked around, and found what he was looking for forty metres away: the head. He rolled it over, and gasped. Blond curls and a strawberry-blond beard matted with blood. The eyes, half-open, were the grey-blue of Tar Sar. It had to be a hostage, or possibly a Chechen fighter enlisted into the Kashmiri *jihad*. If it was a hostage, Haider knew that the political ramifications would be momentous. The militants had broken new ground here, he thought, capturing a foreign tourist and killing him so brutally.

Lighting up a Classic, DSP Haider turned to see his constables arriving in the Gypsy. They shouldered their weapons as Haider rolled the body over. Everyone gasped. 'We all saw right away that the blood on the corpse's neck was still oozing, which meant that the killing was recent,' said Haider. Whoever had done this might still be nearby, watching. They had to act fast. They might be outgunned. Haider saw that a note was pinned to the victim's shirt, and plucked it off: 'We have killed the hostage because the government has failed to accept our demands. Indian dogs, if you do not fulfil our demands, in 48 hours the others will suffer the same fate.' The DSP felt bewildered, incensed and distraught.

He ordered the twitchy constables to make a rapid search of the area while he looked over the butchered corpse for anything that would aid identification. Terrified, the two men ran around, safety catches off, while Haider poked at the cadaver. Although there were brown socks on both feet, there was only one black boot, trademarked

'Micro', on the left foot. The right foot poked out of its sock, and was dirty and blistered, as if the victim had walked a considerable distance without footwear.

Feeling inside the man's torn green *shalwar kameez*, Haider found what felt like a square of paper forced into one of the seams. He wriggled it free, and saw that it was a page torn from an Indian magazine. On one side was a banal cigarette advertisement, some scantily clad Bollywood starlet running across a beach. On the other was an advertisement for 'Arvind Cotton Classics'. Haider was perplexed. It had to contain an important or personal message, since the hostage had clearly gone to the trouble of concealing it. Scrutinising the page more closely, he spotted tiny, handwritten words marching antlike along its margins. On one side was a list of countries: 'Turkey', 'Greece', 'UK', 'Bolivia', 'Brazil'. On the other was a list of local place names: 'Magam', 'Pahalgam', 'Kapran'. On the reverse were the titles of dozens of songs by David Bowie, the Waterboys and Led Zeppelin. Nothing significant, Haider concluded as he shoved the page into his pocket.

The corpse was wearing a green T-shirt. Haider reached for the label: 'Janus of Norway J'. The Norwegian hostage? It had to be. He lifted up the T-shirt, and recoiled. A message had been carved into the dead man's chest in ten-inch-high letters in what looked like Arabic or Urdu script. He called his men, who helped him decipher it. No one was quite sure, but then he got it: A-L F-A-R-A-N.

One of the officers had found a long knife among the deodars. Haider suspected it was an army-issue bayonet of some kind. Covered in blood, it was probably the murder weapon. 'The foreigner had been frog-marched here, before being forced down and sacrificed like a goat for *Eid*,' he thought.

Haider knew they had to get out of here as soon as possible, with the body. As he and one of the constables slid it into the back of the Gypsy, the other constable came back with another trophy: a green rucksack. In it were a handful of colour photos, a small purse containing shipping receipts and credit cards, and a passport that confirmed the dead man's identity: Hans Christian Ostrø. 'I scooped up the head, wrapped it in a strip of cloth and put it on the seat next to me, where it remained, rolling this way and that, all the way back to Anantnag,' DSP Haider recalled.

By the time they arrived at Anantnag, the town's police station was besieged. Amid chaotic scenes, the body was hustled inside on a rusty stretcher. Someone took a photograph showing Ostrø's head propped unceremoniously between his thighs as Haider screamed, 'Get these parasites out of here!' He ordered the stretcher to be taken to a private room. 'Doctor!' he shouted, calling for a police medic. While he waited, he again studied the torn page he had found in the man's clothes. What was he missing here? As he scanned the song titles more carefully, his eyes lit on a phrase: 'Good luck to you all. If I should die, I am wearing a message to my family in my balls.' The hostage, he realised, had cleverly hidden a significant message amid otherwise random writings that he knew the kidnappers would not be able to understand. Instead of waiting for the police doctor, Haider began to manhandle the body. It was difficult, but eventually, feeling along the creases, he retrieved a roll of papers from the victim's underpants.

Inside was a blizzard of words, but frustratingly they were in Norwegian. Just as he was wondering where he could find a translator, an Inspector poked his head through the door to say that a helicopter was on its way. BB Cantt had commandeered the corpse, on the Governor's orders. Ostrø belonged to the army now. Once again, Haider was being sidelined. Growling, he pushed the papers into his pocket.

As they filed into the German Embassy dining room for lunch, Marit Hesby was alarmed to see that she was seated beside the Ambassador, Frank Elbe. What on earth would they talk about? This world was new to her. She was relieved to see Jane Schelly slip into the chair on Elbe's other side. Before the Ambassador arrived the two women chatted for a few minutes, discussing the latest rumours. Someone had heard that the hostages had had their shoes taken away to prevent them from escaping. After Elbe arrived, the meal got under way.

Halfway through the main course, a succession of Embassy staff got up to leave. Hans Christian's sister Anette noticed it straight away. 'The German Ambassador disappeared. I thought, "Oh, it's the press, they've found out we're all here and they're asking for interviews."' But one by one the diplomats filed back in, and said nothing, although their faces looked gloomy. 'We had our dessert, cherries jubilee,' recalled Marit, 'but Ambassador Elbe didn't touch his plate.'

The families were ushered into another room for coffee. 'Our Ambassador, Arne Walther, was standing over in a corner with the British High Commissioner,' said Anette. 'I thought, "That's strange, Arne wasn't invited to the meal." There was also a doctor who I recognised from the British High Commission. They called us all to attention. Then they told us that the body of a Caucasian male had been found, although not formally identified. We should all go back to our respective embassies and wait for news.' The women shrank back in horror, and then the sobbing started.

Marit was stunned. 'I remember looking at the other families and feeling sorry that one of them would soon be told their loved one was dead.' Someone, nobody could recall exactly who, starting weeping and saying that she wanted to go home. Jane remembered the stunned atmosphere as everyone wondered who it was who would receive the terrible news: 'You didn't want it to be your loved one, and yet you looked around the room and thought with horror that you could not wish this on anyone.' Jane felt she had to say something on behalf of all the families. She asked if it were possible that the body might be that of someone else, since all the papers were reporting that Westerners were still trekking in the Pahalgam area. 'Elbe looked at me as if he did not understand my English, and said absolutely nothing,' Jane recalled.

As she walked out, Marit noticed the German Ambassador putting his arm around Jane, and a guilty wave of relief washed over her. 'It must be Don,' she thought. However, when Marit, Anette and Hans Gustav arrived back at their Embassy, the Ambassador called them into a private room. 'There's a rumour,' he said quietly, 'it's Hans Christian.' The family was stunned. Could it be a mistake, Hans

Gustav asked desperately. Walther didn't think so. The police in Kashmir were asking if Hans Christian had any distinguishing marks. Marit immediately thought of the scar running diagonally across the right side of her son's back. When he was six years old and living in Tromsø, a neighbour's dog had attacked him. 'Yes,' she said hesitantly. 'All I had in my mind's eye was a picture of my beautiful boy lying dead somewhere,' she remembered. It was senseless and cruel. How could someone have killed her son, a boy with so much love in his heart? If it was Hans Christian, she needed to know how he had died. Ambassador Walther looked away with an expression that suggested this was something he had not prepared himself for. 'We don't know,' he murmured.

Anette was mute. She idolised her big brother, who had taught her everything she knew about music and poetry, and could not imagine life without him. She made her excuses and went up to her room. For a moment she sat on the bed, trying to collect herself. Hans Christian had always been there for her: 'He just couldn't be dead.' Still unable to cry, she called her boyfriend in Stockholm. He had already seen it on the news. 'Eric told me to prepare myself for something terrible. The reports in Sweden were saying that Hans Christian had been beheaded. I just couldn't get this. I couldn't understand this. I was in complete shock. This kind of thing – in Norway, it was totally unknown to us.'

On the afternoon of 13 August, in the Welcome Hotel in Srinagar, Tore Hattrem was sitting and reading. It was his week on as the duty liaison officer representing the relatives' interests now the families were down in New Delhi. In recent days the British High Commission and the American, German and Norwegian embassies had organised themselves into a more manageable group they called the 'G4', in an attempt to simplify and coordinate arrangements between the four nations whose subjects were involved in the kidnapping. 'Someone called to say a body had been found,' Tore recalled. 'A car was waiting to take me to Badami Bagh, the army HQ.' He would have to inform the G4 straight away, and he was told that General Saklani was preparing to call an emergency meeting of the Indian security forces' Unified Command.

At the military hospital, dozens of worried-looking officials, some of them in uniform, were milling around. Silence descended as the Norwegian diplomat entered, and they parted to allow him through. The sight of Ostrø's mutilated corpse on a gurney in the mortuary room, his head lying between his thighs, made Tore retch. It was the first time he had ever seen a dead body, and the fact that it was some-one he knew made it all the worse. 'It was terrible. Sad. I barely recog-nised him as the young man who'd come into our Embassy. Blood was spattered across his face, as if he'd been in a battle. Only one boot had been found, which everyone was puzzling over.'

A few days previously, when all of the hostages had been alive, the kidnappers had sent a new set of photos to the Press Enclave in Srinagar. The pack comprised single shots of each hostage sitting on the same metal chair against the wooden wall of what looked like a sizeable village house, as if they were in a macabre passport photo studio. At the time much had been made of the fact that Hans Christian was wearing only one sock – his family had hoped that this was some kind of secret sign. Looking now at an army doctor examin-ing the body's blistered right foot, Tore was more inclined to believe the rumour that after John Childs' escape the other hostages had been punished by having their footwear removed.

After identifying the body, Tore was shown the note that had been found pinned to Hans Christian's shirt and the roll of papers that had been hidden in his underwear. Could he translate the hidden writings, asked a policeman impatiently. Tore flicked through the sheets of paper. 'There were so many things to read, letters to family members, poems, stories.' He translated a few passages as the policeman, whose nametag read 'Kifayat Haider', stood agitated at his elbow. 'He wanted to know what all of it meant immediately. I guess they were hoping to find clues about the kidnappers' location. But I found it very hard to decipher what Hans Christian was saying. I told them I would need some time to do it. And I felt that I really should not be reading these private letters.'

But Haider was insistent, and he wanted Tore to get started immediately. 'I could see there was a high level of anger and frustration on the part of the writer, and that he seemed to be reflecting on his own death,' Tore said, but he told Haider he was not going to translate any more: 'This was a job that needed to be done properly, and respectfully, and not standing around a gurney.' Another officer, his nametag identifying him as DSP Gupta from CID, entered the room, and Haider blanched. Gupta stretched out his hand and asked Haider for the paperwork.

Tore had spotted a letter, presumably from Paul Wells, addressed to Catherine Moseley, and tried to get it back too so he could pass it on. 'Not yet,' Gupta said, taking everything, then hustling Haider out of the room and into a neighbouring office, from where Tore overheard a furious row. 'You didn't tell me he was in the army!' Haider shouted at Gupta. 'He had a bayonet, Norwegian army issue. Some of his clothing too. Why was he here? Was he in intelligence, and was that connected to his death?' Gupta tried to shut Haider up, telling him he was 'out of his depth'. Gupta had come to do his job and take photographs of the corpse, particularly the Arabic inscription on the chest. It was not for him to explain to Haider why CID was 'taking complete charge of the case'. He now raised his voice too: 'Just let it go! This is a CID matter.'

Tore predicted that there would be a tussle for control of the remains of Hans Christian Ostrø too. Who would have jurisdiction over his death? 'We wanted a formal post mortem conducted by one of the Embassy doctors,' Tore said, but the Indian authorities reserved the right to take the lead. After twelve hours the body was released with the issue unresolved, but an agreement to get it to New Delhi, where the next stage would be decided. 'We removed Hans Christian's clothes, put him on ice in the coffin and had him flown to New Delhi on a military flight.'

Anette tried to keep the details of Hans Christian's death from her mother: 'I didn't think she would be able to take it.' But some Indian newspapers ran the ghoulish picture snatched at Anantnag police station. The matted hair and the blood spatters told the whole story, as did his parted lips, locked open in an oval of surprise. One Kashmiri newspaper reported that a family living near Seer had seen Hans Christian on the evening before he was killed. 'Militants came with him for food,' said the villager. 'The foreigner would not eat, but he drank some milk. When they left, they took a rope with them.'

When Marit saw the photos and reports, her first thoughts were for her ageing father, sitting alone at home in Norway, watching developments on television. Hans Christian had been his favourite grandson, and she couldn't allow him to find out that way. Ole Hesby was delighted to hear his daughter's voice when she reached him later that day. 'He said, "Oh, you're in India, how lovely, what news of Hans Christian?" And then I had to tell him. It was the hardest call I ever made.'

Hans Christian Ostrø's simple wooden coffin arrived in the Indian capital on 14 August, two weeks after he was supposed to have flown home. His parents could not face the formal identification, so Marit's husband John, who had come to India to support her, stepped in. He arrived at the airport to meet the flight from Srinagar only to find 'journalists crowded around the casket. We couldn't get anywhere near.' Pushing through the crowds, Tore Hattrem identified himself and told John to rendezvous with them at a military hospital. For the rest of that afternoon they played cat and mouse with the Indian press pack. 'Three times they tried to identify the body,' Marit recalled. 'But each time the press burst into the room to get a picture.' Eventually the coffin was taken to the All India Institute of Medical Sciences in south New Delhi, where an argument broke out over who should conduct the post mortem.

The Indian government insisted its medics should preside, since Hans Christian had been killed on Indian soil, and the crime was being investigated there. The G4 weakly argued that as the victim was a foreigner, they should lead. It was decided that Indian doctors would start things off, observed by representatives of the G4. But, enraged by what they saw as the patronising attitude of the Western diplomats, the Indian team tried to shut the foreigners out anyway. 'We met with considerable obstruction and disinformation during the course of the day,' wrote Dr Andrew Reekie, a British High Commission doctor who had been delegated to watch proceedings. 'Every effort was made initially to bar me.'

The post mortem eventually began at 5.30 p.m. on 14 August, with Dr Reekie and an unidentified FBI medic observing. 'Externally, the decapitated body was well nourished and showed no signs of neglect or of torture,' Reekie wrote. 'There were ante-mortem minor abrasions to the knuckles of both hands and a possible minor bruise to one of his calves. Apart from the extensive damage to the neck, there were no other external injuries and no sign of a struggle.'

Next, the neck was examined. Police reports had suggested Hans Christian had been kneeling, with his hands and feet tied behind his back. But the wounds on his body suggested that he had been lying face up when he was killed, with someone pinning him to the ground. Unless he had been asleep or unconscious, he would have seen everything. The post-mortem findings were grim. The first swing of the blade, a Norwegian army knife, had cut only three centimetres into Hans Christian's throat, severing his trachea and some of the neck muscles and blood vessels, without ending his life. The doctors found particles of blood in Hans Christian's lungs that had been inhaled as he struggled for breath. Seconds later, the executioner had tried again, this time cutting across the neck to a depth of four centimetres, the knife stuttering on the spinal cord. The last cut, which caused the third of 'three deep notches', according to Dr Reekie, severed the head completely.

There were a few small mercies. Contrary to some media reports, Hans Christian had not been shot or tortured, and the deep lacerations on his chest spelling out 'al Faran' had been made after death. Reekie found them 'very interesting in that the depth of the cuts was very even and consistent and had almost an artistic quality'. Lastly, the doctors turned their attention to the time of death, concluding that he had died around midnight on 12 August, about the time Marit Hesby had woken from her dream.

*   *   *

Hans Christian's body was repatriated to Norway with his family the following day. 'I couldn't bear to be in India any longer,' Marit said. 'I wasn't angry with anyone, I just wanted to get him home.' Just before they left, Ambassador Walther gave her copies of the letters and poems that had been found hidden about her son's body. The originals remained with security officials in Srinagar. She packed them into her case without looking at them. 'We decided to read them together as a family, quietly, after we got home.'

However, by the time they landed in Oslo some of the letters had been leaked to the Indian press. Anette recalled: 'Even that private moment of sharing his last words was stolen from us.' For her, the worst thing was the publication of a private message of farewell from her brother. 'Little big friend and oasis,' Hans Christian had written, probably sitting alone in the *gujjar* hut. 'My smiling sister, my fair half part. What can I tell you? Know that you are beautiful and don't doubt your own word. Seize the day and if I can tell you anything philosophical remember that everything is to live for. There are positive measures hidden in every shadow. Sister, you are created to bloom and live for the moment. The sorrow is there because you are going to be happier. See all the colours. Separate the colours and breathe stronger than before. I am extremely fond of you. I love you.'

Nine days later Anette gave the eulogy at her brother's funeral in Tønsberg Cathedral, a service attended by the Norwegian Prime Minister and the actress and director Liv Ullmann. 'We've waited for you every day and every night since you were taken in Kashmir,' Anette said of her brother, her voice quivering. 'Some us have felt the thoughts you were sending us, some of us have felt your strength. You will never be gone. You will live and breathe with us each day, each month and each year. You were my protective big brother, but you were also my best friend. For me you will never be some kind of saint or martyr, you will be my handsome brother ... We'll meet again in another world, in a paradise.'

Marit had asked that Hans Christian be dressed in the traditional felt hunting outfit she had bought him the previous Christmas, just before he had gone away. Now, as she stood beside his flower-bedecked casket, she willed her son to give a sign that his spirit was still alive. 'One white rose dipped down, right beside me. I know that it was him, Hans Christian, saying, "I'm fine now, Mummy."'

Marit invited all her son's friends for a pizza-and-beer party at the Tønsberg summerhouse, just as Hans Christian had planned to do upon returning from India. She pasted his last holiday snaps of the Meadow and the road up to Chandanwari into the photo album she had prepared for his homecoming, along with his *kathakali* pictures. Then she chose the words for his granite headstone in the churchyard close to where she had grown up: 'When the moon's veil was lifted, you became the sun's dancing rays.' As she carried his ashes down to be buried, she felt a twinge deep inside. 'It was like the birth pang I had felt when Hans Christian was born. Now I had to give him back.'

THIRTEEN

Resolution Through Dialogue

The discovery of Hans Christian Ostrø's mutilated corpse stunned the families of the other men still being held in captivity. The manner of his death was unimaginably brutal, dragged like an animal into a forest clearing where he was trussed up and beheaded with his own knife. This was the so-called 'show kill' IG Rajinder Tikoo had been worried about. And according to the note pinned to the body, Don, Keith, Paul and Dirk only had forty-eight hours before they met a similar fate, unless the Indian government did something new.

Almost four thousand miles away in Middlesbrough, Keith Mangan's mother Mavis felt tormented. 'Newspapers and TV people phoned all day, asking me, "How do you feel?" I said, "How do you *think* I feel?" and slammed down the phone.' Keith's father Charlie did speak to a reporter, saying, 'If Keith knows what happened to Hans Ostrø, I shudder to think what he's thinking about now.' In Blackburn, Bob Wells, Paul's father, was desperate and resigned: 'Apart from raising a private army and sending it in, there is little we can do. Things were moving along quite positively. Now we are back at square one.' Even John Childs came out to issue a condemnation of the bloody events in India. 'Although I never met Hans Christian Ostrø, I knew something of what he must have gone through,' he said later. After he learned how Ostrø had died, all his worst memories came flooding back: the slaughtering of the sheep, the nights shivering under rough blankets wondering if each hour would be his last, the likelihood that he would never see his daughters again. 'To this day I remain utterly horrified,' he said.

Did the other hostages know about Ostrø? No one could be certain. Those in a position to know, the Indian authorities, were giving nothing away and appeared stunned into inertia by the beheading. Something had to be done to reinvigorate the operation to free the hostages, and to get India to articulate its strategy. 'It's getting desperate up there now,' Bob Wells told the *Lancashire Telegraph*, adding that he wanted the Indians to mount a rescue attempt. Tim Devlin, Charlie and Mavis Mangan's MP, said the couple agreed: 'They would rather something was done, even though they know it is enormously risky.' If India declined, the West should step in, foreign newspaper columnists suggested, calling on their governments to carry out unilateral 'tactical operations' in Kashmir to free the men. The pace was upped in New Delhi, the Ambassadors of Norway, Germany and the USA, Arne Walther, Frank Elbe and Frank Wisner, along with the British High Commissioner Sir Nicholas Fenn, demanding 'crisis talks' with the Indian Home Minister and intelligence chiefs.

In London, Commander Roy Ramm recoiled when he heard the news. He thought Ostrø's killing 'medieval'. In his long career at New Scotland Yard, where he had risen to become head of Specialist Operations, he had never seen anything quite like it. For the past five years he had been the lead on hostage negotiations, roaming the globe in his attempts to talk captured Britons free, and he had followed the Kashmiri hostage crisis since it first unfolded in the heights of the Pir Panjal.

Ramm read a hostage situation, one of his chief inspectors said, like a trashy novel – fast and avidly, and not necessarily taking in all the details. He didn't need to, since he was a master of the judgement call. When he received the first reports of the Kashmir drama, on 5 July, he had been in New York giving a talk at the United Nations. He had 'stuck out a wet thumb to see which way the wind was blowing', and concluded at once that things were 'terrible from the off', writing in his private journal: 'I learned that the rebels were demanding the release by the Indian government of what they described as "*political prisoners*". I was concerned that we would have little latitude in negotiations.' He was acutely aware that having faced down the IRA's bombing campaign for three decades, the British government would never agree to fold before terrorists, let alone condone the release of political detainees, and he presumed that India felt the same.

An emergency bag always at the ready, passport in one pocket, toothbrush in another, for the past five years Commander Ramm had lived a last-minute life. Permanently on duty, perma-tanned, his hair prematurely greying but elegantly styled, he had a penchant for high-collared, open-necked shirts that disguised his thick neck and narrow shoulders. Roy Ramm was a hunting dog, ever alert for the call that could dispatch him anywhere in the world. Back in London after his New York trip, he was summoned to the Foreign and Commonwealth Office (FCO), fully expecting to be on the next flight to India. This incident needed clarity and speed of response. Instead, a junior civil servant 'with a broom up his arse and a Double First in Classics' told him that his services were not needed. 'That was bloody quick,' thought the prickly Ramm. That night his anger spilled over into his journal: 'The FCO seemed to think that the Indians had everything under control.' He doubted it, since from a quick reading of the facts and a little research into the context – a vicious and unending war between two neighbours sharing a disputed 'non-border' – he could see that India needed all the help it could get. 'That's why in hostage situations governments brought in outside teams to mediate a solution: a dispassionate voice of reason unconnected to whatever had set the crisis running in the first place.'

But here he was, Britain's premier hostage negotiator, getting the brush-off while lives were under threat in Kashmir. 'White-collar trade unionism', he called it: 'Civil servants protecting their arses and their assets.' Complacency got people killed, he warned. Didn't they know that? He pointed out that 'people took hostages primarily to get attention'. If you dismissed the kidnappers, as he believed the Indians were doing for whatever reasons, driving the talks into a ditch intentionally or otherwise, al Faran would feel compelled to kill so as to make itself heard. 'A skilled negotiator engages the hostage-takers, listens to their concerns and empathises. Once you have their trust, then you can take control,' Ramm tried to explain, just as IG Tikoo had done thousands of miles away. But the young men with their Double Firsts in Classics had not listened.

It was not as if Ramm needed the work. His hands were full right now. 'Keep me in the loop,' he chirped as he walked out of the FCO, but he was worried that he already knew where this would end up. To him, the FCO was a collegiate supper club that smelled of Mr Sheen. The activities of the Yard, which he had joined in the sixties, 'in the days when it was still a force and not yet a service', as he liked to say, were underwritten by intelligence gleaned and action well-planned. And it was a meritocracy, albeit a predominantly male, white, Christian, working-class one, that had spent several decades defending itself against allegations that it was in thrall to the Masons and in the pay of organised crime.

Ramm was forced to 'watch from the sidelines as in those first weeks the hostage negotiations went round in circles', he wrote. He was shocked that 'there was very little desire to increase the pressure over here, even though two British nationals were involved'. Then his worst fears had been realised with Ostrø's death. Within hours, and with another deadline about to expire, Ramm received a 'sombre' call from Whitehall while he was out on a Sunday walk with his wife. He was called back to the woody whorl of the FCO for a briefing. Twenty-four hours later he was on a plane to New Delhi, with instructions to try to discern the Indian strategy, help shape it and move things forward. 'After Ostrø's death, it was like flicking a switch,' Ramm said of the British government's response. 'It just went at a different speed.' The previous mood of optimism among the diplomats in New Delhi had been 'hammered into the red dust'.

The British team in New Delhi appeared relieved to see Commander Ramm. The High Commissioner, Sir Nicholas Fenn, had dispatched his own white Land Rover to collect the detective from Indira Gandhi International Airport. As soon as he reached the British compound in the manicured Chanakyapuri diplomatic enclave, Ramm tried to impose some order on the situation. The latest deadline had just expired, and they needed to wipe the slate clean and restore proper channels of communication with al Faran. Most importantly, India, a country fidgety about sovereignty and filled with post-colonial anxieties, fighting a proxy war stoked by its neighbour and under the scrutiny of London, had to open up and cooperate with them. 'Our side only had to sneeze to put New Delhi's back out,' Ramm later wrote in his journal. He could see that it wouldn't be easy. From what he had read of the case on the plane, he was also wary about al Faran: 'Jittery, shocked by their own actions, maybe even a little revolted, the kidnappers will be feeling fenced in and frightened.'

An emergency meeting of the G4 was called at the US Embassy. Ramm was invited too. It was, he was advised, the right forum for throwing ideas around. 'Thank God,' he thought to himself. But on the way over he listened incredulously as the deputy head of the British mission briefed him on the philosophy of the G4 set-up. The four concerned nations had agreed to keep only one permanent representative in Srinagar, while a small team of diplomats based in New Delhi maintained daily communication with India's Home and External Affairs ministries. They had also agreed an 'all for one and one for all' policy. All the hostages would have to be released in one group; there would be no trade-offs that saw a dribble of releases, one man at a time. Ramm thought, 'What the fuck is that?' It sounded a lot like socialism. In almost every kidnapping he had resolved, he had done it by gradually whittling away at the hostage-takers' demands. He couldn't believe the G4 had set the bar so high from the start. As far as he was concerned, pragmatism reigned in struggles to the death.

Ramm was glad to find a familiar face at the US Embassy: Gary Noesner, the head of the FBI's Crisis Negotiation Unit, motto *Pax per Conloquium*, or 'Resolution through Dialogue'. Noesner had an excellent record, with one significant *caveat*: Waco. Two years previously he had been the Bureau's chief negotiator at the fifty-day siege of cult leader David Koresh's Texas compound that had ended with a raid that left seventy-six dead, including more than twenty children. These days Agent Noesner used the episode to hammer home the lesson that negotiation almost always won out over tactical operations, bemoaning the FBI's failure to establish proper channels with Koresh. Noesner was a bootstraps agent, just like Ramm, and they respected each other. But no sooner had they sat down with the US diplomats and a handful of State Department representatives than the temperature dropped a few degrees. 'I sensed that my mere presence seemed to offend,' Ramm wrote, concluding that the crowd from Foggy Bottom regarded the FBI and British detectives as 'bottom feeders'.

He pressed on, directing a clutch of questions at Noesner, who was several weeks ahead of him on the kidnapping. How many kidnappers were there? What were their methods of communication? What about the psychological state of the hostages? Had anyone spoken to them directly? Had they debriefed John Childs? No one answered. Noesner looked shifty. Ramm began wondering if he was in the wrong meeting. This was not like any operation he had been on before. 'There was some arse-watching going on here. Or perhaps client protection. It was as if the gathered diplomats were more concerned about feathering their relationship with India than about freeing the hostages.' After Ramm's pressing questions had been ignored, an FBI agent he had never met stood to explain that he would demand that India hand over documents and tape recordings as potential exhibits. He was looking to build cases for an extra-territorial criminal prosecution in a US court. Ramm cringed, realising that this agent was from a so-called witness testimony team that had been formed in the mid-1980s to gather evidence in foreign countries. They had been used in Liberia and Colombia, and their activities had sometimes led to audacious and controversial FBI actions, with foreign nationals seized without the knowledge or consent of their governments. 'Cart before horse,' Ramm later noted in his journal: two FBI teams working the same case, and not together. He worried that the team looking to prosecute perpetrators would alienate India, undermining the operation of the second, tasked with freeing the hostages, whose success hinged on India's cooperation. 'I felt uncomfortable that the element of the Bureau I believed could contribute most was starved of intelligence [by India] whilst another element, of which I knew very little, was likely to make things even harder with the host government,'

Ramm wrote. He did the sums: four embassies, four sets of military advisors, four sets of spooks, and two FBI teams, not to mention a hostile, go-it-alone Indian establishment and the 'all for one and one for all' policy of the G4. 'Things were *not* good.'

Ramm was asked to leave while the diplomats thrashed out the details. 'I know that some of what I said in that first meeting in the US Embassy may have made life briefly difficult for my diplomatic colleagues from the British Embassy,' he reflected. However, much to his surprise, later that day he was appointed to lead a multinational team that he hoped was not already dead in the water. 'On the Americans' part I suspect there was also a measure of "Anything to get that Limey bastard out of our hair" about it,' he said.

Roy Ramm had been in plenty of hot spots, but something about Srinagar appalled him. On the flight up he had been shocked to see foreign tourists clearly intending to go trekking, even with a hostage crisis ongoing. The scene on the streets was even more disturbing: Kashmiris carrying on with their lives as if the overwhelming military presence around them – more than half a million soldiers in a valley not much bigger than Hampshire – was invisible. 'It was on a different planet to New Delhi,' he wrote. Security Advisor Saklani had arranged for the representatives of the Yard and the FBI to be put up in state guesthouses in the complex in Church Lane where Jane, Cath, Julie and Anne had stayed. 'We drove for about half an hour before arriving at a road with a heavily fortified guard post at its entrance,' Ramm wrote. 'We waited whilst soldiers looking for bombs peered beneath our vehicle with mirrors. Our operations base was a large, once-comfortable house with four bedrooms on the first floor and several rooms on the ground floor we could use as offices.' From the back windows, across a lawn dominated by a generator and satellite communications dishes, he could see the Jhelum River.

The house filled up fast: 'There were two negotiators, always a British police officer – usually from the Yard – an FBI agent, diplomats from the USA, Germany and the UK and the odd soldier or two.' Then there were the British and American spooks from MI6 and the

CIA, as well as military advisors from both countries, who wore no uniforms but still all dressed the same: chinos, T-shirts and shades. With all the bedrooms occupied, Ramm unpacked in a ground-floor room, amid a collection of old car batteries used as a back-up power supply when the nightly 'load shedding' kicked in. One of his team, Chris Newman, an old colleague who had flown up ahead of him, gave him 'some helpful advice about bed bugs, lice and sundry other unpleasant insects', and briefed him on the Indian operation being led by Security Advisor Saklani from the villa next door.

Ramm's first meeting with Saklani was scheduled for that afternoon. Philip Barton, the thirty-one-year-old First Secretary at the British High Commission, was also in town, and advised him to tread carefully. But then, British journalists had been critical of Barton too: Tim McGirk of the *Independent* reported that 'some Kashmiris felt the diplomats were far too reliant on the Indian authorities to secure the release of the hostages'. The British diplomats had been assured that a 'massive search' was under way, although there was little evidence of one.

Ramm arrived for the meeting before the appointed time. Saklani's office was already filled with unidentified officials. 'We all sat in cinema rows in front of the General,' Ramm wrote. A marble inkstand and paperweights formed a barrier across the glass-topped desk. Dressed in immaculately pressed military khaki and a silk cravat, Saklani had 'distinguished grey hair, neatly trimmed and oiled in 1950s military style'. For Ramm, the protocols were too elaborate, 'a succession of handshakes and small talk about the food, my journey and the weather, before tea and biscuits were served by a white-suited orderly'. The Yard had its own customs, but they ran more to a pint of Pride and a bag of cheese-and-onion crisps at the Feathers. 'Saklani's English was excellent, his Englishness over-manicured and anachronistic,' Ramm wrote. He had not worked in India before, and had no understanding of Saklani's background or intentions.

Ramm thought they hit it off. 'He rather liked my rank, "Commander". It was comforting, more naval than police.' And after the pleasantries Saklani launched into a 'useful' briefing, and 'told us what he could'. Ramm was surprised. This could work out after all, he thought, since Saklani was 'a decent and fundamentally honest man'.

What could the Security Advisor tell him about negotiations, Ramm asked, referring to the secret talks he had read about in the newspapers. Saklani did not balk. 'Mr Tikoo', a senior Kashmiri police officer, was conducting them. What were their methods and means? 'Conversations with al Faran usually took place on VHF radio, and Tikoo had to deal with them alone,' Ramm wrote later, highlighting the sentence to show his concern. Afterwards he annotated this passage: 'Negotiating is not the battle of two great minds, Karpov against Spassky, chess grandmasters computing every move in their heads. The normal Yard and FBI system was to have more of us than them.'

After the meeting Ramm made the first of many long-distance phone calls: '[A colleague in Colombia] was by now in the foothills of the Andes, trying to get the British soldier [who had been taken while birdwatching on his day off] freed. In hindsight these were extraordinary conversations. Two Metropolitan Police detectives, at opposite ends of the earth, in the remotest of locations, using skills learned on the streets of London to try to save the lives of Britons held by guerrillas and bandits.' Maybe, he would concede later, when he had had time to come to terms with what was about to happen, this had been his first fundamental error, positioning the Yard as the saviour, when all along the answers lay with India.

Over the next couple of days Ramm got used to waiting in line to see Saklani, taking a seat in a fan-cooled antechamber, surrounded by old Kashmiri men and women who came in a steady stream seeking information about missing sons. 'Saklani told me that there was not much he could do for any of them, so he doled out a few rupees, like alms, and sent them away,' Ramm wrote. On al Faran matters too, Ramm could not shake the feeling that while Saklani was attentive, he gave away nothing of importance. More than anything else, Ramm knew he needed to get close to Rajinder Tikoo, the hostage negotiator, if he was going to have any influence over how things progressed. He explained this view to Saklani, telling him that negotiators in the West trained for years before they were let loose on a live hostage situation. Saklani had appeared irritated by this, Ramm recalled, then let slip that Tikoo was not always alone. Every night the Crime Branch IG attended a high-powered debrief with Indian intelligence, the army and the Governor – another meeting to which foreigners were not invited. Ramm saw a crack in Saklani's defences. 'I said, "Look, you have the cream of the world's crisis-management teams sitting on your doorstep. We can help. Let us address the meeting or feed ideas into it." The General said he would have to consult the security agencies, and here was the problem.' The Indian officials in Kashmir were immersed in Kashmir, and believed their perspective could never be understood by outsiders. Murderous things happened in this lawless corner of the subcontinent that only made sense to battle-hardened Indians who were versed in the game. 'This was not Dixon of Dock Green, where the Police and Criminal Evidence Act held sway,' said Ramm.

Frustrated, the British officer returned to Church Lane. He didn't want the keys to the bloody city, just a chance to recharge this flagging inquiry. 'Saklani had a terrible dilemma,' he wrote in his journal. 'The hostage-taking was important to us and, I believed, to him, but it had to be seen in context. There was a war going on that Saklani and his comrades had been fighting for years. Apart from reports of diplomatic activity in New Delhi and occasionally in the United Nations in New York, I suspect Saklani had been isolated from direct contact with representatives of foreign governments for his entire career, and now he had four living in the house next door!'

Ramm's team waited. They were not idle, using the time to transform their Church Lane villa into a forward command post. But they had been unable to get maps from the Indian authorities, as representations of this shifting area of disputed borders had been classified, seen as potentially confirming (or denying) one country's claim over the other. Around the world there were numerous conflicts over statehood and identity in which maps with their defining boundaries were politically toxic, from Israel's dispute with the Palestinian people to the civil war raging between Tamils and the government in Sri Lanka. Any maps, even the most basic tourist version, that showed Kashmir, or India's sensitive borders with China, let alone Bangladesh, had been impounded in the national archives years ago, and the army and its agents had been removing road signs and destroying granite mileage markers throughout the valley since the early nineties, creating a nameless, routeless war in an area that had become engulfed in ambiguity.

Western embassies resorted to US military flight charts dating from the 1950s, single sheets that were overlaid to make composite maps. Having managed to patch together a visualisation of the terrain, Ramm's team could begin to chart the movement of the hostages. In the absence of intelligence sharing, they drew most of their information from the press and the television news, as did Tikoo, using coloured markers and drawing pins to record sightings on their improvised charts. 'In a typical hostage situation, you know where everyone is, and you pick up the phone and you know where to ring,' Ramm said. 'If you're in London, and you have a kidnapping, you're so proximate to it that the policeman says, "OK, let's cordon off the area and kick the doors in until we find this guy."' But there was nothing typical about this crisis.

Ramm would have to be resourceful. He closely studied the short document that constituted John Childs' debrief, and those of the Westerners who had escaped the kidnappers' clutches in 1994. From what Childs had recalled, the original group of four captives were taken on a route that roughly shadowed the Amarnath trek, although they had shunned the regular paths through the Betaab Valley, choosing instead to make a series of punishing u -and-over climbs. For the first three nights they had camped above t e treeline in remote *gujjar* communities, but on the fourth they had camped a few hundred metres above the Amarnath track. The locations from where Dirk Hasert and Hans Christian Ostrø had been snatched, Chandanwari and Zargibal, were both stopping-off points along the way to Sheshnag. Beyond Sheshnag Lake the path split, the Amarnath route peeling away to the north-east, while another, little-used route led south-east towards the treacherous Sonasar Pass and into largely uncharted territory. Which route had the kidnappers taken?

Foreign trekkers would invariably head north-east to Amarnath or north-west to visit sights such as Kolahoi Glacier, Sonamarg and Buttress Peak. But as far as the FBI could learn, there had been no sightings of the hostages towards the north, suggesting that the rebels had gone south, into a wild and remote area about which little was known. Given that Ostrø's body had been found in this direction, this was the most likely theory. It gained ground after Ramm's team quizzed foreign journalists who had been following the story from the beginning, who told them the gossip on the ground was that the hostages were in the vicinity of the Warwan, a wide, isolated valley running north to south between Sheshnag and the villages east of Anantnag, whose only links to the outside world were over a series of treacherous snowbound passes. One of these routes – the Sonasar Pass – split off from the Amarnath Cave route at Sheshnag, and involved a gruelling and dangerous southerly climb of twelve miles. Beyond, the Warwan widened out into a lush plateau more than twenty miles in length, with as few as a dozen villages lining its flanks.

Studying material from the kidnappings of Kim Housego and David Mackie, the team read that Kim and his parents had been seized near the Meadow and taken to Aru on the pretence of checking their passports. The ransom demands were also similar to those in the present case. Kim's recollections, written up for the FCO and Scotland Yard after his return to the UK, referred to himself and Mackie walking for three days before being forced at gunpoint to make a painful climb at high altitude, a route that eventually led down through a birch forest into a long glacial valley. Here, in a village at the foot of the pass, they were locked inside a wooden 'guesthouse' for several days while the kidnappers deliberated. Later they had been marched down through the valley towards another icy pass at its southern limit, only for the kidnap team to change their minds and march them back up again the following day. Eventually they had been taken back over the pass at the head of the valley before joining a rough, muddy track at Chandanwari, from where they were taken by taxi to Anantnag. It all seemed to fit what Ramm was seeing on the map.

Kim said he had overheard the name of the village in which they had been kept for most of their time as hostages: Sukhnoi (pronounced 'Sook-nes'). Ramm's team eventually found it at the head of the Warwan Valley, just south of the Sonasar Pass. Might the hut Kim and David were imprisoned in have been used again, one year on, to hold Don, Keith, Dirk, Hans Christian and Paul? Were they its wooden walls that provided the backdrop to the recently released photos? Ramm thought it possible.

FBI headquarters at Quantico in Virginia chipped in, closely examining all the kidnappers' photos. It was just possible that the flowers visible in one picture of the hostages sitting on a rock might grow only in a certain place. *Gujjar dhokas* also varied subtly from valley to valley, and the lichen, mosses and grasses that roofed them could help to determine elevation and orientation, their exposure to the sun and growth patterns helping create a compass grid for the images. Then there were the missing personal items. The detectives began drawing up a list: Don's yellow-and-black Casio altimeter, Nikon SLR and Tamron lenses; John Childs' Canon, with his social security number etched on its base; Paul's Nikon camera inherited from his grandfather; Julie and Keith's stolen travellers' cheques; and Hans Christian's missing Norwegian Army-issue boot. Five passports. The FBI also called on John at home in Simsbury. 'They would come with photographs of dead militants, who all looked like they'd been in a freezer for some considerable time,' John said. 'They looked like strangers to me.'

Al Faran had killed once. Would it do so again? Roy Ramm wished he had been running the show from the start. An experienced negotiator would have sensed that tensions in the rebel camp had been building to dangerous levels before the killing of Ostrø, and measures could have been taken to ease the pressure. This was the kind of delicate operation Ramm specialised in. It relied on psychological profiling, human instinct, technical intelligence and everyone working to the same purpose.

Once, he tried to talk to General Saklani about profiling, explaining how negotiation teams spent as much time seeking out information on those behind a kidnapping as talking to them. But the war-weary general changed the subject. Like all who served in Kashmir, after a number of years at the front line it had ceased to matter to him where the men he saw as terrorists came from, whether it was Bahawalpur, Mirpur, Kotli or Khost. It mattered even less if they were motivated by religious belief or politics. To Saklani and his colleagues, they were simply a mass of faceless and illiterate *jihadis*, clinging to a false ideology. All of which was unsatisfactory for the foreign teams, who began assembling their own files instead.

Comparing the demands made in 1994 and 1995, they zeroed in on the man at the centre of both: Masood Azhar. The FBI and Scotland Yard made representations to visit Masood in Tihar jail, but as they expected they were refused. Instead they raided Western intelligence archives to discover deep linkages, reports, nuggets and speculation that had remained dormant, but that when put together portrayed a very different Masood to the blethering fundamentalist pigeon his Indian captors represented him as. A copy of his confession from 1994, obtained by the FBI from a friendly Indian intelligence source, showed that he had readily admitted to travelling to Kenya, Somalia and Sudan in 1991 and 1993, describing how he had been dispatched by Maulana Khalil, his mentor from the Binori Town *madrassa* in Karachi, to corral veterans of the Afghan war who had been deported by Pakistan after the conflict ended.

'In Sudan, Masood had met Osama bin Laden and his nascent al Qaeda group, founded in 1988 in Afghanistan,' read one report Ramm saw. The FBI requested more information on both bin Laden and al Qaeda, which in 1995 were perceived as minor players. Reports gathered by British foreign intelligence and its allies' agencies suggested that bin Laden had armed, funded and transported fighters idling in Africa to a new front opened up by the Islamic Union of Somalia that was facing down US forces sent to bolster a failing international peacekeeping mission, with Masood Azhar providing the rhetoric in the field. Through bin Laden, this report suggested, Masood had come into the orbit of Somali warlord Mohammed Farah Aideed, who in 1993 had had a central role in the ground-shaking events that would later be depicted in the movie *Black Hawk Down*. Working with bin Laden again, Masood had travelled to Yemen to redirect yet more militants to the Somali *jihad*, meeting *mujahid* leader Tariq Nasr Fadhli, also an Afghanistan veteran, who was suspected of being behind two hotel bombings in Yemen in December 1992 that had targeted US Marines headed for Somalia.

Kenya, Sudan and Yemen. A trap laid for US forces in Somalia. Osama bin Laden's cash and Masood's invective. Ramm and the FBI were building up an alarming portrait of the man al Faran demanded be freed. French, German and British intelligence had further snippets, as did the Saudis. They warned that Masood's influence extended deep into Europe. During the early nineties he had travelled extensively across Britain, where he was hosted by a *maulvi* in east London. Raising funds and recruits, his oratorical reputation preceding him and packing out mosques up and down the country, Masood had targeted working-class Pakistani expatriates, who maintained strong links with their old homes and had transformed places like Mirpur, in Pakistan-controlled Kashmir, into boom towns.

In Birmingham, Masood befriended Abdul Rauf, formerly a judge in the *sharia* court at Mirpur, who in those days made his money as a baker in Bordesley Green. According to British intelligence, Rauf was a keen fund-raiser, having helped set up Crescent Relief, a charity that sent donations to Pakistan. Rauf introduced him to 'his rootless teenage son, Rashid, whom he said was in need of a mentor'. It would be some years before that relationship would lead to the wayward Rashid Rauf enlisting with Masood in Pakistan, hooking up with Osama bin Laden's al Qaeda too. There were others Masood recruited as well. A file note sent to Ramm mentioned Omar Sheikh, the LSE student who was used by the Movement as the bait in the kidnapping of Paul Rideout and three other Western tourists in New Delhi in October 1994.

Studying Masood's finances, other connections emerged. Not only had Osama bin Laden funded some of his operations, the US intelligence community found compelling evidence that in Pakistan the ISI had been underwriting his organisation, making monthly payments of up to $60,000 to the Movement. In two classified memos circulated to the American embassies in Islamabad and New Delhi, the CIA highlighted how the Movement was also 'discussing financing with sponsors of international terrorism'. The bankers were thought to include the then Libyan dictator Muammar Gaddafi. Masood's outfit had 'new support groups founded across Europe, and head-quartered in the UK'. These groups' strategy was also changing, according to the CIA memo, with Western civilians now a target and self-contained terror groups being ditched for a much more fluid and united movement of like-minded *jihadis*.

There was compelling evidence that this transformation had already started. The CIA learned that the Movement had moved its training camps out of Pakistan-administered Kashmir to Khost, re-establishing them alongside camps operated by Osama bin Laden and protected by the rampant Taliban, Afghan student medievalists wreathed in black who by 1995 controlled nine of Afghanistan's thirty provinces. They had begun to besiege Kabul too, and were emerging as likely rulers of the entire fractured country. 'Masood Azhar was a dangerous emerging force,' an FBI report concluded. Was this, Ramm wondered, why the Indians would not countenance freeing him? Or did they know none of it? There were no answers forthcoming from New Delhi, but what Ramm had discovered was a frightening portal into the future, that reflected grimly on the present crisis too.

An alarming picture of the Movement and its General Secretary Masood Azhar was emerging. But what of the hostages and their captors from the mysterious al Faran, about which no intelligence could be found? The foreign detectives began to examine the letters secretly written by Hans Christian Ostrø, both the ones found on his body and the many others that had made their way by various means into the hands of the police. Working on copies supplied by the Norwegian Embassy, they started with the Arvind Cotton Classics advertisement that DSP Kifayat Haider had found hidden inside the dead man's shirt, the one that he had used to reveal he had stashed a message to his family 'in my balls'. A few lines higher up on the page, unnoticed by the Kashmiri police, was another short message written in minuscule lettering. Dated 'August 6', it was entitled 'Escape Part 2'.

It began with a time. '0.30. I talked with Dirk and shared some thoughts and questions with him. We have been thinking about the same things: about the women and how to get away. If we have not escaped, I think we will do it in the middle of this month if nothing happens. *Inshallah*, if God wills … Light up the flame, sing and be joyful.'

So they *had* been plotting an escape. Ramm's men postulated that they were trying to win over the village women who cooked for them. Maybe it was for this reason that Ostrø had been murdered, Ramm suggested.

Some other notes were dated too. On 'Dag 24' (which for Ostrø would have been 1 August) he referred to trouble brewing inside the kidnappers' camp: 'Here has been a fight and that was good. Now one needs to go carefully because it is a minefield.' Tensions were high, and the kidnap team seemed to be in danger of splitting. 'People are locked in. Other fellows are locked in too. They are left over to other people without weapons and they could not defend themselves.' Ostrø appeared to be referring either to sympathetic villagers being locked up with them, or to Movement men who had been won over by the hostages.

On another page was a similar reference to fighting: 'Holy fight, the battle's just begun. We're melting silver bullets. To be on the run. The dogs are hungry with their tongues outside. Still we try to have fun and be a preacher in the night.' Ostrø was trying to mess with the heads of these men whom he thought of as slavish animals. But then Ramm's team came across a more literal entry: 'I have changed a bit since I wrote the first note and I hope your chances are good.' Ostrø could only be addressing the other hostages, they concluded, which meant he had been separated from the others, although he was still close enough to them to believe he could get this note to them, maybe carried by the women, or by one of the Movement's tame fighters who had been won over. But what had he done to be singled out? 'I can't personally put my faith in these people. I believe it will be harder for the big Kommando [sic] to put a death order on you with me alive.'

One week before Ostrø was killed, he had done something so momentous that he believed al Faran's leader, whoever that was, was considering having him killed. The FBI and Scotland Yard were convinced he had made an unsuccessful break for freedom, and that he was telling the others it was up to them to flee on their own. 'You might get home before me,' he continued. 'I am doing it now because I still have some strength left. I am slowly vanishing and I am of that kind which you can't really see if I am sick.' He was on hunger strike, perhaps intending to become a sacrifice, or to distract attention from the others. 'Good luck to you all,' he had signed off. 'God bless you in the fight!'

More fragments of what he had been going through lay in the pages of a little green prayer booklet, *The Hidden Words of the Baha'ullah*, that investigators established he had bought during a visit to the Bahá'í temple in New Delhi on his way to Kashmir. 'So what has the world to give today?' he had scribbled in the margin. 'A wet blanket, a cold, news in Urdu, good warm tea, bread without health, light from God, rain and blue heaven …' He went on to identify one of the kidnappers, 'Schub, a fighter, but he is only good and kind' – possibly a reference to someone with the Pakistani name Shoaib, the FBI noted.

Here also were poignant reflections on his old life: 'To all the girls I have known, how big a part I am in you, I don't know. But I do know that one kiss from you can put me out of balance, can send me high up in heaven out of control.' But these moments of elation were fleeting, and by the next message his mood had darkened: 'I'm hiding myself. It's turning to evening. There are so many lonely others who will fight God. They are all seeing. Don't stand alone.' Was he feeling the weight of his isolation from the others? Some phrases were filled with a palpable sense of the strain he was under: 'I write this with my hands tied.' Some contained considerable foresight: 'Why such very bad people behind a prophet? The Muslim brotherhood represents pain, fear and hatefulness. Are you going to begin the next world war? Islam against developed countries. Are we going to suffer because of their ignorance? How does one meet hatred and isolation? Don't we have the same right to breathe and do things like they have?'

Throughout, his growing pessimism was palpable. 'To my family,' he wrote. 'If I should die now … I don't die poor … You have been the essence that I have built my life on. A big train of gratitude and happiness is going through Asia to Norway to come and live in the house you have built in your dreams. Think of me. Think of castles, drakes, women with long hair. Think of little puppies, old skinny books, the innocent, growing seeds, rainbows, stars, the sun – and grow?' In a dark corner he had conjured the things that made him happy.

'To my family,' he wrote again. 'If I should die now, there will come bubbles of the tenderest love to those who are going to keep going with this life on earth which I have loved. The warmest hugs … I'm not afraid to die. You should know I'm well. I have had it better, but I'm not in any pain. Inside me there is lots of light. If I should die now, I have to tell you there are lots of things unfinished. My unborn children have missed an exciting childhood and my ocean of love. My family will never see me again. My best friends will put a ring of flowers on the top of a tower. If I should die now, I will not be satisfied. Much time will be wasted. Much suffering for me and mine without meaning … Open up lord, open up my eyes because I see my limitations and I am very silent.'

Then came the last set of notes. 'Now I'm tired. It will be evening. The voice has been reduced and the listeners have become dust.' He had no audience left, just his own imagination. 'The butt has been broken, which dream shall now be dreamed?' All he could hear were the angry voices of his captors. 'Repetition and noisy men repeat themselves and are very boring, monotonous.' They were arguing about how to deal with him. 'One destructive hope, to escape home.' But he feared that due to his hunger strike he no longer had the strength to run. 'The well is empty and the stomach is cavernous. I am tired and stop for the night. The sky is still blue but only very little from outside comes into this cell.'

At the very end, he had run out of paper. He wrote the last message on a strip of bark, probably ripped from one of the silver birches that rose behind Sukhnoi village. It was the hardest to read. 'I'm standing on a swing and grey skies become red,' he began. 'Suddenly it was over without warning. Broken knuckles, every organ breathing for air over the ocean waves. Then, it was over. There was no screaming, no hysteria, women yelling or children crying. Only the silence of old men's stagnation and their peace and their quietness, their stillness of knowledge. Far away the golden castle supported by four elephants, Shiva's temple. Around, shifting horizons. Then, it was over. The river's cosmic fleeting was ended. Old men's dry tears over material loss. Hissing snakes and self-pity. So it was over, a person with black eyes, Allah and My Lord. A pistol. I was not afraid. The End.'

The post mortem found broken skin on the knuckles of both of Hans Christian's hands. His lungs had inhaled a mist of blood after the knife's first, blunt cut. But there was no pistol. In the end they had used his own army knife.

Saklani had barred Commander Ramm from going outside the compound in the daytime, and there had been nothing from the kidnappers since the last deadline had expired on 15 August to prove that the remaining hostages were still alive. Ramm's nights were spent watching bootleg videos with American military advisors and contemplating a small photograph he had tucked in his wallet soon after arriving in Srinagar, a picture of the hostages that he kept close to an important letter from his son. 'I carried the photograph as a kind of reminder that amid the stifling bureaucracy of the G4 and the complications of negotiating, there were *lives* at risk,' he said. But as the days dragged by, Ramm began to doubt that he would be able to exert any influence on this crisis, especially after al Faran issued another warning on 18 August that if the army or anyone else launched a raid, 'we will kill the hostages immediately'. This turned the Indian authorities even further inwards.

Then a small movement in the tectonic plates of state occurred. Inexplicably, Ramm was offered a phone call to Rajinder Tikoo, the

Indian police negotiator he had not met, and whose transcripts of his conversations with the al Faran contact he had never seen. The conversation was brief and uninformative, but jovial. The Inspector General of Crime Branch made it clear he was delighted to talk to Ramm, and admitted that he was struggling in his task. He even asked Ramm for his help, hoping the 'huge and sophisticated' intelligence machine back in London could be made to work for him. He also asked Ramm 'if "from our perches high in the sky" we could see movement in a certain area', suggesting that whatever technical intelligence the Indian Army had, it was not sharing it with the Kashmir police. Ramm said he would find out.

Tikoo approached Saklani and asked if Ramm could be present, as a coach, during the phone calls with al Faran, but his request was turned down: 'This seemed a bit too much like a Western takeover bid,' Ramm wrote in his journal. But he got another call, and another, with Tikoo feeding him anodyne titbits, as he clearly hinted that their conversations were being listened in to, and that he was limited in what he could reveal. 'We gave him quicker and better-prepared analyses than his own people could produce,' Ramm recalled. 'We were good at this. We had resources in New Delhi, London and Washington all working hard to corroborate the information provided by Tikoo. We wanted to help, if only they would let us help.'

Eventually General Saklani seemed to ease up, as Ramm and Tikoo talked regularly. Ramm formulated a strategy. 'Go for proof of life,' he advised Tikoo. The killing of Hans Christian Ostrø had put an end to the dialogue, and there was no proof that the other hostages had not been killed. One way to revive the talks and get away from the kidnappers' demands would be for the Indian side to make some demands of its own: 'Prove the captives are still alive, with the ultimate goal being something groundbreaking – like a live conversation with the hostages.'

Tikoo loved this idea. He felt isolated, even hated, dismissed in the Indian media after Ostrø's death as an 'incompetent unnamed Indian negotiator'. Ramm could see the stress Tikoo was under: 'Sometimes, late in the night when he had been pleading with the rebels on the telephone or having a clandestine meeting with an emissary, he would call me and we would chat on the telephone.' The Commander would sit with his sleeping bag wrapped around him, listening to Tikoo's worries. On 19 August Tikoo called in a panic after Jehangir, the al Faran caller, had rung to tell him he should say farewell to the hostages, as they were about to be killed. 'I felt sorry for Tikoo. He was too often having to absorb the stress and horror on his own, and he badly needed support. He was under very considerable personal pressure. "Oh well," Tikoo would say, yawning down the telephone line to me at three in the morning, "I have Mr Johnnie Walker to give me a hand. Good night, my friend."'

Finally, after many days and weeks of asking, Ramm and Tikoo met face to face at Saklani's office. Each was pleasantly surprised by the other. 'Although deferential to Saklani, Tikoo held his ground when he felt he had a point,' Ramm wrote in his journal. 'He would make his point forcefully, nodding, smiling, stabbing at the air with the end of his good English briar pipe – of which he had a collection.' Tikoo was quick to open up. 'When we were alone with him, in a side room of Saklani's house, he whispered, "Fucking soldiers don't understand coppers. They think differently to us." I found this a very Anglo-Saxon comment, in one way so absolutely typical of police-canteen language and culture, but so incredibly out of place in the foothills of the Himalayas. I laughed out loud, too loudly for Tikoo's comfort, and he quickly "shushed" at me.' Tikoo, Ramm felt, 'could have been dropped into most Met police stations and would have blended in'.

In the early hours of 22 August, the day before Jane Schelly and Don Hutchings' tenth wedding anniversary, IG Tikoo received an unexpected call at his home in Transport Lane. The Movement was making a drop, and he was requested to pick it up personally, in an elaborate and potentially deadly piece of theatre. 'Where?' he asked. 'Khanyar,' replied his contact – the downtown neighbourhood of Srinagar where the previous month the Border Security Force had stormed the house from which al Faran had been making the calls, causing the negotiations to become fraught. 'The crossroads near the Tomb of Jesus.'

The location was a busy intersection in the middle of Srinagar's old city. It had been given its name because it lay near Roza Bal, an ancient shrine to a Kashmiri saint that some ardent, creative Christians believed also to be the final resting place of Jesus, said by them to have gone there after surviving the crucifixion. The small, single-storey shrine building and the nearby Jamia Masjid mosque, Srinagar's largest, were surrounded by traffic, the Iqbal market and traditional wooden shop-houses. The area was always thronged with people, making it, in Tikoo's mind, the perfect location for an ambush. But he came as instructed, in an unmarked white Ambassador, and casually retrieved a dropped envelope, ripping it open as the car made its way back towards Lal Chowk and safer ground.

Inside was a photo: four familiar faces, although they were now visibly tense and numb, skeletal but *alive*. Of course there was no Hans Christian. When Ramm saw them he felt chastened. Don and Dirk sat in the middle, holding a newspaper dated 18 August, their beards visibly longer than before, although they were still wearing the same, now ragged clothes. Keith was at Don's side, dressed in the warm woollen waistcoat he had bought from the *shikara* salesman on Dal Lake. Paul, dressed in a heavy tartan shirt, was hugging his knees despondently. They all wore identical expressions of hopelessness. There was a cassette tape, too. 'My name is Paul Wells. Today is 18 August 1995. I am fit and healthy. I have no problems. Catherine, I love you. See you soon.' He sounded better than he looked. There were similar messages from Don, Keith and Dirk. 'Julie, I love you very much,' said Keith. 'Please pass on my love to my family.'

Prompted by Ramm, Tikoo knew what to do. He would thank Jehangir for the package, but tell him that all it proved was that the hostages had been alive the previous Friday. He would then ask him to provide concrete proof they were alive today. After that, things might get going once more.

Six days later, on 28 August, Tikoo sat down in Transport Lane and checked that the tape recorder was working. A few minutes later his VHF set burst into life, and a hesitant voice enquired, 'Hello?' The accent was unmistakably American. Tikoo closed his eyes to immerse himself in it. That one word made him 'thank the gods' and punch the air. It was Don Hutchings. This was the first direct contact anyone had had with the hostages since they were taken, in Don's case fifty-six days before. There was so much to say that Tikoo barely knew where to start, but the most important thing was to reassure the captives that his side was working hard. Their families were missing them, but were bearing up well, Tikoo said. They wanted them to 'be as strong as they were being'. Were the hostages all in good health? 'Yes, we have no problems,' Don replied, keeping his words to a minimum, talking precisely and without emotion. No doubt someone armed was sitting beside him, listening closely.

They went through a prearranged ritual, Tikoo asking obscure personal questions. 'What are the names of your cats?' 'Homer and Bodie,' came the almost inaudible reply. 'What happened to your twin brother?' 'He died when he was three days old.' It was definitely Don Hutchings. Tikoo read out some questions for the other hostages, and two days later Don spoke to him again, giving all the correct answers. For Keith: 'What is the name of the school that you and Julie went to, and who was Septimus?' Bertram Ramsey School, and Septimus was Keith's grandfather. For Paul: 'Where and when did you first meet Catherine Moseley?' 1 October 1992, at Rock City, Nottingham. And for Dirk: 'Where did you first meet Anne Katrin, and what is the name of your cat?' Anger Kino cinema in Erfurt. The cat's name was Mayer. Tikoo smiled. He felt they were back on track. He was going to win this. He was. Come what may.

FOURTEEN

Ordinary People

Trapped, with darkness all around, Jane Schelly tried to quell the rising sensations of panic. She was sure this was a dream, but leaving it was proving difficult. Her sleep felt treacly and deep. Try as she might, she felt as if she could not wake up. 'We're in a building, in a hallway with these metal steps, ones you can see through,' she recalled. 'The terrorists are in there, and so is Don, somewhere.' She didn't know how she knew it, she just did. But this place disoriented her, the stairs disappearing into a yawning void above. It took a few seconds to realise what the gnawing in her stomach was, but then she did: dread. She heard boots clank on metal. 'What I remember so clearly was that one of the terrorists was sitting on the step above me … and he had his arm round my neck and was holding a knife to my throat.' She felt the cold, gliding motion of a sharp blade slicing across her neck. 'If I moved at all, the knife started to cut in, and the blood was starting to drip down my neck onto my clothes.' Her nostrils filled with the ferrous smell of blood. Was this what Hans Christian had felt?

She heard voices. 'The terrorists were yelling and threatening to kill.' Looking down she saw Julie Mangan, 'a little farther on the steps, just kind of frozen'. Julie was looking up at her, horrified. 'Then suddenly I was facing a guy who had just appeared, dressed completely in black; he was a commando, a rescue guy. Just as quickly there was a shot, and the guy's head went flying through the air. I kept watching it, as the knife dug deeper into my throat and as I looked all around hoping to see Don.'

Jane's eyes flickered open, her trembling hands feeling the soft fret of cotton sheets, not steel banisters or concrete walls. After a few seconds of confusion she realised she was in New Delhi, in the two-storey apartment at the British High Commission that she, Julie, Anne and Cath had been staying in for the past few weeks. Since the horrific death of Hans Christian Ostrø on 13 August, nightmares like this had been plaguing her and the others. For nine days after his murder, they hadn't even known if the hostages were still alive. Then, after six weeks of nothing, hearing Don's voice just a few days after their wedding anniversary had made Jane feel more hopeful than she had in a long time. It had been such a gift to listen to him. The tape recordings of Tikoo's two conversations with Don were the first pieces from the negotiation process to be shared with the four women. There were also now some positive rumours.

After Don had answered the second set of proof-of-life questions on 30 August – the tape was played to the women a few days later – there had been a suggestion that al Faran might even release him as a sign of good will. But the G4 had resisted, sticking to its 'one-for-all' policy, and the opportunity passed. Jane had felt sick to her stomach, knowing she couldn't object, although she thought it unfair. Now she felt as if she was back in limbo: trapped between negotiations about which they were told almost nothing, and the Indian military's refusal to countenance a rescue attempt 'for fear of endangering the hostages' lives'. Every day, diplomatic liaison officers came to brief them just before lunch, reassuring them that 'strenuous efforts' were still being made in Srinagar. Jane did her best to remain positive, but she was struggling. She rolled over and stared, red-eyed, at the bedside clock. It was 4 a.m. The early hours were the hardest. Beside the clock, her journal lay open at the last entry: 'They are going through every possible strategy …'

In Transport Lane, IG Rajinder Tikoo was staring at the bricked-up view from his window. He had had too much time to think in the past few weeks, contemplating his own state of mind, frustrated by the limitations of what he had been ordered to do and by the physical confines of his quarters. Sometimes he had thought he would go mad. Tikoo was an explorer who had not yet travelled, a philosopher who had been ordered to stop thinking. He felt trapped. As the head of Crime Branch he had known instinctively how to handle most situations that presented themselves, being a master of diplomacy and officialese who could write up a storm when it came to requisitioning men and equipment. But, trying to find the word to describe his feelings right now, a mixture of fear, disgust, suspicion and cynicism, he kept coming up short.

Hearing Don's voice had revived him. Roy Ramm and his FBI partners had encouraged him down the route of obtaining proof of life, and it had paid off wonderfully. The foreign negotiators had wanted to press for victory, and there had been a real sense from Jehangir that al Faran was ready to make concessions. But after the great breakthrough, the 'higher-ups' had ordered him back to the starting blocks: 'prevaricate, give away nothing, no prisoner releases, or anything else'.

For the past couple of days it had just been him and his clunky computer, with his golf clubs sitting in the corner, enticing him away. Battleships booming. Clive Cussler occasionally. He wished Commander Ramm were here, to discuss anything, even to chat about the differences between policing in Kashmir and London. But Tikoo was still forbidden from freely mixing with Scotland Yard and the FBI's representatives on the ground, and unbeknown to Ramm the time he spent on the phone with the IG was more closely observed than ever, his input tightly scripted by Saklani and other officials. Although he understood New Delhi's determination to remain in the driving seat, and the higher-ups' desire not to give foreigners access to raw intelligence, Tikoo could not help feeling that genuine British and American efforts to help were being throttled for reasons no one was sharing with him.

Cold-shouldered by the Indians, the outsiders pounced on any detail they could get, milking it for inflections, analysing every word that came from Jehangir (whose code-name had even been withheld from them in one of the many acts of petty control), refining their ever more detailed knowledge of the hostage-takers. Tikoo was impressed with what they had put together: remarkably detailed psychological profiles of both the kidnappers and the hostages, as well as several box files' worth of material on the previous kidnappings. Ramm and co. ceaselessly combed these records for links between the earlier crimes and the present one, expanding, too, their understanding of the jailed *jihad* leaders that this was all about: Masood Azhar, the Afghani and Langrial.

By contrast, Tikoo's bosses knew little about al Faran. They cared not a jot for creating character profiles of the gunmen in the mountains, regarding them as nothing more than a gathering of pseudonyms, hung on unwashed bodies that would eventually be culled and replaced by yet more photofit *jihadis* from over the Line of Control. For the past few years it had been rumoured that those killed crossing the LoC were not even buried, but were left to rot by the thousand in the fields beside the Indian Army camps strung along the border, a carpet of cadavers that served as a constant reminder of what was at stake for those looking over with binoculars from the Pakistani side.

What was the endgame New Delhi had in mind, Tikoo wondered. Even though he had been told many times that India would not release all of the prisoners demanded by al Faran, his previous experience suggested that some might be freed. There was always room for manoeuvre. He had had a hand in several kidnapping cases in Kashmir, and access to the files of many others, and knew that virtually all of them had ended with some kind of compromise. When Rubaiya Sayeed, the daughter of New Delhi's Home Minister, was kidnapped in 1989, five prisoners had been released, including a Pakistani militant. When Nahida Imtiaz, the daughter of a prominent Kashmiri MP, had been abducted in 1991, a Pakistan-trained militant was freed. Later that year a well-connected executive director of Indian Oil, K. Doraiswamy, was snatched in Kashmir, and even though only five prisoner releases had initially been demanded, New Delhi ended up secretly handing over twelve, against the wishes of hardline Kashmir Governor Girish Saxena. During the 1993 siege of the Hazratbal mosque in Srinagar, Tikoo had watched as safe passage was granted to at least seven Pakistan-trained gunmen, and he had personally secured the release of the former politician from Bihar, P.K. Sinha, by secretly acceding to some of his kidnappers' demands.

At the start of the current crisis, al Faran had demanded that twenty-one prisoners be set free. Even Tikoo could see this was far too many for New Delhi to stomach, and was merely a negotiating stance. He had whittled it down to fifteen, and in recent days, through a combination of cajoling and persistence, had further reduced it to four: Masood, the Afghani, Langrial and Omar Sheikh, the British Pakistani who had kidnapped Paul Rideout and three others in October 1994. Tikoo had been jubilant when Jehangir had agreed to this latest, significant concession, and had dashed round to Saklani's office to inform him, expecting the Security Advisor to be just as pleased. But Saklani had sent him away with the instruction 'Just keep talking.'

On 1 September, Day Fifty-Nine, Tikoo's radio set buzzed into life. He was supposed to be the government's guide in all this, but he was no longer sure he knew the way himself. He put on the headphones and greeted Jehangir with his most frequent opening gambit. 'How are you, my friend? I hope you are looking after the tourists.'

'What have you done about our demands?' Jehangir snapped, according to an official transcript of the tapes that would be made by the Intelligence Bureau that afternoon, and obtained by British intelligence through back channels. Tikoo was pitched straight back to the one subject about which he had nothing to say. Clearly the intermediary was in no mood for small talk.

The IG tried to distract him, knowing that today, for once, he had a solid excuse as to why there was nothing to report. 'It was proceeding really fast, but what to do? Beant Singh was killed yesterday.' The previous afternoon, Singh, the Chief Minister of Punjab state, had been assassinated along with at least fourteen others when militants had set off a car bomb in the secretariat complex in Chandigarh, the capital of Punjab, just as Singh was leaving his office. A crucial ally of Prime Minister Narasimha Rao, Singh had been responsible for helping to crush the insurgency by Sikh separatists in Punjab and restore peace to the bloodied state. The audacious assassination had rocked the government in New Delhi, which was now on high alert.

'What are we supposed to do about that?' said Jehangir dismissively.

'Listen to me, my friend,' Tikoo urged, knowing that the hostage-taking in Kashmir was far from the Prime Minister's mind right now. 'You have no idea of how governments function. Why don't you speak to me tomorrow evening, by when …'

Jehangir barged in. 'It can't be done. I've told you, we know how to kill. Last time you found the body. This time we'll discard the bodies at such a place you won't ever be able to find them.'

Tikoo found it hard to suppress a wave of fury. He detested Jehangir's casual cruelty. He was talking about real people. He could not bear to be pushed back into this tit-for-tat game once again. 'Look, we know *what* you are capable of, that isn't in question,' he said. 'So show us something new.' He then threw a bone, one that he regretted as soon as he had let it go: 'Look up. Allah is listening to you.' This was slack. He had promised himself never again to talk about Islam, and he cursed himself under his breath.

Luckily, Jehangir was distracted. 'Are you giving me a date or not?' he shouted.

Trying to talk him down, Tikoo responded calmly: 'I'm telling you, we are working out something. Why don't you understand that such things take time?' He tried one of Ramm's suggestions: move away from dates, and focus on the consequences. 'You and I will both regret the fact that you were not patient,' he continued. 'What will you gain by killing unarmed tourists? You will get a bad name.'

'What bad name will we get?' Jehangir snapped back. 'We are not planning to form a government.'

Tikoo stifled a laugh. Jehangir was so dry, he thought, and he was also on the money. Tikoo knew that all New Delhi cared about was how things appeared, while these men only wanted actions. But he did his best to stick to the script. 'Then why do it? You kidnapped them for a specific purpose? Aren't you worried about the safety of [the jailed Movement leaders whose release the kidnappers were demanding]?'

Jehangir's response floored him. 'As for them, *those people* don't really matter to us.'

Tikoo sat up. If he had heard correctly, Jehangir had just signalled a significant departure, giving him a possibility. Was he saying that Masood Azhar, the Afghani, Langrial and the others were now not important? Was Jehangir prepared to consider a new kind of deal?

Before Tikoo got a chance to think this through, Jehangir barged in again: '*Those people* don't really matter to us.'

Tikoo had not misunderstood. He needed to think how he could turn this to his advantage. He had to report to General Saklani, and sound out Roy Ramm. The prisoners might not be a stumbling block any more. Al Faran had spent too many days stuck in the mountains, the IG thought. The ground was shifting. He said gently to Jehangir: 'Please wait. Speak to me tomorrow at nine in the morning.' He used a voice that he hoped sounded 'knowing and open'. 'I thought to myself, with everyone listening in to these calls, and all parties aware there were ears on the line, everything said had to be encoded to one degree or another. But luckily I understood Jehangir's nuances. I had caught this one just as it popped out.'

Before ending the call, Jehangir returned to a well-trodden path, as if for the benefit of anyone who might be eavesdropping: 'Let me make myself clear, if by nine you don't talk in specifics, by 9.30 a.m. all four of them will be dead, and you won't know where to find them.' But somehow, both of them knew they had crossed a line. There had been a subtle shift in what was being said, and as Tikoo heard the line go dead, he felt his heart lifting.

But on 2 September, Day Sixty, there was no morning call from Jehangir. Tikoo grew more concerned by the hour: it was at times like these, when there was no talking at all, that he worried the most. Just after 3 p.m., the morning national papers arrived, having had to travel a long distance to reach Srinagar. They prominently carried a story that made Tikoo flinch: unnamed sources revealed that al Faran had scaled back its demands to just four prisoners, and that this too might be open to negotiation.

'I just wanted to burst,' Tikoo recalled. Leaks were an occupational hazard and a political indulgence in India, but his volatile dialogue with Jehangir was predicated on absolute secrecy: 'Publishing even a small detail now could send the whole kit and caboodle flying.' Jehangir must not think that he, the government's negotiator, could not be trusted to keep his mouth shut. If Jehangir's thoughts were exposed to his mentors in Kashmir and over the LoC, it would endanger his life. And now, just as Tikoo had been toying with a new kind of offer that took account of Jehangir's radical change of heart about the prisoner releases, details of their secret negotiations had appeared in the press for the world to see.

After the initial shock, Tikoo began weighing up who could be responsible for the leak. Only a small number of individuals knew the hard facts: General Krishna Rao, the Governor of Kashmir, and his Security Advisor General Saklani; the Prime Minister and his inner circle in New Delhi; the top tier of the army, including the Commander of 15th Corps based in BB Cantt; and the higher-ups in IB and RAW, who listened in on his conversations with Jehangir. One of them must have tipped off the press. But why? 'All of us were supposedly working towards getting the hostages released, so who stood to gain from upsetting the applecart?'

He struggled to comprehend what was going on. General Saklani was the closest to the negotiations, the first to learn of Tikoo's successes and fears. He was an extension of Governor's Rule, so his allegiances lay with New Delhi. But over the weeks Tikoo had put his prejudices aside and come to see that Saklani 'played with a straight bat', and often appeared as surprised by events as Tikoo himself was. He seemed sincere in wanting to get the hostages out alive. Tikoo could not say the same about Governor Krishna Rao, whom he rarely spoke to, and who many Kashmiris disdained. But he doubted that even this iron governor, a man on the brink of retirement, would court notoriety by being in charge of an operation that led to the death of five Western hostages, a stain on a much-decorated career.

Any suggestion that the Prime Minister, Narasimha Rao, was giving in to the demands of Pakistani terrorists would be abhorrent to voters and valuable to Rao's massing political opponents. Rao had come to power in 1991 pledging to expose Pakistan's role in state-sponsored terror, especially in Kashmir. But violence in the state had surged, and Rao had been consistently outwitted by India's 'bad neighbour' Pakistan, a country that in Tikoo's mind had a standard operating procedure: do something intolerable, then go on the offensive with diplomats capable of snake-charming London and Washington into believing that India was overreacting and inflexible.

Tikoo reasoned that the Rao government would want to keep its dealings on the hostages secret, and not blurt them out. It would gain nothing, he thought, by bringing about the collapse of the negotiations, which would lead to its being labelled incompetent. Could the Prime Minister's political opponents be the leakers, Tikoo pondered. One thing was for sure: at the moment everything to do with Pakistan was fraught. Just a few days back there had been uproar in the Indian press at rumours that US military hardware, promised to Pakistan in return for its support during the anti-Soviet secret war in Afghanistan, but withheld since 1991 (to punish it for covertly procuring nuclear weapons), was about to be released. 'Pakistan can do no wrong, even when it has done wrong,' was one Indian newspaper's take on it. 'And its reward? Nuclear bombs that will be aimed at India.'

Even if the government was not responsible for the leak, could the same be said about the intelligence agencies and the army? This was much harder to know. The army was slogging away at a brutal and draining insurgency. In the midst of all the bloodshed and intrigue, the hostage situation was a relatively minor irritation. If anything, the problem with the army was getting it to engage with the hostage crisis at all. All the army was really concerned about was rousting out al Faran, so as to eliminate another Pakistani-backed group operating in the Pir Panjal mountains. But in its attempts to do that, would it put innocent Western lives at risk? Tikoo was not sure: the army had committed so many abhorrent acts in the valley since the militancy began in 1989 that five more deaths would be insignificant. As for IB and RAW, Tikoo shuddered. Their strategy in Kashmir was ever-changing, although it was seemingly underscored by two main ideas: to present Pakistan as being to blame for everything, and to cripple the Kashmiri independence movement. In recent days, Tikoo had seen evidence that the intelligence agencies were paying far greater attention to what was going on in Transport Lane. An IB officer, 'Agent Singh', had been installed in a nearby location, from where he listened in on every call Tikoo took from Jehangir.

Tikoo could not be certain of anything. But given the potentially incendiary nature of this case, he was glad he had decided to surreptitiously tape all of his conversations with Jehangir, knowing the state was doing the same. He would also continue negotiating to the best of his ability, but in the knowledge that someone, evidently high up in the establishment, seemed to want him to fail, for reasons that were not yet clear. It was not only the supercharged political climate that worried Tikoo. Winter was coming, and that would soon have a dramatic impact on the kidnappers' mentality.

'Up in the mountains, it would already be sub-zero at night,' Tikoo said. Snow was on its way, and there would be increasingly little food available. The mountain villagers would be bedding in right now, storing grain, counting their livestock and conserving whatever vegetables they had. Many of them would be kept alive over the coming months by the winter rations book supplied by the government for rice and *jaggery*. *Tsot* bread made from flour and water was the only staple, primped with a thumb and thrown onto a hotplate. The kidnappers too would have been well aware that the crunch time was coming. Soon the mountain routes back to Pakistan would be blocked, trapping them in the Kashmir Valley until spring. Tikoo doubted the kidnappers would want this to go on for another six months, or were capable of sustaining it for that long, through a bitter winter, and he also worried about Jehangir himself. The al Faran mystery caller was becoming erratic, and other intermediaries (with no names attached) had stood in for him in many recent calls. 'Stop-gap majors', Tikoo called them, thinking of their clumsy, country voices that could barely string a sentence together. Whenever Jehangir returned to the dialogue, after these breaks, he was increasingly irascible. Facing a fading and paranoid intermediary, with a bruised and defensive government on his back and unseen establishment enemies sniping from all sides, and with even the weather against him, Tikoo needed to find a way out of this nightmare as quickly as he could.

3 September, Day Sixty-One. Tikoo awakened to the familiar gloomy vista. In Srinagar it was a warm morning, but he knew it could be sub-zero in the mountains. Suddenly, his VHF hissed into life. It had to be Jehangir, since the two of them had been taking it in turns to feed one another a frequency that had digits added and removed at prearranged intervals: a straightforward cipher that after some twiddling revealed the right channel. After yesterday's leak, Tikoo had wondered if Jehangir would call at all. Anxious to avoid a slanging match about the news stories and to get the conversation off on the right footing, Tikoo pressed 'Talk' and got in first: 'We have moved ahead, so you should also be patient.' He wanted the words to ring out loud: 'moved ahead'. He was certain that if they could get beyond yesterday's headlines, they could reach some new demand, a trade-off, although he did not know what it might be.

'You are just wasting time,' Jehangir spat. He sounded tired and despondent. 'What are you going to tell us now that you haven't already said in the past two months?'

Tikoo took Jehangir's tone to be an indication that he had seen the leaks in the papers. He came up with a sop to buy himself a little time. 'Why don't you understand? The decision has to be taken six hundred miles away from here [in New Delhi]. Please call me in the evening.'

But Jehangir was not in the mood. 'We told you, we can't give you an extra second. If you give us a date, we wait for a year. But first give us a firm date.'

A date by which some kind of deal would be done was all he seemed to want, but Tikoo did not have the authority to give it. 'So many people are involved in such a decision. Why don't you understand?'

he repeated. 'I have assured you that the government isn't planning any operation, so why can't you just wait?'

'What is the use?' Jehangir was getting angry. He sounded unstable. 'You have been saying the same thing for the past two months. We decided yesterday to kill them, and let me tell you, there is no difference in what *we* say and what we do.'

This straightforward dig about the respective sides' codes of honour suggested to Tikoo that the leak had rankled badly. Jehangir sounded like a disappointed schoolboy, Tikoo thought. He hoped he would not go off the rails. Tikoo would have to up the stakes to get back on top of this. He decided to get his boss, the Director General of police, in on the next call, to show Jehangir that he was sincere, and that the higher-ups were listening. Mahendra Sabharwal, Kashmir's most senior police officer, was 'not easy with words', Tikoo recalled. But Tikoo could borrow the DG's authority to reassure Jehangir. And, as Roy Ramm had told him repeatedly, there was always something to be said for getting a new voice involved.

At 5 p.m. on 3 September, the VHF burbled for the second time that day. Now there were two men sitting and staring at the bricked-up view in Transport Lane: IG Tikoo and his plump Director General M.N. Sabharwal, who always kept a rictus smile fixed to his face. A third man, 'Agent Singh' of the Intelligence Branch, listened in from nearby, his pen at the ready. A fizz and a burr, and then Tikoo started talking with renewed confidence, hoping to set the tone. 'How are you? What about the guests?' Without giving Jehangir a chance to start complaining, he continued: 'Mr Sabharwal, my boss, went to New Delhi by special plane. We are all at it. Why don't you talk to him?'

The DG, clearly uncomfortable with the situation, took the handset. 'Please don't blow it,' Tikoo thought to himself. 'Solutions take time,' the DG began uncertainly. 'If you had not killed Ostrø we would have been closer to the destination.' Tikoo could feel a sense of rising panic. Why was the DG going back there? He had already buried that tragedy, which he was certain Jehangir, who had openly cursed the

Turk on more than one occasion, deeply regretted. But the DG seemed oblivious, and continued, his finger wagging: 'You also know that the tourists are innocent, not involved in your fight. Why don't you leave them first, and then we can carry on with our discussions?' Tikoo heard the line going dead even as the DG chuntered on.

The debrief was cantankerous, Tikoo recalled. 'The DG accused me of not being hard enough on the kidnappers. He seemed to think we had been courting, taking a "walk in the park", while I tried to explain the backstory and how we needed to get on track after the disastrous leak and sound out a new deal – perhaps one that did not even involve prisoners.' General Saklani backed him up, saying that reaching a solution was a delicate art. At the after-meeting with Roy Ramm and his counterparts from the FBI, the Indian team gave little away. 'My hands were tied,' Tikoo said. 'I would like to have told them we were looking for a new solution, but was forbidden, and instead we waffled on about nothing in particular, as if it was the most important thing on earth, wasting everyone's time.'

In the absence of any information from Transport Lane, Ramm and co. had been brainstorming for new approaches that might get the focus off the leak and the subsequent denials from the Indian government that it was responsible. With the PM under fire, and al Faran bitter at its dialogue being made public, the talks had to be redirected. Ramm suggested that in the next conversation IG Tikoo should offer the kidnappers something physical that might also reach the hostages. 'Feed the criminals and you feed the captives too,' Ramm said.

The radio hissed again, for the third time that day. This was a good sign, Tikoo thought as he picked up the handset, primed to go. 'Tell me,' he said, 'do you need any rations or blankets? Some wheat or rice?'

Jehangir's response was deadpan as usual: 'We are not arranging a wedding here.'

Tikoo smiled. DG Sabharwal spoke up, this time taking things slowly: 'In the end there will be a solution. But it will take time. Why don't you speak to your commanders and appeal for time?'

This was Tikoo's idea. For many days now he had wanted to reach out to Jehangir's commander, Sikander, in the knowledge that intelligence showed Sikander's hand had strengthened after Ostrø's death. An intercept by Indian signals had caught an unknown voice from Pakistan, thought to be Farooq Kashmiri, the Movement's military commander, castigating the Turk for the killing and reminding everyone on the ground that Sikander was running things. Tikoo had another thought, too. Unlike Jehangir, who was from Mirpur or somewhere close by, Sikander and he were both from Indian-administered Kashmir, which meant a lot more than speaking the same language. Regardless of the hatred that had come between them because of the conflict, Tikoo believed that as a Kashmiri, Sikander could be made to understand the need for a peaceful solution. 'Kashmiris, however virulent and dogmatic, are not an inherently violent people,' Tikoo said, 'unlike the Pakistanis who were sent over here.'

'It can't be done,' said Jehangir emphatically. Sikander would not be brought to the radio set. 'Speak to IG Tikoo at five tomorrow,' said DG Sabharwal weakly.

'This can't be done,' replied Jehangir, whose tone suggested he felt piqued by the idea of bringing Sikander into the talks.

Tikoo took back the handset, thinking that the Director General's presence only seemed to aggravate matters. 'Call me tomorrow and I'll let you know where we've reached,' he said, hoping he sounded masterful.

But Jehangir was irreconcilable. 'This is our last conversation,' he spat back. Tikoo thought: 'He sounds like we've had a lovers' tiff, but the consequences are far more awful.' He tried to recall the elation he had felt after first talking to Don Hutchings on 28 August.

Before he replaced the handset, he tried one last trick to appeal to Jehangir's humanity: 'Don't act in haste. It is a question of human lives.'

The line was already dead.

* * *

The following day, 4 September, Tikoo was surprised when the VHF started up. Jehangir would not continue to call if al Faran thought there was no deal to be had, he reasoned, despite the recent bad blood between them. But Tikoo felt too tired to joust this morning. 'Things are getting delayed,' he said weakly to Jehangir, forgetting the usual pleasantries for once. 'Appeal to your commander, and please be patient.' Come on, he thought. 'Get Sikander on the line. Kashmiri to Kashmiri, we can work something out.'

Jehangir responded right away: 'There is a limit to waiting. Give me a date, even if it is a year from now.' Tikoo decoded this to mean that he wanted the bare minimum, to know how long it would take to construct a deal – whatever that deal was.

'Why are you talking of a year?' Tikoo replied, hoping to sound reassuring. 'It will take much less. What are you going to achieve by taking a hasty step?' He tried another tactic: 'Give me a few days. So many things have to be decided.'

This sent Jehangir off in the direction Tikoo least wanted him to go. 'Don't teach me things!' the intermediary thundered, before returning to the issue of the wasted weeks spent discussing prisoner releases that were never going to happen. Jehangir was fuming now. 'The government released militants in exchange for Rubaiya Sayeed and K. Doraiswamy [the Indian Oil director], and it took less than two months.'

Tikoo had long dreaded Jehangir raising this subject. He decided to be honest. 'But they were locals. This time four Western governments are involved.' Get him off the subject, he thought, and move this conversation forward. 'Is there any possibility of any other kind of deal?' he asked.

But today, Jehangir wasn't playing: 'There is not. I have told you that this time you won't find their dead bodies.'

Tikoo was sick of this. 'Why do you want to harm them? Why kill poor unarmed guests?'

'Now we have decided to be stubborn. We will show you. I can give it to you in blood. I have told my accomplices.'

'I swear to God we are doing something.' Tikoo tried not to sound rattled. 'Call me in the morning. That way I'll get the whole night to do something. We may even have to send a special plane.' It was a weak riposte, but in these desperate times, sent in to bat with no pads, gloves or box, it was the best a man could do.

The following day, 5 September, Jehangir called again, but the IG was out, caught up in the aftermath of a massive car bomb that had destroyed Ahdoo's, a city-centre hotel that had until a few weeks ago been filled with foreign journalists. At least thirteen people were dead, and after the debris and rubble had been cleared Tikoo fought his way through the traffic to General Saklani's office in Church Lane, where he found the Security Advisor preoccupied with the newspapers. 'The al Faran talks have collapsed,' Saklani said, reading aloud. India had no strategy 'other than obfuscation'. The New Delhi plan was 'to exhaust al Faran while giving away nothing', according to anonymous senior sources. Tikoo said nothing, feeling the warmth leaching from his hands. In his most private moments, he was beginning to reach the very same conclusion. But who the hell had broadcast this to the world? As far as Jehangir was concerned, they were still heading towards some kind of deal. This was not a leak, but it was further proof that someone in authority was briefing against the talks.

Saklani seemed genuinely shocked. He blustered that Tikoo should 'just keep talking' while he investigated the source of these comments and stomped on them. Tikoo went miserably home to Transport Lane, expecting to hear nothing from Jehangir. But the radio lit up right away, and this time Tikoo got both barrels: 'You have broken this relationship!' Jehangir was furious.

'Can this relationship be broken?' Tikoo replied sullenly.

'It has been broken.'

'Tell me,' said Tikoo, 'the papers are saying our contact has snapped, and here we are talking to each other.'

'Forget all of this long talk. I am going.' The damage appeared irreparable for Jehangir.

A long pause. 'Tell me,' repeated Tikoo sincerely, 'what can I do?' He really wanted to fix this. The whole thing was getting under his skin. 'I understand that you are having problems in the mountains. It is getting cold. Tell me what you want – food or grain – and I'll have it sent in tonnes.'

'There is no need,' Jehangir replied. It was his turn to be sullen. 'You will not even find their ashes.'

'Fuck, fuck, fuck, the fucking newspapers,' Tikoo said to himself. 'I knew at that point I had to pull the rabbit from the hat, and really fast.' Money. There was nothing else he could think of at that moment. He told Jehangir that if al Faran was prepared to give up the hostages, he would safeguard the kidnappers' passage out of Kashmir, with money placed in a bank account that would be accessible once the hostages had been recovered. 'It was a straight-up deal, effectively a ransom, although that word could never be used in these fraught times.'

He was greeted by silence. He could hear the man at the other end of the line breathing.

'Good night,' said Tikoo cautiously.

'Good night, 108,' said Jehangir.

6 September: there was no news from the mountains. However, the New Delhi newspapers had another unsourced scoop, this time apparently emanating from the Indian intelligence agencies. Someone had intercepted a letter, allegedly from the Afghani, who was currently in the same high-security ward for terrorist prisoners in Tihar prison as Masood Azhar and Omar Sheikh. According to the newspaper reports, the letter contained an instruction to al Faran: 'Kill the hostages. What are you waiting for?'

Could it possibly be true, Tikoo pondered, aghast. He contacted his Crime Branch team and requested that they get a look at the letter. He felt he was extremely close to reaching a deal with Jehangir, but this 'call to kill', said to be from a man who was universally respected by militants, could undermine everything, and possibly drench the crisis in bloodshed.

Crime Branch's request to see the note was refused. The Kashmiri detectives were told it was being analysed by Intelligence Bureau agents in New Delhi. Without having examined it themselves, the police, Tikoo included, were inclined to be sceptical. This felt like an intelligence-agency plot, designed to destabilise al Faran. Tikoo thought hard. 'Why stop a letter that contains an instruction to kill, and then enable its explosive contents to be known by all?' Now that the contents of the letter had been relayed into the hills above Anantnag, its authenticity was no longer the issue: the safety of the hostages was. Would a tragedy in the mountains better suit the intelligence guys than a victory? Would Pakistan look worse if the hostages died? Of course it would. Tikoo could not stop himself. These flights of fancy would get him nowhere, but someone had to think the unthinkable. Tikoo was fighting for the lives of the four captives, but with every passing day he was becoming convinced that someone on his own side had other ideas. 'It terrified and depressed me,' he recalled.

7 September: still nothing from the mountains. But in New Delhi the adverse reporting continued, the newspapers releasing more supposedly secret details, this time an excerpt from a highly sensitive report said to have come from BB Cantt, the army's 15th Corps headquarters in Srinagar, which Tikoo and his detectives could also not get hold of. It was said to reveal that in recent days an Indian Army patrol had been scouting close to where the kidnappers were thought to be holed up. In the light of this development, the newspapers said, negotiations had been abandoned altogether, in favour of 'tactical operations'. One article concluded by revealing that camped in Srinagar alongside hostage negotiators from Scotland Yard and the FBI was a contingent of US and British special forces.

This couldn't be worse, thought Tikoo as he ripped up the paper. He needed to work on the cash deal, but now he would have to 'waste valuable time dealing with this *crap*' and placating Jehangir. The worst thing they could do now, as al Faran teetered, was to threaten it with a full-scale operation by foreigners. Whoever had leaked this latest fantastical detail knew what they were doing, since not only would it spook al Faran, it would enrage the Indian Army too. Foreign forces on the ground in Kashmir undermined India's authority in a war that was all about sovereignty. Tikoo read in the *Indian Express* that the head of the Northern Command, Lt. General Surinder Singh, had already tendered his resignation in light of the supposed news. Tikoo's morale was steadied a little by an emphatic statement from New Delhi that no tactical operation run by Western governments would ever be permitted in Kashmir. 'First there would be foreign boots, and then foreign mediators, and then New Delhi would be screwed by some deal favouring Pakistan into losing Kashmir,' he said, recalling the army's rationale. 'And anyhow, probably none of this was true, but the debating of it once again undermined the talks, hacking away at the foundations of the process.' Tikoo wondered if his deal was bust.

The following day, 8 September, the kidnappers released a statement that spoke loudly to Tikoo: 'The government should announce the release of our jailed militants *without mentioning a number*.'

Since Tikoo had worn down Jehangir's original demand from twenty-one prisoners to four, they had focused on other ideas, including cash. Tikoo was certain that in this statement, which ostensibly seemed to return to the question of prisoner releases, Jehangir was actually employing a crude code: 'He was asking for a figure through this message, a hunch that appeared all the more likely when I received a call from Jehangir that night.' It was the first time they had spoken in three days. Jehangir aggressively challenged Tikoo, accusing him of being unreliable. While Tikoo had promised them a corridor back to Pakistan, an Indian patrol was reported as having moved within sight of al Faran, with the US Delta Force and probably Britain's SAS also in the area. How could they ever trust him? 'To be honest, I could see Jehangir's point,' said Tikoo. 'Everything I had said turned out the opposite.' There was nothing else for it: he would have to try to reposition the idea of a financial guarantee that no one in this charged climate could ever call a ransom.

Despite the eavesdroppers, Tikoo blurted it out. He offered money. He needed to know how much. Now it was Jehangir's turn to cut things short, saying he would call back the following night.

Twenty-four hours later, he was as good as his word. 'Hello.'

'Hello, how are you?' Tikoo replied. After a long silence, Tikoo tried once again to reach out to Sikander. If they were close to a deal, he would be much more confident dealing with a fellow Kashmiri. 'OK, you tell me, is your commander from here or from across the border?' Tikoo asked.

'He is from here only,' Jehangir replied. Tikoo followed up with a dig: 'Aren't you worried about harming your cause, the Movement, with this prolonged act of cruelty?' It was a constant worry for Kashmiri militants that they risked alienating the very people they were supposedly fighting for.

Another long pause, then Jehangir replied, 'The Movement can go to hell.'

After so many exhausting days shepherding the foreigners in the freezing mountains, concealing themselves from the security forces and attempting to negotiate with a slippery interlocutor who seemed unable or unwilling to concede anything, all ideology had bled from the equation, as far as Jehangir was concerned. 'I was aware that this may not be how Sikander felt, but however hard I tried, I just could not get to him,' Tikoo recalled. 'But Jehangir had now jettisoned the prisoner releases. He had also rejected the Movement. It was all about getting this to an ending we all could stomach. I was sure of it.'

It was Tikoo's turn to take control: 'Call me tomorrow,' he said. He was certain, for the first time, that they could strike a pact. 'Look after the tourists. Good night,' he added.

Until he had it in the bag, this had to be kept from everyone, even Saklani. But over the next few days Jehangir wriggled some more, piling on the pressure cruelly and precisely, dithering over amounts and methods, going back to prisoners and amnesties, making new threats to kill, singling out Don as the first to die. Tikoo asked what sum would end the affair quickly. Jehangir conjured an astronomical number. 'Impossible,' Tikoo replied. On 17 September Jehangir called back. He had a revised figure. He sounded deflated but serious: 'One *crore* [ten million] rupees.'

Tikoo almost laughed out loud. 'After all this time, al Faran was asking for only £250,000. This was an amount so small we could handle it ourselves. I mean, any one of us could sign out these funds and end it all right here and right now.'

'We're there,' Tikoo said to himself as Jehangir clicked off the line. 'We're at the end. Everything's going to be all right. And we've paid a tiny price for four lives, one that New Delhi can live with.' He drained a celebratory glass of Bagpiper whisky and soda, thinking of the long-deserved break from Srinagar he would now be able to take with his wife. Perhaps they could head for the States, or Canada? He fancied San Diego. He did a little jig. 'Imagine the price to the valley if this had gone to hell,' he reflected, 'and the hostages had been skewered in paradise. We would never recover.' He could not bear to think about it. But the valley was saved, as were the foreigners in the mountains. The jubilant Tikoo called his driver and rode round to the Security Advisor. 'It's a deal!' he gabbled. 'We've done it! Hoorah, hoorah, hoorah! I have it on the table! The hostages are ours for one *crore* rupees.' Saklani raised his eyebrows, and repeated the sum, incredulous. He then shot Tikoo a look of delight. 'There is no time to go over it now,' he said as he called his car to take him to the Governor.

Left alone, Tikoo recalled the Saturday night back in July when General Saklani had first handed him the phone. He exhaled, his whole body shaking. 'I had been on tenterhooks for seventy-two days,' he said.

On 18 September Tikoo was woken in the early hours by his phone trilling away in the darkness. 'Go away. It's too early,' he murmured into his pillow. 'Far too early.' The ringing continued. Something must be wrong. 'Damn it,' Tikoo thought, praying that it wasn't the slippery Jehangir calling to cancel the arrangement. He continued to ignore the ringing, and eventually it stopped. But half an hour later it started again. By then Tikoo was up anyway. After a lifetime in service, his body clock militated against lie-ins. He grabbed the receiver, to find it was a colleague from New Delhi. 'He told me, "There's a story on the front page of the *Hindustan Times*. I guess you won't have seen it yet." And I said, "Yes, OK, come on. Tell me." And he said, "It says the kidnappers have abandoned their demands for prisoners." I said, "Yes. OK. Good. That's old news and gossip." He said, "And it says the government has secretly agreed to pay a ransom of one *crore* rupees."

I said, "Holy shit. Oh the gods," and slung the receiver across the room.' Tikoo felt sick. He raged and spat. He might have cried. 'It's blown! The whole bloody shebang's broken!' he shouted at the top of his lungs. He had been humiliated, and Jehangir exposed as a paid mercenary.

He sat down before calling his driver and telling him to take him to Church Lane. 'Who the hell is behind these leaks?' he shouted as he stormed into General Saklani's office without a thought for the usual courtesies. Saklani appeared ashen. 'It was not the Security Advisor – the job was too dear to him. I could see it in his eyes. These leaks had come from some other place. It was disastrous. It should not have been done. Once the *Hindustan Times* hit the valley at 2 p.m., the whole game would be over.'

Tikoo spoke up: 'Once this thing is out ... I have nothing left to talk about.' He could barely string a sentence together. 'It is a full stop. I have just become irrelevant. Once this secret deal is everywhere, humiliating them, they will never trust me again. And, you know, I have wasted my time, too.'

Saklani went to tell the Governor what had happened while Tikoo left for home. By the next morning, the IG's mind was made up. It would not be a formal resignation, since protocol denied this, as did his ambition. 'Look, one of my uncles is dying,' he told Saklani. 'I have to go to Ahmedabad on compassionate leave. I will be away five, six days, so can you kindly ask someone to take over for me?'

Later that day, Tikoo took a seat on a flight out of Srinagar. 'The end is now foretold,' he thought. Before leaving, he had called on the foreign negotiators to say farewell. 'I apologised to the Brits, etc., and told them, "I am leaving this assignment, and I want you to know I am sorry."' But he could not reveal what had just happened. Only a small group of Indian officials had known about the cash deal – he could count their names on the fingers of one hand. All around him was evidence of a profound betrayal that reached to the summit of government, although so many pieces of the picture were missing that he could not fathom what or who lay behind it, or why anyone would have chosen this course, rather than victory, with the hostages triumphantly freed.

Rajinder Tikoo had become attached to the cause of the families, and could not shake the image of the hostages being snatched from their former lives into a new world of terror and uncertainty. 'The problem for them all,' he recalled, 'was that they were just ordinary people.' He stared out of the plane window and down at the Pir Panjal, that was now muffled by deep, fresh snow.

FIFTEEN

The Squad

Somewhere behind the high walls and barbed wire of the Jammu and Kashmir Police's Crime Branch, the old cream-and-ruby-red building set back from the snarling traffic of Srinagar's Jehangir Chowk, lay a bulging secret file, held together with a leather binder and tied with a length of string. It began with three First Information Reports or crime logs: the initial kidnapping report raised by Jane, Cath and Julie on 5 July at Pahalgam police station; followed by another, concerning Dirk Hasert and signed by his girlfriend Anne Hennig at Chandanwari police post on 8 July; and a third, date-stamped 'P/S Pahalgam, July 11', ~~which was when a Duty Inspector had finally got round to record~~-ing the abduction of Hans Christian Ostrø in Zargibal, from where the villagers had taken their time in clambering down the mountain to report the crime.

However, beneath these meagre offerings – the Urdu-scrawled snapshots of a moment in time – lay a mountain of paperwork, the sum total of what Rajinder Tikoo's Crime Branch inquiry team had been doing over the seventy-two days that he had been absent from the office, following his first telephone conversation with Jehangir. Here lay a legion of typed affidavits, each one endorsed with a sheet of court-fee-stamp paper, and interrogation reports, sealed as a true record of who had said what to whom by the thumbprints of the broken, illiterate confessors. Interspersed between these official police documents, written in English and Urdu, were page after page of handwritten observations, rough transcripts of unofficial 'interviews' and pencil-sketched maps of outlying hamlets, villages, mountain routes, arms caches and suspected militant boltholes. There were typed case notes too, and small, cigarette-card-sized photos of straggle-headed militants (alive and dead), intelligence tips and informers' reports, some jotted on torn newspaper pages and others on the backs of cigarette packets. In sum, this enormous Crime Branch file, and all of its ancillary evidence folders and boxes, was bursting with the snippets and double-talk that industrious policemen gather during a major operation.

The FIRs were practically all that the families of the hostages and the Western negotiators like Roy Ramm had laid eyes on. But for the Indian and Kashmiri top brass – police, army and intelligence – the entire file was theoretically available, although the choicest bits had been distilled into Daily Situation Reports. The DSR was like a core sample pulled from a giant oak, a summary of everything significant. A shorter version of it would have been included in the Daily Summary, dispatched to anyone with clearance and an interest in the case.

Here, seen only by a select circle of high-ranking Indian readers, was every last detail of a thorough investigation that no one in the West even knew existed. The unedited bundles and boxes were packed with revelations, just one of which would have rejuvenated the anaemic FBI and Scotland Yard investigations.

The Kashmiri police donkeywork had begun on 5 July, just hours after the first kidnappings, when IG Tikoo, then still based in his pipe-smoke-scented Crime Branch office with its wooden veranda, had called in one of his superintendents, SP (Crime) Mohammad Amin Shah, a garrulous veteran investigator. Regardless of what other security agencies were planning to do to tackle the unfurling crisis, Tikoo had ordered Shah to form a dedicated Crime Branch team. 'We couldn't leave the police response down to the deputy superintendents out in the field,' Tikoo recalled, referring to men like DSP Kifayat Haider, stationed in Bijbehara, for whom he had little respect. 'This was a complex and difficult matter whose consequences were potentially enormous, threatening to blight the whole of Kashmir as a valley of kidnappers and killers, and it demanded investigation and coordination, directed from the centre.'

Savvy and well turned-out, SP Shah knew what kind of detective to put on this case. He called in another superintendent, Mushtaq Mohammad Sadiq, who ranked below him, but was among the most experienced field officers in the department. A master of the unconventional, who was happiest working off-diary on covert investigations, Sadiq was small, moustachioed, grey-faced, and appeared to be all forearms. He was also young, clever and invisible. While many in the Jammu and Kashmir Police spent as much time courting the press as pursuing their cases, getting themselves written up heroically and riding around town in bullet-pocked Gypsies or gleaming Ambassadors, SP Sadiq always remained in the shadows, valuing his anonymity, which was key for a man who was about to rub up against the Movement.

Sadiq had got to understand the value of preserving his anonymity when he served in the counter-insurgency unit, listening in to the militants' chatter, hearing the gunmen identifying individual cops and intelligence agents as targets, drawing up detailed kill lists, locating their stations and homes before laying ambushes. Although SP Sadiq was well known on the insurgents' grapevine, given the number of operations he had run and his tally of kills, and his reputation for savage interrogation and ruthlessness while undercover, they had a name only. Pinning a likeness on him proved impossible. 'Sadiq: he's that thickset one like a pony-*wallah*.' 'No, that's Ghulam Nabi from intel,' ran one exchange he overheard. Or, 'That Sadiq has long, long wild hair like a *pir*.' 'No, it's razored, like Haider's.' And finally he had eavesdropped this: 'Can anyone describe this Sadiq? We're beginning to believe the bastard doesn't exist.'

A Kashmiri Muslim from downtown Srinagar, Sadiq understood the street. He had thrived in the most challenging postings, such as Anantnag, the volatile south Kashmir town that militants had poured into over recent years. There he had melted into the crowds of fired-up Kashmiri youth and Pakistani-backed militias, finding and managing high-value sources so as to feed a steady stream of valuable intelligence back to police lines. But he was under no illusions as to where his real loyalties lay. As well as the ISI-trained Kashmiri and

Pakistani gunmen who took potshots at him, he also hated the Indian chauvinists in the security forces and elsewhere, Hindu hawks who flew in to hoist the saffron, white and green union flag, rah-rah-rahing about 'Kashmir being Indian' before retreating to their heavily fortified camps to watch the valley burn.

Sadiq saw himself as a Kashmir-born Indian – in that order. The alternative, to be a son of Kashmir who rejected India and who chose to fight, was a fool's choice, he believed. To his mind, the fight for *azadi* had become corrupted over the past six years. '*Azadi*' was a fine-sounding catchcry for Kashmiri politicians, but most of them used it to enrich themselves, accepting money from Pakistan while ignoring the plight of their impoverished constituents, opening themselves up to accusations from New Delhi that they were treasonous and corrupt. The young men who actually enlisted with militant outfits were similarly foolish, in Sadiq's opinion, doomed to be little more than cannon fodder, dying in their thousands, their sacrifice going unremarked, while the real aspiration of the Kashmiri people – to be left alone to govern themselves – was crushed between the jostling tectonic plates of New Delhi and Islamabad.

When he got the first call about the hostages on 5 July, Sadiq made few demands: ten men of his choosing, freed from all other duties, who would exchange their uniforms for skullcaps and woollen Kashmiri *pherans*, and would not set foot in a police station unless their lives depended on it. They would be referred to in the file simply as 'the Squad'.

The Crime Branch file showed that the Squad hit Pahalgam hard on 6 and 7 July, brushing aside DSP Haider. Without stopping to introduce themselves or to explain why they were there, Sadiq's plain-clothed officers had scoured the trekking town for information, targeting local hoteliers and drivers, guides and pony-*wallahs*, many of whom regarded the militants as heroes, but whose livelihoods were now in jeopardy. If the kidnapping crisis could not be defused, the Squad warned them, the Indian security forces would relentlessly turn them over, splintering their businesses and smashing their homes.

And if they did not assist the investigation, this formerly charmed gateway to the mountains might appear to have broken its bond with its foreign guests, and be shunned by them for years to come. They need look no further than Aru, which in the year since the 1994 abductions of Kim Housego and David Mackie had been transformed into a ghost town.

The guilt and fear soon got many in Pahalgam talking. One of the first taboos to be broken was the fingering of Sikander, with numerous residents identifying the man who up until this point had been seen by many as a local hero, as the *éminence grise* behind al Faran. The word on Pahalgam's blustery single street was that Sikander, who informers claimed had been in and out of the town in recent months, had been working with his Pakistani controllers to coordinate a kidnapping operation that had its roots as far back as January. Someone said that while Sikander was supervising the operation, the man in charge on the ground was a foreign militant called the Turk, who had been operating in Kashmir on and off for a couple of years, and who 'dressed like a holy man but had a reputation for brutality'. Residents also identified the Turk's deputy as Qari Zarar, a Kashmiri-born militant from the southern side of the Pir Panjal mountains, a man who saw himself as a leader, but whom the Squad marked down as 'second fiddle'.

Under interrogation, former militants and sympathisers named the two most important Pakistanis in the kidnap party as Nabeel Ghazni and Abu Khalifa. Both were said to have trained in Camp Yawar, and to have had lengthy battlefield experience in Afghanistan. Backing up Ghazni and Khalifa were two Kashmiris from Doda district: Sikander Mohammed and Mohammed Haroon. These four veterans made up the tier of command beneath the Turk and Qari Zarar, and were all thought to have been accompanying the hostages from Day One. Sadiq's team sent a report to the higher-ups along these lines: 'It should be noted, that we have identified the core members of the kidnap party etc. etc. ...'

The rest of the gunmen were known only by their fighting names: Shoaib, Waheed, Asif, Yusuf, Jawad, Batoor, Ghazan and Droon, the last three being Pashtun names, suggesting that they originated from the Pakistan–Afghan border. The others, as far as the Squad could ascertain, were mostly Pakistanis from Kotli or Mirpur, in Pakistan-administered Kashmir. Lastly, there were a number of *gujjars* and *dards*, impoverished shepherds and hunters whose hennaed hair and kohl-rimmed eyes marked them as outsiders, and who came and went. Their job was guarding the heights above the hostage party, and acting as lookouts and sentries outside the *gujjar* huts where the hostages spent their nights. A photo of some members of the kidnap team was even procured by the Squad, that a fighter had presumably taken using a camera he had stolen from the hostages, and gone to the lengths of getting developed. It showed five men in battle gear, smiling broadly on a grassy hillside at the height of summer, arms around each other's shoulders, Kalashnikovs at ease, daggers hanging from belts. 'On tour with al Faran,' one of Sadiq's officers quipped. A copy was placed in the file, where it remains today. When it was shown to John Childs many years later, he instantly recognised the tall, smiling militant on the left of the picture. 'That's the one I arm-wrestled,' he said. 'One of the more reasonable of our captors.'

Within three days, the Squad had drawn the higher-ups' attention to its first significant conclusion: 'Al Faran is meaningless.' The Squad believed the kidnappings had been carried out by the Movement, an ISI-sponsored Pakistani militant group mentored by Maulana Khalil from Karachi. A report was sent along the lines: 'It should be noted, that we have linked … etc.' The team also had proof positive of an overlap between those responsible for the 1994 abductions of Kim Housego and David Mackie and these kidnappings, as many in the present kidnap party were known to have worked both operations.

The next task was far harder. The Squad would need to infiltrate the Movement and track down Sikander, who was thought not to be travelling with the kidnap party but holed up in a Movement safe house. Their ultimate goal was to get someone into or alongside the al Faran team, an ambitious task, but one they thought possible. They started with the Movement's allies in and around Pahalgam, trying to see who might be flipped. They also activated their own sources out in the deep countryside, and all the way down to Anantnag town: assets, paid and unpaid, volunteers and those who had been press-ganged, rural people over whom the police already had the clamp, and who could be made to befriend and then betray the men around Sikander – in the knowledge that their lives (and those of their families) depended on it.

It began in Dabran village, with Sadiq's men targeting Sikander's childhood home, close to the village's communal wash-house and general store. Throwing the Bhat family's possessions into the mud, the security officials threatened to return every week and do it again, until they talked. This prompted Sikander's desperate father, Ghulam Ahmed Bhat, to bury what keepsakes they had to remind them of their son in the garden – a school bus pass, ID card and birth certificate. 'I also took the only photo we had, placed it in a bag and pushed it deep beneath a bed of vegetables,' he recalled.

In the first days after the kidnappings the Squad struck continually in Pahalgam, tearing apart Sikander's associations: door-to-door midnight arrests, the lightning application of brutish force. This flushed out the revelation that the kidnap team had not headed higher into the mountains after snatching the first four backpackers on 4 July, but had brazenly descended into Pahalgam at 2 a.m. on 5 July – right into the hive of police and paramilitaries. Could this possibly be true, Sadiq wondered. Sikander was bold, but would he choose such a high-risk strategy while his team was holding foreign hostages? It seemed unlikely, but when several eyewitnesses came forward to describe how a small procession of militants had snaked its way down the mountain and into the slumbering trekking station in the early hours of 5 July, over a small wooden bridge and into the Heevan Hotel, the story began to have a ring of truth about it. Some of those working at the Heevan were already under suspicion of secretly supporting and working for Sikander's outfit.

*   *   *

The Squad raided the Heevan Hotel early on 6 July. Their search led them to a tatty, unpainted attic room with boarded-up windows, a small, airless chamber where it was impossible to stand up straight because of the protruding eaves. It was empty, but there was plenty of evidence that it had recently been occupied: 'The tea in the cups was warm, and breakfast plates and bedrolls were still scattered around,' said an officer who witnessed the scene. In the bathroom, a dank and dirty corner, a tap was still running, and on the floor were foreign food wrappers and scraps of paper. The detectives questioned the hotel staff, eventually finding an old Kashmiri *chowkidar*, or night-watchman, who confirmed that an armed party had turned up at the hotel in the early hours of 5 July. He had shown them to the attic room, and been ordered to look after them.

Were the foreigners among them, the interrogators asked, pressing him hard. The *chowkidar* seemed evasive, saying that it had been dark. All he did know was that he had heard through kitchen staff that the Movement had abducted a group of foreigners from a camp-site in the Liderwat Valley sometime the previous evening. 'It was already the talk of the town,' he whispered. 'Everyone knew.' Later, he had listened at the door, and overheard men speaking about hostages and ransom demands. They seemed to be communicating with others via a two-way radio. 'He was sure those inside the room were leading the kidnapping,' said a member of the Squad's interrogation team.

By now the *chowkidar* was terrified, and he clammed up. In an attempt to clarify the story, the Squad found a young Kashmiri waiter who also worked at the Heevan, and who admitted (under brusque questioning) that he had taken food up to the room several times over the following forty-eight hours. Slowly, the frightened boy drew a vivid picture of a group of men sitting quietly in a darkened room, whispering occasionally, with heads bowed. He had only snatched a few glimpses, as at all times the door had been guarded from the inside by two foreign *mujahideen*, while two more kept watch outside, and others were positioned at the base of the stairwell and around the rear of the hotel, close to the kitchens and refuse bins. To the Squad it was clear: they had uncovered al Faran's base camp, brazenly established in the town itself.

The boy described how the party in the room had repeatedly called for food and drink, and he had brought up trays of tea, *chapattis* and *daal* fry. A string of thickset Kashmiri militants had arrived throughout the night, smelling of gunmetal and goose fat. From the reaction of the guards, the boy said, some of them must have been senior commanders.

The next time the door was unlocked he had caught sight of a clean-shaven man, dressed like a schoolteacher in a shirt and jacket, with an instantly recognisable face: Sikander. 'What did he say?' the police interrogators demanded. 'What was the plan for the hostages?' The boy could not recall much, as he had only overheard snatches of conversation. At one point Sikander had said, speaking quickly: '*Kya tumne dopehar ka khana khaya?*' (Did the hostages have their lunch?) 'No,' a distant voice had replied. 'They are hungry and getting agitated. They keep asking questions about when they will be freed. What should we say?' The boy said he thought he had heard the crackle of a two-way radio.

'*Maze karein*,' Sikander had said, instructing the captors to eat well. The men in the room had then slept for an hour, the boy stated, until their first *namaz* prayer of the day, around 5 a.m. Over the next three hours the room's occupants had spoken on the radio several more times, and slept again, until more food arrived after 9 a.m., oily fried eggs and flat bread that everyone wolfed down, after which they were ordered in Urdu, '*Khamosh raho*.' Silence. Several gunmen raised their Kalashnikovs to their lips as a rumpus started below in the hotel proper. Guests were awakening, and their breakfast babble rose through the floor with the smell of buttered toast, bringing fresh tension into the attic room.

Some tourists had their breakfast on plastic chairs and tables arranged on the lawn overlooking the Lidder River. The Heevan Hotel was the plushest spot in town, its literature boasting 'exclusively furnished rooms and suites with wall-to-wall carpeting'. A grand reception area panelled with pine led to a travel centre, banqueting hall and what was described as a 'multi-cuisine' restaurant, which meant that a few Kashmiri specialities – meats prepared in yoghurt and almond-flecked green tea – were served alongside Indian staples from the Punjabi north and the Tamil south. From the corridor beneath the attic room came a girl's muffled laugh and a man's response. Trekkers were setting out for the high passes, excited and fired-up. If only they had known what was going on just above their heads. Snatches of conversation floated up from the garden. Someone was talking about a walk up to Aru and Kolahoi. A man was discussing the Amarnath routes with his wife.

Later, noises had come from the street outside. The *chowkidar*, who appeared from the file transcript to have undergone many hours of intense interrogation despite his advanced age, admitted he had gone to see what was happening. A group of Kashmiri students who had been camping in the Meadow had arrived in the town and raised the alarm about the kidnapping. The waiter recalled the same incident, and said that soon after, the party in the attic room had moved into a corner, far from the window.

The *chowkidar* recalled another loud commotion outside, which included foreign voices, at around 2 p.m. Again he had slipped out. 'Several women had arrived from Lidderwat,' he said, 'telling everyone there had been a kidnapping up in the mountains.' The Squad had underlined these words in the interrogation report, clearly struck by the image of three Western women out in the street calling for help, unaware that the men who controlled the fates of their loved ones were just yards away, listening to everything that was going on.

By sunset on 5 July the noise outside had died down as Pahalgam settled in for the night, recalled the boy. The party in the attic room stayed put too, while outside a local police inquiry was unfolding, with DSP Kifayat Haider arriving from Srinagar. But by the early hours of 6 July, the al Faran party was fractious and jumpy, arguing among themselves. The next thing the *chowkidar* remembered was around 4 a.m., when he heard the men in the attic room being ordered to dress: 'Get up, take your things, we have to move.' Shivering as they emerged at the bottom of the stairwell, they had made straight for a narrow alley. 'Quick, quick, out of sight!' a gunman had shouted, pushing them into the darkness, away from the Heevan Hotel, out of Pahalgam and up into the silent Betaab Valley in the general direction of Amarnath, where, as John Childs would later confirm, the hostages and kidnappers were holed up.

There, the interrogation notes ended. A second report in the Crime Branch file consisted of a medical statement that sometime on 7 July the Heevan's *chowkidar* had collapsed during interrogation. His questioners' names had been redacted from the official report, their alarm hinted at by the correspondence and the forms they filled in about the incident. A doctor was called for. He took one look at the old man, pronounced him dead and turned on his heels. As news got out about the *chowkidar's* death during interrogation, Pahalgam bridled, with youths pelting a police post with stones, haranguing DSP Haider, accusing his officers of torturing an old man to death.

'A cop among the people', as he liked to think of himself, DSP Haider depended on the good will of the local populace. But on the morning of 7 July, when he had arrived at work to find Pahalgam police station besieged by furious locals, he had had no idea what was going on. He rang SP Mushtaq Sadiq and his superiors for an explanation. An internal investigation was promised, and the Squad called in another doctor to examine the *chowkidar*. He concluded that the old man had had 'a weak heart that could explain his passing'. With insufficient evidence, and one opinion in their favour, Sadiq's Squad was in the clear. They moved on, focusing on Amarnath in their search for the hostages. As Qari Zarar and two others among the kidnappers were from Doda, a district far to the south-east of Pahalgam, the Crime Branch team had a good idea of where they might be headed. Beyond Amarnath lay the wild passes and remote valleys of the Pir Panjal, and little-used nomad routes that led towards an untamed land without electricity or telephones, a place of perma-winter.

* * *

The Warwan, an intimidating, windswept basin whose name means 'green valley', lies hidden in one of the wildest and most sparsely populated corners of the subcontinent, thirty miles' hard trekking to the south-east of Pahalgam, a journey that involves a gruelling ice climb over the Sonasar Pass at fourteen thousand feet. Only a few dirt-poor, isolated *gujjar* and *dard* communities cling to the Warwan's sheer, scarified rock flanks, their simple stone huts, or bivouacs constructed from tarpaulins, looking down onto the turbulent glacial water of the Mariev Sudher River below. Down in the alluvial plain that turns a vivid green with mountain grasses in summer, a series of ancient wood-and-stone villages dot the river's banks, some reached by rotting suspension bridges or large stepping stones across the water. To the north, enclosed by inaccessible snow-clad ridges on all sides, lie the high peaks of Kargil and India's northernmost tip, where frostbitten nomadic Kashmiri tribesmen mingle with Tibetan herders along the long, harsh border with China. To the north-west lies the equally isolated Pakistani region of Gilgit, and to the east the tiny, remote Buddhist kingdoms of Zanskar and Ladakh, with their wind-whipped prayer flags, where the arid cold and heat have reduced the landscape to sand. Warwan has a fierce, primeval air. It is a place where time has stood still for centuries, and where the residents are happy to spend most of their lives cut off from the outside world.

There are no roads, cars, police posts or rules. Warwan's remoteness has made it off-limits to foreign trekkers and unarmed government officials, but in 1995 it was open to hordes of itinerant gunmen. Open a baker's wooden cash drawer in Inshan, the largest village in the valley, and you were just as likely to pull out Saudi riyals or Uzbeki soms as Indian or Pakistani rupees. There were likely to be coins from the Caucasus and Iranian rials, not to mention pesos from the Philippines, indicating how the Warwan h 1 become a stronghold for Islamic fighters of many different nationalities who were pouring into Kashmir from the Arab world, the former Soviet states and elsewhere in Asia, causing the native villagers and herders to live in fear. Twenty miles long and inaccessible for eight months of the year, Warwan was easily defendable by whoever got there first during the thaw.

The only way out of Warwan to the south is via a zigzag track that rises above Inshan, a settlement of hungry farmers, heroin smugglers and arms dealers. When the rain arrives it becomes a treacherous cascade of churned mud. When frozen it is an impassable chute. Even during the dry season, the severity of its inclines spooks the thickset ponies that hack up towards an army outpost at the inhospitable Mardan Top. At thirteen thousand feet, Mardan Top is an angry bowl, barren and brown, nestling in the crook of far higher peaks, leading across and eventually down into the outer limits of Anantnag district. There is nothing awe-inspiring about Mardan Top, and the Indian soldiers unlucky enough to be posted there rarely emerge from their huts, although some have painted on boulders the other name given to this high pass: the valley of death. Gusts of dry, freezing air desiccate whatever they touch, cracking skin, blistering lips, followed by wisps of wet fog that saturate everything and then freeze over, the combined wet-and-dry tools of erosion that reduce rocky outcrops to rubble, and are capable of driving even mountain men mad.

By the second week of July 1995, with John Childs having escaped and two new hostages to consider, Warwan was where the Crime Branch Squad began to focus their search. They had been led there by intelligence picked up in Pahalgam, and also by interviews conducted with Kim Housego after his and David Mackie's release from captivity in the summer of 1994. He had said that after climbing for several days east of Pahalgam, their guards had placed lookouts on the upper reaches of a vast and remote valley: 'We had walked for sixteen hours over high and dangerous passes. At times I thought I would slip down the side of the mountains still thick with ice and snow. We were fearful of being carried away by avalanches. I was badly sunburnt, as I had no protection.' They passed nobody all day, and Kim watched, sickened, as the militants photographed each other with the cameras they had stolen from them. After spending the night in an empty *gujjar* hut, 'where we were soaked to the skin and sat around a smoking fire unable to sleep', the next morning they had reached the pinch-point of Sukhnoi, the northernmost village in the shadow of the Sonasar

Pass. A cluster of stone houses roofed with wood shingles, Sukhnoi is ringed by huge boulders that have rolled down the mountainsides, and looks out over the rich floodplain of the raging Mariev Sudher River. Sukhnoi feels forsaken even in summer. The only manmade materials in view are the zinc sheets painted Islamic green on the roof of the village *masjid* that someone has manhandled over the mountains.

At the edge of Sukhnoi is a wooden guesthouse, built for travellers forced to overnight when bad weather or exhaustion prevented them from completing the up-and-over to Pahalgam. 'It looked like a Swiss chalet, unlike the rest of the houses in the village, that rested on stilts,' Kim recalled. 'Inside were two rooms, each of which had their own fireplace. With the rest of the group, now about seventeen, we shared the two rooms.' They had remained there from 10 to 13 June, according to police files. Kim reflected: 'The weather had turned bad. Mist and rain engulfed the valley. At times we could no longer see the mountains.' Rashid, an English-speaking militant commander, told them that some of the group had been sent out with a hand-held radio to try to establish contact with their leaders in Srinagar, but had failed. 'We felt completely cut off,' Kim recalled.

Inside the hut, an increasingly irritable David Mackie had taunted his devout guards with his atheism, while Kim had told them about the new life he was planning at his English boarding school at the end of the summer. Meals were invariably rice and bread, but 'occasionally, on a good day, some lentils or tough inedible meat were added'. The names of some of his captors had stayed with him: Rashid, Wahid and Suebe, with whom he had been photographed – possibly the same man referred to by Hans Christian Ostrø as 'Schub'. Kim said they had passed the hours 'drinking endless cups of tea brought to us by the villagers on the orders of the group', and that 'the villagers we met looked scared. We had no conversation with them.' Eventually they had been led out of Sukhnoi and down the Warwan, following 'a broad track with walls either side'. Kim had 'vivid memories of the militants descending the valley, their Kalashnikovs held out in front of them as on a raid in a film'.

After walking almost the length of the undulating Warwan towards Inshan, they had frustratingly been ordered to retrace their steps, as Indian forces had been deployed in the area. They ended up back in Sukhnoi in the middle of the night. 'I began to think I might never have a holiday again – and might not even survive,' said Kim. After another depressing night in the chalet they began the arduous journey back to Pahalgam. At Chandanwari they were met by three militants the hostages had not seen before. 'They looked different, more educated, and clearly from the town. They all welcomed us with a big hug, and one said, "*Inshallah*, tomorrow you will be free and with your families."' It was very likely that one of them was Sikander, the Squad concluded. Kim and David were then taken to a hotel and allowed to shower in warm water, but afterwards one militant was offended to see that David had shaved. 'Why?' he asked. 'Your prophet had a beard.' Later, the group had commandeered a taxi and taken the two hostages down to Anantnag, their faces wrapped in scarves to disguise their recognisably Western features. The following day Kim and David had been released into the hands of Yusuf Jameel's photographer friend Mushtaq Ali of AFP.

Sadiq knew that the *mujahideen* were creatures of habit, and the Squad were working on the theory that the Movement would use Sukhnoi again. The village stares down the barrel of the Warwan, and is protected by cliffs on three sides. It is so isolated that it has retained its own dialect, a pure form of medieval Kashmiri that is not understood by city sophisticates whose language has over time become mingled with Urdu and Hindi.

Maybe the hostages were already in the village. But Sukhnoi's isolation made it hard to observe even from a distance. Armed al Faran scouts or their hired hands would be all around, dominating the high ground, as Kim Housego had described. But the location of the village could also be an advantage, the Squad reasoned. Most of the necessities of life had to be brought in, meaning there was constant traffic, with villagers and their ponies coming and going, bartering with their government ration books down in Inshan and even as far away as Pahalgam. There the Squad intended to tap them up, offering small sums of money, courting them slowly, warming them around a fire, buying them tea and bread, drawing out information from poor and hungry men.

By the third week in July, Sadiq's men had pieced together various snippets of information to build up a picture of the kidnappers' movements. After a miserable week spent in the high passes around Sheshnag, losing one hostage (Childs) then snatching two more (Hasert and Ostrø), al Faran had pitched into Sukhnoi on 9 or 10 July. One of the first villagers coaxed to speak to the Squad said that 'a party of eighteen or so fighters with five Westerners stormed in late at night'. The Squad sent a report to the higher-ups: 'It should be noted that we have the likely location, etc., etc. …'

Gradually, as more villagers were squeezed, cajoled and bribed, a fuller picture emerged. The prisoners, the Squad were told, were locked in the wooden guesthouse on the outskirts of the village. This was confirmed when the photos of them sitting against a wooden backdrop reached Srinagar. These matched those taken in 1994 of Mackie and Housego, who recalled how their kidnappers had repeatedly tried to photograph them inside the guesthouse: 'David was asked to take pictures, which he did and then exposed them so that they would not be used as propaganda.' A report went out to the relevant Indian authorities, something like this: 'It should be noted that the location in Sukhnoi is confirmed, as is the house itself etc., etc.'

The Squad now knew who al Faran was, its structure, and where it was hiding the hostages. They even had a makeshift map of Sukhnoi, drawn by a local, on which the location of the hostages' hut was marked. Over the following days, their information was refined with the help of more first-hand accounts. Some travelling members of the village headman's extended family were pressured into talking. They recalled telling the police, 'The gunmen arrived running. They pointed their weapons at our relatives, demanding hospitality. "We are alone here and unarmed," we told them. "What are we supposed to do?"' There was not enough food for the families living in Sukhnoi, let alone to feed the newcomers as well. '"You bringing foreigners here will endanger all of our lives," we told them.' But al Faran had been insistent. 'You *will* do your best. You will *not* speak of this or *talk* to the foreigners.' 'What should we have done? We were outnumbered and outgunned. They would have killed us all.' The headman's family was forced to turn their main kitchen into a canteen, with his wives deputed to cook for the hostage party and bring them endless cups of tea. 'We were terrified.'

Three teams of seven sentries rotated the guard duty, creating three security rings: one in Sukhnoi itself, a second out in the valley among the *gujjar* animal flocks, and a third high above the village, using rocky outcrops as guard posts. The outfit was well equipped, with new Japanese VHF radio sets, Morse-code pads and Diamond antennae, used to deflect their signals off the mountains, confusing any attempts by the Indian military to locate them with direction-finding equipment. The signal from a basic radio would have been blocked by the mountains, but with a Diamond antenna placed on a peak, its range could be boosted by twenty miles or more. A detailed Squad report on al Faran's communications noted how sophisticated it was, making the police certain that this was 'a state-backed operation' funded by Pakistan using advanced communication equipment and practised methods: 'Instead of a single frequency, they jump with their message, relaying them over a number of pre-set frequencies. At other times the data is broadcast in "packets" or bursts. They are highly trained, and have tapped into a sophisticated militant comms network that relays their messages over the LoC. This MC [master channel] that catches their signal is run by operators living in the high Pir Panjal, who have access to sophisticated HF radio sets that can broadcast three hundred miles, easily reaching Pakistan or Kabul.' The only thing that could stop them talking was the weather, as Kim Housego had witnessed in 1994.

The Squad's picture of life in the Warwan became fuller with each new statement extracted from a villager. The Sukhnoi *maulvi* told them how the hostages lived: 'Each morning the foreigners were allowed out to exercise on the grass banks beside the river. Sometimes they played volleyball or football for several hours.' It was an unlikely image, the captives herded onto an improvised sports pitch, but the Squad thought it must have helped to keep them manageable. A woodcutter who frequently travelled in and out of the Warwan said: 'By dusk they are back inside, where they are provided with *lavash* and *daal*. We are discouraged from talking to them. The guards changed frequently. Even if we wanted to reach out to them we would have been prevented. It was strange to have these outsiders living among us and not be able to get to know them.' Another statement came from a family of herders who had passed through Sukhnoi: 'The foreigners called out to us. We felt ashamed. It is not our way to watch people suffering.' A report was sent up the line of command by the Squad, and out via the DSR to all interested parties: 'Location, village, conditions confirmed, etc., etc.'

By the first week in August, the Squad had drawn up basic profiles of the captives from the testimony of villagers.

'The younger British hostage [Paul]: Moody, sits on his own on the floor, to the right of the door. Depressed and scared. Arguing with the guards and his fellow hostages. Won't eat with his hands. Has made a spoon with a stick.'

'The German [Dirk]: Talks with the Norwegian, but otherwise is silent. Sickened by the food. Spends time inside the hut when others are out. Unable to cope? Sleeps with his hands over his head.'

'The American [Don]: Villagers nickname him *sarpanch* [headman]. Has got the guards to back off by persuading there will be no escape bid. Had a *charpoy* [Indian bed] brought over for the captives to use during the day that is placed outside the door. The guards have started coming to him with problems. Treats minor wounds and has helped sick villagers.'

'The Norwegian [Hans Christian]: Villagers call him the magician. Has tried to learn the dialect, making everyone laugh. Constantly irritates his guards by dancing and singing loudly, some kind of south Indian dance. Made a ball. Whittled a bat. Used string and poles to make a net. Tried to catch fish in the river. Asked if they could play baseball and volleyball. Taught children games.'

'The other Briton [Keith]: Solid. Calm. Strong. Gives little away. Called "boulder" by villagers. He makes peace with everyone after a fight. Stops the arguments flaring.'

For now al Faran appeared to be staying put with its captives. The only thing that caused them to move temporarily was hunger, as a teashop owner from the nearby village of Brayan recalled telling the Squad: 'They came here one day, looking for sugar. The prisoners looked depressed. We told them release the foreigners as this is bringing shame on all of us. We said the whole of Kashmir is against this. They said, "It will all be over soon." We saw the foreigners. They wore local dress and plastic shoes.' A villager from further down the valley reported how his neighbours had been harried by an Indian Rashtriya Rifles patrol passing through. Later, one of the al Faran commanders came down to find out what had been said, and seemed 'very tense'.

The Squad had many observations to send back up the line: occasional Indian Army patrols were moving around Warwan, even though 15th Corps officials at BB Cantt categorically denied it. The kidnappers were rooted to a single location, yet the police were aware of no active plans to launch a rescue attempt. 'We are doing what was asked of us. Now what will we do for the hostages?'

Sukhnoi was impregnable, came the reply from the security forces. They asked for yet more intelligence about the positioning of the guards on the hillsides and in the village. What time did the guards' shifts start and end? How many remained outside at night, and how many slept in the room with the hostages? All of these were details that were difficult to ascertain. The hostages could easily be killed or wounded in the helter-skelter of a raid, the army warned in conversations the gist of which was noted down in the Crime Branch file.

Frustrated at not being allowed to move on Sukhnoi, Sadiq's Squad switched tactics. If a raid was out of the question, then another way had to be found to penetrate the al Faran camp. Out in the countryside, the Squad continued recruiting and activating undercover sources. Among them, the file revealed, was a young constable from Ashajipora, a village south of Anantnag, identified by his initials,

'MMS'. Only his aged father knew he had enlisted as a police constable some months back, and now, instead of putting him into uniform, the Squad sent him back out into the countryside to volunteer for the Movement. MMS had the right credentials, since his brother had been a militant and a *shaheed*, having been 'martyred' while fighting the Indian security forces, which gave the family status in the community. Within a few days, MMS reported back to Crime Branch that he had been accepted into a Movement cell operating from Achhabal, an old Mughal town five miles from Anantnag, on the road to Daksum, one of the group's strongholds. The Squad was inching closer to Sikander and to Sukhnoi village.

Then there were the Movement fighters and supporters who were already in custody, most of them facing indefinite prison terms, torturous interrogations, or death in staged encounters upon release. The most vulnerable, with children or large extended families, were offered a deal by which they were released back into their communities to act as double agents. Some of them vanished the minute they were freed. Others did what was asked, in the knowledge that in Kashmir it was impossible to hide from the security forces for long. Prisoner release was a risky strategy, but the Squad argued for it. One of those who worked out for them was a hospital canteen manager referred to in the file by his initials, 'MAT'. After his release from prison he almost immediately gained access to Sikander himself, having been accepted by Movement cadres in Pahalgam and its surrounds as *bona fide*. Equally precious were the police's long-term undercover assets, unmarried officers who had given up everything for the job. Key among them was Agent 'Rafiq', a constable who had agreed to endure a six-year stretch in Srinagar's Central Prison on a terrorist charge contrived to get him close to convicted militants. From there he had reported continually on their dealings with the brothers on the outside. When he was released he used his cell-block credentials to approach the Movement's Anantnag operation, and by July's end he was fighting alongside them.

Mushtaq Sadiq liked to handle some of these assets personally. The best of them included a militant commander and suspected ISI agent from Pakistan who had been captured in Warwan at the end of July. This man had expected to die during interrogation, but Sadiq spared him, offering him an amnesty and free passage out of Kashmir if he worked for him. Agent 'A for Ahmed' agreed, and after being released he told his comrades in the Warwan that he had eluded captivity by hiding in the upper reaches of the mountains. The story was accepted, and Agent A was welcomed back into the fold, stationed in and around Sukhnoi, from where he reported back on the mood and the plans of the kidnappers, and the health of the hostages, giving the Squad a foothold inside the village itself.

Contact with these resources had to be made through message drops or occasional phone calls to pre-agreed public booths. A Squad member would wait around Anantnag, or on the outskirts of an outlying village, in a wood store or a smithy, a copse or a riverbank, often for more than eight hours, until the agent felt safe enough briefly to give his comrades the slip.

There was little the Squad did not utilise. Just as Roy Ramm and co. had prised apart the Ostrø letters, the Squad analysed them too, the Crime Branch file revealing how some of them had reached Srinagar after a villager had risked his life recovering them in the Warwan and getting them to the police. The significant advantage the Squad had over Scotland Yard and the FBI was that they already knew the location of the captives, something kept from the Western detectives. So when they read these pages, written in the Warwan, they not only fleshed out the perspective of the imprisoned men, but also confirmed crucial information about their precise location.

'To note, atmosphere in Warwan changing in favour of the hostages,' read a report the Squad sent to senior officers. 'Villagers are helping the hostages, an important consideration if there were to be an active operation.' While they waited for a response, the Squad tried to find out more about Hans Christian Ostrø's fate from their eyewitnesses in Sukhnoi. A tumble of images and insights came back.

The first conclusion reached by the Squad was striking: 'Ostrø has formed an escape committee. A man with some military training, he has decided the captives have to get out at *any cost*.' Beginning in late July, Ostrø had challenged, undermined, sniped at and harassed the kidnappers, taking the game to them despite entreaties from the other hostages to desist. A villager who still lives near Sukhnoi told the police, 'He has made three hard escape attempts.' On the first, he was said to have got out at dusk and raced up the mountainside behind the village, only to run into a returning al Faran patrol. 'They led him back into the village at gunpoint, with the prisoner shouting, "I'll go again and again, wherever you put me."'

On the second attempt, Ostrø had jumped into the raging river. 'But the freezing water paralysed him,' said the villager. 'We thought he was drowning.' Ostrø had been fished out shaking. 'He was dragged back to the hut and still he screams and shouts. We think he has stopped eating and is tied up inside the house.' On the third attempt, at the beginning of August, Ostrø had knocked over two guards with a branch and pelted off down the undulating path towards Inshan, making it through two villages and over a precarious wooden bridge before militants on ponies outpaced him.

The Squad were now worried for Ostrø's safety. They began picking up signs that the kidnap party was tiring of his unruly antics. A villager from Brayan who passed through Sukhnoi in the first week of August recalled telling police: 'I saw a blond foreigner tied like a goat to the leg of a *charpoy*. He was calling out for water.' In the writings that had found their way to the police, Ostrø had alluded to being trussed up.

In the second week of August, word came from a baker in Sukhnoi that Ostrø had been permanently separated from the others: 'He is in a different house, tied to the *charpoy* night and day. Every night he and it are dragged inside. He doesn't even come off it to go to the toilet. He screams and sings through the night.'

The relentless Ostrø still would not submit. Tied up outside during the daytime, he had spotted something. The villagers saw it too: 'A helicopter. It returned most days. Militants joked among themselves that it was the Pakistanis, keeping an eye on things. We said, "No, look at the markings. Saffron and green. It's Indian. An Indian helicopter."

Most days we heard its rotors whirr, sometimes higher, sometimes lower. It was over us all the time. We thought they were taking photos.'

One day, Ostrø chose his moment when the guards went to wash. 'The hostage managed to break free, and jumped up, waving a scarf at the chopper. "I am here, look, look, we are here. Come and get us. Can't you see, we're prisoners."' The gunmen came running, knocked Ostrø out with a rifle butt and tied him down once more. Afterwards, fights broke out among the militants. 'The chief was angry and frightened of the helicopter, and fuming with Ostrø.' Some villagers protested, only to be beaten too: 'We were told that our lives also would not be spared. In the morning, they took Ostrø away.'

An urgent report went up the line to Sadiq's superiors, along these lines: 'Army surveillance all over Sukhnoi from the air. Ostrø in danger. He has disappeared.'

SIXTEEN

The Game

The Indian helicopter crew must have seen Ostrø waving, the Squad concluded, as well as the Indian intelligence analysts who studied the photos they took. What about the agents from IB, who got to see all the data, along with their publicity-shy partners in RAW? Senior Kashmir police officers pressed the insular intelligence community for information, and the spooks begrudgingly produced a few 'high-quality stills', although they continued to withhold details about the intention of this intelligence-gathering operation or any clues as to its duration.

RAW's leading agent in Kashmir was C.D. Sahay, a loquacious officer from Karnataka in India's south-west who had become a spy in 1970 and would become RAW's director in 2003. He selected the shots to be passed down to the police: 'They were so detailed you could see the sweaty faces of the captives as they played volleyball or cricket on the riverbank. They were pin sharp, and it felt surreal, almost intrusive, to be staring at them.' There were images of all aspects of Sukhnoi village, as well as countless overhead pictures of the hut in which the captives were held. 'There were even shots of some of the al Faran outfit, racing around Sukhnoi and guarding the hostages,' Sahay recalled.

The Squad wondered how widely these images had been distributed, thinking of the politicians and civil servants in New Delhi who fended off daily press questions about what India was doing to rescue the hostages by claiming the search had failed to pin down al Faran or its captives. Here was hard proof that the upper echelons of the Indian security establishment had known of the hostages' whereabouts for many weeks, and were observing them regularly while telling the wider world (and the families) the opposite, and also failing to mount a rescue operation, even though al Faran looked like sitting ducks.

The intelligence services and the military were unused to being cross-examined by the police in Kashmir. Few answers trickled down, apart from a brief statement that 'A raid is unworkable.' Years later, RAW's Sahay still insisted: 'The Warwan *was* impenetrable. We just couldn't move on Sukhnoi because of its geographic isolation, and the high ground that surrounded it. If we came in by air, we would have been heard long before we were seen and the hostages would have been killed. If we climbed over the mountains, their lookouts would have twigged us and the outcome would have been the same: a slaughter in Sukhnoi.'

Privately, the Squad dismissed this reasoning. One member recalled: 'If it had been a matter of days, or even a fortnight, the argument that it was "all too dangerous and difficult" might have held water. But the hostages were there for many weeks. After all this time not to have advanced at all, and not to have thought of something and tried it out, suggests someone, somewhere did not *want* to move on Sukhnoi.' The Squad began to think that the Indian security forces intended to keep the kidnappers and the hostages penned in this remote valley. But they could not fathom why. The Squad now regarded themselves as the hostages' 'last hope', and while they tried to get to the bottom of the official foot-dragging, they redoubled their efforts to free the captives, seeking more information from among the Warwan's terrified inhabitants. They needed to know what had happened to Ostrø, how the remaining hostages were coping after his disappearance, and most pressing of all, what the kidnappers intended to do with Don, Keith, Paul and Dirk.

Some witnesses, Sukhnoi residents or those from nearby villages, believed that the kidnappers' commander, the Turk, was infuriated by the Norwegian's last attempted break for freedom, having already become agitated by the near-continuous presence of the all-seeing eye of the Indian helicopter above Sukhnoi. The same story came back from Agent A, the Pakistani militant who had been put to work as a double agent. He claimed that the regular, distant whirr of rotor blades had gone on 'for more than two months', and had got the whole village on edge. After Ostrø broke free to signal to the helicopter, villagers had watched, horrified, as the Turk took hold of him, telling him in a language he could not speak, '*Tum bhi bahut zahmat ho.*' You are too much trouble. Then the militant leader had appeared to become calm. 'I'm setting this one free,' he announced. He left with Hans Christian the next morning, 11 August, accompanied by two *dards*, nomadic hunters, and several clanking bags of provisions. After they were gone, a villager overheard the four remaining hostages being told by Qari Zarar, al Faran's Kashmiri deputy commander, that their friend was being set free 'as a goodwill gesture' and because 'he was too much of a handful to keep captive'.

The Squad pieced together Ostrø and the Turk's movements, their sources supplying piecemeal accounts from the length of the dangerous Warwan, drawing out good intelligence from increasingly open villagers, convincing evidence that a rescue was possible – if there was the political will. For now, they mapped the Turk and his small procession as they made their way south, following the line of the Mariev Sudher River as it rushed through the valley. First they had passed through the village of Rikanwas, a forty-minute walk to the south, which remained bathed in warm sunlight for an hour after Sukhnoi fell into freezing shadows. Following narrow, stone-walled paths that wove across the steep ups and downs of the basin, they had then passed through topsy-turvy Gomry, reached by an ancient bridge held up by columns of wobbling boulders, and then down into a deep gully the churning river had cut into the valley floor, its water-smoothed stone banks rising like the bowed sides of an enormous tanker. Three hours into the walk they had climbed a path that passed the walled village of Afti, then up and down several more calf-straining inclines towards Basmina, a fortified stone-and-wood hamlet lying near the valley bottom.

They trekked beside the river for another hour before stopping briefly to take on water and bread in lonely Chordramun, where wooden guttering diverted rivulets throughout the village, giving each house running water. By this stage, twelve miles south of Sukhnoi, all was not well in the party, according to one shepherd who saw them. He had been astounded by the sight of a blond Westerner being pulled along the path by a 'furious' militant commander: 'The *angresi* was shouting and resisting, while being hauled like a calf.' A farmer was also shocked to see 'a guest *mujahideen* fighter dragging along a foreigner, his wrists bound with twine'. After Chordramun, the group had left the river, and shepherds spotted them setting off to the west, scrambling up the steep scree-and-grass bank of the Warwan and into a dense forest, following a path that local nomads rarely used, before disappearing over the high ground and into the snow, heading in the direction of Vail Nagbal. There, the Squad knew, having read DSP Haider's report, two days later, on 13 August, Hans Christian Ostrø was beheaded.

Villagers who still live in the Warwan recall that the Turk arrived back in Sukhnoi, alone, on 14 August, 'sullen and irritable'. His comrades already knew what he had done. Qari Zarar, the al Faran deputy commander, was 'screaming'. The discovery of Hans Christian Ostrø's headless body was all over BBC World Service, he said, with reports highlighting how the killers had incised the name 'al Faran' across his chest. Was the Turk insane? Qari Zarar was overheard repeating a line from the radio over and again: 'Global condemnation of the violent men behind such a brutal killing'. A blazing row flared up between him and the Turk, with residents taking shelter, afraid that one would kill the other and then slaughter any witnesses. 'How can this help us achieve our aims, getting our leaders freed?' Qari Zarar was heard to bellow. 'It makes us look like dogs!'

No one could bring themselves to tell the remaining hostages the truth, villagers said later, with the kidnappers maintaining the charade that Ostrø had been released. But with the members of al Faran now deeply divided, their heads hung low, everyone in Sukhnoi suspected that Don, Keith, Paul and Dirk understood something terrible had happened to Hans Christian. While the hostages dealt with that knowledge in whatever way they were able, the Movement in Pakistan publicly distanced itself from the Turk, releasing a press statement condemning the killing and even 'the militant group that had seized [Ostrø]', to which it claimed 'no allegiance'. Was al Faran now out on its own, the Squad wondered.

In Sukhnoi, the nervous kidnappers debated what to do. From the Movement's heartland high in the wooded Anantnag hills, the Squad's agents MAT (the former hospital canteen manager) and MMS (the young police constable) reported back to Crime Branch that in the days after Ostrø's death, al Faran's commanders mounted a damage-limitation exercise. Sikander had sent furious messages over the Line of Control to his contacts in Pakistan, complaining about the behaviour of his commander, 'a man he had never trusted'. Now he sought advice on 'managing' the disaster. 'We need to act. What should I do?' Sikander asked in coded communications sent from his hideout, thought by the Squad to be a safe house just outside Anantnag. Indian signals intelligence intercepted some of the calls to and from Sikander, a barrage of rebukes and recriminations, and some advice. '*Madarchod!* [Motherfuckers] We're losing this game all on our own, portraying ourselves like common *darshit gar* [terrorists],' a known ISI 'voice' in Pakistan said. 'Stay put. Do not travel to the Warwan. We don't need another brother getting sucked into this mess.'

The Squad knew it needed to do something before the remaining hostages fell victim to the emerging divisions in the kidnappers' camp and the rage of the Movement's ISI sponsors. Al Faran was disintegrating. Political will in Pakistan was ebbing. 'In these conditions Pakistan is liable to conceal all clues of its involvement and burn the whole operation,' thought one Squad veteran. The lives of the hostages hung by a thread. But before it could make any contingency plans the Squad lost its eyes.

Agent A went missing. He failed to turn up at a prearranged rendezvous with his Crime Branch handler at the southern end of the Warwan. Soon after, the Squad received reports of a firefight between a Rashtriya Rifles unit patrolling near Inshan and unidentified 'Pakistani militants'. Afterwards, the army, following normal procedure, handed over a body to the police at Anantnag. The Squad identified the dead man as Agent A, and sent a sombre report up the line: Agent A's double dealing had been rumbled, the ISI having worked out that he was in the pay of India. 'Rather than bloodying themselves, the ISI, posing as Kashmiri villagers, had contacted the Rashtriya Rifles base to report a Pakistan spy in the valley, giving away his rendezvous spot,' the Squad reported bitterly. 'Indian soldiers were waiting for our agent when he arrived, not knowing he was one of ours.'

The death of Agent A was a body blow, but it got Squad leader Mushtaq Sadiq thinking about the mess of Kashmir. He dwelled on India's secret surveillance of Sukhnoi, its apparent tactic of keeping the kidnappers deliberately penned in, and how Pakistan had hood-winked the Indian security forces into killing their own agent. India and Pakistan fought each other in the valley by manipulating the lives of others. Everything that happened here involved acts of ventrilo-quism, with traitors, proxies and informers deployed by both sides, and civilians becoming the casualties. Veterans like him and his coun-terparts in Pakistan called it 'the Game'. One leading hand in the Squad said: 'Pakistan tried something, India blocked it and turned it around, or the other way around, and there were so many angles to it, that really when you were playing it you forgot yourself completely, until it seemed like the most beautiful thing in the world.'

The overarching strategy of the Game, the detective said, was to use any means necessary to sow confusion, hatred and suspicion between the different religions, races and competing militant outfits in Kashmir, so that no one group dominated, and all remained weaker than India's security forces. But the Game went far beyond the age-old tactic of divide and rule: 'We slandered and manipulated. We placed words into someone else's mouth to poison friendships. We created false fronts, fictitious outfits, to commit unthinkable crimes. We tapped phones, listened in to illicit lovers and blackmailed them. There was no moral compass. The Game had absolutely no boundaries, and this was some-thing you only came to realise once you were no longer in it. And then you would stand back, sickened by what you had done.'

Soldiers, policemen and spies, the constitutional guardians of the state, became killers or hired them, disguising themselves as Islamic militants or Kashmiri political activists to spill the blood of soft targets, blackening the name of the freedom movement: 'Massacres in a village, rapes at night of women fetching water, morale-sapping shootings and bombings that targeted lawyers, journalists, trade unionists and philanthropists in the high street, their offices or homes. Some of it was accidental, but most of it was done to inflame, poison, erode and terrify all residents.'

There were no rules, only outcomes. The result was a permanent, rumbling chaos in the valley that both prevented Pakistan or the Kashmiris from moulding a resistance that was capable of capturing the state from India, and stopped India from imposing a profound enough peace to be able to incorporate the state into its union.

The Squad began to wonder whether the Indian response to the kidnappings was in some way a part of the Game, a reaction to Pakistan's sponsoring of the terrorist incident. It had happened before, back in June 1994, when Indian intelligence had made a few daring and brutal moves during the Housego/Mackie hostage crisis that had jeopardised the whole operation to free them, but that were later claimed to have been justified since they almost extinguished the militancy in south Kashmir.

Since 1989 the south of the valley had been increasingly dominated by two militant outfits. The home-grown Kashmiri rebels of Hizbul Mujahideen, generously backed by the ISI and steered by Sunni clerics in Pakistan, competed for dominance with the Movement (Pakistan-born, but having recruited Sikander and other Kashmiris to give it grassroots credibility). Alarmed at the power wielded by these two outfits, which had made the region's main town, Anantnag, and the hills that ringed it ungovernable, the IB tried to penetrate both in order to set one against the other. Eventually Indian intelligence turned a senior field commander in HM, known as 'Umar'. As the kidnappings of Kim Housego and David Mackie were unfolding, Umar was fed false intelligence that the Movement's key spiritual advisor in Anantnag, Qazi Nisar, was stealing money from his own mosque, while collaborating with India to actively canvass against the militancy. The embezzlement allegation was an outright lie, but was particularly damaging for an ascetic cleric. The collaboration claim was subtler, and far harder to refute, as it relied on a nasty distortion of the truth.

Cleric Qazi Nisar, who was much respected by Sikander, had been persuaded by the Housego family to intercede to get Kim and David Mackie freed. Twisting this out of context, Umar passed on the false charges against Qazi Nisar to the HM command. Hardliners there ruled that the much-respected holy man was a treacherous double-dealer, and ordered his execution. A few days later, on 19 June 1994, Umar carried out the cleric's killing, bringing a shocked Anantnag to a standstill. Following orders from his Indian handlers, Umar called Kashmiri journalists like the BBC's Yusuf Jameel and blamed the murder on Sikander, telling them that he had been angered at Qazi Nisar's meddling in the kidnapping. Since the Movement was known locally to be responsible for the Housego/Mackie abductions, this claim appeared credible, and Sikander was widely blamed, threatening to wipe out his standing in the district that was his power base. As hundreds of thousands of people massed for Qazi Nisar's funeral, distraught at the killing of such a holy man, the Movement, understanding the danger it was in, declared war on HM for framing it. According to a Squad veteran, 'The Indian security forces sat back to watch the slaughter, months of tit-for-tat killings exploding in the district that drained HM and sapped the Movement, getting rid of a troublesome cleric along the way.' Having lost its intermediary, the operation to free the two Western hostages almost collapsed. Only the perseverance of David Housego saved the day, as he struggled relentlessly to find new ways to pressure the Movement into releasing his teenage son.

Whether it was the recent death of Agent A, or the setting-up of Qazi Nisar, the simple truth was that every tragedy that struck the benighted valley was contrived or manipulated by either India or Pakistan. The Squad veteran concluded: 'For the security forces, winning the war in Kashmir, playing the Game, came before everything else, including the lives of a few unimportant backpackers.'

Pakistan had already played its hand in the current operation, backing the Movement. The Squad was certain, too, that the ISI had helped to form and equip al Faran. Islamabad was keen to see India squirm as it tried to defuse the resulting hostage crisis, drawing international attention to the Kashmir imbroglio, which garnered few global headlines these days. 'Then it had been India's turn to play,' a Squad officer said. 'India responded chaotically at first, letting the abduction meander on while the pilgrimage to the ice cave was concluded.' New Delhi only turned its attention to the captives in the mountains in August, and then took every opportunity to focus worldwide attention on Pakistan's responsibility for the kidnappings, with Islamabad labelled as 'the architect of terror in the valley'. Every day the abduction was allowed to continue, another statement came from New Delhi haranguing Islamabad in a rolling propaganda offensive that made Pakistan increasingly uncomfortable. Thinking about the Indian helicopter above Sukhnoi that watched everything and did nothing, the Squad sent a report along these lines to the higher-ups: 'Are we still trying to rescue the hostages? Or does the state have another plan?'

If India was deliberately dragging its feet on this case, squeezing the kidnapping for maximum propaganda value, someone on the Indian side would have to take the blame if the crisis ended with blood being spilled. The Squad had no intention of being hung out to dry, and branded as incompetent. They needed to do something that did not happen too often in Kashmir: solve the crime. 'We had become attached to the case, and felt for the hostages,' said a Squad officer. 'We feared too for our careers.' They searched for new sources to help them peer into remote Sukhnoi, but unable to replace Agent A, by the end of August they had only gained a partial view, snatches gleaned from brief conversations with itinerant residents coming and going to and from the village.

The little that did emerge, recorded in the Crime Branch file, showed that while all official efforts in Srinagar centred on pushing Jehangir into providing proof-of-life information, the kidnap party sat tight in the Warwan. The Turk remained as commander, quarrelling with his deputy Qari Zarar. Sikander, via his safe houses east of Anantnag and in Pahalgam, was the Movement's linchpin, handling all communications with Pakistan. The four captives remained prisoners in their wooden 'guesthouse' in Sukhnoi.

However, as soon as IG Rajinder Tikoo's hard-won secret cash deal had been blown into the open on 18 September, convincing Tikoo that 'someone in the Indian establishment wanted this rescue operation to fail' and leading him to quit his negotiator role, everything changed. 'Al Faran packed up and fled,' said a villager from Gomry, the settlement two down from Sukhnoi. 'They were gone by the third week of September,' a teacher from the same village confirmed, having travelled to Sukhnoi to visit sick relatives. 'The guesthouse was empty for the first time since late July, although in Sukhnoi villagers remained scarred by what had happened. They feared al Faran could return any time, and were on tenterhooks. They wrestled with the guilt, sickened by what they had been forced to collaborate in. No one would go near the guesthouse. But what else could they have done?' Another local from nearby Brayan saw the gunmen making their way down the valley with Don, Keith, Paul and Dirk. Heavily bearded and 'wearing Khan dress and plastic shoes', these days the hostages and the militants all looked alike as they trudged off south. After eleven stationary weeks, much of them under close observation, they disappeared, throwing the Squad into a panic as they searched for their trail.

Crime Branch agents were sent over Mardan Top and down to Inshan to comb through the scattered lower villages of the Warwan, tramping worn paths that criss-crossed the valley bottom. Given its physical remoteness and its deep connections to the militancy, the Warwan remained a treacherous place. The Squad stayed in the background while their emissaries sat down at smoky firesides, conducting polite conversations that began with tea and discussions about the harshness of life, but then moved on to more probing questions about any militants who had recently passed through with foreigners. Gently, villagers began volunteering information, delighted to be free of al

Faran, and revealing how, despite being terrified of the gunmen and the security forces, they had secreted many things away over the past two and a half months.

Hans Christian Ostrø's writings had been discovered by someone in the Warwan and smuggled out of the valley, and villagers confirmed that all of the hostages had kept themselves busy by writing on anything they could get hold of: scraps of paper, bits of bandage, food packaging and strips of bark. In 1994, Kim Housego had done the same. 'Villagers or herders were passing through all the time, on their way up or down the valley,' he recalled. 'We did not know where they were going, but we felt they were our only chance of getting a message to the outside world.' To increase the chances of this happening, as many notes as possible were left lying around. 'You cannot imagine what you are capable of until you face a situation like this yourself,' Kim said. 'We contemplated writing on the rocks, and on our rubbish, on anything we could utilise.'

This time around, the hostages also appeared to have discarded or hidden their missives whenever and wherever they could. Almost whenever the villagers passed Sukhnoi's improvised volleyball court, or walked along the meandering silt tracks beside the river, they had found scraps of the hostages' writings, paper fragments ground into the mud by passing hooves and plastic sandals. When they trotted on their ponies between the protective stone walls of the bridlepaths, they had discovered pieces of paper jutting out of the dark grey rock or peeking out of the cairns left by European climbers who had mapped the region in the early twentieth century. They had pulled yet more from the fields as they turned the soil with their bullock-drawn ploughs. Many things had also been concealed in Sukhnoi village itself, forced into gaps between the large foundation stones around the mosque, between the rocks beside the riverbank that the villagers used as their night-time toilet, and into the split wooden poles that propped up their houses. Any of this material would have encouraged the partners and families waiting for news, but they got to see none of it. 'Much later, I heard stories that Don had been writing, writing, writing,' recalled Jane Schelly. 'But we never saw anything. Not a single sheet.'

Like the residents of Zargibal, who had been too scared to report Ostrø's abduction immediately, the people of the Warwan feared being found with incriminating papers by either the kidnappers or the Indian security forces. So they had handed most of what they picked up to literate schoolteachers or pharmacists, who then copied their contents, as best they could, into dog-eared exercise books that they stashed with their animals, or beneath the floorboards of their homes. The originals were burned. Unfortunately, some of these copy books had also been deliberately destroyed shortly before the al Faran party departed the area, the hostages' thoughts and fears lost forever, as villagers were panicked by al Faran gunmen trawling through the Warwan looking for supplies for their next mission.

Now, with the valley theirs again, the villagers retrieved what remained to paint a picture of an increasingly isolated and frustrated party of men who could not understand why no one came to rescue them.

'We have been kidnapped,' one shopkeeper read from some spidery notes. He said he had paraphrased the original document, a sheet of paper found wrapped around a ball of mud, getting down what he took to be its meaning, but not the exact words. He had not used English in many years. 'We are being kept in a wooden hut, a four-hour walk north from here,' the notes continued. 'We do not know the name of the place. We are in extreme danger. We need your help. Take this message to the authorities.' There were five signatures beneath a map with a dotted line tracing a route from Pahalgam over the tops of mountains and passes labelled 'Sheshnag' and 'Sonasar', and down into a valley spelled 'Varvan'. The shopkeeper had noted the unusual spelling, a transcription of the strong accent of Sukhnoi people, who pronounce the 'w's in Warwan as 'v's.

This note appeared to have been written soon after the hostage party reached the Warwan Valley in the second week of July, when the hostages had a fresh mental picture of their route. If, like Kim Housego, they had listened to reports about their abduction on the radios carried by al Faran, they would already have had an inkling that search efforts were unfolding. For much of Kim's time in captivity, the kidnap party had been glued to their radio sets, he said, listening avidly to news reports about the kidnapping on Indian state radio, Pakistani channels and the BBC World Service. Kim recalled the delight of one particular night when he heard his father's name mentioned several times in a BBC Urdu broadcast. He also remembered how the kidnappers had become electrified whenever they heard any of the Movement's leaders back in Pakistan referred to on air. 'All the group [would] raise their hands in salute,' then shout the commander's name followed by the word '*Zindabad*', or 'Long live'. Isolated as they were, everyone felt desperate for reassurance. The Squad wondered how the hostages would have felt if they had overheard the reports of the first press conference given by Jane, Julie, Cath and Anne at the Welcome Hotel on 13 July. The detectives themselves had been moved as they listened to Julie's voice, trembling across the airwaves: 'In the name of God, let our loved ones go. We miss them terribly.'

On other scraps of paper, four of the hostages had written brief descriptions of themselves, according to records kept by a schoolteacher.

Don: 'I am a US citizen. I am married to Jane. I am 42 years old. I'm still pretty fit. I was surprised how well I managed the walk over the top from Pahalgam. Spectacular views despite doing it under duress. Now we are resting beside the river. The most frustrating thing is not having language in common. And the microbes. Some of us have been hit by dysentery. We cannot drink the glacier water as its high mineral load gives everyone a raging thirst. The pure water stream behind the village is fine but almost dry. There is very little food. We have organised a rota to forage for wild herbs. The gunmen never leave our sides. They are all devout. They do not seem like killers. Some of them act like kids.'

Kim Housego had picked up Hindi during his school days in New Delhi, and also had a few words of Urdu. Hans Christian Ostrø was the only one of the 1995 hostages who could speak a word of either language, leaving the others powerless to communicate with their captors. Hans Christian wrote of himself: 'I am from Oslo, Norway. I am 27. The villagers call this place Sukh-nis. They speak differently to everyone else I have met. It was a long and difficult walk but if I could get away I would be able to find the way back to Pahalgam. We have drawn maps, using charcoal we stole from the fire. This was our first task. The people who took us are frightened. They do not know how to look after us. Schub, he is good. But the Kommando [sic], he is not a good man. Sometimes he looks like he wants to kill me. We have started a volleyball team. I am also trying to get villagers to learn *kathakali*, but the gunmen have told them not to speak to us and so we have to dance in silence. These are superstitious, stupid men. This place is at the end of the world.' As always, Ostrø had been looking for any way to communicate with and reach out to the strangers around him, unafraid of being somewhere alien and new.

Keith: 'My name is Keith Mangan. I am from Middlesbrough, UK and married to Julie. I am 33. We have started to secretly write whenever we can. We have to do what we can to get the message out. We feel exhausted, ground down. Hans Christian got a pencil from the villagers. We are using charcoal from the fire. I miss you very much, Julie. And my family, please send them my love if you read this note. We talk about what happened, how it happened, why it happened. The main problem is the sickness, which is very wearing. We are vomiting and have diarrhoea. We need medicine. But we are still alive.'

Paul: 'HELP. My name is Paul Wells. I am 24 and from Blackburn, England. I was trekking with my girlfriend, Catherine. I hope she is well. This valley is the most beautiful place that I have seen. There's no light pollution and there are beautiful hawks in the sky but my camera has been stolen. Wild animals are in the forests, but we do not see them. The villagers and our guards are very different from us. Whoever reads this should let the authorities know. We need HELP. We are waiting.'

There was no word from Dirk. The Squad wondered if he might have written something in German that the villagers, unable to understand it, had discarded.

With what they had, the Squad were able to judge that the hostages had probably learned from the radio that the Indian government was negotiating for their release. Their hopes would have been raised if they had heard the reports broadcast on 17 July quoting a senior Kashmiri police officer as saying: 'Serious discussions are going on and we are not rigid. We may release four or five militants – but not the twenty-one they are demanding.' If the hostages had heard and believed this, they would have concluded that al Faran had an intermediary elsewhere, far away from the Warwan. John Childs had thought as much on the first day of captivity, as he watched the kidnappers waiting to receive orders from Sikander on their VHF set.

In a long document found near Mungli village, a hard day's walk from Sukhnoi, the hostages and several members of al Faran were cast as characters in a story based around their predicament. All that had survived of this, the villagers recalled, was the title page, a cast list and a summary of the plot. This must have been written under the influence of Hans Christian Ostrø. Many villagers in the valley recalled the blond hostage who 'danced and sang and shouted' all day long, refusing to be quiet. Even in captivity, Ostrø's theatrical spirit was irrepressible.

A bundle of papers was recovered from various hiding places around Mungli too. They suggested that the hostages had spent a week or more there, possibly while the kidnappers were waiting for some delivery coming up from Anantnag, or negotiating for food supplies. Again, the originals were destroyed after the village notetakers had made an attempt at recording some of what they read:

A Dream Book – in which each hostage had recorded his
    nightly visions and invited the others to interpret them.
Medicine list – updated according to the ever-changing needs
    of the hostages.
Score Cards – used for games such as volleyball, cricket and
    football (separate cards for hostages, guards and villagers),
    as well as notes about rudimentary games played inside
    when the weather was bad, using river pebbles as counters.
Rules and Opinions – set by the hostages for themselves, to
    make living at close quarters possible, including a

complaints page where any hostage could write down
something that was irritating him, for later discussion.

An Atlas of the Mountains – an attempt to map the hostages'
location and possible escape routes.

The hostages were trying to manage their isolation, which had hit Kim
Housego hard too: 'So many hours spent waiting and doing nothing
were agony. We became despondent. In spite of promises of release,
we did not move.' Even though he and David Mackie were held for
only seventeen days, after the first week, relations with their kidnappers had become strained. 'We did not talk with our captors as much
as we had done earlier. They gave us food and walked away. Villagers
were prevented from talking to us, too.' So desperate were they to
regain their freedom that Kim and David had contemplated a multitude of escape plans, including hurling themselves into the freezing
river in the hope that it would carry them back to civilisation.

A sheet of paper torn from a school exercise book was recovered
from under a long, flat *dhona* stone used by the local women for doing
their washing at Margi. Part of what had been a much longer document that had been found by a young boy on the silt riverbank below
the isolated village, perched high on the eastern flank of the Warwan,
opposite Chordramun, villagers had copied it down.

'We the creators of this new world, bored of the old, want anyone
who finds this to understand the rules for citizenship,' an unidentified
hostage had written. '1. Everyone is free to do as they please. 2.
Everyone can be anything they want to be. 3. Every God is great. 4.
There shall be no tyranny under the rule of God and we fight for the
rights of every man to wear what he wishes.'

The rigours of a remote Islamic life, where all anyone talked about
was faith, were grinding the hostages down. There was a constant
religiosity in the mountains that sat uncomfortably with the
Westerners, who viewed faith as a private matter, although Don and
Hans Christian were fascinated by the spiritual. Paul too had read
widely on reincarnation, according to his family, and Dirk had found
himself drawn to Islam, describing it to his girlfriend Anne as a 'real

living religion'. But after their abduction, and so many days of watching the constant rota of daily prayers, and being lectured on the pre-eminence of Islam, they may not have felt the same way.

There followed another list that had been copied by a villager: 'Buildings, cities, natural wonders ... Brazil, Peru, Norway, Israel, France ...' At first it looked similar to the list Hans Christian had written on the back of the Arvind Cotton Classics advertisement recovered from his body, in which he had named all the places in the world he had seen. But underneath was written: 'We, the architects of this new world, are working to bring peace to the valley with a new programme of imaginary building in the style of great countries.'

Alone in their room in the wooden hut for many hours of the night and day, the hostages appeared to have been painstakingly building an imaginary world to inhabit, in an attempt to escape the banality and terror of the real one they occupied. 'We demand a great library,' the writer continued. 'The Committee for a New Kingdom demands a list of books – Great Expectations (or anything by Dickens), Shakespeare, something by Tolkien, John le Carre, Tagore, Gunter Grass and Bertolt Brecht ... We demand a new menu: out with bread and rice.' As Kim Housego found a year earlier, the monotony of the food was one of the things that ground everyone down.

Other hostages have reacted to their captivity in similar ways. Terry Waite, the Archbishop of Canterbury's envoy who was abducted in Beirut in 1987 and held for almost five years, reflected that he came to see his imprisonment as a chance to embark on an inner journey, one as 'complex, interesting, dangerous and rewarding as those I had made externally for most of my life': 'In a situation of extremity, allow your unconscious to come to your aid. Rather than nightmares, my dreams were frequently amusing. Things I thought I had forgotten began to emerge. Mentally, I began to write my autobiography. I drew on memory and language, the books I'd read, the passages I'd memorised, the language of childhood, which, for me, stood in part on the Common Book of Prayer and the hymns I'd sung. These all became invaluable. As does music, these breathe a certain harmony into the soul.'

A 'list of songs' followed in the Warwan papers, copied down by a villager who recalled that it was initialled 'HC', for Hans Christian. 'Fisherman's Blues', he had begun with, a song by the Waterboys, one of his favourite bands; 'War' had followed, a sixties protest song by Edwin Starr; then 'Dum Dum Boys', an Iggy Pop song that had been adopted as the name of a Norwegian rock band he liked from Trondheim. 'People Like Us' was next, a Talking Heads track whose lyrics may have seemed to chime: 'The clouds roll by and the moon comes up, How long must we live in the heat of the sun?'

Then something lighter, 'Always Look on the Bright Side of Life', from the film *Monty Python's Life of Brian*. Was that Hans Christian's idea, or something supplied by one of the British contingent? Next came 'Blowing in the Wind', by Bob Dylan. Had they sung it together while they wondered if anyone was doing anything to free them? The list got more sombre, finishing with several Simon and Garfunkel ballads, including 'Bridge Over Troubled Water' and 'The Sounds of Silence': 'My words, like silent raindrops fell, and echoed in the wells of silence'.

Sukhnoi was their well of silence.

Near Brayan, a child found an empty box of Four Square cigarettes and took it to the shopkeeper there. Inside was a doodle of five stick figures with beards sitting beside a river, and the words 'Our names are Paul, Keith, Don, Hans Christian and Dirk. We are being held hostage.' Clearly this had been compiled while Hans Christian was still alive, although some time had clearly passed, as the wording on the message that accompanied it was becoming more urgent: 'Please help us. Do not destroy this! Hide the box and take it to the authorities. THERE WILL BE A REWARD. Our lives are in grave *danger*. We are kept prisoners in Sukhnoi. We are easy to find, an entire day's walk up from Inshan at the other end of the valley.'

This was followed by some helpful pointers, 'in case the Indians are planning a rescue': 'The guards are not so watchful now. There are some sentries higher up overlooking the village. Perhaps six. Mostly *gujjars*. There are several more stationed in Rikanwas village just below us, perhaps two men. But they do not have the belly for a fight.

No one wants to fight any more. P.T.O.' Drawn on the inside of the box was a detailed map, with a snaking river crawling between tall mountains to a village marked with a cross. A bird's-eye view of Sukhnoi was beside it. 'We are here.' An arrow pointed to a lone building on the village's edge near the river. Written in capitals were the words 'WOODEN HUT'. Next to it were scattered small crosses identified as 'GUARDS'.

Had the hostages seen the Indian helicopter when they wrote this message? If they had, it would have conflicted with reports on the BBC at that time that they might well have heard, which questioned the extent of the Indians' search efforts. In one press conference at the end of July, shortly after al Faran had made its false claim that the hostages had been wounded in a firefight with security forces, General Saklani had been forced to respond to an accusation that there was little evidence of a large search operation. 'My men are invisible,' he had said.

One villager came forward to describe how he had found an eighteen-inch length of gauze bandage, on which the hostages had made drawings and written a commentary. Seven stick men were depicted with beards, turbans and rifles, he remembered. Beneath each was a name: 'Farooq', 'Schub', 'Nabeel-1', 'Nabeel-2', 'Malang', 'Mohammed-1' and 'Mohammed-2': 'These men are from Kashmir, Pakistan and Afghanistan. They are holding us. Please help.'

The bandage evoked the photos of Don and Keith, lying apparently bloodstained and badly injured, that had arrived in Srinagar on 6 August, supposedly evidence of the firefight of 21 July. On it were four signatures, but unfortunately the bandage had been lost.

This was the first evidence that Hans Christian Ostrø was no longer with the others, and dated this message to early August. It was difficult to be sure if he was still in Sukhnoi, tied to the *charpoy*, or had been taken away, but what came next suggested the latter: 'Whoever reads this should help us now,' read another transcribed note. 'Everyone knows our situation by now. Our friend took letters from each of us. In them we asked for help and we do *need* help. Contact the police, the army, anyone you trust and set us free.'

This must have been written after the other hostages had been told Ostrø was going to be released. He had concealed their letters in his clothing, suggesting that they had known his departure was imminent. But only one letter – from Paul to Cath – had been found on his body by DSP Haider. What had happened to those written by Don, Keith and Dirk? Had the Turk found and destroyed them? Or had Ostrø, having realised he would not live long enough to deliver them, discarded them along the path in the hope that someone would pick them up? The Squad would never know.

More writings had been paraphrased in another village exercise book: 'We have some advice for the Indian government. Everyone here wants this to end. Our guards are looking for a way out. We are watching the Indian helicopter. We have seen it repeatedly. But still no one comes.' There were more drawings, too: a helicopter hovering over a village, from which matchstick figures were waving. 'We are waiting. The kidnappers want *money*.'

IG Rajinder Tikoo's talks about a money deal would not begin for several weeks, and would only be agreed on 17 September. But it appears the discussion in Sukhnoi had already turned to a ransom of some kind.

Another message was found on a label weighted with a stone. 'Food is becoming scarce,' it began mournfully, as transcribed by a shopkeeper. 'Traipsing to find some more. We make a daily pilgrimage to other villages for rice and are looking for more wild plants to eat. Morning fogs have started, which the villagers say means snow is coming. They also taught us Kashmiri names for the iced mountains we can just see in the distance to the north – Nun and Kun – they meant visible and invisible. One other peak we can see behind to the north is called the Big Forehead. It shows the way to Kargil and Sonamarg. We are cold. There are only four of us. Villagers have nothing for us. The helicopter is still there. Please help us.'

This note suggests the hostages had found some way to communicate with the villagers, and confirms that they were confused by the constantly hovering Indian helicopter, which conflicted with the countless items broadcast on various radio stations in which Indian officials claimed still to be searching. 'We don't know where the kidnappers and their captives are hiding,' one police official told the BBC on 14 August. 'We think they've been moving constantly up in the mountains.'

A document that might originally have come from some kind of diary contained these words, according to the man who copied them down: 'Menu: Rice, salt tea, biscuits. Rise 4.10 a.m., prayers started early today as some local councillor came to the village and we were hidden away.' Like Kim Housego, the hostages complained that most nights it was so cold they could barely sleep, and that breakfast was always the most disappointing meal of the day: 'Cold bread from last night, hard and tasteless. We cannot drink another cup of salt tea.' According to this record the hostages had been allowed to exercise down by the river for only an hour before being locked up again: 'Played games with stones in the hut. Have listed all our favourite songs and places to visit but Dirk has not talked for three days. He misses Hans Christian.' That meant this note must have been written in late August or early September.

Whoever wrote it was either putting on a brave face, or reporting what Hans Christian had also hinted at in his letters: that some of the fighters in al Faran had bonded with the captives. 'We feel almost like we have become one unit with our kidnappers. We talk to them and they eat with us. We help them when they are sick and they take us with them when they hunt or forage. Let's hope we can see it through to the next stage.' And although Hans Christian was no longer with them, his influence lived on: 'We are telling stories, making up an imaginary world with the best places and best cities, what kind of people would live there, what kind of buildings would it have, who would be in charge, what kind of music would be in the bars and cafes.'

On another page, the original of which had been ripped from the school exercise book, was a passage entitled 'Notes for a "Letter to the world"'. 'Dear World,' it read. 'We want to know when you are coming for us. We thought we would be set free. We thought it was the end. But it has not ended.' There the note finished, as if the writer had been interrupted. Were they plotting to escape, the Squad wondered. Or had they decided to sit tight, having heard on the radio that the Indian negotiator, IG Tikoo, had successfully whittled down al Faran's demands from twenty-one prisoners to four?

'We dedicate this to Hans Christian Ostrø,' began a note found wrapped around some flat pebbles outside Brayan. If the surviving hostages had not heard about the Norwegian's death from the radio or the kidnappers, someone in one of the villages must have told them about it now. But did they know how he had died, or who was responsible? The next few lines of script were illegible, said the villager who had transcribed the message, the page having got soaked before it was recovered, but the last sentence was still legible, and it was chilling: 'We all said a prayer for him – believers and non believers. Now we know our letters reached no one. If you find this you have to help us or no one will.'

The words called to mind the mournful picture of the four hostages that reached the Press Enclave in Srinagar on 22 August, about ten days after Ostrø was beheaded: four wan men, their faces without hope, with Dirk and Don holding up a newspaper dated 18 August 1995. 'It seems that the Norwegian was killed first because he was the most expendable,' one broadcaster had claimed on the day the picture surfaced in Srinagar. 'The kidnappers are calculating that Britain and the United States would be able to apply more pressure on India to comply with their demands.' Were the hostages hearing this kind of analysis on the radio too, the Squad wondered, fearing for their sanity?

A single paragraph on a scrap of paper curled inside a Limca soft-drink bottle was found on the path leading out of Warwan towards Mardan Top, at the summit of which was the camp of the Rashtriya Rifles, whose Victor Force patrolled Anantnag district. 'It has been so long since any of us has moved that we are unfit,' one unidentified hostage had written, according to the man who found it. 'Our muscles are weak but they say we need to go faster since the villagers can smell snow. It feels like we're running out of time. Extra guides have been recruited and the nomads are leaving. It will end soon, the guards have said. We should be pleased to be moving, leaving here at last, but they have told us the same many times before. We do not know what is their plan or where we are going.'

They were quitting Sukhnoi. While Don, Keith, Paul and Dirk should have been jubilant to be getting out of the desolate Warwan, in fact they seemed dazed. They were being led away from a place they had become familiar with, hurried along a goat path into the unknown.

SEVENTEEN

The Goldfish Bowl

In the outside world, all the partners and families of the missing men heard from the mountains was a flood of rumours. Trying to distract herself in Middlesbrough, Mavis Mangan returned to her job as a school dinner lady, but Charlie, who was retired and in bad health, rattled around at home on an endless cycle of DIY jobs, lamenting that his son wasn't there to help him. In Blackburn, Dianne Wells, who was recovering from a serious illness – by chance, she had entered hospital on the day Paul was abducted – was housebound too, filling scrapbooks with newspaper cuttings 'to show my son when he comes home'. Bob, Paul's father, had returned to work at Debenhams department store, but worried constantly about his wife's state of mind and that of Cath, alone in New Delhi. A few weeks into the crisis he had talked to the Foreign Office about going out to India to support her. 'She was under too much pressure. But the message from the civil servants was clear: I'd just be getting in the way.' Julie's mum, Anita, felt similarly helpless: 'We are just waiting, knowing we cannot do anything.'

In New Delhi, Jane, Julie, Cath and Anne were coming to terms with life in what one of them had christened 'the goldfish bowl' – their shared apartment at the British High Commission – as well as their unsolicited roles as 'hostages' wives'. Formerly strangers, they had lived in each other's laps for three months, and had become close friends who relied greatly on each other. Jane and Julie were inseparable, while Julie and Cath had developed a close bond that dated from their first meeting, all that time ago on the Srinagar-bound bus.

Only Dirk's girlfriend Anne, with her limited English and detached manner, remained slightly apart.

In this charged environment, emotions seesawed wildly. 'You sometimes can't help but stew,' said Jane. The early mornings were her own private danger zone, when she woke from chilling dreams, like the one in which she received Don's severed foot in the post. To counter these morbid thoughts, she would rise at dawn and go for a run around the compound that smelled of night queen and baked earth, striding through her fears, returning to shower before the others woke. 'It helps me to focus on what concrete, positive steps I can take,' she told them. When everyone had got up they would sip muddy instant coffee, the best they could muster in a nation raised on tea.

It was only a matter of time before the Indian negotiators broke through, Jane would say almost daily. The women had to remain strong, as afterwards their partners would need as much love as they could give. Julie would ask how long they should wait there, knowing no one wanted to answer that question. But privately they had all thought it, and eventually someone broke the taboo and said it: 'We can't stay forever.' After a fraught discussion at the end of July, they had made a pact: they would leave India when they believed they could no longer contribute. But for now they all felt as if they were the investigation's much-needed conscience.

Morning briefings with High Commission and Embassy staff became their anchor. Usually it would be British First Secretary Philip Barton, Tim Buchs of the US Embassy or the Norwegians' Tore Hattrem who would come over, bringing the latest report from the Scotland Yard and FBI experts holed up in Srinagar, along with statements from the Indian Home, Defence and External Affairs ministries and the G4's own meagre findings. The women searched for patterns in the conflicting reports from the various Indian agencies, worrying that they had no access to anyone working behind the scenes. 'You think that by being closer to it you can get more information,' Jane said. 'But that's not necessarily true.' The diplomats assured them that if they were back home, things would be the same. In Britain, the relatives of crime victims were handled by a family liaison officer, and were not allowed access to an operation, although they did receive privileged briefings – something that never happened here. Privately, Jane was beginning to doubt the Indian efforts: 'I think that each [agency] has their piece of the puzzle, and if we ever put all the pieces of that puzzle on the table at the same time, we just might come close to seeing a complete picture. Instead, it seems as though every group protects their own bit of information, not sharing it with anyone else.'

To stop herself and the others from dwelling on negativities, Jane dragged everyone out on trips organised by Embassy staff: to the Red Fort and the Gandhi Museum, the crumbling fifteenth-century tombs and gardens of the Lodi dynasty. Even then, Don was constantly on her mind, and she picked up little knick-knacks for him, including a Bhima mask from the Crafts Museum, although she was unaware of its connection to Hans Christian Ostrø. The outings sat uneasily with them all, Julie especially. On 3 August she had gone on an exhausting day trip to the Taj Mahal, on the very day she should have been there with Keith, celebrating their tenth wedding anniversary. She returned to be greeted by al Faran's photographs of Don and Keith lying apparently bloodied and unconscious. 'How could I have thought it was acceptable to go sight-seeing when Keith's life hung so precariously,' she cried to Anette Ostrø. After Hans Christian's death ten days later, Julie had almost stopped going out altogether, frightened of missing an important development and wary of the press pack that turned up everywhere, like a cloud of mosquitoes.

Increasingly, Julie found reasons to do nothing. During the day she was exhausted, and at night she was kept awake by visions. In one recurring scene she struggled to arrange Keith's funeral, putting on a brave face and making it to the church, only for him to walk in alive, halfway through the service. At other times he would come back to her injured and bleeding. Corrosive thoughts kept her on edge. Was she doing enough? Had she written him off? Would he still love her when he returned? When Julie started carrying around a cellophane-wrapped Indian magazine that contained a photograph of the beheaded Hans Christian Ostrø, which she told the others she wanted to show to Keith as proof of his lucky escape, Jane became worried. With Anne's help she contacted a psychiatrist at the German Embassy and arranged for Julie to receive counselling. But nothing, not the doctor or the sleeping tablets, could stop Julie's head from spinning back to the Meadow, where among the wild forget-me-nots all their lives had been transformed. 'One minute Julie senses Keith is free, the next that he is dead,' her mother Anita said. 'We are up and down all the time.'

The recording of Don Hutchings speaking directly to Rajinder Tikoo on 28 and 30 August had revived the hopes of all of the women. After listening to them repeatedly, they had issued a joint statement: 'We are grateful … for this humanitarian gesture. It has greatly relieved and comforted us.' But they were warned by their diplomatic liaisons to be realistic. 'We have been told that things could get tough and that there is only a 50–50 chance of them getting out alive,' Jane wrote in her journal following a debriefing after the second tape recording had been played to them. The rest of the families quietly wondered why the other hostages had not been able to talk. Keith's mother Mavis told the *Gazette*: 'I would have been a lot happier if it had been Keith on the radio, but at least it's a step in the right direction.'

Then, in early September, things began to slide once more. It began with the first newspaper leak, a source claiming to be close to the secret talks revealing that al Faran had reduced the number of prisoners it wanted to be released from twenty-one to fifteen. The kidnappers reacted badly to this indiscretion, threatening to kill the hostages one by one, starting with Don Hutchings. Jane was told this news at a morning briefing: 'I was busy writing, taking notes as always, and as I was writing, I heard them say that Don had been singled out.' Al Faran had said that they would kill him at eight o'clock that night if the government did not modify its position. 'I could tell that all eyes were on me,' Jane continued. 'Then I realised my leg … had begun shaking uncontrollably, a violent shaking that made it almost impossible for me to write.' She'd had this experience before, while rock climbing, and pressed her foot down hard on the floor. 'All the while I was looking at my notepad, clenching my pen so very tightly … unable to look up. I'm sure everyone thought I was crazy, but I just couldn't look up and make eye contact with anybody.' The other women asked what they should do, on Jane's behalf. They did what they always did, and issued a modest statement: 'We appeal directly to al Faran to release safely the ones we hold so dear. Indeed we ask all parties involved to do their utmost to achieve this result quickly.'

Back in the US, it was Labor Day weekend. All Jane and Don's friends were having a get-together at their home in Northwood. But all she could think about was the deadline. Eight p.m. came and went. Al Faran remained silent, as did the Indian government, leaving everyone to assume it had just been another cruel but idle threat – everybody apart from Tikoo being oblivious to how he was struggling to reach a cash deal with al Faran. 'It was a rough weekend,' said Jane. 'I can't remember how we knew after that point that Don was still alive, but that was the assumption. At least there was no message to find a body at any given location.'

Then there was a second leak in an Indian newspaper. Coming from another source that claimed to be close to the secret talks, this one stated that al Faran's demands had been further reduced to just four prisoners. The kidnappers were prompted to issue more threats, this time against all of the hostages. The women waited and agonised and listened to the news. Once again nothing came of it, although an Indian government spokesman did emerge this time to reiterate New Delhi's position that no release was acceptable.

After a third leak, the talks purportedly collapsed altogether. After a fourth, they were back on. The fifth leak was the strangest, the women thought, another source telling an Indian national newspaper that the kidnappers had abandoned their demands for the release of any prisoners altogether, and now wanted cash, Tikoo having secured a two-and-a-half-*crore*-rupee deal with the kidnappers. Jane noted in her journal how al Faran had responded. Taking money, they said in a message delivered to the Press Enclave in Srinagar that denied the rumour was true, was 'an obnoxious image' that 'repulsed' them. Within hours, a story had reached New Delhi that al Faran had broken off talks 'for the last time'. Jane recalled: 'It all happened very, very quickly, from the time the [cash] thing was proposed, to the time it was leaked, to the time when it was just out of the question. We all wondered [about the cash deal]. Was this a serious opportunity, one that we would regret missing?' They just did not know.

Kept away from the negotiating process, the women could not understand whether these leaks were misinformation or an accurate reflection of the talks process. Jane couldn't help but agree with a devastating assessment in *India Today*, the country's premier news magazine, that concluded: 'The Indian government limps along from day to day as if in a collective daze, even as the al Faran issues threats that are as ominous as they are sinister.' Jane wished they had contact with government negotiator Rajinder Tikoo, who was himself the subject of a leak claiming he had walked away from the talks for reasons that were not clear. Jane was frustrated and frightened: 'I wish when we had had contact with the group that I had gone in on my own. I wish I had been the one negotiating, because who's going to work harder to get my husband out than me?'

Up in Srinagar, the foreign experts played the leaks down. Roy Ramm characterised it as 'Low-level flunkies on Saklani's team selling off juicy pieces of gossip for a few rupees. He thinks, "Bloody hell, I've never had one of these [snippets] before, with whom shall I share this?"' But after the story that al Faran would settle for a ransom broke on 18 September, Ramm began to wonder. The talks appeared to be finished. Unable to understand why, and not having sufficient inside knowledge to anticipate what would happen next, Scotland Yard and the FBI too were perplexed by Tikoo, who came to bid them 'a genuine farewell' without telling them why he was going. Ramm struggled to remain positive. However, what he did notice as he stared at his map of recent sightings of the hostage party was that whatever had happened in the secret talks had had a dramatic impact on events in the mountains. A rash of coloured pins correlated to brand-new sightings. For the first time in many weeks, the hostages were on the move.

*　*　*

News of the first sighting came via the *Guardian*, whose reporter had made a dangerous journey to Inshan, a village in the southern reaches of the Warwan Valley. There a family of herders claimed to have been approached by a gang of Pakistani and Afghani militants looking for help to get out of the valley, who said they were guarding 'valuable hostages'. The herders tried to strike a deal, eager to elicit information that they might trade for cash or influence: 'We won't just show you the way, we will help you fight also.' The militants became twitchy, and clammed up. As they parted, the herders shouted a warning: 'We have about twenty days maximum before we have to leave this place to migrate for the winter.'

The first heavy snow was falling in the heights, night temperatures were plummeting, and the herders knew that the lush alluvial plain where Hans Christian had danced *kathakali* and Don had played volleyball were about to be covered in a blanket of ice. For the next six months the Warwan would be cut off from the world, and anyone who could get out would soon be on the move. Ramm and co. deduced that the kidnappers would have to move too, which made sense of these new sightings. It also made al Faran vulnerable.

A few days later, the hostage party had been spotted on a path leading over bleak Mardan Top, the 3,800-metre icy pass leading out of the Warwan Valley. It was a dangerous exit route, as there were countless accounts of nomads dying there from frostbite or exposure. After the ascent to this pass, the route cut through the mountains and across an ankle-breaking field of scree. Eventually it led into one of three parallel basins that ran south-west from the Warwan to Anantnag.

Soon, another sighting arrived. It came from nomads who placed the party at Kuzuz Nar, in a valley parallel to Mardan. If this information was correct, they had made it over the pass, but according to a report received by the British High Commission they had been badly affected by the ice climb, with a herder claiming that 'two of the hostages and one of the kidnappers [were] now seeking treatment for snow blindness'. The punishing winter had begun in the Pir Panjal, part of the north-western complex of the great Himalayas that rise behind it. In the New Delhi goldfish bowl the women dwelled on what all this meant. But softening the distressing images of men dazzled and burned by the first heavy snowfall was an apparent destination that had a winning logic to it: the south Kashmiri town of Anantnag. All of the sightings seemed to suggest that the kidnappers were zigzagging in the general direction of Sikander's realm.

In 1994 the endgame had been played out in Anantnag, with Kim Housego and David Mackie released into the care of photographer Mushtaq Ali at the poplar nursery on the road to Pahalgam. Everyone prayed that winter was now forcing Sikander's hand, and that the kidnappers were pushing towards another Anantnag handover. But the Indian Home Ministry disagreed. A spokesman advised caution, warning that the dense hills above Anantnag were a militant heartland, populated by partisan villagers who would give al Faran food and shelter. Most settlements east of the town had been transformed into fortified militant compounds, while subterranean arms caches, tunnels and hideouts riddled outlying forests. Winkling out the kidnappers from this region would be even more precarious than from the Warwan Valley, the Indians suggested. This depressing response, clashing with what local sources were saying and with what Roy Ramm sensed, cast the women into a new depression.

But as the days passed, the sightings continued, many of them extremely detailed. One described an 'al Faran person sitting on bridge' having an unguarded conversation with another militant about plans to move the hostages to 'underground structures' near Hapatnar. Another name, more research for Ramm and co., whose movements were restricted to the government compound in Srinagar. Unable to visit the Anantnag district for themselves, they had to be creative. No A–Z of Kashmir existed, and villages sometimes had more than one name: ancient Sanskrit, medieval Hindu, bastardised modern Kashmiri or Urdu equivalents. Often there were multiple spellings too. The foreign team had to use what local contacts they could muster – a driver, a baker, the shopkeeper who sold them cigarettes. Eventually they found Hapatnar on a map in a remote valley to the north of Kuzuz Nar.

For a couple of days there was nothing. Then a handful of militants were spotted at Brah, a village on the path linking Kuzuz Nar to Hapatnar. According to Ramm's map, this was very close to where Hans Christian Ostrø's body had been found. Two Westerners were also seen there, under the guard of militants. On 26 September they were sighted again, outside Brah in an 'underground bunker' to the east of Anantnag. The foreign negotiators issued a warning. Although al Faran seemed to be moving towards Anantnag, as it had done in 1994, India should act soon, or the kidnappers could feasibly keep the hostages hidden for months to come, with the snow covering their tracks.

A day or two later, a compounder (a village pharmacist) came forward. He claimed to have been forced by al Faran to walk blind-folded for eight miles deep into the forest, to treat some gunmen and two sick hostages. 'One was much worse than the other,' he said, but both were 'deteriorating in extremely cold, unhygienic conditions with a restricted diet and psychological pressure'. He had not seen where they were staying, as he had been told to wait in a copse, and the hostages were brought to him.

For the partners, the hardest day was 12 October, the ninety-ninth day of captivity for Don, Keith and Paul, the ninety-fifth for Dirk. Thick snow now carpeted all of the upper reaches east of Anantnag, and the women, down in humid New Delhi, tried not to think too much about how their loved ones might be facing the milestone of one hundred days in captivity. The day plodded by like so many others, although Jane called home to Spokane, knowing friends there were marking the occasion with a meditation session in her back garden. Her and Don's extended family of mountaineering enthusi-asts, doctors and nurses had kept their home life going, watering the garden, caring for the two dogs, Bodhi and Homer, answering phone messages and dealing with the press. There had been candlelit vigils in local parks, and the people of Spokane had tied yellow ribbons around trees, trekking posts and other local landmarks to remind everyone that Don was still out there. Some had wanted to make more of a public fuss, such as picketing the local airport to warn travellers not to visit India. Jane had stopped them, asking everyone to keep things low-key, in line with the repeated warnings from the diplomatic liaison officers that too much publicity could both scare off al Faran and turn the Indians hostile. In her heart, Jane was starting to think she needed to go home to her close friends and family. Nothing had been heard from the kidnappers in twenty-four days, and she felt as if she could achieve more in the United States lobbying for Don's release than hanging around the oppressive Chanakyapuri compound, going stir crazy.

In Srinagar, Roy Ramm's frustration was also mounting. He sensed al Faran was exhausted – the hostages too, no doubt. A deal was there for the taking, but he knew nothing of the negotiating process, or even if there was one ongoing. If only they could reach out and pluck the hostages, he said to himself every morning as he contemplated the pins blossoming on the map. Then, on 15 October, several eyewitnesses emerged at once. All reported seeing four hostages sitting in the back of a truck in Anantnag. This was tantalisingly close, just a ninety-minute drive from Srinagar. The Indian authorities came forward, but only for a spokesman from the Home Ministry to once again put the kibosh on things, dismissing any talk of a rescue. Militants stalked Anantnag just as they dominated the hills above it, the spokesman said, adding that the time lag between sightings and their reporting made them difficult to act upon. Any sweeps of the city by the security forces would lead to the hostages being killed, he warned, crushing any last remaining hopes that such action was being contemplated.

The foot-dragging and inertia continued, even as evidence of al Faran's increasing desperation grew. A bus driver came forward to say thirty militants had hijacked his vehicle in broad daylight near Hapatnar. Among the party were four Western prisoners, one of whom was limping. The driver had taken them to a village he identified as Langanbal, where the militants had bought painkillers and antibiotics from a pharmacy before taking off east with a Kashmiri trekking guide.

A new pin was placed on the map at Langanbal, six miles from Pahalgam, where all this had started back in July. However preposterous the bus driver's story seemed, Roy Ramm, who kept returning to the Housego and Mackie abductions, found logic in it. Back in 1994, Sikander's men had commandeered two taxis outside Pahalgam to take their footsore captives on the last part of their journey to the poplar nursery. Kim Housego later recounted how this last stage of their journey had become a farce when one of the taxis had suffered a puncture: 'All the gunmen tried to cram into the other car, arguing over who would get a seat, an issue that became so heated that several gunmen had jumped into the open boot, spilling loaded weapons onto the road.' Now, in Ramm's mind, the only logical reason for Sikander to circle Anantnag was to engineer another hostage hand-over and somehow save face. The trick would be giving him some-thing that would enable him to back out gracefully. Ramm hoped India was thrashing out the details in secret.

Back in Middlesbrough, Mavis and Charlie Mangan's local paper, the *Gazette*, leapt on the sightings at Hapatnar and Langanbal, saying they 'provide the first real evidence of [the hostages'] safety after negotiations … broke down a month ago'. But Keith's parents strug-gled to comprehend why things were moving so slowly. In Blackburn, Bob Wells had cobbled together a map of the Kashmir region, using pages he had photocopied at a local library. Like Roy Ramm in Srinagar, Bob had marked all the sightings, and ran his finger along the paths and roads between them, concluding that the distance between Indian-controlled Srinagar and rebel-held Anantnag was infinitesimal. He could not understand why there was no rescue attempt. 'It was so frustrating. But we just kept being told the same thing: the Indians were on top of things.'

On 24 October the hostages were spotted back in Anantnag, clothed in *pherans* and plastic shoes. Again, one of them was said to be limping. Ramm and his assistants wished they could talk directly to the witnesses. Everything that arrived from General Saklani's office was shorn of particulars, making each account a mere waypoint, of little use as evidence in a building inquiry. That was being conducted elsewhere, Ramm was certain. He hoped the Kashmiri detectives, as coppers back home would have been doing, were crawling all over the countryside, even if their political masters were recalcitrant: 'Anywhere else in the world, the fraternity of police would have shared intelligence and war stories. Here *everything* was infused by politics, shrouded in secrecy and predicated by control.'

Something else was bugging Ramm and co. as they stared at the newly crowded map in their improvised operations room. An inconsistency. 'Why were there so many hostage sightings in Anantnag, a turf that New Delhi maintained was completely under militant control? If al Faran was among its own then it would remain invisible here,' Ramm told himself. Something was missing in their understanding of the situation on the ground in Anantnag.

In September, after cautiously interviewing villagers in the Warwan and sifting through the literary moraine left behind there by the hostages, scraps that revealed their desperate attempts to stay sane and their growing interdependence with their captors, the Kashmiri Crime Branch Squad had also concluded that al Faran was heading to Anantnag, and looking to broker some kind of deal. The detectives decided that they would try to intercept the hostage party as they descended from Mardan Top, in a mission they regarded as 'going behind enemy lines'.

For six long and bloody years, the knotted pine forests above Anantnag, with their cascading mountain rivers, abandoned Mughal gardens and corkscrew tracks, the plateaux of paddy and the walnut groves, had cradled the *azadi* movement. Here a field of militant outfits had sprung up like purple saffron crocuses. Some groups were Kashmiri, others created by Pakistan. Most did not consist of battle-hardened *mujahids*, but of students, mechanics, tailors, carpenters, bakers, schoolteachers and the unemployed, an army of amateurs supported by hundreds of thousands of poor country people whose resentment of India kept their lips sealed. All too often the price of their loyalty was a terrible retribution from the Indian security forces: ancient wooden villages incinerated and angry garrisons parked outside the ruins, a corrosive cycle of military operations – crackdown, cordon-and-search and catch-and-kill – that saw thousands of residents detained without warrant, tortured and killed without a trial, their bodies dumped in unmarked graves scattered throughout the district's woods. Despite – and because of – the Indian brutality, outfits like Sikander's Movement and Hizbul Mujahideen flourished. Although they fought with each other, bloodily, over supporters and territory, disagreeing bitterly too about religion and ideology, with HM winning the upper hand, collectively they still controlled most of the villages and hamlets in the Anantnag district, as the Squad knew from bitter experience.

Mushtaq Sadiq's men arrived in the region in the third week of September, pitching up in Lovloo, a remote village of wooden houses strung out along a ridge twenty miles south-east of Anantnag. They had been tipped off that this was an important Movement strong-hold, and they trod gingerly as they attempted to pick up al Faran's trail. Lovloo was one of the last Kashmiri outposts before the hills became mountains, criss-crossed by perilous icy passes that led into the Warwan, and was, as far as the police knew, a dormitory for gunmen who came down from the heights at the end of summer, the village's haylofts providing beds for the night.

However, what the Squad found in Lovloo was a Kashmiri calling himself 'the Tiger', who claimed he was paid by the Indian govern-ment to control all the villages visible on the hilltops above his home. A surly figure, who sat wrapped in his *pheran* in a well-tended garden of neon-yellow daisies in front of his cottage overlooking the routes down from Mardan Top, the Tiger was surrounded by heavily armed bodyguards, and openly carried a rifle. Unlike Lovloo's other inhabit-ants – farmers and woodcutters who scurried away as soon as they saw outsiders – he was not frightened of anyone in authority. But he didn't wear a uniform either.

The predatory Tiger, whose fat fingers have seen so much action over the years that he is barely able to close them in a handshake, still lives in Lovloo. His real name is Basir Ahmad Wagay, and he was formerly a builder by trade. His radio call-sign, 'Tiger', derived from the ostentatious moustache that curls around his cheeks, and from his self-professed 'fondness for a brawl'. He had a vicious temper that got people jumping (including his wife and two daughters, who cowered indoors, he said). 'Fuck with me and I'll fuck you up,' the Tiger bragged as he crushed fresh walnuts in his fist, explaining candidly how he came to be roaming around Lovloo, openly armed to the teeth.

In 1991 his father had been arrested and tortured by '*behanchod* Indian soldiers', he said, calling the troops 'sisterfuckers'. After that the Tiger had gone to war, joining the Muslim Brotherhood in 1992, the same militant outfit Sikander had enlisted in during his college days in Anantnag. At first, all had gone well, with the Brotherhood claiming scores of hits against the security forces, who in the Tiger's words were '*suor ka bacha*', or sons of pigs.

'But things changed in 1994,' the Tiger reflected. 'Our discipline eroded, and the true militancy became no more noble than mugging. We were *gandu* [arseholes], and badly outgunned by the Indian dogs.' Not wanting to end up rotting among the faceless corpses stacked in mass graves all along the Line of Control, and disenchanted by the *azadi* cause, the Tiger and his followers had secretly agreed to switch sides after being approached by Indian intelligence agents who offered them money and protection to hunt down their former comrades. From now on they would be known as 'renegades', allowed to keep their weapons and any spoils they procured.

The existence of the Tiger's group was secret, and vehemently denied by the Indian government. Although the Squad knew about the classified operation to recruit Kashmiris to spy for the security forces, which had commenced in 1994, they had had no idea that it had penetrated this far into the militant-infested Anantnag hills, or that it involved arming former militants as well as using them as informers. From what the Squad understood, the intelligence agencies had modelled the plan on a tactic used by India in Punjab state in the 1980s, when a Sikh insurgency had risen u , and fighters disgruntled with it were lured to the government side nd deployed to crush their erstwhile comrades. The philosophy that underpinned the initiative, turning one community against another, was also a central tenet of the Game.

'I'm the fucking law now,' the Tiger says he told the police. He even has a laminated identity card bearing his photo, which he keeps in a creased red-plastic shopping bag. Stamped by the 36th Battalion of the Rashtriya Rifles, the card describes him as a 'Battalion Commander' and gives the serial number of his rifle, which was bought for him by Pakistan when he went over the LoC to train during the early days of the insurgency. The Squad could not help but marvel at the irony of this. The force that was created to crush Kashmir's insurgency, India's brutally effective RR, had endorsed the Tiger and sanctioned his weapon, both of which had been tools of Pakistan, triggering a new kind of insurgency. According to the Tiger there were thirty-five men under him, spread across six or seven large villages and a number of hamlets, all militants who had flipped to the government side and were authorised by the RR to bear arms, carrying similar cards to prove it.

They were paid 'two bottles of wine a day' by the 36th RR's Colonel Awasthi, for whom they ran a network of unofficial informers, villagers who received small amounts of cash for revealing whatever the Movement or HM was up to. Whenever the Tiger's men got a call from one of these sources, they commandeered a fleet of taxis to get to the fight, since they had no cars of their own. Without mobile phones, they were dependent on the confused copper wires of India's public call boxes to keep in touch with each other. And in a remote and under-resourced region riddled with poverty and petty village disputes, this DIY government hit squad also used their newly-gifted power to settle a lifetime's worth of grudges.

The Tiger boasted: 'I say to my boys, "Go into so-and-so village and start shooting those dog-fuckers." Then we used to leave some of our boys behind.' He dusted off his hands. '*Ragdoo, ragdoo* [smash, smash], they misbehave. And I come back and tell the people sitting in the ruins of their homes, "*Lath choos* [cocksuckers], unless you come over to my way of thinking, we'll be back."' He said the speech normally sorted things out, as did the stories that had reached all of the villages across south Kashmir that government-paid renegades were permitted to do whatever they liked.

Strong-arming, informing and looting soon became wholesale killing. The Tiger said that in early 1995 the 36th Rashtriya Rifles had introduced a cash-for-corpses incentive scheme, in line with another rule of the Game: My enemy's enemy is my friend. 'Now, for every body that I or my men dump at the local 36th RR camp, we are paid between ten thousand and twenty thousand rupees [between £200 and £400], depending on the seniority of the deceased militant. But no one examines the bodies, asks for debriefs or IDs, so we shoot whosoever we choose. And so long as the RR remains in power, no one is going to stop us,' was the way the Tiger told it. He had taken to his task with gusto, carrying fat rolls of five-hundred-rupee notes, testifying to the eighty-nine kills he would personally rack up, most of which he could no longer put a face to. He became so valuable a resource that when he got shot himself in 1995, the army sent him to Srinagar, where he received medical treatment at the military hospital in BB Cantt, Indian Army headquarters. 'Since we took over, we got rid of those *zinheke* [sons of whores] completely,' the Tiger said, referring to the militants from HM and the Movement whom he had once considered as brothers.

This area in the upper hills was no longer a haven for Sikander or his men, the Squad could see. When they asked the Tiger what he knew about the hostages, he said he was sure they were heading this way. He recalled: 'Our sources told us the kidnappers arrived here from the Warwan – end of September – and spent the first few days hanging around the upper forests. We climbed a few mountains and we found some freshly used militant hideouts where the bedbugs were full of blood. They had been there all right. We hung around for seven or eight days, waiting, but did not see them. We did hear them on the VHF sets, chattering, saying the hostages were healthy, but cold and hungry.' He concluded that al Faran was intending to come down into town: 'Those *halamke* [bastards] were heading for Anantnag town. But they would have to cross us first, and then we'd have them.'

Letting rip with a fusillade of shots, to show the conversation was at an end, the Tiger snatched back his paperwork, tossing his photo-ID and other assorted documents into the red shopping bag. 'I only know bits and bobs,' he said, shifting from one leg to the other, appearing to have become uncomfortable with this subject, having thought about it a little longer. 'The hostages are a matter for the higher-ups. You should talk to them. It's their operation. We are not employed to think about stuff. We are wolves.' In any case, he had to go. Every evening at dusk he drove in a convoy of taxis down the mountain to the nearest Indian paramilitary base at Vailoo, thirty minutes away, where he would spend the night in a bunker, drinking Old Monk rum with the soldiers and listening to the thwack and whizz of home-made mortars flying overhead. His new incarnation as a government killer had cost him dear. The Tiger had lost count of the number of relations, friends and neighbours who wanted him dead.

The Tiger's gory grip on the forests and foothills east of Anantnag explained why the Indians had been able to gather so many sightings of the al Faran party in this area – the ones that had been leaked to the press and became coloured pins on Roy Ramm's composite map. Contrary to what the Indian government was saying publicly, it had ears and eyes in villages at the previously hostile top end of the district, informers paid to work its beat, and gunmen to act on the intelligence, tipping the balance of power towards New Delhi. This change would force Sikander into a corner, the Squad concluded. They needed to move fast to secure a deal before he panicked. The key could be the renegade intelligence networks. If they extended across other hilly areas above Anantnag, and the Squad could get them to work for them, the task of hunting al Faran, or communicating with it, would be that much easier.

The renegades would not take orders from Crime Branch officers without being told to do so from above, so the Squad set off in search of the Tiger's boss, Abdul Rashid, a thirty-two-year-old former government employee in Anantnag's weights and measures department, hoping that he would either have the clout to make a decision, or could spill some useful intelligence. Like the Tiger, Rashid had joined the militancy in 1990, becoming a district commander in the Muslim Brotherhood before secretly defecting to the government side in 1994, when his new Indian handlers gave him a call-sign: the Clerk.

No longer welcome in his home town of Guri Draman, a bucolic village whose name means 'colt grass', the Clerk had sought sanctuary among the Indian paramilitaries in Vailoo, a two-street village of mercantile farmers, close to an ancient arched stone bridge over the Breng River. Everyone in the village loathed him. Stories were whispered of how one day he had ordered one of his men to pluck a neighbour's baby from her house, and plunge it into a freezing water butt, holding it under until it stopped kicking, because its mother had given a bowl of drinking water to a bleeding prisoner he had had hogtied to his jeep.

The Squad found the Clerk easily enough, since he had made so much money from his renegade activities that he had built himself a mansion, protected by imposing black iron gates and guarded by heavily armed Indian paramilitaries. Now, the Crime Branch detectives were held at those gates while guards checked their IDs, relaying their details to some distant controller over a state-of-the-art high-frequency radio set. Whatever he did for them, the state was clearly guarding the Clerk well. Finally they were given the nod, and the Clerk, sitting on his wooden veranda, beckoned them over, sipping from a cup of Lipton, but offering nothing to the members of the Squad, a deliberate act of discourtesy that would be understood by all Kashmiris, for whom the offer of tea was a customary greeting, like a handshake in the West, or even a kiss.

The detectives could see that the Clerk was a different proposition to the Tiger. Handsome, dressed in jeans and a crisp shirt, he appeared sophisticated and calm, although if only half of what they had heard about him was true, he was far more cruel than his lieutenant in Lovloo. When he was asked about al Faran, he became hostile. 'Whatever my boys find is passed up the line to the Rashtriya Rifles,' he said. His family, who today still live behind the big black gates in Vailoo, came out to listen. One of them recalled: 'He told the visitors he was answerable only to his army handlers, just to keep things simple. If express permission was given by the higher-ups he could cast his mind back. But he had no such orders from the Indian Army or intelligence.' The Clerk said he was too busy nowadays to talk to policemen: 'Kidnappers and foreign hostages are not my business. That's further up the pay scale. I have only one task here. We have instructions to eliminate HM in Anantnag, wiping them out, leaving no trace, by the winter's end.' With that he stood up abruptly and was gone.

Faced with the renegades' reluctance to talk about the al Faran operation, the Squad knew that they needed to find someone senior enough to be able to assist them without having to seek authorisation from the higher-ups. This was something of an outside possibility, as they were a secret force that in these early days the government wanted to remain obscure. The policemen worried too that they were dabbling in a shadowy world, which they had entered without permission or invitation. That was perilous in Kashmir, where curiosity often got people killed.

Leaving the wilds of Lovloo and Vailoo, the Squad headed down the Sosanwar Hills towards Anantnag, through an undulating landscape of unmade roads and silent pines. Village boys beat the walnut trees by the side of the road with long bamboo poles to bring down the autumn crop, and the Squad's jeeps crunched over the broken branches. Occasionally they passed an isolated army camp or STF checkpoint, marked out by red-and-white fencing and bounded by sandbags, sentry posts and barbed wire. Empty beer bottles jangled from the fences, and signs declared 'Army Helpline', with a mobile telephone number scrawled beneath them. They wondered how many locals dared ring that number. 'Make 1995 A Year With No Human Rights Abuses' read a hand-painted sign just outside Achhabal, the site of a legendary Mughal garden designed in the seventeenth century by Noor Jehan, the wife of Emperor Jehangir. Once it had been a popular picnic destination for all races and creeds, but these days the grass was jaundiced, the fountains dry.

Several hours later, their journey prolonged by roads fractured by heavy military vehicles pounding along them, the Squad eventually reached Anantnag. Militants once controlled the town, and the security forces had had to be careful whenever they ventured beyond police lines. But now, in October 1995, everywhere the Squad turned there was a renegade outpost, from which locals said rose the ferrous smell of blood. A sprawling wooden house once owned by Kashmiri Pandits (Hindus) in the Janglat Mandi neighbourhood had been transformed into a massive interrogation centre. These days no one went near it unless they were dragged in by their heels, neighbours said. The renegades had another such place in Kadipora, Anantnag's hectic market, where above a lintel beneath the veranda someone had scrawled words that remain there today: 'We are proud to be Indians. Get them by their balls, hearts and minds will follow.' Kashmiris who had become Indians for gold, the renegades did as they liked, and had set up their HQ in another illegally occupied Pandit mansion beside Mehndi Kadal (Henna Bridge), brazenly close to the central Saddar police station. Outside the building, the turncoats squatted under anti-grenade netting, and were even guarded by khaki-clad officers from the volatile police Special Task Force, whose bullet-pocked white Gypsy jeeps were prominently parked in front to show who was in partnership with whom. The STF was now almost as unruly as these Kashmiri irregulars, the Squad noted.

None of the mercenaries would talk to Crime Branch. The local cops admitted that they were not in control of them. One officer described how a particularly vicious renegade commander had taken up residence inside Anantnag's Police Superintendent's office, from where he held court with his feet up on the desk, making it impossible for anyone to investigate the six hundred or so killings his men were accused of carrying out: their victims included the town's chief medical officer, a former member of the state assembly and a well-loved schoolmaster. It was the same in other towns too, the Squad heard. A police source in the Anantnag control room told them about a renegade called Fayaz who was known to have personally killed more than a hundred Kashmiris who may have been militants, or their distant relations, neighbours or friends, a kill rate verified by the RR. Now, Fayaz walked the streets of his home village 'like a king', and 'even policemen looked down'. 'Whatever Fayaz wanted he got, apart from Naseema, the most beautiful girl in the village.' When she turned him down, he had her abducted and raped until she became pregnant. 'To prove his power, he then went after her sister too.' The distraught family contacted the police. 'The cops took the details, and then rang Fayaz, who charged into the village market. There he produced the eight-months pregnant Naseema, stripped her and shot her repeatedly in the belly before a large crowd, shouting, "We are in charge, and no one can touch us. This is what you get when you fuck with us." Naseema with her unborn child died. Her sister is still with the renegades.'

In six years of war, Kashmiris, inured to bloodshed, had never known terror like this. The Squad worried that there was nothing they could offer the renegade leadership of Anantnag to get them to work for them. They were the creation of the army and the intelligence agencies, a pragmatic and dangerous arrangement that made life on the ground easier for the embattled Indian security forces. If the backers of these renegades discovered that their hard-won contacts, oiled with bottles of whisky and stacks of rupees, were being utilised unsanctioned by Kashmiri Muslim police officers, the payback was potentially lethal. Twice in the past five years the police had been disarmed by the Indian security services when they had faced each other down over disagreements.

The Squad had already suspected they had been set up to fail in this inquiry. Now, probing the renegades, they felt even more vulnerable. For several days they watched, and discovered that suitcases of government cash were being delivered to the Civil Lines area of Anantnag, where most officials lived. From there the bags of cash were sent into the hills above town.

The detectives followed the money, and discovered its destination was an inconsequential village an hour south-east of town, close to historic Mughal Achhabal. When they arrived in Shelipora, they found the small grid of mud-walled buildings surrounded by living willow fencing and orchards was now striated with freshly dug trenches and bunkers crowned with razor wire. The houses were draped in camouflage netting and fortified with jute sandbags, their windows and balconies taped against blast damage and screened off with tall sheets of corrugated metal to repel volleys of incoming rocket-propelled grenades, as small clusters of militants from HM made regular, but so far futile, attempts to smash their way in.

Shelipora was a bristling fortress. Indian armoured vehicles came and went, with masked gunmen from various government paramilitary agencies riding shotgun, sporting bulletproof vests and cradling automatic weapons. Here, tooled up and dug in, they discovered, was the headquarters of the most powerful pro-government militiaman in the entire district, a man who oversaw everything from the perimeter of Anantnag town to Mardan Top. His name was Azad Nabi, but out in the field he was known by his call-sign: Alpha.

Born Ghulam Nabi Mir, Alpha had once been a 'Constable Driver' with the 7th Battalion of Kashmir's Armed Police, another wing of state security deployed to tame the valley. In 1989 he had deserted and crossed the Line of Control to train as a militant, enlisting with HM and returning to fight the Indian security forces with vigour. Soon he became an HM district commander, before defecting to a breakaway faction called the Muslim Warriors, eventually becoming its chief. This second defection meant he had to fight for survival on two fronts, against India and his erstwhile comrades in HM, who were furious at his disloyalty.

The intelligence services had reached out to Alpha in 1994, offering him sanctuary from HM and arms with which to fight his former brothers. This triggered one of the most ambitious intelligence operations in the valley, the defection of Alpha's entire band of 450 warriors, who surrendered en masse at a secret ceremony on a parade ground, watched by Kashmir's Inspector General of Police, Paramdeep Singh Gill. Alpha's renegades had then been sent to north Kashmir to harass HM. They were credited with two hundred kills there before being redirected to Anantnag, picking Shelipora as their base. Here they had linked up with the Tiger and the Clerk to become India's premier attack dogs in south Kashmir, raping, killing and boozing, running all of the renegade networks in the countryside. Collaborating closely with the police Special Task Force, the RR and Indian intelligence, they specialised in operations that the state could deny, also developing a round-the-clock interrogation programme to keep the general population cowed that was renowned for its brutality and indiscrimination. Alpha was the fountainhead for everything that happened in the countryside, and his proximity to the authorities was visible for all to see. He rode around Shelipora in a bulletproof police STF Gypsy, and was protected by STF bodyguards. He boasted that he 'earned more than a cabinet minister in New Delhi', and his fighters received regular wage packets from the state: three thousand rupees (£60) per month for a rank-and-file *mujahid*, four thousand (£80) for a company commander and six thousand (£120) for a battalion commander.

The Squad had reached the top of the renegade tree. They decided on a dangerous tack. In a highly sensitive operation, they attempted to infiltrate Alpha's Shelipora fortress and his district's renegade network, turning those on the bottom rungs into informers and placing their own people, former militants who had the right pedigree, inside Alpha's units. These sources wriggled, eavesdropped and recruited people who Kashmiris call *nabuds*, a slang term derived from the local word for 'sugary', meaning someone who could be enticed to give up little snippets of information when sweetened by cash: the poverty-stricken or put-upon, the greedy or ambitious.

Gliding like honey through hamlets and small market towns, these *nabuds* courted others, creating a network within the renegade hierarchy that generated reams of intelligence, none of which Ramm and co. would ever see, but that took the police Crime Branch inquiry to another level. As they had hoped, they began receiving countless reports about al Faran, generated by Alpha's spies in the countryside, who saw everything. By the end of October the Squad were aware of sightings of the kidnappers in Hapatnar and remote Brah, in Asharjipora village and Anantnag itself. A report was dispatched, along these lines: al Faran is now completely exposed. The hostages are alive. The kidnappers are hot-footing it around, out on a limb. 'They are exhausted, desperate for a deal, and they will break soon.'

No direction came back from the security forces. But the Squad sensed that if only they could develop their intelligence faster, reducing the lag between receiving the name of a village and raiding it, they could bring this kidnapping to a positive conclusion, and quickly. Whenever they converged on a hideout al Faran was ahead of them, sometimes fleeing only moments before they arrived. In one case half-filled teacups had been left beside a fire that was still glowing, flat breads warming on the stones, and a packet of cigarettes just cracked open, the foil half pulled off.

However, by early November, despite numerous close calls, the Squad had got no nearer. The detectives were also stewing over one undeniable fact: whether it was Alpha's warriors or the Clerk's new Brotherhood in Vailoo or the Tiger's thugs in Lovloo, the pro-government forces ran everything and saw everything. The countryside India publicly claimed to have lost control of had in fact been brutally battened down. This raised one serious question. The Squad sent a report up the line, something like this: If we own the countryside, and wherever al Faran treads it can be seen, how do Sikander's boys continue to evade the renegades and remain at large?

There was something profoundly troubling about the landscape above Anantnag.

EIGHTEEN

Chor-Chor Mausere Bhai
(All Thieves are Cousins)

In the last week of October, Jane, Julie, Cath and Anne took a vote. As far as they could see, nothing was happening. Al Faran was silent, the Indian authorities too. The women all needed to leave India. Julie and Cath missed their families and friends, and Jane was desperate to get back to some kind of regular life. The autumn term was under way, and she could not keep the elementary school where she worked hanging on indefinitely. Don's work also needed to be sorted out. And they had all had enough of sitting around, made to feel useless and pretending to be tourists.

Their collective decision to go was not just based on what they were missing, but also on a growing belief that they could achieve much more outside India. In Britain, the USA and Germany they could lobby their governments to intensify the pressure on the Indians, with Jane planning to use her brother-in-law Don Snyder's political connections in the Pennsylvania House of Representatives. All of them agreed that too much time was passing. 'Can it be possible that one time so long ago I was writing Day 25, Day 53, Day 67 ... How many more will I have to write?' Jane pondered in her journal. She and the others wrote a parting statement: 'It has been 114 days ... for all that time we have waited anxiously for news of their well-being, prayed for their safe return to us. We have now decided to return to our homes to seek the support of our families and to discuss with them ... what is happening in India.'

Before they left New Delhi, they were all called in by their embassies. The search would continue, they were told, but such was its sensitivity that it could be derailed by any ill-judged comment, even from the other side of the world. They should all refrain from talking to the press. Jane agreed. Her greatest worry was that by leaving India they would be cut out of the diplomatic communication loop. One of the best things about being in the Chanakyapuri compound was that she felt she knew what the embassies knew, and not long after they knew it. The US Embassy promised to provide her with a dedicated State Department liaison officer who would call her regularly, daily if necessary. The British High Commission agreed to arrange something similar for Julie and Cath. The Indian Home Ministry reassured the women that they were making the right choice by leaving. Officials confided to them that, for reasons that were not explained, the 'threat to the hostages' lives had receded'. What did that mean? None of them could decide.

Before they knew it they were saying goodbye at the airport, trying not to feel as if they were quitting, although that was all they could think about. They boarded their flights unsure of when they might be back, or if they would ever see each other again.

On 26 October, as New Delhi disappeared beneath the autumn smog, Jane thought how she and Don should have been making this homeward journey three months back, their rucksacks stuffed with gifts and snapshots, their heads filled with stories to share with friends. Instead, she was returning with an album of harrowing photographs that charted the descent of five smiling figures in newish trekking gear, weathering some bad luck but with a great adventure story to tell, to four, despondent bearded wraiths.

Cath's suitcase, originally packed for a six-week adventure, now bulged with paperwork. In her hand luggage was a bundle of Paul's holiday photos: Julie, Keith and Cath laughing as they struck out along the path from Pahalgam in T-shirts and shorts; Julie and Keith chatting beside their tent just moments before their lives were changed forever. Recovering some possessions she and Paul had left behind on the houseboat, Cath had found the postcard Paul had written but never got round to sending: 'Dear Mum and Dad, It took us 30 hours to get here and I (oops!) *we* are now staying on a houseboat for £3 a

night. I'm sitting on the roof of the houseboat writing this to you …
The houseboat owner Bashir is taking us on a trek tomorrow to
Kolahoi Glacier with two British people and a Canadian. It should be
fun! Love from Paul.' Now she would have to deliver it to Bob and
Dianne Wells personally.

When she was back on British soil Julie held a press conference, wanting to head off the newspaper and TV reporters. Charlie and Mavis
stood by nervously as she explained why, in need of a different kind
of support, she had left New Delhi. 'My source of that support is here
at home with the community, my friends and my family,' she said.
Mavis, buoyed by Julie's return, also said a few words. It felt good to
be face to face at last.

Then Julie fell to pieces. She couldn't work, wouldn't eat, and was
consumed by guilt at having abandoned her husband to his fate. She
moved in with her mother in Eston, but was kept awake by horrific
dreams: Keith falling through the ice, or locked up somewhere
beneath the forest floor, or shackled and injured in the snow, or
suffering and frightened in some isolated herders' hut. Kashmir
seemed so far away. The local Kashmiri community on Teesside got
in touch, offering to help, and a couple of times they got together.
But Julie left those meetings feeling as hollow as she had in Srinagar.
As far as she could see, they just wanted to use her predicament to
highlight their woes: 'The sheer negativity of those people shocked
me.'

Jane's return was also low-key but fraught. She spent a week 'crying
on the settee' with her parents in Orefield, Pennsylvania, before facing
Spokane. Everyone rallied around, arranging a potluck dinner, filling
her in about everything the city was still doing to keep Don's memory
alive. But the home he and she had packed with mementos now filled
her with a crushing feeling of loss, whether she was sitting in his study,
or gazing out over the back garden, or looking up at the moon and
'wondering if he could see it too'. There was one gift he had not yet
seen: a crystal ball she had bought for his forty-third birthday. If only
she'd given it to him before they went to Kashmir, he would have

joked. Not wanting to fester, Jane returned to work, and got on with her life straight away – shopping, gardening, running, teaching, cycling, sleeping.

Then, after forty-nine days of silence, al Faran re-emerged on the other side of the world.

On 9 November a handwritten message was dropped at the coop of smoke-filled offices that made up the Press Enclave in Srinagar. Still without access to the official inquiry, and with nothing to do in Kashmir, many of the Scotland Yard and FBI investigators had returned to New Delhi. But now that there was something to analyse, the Church Lane guesthouse quickly filled up again, even though the contents of this long-awaited al Faran communication were troubling.

One of the hostages had suffered 'bad injuries' after a fall, it claimed, while another was 'ill and being given medical aid'. No names or details of the accident were revealed, in a calculating disclosure that could not be verified. While Roy Ramm and co. remained sceptical, a new eyewitness claimed to have seen Don being carried around 'on a militant's back'. Given how many weeks the hostages had been in captivity, and the harshness of the terrain and the climate, this report could not be ruled out either. The investigators were struck by another thought. The last time this kind of card had been played by al Faran – the theatrical images purporting to show the wounded Don and Keith after a firefight – it had presaged a breakthrough in the secret negotiations. While everyone was certain the photographs had been rigged, they accompanied al Faran's first major concession, a dropping of the prisoner numbers from twenty-one to fifteen. Would this new letter, after so many weeks of silence, also be accompanied by a move, perhaps towards a deal? Hopefully, Ramm and the other negotiators told each other, the Indians were working on something special.

They got nothing from General Saklani. Instead, an uncompromising Director General of Police, Mahendra Sabharwal, Rajinder Tikoo's boss, his hair lacquered and neatly cut in a short back and sides, emerged to face the press. He had nothing to say about the government's progress. He could not even confirm if any negotiations were taking place. Instead, he warned al Faran that the hostages' welfare was solely their responsibility. The whole world was watching, he said, and they should release the prisoners unconditionally if they were concerned about their health. 'The DG was on the money,' Ramm thought, but being so utterly uncompromising was not necessarily a good tactic in hostage negotiations. He wished he knew what was going on behind the scenes.

Back in the USA and Europe, the women began questioning their decision to leave India. Responding to al Faran's message, Jane in Spokane issued a measured statement that concealed her mounting anxiety: 'I will return to India when events indicate my presence can contribute in any way to Don's safety or to his release.' She would not be indulging in any mudslinging: 'The governments of India, Germany, Great Britain, Norway and the United States have worked tirelessly to win the release of the captives. I am most grateful for their efforts.'

Five days later, al Faran surfaced again, this time to claim that the hostages' condition was worsening: 'One of them is struggling for life. If one of them dies, the government will be solely responsible.' Don and Jane had always stuck to their plans, and the current plan Jane had formulated was to stay put in the US. But if Don was on his deathbed, how could she sit by and do nothing? The cruelty was unending, she thought, angry at what al Faran was putting them all through and disgruntled with the Indian authorities for not doing more to end this standoff.

Then, on 16 November, Srinagar's Press Enclave emptied as the journalists headed to Anantnag following a tip-off from a reliable conduit that Don was about to be released. But the BBC's Yusuf Jameel wasn't there to join the procession. Two months back, on 7 September, a woman wearing a *burqa* had come to his office. Every day, many mothers and daughters came to beseech him to investigate the fate of their missing relatives, and she had joined the line of petitioners, eventually leaving a packet on his desk, since he was busy on the phone. Yusuf's friend, the photographer Mushtaq Ali, had ripped it open, detonating a bomb that blew him to pieces, strafing Yusuf with shrapnel and injuring another photographer.

The BBC had flown the distraught Yusuf to London for emergency medical treatment. Haunted by the loss of his friend and by the knowledge that he had been the intended target, he had been told to stay put in London while his contacts in the establishment and at the Press Enclave investigated a conspiracy to kill him that appeared to involve senior members of the Indian Army and their dupes – although the military weakly denied it. Everyone knew that Yusuf's report of eyewitnesses' claims that Indian soldiers had torched the ancient city of Charar-i-Sharief in May had so enraged the military that they accused him of treasonous incitement. Even now, as Harley Street doctors attended to him, anonymous threats continued to be levelled at Yusuf, passed to the BBC bureau in New Delhi and through his colleagues in Kashmir.

The parcel-bomb attack had stunned the Srinagar Press Enclave. If the army could do this, committing an overt act of terrorism against a BBC employee, indifferent to the ramifications, what else was it capable of? Ever since, Kashmir's journalists had been treading extra carefully, especially when it came to the hostages. They too were scep-tical about the authorities' apparent lack of urgency in resolving the ongoing crisis, but knew better than to probe too deeply into what lay behind it.

The tip about Don Hutchings' release was the only uplifting news they had had in many months. Mushtaq Ali's death had taken its toll on everyone. The Press Enclave wanted the story to be true. To Yusuf it seemed entirely plausible that, unable to cope with the freezing weather, having failed to strike a deal with intractable New Delhi, and possibly with the Westerners' health worsening, al Faran was looking for any way out. Four months was a long time to hold hostages. The Muslim Janbaz League had held the previous record for the longest kidnapping in Kashmir, having imprisoned two Swedish engineers in western Kashmir for ninety-seven days in the spring of 1992. Shaking his head and wincing, their field commander, Qadir Dar, recalled: 'It was really one of the most stressful operations we ever mounted. They ate more than we could afford. They wanted to drink things we could never find in a Muslim country. And they played on everyone's mind all the time to such a degree that our *mujahids* felt destroyed. We could also never really communicate with each other, as poor English, theirs and ours, got in the way.' The al Faran team was 134 days in, and facing a long winter ahead, during which nothing could move. Yusuf could almost imagine the conversations he would have been having with Sikander if he had remained in Kashmir.

Despite the journalists' hopes, there was no sign of Don in Anantnag. The next day, 17 November, another message was dropped off at the Press Enclave. Its tone struck everyone who read it. 'The sick hostage's condition is deteriorating and he can die at any time,' al Faran warned, turning the knife. His family should 'rush to Srinagar immediately' so that in the event of his death they could collect the body. Ramm and co. concluded that al Faran was deploying cod psychology, sending a pleading note loaded with pressure points to disguise the fact that its operation was on the ropes. But local journalists had a subtly different reading. This may have been pure theatre, the Kashmir media huddle concluded, but it had a concrete aim. Desperate for a deal after all these months, Sikander could see things dragging on interminably, with India relishing the kidnappers' and Pakistan's mounting discomfort. 'Without the families present,' Yusuf calculated, 'there was no pressure on New Delhi to conclude the negotiations. This was Sikander's stab at getting the women back to Srinagar to force the pace.'

No response came from New Delhi. But in Kashmir, Director General Sabharwal held another press conference. It was a one-line affair, with the police chief warning al Faran that trying to blackmail India and the hostages' partners only served to expose them as savages. To ram this point home, and grab more column inches in the Indian media, External Affairs Minister Pranab Mukherjee commented: 'This is a question of principle. We cannot subject ourselves to a situation that would encourage more kidnappings.' In Church Lane, the Scotland Yard team was worried. 'He's right, but what is he saying to them in private?' Roy Ramm recalled thinking. 'We hoped he was saying something, otherwise he'd just slammed shut every door.'

In Spokane, Jane felt as if she was on the rack. The State Department advised her to stay put, its spokesman Nicholas Burns telling reporters at a White House briefing on the kidnapping, 'We support the Indian government. We share its views that this hostage-taking cannot be condoned, cannot be justified and must be ended.' Nobody had forgotten Don or the other hostages, he said. 'We are hoping and praying for his release.' Jane hoped they were also doing significantly more. In London, the Foreign Office was as inscrutable as ever, telling the *Gazette* in Middlesbrough: 'It is very difficult to distinguish fact from fiction.'

IG Rajinder Tikoo, back in the Crime Branch hot seat, having returned from his compassionate leave of absence following the collapse of talks, was keeping his distance from the case. Nevertheless, he winced when he read Pranab Mukherjee's statement, suspecting there was now no back channel to al Faran, and nothing was being said about the case at all, other than 'public platitudes'.

'What did Mukherjee know?' Tikoo huffed. 'Kashmir was nothing to do with principles, and all about managing threats by making concessions.' Other kidnapping incidents had been ended after India had released prisoners, paid cash or provided some kind of collateral to militants who had then given up their captives. 'So why not this time?' His mind wandered back over the seventy-odd days he had spent holed up in Transport Lane attempting to resolve the crisis, only to come to the realisation that rather than trying to win, those above him were happier allowing Sikander and Pakistan to endlessly lose.

Jane spent Thanksgiving with Don's family. Although she anguished over her decision not to return, she didn't want to give al Faran the satisfaction of 'jerking me back and forth between India and Spokane'. Since the alarming message on 17 November there had been nothing from the kidnappers' camp. She used the holiday to fashion a joint statement with Julie, Cath and Anne that backed the position being maintained by the G4 nations in New Delhi. 'You are punishing us for something that is out of our control,' the women said, addressing al Faran directly. 'Our governments have said that they will make no concessions to those who hold their citizens hostage, and that they will not urge *other* governments to make concessions.'

In the news vacuum, a few reporters headed along National Highway 1A to south Kashmir to see for themselves what was going on. Among them was Suzanne Goldenberg of the *Guardian*, who filed a report from Dudwagan, a bedraggled village twenty miles south-east of Anantnag, just south of Verinag, a natural spring around which the Emperor Jehangir had constructed a holiday retreat in the seventeenth century. Apart from a brief scramble over some rocks, reaching the village wasn't that hard, Goldenberg reported. It didn't take her long to get the locals talking either. 'In this mountain hamlet ... where white patches on children's faces speak of chronic illness and malnutrition,' she wrote, 'the Britons Keith Mangan and Paul Wells spent Day 138 [19 November] as captives of Kashmiri separatist gunmen.' The villagers told her that a few weeks previously, all four hostages had spent a night in the nearby hamlet of Kamar, on the other side of the Sandran River. For the families reading these reports back home, it seemed absurd. 'If the journalists could find out the hostages were in such and such a village, why couldn't the army or police do the same?' asked Bob Wells, who simply could not understand what was holding the Indians back.

Something worried Goldenberg, who had made most of the running on this story. Dudwagan was close to an outpost of the Indo–Tibetan Border Police, an arm of the Indian security forces. The villagers told her that in recent months insurgents operating in their district had been on the run from 'renegades', some kind of secret armed force in the pay of the government. 'What is so extraordinary about the hostages' perambulations around Anantnag is that south Kashmir, once a hotbed of militancy, is now firmly in control of Indian security forces,' Goldenberg reported, casting back to a recent statement in which al Faran had accused the Indian government of 'throwing dust in the eyes of the world'.

* * *

Towards the end of November, the first heavy snow fell in Srinagar, and everything to do with the investigation became harder. Travelling even small distances in the valley took an age, while army *jawans* retreated to their braziers and the police and military top brass headed over the Pir Panjal mountains to their alternative headquarters in Jammu, the state's milder winter capital, and villagers huddled indoors, having stocked up on firewood, kerosene and charcoal.

Just as the Squad thought they might, the kidnappers broke cover. In the last week of November, Sikander's team contacted the Hurriyat Conference in Srinagar, an influential but prickly umbrella organisation representing Kashmiri separatist parties, asking it to get the Indians around a negotiating table. 'How much clearer could they be?' Yusuf Jameel recalled. 'They wanted some kind of deal.' For months, politicians aligned to Hurriyat, some of whom had links to militant outfits in the valley, had faced mounting pressure from the G4 group of nations to help end the hostage standoff. So far Hurriyat had refused, wary of being made to look like co-conspirators and having their movement tarnished by a criminal enterprise, aware of the Hindi proverb '*Chor-chor mausere bhai*' – all thieves are cousins.

But al Faran wasn't giving up. It issued a statement trying to force Hurriyat's hand: 'If the Hurriyat desires to save the lives of the four foreigners, it should come forward to mediate.' Hurriyat leader Syed Ali Geelani, a wily strategist, privately wanted to end the crisis, which he could see was damaging Kashmir's standing internationally. But publicly he wriggled, telling reporters his organisation could not mediate about the hostages' release with a government that held tens of thousands of innocent Kashmiris prisoner too.

Two days later, al Faran ratcheted up the pressure, sending an emissary to Srinagar to meet with Hurriyat leaders and issuing another statement: 'Until today we have faced a lot of difficulties ourselves and kept the four tourists as our esteemed guests. But we cannot keep the foreigners safe for a long time.' They claimed that they were under intense pressure, having recently suffered two fatalities in a firefight with Indian security forces, a story New Delhi vehemently denied. A second time, Hurriyat turned down the kidnappers' request to act as mediators. Al Faran had started this, Hurriyat announced, 'and al Faran could finish it'.

In Church Lane, Roy Ramm believed that all the signs pointed to al Faran being ready for a handover. They wanted out. If the reports from down south were true and the militant network had been secretly throttled by India, that handover was more likely to come sooner than later. A way out could be found, Ramm was certain, as long as India wanted one too.

By mid-November the Squad's undercover agents had wriggled into Alpha's inner circle in Shelipora. Most nights they sat drinking rum with Alpha's field commanders and listening to the renegade strongman lecture his men about their priorities, in conversations that were relayed back to the detectives. 'We are guns for democracy,' Alpha told them without irony one frosty night. 'Our task is to squeeze the remnants of the militancy so that the elections can go off without a hitch. *Nothing* else matters.' Alpha was referring to India's impending national polls, commencing in April 1996, in which the security situation in Kashmir was emerging as a key issue. Indian Prime Minister Narasimha Rao had promised to quell the insurgency when he came to power in 1991, only for violence in the valley to have exploded. Then there was the Jammu and Kashmir state election, slated for the following September. That would end the much-hated Governor's Rule, and would be the first poll Kashmiris had participated in for seven years. It would be a defining moment for the beleaguered state, one that politicians in New Delhi wanted to use to show that they had brought normality to the valley.

But for both elections to run smoothly, the militancy had to be kept tamped down and the voters marshalled in New Delhi's favour. 'When the election opens, our job is to get the vote out,' Alpha explained to his men over plates of steaming rice, mutton gravy and sour walnut pickle. 'Village by village, we are going to march people into the polling stations with our guns in their backs.' He claimed they had been paid by Congress to keep the countryside calm and get the vote out, with cash also coming from Rao's local political partner in

Jammu and Kashmir, the National Conference. Alpha bragged that between them the two parties had stumped up two *crore* rupees (£400,000), and that the mission had the blessing of some political heavyweights, including Rajesh Pilot, Minister for Internal Security, whom Alpha claimed to have met. 'We are going to give you what you want, whatever the cost,' Alpha said he told Pilot, to which the Minister was said to have responded, 'Together, we'll free Kashmir.'

At the top of Alpha's pre-election priorities, he told his commanders, was breaking Hizbul Mujahideen. The Kashmiri insurgent group he had once fought for had in the past four years become Rao's biggest headache, transformed by Pakistan's spy agencies into a major force in the valley. Lavished with Islamabad's matériel, HM had opened its own press agency, a women's brigade, and five divisions of several thousand militants each that savaged the Indian security forces, calling for Kashmir to be united under Pakistan and culling any militants who said differently. Although HM units had taken a drubbing in the towns of south Kashmir like Anantnag as a result of the renegade programme, it was still strong out in the countryside. Alpha now instructed his men to redouble their efforts to winkle HM's cells and arms caches out of every remote village.

The Squad's agents also reported that Alpha intended to participate in the elections personally, forming his own political party that would, of course, be backed by Congress. He could see that a career based on betrayal had a lifespan of moments, whereas becoming the chief of his new People's Patriotic Front might secure him many comfortable years to come.

The Squad was baffled. Nowhere in any of these discussions of 'priorities and duties' was there any mention of al Faran, of cornering Sikander or of finding Don, Keith, Dirk and Paul, which New Delhi was saying were the local priorities. Previously Alpha's men had at least channelled intelligence on the kidnappers to their handlers, bursts of detailed information that the Squad had tapped into. Why was he focusing elsewhere, and why had his men made no attempts at ambushing the kidnappers, even though they were obviously aware of their every step?

Worried and puzzled, the Crime Branch Squad sought advice from their superiors in a report that went something like this: Freeing the Westerners would be a good-news story that would benefit everyone, especially the government, which could use it to show that Kashmir was under control. 'And everything is tilted against Sikander and al Faran, who have demonstrated that they want out. The renegades could finish them off, but instead they are, inexplicably, holding back. Alpha has now been reassigned other duties.' Why was everyone ignoring al Faran? Why was there no talk of winning the hostage crisis?

The questions went unanswered until the end of November, when one of the Squad's agents in Shelipora engineered a candid admission from Alpha's most prized commander, a heavy-set, hard-drinking Kashmiri who is known to this day by his presumptuous call-sign, Bismillah – the Islamic shorthand for the opening phrase most commonly used in every Muslim's spiritual life: 'In the name of God the merciful and compassionate.' According to the Crime Branch file, Bismillah was, despite his name, personally responsible for the deaths of 'a colossal number' of Kashmiri villagers and militants, and had acquired a reputation as 'Alpha's chief strongman'.

Like most renegades, Bismillah had joined the insurgency in 1989. He had fought with HM before joining Alpha's new Muslim Warriors, jumping with Alpha again when the Indian security forces had brilliantly engineered their mass surrender in 1994. 'These days only greed and power move him,' the Squad wrote. Most nights, Bismillah sat in his silo-like bungalow in Shelipora, completely enclosed by high corrugated sheeting, its doors protected by sandbags and its roof converted into a machine-gunner's nest, holding court, slugging back army-ration Whyte & Mackay whisky from a bottle gripped between stubby, nail-bitten fingers. 'Often he is drunk by 7 p.m.,' the Squad's agent reported. 'Then he starts playing cards, cheating his colleagues out of their money, or simply robbing them.'

At the end of one long night of gambling and drinking, the fate of the Western hostages had finally come up in conversation, and a stony-faced Bismillah had asked the Squad's agent whether he was

411

curious to know why the renegades had never caught Sikander. The agent had shrugged, pretending to be uninterested, and Bismillah, keen to share his secret, had told him, 'It's because Alpha has signed a secret ceasefire with Sikander, an agreement that predates the kidnapping.'

The police agent was stunned, and struggled to retain his composure in the half-light of the smoky, candlelit room. If Bismillah's extraordinary claim was true, it meant that the men who should have been hunting al Faran were actually in league with it, and were also in the pay of New Delhi, which raised worrying questions about the Indian government's role in all of this.

'We became brothers of sorts,' Bismillah, who still lives in Anantnag district, recalled. 'We turned a blind eye to their affairs. We stopped hunting them. And Sikander kept away from us.'

This revelation shocked Sadiq's detectives. A deal between the renegades and Sikander was the last thing they had expected. They needed to confirm the existence of this pact before breathing a word about it. Being Kashmiris, raised on conspiracies, they believed it was quite likely true, and they wanted to know who was behind it: 'We had all played the Game,' said one of them who analysed the statement, 'and we knew it had no rules. But this pact was politically explosive.'

If the agreement between Alpha and Sikander was genuine, then Alpha's handlers in the security forces, the police STF and even the intelligence agencies were all potentially implicated in Sikander's activities too. Were they a party to the kidnapping? The more the Squad learned about this case, the more dangerous it looked. The police wanted the hostages free, and their own careers saved. They did not want to shine a bright torch into the rotten cavities that underpinned the Kashmiri state.

There was another possibility. Men like Bismillah and Alpha had become manipulative thugs who took advantage of their government backers, unleashing a reign of terror over Kashmiri villages in the knowledge that they could do exactly as they pleased, without fear of reprisal or arrest. In engineering this truce with Sikander's Movement, there was a possibility that they were freelancing, dusting off their old militant contacts to make a profit or create some kind of advantage. The renegade–al Faran ceasefire might have nothing to do with the authorities at all.

Finding out would involve stealth and discretion.

The Squad went back to their agents within the renegade network and its informers close to the Movement, fishing for anything that could help clarify the nature of the pact. What came back were worrying claims from multiple sources that the police STF, backed by a faction within Indian intelligence and with the knowledge of counter-insurgency specialists of the Rashtriya Rifles, had known about the deal from the very beginning: in fact it had been brokered at their suggestion, having first been mooted in the late summer of 1994.

The idea had originated with the security forces, it was said, after the state-inspired killing of the cleric Qazi Nisar in Anantnag in June 1994, blame for which had been falsely foisted on Sikander's Movement by HM, leading to a war between the two militant outfits. In Anantnag, where HM's role in the cleric's assassination eventually came out into the open, residents had turned against the group, ending its domination in the town, much as the Indian intelligence agencies had hoped.

Bismillah recalled the fallout: 'But HM remained a brutal force in the countryside, so our commanders and their security-force handlers insisted that throttling HM should remain our prime focus.' The Indian security forces had an idea. 'Now that HM was weaker, they suggested we form an alliance with HM's main enemy, the Movement, so that we could finish them off rather than fighting each other. "Don't worry about Sikander," the STF and intel guys told us. "Use him to crush HM. We'll mop him up and the Movement later."'

The logic of a truce between all the sides that stood to benefit if HM was neutered was familiar to anyone who played the Game: My enemy's enemy is my friend. HM's killing of Qazi Nisar had incensed Sikander, who was intent on taking revenge. The government wanted HM culled so it could begin to prepare for elections in Kashmir. Alpha wanted money, and given enough he would do anything, including wooing the Movement to help annihilate HM. But how could Sikander, a loyal, principled *mujahid*, be befriended when Alpha stood accused of having betrayed Kashmir and the militancy? Renegades were traitors, while Sikander remained true to the cause.

Many years later, still drinking, gambling and killing, protected around the clock by a dozen hard-bitten Kashmiri gunmen, Bismillah recalled how Alpha's connection to Sikander had been rekindled to bring him into the renegade fold. 'They shared a radical background. Alpha and Sikander started off together in the J&K Students Liberation Front, before joining the Muslim Brotherhood at the same time and crossing the Line of Control for training in Pakistan and Afghanistan. After that they returned to Indian Kashmir, with Sikander recruited by the Movement while Alpha flip-flopped to the government side. They were adversaries, but still Kashmiri brothers who even talked to each other on the VHF set.'

In September 1994, Alpha got a message to Sikander outlining a secret offer: if he took part in a new front against HM, the renegades would stop hunting him and the Movement. The security forces would back off too. The timing was crucial, Bismillah said. 'Sikander was in a tight spot, chased by the Indian security forces, and bush-whacked by HM, with the top tier of his organisation jailed: his *emir* Masood Azhar, his military commander the Afghani, and his pre-eminent field commander Langrial.' Sikander could see the advan-tages to gaining protection by coming under Alpha's umbrella. 'We just had to push him into it by sweetening the pact,' remembered Bismillah. 'That winter, Alpha was told by his STF, army and intelli-gence handlers to pass weapons and explosives to the Movement, with which Sikander could better pound HM. The intel guys said it would work in their favour in the end.' They traded fighters, too. 'We sent him a few of ours as a vote of confidence. He sent us a handful of his, so that we were bound to each other.' It was a Trojan horse, with infor-mation passed from Alpha's men within the Movement to Indian intelligence, who were now able to see right inside Sikander's outfit.

The Squad realised that the timing made the Sikander–Alpha ceasefire deal even more controversial. It had been negotiated shortly after Kim Housego and David Mackie's release in the summer of 1994, and was probably in place during the bungled kidnap operation mounted by British student Omar Sheikh in New Delhi that October. There was no doubt it had been up and running well before this current hostage crisis, and all the way through Rajinder Tikoo's failed negotiations.

While there was no suggestion that Alpha was directly implicated in the al Faran kidnapping, it was likely that his pact with Sikander had provided the Indian security forces with a vital portal into the al Faran camp from the very first day that Don, Keith, Paul and John Childs were seized in the Meadow. Was this why they had been so quick to locate al Faran in the remote Warwan, and pin it down there for eleven weeks, before following it all over Anantnag district with pinpoint sightings in every village? But why hadn't they used the pact to rescue the hostages? Kashmir was a swamp, the Squad concluded. And as they contemplated these riddles, wondering if they should walk away before getting sucked in any further, everything fell to pieces.

On the first frostbitten day of December, with the pine forests above Anantnag heavy with snow, the thin wisps of smoke emerging from the canopy the only evidence that anything out there was alive, the Squad received another message from inside fortress Shelipora: al Faran had given up the hostages.

They were gone. 'The rope has been passed on,' were the words the source used.

Astounded, the Squad relayed a report up the line that went something like this: 'Al Faran are out of it. The kidnappers have *traded* the hostages with an unidentified third party. Don, Paul, Keith and Dirk are no longer travelling with the Turk. Sikander's whereabouts and that of the al Faran party are unknown. Hostages last seen heading for Lovloo.' This was the village where the Squad had found the Tiger and their chase for al Faran had intensified.

After tracking the hostages for six months, getting to grips with Sikander and al Faran, working out how the renegades fitted into the complicated picture, unearthing the secret pact between Alpha and Sikander, the Squad had been cast back to square one. There was not a scintilla of information about who now held the hostages, where they were, or even that they were still alive. Mushtaq Sadiq and his ten-man team despaired while they pondered why the hostages had not simply been freed, with everyone coming out as a winner.

When the news reached Kashmir police headquarters in Batamaloo, Srinagar, the Squad were showered with questions that they could not answer. But they stood their ground. The source was unimpeachable, they said, and also pointed to recent statements made by al Faran itself. After unsuccessfully seeking the help of the separatists of the Hurriyat Conference in mediating a peaceful resolution, the kidnappers had hinted at what would happen: 'Until today we have faced a lot of difficulties ourselves and kept the four tourists as our esteemed guests.' 'Until today', they had said, suggesting that meant 'but not for much longer'.

As the Squad contemplated a whole new, exhausting round of negotiations with a new and as yet unidentified kidnap group, an act of savage bloodletting slowed them down. Agent MMS, the brave young constable Mushtaq Sadiq had sent to infiltrate al Faran in the Warwan, was hauled out of a sewer in downtown Anantnag, killed and gutted, with a note pinned to his bloodied shirt denouncing him as a traitor.

Then the Indian Army struck too.

Late on Monday, 4 December, Kashmiri journalists were called to a hastily arranged press conference at the army's headquarters in BB Cantt, Srinagar. Whenever Badami Bagh called, the Press Enclave ran. Shri Hari Haran, the army spokesman who took the rostrum, appeared to be in a good mood. The Rashtriya Rifles had just concluded a major operation, he said, and after an intense firefight involving several thousand men, a cell of battle-hardened militants had been shot to pieces in the paddy just beyond the village of Dabran, five miles south of Anantnag. A map was passed around, on which Dabran was circled. The gun battle had blazed for seven hours, during which one civilian had unfortunately died, but three foreign militants had also been killed, with two captured alive. A picture was handed around showing several blood-spattered cadavers lined up on the ground, dressed in army-style coats over *kurta* pyjamas. The army had also recovered a large cache of heavy weaponry, Haran continued, showing photographs of six battered AK-47s, several machine guns, two high-powered VHF radio sets, a sack of grenades and coils of ammunition belts.

A current ran through the room as the journalists whispered among themselves. Everyone knew that Dabran was Sikander's native village, and that for the past twelve months its residents had been forced to undergo a humiliating cordon-and-search operation every Wednesday evening as punishment for its most notorious son. Was the Movement's southern commander Sikander among the dead, someone asked. No, said Haran emphatically. The three men killed were foreign fighters. The two taken alive were Kashmiri militants, but they came from Doda, in the state's south, and were currently being interrogated. The journalists did not need to see a picture this time, as they knew what Haran meant: beatings, electrocution, cigarette burns, praying for death, with families left to wander between army camps searching for their missing loved ones. The press pack left to file identical brief reports. These sorts of encounters, even with this number of fighters involved, were run of the mill, and rarely made headlines.

Five days later, on 9 December, the army called the journalists back to BB Cantt for a significant update. One of the three militants killed in the Dabran gun battle had been positively identified as Abdul Hamid al-Turki. The journalists sat up. Al Faran's famed commander, the Turk, a man who had had a reputation as one of the most austere and unpredictable *mujahids*, the kidnapper who had personally beheaded Hans Christian Ostrø, was dead. This was a *real* story. Army spokesman Haran beamed as the assembled journalists worked themselves up into a lather of questions. If the Turk, who had been in day-to-day charge of the hostages from day one, was dead, then al Faran was surely scuppered. What about the hostages? What could the army say about their location? Haran shrugged. The hostages were still missing. But he could confirm that two senior al Faran fighters, Pakistani nationals Abu Khalifa and Nabil Ghazni, who newspaper men identified as members of the original al Faran team, had died alongside the Turk in the paddy. Four other unidentified men had escaped. Large amounts of cash, bogus passports and several 'partially damaged' Japanese SLR cameras had been recovered from the bodies, along with a standard field communications kit: two Morse keypads, a Chinese-made antenna, Japanese-made headphones and a VHF radio set.

What about the hostages, someone asked again. They had not been found, Haran replied. However, one of the captured militants had cracked: either the hostages had been abandoned 'somewhere in the high ranges', or they had been 'handed over to some local militant group'. Either way al Faran had got rid of them before they were pinned down in Dabran. Haran had one more headline. The captured militants had admitted to being part of the group that burned down Charar-i-Sharief in May, a confession that finally placed the army in the clear over one of the most controversial incidents of the entire insurgency.

Handed over to some local militant group. The journalists could not get back to the Press Enclave fast enough. 'Indians Kill Leader of Kidnap Group' ran the first wire story from AFP. As the day wore on, the headlines got worse: 'Western Hostages Dumped by Captors'. And then: 'Worry Rises for Hostages Seized in India'. Woken by a phone call from India in the middle of the night, Jane in Spokane got straight on to her liaison officer at the State Department. Reading between the lines, it sounded to her like a rescue attempt gone wrong. In Middlesbrough, Julie's heart was clattering as she called the Foreign Office. If several of the kidnap party were dead, and the hostages had not been with them, where were their loved ones now, and who was holding them? She could barely bring herself to contemplate Keith, sick and weak after six months in captivity, locked forgotten, inside a *gujjar* hut, starving as the snow drifted against the door.

The Indian Home Ministry was deluged with urgent demands from London, Washington and Berlin. The Indian Defence Ministry too. Why had no one been informed a rescue attempt was in the offing? But when General Saklani addressed the press, he made a spectacular backtrack. First, he wanted to make it clear that the Turk and the other militants had been killed in the course of a 'routine' cordon-and-search operation, and not during some secret manoeuvre to free the hostages. Second, al Faran had not been destroyed as a result of the Dabran operation: in fact, since the encounter its numbers had swelled. 'Over a hundred al Faran militants are still guarding four Westerners in the forests of Kokernag in south Kashmir,' an uncomfortable-looking Saklani said, to the consternation of everyone listening. Around the corner in Church Lane, for once Ramm and co. did not put a pin in their map. How could al Faran be on the ropes, and then suddenly be rejuvenated after its field commander and his deputies were killed? Only a short while back al Faran was beseeching the Hurriyat Conference to get India to the negotiating table, having also tried to get the women back to India in the hope of forcing New Delhi's hand. And now it was claimed to be resurgent once more. Saklani's story was nonsensical.

In response to the mutterings of disbelief in the media and diplomatic circles, the military establishment came out for a second go. A senior Defence Ministry spokesman in New Delhi said he wanted to downplay the intelligence gleaned from the interrogation of the two captured al Faran fighters. 'They are hard-core militants, and can change their statement any time,' he said, relegating what had previously been presented by the army as a certainty into no more than a possibility. By day's end, a government spokesman in Srinagar was claiming that the hostages had just been spotted near the Mughal gardens of Noor Jehan, at Achhabal, six miles south-east of Anantnag. 'All of the four were visibly healthy,' he said.

Al Faran broke its silence. A fighter known to journalists contacted the Srinagar Press Enclave. Praising the Turk as a *shaheed*, he confirmed that his field commander and two other *mujahids* had been killed at Dabran, and that two others had been captured alive. He added that the statements extracted under torture were accurate. It seemed that the army had been telling the truth first time around.

Then al Faran confirmed what army spokesman Hari Haran had initially told reporters: it was no longer holding the hostages, three of whom had been 'arrested' by the Indian Army, while the fourth was 'missing'.

If the spokesman was to be believed, this was a hugely significant moment. To a casual observer, the remark that three of the hostages were now in the Indian Army's hands after six long months with al Faran would have seemed to be fantastic news. But why had the army not confirmed this? Those who knew Kashmir were worried. As far as militants were concerned, the word 'army' could also include its proxies, the renegades. Did the statement hint at some kind of murky deal behind the scenes, involving the ungovernable renegades? And where were the hostages now?

Three Arrested. One Missing. No sign anywhere of Don, Keith, Paul or Dirk. The Press Enclave speculated feverishly about whether al Faran was lying, putting up a smokescreen or embellishing the truth, as it had done on so many previous occasions. Or was the army hiding the truth, the establishment issuing statements and revisions, corrections and addenda that had a whiff of panic about them? Journalists who had covered many surreal events since the militancy first sprung up knew not to rule anything out, including a militant propaganda exercise or a government plot. They knew all too well that Yusuf Jameel had only narrowly survived a sophisticated parcel bomb that an officer in the Indian Army stood accused of commissioning, and that had killed his best friend. To local ears practised in interpreting the conflict in Kashmir, the rapid succession of conflicting official statements suggested there was a dangerous game on somewhere in the valley.

Watching the army's clumsy reversals, the Crime Branch Squad had at least felt vindicated that they had got to the heart of the action. Their source in Shelipora had revealed that al Faran had dumped the captives several days before the BB Cantt press conference. Al Faran had hinted at it in their statement after Hurriyat rejected them, the two captured militants had volunteered the information to the army, after which al Faran confirmed it to be true. Now al Faran had put forward an altogether more worrying scenario, one that the Squad had already been contemplating for several days. But the Squad was still left with two key questions, amid the scores of smaller ones. Where were the hostages now? And what had happened to the deal between Alpha's renegades and Sikander's Movement that had assured al Faran protection from attacks by Indian security forces?

While the families fretted, not knowing what to believe, al Faran remained silent. But one week after the firefight at Dabran, the Squad made a breakthrough. Their agent in Shelipora called for a face-to-face meeting. What he had just learned could not be trusted to any messenger. It took days to set up, while the Squad worked out how their man could give his renegade associates the slip and get out of the fortress to talk to them. When he finally emerged it was to make a bold new claim: the hostages were still alive. Alpha, the paid-up government agent and wannabe politician of Shelipora, had personally taken control of them, and was concealing them at an undisclosed location.

Not knowing whether to be alarmed or relieved, the detectives tried to find out if the renegade commander was doing this on his own initiative, hoping to extort money from the government, or was acting on the orders of his handlers in the Special Task Force or Indian intelligence, as a precursor to a theatrical, headline-grabbing release. Was it all over? Had the Indians finally secured the hostages' freedom? Or was this the start of something new and particularly cruel? One theory was that the hostages' freedom was now close. 'Another was that a monster who was much less predictable than al Faran now had the backpackers in his grip,' a veteran Squad detective recalled grimly.

Then, nothing happened.

There was no public statement from the Governor's office revealing the triumph of the security forces over al Faran, with the kidnappers tricked into handing over their prisoners. The Squad went back to its source, but the same story came back: Alpha was holding the hostages somewhere high in the frozen Anantnag hills, beyond his domain at Shelipora. The police squeezed all of their agents and sources, securing only one more detail: Alpha had supposedly 'bought' the hostages from Sikander for four *lakh* (400,000) rupees, the equivalent of £8,000, a fraction of the sum Jehangir and Rajinder Tikoo had been negotiating their way to in September.

The Squad was incredulous: 'We struggled to get the pieces to fit, but were continually told that Alpha was acting on orders.' It had been established beyond doubt that al Faran had been ready to quit by the end of October, worried about being trapped in the valley over winter and preparing for a handover. 'By mid-November, the kidnap party was spent and desperate to go home to Pakistan, giving up the operation,' the Squad veteran said. With al Faran weakening and Sikander willing to consider any way out, the kidnap crisis was about to come to an end. But then Alpha was contacted by his handlers in intelligence and the STF, with orders to 'approach Sikander with a deal' to keep the crisis rolling.

The veteran said: 'Everything pointed to the unthinkable, that some of Alpha's hard-line government controllers told him to propose to Sikander that he should "take a break", telling him al Faran "could regroup". A few of Alpha's most trusted men, led by the Clerk in Vailoo, would meantime take over the hostages, handing over a financial surety as proof that the captives would not be harmed. At the end of December, Sikander could decide if he wanted the hostages back, to recommence his al Faran operation, and if not they would be released.' It appeared that there were some in the Indian establishment who did not want this never-ending bad-news story of Pakistani cruelty and Kashmiri inhumanity to end, even when the perpetrators themselves were finished.

The Squad reported some of its thoughts to its seniors, using these kinds of words: 'Sikander's men handed over Paul, Dirk, Keith and Don to Alpha's renegades in the third or fourth week of November, around the time when the final sightings dried up. Sikander has given up. Al Faran is finished. Embarrassingly, India controls the hostages.'

Now that they had this intelligence, the Squad looked differently at the army operation in Dabran. They recalled what Bismillah, Alpha's drunken number two, had related inside fortress Shelipora: that the security forces had, right at the beginning, assured Alpha that when the time came they would 'mop up' the Movement and its commanders.

That time had evidently come at Dabran. The Squad's agent dug some more, coming up with an outline of events. The firefight had been a straightforward ambush, with the Indian Army intent on eliminating al Faran the minute they had let the hostages go, before they had a chance to get over the Line of Control: 'Alpha had called the meet with the Turk, suggesting Dabran as a rendezvous, getting the information to the Turk's men and making it look as if it was Sikander's idea.' The Turk had set off thinking he was meeting his commander to discuss their passage back to Pakistan. However, the army had been tipped off and was lying in wait, having staked out the *chinar* trees surrounding Dabran's terraced paddy. 'There was no need for the peace pact any more,' the Squad concluded. 'HM were crushed. The elections were pretty much a certainty. And the hostages were with Alpha, the government's man. All of which made al Faran a mess to be tidied away.'

The Squad were convinced by this version of events, and passed it on to their superiors. They now fully expected the renegades to go after Sikander too. With him dead, the renegades would have destroyed virtually all of the living evidence of India's connections to the Movement and al Faran. Apart from Don, Keith, Paul and Dirk.

In the second week of December, temperatures in downtown Srinagar slid to minus 3°C, which meant it would be deathly cold in the high mountains. On the 10th, a Crime Branch source, also well known to the STF and the renegades, emerged with a possible location for the hostages. According to the Crime Branch file, they were being held in a house in one of two remote twin villages, Mati and Gawran, the last settlements before the treacherous zigzag track up to the icy pass at Mardan Top. Consisting of only a few score stone-and-timber houses a five-hour hard drive from Anantnag, they clung to the Himalayan foothills like limpets on a storm-blasted rock.

In summer, the upper village was a destination for *mujahids*, local and foreign, who emerged from the woods to call on families that supported the insurgency. From there, the track carved through the treeline and bled away into steep scree slopes, marking the end of all plant life and the start of the stony higher mountains. Above, white vultures circled, while in the trees black bears coughed and barked. A hairpin path ran through the wild woods, strewn with boulders and criss-crossed with snowmelt streams. It eventually reached Mardan Top, from where the up-and-over into the Warwan could be made by anyone with the inclination and the leg power. In winter, the village was cut off from the outside world for months at a time.

Below, in the lower village, with its small unmade high street and a dozen shop-houses selling coils of rope, nails, hard biscuits, oil and soap, it was a different story. Since 1994, it had been colonised by the security forces, which used it as a gateway to control the flow of militants descending from the high passes. Several bullet-pocked white jeeps of the STF dominated the entrance to the village, and there was a well-guarded checkpoint, an STF garrison and a lodging house manned by Alpha's men, who locals said had arrived in late 1994. The police and the renegades had warm shelters, with generators and braziers, and were well stocked with charcoal, food and booze. A cantilevered barrier, weighted at one end with smooth stones fished from the riverbed, blocked the road. No one passed without going through it, and men with rifles and hunting dogs patrolled the fields and woods on either side, day and night.

Although they had never been there, the Squad knew exactly what kind of place Mati Gawran was: a distant no man's land, one of Kashmir's secret killing grounds, where stories of atrocities committed by militants or, as often, by the security forces (or their paid proxies), were occasionally reported in the pages of *Greater Kashmir* but never in the *Times of India*. Serial rapes, punishment beatings, interrogations, humiliations and deaths – everyone understood that the crimes would never be investigated. The Squad knew that the scrubby hazelnut groves scattered around Mati Gawran's lower reaches and the woodlands around its upper parts would be pitted with soft earth mounds, the undulating evidence of hundreds, possibly thousands of killings, bodies dumped in unmarked graves, a legion of Kashmiri civilians who had fallen victim to Alpha's men or their partners in the Indian security forces, who had become accustomed to processing their prisoners without even a nod to the law.

It was a grim place for the hostages to end up. Cruelty had turned the local populace mute. The Squad sought guidance from the higher-ups, and were granted permission for their informer to be sent back to Mati Gawran immediately. He drove south-east of Anantnag, through the Sosanwar Hills and into thick snow. After four hours he reached Vailoo, with its arched stone bridge over the Breng River. He passed the Clerk's fiefdom and those black iron gates that concealed a mansion built on blood money, and the Indian paramilitary base where the Tiger hung out at night, anaesthetised with rum. These days, countless families stood around outside, pathetic huddles of women and children petitioning for the return of husbands, fathers, sons and brothers who had vanished. On went the informer, slipping and sliding in his battered Tata Sumo jeep along the pitted road into the mountains, the snow beaten into slush by convoys of military vehicles. Eventually he reached the turning for iced-over Lovloo, where in summer the Tiger sat in his garden, crushing walnuts as he took confessions from men who prostrated themselves in his garden of daisies, their last view in this life being of the dirt at his feet.

Sliding down the other side, the Squad's source drove on, between terraced paddies and poplar trees, weaving from army camp to STF picket, towards Larnoo. In summer, a carpet of green pasture and wildflowers rolled from here into the forests, but now every village was hunkered down for the winter, the inhabitants sheltering behind felt-curtained windows, blankets pinned over wooden front doors. Many of them, no doubt, caressed laminated photographs of missing loved ones: Nazir Ahmed Deka, a vendor of perfumes; Ghulam Nabi Wani, the cloth hawker; Ali Mohammed Padder, small-time government employee; Abdul Rehman Padder, the village carpenter. And scores of others: Hassan, Imtiaz, Rashid, Javid – cobblers, shepherds and poultrymen who now existed only as passport pictures that had been pinned to hoardings, doors and trees. They were so numerous that from a distance these images of the missing looked like stained glass.

The agent drove on, passing Gudraman, the scene of many violent clashes between militants and government-paid gunmen, until the drivable road reached lonely Mati Gawran. Arriving at the cantilevered barrier, he introduced himself at an STF picket in the lower village, where he was greeted with Lipton tea and embraces. Known by the police and Alpha's men, he was waved inside a nearby house, half covered in snow and guarded by a heavily armed group who lounged in the back of an armoured Gypsy. Inside, 'Alpha's men sat around a fire, drinking from a quart bottle of Honeybee brandy, playing cards'. He exchanged greetings, and said he was tracking fugitive militants who were known to have come over the top. And then, as he went to go out of the back door, saying he needed to urinate, he saw them, just as he had been tipped off that he would: a group of weary, white-faced figures, huddled together in a corner under blankets: 'No one had tried that hard to hide them. I stared and stared. There is no doubt in my mind, it was them, though I don't know how many exactly. At least three? Maybe four. With long beards and matted hair, they were shivering in thin, dun-brown *pherans*, hugging *kangri* pots [braziers]. But then someone called me and I had to go back to the card game.'

How did the hostages seem, the Squad asked. 'Exhausted, resigned and empty.' He searched for the right words, or an image. 'They looked like *bears*,' he said after a long silence.

This man was one of their best agents: reliable and practised. Like *bears*. The Squad wrote it into the file. They believed his story. Having dispatched a report up the line, they were told to go to Mati Gawran immediately. They left Srinagar in the third week of December, beneath a smudged, snow-bearing sky. There was much to think about on the tortuous journey of bumps and skids, twists and turns. Taking the right fork after Vailoo and following the riverside road, the once livid-green waterway now sluggish with ice, they turned left at Badihar to reach Iqbal Town, passing through the mourning village of Larnoo, before finally spotting the glimmer of burning braziers beside the cantilevered barrier that marked the outskirts of Mati Gawran.

It seemed peaceful enough. The river chuntered, trees crackled and hawks whistled high above. The Squad found the house beside the STF checkpoint, exactly as the informer described it. The door was bolted from the inside, and fresh snow was pressed up against it. Kicking it in, they rushed inside, lighting it with their torches, only to find the back door wide open, gusts of snow spilling across a concrete floor littered with empty cigarette packets and Honeybee brandy bottles. Having searched the house and found nothing significant, they knocked on the doors of neighbours and shopkeepers. No one seemed capable of recalling who had until recently occupied the building – as if, in this tiny tick of a village, it was possible for a group of strangers to pass unnoticed.

Frustrated, the Squad skittered back across the ice to Anantnag. For the next fortnight they returned to Mati Gawran many times, talking and checking, walking among the trees and fording a brook to search the dense and dangerous wooded slopes beyond, leading to wild Mardan, that no one controlled. But there was nothing to see, and still nobody could be persuaded to talk. A few spies remained behind to maintain a quieter surveillance. Some of the Clerk's men swung by, the Squad heard. Bismillah was spotted a few times too, as were Alpha and the Clerk. But there was no sign of the hostages, although the STF remained a constant presence, its khaki-clad constables, clutching machine guns, arriving for unspecified operations, sometimes bundling terrified, hooded Kashmiris out of their Gypsy jeeps and into their closely guarded netted shelter.

For once, no report was sent up the line. Nothing would be said of this until the Squad had finished its investigations. They had travelled so far that they could not give up without discovering what had become of Don, Paul, Keith and Dirk, who after such a protracted case felt almost like brothers to them. As far as they knew, the four

Westerners were still alive, bargaining for their freedom or resigned to their deaths. The detectives of the Squad could not abandon these vulnerable men at such a critical moment.

Before winter's end, the Squad at last got some real news, shocking intelligence that came close to breaking agents and sources who had not stopped working since they were first engaged in July 1995. Finally their contacts, who had risked their lives to become deeply embedded among the renegades and militants, had found an eyewitness to the hostages' fate whose credentials checked out.

The source was one of the few Kashmiris who could come and go from Mati Gawran as he pleased. He was connected to the renegades, known to the police STF, and had worked as a scout with the army's Rashtriya Rifles. Trusted, feared and (if he was honest) compromised too, having got his hands dirty fighting the militancy for many years, he proved his access by telling the Squad's agents things about Alpha that only his closest aides could know. He went on to divulge that until very recently he had been working as a gunman for Alpha, a dogsbody stationed in and around Mati Gawran, where he had also served the Clerk. He claimed to be one of the last to see the hostages alive, and was prepared to meet the Squad and tell them what he had witnessed.

Once again the Squad converged on isolated Mati Gawran, finding the eyewitness waiting for them, just as he said he would be, in a clearing in the woods, snow settling on his shoulders. The hostages had returned to the village one more time in December 1995, he told them: 'The foreigners were hustled into a house by some STF boys and renegades. Since everyone knew me, they let me in too, and I hung around, drinking and talking late into the night. At last, one of the Clerk's top boys came in, saying they had received new orders and my duty was about to begin. We gathered up the hostages and walked them out into the snow. There was only one end waiting for them, and we all knew it. No one could risk the hostages being released and complaining of collusion, having seen uniforms and STF jeeps, possibly hearing things too that they understood. We led them into the trees, a good, hard walk behind the lower village. I remember that the snow was heavy and deep. And there they were shot. I did not do it, but I saw it with my own eyes. Afterwards, village men were forced at gunpoint to dig a hole down through the frozen earth in which to bury the bodies.'

The Squad asked for a date. '24 December 1995.'

Wanting to check out the location, the Squad escorted the man through the woods. 'He walked briskly, illustrating his story, tracing footsteps in the snow: convincingly, authoritatively. The details were compelling,' one Squad member recollected. 'But one tree looked like another, and although he tried for several hours, he could not pinpoint an exact burial.' Was there money to spend on a search, the detectives asked their superiors. Could they hire sniffer dogs and thermal-imaging devices or ground-penetrating radar, and draft in foreign search teams? 'If we deployed resources, the grave could have been found. We were all certain. But who was going to explain this story of broken allegiances and betrayals to the Western agencies who would be needed to assist with such an operation?' the Squad member asked. No search was sanctioned. The request lay on file.

Haunted by what they had discovered, the Crime Branch team debated among themselves. It did not matter how many times they juggled the facts, looking back over all of these arduous months, they always came back to one unpalatable conclusion, says one of the detectives, a senior serving officer who agreed to talk at his government house outside Srinagar. Over *masala* omelettes and lime soda, he described the dawning realisation that their desire to solve the crime was at odds with the goals of some senior figures in the military and the intelligence services who could have saved the hostages, but chose not to. 'Wrapping up the kidnapping quickly had suited Crime Branch and the desperate families, who we never met,' he said, pushing his food around his plate. 'For us this was a cruel, needless crime that had to be solved. However, for Alpha, who had become unimpeachable, and a few rogue officers in the STF who by now were behaving like gangsters, and for a hard-line clique of agents in Indian intelligence and the army, all of whom had come to operate outside the norms and with absolutely no oversight, there had been no virtue in ending the hostage-taking at all.'

The detective abandoned his lunch and held his head in his hands, before sending his heavily armed security detail out of earshot. 'I have never talked about this case before,' he said, tears welling in his eyes. 'For years we've felt guilt-ridden. I have wanted to say something, and I have waited for this moment to come – even after a decade and a half.'

Pulling himself together as a batman arrived bearing a bowl of freshly picked apples, he waited for the man to leave before continuing: 'This was the harshest version of the Game that anyone could imagine. All the time New Delhi said it was trying to crack al Faran, a group within intelligence and the STF was letting them dangle, happy to let the militants portray themselves as savage criminals.' At every turn, these few agents and operatives had worked to prolong the crisis, hacking away at Rajinder Tikoo's dialogue, unnamed sources leaking the details of the process, using al Faran's every concession to humiliate the kidnappers. There was no way those playing the Game would allow a fading militant like Sikander, demonised by his misjudged kidnap plot, to rehabilitate his own reputation and that of the insurgency by freeing the backpackers: 'Why give Sikander the chance to square this one off, when bad news and the kidnapping could be made to prevail, the hostages vanishing into thin air – blackening the name of the Kashmiri struggle and further blackening the reputation of Pakistan, the country that had backed it?' When Sikander had tired, Alpha had been ordered to take over, to make the kidnapping cruelly roll on, making it a crime that would be remembered by generations to come. The officer wiped tears from his eyes. 'We really have lost our humanity,' he said. 'This is the price of so many years at war.'

Furious and frightened, the Squad kept these dangerous, treasonable thoughts to themselves. An approximate date of death and a rough location for the bodies were entered into the al Faran file. A memo was passed up the line. But there would never be a public outing for the details of this most sensitive of cases.

* * *

Others close to the hostage inquiry would never forget it either. Right from the start, Rajinder Tikoo had smelled something foul about the authorities' al Faran strategy. For a long time afterwards he refused to talk about anything connected to the 1995 kidnapping, or to revisit his days spent waiting for Jehangir to call. But in one unguarded moment in the summer of 2010, a few months after he had retired, he reflected on the slow throttling of his negotiations with the kidnappers' intermediary: 'Believe me, when these leaks came in the summer of 1995 we all felt, this is unnecessary. It should not have been done. It was disastrous. They were a full-stop. They made me irrelevant. You have wasted your time doing things, and with a very sad heart you think it is all in vain. In the end, we had it in the bag, for a small cash sum, but even this was sabotaged.' After a peg or two of Bagpiper whisky, Tikoo toyed with the possible motives behind the sabotage of his negotiations: 'The people who did this wanted to prove to the world that these fellows are mercenaries, no respect for anything, no cause, and are basically here to commit terror, and have not even spared the foreign visitors.' After another peg, he touched on the authorship of the leaks that frustrated his shot at ending the crisis: 'Somebody in intelligence did this, and he should be whipped and shot. They got their mileage. But it was so very callous.'

The force's top brass was required to seek judicial permission before closing the al Faran file. A Case Report was finally submitted to a court in Aishmuqam in May 2002, stating that the investigation was 'unresolved' and that the abducted men had not been traced. That report is still 'pending disposal' at the court, with no hearing to test the police claims. In Kashmir, where many emergency laws have been promulgated to sidestep the judiciary entirely, some shielding the security forces from prosecution, others enabling suspects to be detained without trial, while all of the practitioners of the Game existed in the shadows, the law had become anaemic. And the rigorous, incendiary al Faran file was quietly closed and placed on the shelf in the Jehangir Chowk Crime Branch headquarters.

Tied up tight, it became a real Kashmiri story, the kind that emerges like a glistening soap bubble, only to vanish.

NINETEEN

Hunting Bears

Unaware of the Crime Branch Squad's deliberations in the snowfields of Mati Gawran, the families of Don, Keith, Paul and Dirk spent the run-up to Christmas 1995 doing what they could to remain cheerful, marking the occasion by buying gifts and recording greetings for their missing loved ones, sending them to Kashmir, addressed 'c/o al Faran'. At best, a sympathiser might pass them on, Julie and Mavis Mangan thought as they posted Keith's package in Middlesbrough. At worst, the Kashmiris would be forced to think about a group of innocent men who could not be found, thought Jane Schelly, wrapping Don's presents in Spokane: a harmonica, a recorder, how-to-play manuals for both, a sweater, socks, a scarf and mittens, a toothbrush and sunscreen. 'Dearest Don,' she wrote in the accompanying card, 'Be positive. Keep your hopes up. And dream of the day when we will be together again.' She wrote in her journal: 'Cautiously hoping.' Could Don be home for Christmas? 'I really don't think so, but I can't help but to allow some small hope.'

A few days before Christmas, Tim Devlin, Mavis and Charlie Mangan's local MP, announced that the Indian authorities had given him assurances that the presents and cassette recordings had got through to the hostages. This delighted the families. 'We were all on cloud nine,' said Mavis, who felt as if the whole of Middlesbrough was celebrating with her. She told everyone the Indians were getting things done at last. Jane spent Christmas morning sitting with her parents on their sofa in Orefield, talking about her hopes for Don's imminent release: 'Mom took me into her arms and was hugging me, and we were all hoping for the best.'

But on Boxing Day morning, Sheikh Mushtaq, a Reuters stringer based in Kashmir, struggled through the snow to Pahalgam, where he discovered that the families' packages, together with hundreds of letters and cards from well-wishers, had simply been stuffed unopened into a cupboard in the local post office. 'Up on the snow-clad peaks of Himalaya, Santa Claus will come to help you,' read one signed by 'the children of Darlington'. When Mavis heard the news, she collapsed: 'Yet again, we were simply crushed to the floor.'

IG Crime Rajinder Tikoo, who was by now back behind his desk, was fond of saying that Kashmiris told you only what they thought you wanted to hear. Wasn't that how Don and Jane, Julie and Keith, Paul and Cath, Dirk and Anne, Hans Christian and John Childs had ended up in the hills above Pahalgam in the first place? Confirming that someone's gifts had been received when they had not was the same people-pleasing coin that led tourism officials to pledge that Kashmir was safe when it was a beartrap.

Then good news began to trickle through again. In February 1996 a photograph emerged that India trumpeted as proof that al Faran was still functioning, and the hostages were still alive. Four unkempt, bearded men had been captured on camera, against a backdrop of a pine forest lacquered with snow. The picture was blurred, the women were told, as it had been copied numerous times. But there was no mistaking the faces. Everyone was ecstatic. For more than two months, since the confusing army account of the Dabran firefight of 4 December in which the Turk and two others had been killed, the hostages' families had been in limbo. Then there had been al Faran's cryptic statement of 11 December, in which they had claimed the army – a word that to a militant also meant renegade – had 'arrested' three hostages while the fourth was missing, only for New Delhi to dismiss this as a wild lie.

Finally, out of the frozen hush of a snow-filled landscape came this photo, cutting through all the terrible scenarios that had played in the families' minds, a straightforward picture that represented a specific moment in time. The Indians dated it at some time in January 1996, several weeks after the Dabran firefight. The newspapers in the subcontinent were filled, for once, with news other than the Prime Minister's poor prospects in the impending election, for which voting would start in April. The Kashmir hostages were still alive.

But there was something strange about the photograph. The authorities would at first only describe it, refusing to hand over copies. The image had been procured very recently, and under difficult circumstances, it was said. To publish it, the Indians claimed, would endanger the source. After mounting protests, it was briefly shown to the Scotland Yard and FBI agents who remained in Church Lane, before also being shown to the families. 'We were warned not to breathe a word,' Bob Wells said, recalling the secrecy that surrounded the picture.

The hostages looked remarkably well – almost too healthy, the women thought. Everyone who saw it said the photograph was a long way from the last images they had received, in August 1995, in which the men's air of bleakness had been painfully apparent.

Keith still wore the jogging trousers he had been wearing the day he was seized in the Meadow, only now they were faded and grimy. He had someone else's black padded coat on his shoulders, and what looked like an Afghan *pakul* cap. He was clutching an assault rifle, in a bizarre pose that his family thought he must have been put up to. They read much into the fact that his face was turned away from the camera, as if he was an involuntary participant in whatever this was.

All four of the captives looked relaxed, a clubbable huddle that suggested they were 'in it together'. There were no signs of injury or disease, bandaged feet or scars. Some pondered whether, after all these months, they might have bonded with their captors and become indivisible from them. With the passing of time, the clear distinctions between hostages and kidnappers were blurring; the jarring differences between West and East that had stood out in the first photos were much less evident. Many years later, when John Childs saw this photograph for the first time, he physically recoiled. How easily it could have been him in that picture, he thought as he lingered over the image. He recalled that one of the original kidnappers had carried a Kalashnikov identical to the one Keith was holding: 'I remember that folding stock and pistol grip. It was most unusual,' he said, adding that the large 'cap' covering the end of the muzzle in the picture reminded him how the militants had always taken care to seal their gun barrels by stuffing a piece of cloth in their ends to prevent snow and dirt from getting inside.

To Keith's left was Don, visibly more muscular, his beard more grizzled, and still wearing his blue Gore-Tex Moonstone walking trousers, now worn and dirty above the knees. The most striking change was a Palestinian-style *keffiyeh*, or checked scarf, wound loosely around his neck to ward off the cold. Jane, who pored over the photo in Spokane, was relieved to see that despite all the rumours about the hostages having their possessions pillaged by the kidnappers, he was still wearing his wedding ring, the one she had had inscribed 'DFH/JES 8/24/91'.

To Keith's right was Dirk, also wearing a *keffiyeh*, his wrapped around his head in a similar fashion to how the kidnappers wore their turbans. He was wearing a grey-and-red patterned sweater, the Chinese nylon variety available in most Kashmiri winter markets, the V-neck pullover and long-sleeved white T-shirt he had worn back in the summer clearly inadequate for a Kashmiri winter.

Paul was squatting in front, a *keffiyeh* tied around his head too, like a bandana, and wearing his own maroon-and-navy fleece. His once angular cheekbones were filled out with a layer of winter fat, suggesting he was well fed and rested – his mother Dianne commented that she had never seen him looking so plump.

General Saklani described the photograph as 'solid proof' the hostages had survived Dabran, and that al Faran was still holding them. The government had not been idle, he said, and 'direct and indirect contact' with the kidnappers continued. Hostage negotiators Ramm and co., also unaware of the Crime Branch Squad's findings, had grown tired of Saklani's clip-clopping tone, the way his sentences clunked together like a field-gun assembly. They wanted facts. Too much time had been spent attempting to decipher the security forces' ambiguous rhetoric.

One thing immediately struck everyone who saw the photograph: a fifth man, standing next to Dirk, had been cropped off the print. On Bob Wells's copy, a ruled biro line crudely revealed where the scissors had run, leaving behind the shoulder and upper arm of a short, stocky figure, wearing brown or maroon clothing.

The kidnappers had sometimes concealed their identities by scratching out their faces in photos dropped off at the Press Enclave, but this man had been cut off altogether. Ramm and co., who still knew almost nothing about the Squad's inquiries, wondered if he was an Indian intelligence asset who had worked himself into the group and persuaded them to take this shot. 'Allegedly, the photo had been altered to protect the identity of the photographer,' advised the British High Commission in New Delhi, regurgitating what it had been told by the Indian Ministry of External Affairs. Julie Mangan suggested that the man had been edited out because she might recognise him. But it was hard to draw any solid conclusions about why the image had been cropped. Jane Schelly wanted to believe that the picture was recent, but her State Department liaison warned her it could have been taken any time after September 1995, when the first snows fell in the Anantnag hills, which was where it seemed the image had been shot. In their headquarters at Quantico, Virginia, the FBI were studying the background, flora, light and shadows before offering any opinion. On 8 February Julie and Cath appealed via the Foreign Office for 'direct proof' their loved ones were still alive. No one was prepared to take the assurances of the Indian authorities at face value any longer.

Suddenly, a whole string of new sightings emerged, at such a dizzying pace that it seemed as if someone was answering them. The accounts of these 'credible eyewitnesses' suggested that all four hostages were wintering in what India described as Movement-friendly villages south-east of Anantnag. The sightings had been passed on with General Saklani's personal annotations as either 'accurate' or 'unconfirmed', giving the impression that there was some kind of qualitative process going on behind the scenes. Some material came via the army, relayed from the office of Brigadier P.S. Bindhra, the head of 15th Corps, the most senior operational commander in the valley. Saklani was not able to say much about the rest, only whether it was a 'direct' or 'indirect' account, first-hand or hearsay. All the time he warned of the need to protect undercover sources.

Seeing the weight of military brass attached to these statements, the seniority of the officials who backed them, and unaware of the contents of the police file, Roy Ramm and co. began adding coloured pins to the composite map in Church Lane once more. The hostages had been spotted in Hakura village on 29 December; at Kapran village on 2 January; twice in one day on 9 January, at Doru; then at Gool, in Achhabal, nine days later; and in Singhpora, in Kishtwar district, on 30 January. A pin for Liakbat village at the beginning of March. Another for Desue, where a farmer said he had turned the group away on 3 March. And one more for a sighting of all four captives, near Kokernag on 7 March. Most of these places lay in or close to the Sandran Valley, that ran south of Anantnag, the area Suzanne Goldenberg of the *Guardian* had visited back in November 1995, concluding that it had become a militant-free zone, completely under Indian domination. Back then her story had puzzled the FBI and Scotland Yard, making them question the veracity of India's accounts, but now, starved of intelligence, they were eager for something positive to work on.

In the United States, nothing could dampen Jane's growing feeling of optimism. A difficult Christmas was behind her, and for the first time in a while she felt upbeat about herself. Returning to her teaching job at Arlington Elementary had been a godsend: the children kept her distracted, and also meant she was engaged with life once again. From time to time she would sit down in the gym with her class to explain the latest developments in the hostage story. Her nights remained troubled, but she powered through, sitting in Don's upstairs study, writing letters, calling India, sorting through newspaper cuttings and keeping her journal updated.

She had spent the winter months reading accounts of former hostages, and contacting some survivors, including David Mackie, who was now living and working in Los Angeles. Jane found his account of being held captive by the Movement reassuring. He told her that he and Kim Housego had been well looked after, staying for several days in a 'wooden guesthouse', before walking down a long, lush river valley and then staying at the home of an important Movement benefactor in Anantnag town. There they had been allowed to sleep in proper beds, take showers and watch television. Speaking to David felt like a turning point for Jane, and reassured her that hostage situations didn't always end badly. She read how Hezbollah in Beirut had held John McCarthy, Brian Keenan and Terry Waite for many years before releasing them. In England, Cath and Julie contacted them too, and heard from them how important it had been to hear on the radio that their families had never given up.

Jane could feel herself healing, and Kashmir pulling her back. Although State Department officials phoned her several times a week, often during the half-hour before she headed off to school in the morning, she felt she needed to be closer to the action once more. The snows were receding in the Pir Panjal, and the first anniversary of Don's abduction was approaching, as was her long summer break. But the plan she was starting to mull over could not be carried out without consulting Julie, Cath and Anne.

After surviving the double hell of Christmas and Keith's thirty-fourth birthday on Boxing Day, going through the charade of opening cards and presents from his friends, then finding out that the ones she had sent to him in Kashmir had not been delivered, Julie Mangan had attended the wedding of Keith's youngest brother David, who married his long-term girlfriend at St Barnabas, the same church where she and Keith had been married in 1985. For months the family had put back the date, hoping Keith would make it back in time to be best man. But finally they could hang on no longer, and on 30 December Julie had struggled through the service.

That spring she spent much of her time with Keith's parents, usually going round for a cup of tea and a catch-up at the time the Foreign Office liaison officer made his daily update call. A large framed photograph dominated the living room these days, a shot taken by al Faran of the five hostages smiling and sitting on a rock in the Warwan Valley. It comforted Mavis, who could sometimes make herself believe that Keith and the others were off on a trekking adventure of their own choosing. She chatted away to Julie, conjuring up the imaginary everyday lives of the captives in the Kashmiri heights: 'How are the boys sleeping? What are they eating?' These family conversations made Julie feel closer to Keith. Charlie would chip in, commenting how he needed Keith back to help put new lights up in the porch or with some other household job. Julie understood her mother-in-law's determination: 'I had been his wife for ten years when he was taken, but a child is a special gift, and that must be the hardest part.' Occasionally it felt as if Keith had only popped out for a pint, and Julie's hopes that one day he might just walk out of the snow revived. 'I love Keith and miss him so very much, and so do all our family,' she said at a rare press conference. 'We just keep hoping and praying that this nightmare will be over very soon. The longer it goes on, the harder it gets.' The regular updates from Srinagar helped them all remain hopeful. 'At least nothing has happened to any of them,' she said.

Cath too was levelling out, although no one can ever fully recover from a crisis with no end. After leaving India she had returned to Nottingham, where she and Paul had first got together, and had his photographs from Kashmir exhibited in the lobby of the city's Theatre Royal, along with those of other students on his course. It was a testament to the unfulfilled potential she saw in him. Afterwards, she packed up her Nottingham flat and returned to East Anglia, closer to where she had grown up, before accepting a place on a fine arts course at Colchester University. She went to Blackburn to visit Bob and Dianne Wells, who had just got through Paul's twenty-fifth birthday on 13 February. She confided in them that she wasn't moving on, as Paul was always in her thoughts. 'Whatever you need to do is fine with us,' Bob told her. 'She was still very young, and had her whole life ahead of her. We didn't expect her to just sit at home and wait for Paul.' But none of them had given up, Bob added: 'We decided as a family we would go out to Kashmir as soon as there was something for us to do.' In the meantime he and Dianne would keep their son's memory alive, Bob framing some of Paul's photographs from Kashmir, and Dianne getting involved in a petition to lobby John Major's government for more action to help secure the hostages' release.

In Germany, Dirk Hasert's family were feeling embattled. His mother Christa was approached in January by two men who claimed to have the ability to rescue her son, and who asked her to sign a contract giving them the right to market their story once they had brought him home. Desperate, Christa had agreed. The two men had travelled to Kashmir, where they crashed around, sparking animosity and achieving nothing, then sold their story upon their return. From then on, Christa had refused to speak to anyone outside the immediate family. 'We heard so many lies,' recalled Berndt, Dirk's elder brother, who remains cautious even today. 'Always there was a new hope. A new rumour. But time was running, and my mother could never overcome the tragedy of Dirk's disappearance.'

Meanwhile, in Kashmir, Sikander had surfaced at last. Several Crime Branch agents, including 'Rafiq' (the policeman who had served time in prison to ingratiate himself with the militants) and MAT (the hospital canteen worker who had dallied with the Movement), had got close to finding him, filing quality intelligence about his location. 'Our business,' a Squad member said, 'was getting to Sikander first, so we could find out more about his contacts among Alpha's renegades, to build a more detailed picture about Mati Gawran and to locate the graves.'

But Sikander always seemed to be a few hours ahead of the Squad. He had become especially paranoid after losing the Turk and the others at Dabran, their deaths announcing a clear end to the no-fire agreement he had struck with the treacherous Alpha in 1994. Then, on 17 February 1996, a call came over the police radio that Sikander had been run to ground. However, when the next message came through, it was not to alert detectives anxiously waiting to interrogate him. It was a death notice. The worst had happened. The elusive Sikander had been killed, apparently in an accident of his own making. An explosion had ripped through a house owned by a Movement supporter, close to Anantnag, and Sikander's body had been among those pulled from the wreckage. The army released a statement saying that a bomb Sikander had been working on had detonated, killing them all.

The Crime Branch Squad were sceptical. With his engineering background, and many years' experience as a bomb-maker, having learned his trade at Camp Yawar, where the ISI and Arab technicians had been his teachers, Sikander was unlikely to have done anything so stupid, although an accident could not be totally ruled out. What the Squad focused on was the story behind this death, which only they – and those above them – knew, one that made them view this news differently to their comrades who were punching the air, celebrating the elimination of a most wanted man. For the Squad, they had just lost one of the few witnesses to the Movement/renegade pact and everything it entailed.

Inside fortress Shelipora, Alpha's heavily guarded domain, it was drinks all round. Bismillah, Alpha's go-to man, recalled how everyone celebrated when they heard the news over the radio. They had played their part, and expected to be richly rewarded: 'That morning our people had traced Sikander and several others from the Movement to a house outside Anantnag. A double agent, a man who was alongside Sikander but working for us, gave us the nod.' This man had specific instructions: 'He was told to lead Sikander to a secret arms dump.' The Movement were looking to take revenge for the ambush that had killed the Turk, by setting off a string of bombs aimed at the army and Alpha's network. 'This cache was one of those originally gifted by the renegades to Sikander, the sweetener that had tipped him over to our side in 1994, showing him our intentions were supposedly honourable,' said Bismillah. 'But in fact the explosives and timers had originated with the army, that had pre-set the frequencies for detonation, waiting for the moment to strike.' Once Sikander was inside the house, soldiers had remotely set off the explosives, killing everyone inside, including Alpha's double agent.

In Dabran, the villagers had long expected to hear of the death of their most notorious resident, but everyone buckled all the same. The Bhat family claimed his remains. They could not risk burying him in the village graveyard, since the security forces still called by every week, breaking crockery, smashing pictures, stealing flour, oil and money, warning Sikander's father that they would dig up the corpse if it was interred there, as they would not let his headstone become a place of pilgrimage. Instead they buried him behind their new yellow brick and concrete home overlooking the paddy. Once again Sikander became Javid Ahmed Bhat, the long-legged pace bowler. Not much remained of him, though: no photos, keepsakes, schoolbooks or reports. Almost everything had rotted after being buried for years in the mud of the back garden. The only thing his father managed to save was a copy of a First Information Report lodged against Javid when he was arrested during a student demonstration. Now he carried it in his pocket, fingering its creases to remind him that he had once had a son.

Sikander's death made a few column inches in Indian newspapers, the story spun as evidence that the ailing Rao government was at last winning in Kashmir. But what made headlines everywhere was a press conference given on 10 March by the Kashmir police chief, Director General Mahendra Sabharwal, in Baramulla, a former militant stronghold in north Kashmir where pro-government renegades now ruled. Sabharwal told the Press Trust of India that the hostages were 'alive and well', creating headlines for the next morning's papers, which were once again full of scorn for the Kashmiri militancy that had given birth to al Faran, giving the embattled Rao government in New Delhi a fillip. The resurgence of violence in Kashmir was portrayed as the result of a sustained assault by single-track Pakistan, rather than a matter of political incompetence or venality, charges that had long been levelled at the Rao administration: the previous

August a commission had reported that a nexus of politicians and criminals was 'virtually running a parallel government' in the country.

Several weeks later, in April, the hostages issue rose again. This time, with the start of the elections only a week away, General Saklani contacted 'the hostage wives', as he called them, suggesting they publish a new appeal for information. Now was a good time, he urged, as an appeal would coincide with the start of spring in Kashmir. With the snow melting and the higher passes becoming accessible, the message would reach villagers up in the heights, and the authorities might discover important new clues. To those who knew nothing about the internal workings of the al Faran inquiry, the argument seemed plausible. The women agreed. 'We are confident the sympathies of the Kashmiri people are with us,' they wrote in a letter published in Kashmiri newspapers. Julie, Mavis and Charlie Mangan held a press conference in England. 'We feel in ourselves, it is looking up,' said Julie. Sticking to General Saklani's script, she continued: 'People will be going further into the mountains. People like the shepherds will see more and word will get around faster.' The press was more interested in when she was going back to India. 'If there was anything I could do I would be there straight away,' she said.

Soon the sightings started again, each account triggering a media debate in India that boosted PM Narasimha Rao. In Srinagar, pins were stuck in the map (and stories written up) when the hostages were reportedly spotted at Hillar village south-east of Anantnag on 10 April, and for another sighting two days later. On 20 April the hostages were supposedly seen again at Andu, a village five miles north of Kokernag.

In Bahawalpur, Pakistan, the neighbours of Masood Azhar's father, Master Alvi, recalled how he read these reports 'fuming'. The retired schoolteacher and secret patron to a generation of *jihadis* was 'filled with rage', having been advised by his contacts in Pakistan intelligence that al Faran was finished, most of its members betrayed and killed after the hostages were handed over by Sikander's men back in November and December 1995. 'We set out in January 1996 to get

Masood back,' he told a close family friend, a religious teacher at the Binori Town *madrassa* in Karachi. But the Indians were now manipulating the crisis for their own ends, running what he described as a 'ghost plot', leading him to fear that it would be many more years before his son was freed from jail.

Without consulting any of his contacts in Pakistan's intelligence service, according to a senior Pakistan government source, Master Alvi travelled to Islamabad and called a press conference, in which he played the doting father. 'I know how the families of the hostages must be hurting,' he said, seeming to fight back tears. 'I feel the same for my son. I know their agony.' Claiming that his boy was simply a journalist who had also gone missing in Kashmir, Alvi continued guilefully: 'One hundred times I appeal to the al Faran to release the hostages.'

Jane, who was on her way to Washington with her brother-in-law Don Snyder, could not believe this performance. They had been invited to the White House to watch President Clinton sign a Bill committing the US government to a very modest $1 million extra funding to fight terrorism at home and abroad, an issue that while becoming pressing, was not yet an international priority. Jane was certain Master Alvi was lying. 'The most difficult thing about this situation is just waiting and finding the one thing that will bring [Don] home,' she told a waiting crowd of reporters when she arrived at the White House. Flanked by her brother-in-law and other guests, including relatives of those killed when Pan Am Flight 103 exploded over Lockerbie in December 1988, in the World Trade Center attack of February 1993, and in the Oklahoma City bombing of April 1995, Jane continued: 'I don't set my heart for any particular day. I just feel comfortable enough that some day he's going to be returned to us, and I hope it's safe and soon.'

After the ceremony on the South Lawn, Jane spoke of the impact of meeting other victims of terrorism: 'It used to be that those things were unheard of, but more and more you know somebody else who's a victim. Sooner or later, that becomes your neighbour or your husband. [Terrorism] is affecting all of us.' At the end of the afternoon she was ushered into the Blue Room to meet President Clinton and Vice President Al Gore, who promised they were doing all they could to secure Don's release. That night she reflected in her journal: 'I couldn't help but think how ironic it was that here I am sipping fresh orange juice at the White House while Don is probably eating lentils and rice in some shepherd's hut.'

Barely three weeks later, on 13 May, six days after voting closed in one of India's most fractious general elections in living memory, with corruption, Kashmir, security and public integrity the key issues, Prime Minister Rao was out of office, and other party leaders scrabbled to form a government in an unstable hung parliament. Jane took a call from the State Department. 'A new report just came in that contradicts everything,' she wrote. 'The Indians have captured a high-level militant ... he has said all the hostages were killed last December.' Having spent the first four months of this election year building up the families' hopes that the hostages were still alive, highlighting the story to show how Pakistan destabilised the subcontinent, the Indian authorities now changed course, claiming that they were dead.

Up in Srinagar, Ramm and co. were wondering what this 'report' was. The Squad thought it could not possibly have been theirs, which was far too raw. 'There were so many things that no one could ever admit to,' a Squad member recalled. 'And as to the militant? Al Faran was gone, Sikander too, and most of his inner circle. Who was this man they had found, we wondered.'

As more details emerged, Jane struggled to remain composed: 'I was really shook up when I heard this, but as much as I fear them being dead, I am very, very angry that we are now back in the garbage of last summer,' she wrote in her journal. The State Department warned her that although the story had not been made public, she should prepare herself for a media onslaught. 'I am going to say that I am aware of the rumour, but regard it as unconfirmed,' she decided.

Over the next few hours, as she sat in Don's study waiting for information to be phoned through, she could think of nothing but his death. Could it be possible that he was really gone? She was not willing to give up. How could so many people have seen the hostages this year, if they were already dead? 'It's hard to believe, as the last reported sighting was just two days ago,' she told friends.

Gradually, Jane learned more about the source of this story. He was a thirty-one-year-old Movement commander from Pakistan-administered Kashmir who had been caught three weeks back, and had revealed the hostage story after 'several days of interrogation'. He had not witnessed the killings himself, the authorities conceded, but had heard about them, and gave a specific date: 13 December 1995, two days after the last al Faran communication, which said it no longer held the hostages. That, he said, was a lie, as the kidnappers had continued to hold the four men, having taken them south-east straight after losing their leader, the Turk, at Dabran on 4 December. On 13 December the four had been shot by the surviving members of al Faran in a dense forest close to Magam, a village south of the Clerk's eyrie in Vailoo, on the banks of the Ahlan Nala River. The bodies had been disposed of in a local forest known as Ahlan Gadol, which was roughly twenty miles south-east of Anantnag, or a hard three-hour drive.

Jane began to panic. The account was detailed, and the Indians appeared to be taking it very seriously. In Srinagar, the Squad were incredulous. Elements of the real story had been combined with another, entirely new and fallacious, account, one that erased a far more scandalous run of events that had involved Sikander giving up his hostages to Alpha, acting on orders from his state handlers. 'Now Pakistan and al Faran had been thrust back into the frame once more,' a Squad detective said, 'and we all wondered some more about this Movement commander who was supposedly spilling his guts.'

Two mornings later, on 15 May, as a new Prime Minister from the Hindu nationalist Bharatiya Janata Party was sworn in to try to form a government, one of Jane's friends called as she was getting ready for school. The woman had just heard the story on the radio: Indian officials were publicly conceding that the hostages might not be alive. Almost immediately Jane's phone began ringing, everybody wanting a comment. She went off to work to avoid it. 'So many of the students wanted to know why our army just didn't go in, have a big shoot-out and rescue them all,' she said. 'Got a lot of hugs,' she wrote in her journal. 'Spent a lot of time talking. I'm so very glad that I had the lead time to prepare myself mentally. To deal with the phone calls and the emotions all in the same day would have been too much.'

'Give us Proof,' screamed the headline in the Middlesbrough *Gazette* the next morning, over a picture of Keith sitting on a chair in the Sukhnoi guesthouse taken by al Faran the previous July. Julie gave the same statement as Jane: 'We know about the situation, but we've had nothing confirmed.' The British Foreign Office was also circum-spect, a spokesman saying it was looking into the reports 'as thor-oughly as we can with the Indian authorities'.

The drip-drip of news continued, as if the Indian establishment no longer needed the men alive, and was now determined to kill them off. The captured militant was named as Naseer Mohammed Sodozey, said to be the Movement's banker in Kashmir. He was from Palandiri, a town in Pakistan Kashmir. The Srinagar Press Enclave (recently renamed the Mushtaq Ali Press Colony, in memory of Yusuf Jameel's friend) was briefed that for the past year Naseer had travelled back and forth across the Line of Control, distributing cash from Pakistan's spy agency. He allegedly told his interrogators that during his travels he had learned that the kidnappers had become jittery at the end of September 1995, worried about getting trapped in Kashmir for the whole winter.

After two more months of failing to nail a deal with the Indians, and with the weather worsening, the ambush at Dabran in early December had been the last straw. Under pressure, Sikander had ordered the hostages' executions a couple of days later. Naseer said he had been involved in putting out al Faran's statement of 11 December, saying it no longer held the hostages, but that this had been a red herring. More than 120 pages of interrogation transcript were leaked to key Indian journalists in Jammu and New Delhi, who quoted Naseer telling his captors that he had learned about the killings in January 1996 from Parvez Ahmed Baba, a militant who sat on the Movement's Kashmir *majlis*. Naseer also claimed to have an insight into the execution of Hans Christian Ostrø, saying he had been killed because the Turk had received 'a message from God that came to him in a dream', resulting in the Norwegian being shot dead, before he was beheaded.

The families felt sick and suspicious. The confession was unfeasibly detailed and complete, and it had been leaked to the press two months before Naseer was even charged with any crime. Naseer had also got important details wrong, claiming that Ostrø had been shot, when he had not. 'We didn't know the first thing about this guy,' Bob Wells recalled. 'All we were being told came third-hand. He was a Pakistani militant, so how could we trust him to be telling the truth? But then again, we didn't trust the Indians either.' There was no physical evidence, Bob argued, only a prisoner's lengthy, self-incriminating statement (in a valley where confessions were normally obtained through torture). Jane shared his doubts. 'I imagined [Naseer] was under considerable physical pressure,' she said curtly. The G4 were sceptical too, coming back to the issue of timing, wondering if the hostage story had served its purpose during the election campaign, raising the spectre of a Pakistani hidden hand unsettling the valley, but now had no purpose, as the new government needed stability (and peace in Kashmir, where elections were due).

The G4 tried to find corroboration. The two militants captured alive by the army at Dabran, whose interrogations revealed that al Faran had abandoned the captives, had somehow 'disappeared' in custody. Parvez Ahmed Baba, identified by Naseer as his source, had also vanished, and was being described in intelligence circles as having become an 'Indian asset'. In Islamabad, American and British diplomats brokered meetings with the ISI, demanding access to Maulana Khalil, the founder of the Movement, and Farooq Kashmiri, its military commander. When the two were eventually produced at ISI headquarters they denied responsibility for the hostages' deaths, pointing to previous al Faran statements that the kidnappers had given the Westerners up by the time Naseer claimed they were killed. If they had died on 13 December, said the two *jihadis*, the Indians must have done it. As if to drive home this point, an anonymous phone call came in to the British High Commission in New Delhi, traced to Baramulla in north Kashmir, claiming that Naseer knew nothing about the kidnappings at all.

But India had invested a large amount of moral capital in Naseer's confession, and had to see it through to the end. It needed physical evidence if it was finally to close the case neatly – or at least it needed to be seen to hunt for it. On 3 June, three days after the first prime minister to be anointed had resigned, unable to form a government, and as a second emerged at the head of a new fractious coalition, five hundred Kashmiri policemen with sniffer dogs were unleashed on Magam, a dank cleft between two mountains, hoping either to find the bodies, proving Naseer was right, or more likely, according to one member of the Squad, 'finding nothing but showing the world that India had given this story a run at, before it put it to bed'.

The captured militant had been flown in by army helicopter, and according to Indian officials had helped narrow down the search area to a few square miles of heavily wooded hills. Warning that they could not afford any more kidnappings in what they described as dangerous, rebel-held territory, General Saklani and police chief Sabharwal laid on an impressive escort of fifty heavily armed soldiers to take foreign representatives, their numbers swelled at the last minute by diplomats including German Ambassador Frank Elbe, to the site. Terrified villagers turned out of their ramshackle houses by the security forces watched as dozens of white-and-green Gypsy jeeps, armoured personnel carriers and VIP Ambassador cars clattered by, clogging the hairpins usually plied by goat herders and pony convoys. At one point, so much traffic was on the road it was feared that the ancient arched bridge over the Breng River would collapse, and an engineer was sent from Anantnag to assess the damage.

As the search teams spread out into the forest, the silence punctured by the 'thwack, thwack' of bamboo *lathis* beating a path through the undergrowth, soldiers held back the press pack, who were straining for a glimpse. The spectacle was also watched by a handful of officers from Scotland Yard, the FBI and the German federal police. Thousands of miles away, Jane Schelly tried to distract herself, spending her day immersed in work at school. Charlie Mangan got on with things, feigning indifference, telling the local press, 'We don't know much about what is happening.' Bob and Dianne Wells waited for news with Paul's siblings, Stuart and Sarah. 'We had been unable to find Magam on any map,' said Bob. 'We just sat at home thinking about a village we could not locate, wondering about a man whose evidence we could not trust. Where in any of this horrendous mess was Paul?'

TWENTY

The Circus

The search at Magam was called off after seventy-two fruitless hours. A week later, Paul and Keith's families travelled to London for a three-hour briefing at the Foreign Office, where civil servants dismissed Naseer's confession as unreliable. 'So yet again we were back to square one,' Bob Wells recalled. 'No Paul, no body, no sense that anyone really knew what was going on. The only good to come out of this was that in not finding him, we could tell ourselves he was not yet proven dead.'

In Spokane, Jane came out of the Magam experience determined to assume control: 'I was in a shambles. But you pull into the parking lot and dry your tears.' She finally understood why Kim Housego's father David had ignored his government's plea to stay quiet, choosing instead to set fires under old newspaper contacts, reaching out beyond the Indian establishment and making as much noise as he could on his own. It was time for her to do the same, although she worried it might already be too late: 'If I had intervened sooner, there are so many more things I could have done.' She had always been her own woman, and over the past nine months she had got used to deferring to no one. The thought of returning to Kashmir by herself did not frighten her any longer. She wanted to get into Pakistan too.

Jane decided to grab the investigation and shake it until the truth dropped out. If nothing did, she could live with that. She called a small press conference in Spokane. 'The year has not produced anything. Something has to change,' she said. She also, with bated breath, had a conversation with John Childs, to whom she had not spoken since meeting him at the government guesthouse in Srinagar on 9 July 1995, the day after he escaped from the kidnappers, when she had challenged him about why he had left Don behind.

John recalled: 'We had both realised that keeping quiet was a bad idea, and that we had all been mistaken in going along with the demands to stay silent.' He also remembered how the US State Department had dissuaded him from going back into the mountains in the hours after his rescue, while his memories of the hostage party's location were fresh. 'I tried and tried to get them to fly me up. I could have found the hut, and the route too. But they were adamant. They didn't want to rock the boat: "Leave it to the Indians." I guess none of us were important enough to go the extra couple of yards, to unhinge a nation's diplomatic strategy.'

There were many regrets on both sides. But John agreed to do all he could to help Jane's campaign for the truth. Irrespective of how painful it was for him to rake over the past, he knew he owed it to her, as well as to Don and the others.

Two weeks later, in late June 1996, almost a year to the day since she had flown to India with Don, Jane was back on a plane to New Delhi, alone and armed with a lengthy wish-list of meetings: with the Indian Army, police, politicians and prisoners. She'd learn how to do it: knocking on doors, holding press conferences and whatever else it took. She knew she was capable of it, and she was done with beating herself up.

Within hours of landing, having worked hard to set it up, Jane was in the governor's pristine office inside an Indian prison, sitting opposite Naseer, the Movement militant who had claimed al Faran had killed her husband. Dressed in a clean, knee-length *kurta*, his hair and beard neatly trimmed, he mumbled in English, 'I am sorry, I am sorry.' Jane explained that she wanted hard information. Naseer nodded, but stuck closely to his previous statement. The hostages had been executed in Magam forest on 13 December 1995. He repeated the same inaccurate claim as before about Hans Christian Ostrø being shot. Everything was delivered as if it had been rote-learned from the 120-page so-called interrogation report leaked by the authorities. At the end of their interview she watched as Naseer hobbled out of the room, his shackles clanking.

The moment Jane had arrived in India she had felt closer to Don, but already she could sense him drifting away. She had been unable to prise anything from Naseer, who was clearly preoccupied with saving his own life. He faced a death sentence for an enormous roster of crimes supposedly committed in the valley and in New Delhi. Some of them he was undoubtedly responsible for, but there were many others of which even the prison guards said he was innocent. It would take many years for all the multiple cases to be heard in court: prison officials expected his trials to run well into the new millennium, meaning there was a long time for a deal to be struck between the state and the defence. During this protracted period, Naseer could ill afford to rock the boat.

'I found the prison experience draining, upsetting and emotional,' Jane recalled, thinking that in spite of everything Naseer had seemed sincere, even if his precarious situation on death row had prevented him from coming clean. She took a walk around a park, trying not to get swept up in a wave of pessimism. But the day would get no better. Her next visit was to the normally positive Ambassador Frank Elbe at the German Embassy. She found him in no mood to cheer her up. Up until now everyone in the G4 had maintained an optimistic outlook. But following the Magam débâcle, Ambassador Elbe had had a change of heart. He told Jane that Dirk Hasert's brother Berndt was on his way to India, and that he was going to warn him to 'prepare for the worst'.

Jane left the Embassy feeling as if she had been slammed into a wall: 'I felt so very alone. I walked around with a big knot of tension. It took me back to the summer of 1995, to the reports that Don had been killed, could be killed any day, would be killed, unless … I didn't have anyone to talk to about it. I couldn't talk to a diplomat, and my family and friends didn't have the background. It was the most traumatic event of the summer.'

* * *

Back in Spokane, Jane and Don's friends were preparing to gather at the city's Riverfront Park for a candlelit vigil to mark the first anniversary of the kidnapping. Some had prepared posters, including one that read, 'Climb On, Climb Out, Climb Home'. But here in India, Jane felt as if she was falling apart, even before she reached Srinagar. Distraught, she called Julie Mangan in the UK. From the tone of her voice, Julie knew her friend was in trouble. 'I couldn't bear it,' Julie recalled. She flew out to India that night, cancelling an appearance on the BBC World Service hosted by former Beirut hostage John McCarthy, scheduled to mark the eve of the Kashmir kidnapping anniversary. Cath, Bob Wells and Paul's sister Sarah appeared without her.

Reunited at the US Embassy in New Delhi on 4 July 1996, a year since their lives had been thrown together in the Meadow, Julie rallied Jane. They had both been thinking they needed to claim their lives back, and flying to Srinagar would mark the start of that process. The flight must have had them on tenterhooks, as they looked down into the jaws of the Pir Panjal. But on landing, both of them found themselves feeling relieved. 'I thought I would be very upset,' Julie recalled. 'But actually I felt much closer to Keith.'

Their first stop was Batamaloo, the Kashmiri police headquarters, where Director General Sabharwal was waiting for them, smiling nervously, his hair slicked down. Pens hovering above blank notebook pages, Jane and Julie had decided to comprehensively document everything, and to make it known to everyone they saw that whatever they told them was on the record. There was something they needed cleared up, Jane explained to Sabharwal. Either the authorities had believed the sightings of the hostages moving around Anantnag throughout the spring of 1996 (not to forget the DG's own statement in March that Don, Keith, Paul and Dirk were very much alive), or they accepted Naseer's story, that they been shot and buried in the forests of Magam in December 1995. It was one or the other, Jane said.

The DG paused, then winced and pursed his lips. 'Money may have exchanged hands,' he mumbled. What exactly did he mean, Jane asked. 'Eyewitnesses may have been paid to make statements,' he expanded. Then he bulldozed on, leaving this provocative thought hanging, as if he had never expressed it. But Jane and Julie were already taking its implications in. Every sighting they had meticulously plotted on the trekking maps since January 1996 was potentially unreliable. They left Sabharwal's office enraged by his casual admission. Out in the streets of Srinagar they tried to digest it. Coming back to the city now, armed with all the knowledge they had gained over the past year, Jane could not believe she had once considered it a holiday destination. Yet everywhere she and Julie went they saw young trekkers and backpackers, on their way to the mountains.

General Saklani was next. They expected the Security Advisor of all people to toe the line when it came to backing Naseer's account. But from the moment their meeting started, Saklani distanced himself from the Movement's financier. Naseer 'could not be trusted'. There was plenty of 'room for hope'. All this despite the hundreds of police who had been ferried to the hunt in Magam woods, and the weeks of hoopla surrounding Naseer's confession. Jane and Julie were thrown, as they tried to understand how the General could have flipped so completely from believing in the deaths of the hostages to championing a continuing search. Saklani recited a gamut of new sightings, explaining how the police had come by the information, whether they were thought to be reliable, and plotting the hostages' movements on a map. Jane and Julie concluded that it did not really matter what he thought – he probably did not have a personal view on anything that he was prepared to share. Saklani dutifully represented the opinions of others, and presumably these others had performed a volte-face on Naseer for some reason that was not clear. The women decided to take advantage of this apparent change of heart. They asked Saklani if he could help them to visit some of the key locations, and he agreed. Soon he was driving them to an airstrip, where they boarded an army helicopter. On 1 August they were flown to Kokernag, the scene of several reported sightings over the winter. However, as they landed, they were greeted by a press pack that Saklani had called to record every moment of what they now realised was a whistle-stop tour of Pakistan-backed terror in the valley.

Another election was coming, this time for the Kashmir state legislature, a key vote that would, if successful, see Governor's Rule replaced by an elected Kashmir assembly, and release Saklani from a duty he had never wanted, but that had lasted four long years. Jane could feel the tension rising as people came out of their houses and spotted Indian military uniforms. No one wanted to talk to them. On 5 August Saklani flew them south again, heading this time for Magam, where the Naseer-inspired search had foundered. The helicopter landed in the village cemetery. The local *maulvi* scowled. People bolted. It was raining. Jane and Julie asked if they could walk alone, but here too the press pack thronged forward while the locals hung back. 'The villagers said they knew nothing and had seen nothing,' Julie said, frustrated. Some of them were baffled by the women's presence, as the whole village still lived in fear of Alpha, who dominated the region, and who, as far as everyone knew, was a paid-up government ally.

After their visits had been completed, Jane and Julie felt they had been manipulated, and when they left Kashmir it was with Sabharwal's gaffe about sightings elicited by cash ringing in their ears. They had resolved nothing. Naseer was a stooge, the sightings unreliable. But they had proved to themselves that they could go out into the deep countryside and meet people for themselves. As Jane saw it, this was the only way they would ever discover the truth. Next time they would do it with less fuss, and no escort. They would get people talking. As they said farewell to each other in New Delhi, they agreed to return after the local elections were wrapped up in October.

By October 1996, Jane and Julie's low-profile trip had become something very different from what they had imagined, with Cath Moseley, Mavis and Charlie Mangan, Bob Wells and a British documentary film crew all wanting to come along. Jane had no desire to be filmed, but she was not the only one involved, and she respected the wishes of the others.

Bob Wells in particular wanted everything to be highly visible, having come to the same conclusion as David Housego: 'The Foreign

Office had told us repeatedly that hostages never get released in a blaze of publicity, but we'd had enough of waiting for them to sort this out.' He also wanted to go to Kashmir because he and Dianne had been talking about having some kind of memorial event for Paul, although they could not bring themselves to make it a funeral. 'I would never be able to live with myself if we did that and then Paul came home,' Bob said.

Things had got off on a sombre note when David Gore-Booth, the British High Commissioner, picked Bob up from Indira Gandhi International Airport and told him not to get his hopes up, as Paul was almost certainly dead. Even if the news was discouraging, Bob was pleased to hear someone speak his mind: 'After so many lies, I was grateful that Gore-Booth was able to be straight. It set me up well for all the disappointments that were to follow.' Mavis and Charlie's visit, their first to the region, had been reported by the Middlesbrough *Gazette*, which made much of their working-class roots, describing them as 'just two ordinary everyday Teessiders, she a dinner [lady], originally from Brambles Farm [council estate], and he a steel worker for forty-five years'. Until the previous year they had never even heard of Srinagar, Jammu, Islamabad or Muzaffarabad, but they had overcome their fears and saved up every penny to see things for themselves. Like the other families they were tired of being dictated to from afar, run ragged by people they had never met.

Arriving in Srinagar, the families, film crew and a G4 liaison officer were put up at the Welcome Hotel, overlooking Dal Lake. The previous year it had been crammed with journalists and photographers pursuing the hostage story, but now it was empty. Taking a look around town, Bob hardly noticed the mountains or the shimmering lake, the kestrels that swooped down from the hills to snatch fish from the water. Instead, he was overwhelmed by the militarised and decaying city: 'The building next door to us had been commandeered as a police barracks. We were surrounded by bunkers. It was a bloody war zone, and yet these little rowing boats were going around the houseboats as if everything was normal.' Julie was worried about how Keith's parents would cope. 'We feel quite guilty going to bed in a nice duvet, thinking what are the boys sleeping on,' said Mavis, as the film crew recorded their initial impressions. 'You sit down at a table to eat, and think, what are the boys eating?' That night she lay awake, listening to the sound of gunshots echoing across the lake: 'I'd never even seen a gun before, and now they were going off all around me.'

The families kicked things off in the morning with a press conference, Cath, Julie and Jane announcing a ten-*lakh*-rupee (£20,000) reward, funded by the US State Department, for information leading to the hostages' release. The British government had refused to participate, as it did not condone giving money for information, and Jane had worried that the cash might elicit more false rumours, such as those the Kashmir police had admitted disseminating in the first four months of 1996. Charlie Mangan made a poignant appeal: 'We hope and pray to all the people in this country and Pakistan that they must know, they have sons of their own, they must know how we feel.' He hesitated. The word 'sons' rattled in his throat. Cameras snapped, catching the moment his composure broke. 'I just hope and pray that you get them out quick,' he managed to say, before giving up.

Next, they trooped to police headquarters for an update from DG Sabharwal, who welcomed them in a darkened conference room. For Mavis and Charlie, it was their first experience of Indian officialdom, but Cath, Jane and Julie got their notebooks out. Sabharwal smiled, but looked uncomfortable. 'Indirect reports sometimes emanate from quarters,' he said, 'but unless they are fully verified and corroborated, we are not pursuing them.' He was picking up on what he had told Jane and Julie before, only now he was claiming that the process was vetted to rule out false positives. The women wrote his words down. Sabharwal straightened his collar. The hostages would soon be returned to their loved ones, he said. Someone asked if he could tell them straight, whether the men were alive. 'Certainly, most certainly,' he replied, appearing to have dismissed the Naseer episode and gone back to his position of March. The families said they were hoping to distribute reward posters around the valley, but they wanted to be discreet. The DG said he could help them do it without a fuss.

Their next stop was the offices of the newly-elected Chief Minister Farooq Abdullah, the first civilian administrator in Kashmir since the militancy had taken hold, whose appointment had meant Saklani could head back at last to his modest apartment in the military cantonment of Mhow. After they had taken their seats, Abdullah made an announcement. 'There are certain things I cannot say on record because it's better and it's for their safety,' he said, plumping himself up as the new master with his hands on the reins in Kashmir. 'But in ten days we will give you *proof.*' Of what, someone asked. 'That the hostages are alive,' he replied. 'He's given us quite a significant promise,' Cath said quietly.

Finally they were ready to make an unobtrusive sortie into the countryside. They stepped out of the Welcome Hotel, only to be met by a convoy of Ambassadors led by armoured trucks and Gypsy jeeps with paramilitary police and soldiers with submachine guns hanging out of their gaping doors. Pony carts and civilian vehicles were forced off the road as they sped south, heavily armed specialists from the Rashtriya Rifles riding the roof of the lead truck, their black bandanas flying as the vehicles barged and hooted through Kashmiri lives. Jane quietly fumed, until she was introduced to one of her travelling companions, Group Captain Jasminder Kahlon, the ace helicopter pilot who had plucked John Childs to safety. She listened eagerly as he gave her one of the only first-hand accounts of anything connected to the hostage crisis she had heard in sixteen months.

They approached Vail Nagbal village, the scene of Hans Christian Ostrø's beheading. 'I feel in a way we ought to go,' said Cath, welling up. 'To pay our respects,' said Bob. 'Yes,' said Cath. 'For Anette and his parents.' Charlie was haunted by his imagination: 'It was awful. The body in one place. His head in another.' Bob took photographs, wishing he had any kind of certainty about Paul, even if it was a brutal one.

And then they were off again – whistles, canes, lights, sirens and balaclavas – until they came to the semi-deserted trekking station of Pahalgam, where it had all begun. Taking in the scenery, the densely wooded mountains carved up by two gushing rivers, Mavis understood the scale of the crime scene for the first time. 'It breaks me up, actually, just wondering where he is,' she said, gazing at the Pir Panjal. 'It's just so vast. He could be anywhere, couldn't he? I'd walk every inch of it if I could.' Later, Jane confided in her journal: 'We were required to check in first with the local authorities, who informed me that I would be allowed to walk up the valley only one or two kilometres in either direction. Trekking no longer occurs in this seemingly idyllic valley. I was angry. If only they had been this cautious before, instead of telling us, "No problem. Have a nice holiday."'

Broken Dabran was next, Sikander's village, where al Faran's commander the Turk had been killed out in the paddy. 'This is my husband,' said Julie, standing in the mud and pointing at a laminated photo of Keith, hoping to make the villagers understand their plight. 'He's missing. It's been a long time now.' Women with their own missing – children, husbands and fathers – trudged past, shaking their heads. 'How could they feel sorry for this handful of foreigners escorted by the security forces that they accused of having killed, detained and vanished thousands of Kashmiris without the world caring a jot?' one customer mumbled to a shopkeeper. Eventually, Sikander's mother was rousted from her house. Terrified, tears streaming, she recalled that afternoon: 'I asked them if they knew I had lost a son too. The Western families had no idea.' Bob winced seeing the old woman break down. 'It was terrible,' he recalled, crushed between his own desperation and the villagers' tragedy.

Finally they were taken to Magam, stacked along sharp ridges and around hairpins, surrounded on all sides by hills and forests. Naseer had claimed that here, in a village under Alpha's control, where he placed sentries by day and informers all night, the hostages had been concealed and then killed by the Movement. Earlier that day soldiers had poured into the village, and every man and boy had been forced out of their houses at gunpoint and ordered to squat down in the road and wait for the foreigners to arrive. They had been kept like this in the rain for seven hours, and now they were exhausted, sodden and angry.

Jane and the other women refused to get out of the car. Bob and Charlie were furious, and felt they had to go and talk to these people who they feared had, by this single thoughtless action, been turned against their cause. 'We're so sorry for this,' Bob told them. 'We wanted to come quietly, see you and ask for your help.' Charlie struggled to retain his composure: 'They came here as holiday-makers, tourists in your country. They should have been allowed to go.' He dried up. The villagers stared, filled with bile. A local student pushed his way to the front, shaking with anger. 'What is our sin?' he asked, barely able to hold back tears of frustration. The village had been repeatedly swamped, by militants and now by renegades, he told the Westerners. After that, Naseer and his procession of searchers and soldiers had come too. And now here were the families and their convoy. 'Kashmir is very big,' he stuttered, waving his arms to show the extent of the valley. 'We have never seen them.' A flurry of flashbulbs caught the moment. His heartfelt rage at having been humiliated was described by an army press attaché as 'surly, disrespectful behaviour' of the sort that justified the military's overwhelming presence. With that vignette the family members understood why India had revived the hostage story, embracing their trip wholeheartedly.

There was nowhere else they wanted to go, other than home. Chief Minister Abdullah never came up with the news he promised. Nor did police chief Sabharwal.

The families did not give up when they arrived back in their own countries. They would never let go until they had proof. 'Bones or a body', as Bob put it. 'I don't want to think that they're dead,' said Mavis. Julie was the same: 'I strongly believe Keith is alive. I want to believe, I am going to keep on believing. Otherwise I don't think I could carry on.'

Jane was less certain. After Kashmir, she had made it to Pakistan, and talked to the Movement's military commanders, picking up nothing other than a bad case of giardiasis. Her stomach in spasms, she had returned to the US to spend Christmas alone, opening a few presents, including a gourmet recipe book from her sister and brother-in-law, Nancy and Don Snyder. But even this act of kindness nettled. Who did they think she would cook for now? She read and reread all the messages their friends had written the previous Christmas morning, almost six months after Don had been taken, having gathered at the house to light a candle. 'Back then, I really didn't think that he could ever be killed,' she said. But twelve months on, she was struggling to stay positive. A couple of nights later she summoned up the strength to write down in her journal what she was really thinking: 'In my heart I don't believe he's alive, but I've been wrong so many other times that I have no faith in gut feelings now. We had planned on growing old together.' She finished off by addressing Don directly: 'I love you sweetheart.'

In July 1997, the second anniversary of the kidnapping, Jane returned to Kashmir for one more try. This time she was alone, having secured an offer of a US$2 million (£1.2 million) reward from the US Department of Justice. 'I realise at some point, if Don doesn't come back, I will have to concede that my life goes forward,' she wrote. 'I want to be able to look back and know I did everything. I don't want to say, "I should have done that," because it will be too late.' In her luggage she had brought along thousands of lavender-coloured fold-up matchbooks, printed with details of the reward, in the knowledge that 'almost every Kashmir man smoked'.

Travelling with a Kashmiri politician on his campaign trail, Jane flew over the snowcapped crags to the Warwan Valley. Escorted everywhere she went, she found the villagers fascinated by her story, but wary of eavesdroppers, as the militancy still held the valley in its grip. 'We dropped down after crossing spectacular and rugged terrain in the Indian Army five-seat helicopter,' Jane wrote. 'We saw caravans of ponies, sometimes twelve to twenty-two in a group, heavily loaded with supplies, travelling amongst flocks of sheep being herded by their nomadic *bakarwal* shepherds from the desert areas. We were in the heart of militant country, I was told. Hans Christian Ostrø's beheaded body was found on 13 August 1995, just fifteen miles due east of here.'

At Inshan, the southernmost village in the valley, from where the treacherous track reached up to Mardan Top, the pilot brought the helicopter down on a white 'X' in the middle of a field near the mosque. Hundreds of villagers were waiting. 'Army commanders escorted me to where most of the women and children were assembled. In just moments, the crowd overcame their hesitation and pressed close to me. As I talked about the reward for information and began to hand out posters and matchbooks, reluctance disappeared and hands shot out, snatching the papers right out of my grip. My three photo books were pawed over. I heard exclamations as they saw the pictures of the hostages tied up. I asked if they had ever seen these men. Yes. They said the hostages played cricket and soccer "Right here," as they pointed to an open grass field. I asked if they were ever tied up. No. They were free. The captors washed their clothes. Did the hostages ever speak of their families? No. They said they just wanted to be free.'

There was no time to linger in the village. The helicopter was waiting to take them further south. 'In Dachin,' Jane wrote, 'two medical assistants said they treated the hostages on 5 and 7 September [1995] six hours by foot up the valley at Afti. Don had conjunctivitis for two days, and influenza. Paul Wells had dysentery. Twenty-five militants were with them. Very tall kidnappers, long beards. Foreigners. They didn't understand the language. They were heavily armed.' Jane struggled to take notes, worried to be relying on an Indian Army translator she did not trust: 'I would hear two minutes of talk, then get a twenty-second rerun,' she wrote later in her journal. 'What had I missed? These were people who had been in contact with Don, who were in the midst of telling me about him, when suddenly … the helicopter blades were warmed up and whopping at full speed, and I was being called to leave. I was so close. I had a taste. I want so much more.'

But this would be as near as she would get. The remainder of her trip turned into a fug of illness, insects, humidity and cancelled appointments, leaving her yearning for Spokane. On 8 August she wrote in her journal: 'I'm sick and tired of it all and I want to go home. Be done with the whole thing. I'm tired of the water tap not working, sick of all the flies sitting all over me. Tired of waiting, honking horns, dirty and smelly diesel fumes, stupid traffic jams, idiotic security who are afraid a raisin will explode, and so on ... But at least one of these days I can go home.'

Bob Wells would return to Kashmir one last time that November, travelling with Jane, Julie, Cath, and Dirk's sister Birgit in a trip facilitated by the Indian authorities. Mavis Mangan was supposed to have come too, but she had suffered a heart attack after her previous visit, and Charlie had recently been diagnosed with angina. Losing Keith was destroying them both.

Arriving in Srinagar, Bob was immediately pulled aside and told the valley's police chief wanted to see him. Paramdeep Gill, Inspector General (IG) Kashmir Zone, an officer who had been closely connected to the universally feared STF, the man who had personally overseen the defection of Alpha's men back in 1994, leading to the creation of the hated pro-government militias, had something private to discuss.

Taking a family liaison officer from the British High Commission with him, Bob was ushered into a wood-panelled room with blacked-out windows in a large, heavily guarded police complex in the Srinagar district of Batamaloo. Gill told him he had started his own inquiry into the hostage crisis, an unofficial diversion that he was certain, with his abilities, would get to the truth. The al Faran Crime Branch probe – which had been sealed – was, Gill felt sure, incompetent or inadequate, or both. Then, without warning, he pushed a couple of photographs across the table. One of them was a graphic image of a decomposing head. 'We've found your son,' he said. Bob was horrified. He forced himself to look, trying to see beyond the rendered flesh and flaps of hair, and wondering what kind of way this was to break the death of a child to a father. 'That's not my son,' he said at last, tears of rage stinging his face. Paul had undergone extensive dental work before heading off to Kashmir in June 1995, but this head did not have a single filling.

Gill was not listening. For six months, he said, the STF had been following up leads that had led them to a grave in the cemetery of

Akingham, a small town just south of the Mughal gardens at Achhabal, in the hills above Anantnag town. There they had dug up a body wrapped in a grey shawl, buried without Islamic rites. It was Paul Wells, he claimed, tapping the photos on his desk. 'You know nothing,' said Bob, reddening and standing to leave. 'This is a disgusting circus!' he shouted.

An official from the British High Commission lodged a complaint about Gill's behaviour, but the IG was not easily floored. He sent hair and bone samples to the Central Forensics Laboratory in Ahmedabad, and another sample to a lab in Calcutta. A third batch of DNA was examined at a police forensics facility in Hyderabad, while experts from New Delhi were flown up to Srinagar to examine fragments at the Government Medical College. The story rumbled on until January 2000, when Gill finally announced that scientists at two credible Indian labs had concluded that the DNA they tested was indeed from Paul Wells. Reading the news in Britain, Bob and Dianne were devastated. This was all about international recognition for the Kashmiri police, Gill told reporters. However, he believed that the force was now entitled to claim the $2 million reward from the US Department of Justice and two more rewards of ten *lakh* rupees (£20,000) each from the US State Department and the Jammu and Kashmir government.

The British Foreign Office had had enough. It requested a DNA sample from the Akingham corpse. Three months later it issued a terse statement: 'DNA tests in this country have established that the remains brought back to the UK ... are not those of Paul Wells.' The sample belonged to a man of South Asian origin. The Foreign Office suggested that what had been tested in the Indian labs might have been the reference sample provided by the Wells family, against which the remains were supposed to have been matched. Whether the two had been switched or accidentally mixed, no one could say. Either way, it reflected gravely on the Indian authorities, and the sense of distrust caused by the affair was compounded by statements from Akingham residents, who said that they had told the STF search team that the grave they had dug up belonged to Ziauddin, a fair-skinned

Afghan fighter slain by security forces during an encounter in late 1995. They had buried him themselves.

By the decade's end, the physical search was over for Jane, Julie, Anne and Cath, who between them had been back to Kashmir more than a dozen times, racking up over eighteen months in the region, but discovering nothing definitive, all of them still kept from knowing anything of the Squad's findings. IG Gill had produced two more bodies, both of them supposedly identified by inconclusive DNA evidence, and the women had decided they did not want to see any more. Soon after the November 1997 trip Julie began talking about Keith in the past tense. 'It's hard to admit to myself, but I feel we may not see each other again,' she said. 'I would carry on the fight for ten years if I thought he was alive.' But she was beginning to accept that he was not. After a third body, presented as Keith's, turned out not to be, she knew she was done with Kashmir. She got a job, and bought an Alsatian puppy. For a while she returned to the London flat she and Keith had shared before leaving for South Asia, before fleeing the memories to return home to the north-east, where eventually she began to build a new life with old friends, her family and a new relationship that became a marriage.

For a long time Cath refused to let Paul go, holding on to what she saw as a simple truth: no crime could be hidden forever, and sooner or later somebody, somewhere would give something away. As far as she was aware, nothing had ever been proven: 'That's what makes me feel they're still alive.' However, Cath's hopes eventually faded, as she came to terms with the realisation that Kashmir was comprised of secrets, buried so deeply they might never come to the surface. She too found another partner whom she eventually married, and together they had a child.

'We gave her our blessing,' said Bob Wells. He and Dianne struggled to break free from the past too. For a long time they wanted to leave Blackburn. 'There were just too many memories in that house,' Dianne said, but she couldn't quite bring herself to move, irrationally worried, as any loving mother would be, that if Paul did come home alive and they were not in Feniscowles, he would not know where to find them. But in 2001 Bob and Dianne managed to let go, selling up and heading out to an isolated semi on the edge of a village near Carlisle, with a view over a meadow grazed by sheep. Gradually their sitting-room walls filled up with photos of new grandchildren, hanging alongside the old shot of the teenage Paul in his hiking boots and Aertex shirt halfway up Scafell Pike. 'We had to keep on living,' said Bob, who boxed up all Paul's possessions and piled them at the back of the attic, along with Dianne's scrapbooks about the kidnapping. 'We had to face the inevitable. Our son was dead. Paul was never coming home.'

In Oslo, Marit Hesby and her daughter Anette Ostrø, Hans Christian's cherished younger sister, sponsored a memorial fund to put promising young actors through theatre school, backed by the Norwegian government and supported by the Swedish actress Liv Ullmann. Anette finished college and became a successful film-maker, moving back to Norway, where she bought a wooden house on an island in the silvery Oslo fjord. She filled it with photographs of Hans Christian, keeping his Bhima costume, a big black-and-red notebook recovered from Kashmir, and all of his fantastical, nonsensical, mystical and passionate letters parcelled up in a large cardboard box. Every weekend Marit went down to the black-timbered cabin by the water in Tønsberg, which was kept exactly as it had been when Hans Christian visited it as a child. She would dust and clean his souvenirs before driving over to the churchyard and placing blue flowers at the spot where she had buried his ashes. Every year she and Anette exchanged Christmas cards with Paul, Keith and Don's families. Occasionally they exchanged news too, although, however irrationally, Marit and Anette could not shake off their feelings of guilt. They were somehow better off than the others. They had learned the grisly, horrible truth about Hans Christian's fate, and had been able to physically bury him. Almost every day, their minds slipped back to that day in the German Embassy when Ambassador Elbe had turned pale before telling them that a white-skinned body had been discovered. At the time they had felt secretly jealous of the others, but over the years that followed they had learned to be grateful.

John Childs rarely talks about the events of 1995, even to his family. He did not wish to take his unresolved feelings out of their box too often, although he kept coming back to them privately, churning them over. Did the kidnapping change him? He claimed not, but increasingly he sought out his own company. Eventually he left his job with Ensign Bickford and moved away from Connecticut, to the North-East Appalachians in the wild and wooded far north of the United States, settling in a modest slatted house in the small farming community of Shelburne, Vermont, where locals were more likely to cross into Canada to shop for wood-fired bagels than to drive down to New York. Here, among the gnarly orchards and lakes, he embraced the outdoors once more, spending his weekends skiing or climbing, and running with his new girlfriend Jackie. On his walls were antique maps and mementos, the signs of a well-travelled man who appreciated the span of the globe and human efforts to chart it, so much so that he had a hobby trading in digital maps. Professionally, he had remained in engineering weapons systems, although now for General Dynamics, in a job that took him on frequent foreign trips. But something about John Childs, a reader of Aleksandr Solzhenitsyn, a man who had studied the Beirut hostages, suggested that most of his exploration was internal.

'I didn't avoid India,' John reflected in November 2011, his eyes cast to the floor just as Jane and others remembered him. 'I just had no cause to go back there.' John Childs was not the kind of person to duck anything. Over the years he had become even more self-reliant. 'I am not evasive. I guess some people might see me as distant. But they would be totally wrong. Myself and Jackie are deeply private people. That's all. People don't get it. We just don't go out much,' he said, laughing. Behind his armchair was a wall of books, some guitars and an amplifier, all he needed to keep himself entertained. 'And perhaps I was always like this. A fatalist. Someone who suspects the worse. Or is it more so now? I'm just not sure, but I have never forgotten for a second what happened to me all those years ago.' He went on to recount in intimate detail the days he spent as a captive, recalling touches, tastes, smells and distances, redrawing the route through the

Kashmiri mountains, recalling the characteristics of his captors and his fellow captives, and how his growing sense of doom made him bolt, climbing hand over fist up into the dark Kashmiri heights.

John Childs was full of small inconsistencies: certain the Meadow had not traumatised him, but needing to talk about it; dismissing the weight he carried as the only hostage to escape, while probing the reasons for his good fortune. 'My belief, after all this time, is that I was lucky on *that* day,' he said, interlacing his large hands, steadying a tapping leg. 'For once my planets lined up, if that's how you want to put it. I picked my strategy. I leapt and got away. But on any other day, the same choice would have failed, and I would have been caught, hauled back to the hut.' He held his head in his hands. '"Why couldn't you just bring Don with you?" Jane asked me.' The impact of those words had never left him. The last image he had of Don, Keith and Paul was of them sleeping, exhausted, in the hut as he slipped away. 'From the start, I knew I had to escape. I sensed we would all die. My time came, and somehow it worked out OK. In a struggle there can only be *you*. But, you know ...' He paused, half-closing his eyes as a large grey-and-white cat rubbed against his legs. 'Even today, I can't sleep between sheets. For the past sixteen years I've slept on top of my bed, under a rough blanket, like the horse throws we slept beneath in captivity. I don't know why. Maybe it makes me feel closer to my comrades who were left behind.' He looked shocked to have uttered these words, as if he had never planned to reveal them, but still thinking of the men who would never be found. 'Oh, God. I've never told anyone that before.'

Recently John had lost a close work colleague to cancer, he said. Then Helen, his much-loved mother, died too. These events shook him up, bringing back memories of the Meadow anew. 'My mother's passing made me realise that paying respects and appreciating the person who has gone, the saying "Goodbye," is very, very important. So if you can't, if there is *no goodbye* ...'

Jane Schelly wasn't the sort ever to let go. As Don used to say, if she had a plan, she stuck to it. Don's mask collection still adorned the walls of their red-and-blue-painted sunken living room. His study remained cluttered with his books, and his coat still hung by the front door. She did not remarry. She did not forget. But eventually she did pack away most of Don's possessions, placing them in the attic alongside her Kashmir journals, the maps, the newspaper cuttings and photographs. 'I did not want to have to go back there constantly for the rest of my life,' she said recently. She was not talking about leafing through the physical keepsakes, but about a place in her head where she had stored everything she knew about her Kashmir nightmare.

Fill Your Arms with Lightning

On Christmas Eve 1999, an Indian Airlines plane carrying 178 passengers was hijacked en route from Nepal to New Delhi. It was forced to land in Kandahar, Afghanistan, the birthplace of the Taliban, the austere Islamic fundamentalists who had seized control of the country three years before. The Indian government was faced with an extremely difficult and sensitive situation, as it did not recognise the regime and had no diplomatic presence in Afghanistan.

That night, the Taliban contacted the United Nations to pass on the hostage-takers' demands. They wanted thirty-six Muslim prisoners released from Indian jails, and $200 million in cash. At the top of the list was Masood Azhar, General Secretary of the Movement. Indian newspaper readers were reminded that kidnappers had tried three times already to free him, twice in 1994 and once in 1995, when they had seized six Western backpackers in Kashmir, one of whom had been beheaded, while four had vanished. Masood was currently lodged in Kot Bhalwal high-security prison in Jammu.

Worried relatives of the Indian Airlines Flight 814 hostages, aware that their government's previous negotiation strategy had been criticised as being 'ramshackle and opaque', took things into their own hands. Storming a press conference attended by Foreign Minister Jaswant Singh, they demanded that the government 'do whatever is necessary to ensure the safety of all of the IC814 passengers'. There were less public pressure points too. Sitting in seat 16C on the grounded jet was a senior Indian intelligence operative posted to Nepal, who had been returning to India to visit his sick wife. She was the daughter of a powerful official in the Prime Minister's office, and her elder sister was married to a former director of the elite National Security Guard, a force that dealt with hijacking incidents. These important voices now resounded around the marble palaces of government.

In New Delhi, C.D. Sahay, a veteran agent who had run RAW's Kashmir operations in the nineties, which included working on the al Faran case, was surprised when he got a call asking him to negotiate with the hijackers. Agent Sahay was aware that Masood had been due to be repatriated to Pakistan earlier in the year. However, inexplicably, the plump prisoner had tried to break out of jail on 14 June, jemmying himself into a narrow twenty-three-foot-long tunnel excavated by other prisoners, but becoming stuck. The Afghani, Masood's constant companion over the past six years, had been trapped behind him, and was shot dead by Indian paramilitary police as he reversed out of the hole. Masood was led back to his cell uninjured, and his sentence was extended.

On 27 December Sahay and two other Indian negotiators touched down in Kandahar, where they learned that one of Masood Azhar's brothers was among the hijackers, and his brother-in-law was in the back-up party in Nepal, which supplied the terrorists with cash and weapons. Seven agonising days later, with Indian television running back-to-back coverage of teary relatives camped outside the Prime Minister's house in New Delhi, a deal was struck, India agreeing to give up three prisoners: Masood Azhar; Omar Sheikh, the Briton who had been the lure in the New Delhi kidnappings of October 1994; and Latram, the militant behind the Rubaiya Sayeed kidnapping in Kashmir in 1989.

In Vermont, John Childs was incredulous when he heard the news: 'I was devastated, and really angry. All the time we had been held, the Indians had said they couldn't release any prisoners. And now, just like that, they had keeled over. That was when I finally realised we had all suffered unnecessarily because we were not famous or influential.'

* * *

In the early hours of 31 December, Masood, in Ward Nine of Kot Bhalwal jail, woke to find prison officials swarming into his cell. By 11.30 a.m. he was sitting blindfolded and handcuffed next to Latram, in a helicopter piloted by Captain Jasminder Kahlon, who four years before had rescued John Childs from the mountains above Anantnag. Boarding a civilian jet in New Delhi, the two were joined by Omar Sheikh. 'The plane taxis and within minutes takes off,' Masood wrote later in a journal. 'Startled, I listen to the announcement, "Ladies and gentlemen, we welcome you on board the flight to Kandahar."'

The three prisoners shouted for joy: 'Allahu akbar!' Waiting to greet the prisoners at Kandahar was a senior representative of Mullah Omar, the Taliban's one-eyed emir. That night, Osama bin Laden, the Saudi millionaire who was also a guest of the Taliban, having fled his bolthole in Sudan in 1996, threw them a banquet, recalling how he and Masood had first worked together in Sudan in 1993. 'The Believers are getting ready to celebrate,' Masood wrote. 'The preface to a new chapter of history is being written.'

On 5 January 2000, Masood arrived back at the Binori Town madrassa in Karachi, where thousands of supporters gathered, chanting 'Naraay takbeer, Allahu akbar [Shout out aloud, God is great]!' He told them: 'My dear friends! What India wanted to destroy has reached glorious heights. Oh agents of RAW! You will not be able to catch us until we are sitting upon your own chest, waiting to slit your throat with our knives.' Intentionally or not, his words evoked the slaughter of Hans Christian Ostrø. They were also a foretaste of what was to come. 'My dear friends! My Musulman brothers! Greet me not with cries of "Zindabad" [long live]. For what is the use of living when a gun is hanging above the heads of unarmed, helpless Muslims of Kashmir? Raise the slogan of "Murdabad" [death be].' With a flourish, Masood concluded: 'We haven't come to this world to lead comfortable lives. If you do marry, marry for jihad; have children, but for jihad; earn wealth for jihad; bring up your sons for jihad. I have come alone ... but I will leave here with men who can fight a war.' His followers moved through the crowd, enlisting recruits to join a new outfit: Jaish-e-Mohammed (the Army of Mohammed).

Masood's Army struck three months later in Kashmir, launching the first-ever suicide bombing in Srinagar, outside the army headquarters at BB Cantt. The bomber was Asif Sadiq, a twenty-four-year-old student from Birmingham who had been recruited through contacts Masood had forged during his trips to the UK in the early nineties. More European volunteers were waiting to do the same, Masood warned before heading back to Bahawalpur, where the following year he watched in awe as the Twin Towers fell, following the live television coverage with his father, Master Alvi.

In Spokane, Jane Schelly watched too, sickened and horrified by the al Qaeda attacks on New York and Washington DC. They came just four days before a final memorial ceremony she had arranged for Don: accompanied by fellow climbers from Spokane Mountaineers, she would scatter wildflower seeds on the summit of a local peak, in lieu of her husband's ashes, Don's grave never having been located. As America mourned its dead, Jane decided they should go ahead anyway, paying tribute to a man whose abduction had, it now appeared, signalled the commencement of a new kind of war. 'I would hope we don't do something retaliatory and foolish,' Jane told a local newspaper reporter who asked her, as a victim of Islamic terrorism, what the US should do next. 'In spite of my husband's murder, I don't think violence is the solution.'

America did not listen. Masood too was planning more attacks. Three weeks after 9/11, his Army of Mohammed set off a devastating car bomb in Srinagar, killing thirty-eight people. India claimed that this was just a warm-up for a headline-grabbing spectacular on 13 December 2001, when Masood's outfit allegedly sent five men on a suicidal mission to attack the Indian parliament in the heart of New Delhi, knowing that footage of the event would be seen around the world. India, that would be accused of failing to adequately investigate this raid, in which twelve people died, including the gunmen, described it as 'a wake-up call'. The Army of Mohammed was outlawed by the US, and banned in Pakistan too. Masood was briefly put under house arrest, before being freed 'for lack of evidence'.

On 23 January 2002, *Wall Street Journal* reporter Daniel Pearl was exploring the connections between Pakistan intelligence agencies, Masood's new breed of British-born *jihadis* and their spiritual guides in Karachi, when he vanished. The next time he was seen was in a photograph, with a gun to his head. Emails from his captors were linked by investigators to Omar Sheikh, Masood's British recruit. Since being freed as a result of the Flight 814 hijacking, Sheikh had been working with Masood's Army and also al Qaeda, drawing Pearl into the kidnappers' trap just as he had done with the tourists in New Delhi in 1994. Sheikh was arrested in Pakistan three weeks after Pearl disappeared, and admitted to his role in the abduction, but claimed the American journalist had been passed to another gang, whose members included Amjad Farooqi, a former Masood bodyguard who had helped hijack Flight 814.

The kidnappers released a video showing Pearl reading from a forced confession. Then, in a reprise of what had happened to Hans Christian Ostrø in the snowbound forests of the Pir Panjal, a masked figure was filmed cutting off Pearl's head. His dismembered corpse was found three months later, north of Karachi.

Omar Sheikh was convicted of murdering Daniel Pearl and sentenced to death in July 2002. He appealed, but is still awaiting a hearing. In 2007, Khalid Sheikh Mohammed, a senior al Qaeda operative who was captured in Rawalpindi in March 2003 and transported to Guantánamo Bay, confessed to the FBI that he had slit Pearl's throat while the hijacker Amjad Farooqi had held him down.

Masood's network orchestrated two more suicide bombings in Karachi, and was connected to twin suicide attacks in December 2003 on the motorcade of President Pervez Musharraf of Pakistan as it passed through Rawalpindi. The alleged mastermind, who had a twenty-five-million-rupee (£200,000) reward placed on his head, was

Masood's protégé Amjad Farooqi. Masood was tracked down and placed under house arrest in Bahawalpur, only to be released yet again on the grounds of 'insufficient evidence'. By this time he was thinking about targets further afield.

In September 2004 Pakistani forces cornered Amjad Farooqi in a house in Karachi, where he died in a gun battle. Two months later two young Muslims from Leeds, Shehzad Tanweer and Mohammad Sidique Khan, arrived in Pakistan, ostensibly to attend an Islamic studies course in Punjab. Instead they met a member of Masood's Army, who took them to the LeT for three months' terrorist training. Back in the UK in February 2005, Tanweer and Khan teamed up with a third British Pakistani, Hasib Hussain, and Germaine Lindsay, a British convert to Islam. During the London morning rush hour of 7 July 2005, the four blew themselves up, killing fifty-two people and injuring more than seven hundred.

Masood was still not satisfied. Thirteen months later, in August 2006, Rashid Rauf from Birmingham, whose father had been courted by Masood during his British tours of the nineties and who had married into Masood's extended clan, was arrested in Bahawalpur. Rauf was wanted by English police in connection with the murder of an uncle, but had also been inducted into Masood's burgeoning terror front, assembling an operation to bring down transatlantic airliners with liquid bombs smuggled on board in soft-drink bottles.

After Rauf's arrest, two dozen further suspects would be picked up across the UK, with three men eventually being convicted of conspiracy to murder. In December 2007 Rauf escaped his armed guard in Pakistan, vanishing into the cauldron of the tribal areas, where the US claimed he was killed in a drone strike in November 2008, although his body was never found.

Masood Azhar vanished too. He has outlived almost all of his contemporaries in terror, including Osama bin Laden, while many more are now in jail, among them Omar Sheikh, in Hyderabad in Pakistan. Others, like Langrial, who was released in February 2011, having spent eighteen years in custody without trial, are broken figures. Not Masood. Videos of his recent sermons continue to appear on YouTube and are debated in blogs, while his writings on *jihad* are disseminated via chat rooms. Click a mouse and download his call to arms: 'Will you accompany me in this field? *Inshallah!* Instead of shaking hands with each other, fill your arms with lightning.'

Today, the plump preacher from Bahawalpur has attained the kind of immortality he was seeking since childhood, while the four Western hostages who became both a spur and a benchmark for his organisation – Don Hutchings, Keith Mangan, Paul Wells and Dirk Hasert – are long forgotten, buried in graves that no Kashmiri has dared to identify and no Indian agency has been empowered to locate.

That may change. In murky Kashmir, after two decades of rumours about the fate of an estimated ten thousand missing people (including the four Western backpackers), at least three times the number that vanished under Augusto Pinochet's regime in Chile, a rare moment of clarity has recently emerged.

It followed a five-year slog by Kashmiri activists led by Parvez Imroz, a courageous lawyer from Srinagar who began, unpaid and under threat from the security forces, to elicit secrets from villagers, persuading them to identify and map secret graves scattered throughout the valley that contained, Imroz believed, some of the disappeared.

On 2 July 2011 a Senior Superintendent of Police, Bashir Ahmed Yatoo, whose career had hitherto been distinguished mainly by his loyalty to the state, revealed the results of the first official inquiry into Imroz's claims, before the State Human Rights Commission (SHRC), a government body not known for being outspoken. SSP Yatoo's team said it had identified thirty-eight unmarked mass graves in north Kashmir, scattered through the pine forests and mossy mountain pastures. In them, according to eyewitnesses, lay at least 2,730 bodies. Of these, Yatoo said, 574 had already been identified as civilians unconnected to the insurgency, people who had been plucked from their homes, vehicles or workplaces by the Indian security forces and killed.

Leaked to the press, Yatoo's findings thundered across the valley, prompting villagers to do something no one had done since before 1989. They began to talk openly about how corpses, sometimes burned, headless or mutilated, had frequently been foisted on them by the Indian security forces. 'Bury them somewhere, and don't say a word,' was how Atta Mohammed, a sixty-eight-year-old apple farmer from Kupwara in the north, recalled the Indian security forces putting it as they pulled the canvas back on their olive-green Ashok Leyland truck to reveal the first batch of bloody cadavers. Over the years, he says, they delivered 203 bodies, which this pious man had washed and buried in a copse. All of them were Kashmiri men and boys, not militants from Pakistan, as he was told.

The truth-telling would continue. On 16 September, retired District Judge Javed Kawos, the SHRC's chairman, blindsided the authorities in Srinagar and New Delhi by ordering a widespread programme to identify all of the dead, using DNA analysis and other forensic tools, and an inquiry aimed at finding those culpable in the security forces. 'Prosecutions to bring to justice perpetrators of crimes, shall be undertaken,' he ordered.

SSP Yatoo was called before the SHRC in the last week of September 2011. He was not retracting his report, he said – in fact he had more to add: 'There is every possibility that [all of these] unidentified dead bodies buried in various unmarked graves may contain the victims of enforced disappearances.'

The news of mass graves being uncovered, and the prospect of at least some of the truth about what had gone on in Kashmir being revealed at last, electrified much of the subcontinent. TV crews and their satellite vans were dispatched to report on the unfolding events. Plain-clothed government intelligence agents closely monitored the activities of big-name Indian journalists, the shiny household faces of the cable TV channels who were now followed all over the valley. Other arms of the state tried to threaten eyewitnesses in remote rural areas, but the villagers and farmers refused to be cowed, one schoolteacher brazenly telling reporters: 'We told the thugs who approached us that the times are different. Better watch out.'

After so many years of silence, and with the militants having dwindled, by the army's reckoning, to a band of just 119 active foreign fighters, there was suddenly a rush of eyewitness testimonies. These enabled lawyers to put together a second submission to the SHRC, covering two more Kashmiri districts, Rajouri and Poonch, and another four thousand unmarked graves. One was said to stretch across an entire field, and contained more than 2,500 corpses, according to those who had been forced to dig it, with no one able to say who these bodies belonged to.

SSP Yatoo called on the SHRC to sanction a survey of the entire state, a mass investigation that would reach across the southern Pir Panjal, above Anantnag, and into isolated villages like Mati Gawran, the gateway to frozen Mardan Top to which Don, Keith, Paul and Dirk had been driven, and where they had been executed.

Once the renegades' domain, this area is now almost free of them. The Clerk was cut down in a machine-gun ambush on the road to Vailoo in 2000. He was buried in consecrated ground by his family, only for villagers to repeatedly dig him up and cast his remains out. Alpha, who twice unsuccessfully stood in elections, was shot dead outside his home in Shelipora by unidentified gunmen in 2001. Bismillah survives, guarded by gunmen and elected as a local politician. He jokes: 'No one dared *not* vote for me.' The Tiger, too, somehow outwitted his many enemies, but is now unemployed, and spends his days in drunken penury, sleeping in a paramilitary police camp.

In their place, a building movement for reconciliation is emerging, that might just come up with the truth, and locate many more bodies. As a result of the thaw in Kashmir, for the first time members of the old al Faran Squad have spilled secrets they had been forced to sit on for sixteen years about a case they believed they had solved but whose conclusions were so stark that they too were buried. Their sources too have come out into the open – the agents and informers who helped piece together the complex Crime Branch investigation that can only really be laid to rest when Don, Keith, Dirk and Paul's remains are found.

Searching for the appropriate words with which to address the silent masses in the security services, the villagers in the deep countryside, the law enforcers and policy-makers in Srinagar and New Delhi, SSP Yatoo eventually found some that applied just as well to the many vanished Kashmiris as to the abduction and disappearance of five Western trekkers, a crime that transformed this Himalayan paradise, in the eyes of the West, into a cauldron of Islamic terror. 'Show me the manner in which a nation cares for its dead,' Yatoo said in September 2011, quoting William Gladstone, 'and I will measure the tender mercy of its people, their respect for the law of the land and their loyalty to high ideals.'

ACKNOWLEDGEMENTS

We began working as foreign correspondents in India during the hostage crisis in Kashmir. Returning regularly to the valley, we built long-standing relationships that would enable us, in 2008, to start researching this book and to attempt to exorcise the ghosts of 1995.

Fastidious reporting by a close group of Western journalists based in New Delhi, especially Suzanne Goldenberg of the *Guardian*, went some way towards the truth. We have gone back through the contemporary press cuttings to show what was known publicly, and to compare this to what was recorded in the covert police and intelligence files that would not surface until recently. In our attempts to create an accurate time line from the perspective of the Western authorities, we were assisted by internal documents from the so-called G4 countries – Britain, the USA, Norway and Germany – whose diplomats came together to attempt to gain the hostages' freedom. Particular thanks go to Tore Hattrem, then a political officer in the Norwegian Embassy in New Delhi, and today Ambassador in Khartoum, and to Arne Walther, then Norway's Ambassador in New Delhi, and today its Ambassador to Japan.

Back in 1995, the police and intelligence agencies in India were largely unapproachable. But over the last three years, serving and retired senior police officers from the upper echelons of the Jammu and Kashmir force have generously given us many hours of interviews, recollecting events from 1995, playing us tapes, showing us documents, notes and diaries. Rajinder Tikoo, who conducted the hostage negotiations until they collapsed in mid-September 1995, can still recall sharply what it was like to deal with al Faran, and contributed greatly to the chapters that relate to the talks and their collapse.

Key to helping us understand the STF and the operation of the renegades was Deputy Inspector General Farooq Khan, who as a Superintendent of Police ran the first STF unit. Senior Superintendent of Police Ashkoor Ahmad Wani, who while stationed in south Kashmir worked closely alongside the STF and the renegades, explained his take on both outfits, and their failings. Countless former renegades talked to us too, in south and north Kashmir, including Ghulam Muhammad Lone ('Papa Kishtwari'), Ghulam Nabi Mir ('Alpha') and Abdul Rashid ('the Clerk'), in interviews that began in 1998, with the last taking place in 2011, by which time many of them had been killed or jailed.

We thank those still serving in the J&K force who worked on the al Faran investigation, and who later had access to the detailed summaries and analyses of the case prepared for the police, the intelligence agencies and counter-militancy agencies, who took an enormous risk in opening up their files, sharing copies of their case diaries with us, allowing us to study key witness statements, maps and notes. In return for a guarantee of anonymity, they also helped locate their old confidential sources and agents, whose lives would be at risk if their identities were revealed. Thanks also to the J&K police officers who witnessed the events of 1995 at first hand while serving in Pahalgam, Bijbehara and Anantnag.

In Britain, Roy Ramm showed us a draft of his unpublished memoirs, which incorporate a journal he kept at the time of the hostage crisis.

In Pakistan, the late Benazir Bhutto spurred the writing of this book, as she was in government at the time of the crisis and suspected that the development of al Faran marked a significant step in the growth of global terrorism. Special thanks go to Pakistan's erudite High Commissioner for Britain, Wajid Shamsul Hasan, the last indoor cigar-smoker in town. We are especially grateful to specialists, agents and federal investigators in Punjab, Rawalpindi and Khyber Pakhtunkhwa (formerly North-West Frontier province) who gave us access to exhaustive files that chart the rise of Masood Azhar. They also introduced us to veteran intelligence sources in Karachi, Pakistan-administered Kashmir and the tribal areas who were close to Masood's operation. Members of Masood's various *jihad* fronts talked too, as did those close to them, sharing documents, speeches, diaries and recollections. It took a leap of faith for them to sit down face to face with us, as it did for several retired senior officers in Pakistan's Inter Services Intelligence directorate.

In India, among those who have retired from the intelligence community (assuming an old spook is ever let off the hook) was C.D. Sahay, who provided the most complete account of Masood Azhar's interrogation and the decision to release him in 1999. He was also frank about the intelligence agencies' perspective on the events of 1995, and the decision to let the al Faran kidnapping operation 'run long', so as to allow India to secure a moral advantage over Pakistan. C.D. Sahay was equally insightful on the priorities of the Rao administration in 1995, the role of intelligence during Governor's Rule in Kashmir, and the significance of the *yatra* and the 1996 elections on government thinking about the kidnapping, although he will not agree with this book's conclusions. Similarly, A.S. Dulat, who ran IB operations in Kashmir in the late 1980s and returned throughout the nineties, and who would go on to run both the IB and RAW, was insightful on the rise of the militancy and the shortcomings in New Delhi that led to the explosion of violence in the valley, although he does not agree with the J&K police assessment of IB's failings. A.K. Doval, a veteran IB agent and brilliant field operative who went on to lead the Bureau, watched the Pakistanisation of the militancy from close up, monitoring the growth of infiltration from over the LoC, designing some of the most far-reaching counter-measures to contain it, and working to expose Pakistan's hand using pro-government renegades. He also led operations on the ground during the Kandahar hijack fiasco of 1999, working with C.D. Sahay, and his candid reflections on this operation proved invaluable. Neither he, C.D. Sahay nor A.S. Dulat ever discussed with us the police's findings concerning the transfer and killing of the hostages, and they are in no way linked to these events.

There are many in the Indian foreign service who provided tantalising details about dealing with the Western embassies that besieged them during the crisis, but all of them still work in government, and cannot be thanked by name. The Indian Ministry of Defence and the Indian Army declined to cooperate officially, but individual senior officers in the Rashtriya Rifles gave considerable time to reflect on counter-militancy activities and their work with the renegades. Thanks especially to Lt. General (rtd) D.D. Saklani, who talked frankly and at length about his dealings with al Faran. Late to the book but well worth the call was Nalin Prabhat, Deputy Inspector General for the Central Reserve Police Force in Srinagar, an unflinchingly honest commentator on the insurgency, the state's successes and its profound failings.

Key among the former militants we interviewed in Indian jails was Naseer Mohammed Sodozey, in Ward 2 of Tihar prison, New Delhi, whose family were also generous when we visited them in Palandiri, in Pakistan-administered Kashmir. Naseer explained the background and training of Masood's fighters, detailing his own induction into *jihad* and Kashmir, and maintained, in stories backed up by multiple sources, that he was compelled to create a fictitious 'ending' for the hostage drama, about which, in reality, he knew nothing. Weeks of torture, and the promise of clemency, he still maintains, elicited his cooperation in this deception.

Nasrullah Mansoor Langrial, aka Langrial Darwesh, who until February 2011 was held in Agra jail, gave permission for us to see his files and notes, helping us to understand the character of the men he served with, especially the Afghani and Sikander, whose family in Dabran were patient and welcoming too. In Baramulla, we also spent many days with Qadeer Dar, the retired commander of the Muslim Janbaz Force, who provided insight into his group's kidnapping of Western engineers working in Kashmir in 1991. Today Qadeer is chairman of the People's Rights Movement, a group of many thousands of former Kashmiri militants seeking rehabilitation into mainstream society. The recollections of many of his members were invaluable to our book.

Much help was given by two Kashmiri human rights groups, the Jammu and Kashmir Coalition of Civil Society (JKCCS) and the Association of Parents of Disappeared Persons, which have opened up many previously remote and closed communities through their ongoing work to locate and map a network of mass unmarked graves scattered across the valley, and to chart cases of state-sponsored disappearance and torture.

A big thank you goes to Kashmiri human rights lawyer Parvez Imroz, president of the JKCCS. Winner of the eleventh Ludovic-Trarieux International Human Rights Prize, awarded by the European Bar Human Rights Institute, Imroz has continued working despite several attempts on his life and the murder of many colleagues. Thanks also to the indefatigable Khurram Parvez, the JKCCS's programme coordinator, who could have quit when he lost a leg in an IED attack on his car, which claimed the life of a young female colleague. Thanks also to Parvaiz Matta, who accompanied us on many of our journeys into the mountains. The intrepid journalist Yusuf Jameel has always made time to listen and advise; and from the new generation of journalists, special thanks go to Showkat Ahmed and his excellent *Conveyor* magazine, Masood Husain and his incisive weekly *Kashmir Life*, the photographers Javed Dar and Faisal Khan, and especially to Yawar Kabli, who helped source photos despite the snowfall. There are many other Kashmiris we would like to name, who over the last sixteen years have advised and assisted us, but most of them would be embarrassed to be singled out, as hospitality remains the norm throughout the valley, despite what this story teaches us.

One of the first people to understand what we were trying to achieve with this book was David Housego, who still lives in New Delhi despite his family's experiences in 1994. Special thanks also go to Kim, who we met in France, and to his mother Jenny, who has a business in Kashmir. They all spent time with us, studying maps and dredging up memories, matching the events of 1994 with those of 1995.

Special thanks go to Anette Ostrø and Marit Hesby in Norway, who welcomed us, and made the difficult decision to open up Hans

Christian's diaries and letters anew. Also to John Childs in Vermont, who withstood many requests before finally agreeing to see us. He proved to have a near-perfect memory of all that he endured, and was straightforward and painfully honest.

At first we were nervous about contacting the families of Don, Keith, Paul and Dirk after all these years, aware that they had been hounded by the press in the past, and dragged through countless versions of the case, without ever knowing the truth.

We have huge admiration for Jane Schelly, who helped us immensely and who remains a force of life, retaining command over all of the details of the case, and whose journal throws light on the months and years of turmoil. Jane was our primary fact-checker, and also pointed us towards Ann Auerbach, whose book *Ransom: The Untold Story of International Kidnapping* contains a thorough account of the Western reaction to the crisis, and provides an invaluable reference point, capturing the desperation of those waiting for news in New Delhi and back home.

In Britain, Bob and Dianne Wells opened up their home to us, bravely sorting through many of Paul's albums and letters to help us understand their son, spending hours recalling phone calls and newspaper articles, and the visits Bob made to India in search of the hostages.

Charlie Mangan died in 2010 without finding out what had happened to Keith, on whose behalf he travelled to Kashmir – a trip from which he never recovered. Mavis Mangan, who survives Charlie, and Julie Mangan kept in touch with us through the writing of this book but did not want to actively participate in it.

In Germany, the family of Dirk Hasert were helpful, placing his journey into a sharper context.

We respect too those relatives and friends of hostages who did not want or need to talk to us, having built new lives for themselves, and learned to cope with a crime with no closure.

Thanks also to the Middlesbrough *Gazette*, especially Paul Delplanque, who allowed us to spend hours reading cuttings.

Finally, we are grateful to all at HarperCollins, especially our editors Arabella Pike and Robert Lacey, whose pin-sharp suggestions and revisions whipped the manuscript into shape. Thanks too to David Godwin, our agent, and all at DGA who pushed to get the book to a wide audience.

A NOTE ON SOURCES

The greatest challenge presented by this book was to write about something that could never be known. At its heart is an event that only one person survived.

We sought to fill the silence at the centre of the story by seeking out new eyewitness accounts from villagers and *jihadis* who came close to the hostages and their guards. We have also relied on a rich vein of material written by the hostages themselves, especially Hans Christian Ostrø, whose letters, annotations, doodles and poems evoke the atmosphere in the hostage camp. Villagers in remote areas of Kashmir, where the kidnappers stayed for several months, discovered many items – scripts, letters and appeals – written and then abandoned by the hostages, which they transcribed or committed to memory, and later shared with us.

Outside the world of the five captives, we sought out primary source material, including first-hand recollections of those directly involved in the hostage crisis, on both the police and the *jihadi* sides in India and Pakistan. We also made extensive use of intelligence and criminal reports, as well as transcripts of taped interviews made by the police and intelligence services in Kashmir.

The dialogue, and the quotations ascribed to individuals, have been drawn from the memories of those involved, and shown to as many parties as possible to ensure accuracy.

Some quotations ascribed to the hostages' families have been compared to or directly extracted from interviews they gave at the time to Indian, American and British newspapers, so as to capture the authenticity of that moment – the thoughts they had back then, rather than with the benefit of hindsight.

When we have not been able to see a specific report, letter or memo mentioned in the book, but have spoken to its author – as was the case with the many papers and memos from the al Faran file – we have indicated this by using a specific form of words, so it is clear that what is being quoted is a recollection of what was written by its author, rather than being taken directly from the paper itself.

INDEX